Bisexual and Gay Husbands
Their Stories, Their Words

HAWORTH Gay & Lesbian Studies
John P. De Cecco, PhD
Editor in Chief

Military Trade by Steven Zeeland

Longtime Companions: Autobiographies of Gay Male Fidelity by Alfred Lees and Ronald Nelson

From Toads to Queens: Transvestism in a Latin American Setting by Jacobo Schifter

The Construction of Attitudes Toward Lesbians and Gay Men edited by Lynn Pardie and Tracy Luchetta

Lesbian Epiphanies: Women Coming Out in Later Life by Karol L. Jensen

Smearing the Queer: Medical Bias in the Health Care of Gay Men by Michael Scarce

Macho Love: Sex Behind Bars in Central America by Jacobo Schifter

When It's Time to Leave Your Lover: A Guide for Gay Men by Neil Kaminsky

Strategic Sex: Why They Won't Keep It in the Bedroom edited by D. Travers Scott

One of the Boys: Masculinity, Homophobia, and Modern Manhood by David Plummer

Homosexual Rites of Passage: A Road to Visibility and Validation by Marie Mohler

Male Lust: Pleasure, Power, and Transformation edited by Kerwin Kay, Jill Nagle, and Baruch Gould

Tricks and Treats: Sex Workers Write About Their Clients edited by Matt Bernstein Sycamore

A Sea of Stories:The Shaping Power of Narrative in Gay and Lesbian Cultures—A Festschrift for John P. De Cecco edited by Sonya Jones

Out of the Twilight: Fathers of Gay Men Speak by Andrew R. Gottlieb

The Mentor: A Memoir of Friendship and Gay Identity by Jay Quinn

Male to Male: Sexual Feeling Across the Boundaries of Identity by Edward J. Tejirian

Straight Talk About Gays in the Workplace, Second Edition by Liz Winfeld and Susan Spielman

The Bear Book II: Further Readings in the History and Evolution of a Gay Male Subculture edited by Les Wright

Gay Men at Midlife: Age Before Beauty by Alan L. Ellis

Being Gay and Lesbian in a Catholic High School: Beyond the Uniform by Michael Maher

Finding a Lover for Life: A Gay Man's Guide to Finding a Lasting Relationship by David Price

The Man Who Was a Woman and Other Queer Tales from Hindu Lore by Devdutt Pattanaik

How Homophobia Hurts Children: Nurturing Diversity at Home, at School, and in the Community by Jean M. Baker

The Harvey Milk Institute Guide to Lesbian, Gay, Bisexual, Transgender, and Queer Internet Research edited by Allen Ellis, Liz Highleyman, Kevin Schaub, and Melissa White

Stories of Gay and Lesbian Immigration: Together Forever? by John Hart

Bisexual and Gay Husbands
Their Stories, Their Words

Fritz Klein, MD
Tom Schwartz
Editors

Harrington Park Press®
An Imprint of The Haworth Press, Inc.
New York • London • Oxford

Published by

Harrington Park Press®, an imprint of The Haworth Press, Inc., 10 Alice Street, Binghamton, NY
13904-1580

Notes for Professional Librarians and Library Users: This is an original book title published by
Harrington Park Press, an imprint of The Haworth Press, Inc. Unless otherwise noted in specific
chapters with attribution, materials in this book have not been previously published elsewhere in
any format or language.

Conservation and Preservation Notes: All books published by The Haworth Press, Inc. and its
imprints are printed on certified pH neutral, acid free book grade paper. This paper meets the
minimum requirements of American National Standard for Information Sciences-Permanence of
Paper for Printed Material, ANSI Z39.48-1984.

Cover design by Jennifer M. Gaska.

Library of Congress Cataloging-in-Publication Data

Bisexual and gay husbands : their stories, their words / Fritz Klein, Thomas Schwartz, editors.
    p. cm.
    A compendium of e-mails sent 1998-99 by "men who had belonged to a Bi and Gay men's
list-serve and were out to their spouses about their sexual orientation"—Introd.
    ISBN 1-56023-166-1 (alk. paper : hard)—ISBN 1-56023-167-X (alk. paper : soft)
    1. Bisexuality in marriage—Case studies. 2. Bisexual men—Attitudes—Case studies. 3. Gay
men—Attitudes—Case studies. 4. Bisexual men—Family relationships—Case studies. 5. Gay
men—Family relationships—Case studies. 6. Husbands—Sexual behavior—Case studies. I. Klein,
Fred, 1932- II. Schwartz, Thomas, 1939-

HQ74 .B533 2002
305.38'9663—dc21
          2001039559

CONTENTS

ABOUT THE EDITORS

Fritz Klein, MD, is a psychiatrist who lives in San Diego, California, and is editor of the *Journal of Bisexuality* (Haworth). His former positions include Clinical Instructor at the University of California at San Diego and co-leader of the Bisexual Forum in New York City, which he founded in 1974. Dr. Klein also established the Bisexual Forum in San Diego in 1982. He is the author of the book *The Bisexual Option* and co-editor of *Bisexualities: Theory and Research* (both from Haworth Press) and co-author of *Man, His Body, His Sex.*

Thomas Schwartz is a gay married man who is out to his spouse, children, family, and friends. He has been a member of several e-mail lists and compiled the original compendium of e-mails from one specific e-mail list for husbands out to their spouses, which is the basis for this book. In addition, he was for many years a member of GAMMA, a men's support group, and he has befriended and corresponded with many men in similar situations around the world.

Introduction

Last year Fritz Klein and Thomas Schwartz met at a "Guy Gathering" in Seattle. For the gathering, Tom had compiled a compendium of e-mails sent in by men who had belonged to a bi- and gay-men's list-serve and who were out to their spouses about their sexual orientation. The group at the gathering agreed that this compendium would be a most important addition to the literature and should be transformed into a book. This is the result.

Fritz Klein has been a sex researcher for over twenty-five years. His main body of work has been in the area of bisexuality. For years he has investigated the fact that although there are anywhere from two to five times as many bisexual men as there are gay men, these bisexual men are completely hidden in our society.

Why is that?

The answers are found in this book. Many bisexual/gay men are married and live a "heterosexual" life. The fact that these men might be bisexual or gay is a secret. This invisibility manifests on many levels: in the society in general, in the gay community, in the marriage and family itself, and, in many cases, in the man himself.

It is only in the last decade that the situation has changed—and it has changed dramatically. The catalyst for this change is the Internet becoming available to the average man. Chat rooms, newsgroups, and list-serves have revolutionized the lives of many people. The men in question have been able to "come out of the closet." They have been able to talk and correspond to other men in the same situation—namely, being married to a woman while at the same time having attractions to and/or sex with other men. For the first time in their lives they have now been able to share their stories safely and anonymously.

So at the start of the new millennium, we now have thousands of men communicating with one another. There are now in existence bi-men lists that have over 1,000 members. Altogether there are at least 15,000 men who belong to these bi-lists. This does not include the bi chat rooms and newsgroups that contain thousands and thousands more. In addition, many thousands of married bi/gay men belong to Internet *gay* lists, chat rooms, and so on. They present themselves as single gay men, and some straight, curious, married men frequent these Internet gay lists, and so on, out of curiosity or titillation! These men are not found in the bi/gay married lists or the bi lists.

E-MAIL CONTENT

These e-mails (which were sent during the two years of 1998 and 1999) contain the intimate feelings, understandings, and excerpts from the personal lives of bi and gay (bi/gay) men who are/were involved in a relationship with a female. Most of these men lived in the United States, but some resided in Canada, Ireland, Denmark, Italy, Brazil, Australia, New Zealand, Thailand, the United Kingdom, and Israel.

Although the list does include some "blue-collar" men, most of the men on the list are well educated—graduate degrees are quite common—with many being in professional fields. Many doctors, lawyers, educators, computer specialists, corporate senior managers, therapists, engineers, ministers, visual artists, and musicians are all well represented in the list. Most of the men have one or more children, love them dearly, and enjoy the challenges of fatherhood and family life.

Some of the men have been "out" for years. Many of the men are just coming to terms with their sexuality and are dealing with the unique stress this places upon themselves, their spouses, and the people they love. Most of the men are husbands out to their spouses, though a few of the men were just contemplating coming out. The exciting thing is that these e-mails give each man hope and assurance that he is not alone. Not only that, it gives the man a better understanding of himself! These e-mails may help them improve their relationships with their spouses or can give solace and support to the men whose course in life is separation or divorce.

Most of these men are trying desperately to improve the quality of all their relationships through the process of reaching out and sharing themselves with others. There are numerous reasons that these men join this list—the following two e-mails describe what many of them feel:

From: Ted

When I joined this group, I thought that I was the only person having this problem (being a gay married man), in a marriage of many years that was dissolving. It saddens me to learn that I am not unique.

However, having this group for support is a great blessing!!!

This is the real benefit of the Internet. Frankly, who cares about all this e-commerce crap & porno sites? The major benefit of the Internet is the ability to create virtual communities where people of similar interests/problems can get together.

It is said that computers create isolation. I think it is just the opposite. They allow us to express thoughts, that we would be reluctant to tell our brothers or best friends, to others with whom we have very much in common. The openness and honesty of my brothers on this list brings gladness to my once isolated heart.

Thank you all for being here!!

From: Brandon

. . . But how do we struggle for our place in the sun? The sun doesn't shine in the closet. Demanding to be considered equal to my brothers endangers my family and makes us all outcasts. Lucky are we to have one another through the Internet as well as face-to-face support groups. All of us in this complicated world struggle with one thing or another. It's just doing it in the closet makes it seem we are very different. But I don't think we are. It just seems that way.

E-MAIL INTERPRETATION

Each e-mail must be interpreted by the reader with the understanding that it is only one man's feelings, thoughts, or comments on a specific topic at a specific moment in time. As each man grows more confident concerning his bi/gay sexuality and the changes that this brings to his relationships, his thinking on any topic could change 180 degrees. Views in a specific e-mail written yesterday may no longer be true or relevant to that individual today or tomorrow. The dynamic nature of e-mail is the media's great strength but also its major fault. The truth in an e-mail may be fleeting.

Dates and times of each e-mail were not included in order to help maintain the confidentiality of the list's individuals, even though this information would have helped to retain the sense of that designated moment in time. Each thread or individual e-mail is a unique story within itself and one can read at random within this compendium to learn who these men are. However, only by reading all the e-mails and really understanding the total picture does the life honesty of the bi/gay married men on this list become apparent.

E-MAIL EDITING

After two years of collecting these e-mails, the decision for organizing them was not an easy task. We included within this compendium only the most representative e-mails (about 20 to 25 percent of the nearly 3,000 posts written by approximately 350 men).

An e-mail submitted by one person receives many responses, and these e-mails are referred to as a "thread." These threads often took on lives of their own. Some of these threads even diverted into other threads as the original subject was expanded or the topic moved on to other related issues. These e-mails with multiple threads, subjects, and topics arrive from cyberspace and are displayed on the browser chronologically. Some of these threads, along with other threads, took weeks to play themselves out—creating confusion about subject flow and interfering with readability. Printing all the e-mails in sequential order would not have lent itself to logical thought processes for the reader of this book. The threads were combined under specific headings. Not all e-mails associated with a specific thread were included. We titled these threads using some of the more clever titles of the original e-mail. We then combined them into specific chapters such as: Coming Out, Sexual Orientation, Male Relationships, and so on.

Even though we decided to follow this "natural" organization, be aware that many of the subjects are interrelated and intertwined. Each e-mail occurs only once—even though it may have addressed other topics or other threads. We often made arbitrary decisions as to where to place a thread or a specific e-mail.

The editors have eliminated opening greetings such as, "Hi Guys," "To Joe," and so on, to save space and be able to include more actual correspondence. For the same reason we omitted most closing remarks such as, "Love to all of you" or "Hugs." The integrity of each e-mail's colloquialisms and "e-mailese" (hetero for heterosexual, <G> for grin, TGT for The Gay Thing, and so on) have been maintained. Editing included some obvious spelling and punctuation errors. Some e-mails that included similar thoughts were merged. Many e-mails were edited with the objective of maintaining the integrity of each individual's thought process while filtering out extraneous verbiage.

To protect each man's confidentiality, all names have been changed, specific references to times and places modified, and all personal biographies discarded. The "from" names have been changed to an alias to protect confidentiality. Likewise, each e-mail address of the group's members has been removed. However, the e-mail address of one of the professional members on the list has been retained. The editors, in addition, deliberately chose to eliminate most e-mails dealing with religion and politics (for obvious reasons).

A SPECIAL THANK-YOU AND CONCLUSION

Thanks to the hundreds of courageous men (and some of their spouses) for sharing themselves so openly and honestly with their bi and gay married brothers. We marvel at the integrity of so many like-minded men, from all over the world, brought together by the miracle of e-mail for the first time in human history. The depth of knowledge, self-acceptance, spirituality, and openness of these guys is truly amazing! We created this book of e-mails out of our love of the honesty contained in them and our deep respect for our Internet brothers in the hopes that this material will help other men struggling with similar issues. We also believe this book is important for historical purposes.

The editors have purposely not commented on the e-mails, as we strongly believe they stand on their own and our words would be superfluous and detract from the strength of the men's words and stories.

A very special thanks to a very special, loving man, Larry Peterson, for having the wisdom to begin the list and for the hundreds of hours he has spent helping his brothers understand and accept themselves. He recently published an article in the *Journal of Bisexuality* (Vol.1, Issue 2/3, The Haworth Press, Inc.) titled "The Married Man On-line." We wish to quote from his conclusion, as it most certainly applies to this book:

> ... (Lists) have dramatically changed the lives of the married bisexual and gay men who have access to them. They now have a ready mechanism to receive information; establish networks, friendships, and male families; seek dates; and even find love ...

> For men who live outside of urban areas or who wish to keep their sexuality confidential, the Internet provides opportunities to meet other men with similar experiences that would be unavailable or inconvenient otherwise. As one list member commented, "I have had more 'real' communication in the past couple of weeks reading the posts on this list than I've had (total) in the past ten years." ...

> Through the Internet, married bisexual and gay men have been able to create families, find brothers, and discover mentors who can help them cope with similar challenges. To use the nomenclature of the Net, men now speak in terms of cyber-friendships, cyber-families, and 'virtual' communities, all of which serve a critical function for men who had previously felt isolated and 'weird.' The [e-mails on this list] just scratch the surface of bisexual and gay married men's on-line conversations, but I hope that [they] demonstrate the richness of this material and will spark further studies.

Chapter 1

Coming Out

THE WAY I DID IT

From: Gripp

You are doing it the way I did it. That is, I joined the group, read the posts for about 8 months, then came out to my wife. I had the support of the entire list, plus the benefit of their experiences. Before coming out, I read all the bios, all the 7 or 8 months of posts, plus "When Husbands Come Out of the Closet" by Gochros, "The Other Side of the Closet" by Amity Pierce Buxton, and "Uncommon Lives" by Catherine Whitney. These books deal with mixed-orientation marriages. The case histories they tell do not make for very encouraging reading for a mixed-orientation marriage's likelihood of success, but they do give very valuable help on how to deal with the grief of the straight spouse when she learns of her husband's sexuality.

Additionally, I worked with my wife to improve the intimacy in our marriage before coming out to her. I read, to me, and then to my wife, a book called "Getting the Love you Want: A Guide for Couples" by Harville Hendrix, Harper Perennial. It discusses "The Unconscious Marriage" and "The Conscious Marriage," giving valuable exercises for how to get the love you want—how to develop more intimacy. It made a lot of sense to us. It did not deal with mixed-orientation marriages but was an invaluable tool in improving our intimacy.

Next, I analyzed my motives. I was already in therapy for suicide, so I discussed my motives with my therapist. (The suicide is another issue, but it affected my relationship with my family.) I believed that I wanted to be honest with my wife, truthful; I wanted to quit hiding the life I was leading. Yet I loved her, still do! I wanted her to know and love all of me, the real me, the one she did not yet know. And I wanted to stay married and in a sexual relationship with my wife. This was VERY important to me. I began to tell her regularly that I loved her. I showed her regularly that I loved her. I even began to do the little things, like cards and flowers, that were not a regular part of my repertoire before.

I planned a time when my wife and I could be alone together for several days, when the children were gone. About two weeks before, I told everyone on the list the date that I was planning it, and asked them to pray for me and for us. They did, and immediately began sending posts reviewing their stories with me.

I think that there are several categories of men on this list. There are some men on the list who are no longer married. They relate to their wives and children as a divorced father. That was not what I wanted. I think there are men on the list who identify as gay but are married. Some of them do and some of them don't continue to have sex with their wives. That was not me! I think there are men who identify as bisexual (the word they use to self identify is not important), who want to continue to have a "normal" hetero-sexual life with their wives but want to allow their "not straight" side to be expressed. That was me!

Within each category there are many different expressions of ways of acting/reacting/coping/living. What I found was that the men who had gone through this process and were coping successfully, did not post very often. They did not need the help of the list! These were the ones I needed to hear from. When I actually got to the point of coming out and told everyone, they came "out of the woodworks" and responded. I, also, sometimes posted to individuals on the list privately; but I learned that if I posted to the entire list, I was more likely to get a wonderful variety of responses, each of which would relate somewhat to my situation and be helpful. They also pointed out that there were other men in a similar place to mine who wanted to know how I was dealing with issues, and that I was denying a few men on the list some help if I posted only private e-mails. One guy would gently say so, by asking my permission, by separate post, to post my letter to the list. After a while I caught on. Then I got more responses that were helpful to me.

Tell us your story! Don't be afraid of confiding in us. Some of us will have good comments for you. Ask questions! Say what you are thinking or planning! Ask for comments on your thoughts. Examine your motives. Begin thinking about your wife and how she will respond to your coming out. Try to think all around every issue. Then make up your own mind. It can be worth it.

I have been out for about 8 weeks now. Our marriage is better that it has been since the first few months. It can be that way for you also. Best wishes. I'll start praying for you.

COMING OUT

From: Dave

In revealing my situation to my kids and parents a couple of years ago, my catechism of facts and principles was as follows:

"I'm a bisexual man, and I'm having an affair with a gay man [my child had met him]. I've been sexually active with men for the entire time that I've been married [30 yrs.].

In that time, we've had a great family life, in spite of a lot of self-despite that I've inflicted upon myself, and which I don't need or want to do anymore. Nevertheless, I'm the same person whom you have loved and who has loved you all of your life.

The only thing that's changed today is ideas, i. e., YOUR KNOWLEDGE, and you must adjust to your new awareness. Whether you like THIS knowledge or not, we are in a lifetime relationship with each other.

Relationships are two-way streets, and the quality of the relationship depends upon you and me both.

I love you and I want the relationship to be as good as it possibly can be. (In my case I could say, "I'm not leaving, going anywhere.")

Today, the family relationships are better than ever.

COMING OUT TO WIFE

From: James

My wife gave me permission to forward this post of hers on spouse support to all of you. A couple of you guys are about to come out to your wives so I think you'll find this useful information. My only caution is that Amity Buxton's book is best not read by your wife right after the coming out. The statistics often frighten the wife who is seeking reassurance that the marriage will last or has the chance of lasting. Save Amity's book until much later when she has some objectivity and then can deal with the book better. (I'm referring to my wife's item 1 below.)

Hi,

What an awful burden you are carrying—I hope that talking with your wife will relieve some of it, while it will of course bring much else down on your head to deal with. Your wife is lucky . . . that you are willing to come to her voluntarily, not because you have been "discovered," and that you have been faithful to this point, so she is not being hit with betrayal on top of everything else. You asked for advice; here is what little I can suggest:

• Before you talk to her, read "When Husbands Come Out of the Closet" and "The Other Side of the Closet" and have both available to give to her.

- Talk to her at a time when you can make yourself available on a continuing basis for a couple of days—at the beginning of a weekend, etc. Be ready to stay home from work if you need to. Sometimes people seem to need to just process and process and process for a couple of days.
- Try not to concern yourself about what her reaction is—know that she is being hit by a truck, and how she reacts initially says very little about what she will feel over time and what you both will do.
- Give her at least a couple of weeks to just let it hit her, and don't look for acceptance, understanding, forgiveness, or coping with the future until she is ready to turn to that.
- Tell her everything—don't hold back. It is important she knows there are no more surprises coming down the road.
- Let her know about the str8s list, and that there are ways to find spouses to talk with in person or on the phone through the Straight Spouse Support Network. There are also support groups in many
- areas. But mainly—really suggest that she at least listen on the straight spouse list.
- She will want to know what this means in terms of your intentions/wants toward her—be honest. If you hope to maintain the marriage, say so. If you don't know what will work out, say that.
- Suggest to her that it will take a lot of time to let the dust settle and decide where to go with this . . . sometimes people jump to immediate "I must change my life tomorrow" assumptions and do themselves and their marriage unnecessary damage. If you are willing to take time to work out where to go with this, be sure that she knows that.
- For yourself—subscribe to this men's list and SOTTS lists (Husbands/Spouses Out to Their Spouses).
- I know this can be incredibly difficult, but, more than anything—hear and accept her pain. Let her be in pain, as guilty and terrible as it makes you feel. Face it, don't abandon her because you can't take it. Let her be angry at you, let her despair, let her mourn. Hold her if you can, but at least listen and give her feelings validity and understanding.
- Say you're sorry (which is not to say that you are in the wrong—just that you regret causing pain, that you recognize the losses involved).

Let us know how it goes . . . and good luck.

From: Moris

I know that the spouse is supposed to talk to the spouse support list; however, some of you have asked to hear it from "her own lips." So those of you who don't want to hear from my wife, press delete now.

Otherwise just read away!

Dear guys,

It has been brought it to my attention that some of you think, or maybe, fear, that I am living in a fairy tale in believing that he, his male partner, and I will be able to live together as a triad. Believe me, this is no fairy tale!! Sometimes it's a veritable nightmare. We have experienced some very difficult times over the past almost-eight months and will very likely experience more, but mainly through my husband's love, persistence, and understanding, we've managed to go on. It's not been all "peaches and cream," but it has been something I'd do over again if the opportunity came up. I've known and loved my husband in various ways for a little over 23 years now, and I WANT HIM IN MY LIFE!!!! Because of this I am willing to make sacrifices, change my way of thinking if need be, and become totally accepting of his way of life as it relates to me and his future male partner. Just so you know, I'm not the only one who has made sacrifices and changes. My husband has gone through a lot in just accepting who he really is and in dealing with me. When he finds his true male love, that man will be going through some changes, too, as will My husband and I. We will ALL have to work together to make our triad a loving and lasting relationship.

Any relationship takes a lot of effort to make a go of it, but you won't know you can do it—until you do it. There were many, many times when I felt my husband was more concerned about pursuing his male love life than in keeping our relationship alive and loving. When I was finally able to put my feelings into words, I talked to my special man, my husband. I think that talking about our feelings has been THE most important factor in getting us as far as we are now. I'm not a saint (just ask my husband) by any stretch of the imagination, but I also couldn't be as far along in this new relationship without a LOT of prayer and without the love and support of some of my family members (the others I have not told yet) and of a lot of friends.

If I would ever tell my husband that he could only have one partner or the other, he would not be happy, I would not be happy, and our relationship would die. Besides, because of his sexual orientation, I do not have the right nor the inclination to tell him that. I don't want our relationship to die. By the very definition of a bisexual, he needs both a male and a female for fulfillment. His love for a man in no way lessens his love for me. In fact, over the past couple of weeks, it has grown. I can FEEL it in my heart.

You know, the "ole gut feeling"?? Well, the past couple of times when my husband has brought the same man home either just to visit, or whatever, I have been "OK" with it. My stomach hasn't been in constant turmoil. In fact, I've been downright accepting of it. I visit with him, eat meals with him, and when my husband needs private time with him, I'm still OK. I don't feel totally comfortable in joining them when they are in the pool or on the patio. We talked about this, and now my husband has been making the effort to invite me. He is one wonderful guy!!! I've even asked him to give his man a hug in front of me, although his man is not totally comfortable with that yet. If I never see them hug or kiss, I'll never get used to it, and I want to get used to it. My husband and I hug and kiss in front of him, so why not the other way around? I am finally realizing that just because my husband hugs and kisses a man does not mean he loves me any less. After all he is a bisexual and has enough love for both of us. I know everyone is used to seeing a man and woman together in public, but I want to get used to seeing my husband and his man together, if not in public yet, at least now in our home. My husband should have as much freedom with him as he has with me.

I assure you, I am being very realistic about this new venture. I am in it with open eyes, an open heart, and open arms. This venture has not always been easy, has not always been what I thought I wanted, but it has definitely always been exciting and challenging!!!

If any of you would like me to answer specific questions, I will do my best. Just write to my husband, and he will see to it that I get your message.

Take care, and may God bless you and give you courage to live your lives to the utmost.

From: Mike

Thank you and thank your wife for sharing your story with us.

For those who would say it cannot be done, or SHOULD not be done . . . please just relax and let these people find their own path to love and intimacy, just as you must find your own.

It seems clear that there is no deception, no denial on your part. These are adults making fully informed decisions. No decision is without risk. These folks, like my wife and I, are taking risks every day to live authentically, going against the social grain with dignity, respect, and love for one another. I know there are many more like us who are silent because they don't want to spend their energy defending themselves against the judgment of others.

Each of us must follow our inner wisdom about these things. Let us honor each other on this most difficult journey.

From: Melissa

My husband shared an insight with me that came from his counselor, and it has really helped me deal with accepting that, at present, he might like his life alone better than his former life with me. He doesn't say that he has never loved me, in fact, he says that he still loves me, but he knows that he needs to be apart from me. Here is the insight. (Forgive me, those of you who have studied a lot of psychology. I'm sure this is old stuff to you, but to me, it was so helpful.)

The counselor explained to my husband that the reason he is enjoying himself so much in his new house, even though he has to cook for himself, the bed is cold at night, there's no one to sit and cuddle with in front of the TV, etc., etc., etc., is because he never has experienced the second instance of "individuation" up to this point in his life. There are two stages of learning how to be an independent person, one who is in the world, in a family, but still psychologically separate from those who are significant. The first step toward individuation is taken when the young toddler realizes that he is not his mommy. The second usually comes in adolescence when, through making choices different than one's parents, a teen asserts independence and realizes the power of being who he/she really is. Often this is a step the whole family notices as the teen rebels. Sometimes the change is more subtle, as the teen makes his own choices about which college to go to, how to spend his own money from his first job, etc. But, the "normal" pattern is for individuals to take a big step toward individuation during the teen years or early twenties.

Well, my dear spouse, who was having attractions toward (horrors!) other boys when he was in junior high school, and who was unable to change the pattern in his teen years (even though he secretly went to a psychiatrist) has always had to act in a way which to him was not "normal" but which was a way that others expected him to act. He could not rebel against the expected behaviors because the way he really wanted to act was considered "monstrous" in the Christian evangelical world he was living in. He could not/did not individuate. For many years, he has not known the freedom of being a REAL HUSBAND.

So, now, in his 55th year, he must go through the sometimes adolescent behavior of stepping over boundaries, saying hurtful things just to see what they sound like coming out of his mouth, spending money a bit carelessly, and seeking the friends and lovers he wants. This is the way he will finally find himself, and will probably lose me. But finding himself is so important. Imagine not being truly yourself during your whole life!!!! Years ago, my husband and I bought three Hummel figurines in Germany. One of them is a wistful boy, about 10 or 11, looking over his shoulder. The other two are boy musicians, one playing the accordion and the other the string bass. The energy and musicianship and harmony of these two are evident to even the most casual observer. For years I have grouped the two musicians together on the shelf, and set the wistful boy to the side, glancing backward at the other two, uninvited and unwelcome in the song.

As I dusted the figurines last week, it occurred to me that my husband has always been the little boy apart. And that maybe, just maybe, now he'll have an opportunity to join the orchestra, learn the melody, and be able to live the rest of his life with a light heart. This thought makes me happy, even joyful, in spite of the unwelcome changes in my own life. When I sense him pulling further and further away, I need to listen hard for the song he is learning to sing. It's a wonderful melody, one the universe has been waiting a long time to hear.

GOD MADE HIM THAT WAY, SENT HIM MY WAY, SO I COULD FIND MY WAY

My life began with this man 24 years ago at the tender age 14. This hand-some young man sat behind me in the movie theater and eventually was sit-ting by me giving me my first kiss. I dreamed about him that night and knew I wanted to feel this way forever. I was having trouble believing he actually wanted to see me again. My only problem was convincing my parents to al-low another meeting. They gave permission to invite him to Sunday dinner and I was thrilled.

The rest of our dating relationship was pretty much a struggle as my fa-ther did not approve of his long hair. He was convinced there could be no good in a boy with long hair and I found myself standing up to my father for the first time in my life. I knew my father was wrong about this boy. He could not convince me differently, for I was in love, not blindly but with my eyes wide open. I soon began to realize that my father could certainly use some of my boyfriend's tenderness. This was a milestone in my life. The one we all go through the day I realized my parents weren't God. The day I realized they didn't know it all, and that I was a separate person from them no longer allowing them to think for me and make my decisions for me.

When I was 16 my father took his belt to me for the last time. He whipped me like I was some animal with tough skin that had to be hit with all his force for me to be able to feel the pain he was trying to inflict on me that day. The beating was for something I'd seen him do himself all my life. I smoked a cigarette. I lost a lot of respect for my father that day and replaced it with the deepest respect for my now husband. You see, I received these beatings on a regular basis all my life but I never told any one, as I thought I was so bad and deserved them and so would anyone I told. Not true, I later found out. My boyfriend knew something was wrong when he saw me and insisted I tell him what happened. When I finally relented, knowing this would be the end, that he also would think I was a bad person and would never want to have anything to do with me again. I was blown away by his response. He told me my father was so wrong and that I should never be hit by anyone. He held me and wiped away my tears and told me all the wonderful things I needed to hear to mend a broken heart and spirit.

I started making plans to leave home by attending a college away from home and that began my independence from my parents. However, I wasn't ready to be dependent on myself because I had little self-confidence, so I depended on the one person I felt I could trust. This man was my world, my ticket to freedom (a freedom I wanted but was terrified of) but you know, he didn't allow me to depend on him, instead he told me all my wonderful qualities and taught me to love and depend on myself. How unselfish. He could have had a puppet on a string but he loved me enough to give me the tools I needed to love myself. That's when I knew for sure I would marry this man.

So we married 6 years after our first encounter. We moved to a different state and he started school as I worked 3 and 4 jobs at a time just to stay afloat. We didn't have much but we were so happy. To make a long story short for the next 7 years we worked very hard to reach our goal of buying a house, for we knew we wanted that before children so we would have our own place and yard for our future children to grow and play. After reaching our first goal we went to work on our 2nd goal (our first child), and I became pregnant after a few months in our new house. We were delighted. I gave birth to the most beautiful 5 pound baby girl I had ever seen and my husband cried tears of joy as he gently held that tiny little girl to his face and thanked God for such a blessing. He loved that child as much as I did and wanted nothing but the best we could give her. He walked the floor with her when she had colic, he kissed her "owies," read her stories, and hugged and kissed her and told her he loved her many times daily. But the greatest thing: he allowed her to dominate my time and attention, never complaining that he no longer came first in my life. Believe me, I went overboard. I wanted things to be so perfect for her I nearly forgot he existed. I know that hurt him, but you know what, he kept right on loving me anyway. He not only took the back seat, that man was in the trunk.

Five years after our firstborn I gave birth to another beautiful baby girl. Again my husband cried overwhelming tears of joy as the little baby girl reached up and grabbed his finger with a grip that shocked him. They looked into each other's eyes and were bonded for life. Again he was very much a part of the girls lives, always willing to lend a helping hand—only to hear them rebel and say, "no mommy do it." How that must have hurt but he loved them anyway and continued to help.

Well I wasn't doing well physically after the birth of our 2nd child. I had a curve in my spine that was progressing after the birth of each child.

I was in a lot of pain. I did everything I could to try to end the pain. I started eliminating my physical activities. I went for physical therapy. I went to chiropractors. I had injections in my spine to try to block the pain and that turned out to be a very temporary fix to a major problem. I finally had to relent to take pain medication daily and that really got to where it didn't even touch my pain. My husband had to do it all: care for our 2 daughters, do the housework work full time and take care of his mother. It finally became apparent I would have to have the surgery. I had dreaded my whole life to keep from being a total invalid. It scared the hell out of both of us, but we had no choice. We both knew the risk of paralysis but we had to take it. There were no guarantees the surgery would even relieve my pain, but without it, I would be in a wheelchair within 5 years. We scheduled the surgery and made plans for my mother and sisters to take turns helping us with my care and that of our children.

Well the dreaded day arrived and I don't know who was the most frightened. When they came to take me to the OR my husband held my hand and trying to hold back the tears tried to assure me I was going to be OK. I was told he paced the floors the entire 10 hours it took the doctors to complete the surgery. His eyes were the first ones I saw when I woke up. He looked so tired and I hurt so bad I just wanted to die. I was unable to do anything for myself. It caused excruciating pain just to try to feed myself ice chips. I heard him tell my sister "God I wish I could take her place." From that moment I tried not show how much pain I was in and I felt so blessed to be loved that much.

For the next year all focus and attention was on me and the girls. Again, he was in the trunk. Loving, supporting, and encouraging me the whole time. Making sure our girls' needs were met. So we got past that and it did help my pain.

Exactly 2 years and 1 day after my surgery I gave birth to our one and only son and I've never seen a happier man. He told me he was very happy with his girls but that he felt he would be able to relate more to his son. That is when I realized that I had taken for granted the same feelings I had for our girls. How we each had so much to offer both genders and our love for them was unfailing—but something happened after this beautiful story that almost destroyed what I thought was the most loving home, 2nd to none.

All the while playing the good husband/father role, he had betrayed me. I found out by mistake while trying to learn our new computer that my husband was bisexual. I would sneak and read his mail of the affairs he had with men. I was crushed and I hated him for doing this to me. I talked to my friends before confronting him, looking for advice and guidance. They convinced me for my children's sake I should leave him. When I asked what will I tell my kids, I was advised to make him tell the kids. So I made my plans to divorce him before I confronted him so I would have all the power. How could he do this to me after all we'd been through? I was going to make him pay. He killed the love I had for him by betraying me. I was really hurting inside but I had to act normal. What he did was unforgivable and my friends all agreed. Then something happened that made me think differently. Our song came on the radio, BECAUSE YOU LOVED ME.

Thank God for that song. I now had a totally different picture of betrayal. What he did was minor compared to what I was about to do. How could I even think of allowing my friends to decide what was best for me? Then I asked myself, "What is bisexuality anyway? Does a person choose to be bisexual? Do they really betray anyone by acting on their need to be with their own kind?" I needed to find the answers to these questions before I did anything else. I chose to stop seeking advice from people that knew no more about it than I did.

I needed to find bisexuals to talk to, but where would I find one because apparently not many tell. Then it occurred to me to go to a BI site on the net and enter a chat room. I must say I wasn't impressed by the conversations, as I was lost. Then I started pulling up profiles of the people in the chat room seeking married men to communicate with by immediate messaging. I found and talked to several. They all told me the same thing and answered each of my questions the same. When I asked what is bisexuality they explained that to them it was a gift and a curse. That they were born with the desire and ability to love both sexes and actually needed both in their lives to feel complete. Even though my first question kind of answered my 2nd question, I wanted more detail so I asked it next. Does a person choose to be bisexual? The answers blew me away and left me feeling very guilty for what I was about to do to my husband. It absolutely is not a choice. Why would anyone choose to live hiding part of them from the world and the ones they love? Because they fear losing the people they love most—because they are so misunderstood. Most of us have suppressed and tried to deny it, even to ourselves, only to have it come back stronger than ever right when we think we are the happiest.

If we don't fulfill our needs and desires we go into deep depressions that we can't explain to those seeing us hurt and not knowing why. If we do act on our need to be with another person like us, we must deal with overwhelming guilt, so we are damned if we do and damned if we don't.

NO I DON'T KNOW ANYONE THAT WOULD CHOOSE TO
LIVE LIFE THAT WAY.

Now I'm beginning to see just a little of the pain my husband bore in silence while nurturing others' pain. Now my final question to the guys was:
"Do they really love their wives or just hide behind them so the world won't
know?" Most bisexuals love their spouses with a passion few hetero husbands can offer. They shower them with unconditional love, knowing their
spouses could trample on that love if they knew the hidden them. They will
go to any extreme to protect them from knowing, as they realize their
spouses will hurt deeply because they don't understand, and they fear what
the world will think. They know their spouses will feel betrayed, even
though the truth is the bisexual has betrayed no one but his or her self by not
being able to share all of themselves with their mate.

I left this chat feeling so ashamed that for years I never saw my husband's
inner pain because he did such a great job protecting me. I suddenly realized
his bisexuality is part of what made him what I needed. I realized I loved everything about him and if I could change anything about him I wouldn't
change a thing. I had spent our lives together singing his praises. What's
changed? Except now I have the opportunity to help take some of his inner
pain away and assure him love of the purest unconditional form. Now all I
wanted to do was replace those years of pain with love.

I'm so glad I heard that song that day, as now my husband and I enjoy a
love few people have the privilege of knowing. We look forward to each
day and can no longer get enough of each other. We will forever be grateful
for what we have found in each other. Yes, he's still bisexual and still needs
to share a part of himself with his own kind and that's OK BI me. He gives
me all I need. I owe the same to him. Because:

GOD MADE HIM THAT WAY
SENT HIM MY WAY
SO I COULD FIND MY WAY
THANK YOU GOD

From: James

My wife wrote this response on wives' feelings . . . I thought it might be
interesting for us and/or our wives.

Re: What a Wife Feels

My husband showed me this post of yours—I thought it was a lovely,
compassionate, thoughtful portrayal of a wife's needs. There were two

things I wanted to add, from my experiences with the spouse support list, in answer to the "Why can't some wives accept . . . ." question.

1. It seems that for many couples, the marital relationship DOES change when the husband comes out. For example, many men seem to stop having sex with their wives. Often, this coincides with defining oneself as "gay, not BI." It seems a central issue for wives is—If my husband desires men, does that mean he DOESN'T desire me, or desires me less than I would want? You've got to remember that there are two people here with a need for intimate/romantic/sexual relations with a man—the husband AND the wife—her sexual identity is just as important as his . . . so I think many wives are not content with a sexless or romance-less marriage (if that's what is being offered).

2. Many straight spouses (I'm not one of them) would turn the question around, saying —- "Why SHOULD a spouse accept infidelity with a man, if they wouldn't accept it with a woman? How does the gender of the partner make a difference?"

It seems to me that for spouses to renegotiate a more "open" marriage contract which allows some homosexual expression on the husband's part, the following issues are important to work out:

a. Trust/Honesty—Having an open marriage shouldn't mean not being able to trust that your spouse will stick to whatever you agree to, worrying that things are being hidden from you, etc. The wife needs to know why she should believe that she can trust the husband again, if there has been betrayal or deception.

b. Mutuality/Equality of Needs—Spouses need to know that they aren't just "giving in" to WHATEVER their spouse wants, that they are "doormats" who will do anything to maintain the relationship, whatever the cost to them. In other words, they need to know that BOTH spouses take each other's needs and the needs of the relationship seriously, that the husband is also willing to make sacrifices and compromises.

c. Sex/Romance/Love in the Marriage—Does the gay/BI husband offer the wife a satisfying sexual and romantic relationship? Or is he asking her to accept having something else—perhaps a compassionate and domestic relationship which is loving but not sexual/romantic? If so, is she happy to live with that? (Don't forget, that is exactly what he ISN'T willing to live with and is why he wants to be with men!)

d. Understanding of why the need for homosexual expression is different than other "needs" which can't be satisfied by the marriage—Most people in our culture accept that everyone has "needs" and "wants" which can't be satisfied by one's spouse. We see it as an expression of love and commitment—and morality—to give up satisfying those needs to be married. It seems to me a wife needs an answer to the question: Why is this different?

How is this different from my wanting to screw the guy next door, or a husband wanting to screw around with different women? Why should I treat it differently? Coming to understand this difference is crucial, I think, for the wife not to feel "abused" in the relationship.

Immediately after learning the fact of her husband's physical involvement with another man/men :

1. The wife needs time. She has to come to terms with a whole raft of challenging new "facts" in her life. She has to learn how to cope all over again with her husband in all his moods/needs. How should she treat him in bed ? Is she repulsive to him sexually ? Is she repulsed by the thought that he has had sexual contact with another man/men? Is he or is she at any risk at all from AIDS or other disease? Should she start insisting that he wear protection when they have sex? Has she not satisfied him sexually/otherwise? For how long? Was he always like that (i.e. did he enter marriage like that)? What would/will the family think? What would/will friends think? Especially if they are like her and are homophobic etc.

2. The wife needs understanding. She is suddenly adrift (feeling alone) on a whole new sea where there are no landmarks. She feels desperate. And to whom can she go to? It is all a dark secret and those she talks to may be homophobic, even if she isn't.

3. The wife needs love. Especially from her husband—warm understanding love which lays its life down for her. Kind and gentle love which doesn't demand answers. A sexual love which cherishes and enfolds her—and is willing to give her time in that area if necessary. But of course this is also the time the husband is feeling different : he at long last has unburdened himself of a huge weight of secrecy—he feels free—perhaps almost exultant in his freedom—totally at odds with the weight his wife now feels on her shoulders. So while he can try to be very understanding of her, it is not easy because he too is undergoing a change of outlook/direction. It is perhaps true to say that the knowledge by his wife (whether he told her or whether she discovered it) marks a huge turning point for him. He is unclosed to a person who has meant so much to him. He feels a new man.

4. The wife needs good advice. Over the months it has become so apparent from the postings that those who have gone through this experience say, again and again, that there needs to be some counseling/helping by others who have weathered this particular storm. There is the list for spouses, but often wives are not computer-active, like the men. Help via sympathetic and understanding others (especially wives) seems essential. At stake is the future of the marriage.

Please hear me—I am not suggesting that the above thoughts cover all cases or all aspects—only that there are some considerations that occur to me, a mere male, as to why it is that some wives find it difficult to live with the situation once they have learned of their husbands sexual involvement with another man. All thoughts are offered IMHO!! Would any wife like to correct me or add to these thoughts?

Please also note I am not offering any ideas as to whether it is good or bad to come out to one's wife. IMHO that depends entirely on the two people concerned and the situation—there is no blanket answer.

OUTED YOURSELF TO PARENTS

From: Brandon

Orrin wrote: > *. . . I guess this e-mail is directed toward those of you who have outed yourselves to one or both of your parents. Any advice? Just blurt it out and get it over with? Give them the whole background about hiding from the truth all of my life first and lead her into it slowly? . . .<*

I came out to my mother 6 years ago and things have not gone well. Before I give you all the bad details, let me assure you that life has gone on and I am OK with the fact that my mother, father and 4 siblings have disowned both my wife and myself.

I hadn't planned on coming out to my birth family, as they all live in a small rural community in Minnesota and I have lived away from them for going on 41 years—at that time. Only time that I would see any of them is when I would pack up my wife and kids and drive or fly back "HOME" to be with the "FAMILY." Mother and Dad did visit us at our home (I've lived in 7 States) on 3 occasions in these 41 years and Mother did come and visit us once by herself on one of the occasions that Dad kicked her out of their home. One sister has visited in our home twice. Another sister—once. Two brothers—never. On the second time that Dad kicked Mother out of the house, my siblings decided to send Mother to stay with my wife and I for a while—for "things to cool off between them." Mother arrived in at our home all depressed and pissed off at the world. I was in the hospital having back surgery. When she got off the airplane my wife picked her up and brought her immediately to the hospital to find a room full of my gay friends and my partner all having a wonderful time. At this time in my life my wife and all my kids knew I was gay and we had discussed my coming out to mother. It was decided that it was the right thing to do as "how do I explain my man partner to Mother? How I explain my absence from the house on Tuesday and Thursday nights? How could I ever ask my kids to lie to their grandmother, or my wife to lie?

As soon as I got out of the hospital, my wife and I took mother aside and I "CAME OUT." She was shocked and visibly shaken. She did ask some questions and I was truthful and direct in my answers and tried to be as gentle as possible without being too graphic. Some of her questions (such as AIDS) I answered very poorly and got way too technical but assured her that I only practice safe sex until I met my partner and that he an I were in a monogamous relationship. My wife was a great support and very positive and assured her that all was well with her. Yes, I most definitely came on too strongly at times on the gay issues and some of the growing up problems that I experienced because of being gay. Mother stayed with us for a month and during that time we discussed the issues and she eventually met my partner. My wife, Mother, my partner and I even went out to dinner a couple of times during that month and my partner was even to the house for a family dinner. By now I had called and told all my siblings about me being gay and about coming out to mother—I got only minor (my guess at the time) reactions from them over the phone. When Mother left our home, we knew that all was not well with her on my being gay or her assumptions on my relationship with my wife.

When she hit the tarmac when she got home to Chicago (where my youngest sister lives) all hell broke loose. I immediately received a damming phone call from my youngest sister where I was called all the names in the book. I was told that I was never to speak to any of my family again and that I had destroyed an old woman (She was 71 at the time). I was going to burn in hell!! This she followed up with a damming letter. I did try to call Mother (and Dad) three times after that and I was shut out and Mother hung up the phone. My wife has tried calling and gotten mostly a deaf ear. I have written a couple of letters to all and have received nothing in return. Even though we sent Christmas cards (first couple of years)—we have received none in return.

The rest of the story: My wife loves me and we have an excellent and thriving relationship. My three kids and I have a good relationship and we are open and honest with each other. I have a loving male partner that supports me and my GAY needs (emotional, spiritual and physical need to be an integral part of a male) are getting met. I have many wonderful and loving gay and straight friends that I am out to and they remain a beautiful part of who I am. I have made my peace with God and know that I am loved for whom I was created to be. My birth family has NOT been a significant emotional, spiritual, or physical part of who I have been for 40 years now. I am not responsible for any of their happiness nor do I take any blame or responsibility for their problems. My father is now nearing death—but even in this I have made my amends. And the truth is—I have always known about the deep homophobia within my birth family and I understand that it is their problem. I grew up understanding that "if the truth were ever revealed about my homosexuality"—I'd be disowned and cast out of their lives forever—and it is for this reason that it took me 38 years before I accepted my true nature and another 10 years to come out to my beautiful, loving wife and children. I love and respect myself and my integrity too much to turn the clock back and I refuse to ever live my life as a lie to anyone—especially my own mother. I do remain open to the phone call, card, or letter from any of my birth family and when such arrives I will be as gentle and as loving a son and brother that I can be.

Now, this is probably much more than you were asking—but as you see things don't always go as we would wish or pray them to be. Do have "Loving Someone Gay" to give to her and (depending on your relationship with your wife) it might be advantageous to have her there also. My heart goes out to you and I hope that you will find love and support from your mother. Be advised that your love for yourself and your integrity are of the greatest importance and without these nothing else can survive!! Please let me know how your OUTING goes—I care.

From: Orrin

All I can say is "Wow!" I thought I was reading my own story here. Incredible! I joined the military and married at 18. I also knew the truth about myself but hoped I would change. I went to Officers Training School and am now retired. I have stayed in, but knew that if I were ever faced with having an airman tell me "I'm gay," I'd have to go against AF policy and NOT process him for a discharge.

Still married to the same woman. I also thought suicide was the only way out. But instead, I told her this last February. It's been hell ever since. She's accused me of lying to her, ruining her life, etc . . . It's been tough. I'm absolutely in love with her and don't want to spend a day without being married. She says she wishes she never married me. Because of my revealing this to her, we moved so she could be closer to her family. No one else knows except her mother. She hadn't intended to tell her, but her mom guessed. Smart woman. We have three great preteen kids and one on the way. I've been scrambling to get back into the closet and pretend this never happened, but it's always there in the back of our minds. Anyway, I didn't intend to write all this, just wanted to say "hi" and that I was touched by your post.

BUCK'S COMING-OUT LETTER

From: Buck

Gosh, what an overwhelming response of interest in "the Letter" to my parents. So, I thought I would just post it for all. . . . Would be happy to comment privately to those who have questions. As background, my parents and I are not close; we live on opposite sides of the country. They have had a rocky marriage themselves and have lived separately for nearly 22 years (though never divorced), I grew up in a abusive household (between them, not the kids), alcohol, and my fathers numerous "not so secret" affairs, and never went home after I left for college. My parents are in their 70s and part of my reason in sharing this info with them was to try to begin the reconciliation and closure process to years of withdrawal. This letter was written four months after I moved out of my household, and my mother, being the good gossip that she is, just wouldn't let up until she could figure it all out. Hope it helps:

Dear Mom and Dad (in two separate envelopes of course),

I have sensed an increase in your level of concern regarding my well being and wanted to go ahead and share with you some information regarding my divorce and the future. I had hoped to make a trip to see you in the early fall to share this information with you face to face, but due to my schedule, that doesn't look like it will happen, so I decided to write this letter instead. Rest assured, everything will be fine, things are a bit strained at the moment, but your grandkids are doing well and I have never felt better.

I know the news that I am getting divorced came as a shock to you, but perhaps that is only because we have kept our personal issues to ourselves. In fact, we had both been seeing a psychologist for more than a year prior to my moving out of the house to help us understand and attempt to reconcile our relationship. Over the past two years, my wife has been struggling with clinical depression, which was so severe that it required antidepressant medication for a period of time during treatment. During that period, we began joint counseling to learn techniques to help her with her depression. At the same time, I went for individual counseling to resolve issues that were uncovered during our joint sessions. Specifically, I suffered from anxiety that caused me to display a behavior that was very withdrawn and isolated from my wife and the kids. This was a behavior that had invaded our relationship and was a major cause of my wife's depression. This, I have accepted, was the result of consciously and unconsciously denying feelings I had deep inside of me. Over the years, I have attempted to live the "stereotype" of what I believed was the "perfect husband/father/son," knowing within me that I was not being true to myself. I had built a shell that insulated me from my feelings. That shell damaged me and hurt my relationships with those close to me. This slowly eroded my mental health until I was at the point of breaking down myself.

Through the counseling process, I learned to accept that I am homosexual. It is a fact that I have known since I was a teenager, but kept deeply buried within me. It was not an easy process to finally admit to myself that I was gay. It has taken me a long time to build the confidence and self esteem to know that I am still the same good person I always was and that there is nothing I should feel guilty or ashamed about and nothing to hide. I am now comfortable in accepting the fact that I am gay and have worked hard to discover how I can live honestly with myself and acknowledge the impact it has on my family. My wife and I worked hard with the help of our therapist to try to reconcile my homosexuality with our marriage. After a lot of pain and tears, we admitted that my need to be emotionally stable and live true to myself was not compatible with what we both felt our marriage should be. Divorcing and pursuing our lives independently was the healthiest solution for us. It was a very difficult decision to make and you must accept that we explored many compromises, options, and alternatives along the way.

The kids were told that I was gay when I moved out of the house. I felt it was important to know that they were in no way to blame for the fact that I was no longer living with their mother. I'm not sure that they really understand what being "gay" really means, but they at least have the information when they are ready to understand it more. They have been to see our therapist to ask questions about the divorce and sexuality and he is comfortable that they are reacting in a healthy manner.

So, now we move on. I still struggle with how to allow myself to grow with my new acceptance. As I'm sure you're aware, there is still a lot of bigotry and prejudice in the world against gay men and women. This is of course a great concern because it not only effects me, but carries over to my wife and the kids as well. I am aware of that, and have decided that as I learn more about what it means to live as a gay man that I will become more confident in confronting these biases directly. I do not intend to hide my evolving lifestyle from my children and can only hope to give them a good role model that breaks down unfair stereotypes and the strength to confront prejudice should it present itself to them. They know that I will always be their dad who loves them.

I hope that I can depend on you for support as well. Being homosexual is nothing that you caused. It is the way that God made me and I am a good person; the same good person I was before you knew this information about me.

This information is nothing you need to hide. It is who I am. I have told my sisters everything I have told you in this letter. If you want to talk about it in more detail, I'd like to spend the time. I also have several books on related topics that I would be happy to share with you. I'd have preferred to have had this conversation in person or even on the phone, but frankly, I finally decided that this was the best way for me to share my feelings in a clear, concise fashion. After talking with you and hearing from my eldest sister how concerned you both have been, I felt that sharing this information with you now was important. I didn't want to watch you both worry and project negatively without having the accurate information.

Rest comfortably, we will all survive. The kids will spend every other weekend and 10 weeks in the summer with me. My wife and I have gone through divorce mediation and have successfully reached an agreement on the divorce settlement, which will be presented to the court. (The divorce was finalized with very little public animosity.) My wife has found a smaller house and will close on it soon. We are still trying to sell the big house and have had lots of interest, but no contracts. My job keeps me busy and I am participating in a couple of support groups (thank God for my ability to correspond with similar men on the Internet and I have support through a group of fathers called Gaydads) and have met several new friends. And life goes on.

Hope this letter finds you well, alleviates some fears, clarifies some issues and finds your acceptance of the facts.

From: Brandon

I also live 2000 miles away from my parents. I came out to my parents and siblings 4 1/2 years ago and they all disowned both my wife and myself. About a year after his happened I wrote this letter to them—here it is to also share:

Dear Mother and Dad,

This is the hardest letter I have ever written. Throughout my whole life I have loved both of you unconditionally and I have always known that your love was reciprocated. Over a year ago, I shocked you. I told you that "I'm gay." I did not tell you this because I'm sick or because I wanted to hurt you. Rather, I told you because the stress of my silence was tearing me apart and I respect the two of you too much to continue to hide the truth. When you, Mother, came to spend time with us, it was the first time in my life that I would have had to deliberately lie to you, and I just could not bear that dishonor. I would have also had to ask my wife and my children to lie and that was unthinkable! The only choice was to be open and honest and offer to you all the support and education necessary so you could understand that I am the same son that you have always loved.

This has been a very difficult issue for me to resolve. I have been tortured with this inner conflict since I was 4 or 5 years old when I first understood that I was "different." (Yes, that is 50 years of torture.) I learned early to hide my true feelings and needs. As a matter of fact, I will probably spend the rest of my life coming to terms with my homosexuality. But since I am gay, I have over the years accepted that fact. I am even learned to be proud of who I am and love myself. I have made amends with my wife and the three beautiful children that God has blessed us with. We are and, God willing, continue to be a mutually supportive, loving family and each member within has grown to accept me for who I really am and not who they would like to believe I am.

Overcoming my fear of telling you, and my brothers and sisters, was very difficult. Considering society's propensity toward homophobia, this was a most heart wrenching decision. Indeed, I would not have been able to tell you if I did not have an incredibly loving wife, a supportive partner, accepting children, and a group of gay and straight friends here in the city and throughout the country. I hope eventually to share parts of my life that were previously hidden from you yet were a very real part of my growing up years.

It's not a decision to be gay, it's a revelation. I just am. No amount of prayer (and believe me I tried) will change who I have always been. No amount of counseling can "deprogram" me. No one can be recruited into homosexuality—either you are or you are not. I spent 5 years in intensive counseling after years of anguish only to learn to accept the truth that I am me and there are just some things that can not be changed—such as one's sexual orientation. You should also be assured that homosexuality is not a disease, but a basic, God-given personality trait that cannot be changed. If you think about it rationally, no one would choose to be gay. Who would want to risk the rejection of loved ones, family, and friends; condemnation by most organized religions; and potential exposure to loss of one's career. None of these rejections has come to pass, with the exception of the loss of you two beautiful people within my life. The loss of my brothers and sisters also causes hurt. I miss you all very much.

So what is next? For me, I will keep living, I will keep loving my wife as I have for 35 years and my commitment to her well-being is secure. I will love and emotionally support my children and grandchildren. I will continue to live my life with dignity and pride. I will continue to be a caring, loving, compassionate person knowing that a major hurdle has been surmounted and a beautiful phase in my life based on honesty and openness is unfolding.

How my future life unfolds will also be determined by you and your acceptance. I love you both dearly and your loss deeply saddens me. I also feel your hurt. I do understand that this is an extremely difficult transition for you and will take lots of time for resolution. I will give you that time and all my help if you choose to accept that help. This has been a 50 year ordeal for me and I have learned a great deal of patience with this issue. If you would like literature to read, I would send all that is available.

Here is my suggestion for you. Please write or pick up the phone and call. Just tell me that you love me. You aren't being asked to approve—just learn and accept. Remember that only through dialogue can hurts and misunderstandings be resolved. I am anxious to resume sharing the joys and sorrows of life with you and you with us.

Here is what I hope you will not continue to do. Please do not continue to cut me out of your life. Do not continue to cut my wife and especially your beautiful grandchildren out of your life. You will hurt yourselves at least as much as you are hurting us. Don't lecture me. There is nothing you can say or do that will change the truth. Also please, do not blame yourselves. My sexual orientation is not either of your faults and indeed there is no fault at all.

No matter how this plays out, always remember that I love and need you both. We all need you.

Your Son, Brandon

Note: This letter didn't do any good, as to this day I have received no response from them—SAD

AN END TO DENIAL

From: Brown

My wife and I continue on this journey. More to the point, my own coming out process proceeds with my dear wife bearing the pain left in the wake. Not that I haven't experienced hurt, confusion, and pain. Everyone gets their share in this deal. And it's not over. But we have come to a watershed moment.

It is clear to both of us that we can't continue to look for some reasonable solution or accommodation to present itself to us. When the truth of my sexual involvement with men came to light, the emotions unleashed proved to be searing for both of us. I made a commitment then to expose myself as well as I could to my wife. I thought we both needed to hear what was going on with me. I also promised not to bed another man while we were attempting to come to terms or until we better understood what we were dealing with.

I quickly discovered that my answers to her questions were, more often than not, statements she really didn't want to hear. When I took a stance to not be so open (I felt I causing too much pain), she felt I was hiding things. Damned if I did and damned if I didn't. At times I had to step back and examine my own responses, because they were revealing things to me that had only been vague before. Did I really just say that? However, I have been determined to allow the truth to come to light.

My wife has made the connections. She tells me that I am in denial. After all that has happened over the last months, I am still not willing to fully accept that I am a gay man. While I have become more comfortable calling myself gay, she says I'm still not ready to face the facts. A few days ago she let me have the facts from her perspective. She wants to have a monogamous relationship with a straight man. This guy, her husband of over 21 years can no longer fill that bill. Any suggestions that she accept some sort of arrangement allowing me freedom to express my homosexual desires are abhorrent to her. She also feels that I should not have to deny myself intimate male contact. I have not been willing to promise never to have sex with a man again. As we on the list know, how could I?

Is my wife giving me tough love? Yes, to a point, but she is also looking at her own personal survival. I can only agree with her. Forcing anything that causes more damage is not my intention. Even though we had resumed our love life, the pressures she has been experiencing are inhibiting to her. In so many words, increasingly painful as we continue on. So, our love life and marriage are ending starting now.

I understand why we can't go on. But I'm sad nonetheless. In mourning for my marriage, feeling down about the harm I've caused my wife and children, and wondering what shape my life will take in the future. Somehow my wife and I have been able to act with respect and love toward each other. There have been rough times, no question about that. I hope we can continue to care for each other as we break us apart. For us there can be no having my cake and eating it too.

I'm becoming the gay man God may have intended me to be all along. If there could have been some other way to reach this place, I would gladly have paid whatever price. My wife says, "It's better that we experience more of this as the result of the truth. Nothing hurts like the lies and deceit." The list has reinforced the idea that the truth is the better way. I pray I will reach the peace that some of you have achieved.

From: German

Your letter struck a strong chord with me, and I want you to know that I deeply admire your courage, as well as your wife's. You may be further down the path, but your situation seems to echo mine in a number of ways.

For some of our spouses, their deep-seated personal needs (and the fear/anger that emerges at the prospect of those needs not being met) bang up against the new-found expression of our OWN very valid needs and desires for deep connection to other men. The picture that comes to my mind is one of a rising stream that has suddenly become too deep and swift for either partner to safely cross. At some point, the risk that one or both individuals will be swept away and lost in the act of trying to remain a "couple" is just too high.

I began the process of coming out to myself nearly two years ago and (for better or worse) my wife [came aboard] some ten months later. (Yes, there's been a LOT of good solo and couples counseling involved; my only regret is that I didn't buy stock in the company!!)

Early on, in the name of consoling her, I made a number of promises that I now realize I may not be able to keep. Vowing to be monogamous was relatively easy when my closest confidants (online) were in far- off places like Flagstaff or Providence or even Oxford. But as time has gone on, I've found that the level of emotional sharing we can do here—for which I will be eternally grateful to Bill Gates & Co— is simply NOT enough all by itself, at least not for me. I've tried to pursue companionship via some "safe" avenues that my wife is comfortable with, e.g., by pursuing an "over the back hedge" friendship with a very open and loving (and yes, ATTRACTIVE!) gay couple who moved into our neighborhood last year, and even though I'm not all that religious, by joining a central Lutheran church where my wife & I were married 11 years ago. Ironically, it transitioned into an "open and affirming" congregation that welcomes gay and lesbian couples. But somehow, in both of those settings, I have had the feeling (perhaps coming as much from ME as anyone else outside) that I will "always" be seen as a Married Man, one thus requiring a certain buffer of emotional/personal space between me and what I crave so much from another man. There is one man—a lonely and gentle guy an hour's drive south of me whose wife is in extremely poor health—who has played a very special role in my life during this period, but I just learned he is moving back to Atlanta in the near future. What's more, I've come to realize that I reached out to him more-so because I regarded him as SAFE than because he was emotionally/physically attractive to me and thus truly a good match for my needs. . . .

So after a year of basically denying myself any meaningful face-to-face contact with men like us, I've just recently begun to reach out again. For lack of a better way, I've done it through a local chat-room. Assuming things work out I'll be having a glass of wine with a male friend tomorrow evening and coffee with another guy later in the week. (And if both are administered in the correct doses I'll come out on an even keel!) Even if things don't click with either of them, I don't see myself crawling back into my shell. What's scarier though is what if things DO click? Will I find myself content with the emotional connection that comes with two kindred spirits entering into "friendship," or am I taking that first step onto a steep and slippery slope that will bring me to the end of MY road of denial? If any of the other guys out there have had experiences with this dilemma, I would really appreciate hearing from them.

To some degree I suspect many of us are here because we hope to avoid the pain of separation that you are going through, but I think we need to be careful not to conclude that the outcome you are facing is necessarily the wrong one. For some of us (together with our particular partners), it may be the only viable way. I'm still fighting my internal battle, but I want you to know I will keep your letter and think about it more deeply as I try to find the answer that's right for me. My hope is that by sharing this you will glean some sense of solidarity and support from the fact that I think I understand at least *some* of what you are feeling, and that I admire your courage in taking these difficult steps.

COMING OUT (FRIDAY NIGHT)

From: Gripp

Thank you, thank you, thank you, for your letter and for spending so much time recalling your own experience. I appreciate every sentence. I want to respond to your comments so that I may reinforce them in me and practice what I may be saying and doing beginning this weekend.

Danny wrote: >*Please understand that is not the end of the world. If we were to take a poll of the 200 somewhat guys on this list, I would venture to bet that 75% of them will say that the difficulty and problems they expected when they came out did not materialize. You cannot predict how she will react.*<

This is an interesting comment, and I HAVE felt as if telling her is going to change the world beginning then (for the better). I do expect to feel some relief; I am also preparing to handle with her all the difficulties that she may be having that she shares with me. I have Gochros and Buxton with me and I am rereading and underlining pertinent issues. I am concerned about my wife's emotional health and am prepared to offer her the support that she has offered me this last year, without knowing why I was depressed and suicidal. I know that she is level-headed and I think her reaction will not be as bad as my worst imaginations. Thanks for pointing out that her reaction may not be as bad as my worst fears.

>*Based on my experience in coming out (I too came out voluntarily), I might suggest a few things for you. The first is to arrange therapeutic help*

for her. She will need someone to talk to about it besides you. The more she is able to talk, the less stress will be bottled up inside her.<

We have been working on improving our marriage. I have initiated it. Just yesterday we were in therapy together. The therapist asked her how I had been since having quit drinking (1 1/2 years ago). She made wonderful, positive comments about how I was now THERE, PRESENT, for her and the children, while before I was distant and withdrawn. She continued to say how she thought she had something to look forward to after the kids left home. I will continue working the Harvill exercises with her right up to disclosure, then, when appropriate, afterward also.

At any rate, we have a therapist already on board that we can see together and individually. Additionally, the president of PFLAG is a personal friend of my wife's (mine also). I have been confiding in her, and she is ready to talk to my wife about the "gift" of my sexuality. There are two other gay, previously married, but now divorced, friends with whom she may talk. They are ready for her to call. They are prepared for us to call and have even told me that if my wife wants, we may come spend a weekend with them. They have experience working with couples in this process, as I'm sure you know. Many other of my Internet brothers have offered their telephone numbers for either of us to call, to talk either with them or their wife. I have saved those numbers in a readily available place. I am committed to my wife as I know she is to me, and we are also committed to the institution of marriage. Therefore, it is in our best interest to work on this fine marriage after disclosure to help it continue to grow when I am able to be totally honest with her. (Pray for me that I can be honest. I have 50 years of experience hiding and withholding information. It will be a new experience for me.)

>Do not tell her any more than she need know—at least in the beginning. She can choke on too much information.<

Thank you, I will start by telling her about my "gift" of sexuality, and that I have been afraid to let my gift operate as God has intended, that I want to be true to me within our marriage. I will elaborate as seems appropriate based on her physical cues and responses. From then on I will let things happen and listen to her comments, answer her questions, with the caveat that she should be sure that she wants to know the answer to the question that she may be asking. I want to be able to explain me as much as possible without being hurtful.

>Don't attempt to cleanse yourself by "confessing" m2m experiences (if you've had any) or fantasies (and with whom). Don't forget, you are dumping a ton of bricks on her head by coming out. I did the above and it only came back to hit me in the face.<

This is a good one. Thank you. I know that just looking forward to confessing has already had a cleansing, therapeutic effect on me. I must be careful here, judicious, tell the truth but only what is necessary for an initial disclosure. I have been "confessing" to my therapist, psychiatrist, the PFLAG president, and my Lambda AA group. So I should not have to unload the entire shebang at once just for my healing. I will try to remember to be gentle, loving, and cautious. (Comments?)

>*When you come out, she will get hung up on the sexual angle. Try not to lie but rather to steer her away to another facet of your preference—like the emotional connection you need with another male—not necessarily sexual.*<

I imagine that she will almost immediately focus on my boyfriend, my bearcub who has recently moved away. So I am almost positive that I will have to deal with her immediately guessing that my boyfriend and I have been physically and emotionally intimate. She knows him as my best friend after sobriety, when I have NEVER had a good male friend before, when I was drinking. (I was homophobic, afraid to acknowledge gay and bisexual people for fear that I might be disclosed.) My daughter does not like my boyfriend and is very cool but not rude to him. Our wives have probably already had discussions about my male lover and his relationship to me. I am glad that I am not now in a relationship with anyone. It may make it a bit different, easier. Right now I am still grieving over his loss and am not open to another relationship. However, I will NOT tell my wife that I will not ever have another relationship with another man. I can't make her that promise and I intend to begin by avoiding that lie right off. I will do as you suggest and be delicate. I will be very surprised if she does not make the boyfriend connection because she knows him very well and loves him. She talked of him fondly just yesterday and at great length. (What a wonderful triad we would have made!)

>*Be aware that after you come out, she will go through every emotion there is from "Why me," denial, anger etc., etc. During the anger stage, she may throw some shit in your face that you had confessed to her. During the anger stage is when you may find it advantageous to listen with both ears, don't defend yourself and let her get it all out.*<

Buxton and Gochros go through these stages very well. I have been only an average listener, although we have had good couples communications skills classes. Lately we have been very attentive to each other and worked on verbal and physical intimacy. I have been VERY diligent about this, knowing what I was planning. She has been very appreciative of my attention and discussed it positively, at length, with the therapist yesterday. If only I can continue to use those good skills under stress. I want to be there for her in a loving fashion. Her self esteem is rather positive without being egotistical; I hope that she does not feel unbearably hurt over issues of not being everything for me. I can tell her that she has never had to "compete," that my love for her has actually been greater and I have been more sensitive to her because of my love for and sensitivity toward him. I will tell her this if there is an appropriate time.

>*You will feel better for having come out and once you come out, there is no turning back. It may make you feel better and lighter but you have now turned her life upside down. With the help of both of you, you can turn it right side up again.*<

Yes, I have know about me all of my life, but there is a major part of me that she has never known and she has been married to me and verbally, emotionally, and physically intimate for 28 years. How can she fail to have known "this very important fact" about me? Besides, she may feel social and familial stigma for being married to a bisexual man. She may feel isolated if the resources I have tried to set up for her are rejected by her or not felt as being adequate. I think her sister is her best friend and confidant. I imagine she is going to want to discuss things with her. Her best local friend is probably not going to be very empathetic. I have done the best I know how to help her not to feel isolated. She is strong emotionally, so there should be minimal problems with depression. She has never been bad off emotionally and I am sure that feelings of suicide will not be an option for her. I don't know if she has ever heard of the "fag hag" syndrome. She is not one. I do not expect her identity crisis to be very serious, but who knows! The therapist is ready. I'm sure there will be the "why me?" thoughts. Life is not fair, is it? I don't know how to respond to that. (Any ideas?)

I suspect that the conflicting religious thoughts, especially issues of monogamy, will be difficult for her—us! Also, she will immediately be concerned about health. I will reassure her of my concern for her in my approach to safe sex. She will have the right to make some demands here. (What are your thoughts here?)

>*She may now feel a bit insecure that she will lose you. She will be watching your every move (body language) so be careful. She will listen to every word you say, seeking a message. Try to impress upon her (when she shows insecurity) that you still love her and that's why you are coming out to her—not*

*because you want to leave her and start another life. Repetition doesn't
hurt.<*

I will reassure her verbally that I intend to stay with her, that I love her,
that I am committed to her and to the institution of marriage. Those are my
true feelings. I am coming out to her because I love her, I trust her, and I
need her to know me—all of me, just as I am, just as God made me, with the
gifts and deficiencies that I have. I need to be truthful, honest, for my integrity and social and emotional well being. I believe that if we are able to work
through this healthily, I will be on the road to my emotional recovery. The
psychiatrist seems to agree.

*>If your children are real close to your wife, they will sense that something
is wrong as they note a change in her behavior—You must seriously consider coming out to them if they get concerned about your wife's behavior.<*

My eldest is very close to my wife. I fear that she will have much more of
a hard time than my wife. I have not really worked out how to tell my daughter. I hope that that will not be a unilateral decision, but that my wife and I
can do it together. My wife will have a lot to say in what happens after my
disclosure.

*>all of the above is based on some of the mistakes I made and some of the
constructive things I did. I came out to my wife after a couple of years of
marriage<*

Thanks for your wishes and prayers. I am sending this letter to the open
list. Guys—my brothers—I want and need your help and prayers. Respond
as you feel you can.

From: Gripp

Thank you for your prayers! I appreciate them and all your letters of support. Last night, Friday, about 8:30 PM my wife sat down on our sofa and I
put my head in her lap, as I have done many times before. Then I told her
about God's hard gift to me, the gift of sexuality, the gift I didn't want, the
one that had turned and bit me, and that I had to accept reluctantly. She listened and asked questions, calmly. I wondered, "When is the ax going to
fall?" For about 30 minutes she listened and said that she understood and
thanked me for my honesty. I told her that I intended to be truthful to her
from that point on. The rational, calm part of her reigned for that time.
Then she began putting facts together and drawing conclusions that she
did not like. But the shock controlled for almost a couple of hours while she

sorted out facts, asked questions and made correct conclusions. She did not like it, but guys, "she still loves me and wants to stay married." Thanks for your prayers!

She DID immediately bring up my boyfriend with the fact that we had been lovers. I did not deny it. She recognized that all the symptoms were there and that she might have suspected, but she does not have a suspicious bone in her body, although she may have grown one overnight. The boyfriend facts hurt. She had loved him, and it hurt that I have also loved him—and still do. She cried! Then she sobered up and we talked some more.

I listened, guys, listened and confirmed her feelings as well as her facts. I answered her questions and again promised to tell the truth. I reiterated that I love her, maybe a thousand times. She stated that she loved me and always would.

Finally she began to sort out the assumptions of monogamy. She said that she didn't like it that I related sexually to men, but that she would try to accept. That she would work on it. I told her I would help, by being honest, but still being me. She does seem to understand, God bless her.

At an appropriate time I told her about you, my brothers, and this support group. I told her about those of you who stated you would talk with her. She isn't ready yet. I had set up as much support for her as I could think of, local people she can call, friends she knows that she may call, as well as the fact that many of you and your wives have offered to talk. When she is ready or needful, I hope she will accept your help. I don't want her to feel isolated.

About midnight, we went to bed, but sat on the side of the bed to talk more. She cried piteously for a long time. I held her and talked to her through her crying, asking that she tell me what she was thinking when she could. (She has said many times that I am her best friend.) She was able to verbalize her fears. I listened, repeated her fears, saying that I understood them. I said again and again that I loved her, that she was first in my life, that I had always come home to her, that I had NOT moved away with my male lover. She seems confused, but doesn't seem to hate him. Those fears that I could rebut, I did; those I couldn't, I told the truth and said that I could promise nothing. Many times I told her that I was sorry for what I was putting her through.

We went to sleep sometime around 2:00 a.m. At 5:30 this morning I awoke, and she was practicing the piano. I'm sure (I hope) that it was good therapy for her. She was back in bed asleep at 9:00 this morning when I awakened—where she is now. She knows about this list and I intend to show her some of your stories at an appropriate time. We talked about a close married couple and about whether to tell them. The conclusion was, not at this time. I told her about the few people she knows who know about me. She promised to tell me about anyone she discusses me with so that I can behave truthfully with them.

Guys, I got off easy. She has the depression now. I pray for her, for us. Please continue to pray especially for her as we start this new, but honest journey through uncharted waters. I am relieved but worried. Pray that I will listen and always be there and alive for her.

Thanks again for your continued prayers. More later, I'm sure!

From: Gripp

I showed my wife your letter, thinking she would perceive of it as something positive. I certainly did think that your discussion of a rewarding end was positive. When she read the "roller coaster" she burst into tears. She cried that she did not bargain for this. She wanted to back up to yesterday and start all over without disclosure. She made other comments of denial. And cried piteously. I knew how she felt, because I had cried that way the day my lover left. I followed him for about 40 miles out of town, crying all the way. Intense grief. Unbearable pain. Irreparable damage. I held her, cried with her, and let her grieve. I had very little to say to help her. "God was not with her anymore." She didn't want to live. My lover's wife was right to leave him; that's what she should do, etc. I wished then that I had not come out. It lasted about 30 minutes. Then she slowly calmed down. I stayed very close till she was totally calm. Then we went out shopping for about 4 hours. Now we are exhausted, but still calm. I expect more to happen tonight at bedtime. We talked about disease, specifically AIDS. A while ago, she asked if I had a condom. No, I hadn't needed one since she reached menopause, and all my sex for the last year and a half has been with someone whom I was certain about, disease-wise. I'm sure that the health issue is one that will never be ended. She wanted sex tonight but she wanted me to have a condom. I'm glad she wanted sex with me. That is intense relief. I'll go get some condoms in a few minutes.

At any rate, that was one hell of a roller coaster ride. The bottom dropped out for about 30 minutes. My stomach is still trying to catch up with me.

The afternoon however was very pleasant. She loves for me to shop with her. I don't particularly enjoy it, but I did it gladly today. I didn't want to leave her for a minute.

Thank you for your encouraging letter. I need lots like that.

God Bless you and God Bless your wife. What a courageous couple!!! The roller coaster ride has begun. Please hang tight and buckle up . . . it will surely be a bumpy ride . . . but well worth it. If you can keep the communication open and honest, you and your wife may find a level of intimacy in your marriage that neither of you imagined. That's what has happened with my wife and I. It is by no means easy for either of us, but it is certainly rewarding in many ways both personally and as a couple.

We'll continue to keep you in our prayers.

From: Ken

From reading your account of Friday evening, it is obvious to me that your wife is extremely lucky to be bound to such a fine man. To the extent she may momentarily lose sight of that in these first days, I hope and trust she will realize it all over again.

I certainly don't want to appear to be equating personal situations, for each of us (and our spouses and hence our relationships with them) is quite different. But I have found that, even though I am "out" with my wife, she gets VERY uncomfortable when she learns that I have support out here. (Even to the point of having forbidden me to chat on the Internet, that only after I acknowledged the overtly sexual side of some of those earlier chats— "sigh"). These days I am effectively testing her limits by reaching out/coming out to some friends face-to-face. To me, both are valid forms of sharing and expression but I'm afraid she doesn't agree, at least not thus far.

I guess all I am saying is that if your wife isn't comfortable with the knowledge that you have support "out here," you are not alone. I hope she will warm to it. It's ironic, because women are well known for their keen ability to network and share, yet when we step out of our culturally-mandated stoic character and do the same it can be very threatening to them. My own wife has been VERY sensitive to her perceived loss of privacy, hence my choice not to use a last name here.

I am also truly relieved to hear you bring up the issue of HIV, in my brief time here I had begun to wonder if it was taboo. Of course, like you, I am familiar with safe sex practices, yet short of absolute monogamy NO precautions are "100%" safe, and that is an issue with which I have struggled deeply.

Anyway, thanks so much for your heartening messages.

From: Gripp

Today has been a rather calm day. We got up and went to our respective churches where we play the organ, me at one church, my wife at another. After my services (2) I went to her church to help her move filing cabinets and change her choir room around. Then we went home to eat, just the two of us. We had time to talk more; things were calm, rational, and very loving.

We repotted plants, and cut basil in the garden to make pasta for supper. Then we went to pick up our daughter. She had been on a weekend retreat orchestra—she plays the flute. Just before we picked her up, we agreed that we make a good team. And I said that I would not come out much without discussing it with her. It wasn't important to me to make statements, and I would probably not do that unilaterally anyway. We got our daughter, took her home, and went to church again, just she and I, just to worship, not be musicians. While praying before the service, I looked at the hymn "Just As I Am," a soupy, romantic, hymn from the 19th century. But it said so much for me. Vs. 2: "Just as I am, though tossed about with many a conflict, many a doubt; fighting's and fears within, without, O Lamb of God, I come, I come." I read those verses and cried because they reflected the way I was feeling and brought out some of the emotions. After communion we were prayed for, anointed with oil that the bishop had blessed for healing. It was a very emotional time for us both, the weekend having been very emotional.

We went to pick up my wife's elderly mother for supper. No, I was not going to come out to her. That was very unimportant to me. We had a great time, our family of four plus mother-in-law. No tension, no cryptic messages, just a good, normal, regular time. We behaved as we always do.

I would not say that the weekend has been easy, but it has certainly been constructive, and much easier than my worst fears.

Now home and trying to finish the pasta with the fresh basil and garlic from the garden. I came to the computer to write you and she began to get anxious. I told her that I no longer had any secrets from her and she should come see what I was writing. She didn't want or need to.

Soon it will be bedtime. No sex last night nor night before—not unexpected! Maybe not tonight either, but it will return. I think she is hung up on visualizing what my boyfriend and I may have done together. (I have never told her anything, but I think that is what is the hold back.) That's all right; I can wait. She is working hard, but is not yet ready to talk, especially to strangers she says. I hope she will go to therapy with me on Tuesday.

Well that's it for today, guys! Don't stop praying please.

From: Gripp

Thanks for the kind comments that suggest that we may be doing things sensitively. That is a must for me and I'm glad that you see it. That reassures me that I am being as sensitive as possible without being needlessly hurtful. Maybe my wife notes it also. It is indeed interesting that our stories correspond so much, as you point out! Yesterday was rather calm at our house. My wife and I talked, in bed, (no sex) from 8 a.m. till about 9:45. It was calm, loving, and respectful on both sides. My wife has already become amazingly accepting; beautifully so! I love her for it and appreciate the sacrificial thinking that is going on inside of her. She respects, and seems to understand, my needs to relate to men. My male lover came up in our conversations several times, always with a clear head, and no overt bitterness. She did say that she appreciated his help with my depression several times, especially when I had a dissociative episode. He responded immediately and effectively on that occasion, bringing me quickly out of that lost space I was in. She was relieved and still appreciated his help.

We worked hard together on Monday, my wife and I, housework and party preparations for our daughter's birthday party. We are always behind because we try to do too much, but we got everyone fed and desserted at a logical time. After cleaning up and tending to other familial issues, we went to bed, fairly early. My wife was expressing physical neediness, and I was also. Sex was a beautiful experience, different, full of imagination and creativity. Mutual orgasms (not at the same time, guys!) were experienced and during the subsequent lethargy, we debriefed the episode. She said that she had thought of my boyfriend and I and wondered if I had. I could truthfully say, "no, I had not!" In retrospect, I was surprised that I had not, because I usually did. I had had other fantasies during that sexual episode, of both sexes. I did not volunteer that information, however. At any rate, I think we are well on our way to healing our relationship, forging new paths, and continuing our lives together. There have been no roller coaster extremes Sunday nor Monday. For that I am grateful, and I'm sure that my wife is also.

We slept well and till 7:30 this morning, without awakening during the night to agonize over the past days. We were lucky to awaken when we did—the alarm did not go off—the stem was not pulled out far enough, my fault!

Thank you for your prayers; continue to remember us as well as others who are newly on this journey. My wife reiterates that she is glad that I have told her. She says that she wants the truth and honesty. I want her to have them also. I had a short period of depression on Saturday which was very light and occasioned none of the usual uncontrollable crying over the loss of my male lover, which I still deeply feel. I feel that this coming out is a major factor in the lightening of my depression. (I have had a diagnosis of Bipolar II.)

From: Stephen

I've been finding this biography of D. H. Lawrence so fascinating. This following passage is such a good example of how he complicated the notion of intimacy between men (esp. in the context of heterosexual identity/marriage still being primary). There's a lot of speculation that Lawrence, though married, was "gay" in the simplistic sense we use it today. But Lawrence warned against this notion, thought it limiting, believed that it distracted from the rich possibilities of intimacy between men.

"All my life I have wanted friendship with a man—real friendship, in my sense of what I mean by that word. . . . Not something homosexual, surely? Indeed you have misunderstood me—besides this term is so embedded in its period. I do not belong to a world where that word has meaning. Comradeship perhaps? No, not that—too much love about it—no, not even in the Calamus sense, comradeship—not manly love. Then what Nietzsche describes—the friend in whom the world standeth complete, a capsule of the good—the creating friend, who hath always a complete world to bestow? Well, in a way. That means in my words, choose as your friend the man who has centre."

D. H. Lawrence, New Mexico, 1922

What do you think? How much of our pain is caused by thinking that we have two options—gay or straight, sexual or nonsexual—when there is a rich rainbow of possibilities to satisfy one's need for connection? How many of us wouldn't be struggling with the gay/straight divide in our marriages if we had rich, satisfying, loving relationships—nonsexual in the genital sense—with our male friends? How much of our urgency, which can become so sexualized, is because we have been starved for it?

WIFE ASKED ME

From: George

As I mentioned in the profile I recently posted, I came out to my wife, only because she asked me point blank if I was gay or BI, and I answered truthfully.

Obviously she wanted to know. She said she suspected because of the way my best friend and I interacted with each other. She said she just felt that we seemed to be very considerate and caring of one another, more so than she expected men to be with one another. Neither of us are fem in any-way, nor have we ever openly embraced or shown any emotion for each other, but somehow she detected the special feeling we had for one another.

In a way it was a relief to be out in the open about my orientation. I have wanted for years to discuss it with her but have always been afraid of losing her. I admitted to her that, yes I have a special feeling toward a very special man in my life, my best friend, and that in fact I am in love with him. I had to emphasize that it didn't mean that I was not in love with her. That I love her now as I always have, very deeply. It was difficult to explain that a man can be in love with another man and yet still be in love with a woman. I am not sure I really did do a good job of explaining it. I guess I am not sure I even understand it myself.

Both he and I want to stay married to our wives. While we fill a very special place for each other we do not want to abandon our wives and families. His wife does not know about us or his orientation. It makes it difficult in a way now that my wife knows because we have been friends as couples for many years now. Since my orientation and the fact that I am in love with him is out in the open to my wife it has made it awkward for her when we are together as couples. I only came out this summer. We went out to dinner now twice with them since I came out to my wife. Each time my wife was quite subdued, in no way her normal outgoing self. His wife is convinced my wife is ill. When we leave the restaurant to drive home tears well up in my wife's eyes.

I have suggested many times that she talk with the wives of other BI members of this group, or see a counselor, but she wants no part of discussing it with anyone. In fact, after our initial conversation on the subject, I can't even get her to discuss the subject with me. I try to in many ways. When we are alone and I want to talk about it I openly refer to him as my boyfriend so as not to hide my feelings towards him. When I tell her that I'll be out for the evening with my boyfriend she will say, say hello to his wife for me, really knowing full well that I won't be running into his wife. I think it is my wife's way of denying that my boyfriend and I will be alone together.

She is obviously in a "don't ask, don't tell" mode but I am not sure how healthy it is for her to handle it in this way. For all I know maybe it is the best way for her to handle the situation. In the last two weeks she has been more like herself when interfacing with me in day-to-day husband-and-wife relationships, but when I try to suggest that she and I and my boyfriend and his wife should go out for dinner or something her personality immediately seems to change. She is the same when our married children come to see us. Like my boyfriend's wife, they think that she may be physically ill.

Sorry for the rambling. If any of you have experienced the same situation with your wife please let me know the outcome. I have only been out to my wife since mid-summer. Hopefully time will heal her enough that our relationships with friends and family can return to at least near normal.

From: Mike

As one who has been dealing openly with my sexuality for 3 years in the context of an otherwise "traditional" marriage, I understand your frustration. I have to admit, even I have been tempted to go back into denial on occasion . . . fortunately I snap out of it quickly ;-). And my wife, who has been nothing but supportive and courageous throughout our journey, is also tempted to "pretend" that she has a "normal" marriage. We just recently went through another short period of pretending. But we are getting better at recognizing it before it goes to far. One or the other of us usually brings it to a head. We have a tense but productive discussion. We both express our own frustrations with our situation, but eventually through the process we realize that every married couple we know goes through these periods of tension and release. Many more so called "normal" marriages do not have the level of intimacy and intensity ours has taken on since we began integrating my sexuality into our marriage.

I believe that people who decide to live together intimately must encounter conflict . . . hopefully they are aware enough and skilled enough to turn it into creative conflict . . . productive, growth fulfilling conflict. That's what my wife and I are trying to do these days.

So, there are times when my wife, like yours, needs some space from this "experiment," and so we don't talk about it as much or as deeply. But so far, she has always come back to "reality" and we have been able to continue our journey together, in full awareness. What seems to help us, is that when we ARE connected and talking, I try to reassure her of my commitment to our marriage and family life, AND to my responsibility to myself to live as I was created . . . a bisexual man . . . fully expressive. I do this as sensitively as I can without sugarcoating the reality. It helps us both stay "real" in this situation.

I am happy to say that 3 years into this, we spend MOST of our time in balance, in equilibrium, around this issue. And my wife is showing a capacity for growth and love I had not fully appreciated before all of this. In many ways she has been stronger than I have been in accepting myself as I am. I am blessed.

NATURE OF BISEXUALITY

From: Mandy

Boris wrote: > *I just turned 39. I came out to my wife (we've been married 11 years) 3 weeks ago and am having a very, very hard time dealing with my feelings and what to do. I love my wife very much—even after all that has happened these last weeks we both agree that we've had a really wonderful marriage—we think ours has been better than most others we know, except for the lack of sex. I'm very torn between wanting to stay and make our marriage work and the desire (which I really never considered before) to be with a man.<*

You're joining the list at a very interesting time for me, as I've been posting messages recently, questioning the very nature of what we collectively call "bisexuality," which is the stated group (married bisexuals) this list is intended to support. I notice that you say you "came out" to your wife—came out as what? Gay? Bisexual? (Of course we then get into a discussion of what those words even mean <grin>).

I am a once-married but now divorced gay male (and father).

I agree with much of what you say about your situation and relationship. For many years, I wanted my marriage to work as well (for a variety of reasons), though I was not interested in sex with my wife. But, I was not "out" to my wife all that time, so it was a secret, internal struggle—trying to "make a marriage work" that seemed to have some obvious shortcomings—sex!

Though my then wife (my now ex-wife) and I were great friends and partners and coparents to our child (and we continue to be best friends and she is a great supporter of me, and I of her), I think neither of us wished to continue a sexless marriage. Because I am not bisexual, that was not an option (a sexual relationship with my wife) for me. For many (most?) on this list, their bisexuality does allow them the option of a satisfying sexual relationship with their wives, so for them, maintaining the marriage is very possible and desirable. I'm sure that there are even men here who do not have or do not wish to have sexual relationships with their wives, but who choose to remain married. This may be your situation. And if so, you should be able to find some similar people here, and find out what makes their arrangement work.

I have received some criticism of late, people asking me why I'm "hung up" on the sexual issue. The reasoning being that sex is only part of a relationship. I don't think I'm "obsessing" on the issue, but *for me,* sex is a critical element of a relationship, if we're talking about a marriage or marriage-like relationship. Without sex, then, *for me,* it's like we're talking about just a "friendship" type relationship. I certainly have nothing against platonic friendship, I'm just not sure why one would want to be (or continue to be) "married" to a platonic friend, especially if there were an opportunity to have that friendship relationship *and* a satisfying sexual relationship, all rolled up into one person, as opposed to finding those two elements through mutually exclusive persons. But again, I'm just talking from my own experiences and preferences. There are surely many people who can and will disagree—and who see no conflicts or problems with finding what they need through multiple people in their lives—a smorgasbord approach to relationships. And there's certainly nothing "wrong" with that, for those for whom these kinds of arrangements make sense and work.

From: Boris

Thank you for articulating so well what others of us on the list feel and have experienced. So much of what you say exactly parallels my own experience.

I am not (yet) divorced, though I think my wife and I will probably divorce when one or the other of us feels we need to. Right now there's no need. We live separately, though. I was married for 20 years and have been gay from the beginning (and knew it). Before I married my wife, I was in a ten-year partnership with my first lover, who is still my oldest and best friend.

Even after I came out to my wife fully (she married me as a gay man, but not as one who would continue to have fully developed relationships with men—I mean erotic and sexual relationships), I still wanted my marriage to work, also for a variety of reasons. I enjoyed sex with my wife, but once I returned to my true nature I lost *all* interest in sex with her. And even when we were sexual together, there was *no* erotic interest or arousal whatsoever—only sexual arousal (and love, which is what made it work, when it did work).

I was out to my wife in that she knew all about my orientation and my sexual and erotic history. I was not out, in all those years. I abstained from sex with men (but not from the desire!), and for a variety of reasons on both sides, after our children were born our sex life evaporated.

My wife and I have always been and continue to be the best of friends and parents. She supports me completely in my final coming out because she knows that is who I am and that's who she loves. As I support her decision and action in moving out to live on her own (for the first time in her life, I might add), because it is who she is and that's who I love.

Nor was this (a sexless relationship) an option for me. And a sexless marriage was not acceptable to my wife. I thought I wanted to do this for a couple of years. Now that I'm single again (living at home with my younger child), I'm less certain about wanting it. I think ultimately our separation was right for both of us, even though it was my wife who took the initiative. I had no need or desire to move out.

My experience is that a relationship with a man I love is so wholly fulfilling on the feeling, emotional, erotic, and sexual planes, that there is *no comparison* with the (admittedly very valuable and cherished) spiritual, intellectual, feeling, and emotional relationship that my wife and I had and still have. But she and I can relate to each other so much more really now that we aren't confusing that relationship with the erotic plane (which *never* existed for me, whereas it was *very* important and real for her [which is her tragedy, sadly] or the sexual plane (which we both agree makes no sense now).

From: Kenneth

You have said beautifully what I have so recently come to believe with regard to my own experience. Thank you. With my first erotic kiss from a man, I felt as though I had "come home"—a home never known before, as if I were an orphan who is greeted by his natural father and welcomed into his arms. (I am 50, with 27 years of passionless sex with my wife behind me.) My wife just told me a couple days ago that the only real anger she felt toward me—and this was in May right after I told her I wanted to find a man for my life partner—was for having to give up sex. So your words really hit home.

IT DIDN'T FEEL GOOD

From: Max

Since my wife and I had our "watershed" things have more or less been at a lull in terms of my sexuality. I've still maintained contact with the BI/gay friends I've met online. In fact, two of them I've met face to face . One of went with me to a gay pub. It was great.

I had, during the week, been invited to one of these guy's birthday party. I was reticent about going. Mostly because I'd never been out socializing as part of a predominantly gay group. However pathetic this may sound, I didn't know how to conduct myself. Christ, that does sound awful. Anyhow, in the end, I decided to go.

When I got back to my sister's apartment, I phoned my wife to see how she was (she had gone out for the night with a few from work). She had said that she was ringing my mobile phone but that I hadn't answered it. (Genuine concern more than checking up on me, as I'd only been released from the hospital a few hours previously [went from the hospital to the train :-)]). I started a string of lies about where I'd been. It was the first time I'd done it and it didn't feel good. It was an option I felt I didn't have as to tell the truth was to land me back where we were last July. There is a risk of being caught out, as I made a cash withdrawal which will more than likely be identified on the Bank Statement. This didn't cross my mind until this afternoon.

Coming down on the train this afternoon gave me quite some time to think. The pain that went through my heart just twisted it for the following reasons:

1. I thoroughly enjoyed the party and would have stayed longer.
2. It's something I'd so much like to have as part of my normal social life. (Well, OK, not a party every time, but rather the ability to be with a group which was either of a mixed or BI/gay orientation)

3. This "security of silence" is making our marriage cold and I've no idea where that's going to lead for certain. . . . but!
4. I didn't want to break with my wife because I love her. I do find that being stressed at the moment. Not in it's depth but rather in it's security.
5. I also didn't want to leave my kids, as I adore them and I know they need me, and also because it was said by others that my breaking up the family was being selfish which in a way I could understand.
6. I feel I'm at a perpetual junction with three options. None of them is preferable over the other, in that the losses for each turn seem to equal or outweigh the gains from such a choice.

I don't really have a question at the end of this. Just kind of wondering if this would relate to anyone else or if anyone had opinions on it.

Behavior: That of a rabbit caught in the glare of headlights of an oncoming car?

From: Mike

When I came out to my wife 3 years ago there was NO WAY I wanted to split from her. In fact that was the main reason for my coming out to her. I wanted her to know ALL of me and love me for the person I am, warts and all. (Ahem, that's a metaphor BTW! Just in case !) :-) . The idea of separating was something I did not want in any case, shape, or form.

I would agree that it does seem a backward step to go back to the bad old days of lying. Culture thing is not an issue. Believe it or not, though I initially thought different, my experience has been that those whom I've come out to have accepted it damn well. And that includes my in-laws!

Well, with regard to confessing everything, I'm now in the situation where to confess everything would be to break down the "trust" (honesty?) that existed heretofore. I had been completely honest and open with my wife right up until last July. This was torturous. It hurt my wife and made her "cold" toward me as a method of self-protection. It's for this reason that I'm now lying.

The thing about telling my wife the truth was that she DID imagine all sorts of things. None of which ever happened I might add. She'd tell me of what was going through her mind and no matter what I said to the contrary, she'd still go on with her imagination having a field day.

Lying about my time spending is something which I'm "learning"—as it's something I've never done. If I could point out my main weakness it would probably be that I'm too open and honest with people. Some take it as being too forward, others take it as giving them the chapter and verse when all they wanted was the precis (Pressay).

It was not my wife who said it would be selfish of me to split. It was others, both on her side and mine (in terms of friends and relations). My wife does accept my having a gay side. I'm confident of that. It's what I *do* that becomes a problem :-). She has no problem in my watching a program on TV that is gay related and she will even sit with me—though she would be somewhat uncomfortable in discussing it. It's my meeting up with gay guys that she has a problem with. She wants a completely monogamous marriage in every sense of the word. I cannot give that in terms of my gay side but I can in terms of my heterosexual side. That doesn't mean that I don't fancy other girls. I do. But my wife would beat the socks off them any time, day or night, and I do love and care for her.

From: Carpenter

You remind me of myself a year ago. My first few gay social events were exhilarating, validating, and stressful. Wait until you go to your first gay swim party. I didn't even know how to dress! I've always been open to the people I meet about being a "newbie" at all the gay stuff. Both men who have been out all their lives and men who are only recently out have been very understanding. Once they know you are gay, there is an unspoken bond between you.

The thing I had the hardest time with was learning how to cruise and be cruised. At first, it scared the shit out of me to have a guy come on to me, or even give me more than a passing glance. Now, even though I'm in a relationship, I enjoy the flirtation, and often reciprocate.

Like you, also, I wanted to stay in my marriage—partly out of love, partly out of guilt, partly out of fear of the unknown. I knew that ultimately, we would have to go our separate ways, but I wanted another couple of years with the kids. It just wasn't working. The stress was too much for either of us. We were both riding 2 emotional roller coasters—our own and each other's. My wife filed for divorce about 5 weeks ago. I can write and talk about it now without crying, so I know better days are ahead. We're going to continue to live together until her house is ready, so I suspect she and my kids will be gone some time during the holiday season. It's all very civil.

Anyway, I wish you the best of luck on sorting out your marriage. I won't wish you luck on either maintaining it, or on an amicable breakup, since each marriage, like a snowflake, is unique! By the way, this was a clothing-optional party :). That solved the problem of what to wear.

From: *Sidney*

This is a wonderful statement by my wife who I am very out to. I thought you might like to read this.

> My view of people is very very liberal, people are who they are, and either they are worthy of my attention or they aren't. The only exception to this is family. If they are worthy, then their sexuality, orientation, clothing, lifestyle, job, etc. are only more interesting things to be around. That is life in it's utmost—not controlling, simply accepting and enjoying things that are not common every day white bread generic. Things like that create energy because they make me examine myself for who I am and where my values come from and what I will do with them. I like that. I like the unexpected and the different, so long as it is safe—and it is my intuition that determines what safe is or isn't.

OUTING TO PARENTS

From: *Carpenter*

Something happened today that blew me away. I had been putting off telling my mother about our pending divorce, not being able to decide whether to tell her about the divorce and the reason why, or save the gay thing for another day.

I decided that I would be completely open, tell her about the divorce and exactly why. When I told her that we are splitting up because I am gay, her response was "I have always known you are gay; I'm more concerned about the effects of the divorce on the kids."

That would have been the end of the gay discussion had I not pulled her back to it. I asked her how she knew. Her reply is that a mother always knows these things. I then asked her who else in the family knows. She said that no one will be surprised. It's been a topic on and off for years between two of my brothers.

She also surprised me by saying that my close friend's parents would be better off if they would come to terms with their son's homosexuality. I didn't have a clue that she knew my friend of 27 years is also gay. He has never officially come out to his parents, or anyone else for that matter, not even me!

Anyway, a real load came off my shoulders today. Maybe now I can start reconnecting with my family. My attitude is that I will move forward either with them or without them.

From: Patty

I have not really come out to my mother yet . . . but I know she knows as well. I am in the process of divorce as well. My wife insists that either I or she tell everyone that that is the reason for our divorce. Well, it is only part of it. She is also a very manipulative and controlling person. I have been dealing with a lot of depression and suicidal tendencies as well. Much of which has caused me to lose my identity and self. My wife comes from a dysfunctional, abusive family. You name the abuse, she has experienced it. She has brought many of the same dysfunctions to the marriage. It has taken me over twenty years to realize it.

In losing my self-identity, I have also become confused as to my sexual orientation. I know I have always had a gay side, but have been able to "control" it. During this time of depression, I have not. This of course has caused a number of problems with our relationship. The fact that she wanted to talk about her sexual abuses and the way they made her feel, made me feel like I was abusing her too, even though I was not by any means.

My wife a told me that she would be supportive of me as well . . . but that is only if things turn out the way she wants them to . . . me coming back to her and her alone and her control. When she feels that I am not going her way . . . she is hell to live with. As soon as our house sells I am out of here!

P.S. I have four kids . . . . They all know about my gay side as well and have told me that they support me in whatever I do. The older kids have fought some of the same controlling issues that I am still dealing with.

From: David

I have said this before but my Mom knew, too. Never said anything to me! But when we set the wedding date, she talked to my wife and told her that she should not marry me since I was not the marriageable kind of man . . . at all costs leave off marrying me! With her "in a family way" I am pretty sure "nonmarriageable kind" meant "queer"!

She also deliberately split me off as a young teen from my sexperimenter buddies by sending me off summers to a farm . . . where, of course, I found one anyhow!

Although I did not find out until after her death, her eldest brother was homosexual and had his brain fried by some sort of electric shocks and wound up in State Hospital the rest of his life. I was very close to him on visits out . . . as I was to their bachelor uncle (my great uncle) who also was apparently gay . . . from whom I inherited my beautiful pink-stoned ring. We just never discussed any of these things and I have had to dig them out of their stuff left behind. DUMB! Dumber. And dumbest.

I do suspect our mothers know deep inside, whether they can/will admit it or not. And, of course, when I did come out, my wife had to admit that she, too, did know . . . but was in denial!

Life "on the funny farm"!

From: See

Reading these have been incredible for me. I just had to respond on this. I decided to tell Mom before I told my wife. I was pretty sure my wife would call my mom first for support, and I didn't want Mom to hear it first from my wife. (I'm 36, married 10 years). Similarly to your mothers' responses, she said, "I always knew, I just didn't know *you* knew." After a few minutes of talking, she explained that she was a lesbian, and discovered this several years ago, and is working with her husband on their second marriage each. Unbelievable. Not only did she know, she's been a tremendous source of support for both my wife and I!

HOMOPHOBIA

From: Kramer

Please bear with me. I want to share with you what happened to me yesterday. It was one of the most difficult days I have had since my coming out almost two years ago. As most of you know, my wife and I have decided to set the wheels in motion to end our 20-year married relationship. We have decided that we love and respect each other enough to let one and other go. Our ending is a very loving ending. We plan to be very much a part of one and others' lives. We will coparent, have joint custody of the children, etc. Nothing ugly or nasty. This is the way we want it.

However, yesterday I called my parents to let them know where we were at in our journey to reconstruct our lives. My eldest brother happened to be there at the house when I called. Check this out guys: they (all the men) were all asleep in the living room while watching a football game. Anyway my brother is a very religious person, of the Pentecostal faith. My brother had some very hurtful and potentially self-esteem destroying things to say. In a nutshell he stated that I am destroying my children, my wife, myself, and everything around me. He said that God could not have created me the way I feel he has. He asked me if God also created the Jeffrey Dahmers, murderers, rapists, etc., in his loving way as well? Frankly I was stunned and really did not know what to say. He continued to tell me that although he can love me as his brother, he could not love me for who and what I feel I am, and that in the end I will crash and burn—and then and only then to give him a call. He said although I have given my heart and soul to the Lord Jesus Christ, and that our God is a loving and forgiving God, when I walk up those stairs and the angels look for my name in the book, don't be surprised if my name has been blotted out.

Guys, this all hit me pretty hard. I let my guard down, was at a very weak moment, and basically fell apart for a few hours yesterday afternoon. With the help of my wife and a good gay friend who had just happened to call shortly after my conversation with my brother, I was able to get back on my rainbow and get my head together. Make no mistake, I love who and what I represent. I am a very decent and loving human being who trusts his God. I have never been prouder and happier with who I am. It may take some of us longer than others to self actualize who we are, but baby I've arrived.

I realize it is people like my brother who claim to be "right" Christian people, but it is these people that have the capacity to judge and hate. I do not have that capacity—as the license plate holder I saw said; "Hate is not a family value." Only my God has the right to judge. I trust my God has a special place in his heart for me when my day to walk those stairs arrives.

Thanks for listening guys. Life is great "somewhere over the rainbow."

From: Rodney

Hmmm . . . Reading your exchange with your brother helps me remember why when I was about 12, I stopped belonging to an organized church, though I continue to consider myself a very religious person (with a few nonmainstream attitudes for a "Christian"). I understand how especially hard this must be to hear from a brother, and that your reactions to him are conditioned by your love for him. But I would like to make a couple of comments as an outsider.

It never ceases to amaze me how Christians have such strong opinions about homosexuality when Jesus himself seemed not to think very much about it. Was this an oversight? Or perhaps Jesus just thought that the queer case was sufficiently handled by the concept that God is Love?

Now the situation, from my point of view, is that it is presumptuous (if I believed in damnation in the traditional sense, I'd go so far as to say "damnably presumptuous") for us to suggest that God didn't know what he was doing when he created Dahmers, just as he created your homosexuality and your brother's heterosexuality. He also permitted the Holocaust to occur and continues to permit the most mind-bogglingly awful forms of genocide in Africa and the Balkans.

Now, I don't understand God, I must admit. That is why we have people like Jesus and St. Paul (and the Buddha and the rest): to try to get us a little bit more in touch with how all this horror COULD make any kind of sense.

Pretty typical of the New Testament take on love is this passage from 1 John: "My dear friends, let us love one another, because the source of love is God. Everyone who loves is a child of God and knows God, but the unloving know nothing of God, for God is love."

God is love. Hmm. What might the OPPOSITE of love be? Violence? Dahmers' violence? Rape (because rape is an act of violence)? Genocide? Rejecting a brother?

From: Max

I'm so sorry to hear what you went through recently with your brother.

I hope I don't offend folks here or let people down in some way. Kramer, it's too easy to try to rationalize what your brother said, or try to follow what he said with an argument to counteract or countermand what he said. There's no point. When someone is so set in their ideals and opinions then to argue the point with them will just add fuel to their fire.

You are a good and dear person. You don't need me to tell you that, but it's nice to have it reaffirmed now and again.

Go live out your happiness in the full knowledge that God loves you just as you are.

Your brother may never see the light which shines from people who, in being OK with themselves, are OK with others. All you can do is let him see that you're enjoying that light. The warmth of friendship you have will support you and may, in time show your brother that what you've got is good for you.

Don't fight with him. Don't argue with him. Just leave him be in his lack of understanding. Take care my friend.

From: Brett

I am a religious person and have been brought up to respect the WORD. But Kramer, I also share with you the hurt that has come from religious people. I have a sister to whom I am not out to yet—when I told her how hard it was living with my wife (she had just witnessed my wife's behavior) and despite the fact I said nothing about leaving my wife, she jumped on me and said I had said vows before God and had an obligation to stay with my wife no matter what. She was saying that because of her religious convictions.

One of my sons is in a religious profession but he has been much more understanding than I had thought he would be—maybe he has been trained in his pastoral counseling courses. I have much more difficulty with my middle child, who has also told me to stay with my wife no matter what (he is also the one on whom she will lean) but he says it as a judgmental religious individual.

I noted one poster in responding talked of having left organized religion when aged 12. I try to work from within for more of the Love which is demanded of us in the New Testament. It makes me sick when people evangelize with hatred and when they denounce people—that is not what the Bible teaches—it teaches that we are to love, even if we consider what the person is doing is sin. Really, only God can judge—so why do humans try? And fail?

From: Rodney

I was the person you mention. If there had been people like you in the church I was going to when I was 12, I would not have left. As I have aged, my issues with organized religion have gotten more complicated, so I would probably eventually have left, anyway. But it continues to be a source of almost unspeakable pain to me that so many Christian churches (fortunately, not all), which COULD be a source of such healing energy, have taken such a radically different path.

TELLING WIFE/IMMEDIATE FAMILY

From: Rodney

Washington wrote: > *we plan to tell immediate family and are thinking seriously about telling most people through a carefully worded letter (this would not include parents).*<

I'm interested in what kinds of responses you get to your query. I am recently out to my wife and children, and things are much too unsettled for me to know as yet who else I will come out to, and when. As you will see in my comments, I have VERY mixed feelings about it.

As confusing as it is, I've found that the "general coming out" issue focuses a lot of things for me. My older child (who doesn't live in the same city, but who is gay), for instance, interestingly enough, doesn't want me to come out to our closest family friends—even though she is out to them and even though one of their own children is gay!

I myself don't particularly want to come out to the parents of the friends of our younger daughter, who is straight and is still living at home. In her case, I just don't want there to be a reason for the other parents to stop letting their children come to our house. This issue will vanish in two years when she leaves home.

If I didn't have children, I think I would systematically, but slowly, inform EVERYONE about my orientation—everyone, that is, whom I consider to be a friend. I would want to weed out the "friends" for whom my orientation was an issue. But I have the luxury of doing so without affecting, for instance, my income.

But there's an existential question here, isn't there? On the one hand, it's LUDICROUS that one should feel obliged to talk to other people about one's sex life. There is, after all, a sense in which it's nobody else's business. But, on the other hand—since sexual orientation IS, for whatever reason, an "identity" issue in our culture—isn't it odd that we should feel somehow obliged to lie about it?

For me, this is all related to my "other" issue—my current status of being homosexual abstinent. I haven't actually found abstinence that hard to bring off, but I'm reaching a point where the LIE implicit in abstinence is beginning to bother me.

It's very much like that sense of "invisibility" people in other minority groups complain of. You're just not somehow fundamentally REAL if you don't "fit" a very narrowly defined concept of "normal" humanity.

So basically it's OK to be bisexual—as long as I don't DO bisexual things or TELL anybody that I'm bisexual.

I'm reaching the point where if, through some miracle, I suddenly lost all interest in having sex with men, I think I would STILL think of myself as bisexual and work toward openly identifying myself that way. Things have to change, and being closeted doesn't produce change. First of all, are you excluding parents from your "outing letter" strategy because you're not planning to out yourself to them—or because you think the letter is an inappropriate strategy? A letter to PARENTS is CLEARLY an inappropriate approach, I think—but I suspect you agree with this.

If I were outing myself to FRIENDS for personal, rather than political, reasons, I don't think I would do it in a letter to ANYONE—or on a wholesale basis AT ALL. I think I would take the attitude that coming out to someone is a very intimate act. It is a discussion of your sexuality, after all. Do the people you're coming out to discuss THEIR sexuality with you?

And what's the rush? To get it over with? To prevent the "rumor mill" from outing you inadvertently? Those MIGHT be legitimate concerns, but right now I think they're outweighed by the concern for handling all this in a dignified fashion. I also SUSPECT that most of your friends will respect your request NOT to spread rumors, as long as you make it clear that you believe the outing process IS an act of intimacy and trust.

Outing yourself in a dignified way, after all, might very well—with some of your (real) friends—greatly INCREASE your sense of intimacy with them. I wouldn't throw this opportunity away by acting as though you have this "shameful secret" to tell them. Why not take the attitude that you're outing yourself to them BECAUSE you think of them as your friends? Otherwise, why would you bother?

One guy in this group wrote a very interesting post a couple of weeks ago in which he described coming out, very gradually, to selected straight co-workers. He worked in a very male environment (I think it was the auto industry). He clearly chose his timing carefully. And, generally speaking, he seems to have remained on good terms with the folks he came out to. But I think part of his success was due to the fact that his approach communicated the desirable message that coming out IS an act of intimacy and trust. It's not like a news flash. The "success" he had, by the way, was the best kind of success—his acquaintances continued to associate with him AND EVEN STARTED TO TALK WITH HIM ABOUT HIS SEXUALITY, in an effort to understand it. So his coming out produced, apparently, some valuable consciousness raising.

That's the sort of success I'd like to achieve when the time comes.

From: Dale

There's a lot more to my story, but . . . the "Reader's Digest" version is that my mother was visiting. It was a special visit on borrowed time. Earlier in the spring she had been diagnosed with ovarian cancer. Her trip to our home was her last visit away from home before she died.

There was only one time in my life when my mother and I ever even got CLOSE to discussing my sexual orientation. I can't remember whether it was while I was in college or not long after I was married . . . at any rate it was a very brief, oblique reference. Imagine my surprise, then, when within 24 hrs. of her arrival here for her week's visit, she initiated the topic of my sexual orientation! Come to find out she felt she had known since I was a junior in college but had never discussed her perception with me or anyone else. It felt important to her to assure me that she had loved me no less all through the years in spite of her knowledge that I was probably gay or BI. It also seemed important to her to communicate to my siblings her unswerving love and support for me in spite of her knowledge. What she wanted to say to them, I guess, was "If I have loved my son the same in spite of his sexual orientation all these years, you can, too!"

Just before my mother's visit, a variety of circumstances traveling through a network of friends and church contacts had resulted in a kind of low-level outing of me. I wasn't sure how to respond to what had happened.

I didn't know how widespread things were, nor how to respond so I waited. One of my options certainly was something written to my siblings to make an effort to provide them proactively with information directly from me rather than whatever hearsay might float to the surface. With my mother's interest in communicating with the family anyway, the balance was tipped while she was here to write a letter myself and have her edit it.

It was a fairly long letter covering a list of issues. My wish was to have my family be on the same page at the same at least once in recorded history. The responses I got were varied and diverse. My next oldest sister's immediate concern was finding some way to reassure me of her ongoing love and support. Two of my brothers and a sister didn't respond directly in any way. One brother's message was of support but also "What took you so long to admit something a lot of the rest of us have known for a long time?" A brother who is a missionary engaged in a fairly involved series of correspondences with me until I acknowledged to him that it felt as if we were moving to a position of being adversaries. I finally requested we put the topic aside rather than progress further on THAT path! My youngest sister, also a missionary, acknowledged receipt of my epistle, but declined to make any kind of direct, substantive discussion of the issues.

All this diversity of response seemed to defeat my mission of getting everyone to be at the same place at the same time. I discussed this with my youngest sister who wisely pointed out that however worthy my goal might have seemed it wasn't really a very possible one. She pointed out each of our brothers and sisters received my letter at their own place in life, in experience, in openness to the issues, etc. In spite of my wish to bring the family to a point of commonality and unity, each still needed to process the information (or deny it) as they had ability, time, energy, and interest.

From: Kenneth

My wife and I decided to divorce. We proceeded slowly, as it sounds like you and your wife are doing. We began by telling our closest friends and children, individually and face-to-face. I really believe face-to-face is best, as it allows for you to observe their reactions and can offer support and receive support from them. Our eldest, for example, who is 21, let down her guard for a brief few seconds and teared up. She pulled herself together immediately and has never allowed us to see her vulnerability over this issue since. But it let us know that she was affected and touched by the news.

We didn't tell my wife's father (the only surviving parent) because he was in failing health—and a devout Catholic—we figured the news of our divorce due to my being gay would be beyond his understanding. Besides, there was no need for him to know. Shortly after his death, we told my wife's two siblings and their families. In October (on National Coming-Out Day), my wife and I made a joint announcement to our church congregation, with the support and cooperation of our minister. I have also come out of the closet completely at work and have told my favorite relatives and oldest friends.

The wonderful thing is that, despite some shock and sadness over the breakup, everyone—but one—has been entirely supportive. My wife's younger sibling is a fundamentalist Christian, and narcissistic to boot. He let us know that he does not "condone" homosexuality, and is very much in the minority.

My advice to you? Be as open as you can. Let your unique story be told—many can benefit from seeing firsthand the level of caring you and your wife share. Be receptive to the support you are offered by others. Don't put much stock in the negative opinions of others. You don't need their approval or judgment. Tell only when it feels comfortable and you have a support system in place. Continue to allow yourselves to feel what's going on inside and talk about it. Expect to make silly errors and have bouts of forgetfulness. Be kind to yourselves and forgive yourselves daily. Promise not to hurt yourselves or others (I say this from experience—shame often manifests itself as anger toward ourselves or one another). Most of all know that you deserve all the good things life has to offer and that you will surely have them if you are receptive, open of heart and mind, and work for it. Best wishes and welcome to the future.

From: Crawly

I just wanted to tell you that I really enjoyed reading your response about how to come out to everyone. I have moved out as well (although I'm still here, just my stuff isn't) and for now no papers are being drawn up. I entertained the idea of a "coming out" letter too. I think just because it would get a lot of information out fast, sometimes the idea of having a heart to heart with everyone on my Christmas-card list is too dam daunting.

My question to add to the mix is, "At the end does everyone wonder if they are doing the right thing by acknowledging this gay self?" My wife has been so supportive, but now that I'm almost out of the house I find myself being torn and so is she. We've been together all of our adult lives, and while the thought of being single again can be pretty exciting, there is a part of me that can't believe I've chosen this road.

Before anyone says I really don't have to move, let me tell you that my wife has been very clear that she doesn't share that thought. I feel that I've got to figure this out away from my family too. Time to grow up . . . again.

The idea of being a gay man is feeling more right, but I still have days where I'm confused. Not so much about who I am but rather how I ended up here. SO Anyway . . . Thanks again for such a thoughtful response. Guys, any thoughts?

From: Marlin

Thanks for your thoughts on coming out. What is scary to me is that so many of the guys here who have come out to their wives are all moving out or are divorcing. The ones staying in their marriage seem to be a small minority. It is this which has made me hesitant to speak to my wife about such issues, lest a turn of conversation result in my life as I know it coming to an end.

Until I am ready to accept that separation and loss of my family, which is all I have, as a possible consequence of "the gay thing," then I see no alternative but to try to stage-manage this double life I find myself in. I also have no self-assurance that being honest with everyone will bring me any peace of mind, but might well be the end of me. It is 8:00 a.m. as I write this, and mornings are when I'm usually at my lowest, so, who knows?

From: Rodney

I'm still hoping I can patch my marriage up, but I've had the strangest thought lately. If my wife and I were to split and I were to "reconnect," I think there's a high probability I'd reconnect with a WOMAN (though, of course, one who could accept the idea that I'd continue to have gay relationships on the side).

Why with a woman? Well, I like hetero sex and I KNOW HOW TO RELATE to a woman romantically. I've never had an intense romantic relationship with a man; I'm not sure I could even DO it.

But the thought has crossed my mind that my family might eventually be able to accept the idea that I left my wife and connected with a MAN (you know, the Thanksgiving dinner scene with Mom, Dad, and his boyfriend). BUT I THINK I MIGHT BECOME ALIENATED FROM MY FAMILY IF (INSTEAD) I HOOKED UP WITH A WOMAN.

From: Kenneth

Coming to terms with being gay or bisexual is probably the most difficult thing a human being can be expected to do. First of all, it must be done by oneself. Second, it usually must be done without so much as a role model to emulate. Third, being a homosexual is, in the deeply held opinion of many, the most egregious sin of all, more than incest, murder, or rape. (The possible exception is child molestation.) Fourth, even child molestation—the act, not the attraction—is a voluntary act. Just acknowledging that one is homosexual is enough to incur approbation, even without any act being committed. So, we must be gentle with ourselves. The payoff, as I am experiencing now, is to feel integrated, whole, wholesome, and deliciously alive! It is worth all the doubt and anguish. It is a feeling I would not want to die without knowing.

From: Washington

First, I appreciate all the ideas people have shared with me, on the list and privately. Your ideas are very thoughtful and I will share them with my wife as we decide how to navigate this next process.

I would also like to qualify a concern raised in the last digest. The divorce is my desire, and not that of my wife. She does not completely support my desire (as it is not her own) but understands that, given what I now know about myself, it is how I need to proceed. My point here is that outing does not equal divorce or separation. The irony of the outing is that, not only do I feel 100 times more whole, more real, and more alive, but that I am closer to my wife than I have ever been. It is a paradox that is difficult for me to understand but one that I feel in my heart. I only hope that we are able to stay close as we move forward. Time will tell.

From: Kenneth

I feel quite differently about the effect that coming out has on the balance of power between myself and those to whom I reveal myself. Rather than giving the "outee" a tactical advantage over me, I see it as taking back the power that is rightfully mine. I feel that the person who keeps a secret, especially a shame-based secret, is living in the constant fear of being discovered. Therefore, those who may stumble upon the secret know that it is within their power to deny the subject of that knowledge the thing they value most, their need for acceptance and love (and, in the old days, their liberty or even life). When you owe your happiness or success to withholding the truth, the truth doesn't set you free, it imprisons you.

When I have come out of the closet with co-workers or family or friends, it has not been a political act, but a personal one. I say this because I did it not by way of demanding respect, but because I wanted them to know me in the same way that I knew them. After a while, it wasn't even an act of faith or trust—frankly, I realized that in most cases, I didn't really care whether they approved or not. What I usually found after coming out was that they went right on relating to me just as they had before, only more so. What I mean by this is that I believe that I was more open with them—friendlier, less closed off, as it were—so they responded in kind. They realized (I hope) that: (1) they knew a gay person, (2) that a gay person could be "real," hard working, honest, and a family man, and (3) that I wasn't going to have expectations as to how they were to behave (the last one comes somewhat belatedly).

I am very serious about being a role model at my work place. I work in a very large office building with 4000 employees. I know of 6 gay people in my building. Before I came out last February, I knew of only 1 other gay person, a lesbian. I have come to know the other 5 because I am out. I, too, am very "straight appearing and acting." I am married (soon to be divorced) and have three kids. I'm about as normal as a bedrock democrat and liberal can be in a basically conservative enterprise (the auto industry). When I came out, I'm sure I shattered some stereotypes! That's what role models are supposed to do—make it easier for the next guy or gal.

From: Mike

I guess I am one of the "small minority" you mentioned who are out to their wives and still happily married. I am "duogamous" . . . that is, I prefer to be intimate with one man and one woman (my wife) in my life at any given time. Unfortunately, at the moment I do not have a significant M2M relationship going . . . but I'm working on that ;-). My wife my and I are closer now than ever in our 20+ years together. The openness and courage we've been able to find has strengthened our respect for each other and our SELVES. We are each making fully informed decisions about our lives together and individually. Neither of us takes responsibility for the other's decisions to stay or not stay in this relationship. As long as we are honest about the situation, we have all the information we need to make our own decisions. So far, we've decided to stay together and accept each other completely as God made us. We both know that we are free at any time to come to some other decision.

I've gotten very comfortable with my "minority" status . . . having been an invisible minority (BI white male), passing in the dominant heterosexual culture all of my life. There are more of us on this e-mail list than you might think based on the public posts. I was just having lunch with James and his wife (another happily married couple . . . he's out too) and I was commenting on how it seems that the announcements of divorce on the list seem to come in waves . . . and often around the holidays. I have been on the list since the beginning (3 years?) and this is a cyclical thing. I guess the holidays and the end of the year cause many of us to re-evaluate our positions and make decisions to change things, going forward. That's life.

In the end, we must all follow our own inner wisdom. Trust your SELF. Come out when/if you feel ready. As one very wise brother on this list once told me, "Go tell it in your heart . . . before you go tell it on the mountain." Self-acceptance is fundamental.

From: Marlin

Thanks for your letter. Perhaps it is simply the timing of all this that is so upsetting. My mother died suddenly last month, my best friend died of cancer on Sunday, and I've been out of work for sometime and our economic situation has been very stressful, especially with X-mas and all the expectations that go with that. Even in the best of times, all the foofarah surrounding capitalism's holy day of obligation gets a bit much. Fifteen years ago, it was my usual pattern to drink myself into a stupor and stay there from Thanksgiving until after the new year, and that idea seems mighty tempting right now.

I think that I will eventually come out to my wife, but right now it seems like a tall order. What happens with my boyfriend depends upon a lot of things out of my control. As he grows in sobriety, he may feel the need for a partner who can commit to him, rather than a friend he occasionally has sex with. I feel I can give him up on those terms. Having sex with a man, as an adult, within the context of my own coming-out to myself and the gay community, was totally exhilarating and life-affirming for me, like finding an oasis after 25 years (literally) in the desert. I have no regrets. I only wish that doing so did not thrust me into a state of sin which I am fully conscious of. Whether this was by my rational decision, or the result of simple lust fueled by emotional stress, only time may tell.

From: Jud

Isn't it weird that this terrible secret that we've kept from our wives would actually serve to bring us closer together? Its confusing the hell out of me, but I think it comes from the fact that we actually married decent, loving women who care deeply for us too. But yes, it is ironic yet again that we are starting on the path of divorce. We both realize that "rewriting the rules" so that I can explore my sexual desires outside of the marriage is against both her and my sense of what could work. Yes, I would love to continue to have her love and support for the rest of my life, but I can't do this living under the same roof with her. Moving out and divorcing is, for me personally, a way that we can both try to find someone else that we can fall in love with: Mind, BODY, and soul.

From: Gripp

Having recently come out to my wife of 29 years, I too have worried that there seem to be so many separations and divorces among those who are now out to their wives. There are probably some generalizations which can be stated which will be true to a small extent. One of them is that the choice to stay married to a BI or gay man is up to the wife. She has to decide whether she can share a spouse emotionally with another man, or stay with a spouse who emotionally/sexually identifies with men. What I am saying is that regardless of how I feel about remaining married, my wife has to want it also. She has to feel that her love for me is going to be reciprocated enough to make a satisfying life for her. There are so many major and difficult issues to deal with and some women cannot, do not, or will not find the time or effort worthwhile. Among other issues are emotional sharing, sexual sharing, fear of disease, recurrent fear of abandonment, and fears of inferiority and comparing badly with the other SO.

We are such a diverse group of men and our solutions are all different to one extent or the other.

One comfort to take, however, is in knowing that those of us who are NOT having major problems in finding and working out the solutions to our marriages do not post to the group very often. If things are going well for us, we do not have the need to post for support and advice that others who are going through emotional trauma seem to have. I learned this from James when I, too, wondered where were the men with happy and satisfying marriages.

I hope that the posts that you read do not unduly discourage you. Your marriage is worth working on. Use the examples of those of us who are having problems as a demonstration of pitfalls to avoid in your situation, and pray for them.

I was a member of this list for about 8 months before I came out to my wife. I had those 8 months to read, digest, and save letters that I wanted to keep to help support me in the way I wanted to proceed. It was surely helpful. I am now more aware of how much my wife loves me, and unconditionally. I still constantly tell her how much I love her and reassure her that I will not place us in compromising situations as far as STDs and AIDS are concerned. She appreciates my constant reassurance. We both love the new sense of trusting and truthfulness.

From: Joey

One of the pieces of advice that I received about informing friends and family about situations like coming-out or divorce is not to do it at holiday time. People who are close to you will associate your news with that time of year. My plan for telling people about my orientation has become very individual. I plan on who will be told and at what time based on their situation. This news is the center of our existence at this time in our lives, but it is not necessary to force it to be the center of someone we love's existence until it is a good time for then. Yes, it requires a little planning, but I think in the end all will appreciate our consideration of their feelings. Just a thought.

From: Rodney

Gripp wrote: > . . . *the choice to stay married to a BI or gay man is up to the wife.*<

I think your point is fundamentally valid (you're drawing attention to the large demands placed on a straight woman in a mixed-orientation relationship). But in my case an awful lot of time seems to have passed (nearly three months now) with little apparent movement on my wife's side as yet toward a mature DISCUSSION of the situation, let alone resolution of it. And I must say that, after 29 years of marriage, I had expected a little more than this.

No, it's not quite THAT bad—we have finally started couples counseling. But so far we've only begun to "fill in" the analyst on what's happened in the past, so it's too early to tell yet what will happen.

But I have to say that the husband my wife tells the therapist about (I being, of course, the husband in question)—this man is an incredible asshole. His queerness is the LEAST of his failings. And I feel almost as though I hardly know the woman I hear talking. A tremendous fatigue overwhelms me. I certainly am not going to try to DEFEND myself. I don't really think the role of the therapist, after all, is to JUDGE me.

But I ask myself, to return to your point about choices in the marriage, whether maybe the real choice is MINE and whether I've been deluding myself for years about what was going on in my marriage.

I keep feeling that my wife is operating as though it is OBVIOUS that she deserves some sort of enormous, groveling apology followed by, what? years of abject penance?

But, as I've told her before, it's a little hard for me to say I'm sorry about what I did when what I'm asking her for is TO LET ME KEEP ON DOING ALL THE SAME THINGS, BUT WITH ONE DIFFERENCE—NOT HIDING WHAT I'M DOING. Now, I AM sorry that all this causes her pain—but only if the pain was AVOIDABLE. If the pain is due to the fact that I'm bisexual (when she thought I was straight) or that my queer side has brought us face to face with problems in our relationship more generally—well, in those cases, I'm not even sorry for the pain. I'm sorry only that the pain didn't come many years earlier, so we could have gotten on with our lives when we were younger and more resilient.

I'm sorry this post has ended up being so bitter. But I keep confronting in myself and in posts I see on this list this sense that somehow we owe our wives and/or our children and/or the world an apology for having lied about what we are. There is this generalized sense that everyone else has been somehow "victimized" by our difficulty facing something about ourselves—when the price of truth is potentially losing our families and perhaps even our livelihoods. Or, if we're REALLY unlucky, life itself.

The remarkable thing, I keep reminding myself, is NOT that at one point in my life I ever lied to myself or to others about my orientation. The remarkable thing is that I finally told the truth. Sigh.

From: Travis

Our posts invariably reflect our states of mind and colored by them; how could it be otherwise? I do not believe, reading into our posts, that we somehow have to apologize to anyone completely captures the intent, even if at times the posts may sound that way.

I believe that there is no need for apologies to anyone because of who we are—that goes without saying.

But the truth of the matter is that the responsibility for making ourselves "known" symbolically or otherwise "explained" (if more logical terms are required) to our wives, is ours. I believe that is what we struggle with. Being BI, as someone recently said, is difficult. At the same time, it is wonderful. And none of us would go back whence we came from. As long as we have our loved one's ear, there is hope.

To dispel, perhaps, some of the Holiday Gloom, I will report that my wife and I are still quite committed to one another. There are obvious limits on my exploration of bisexuality; but the frontiers keep expanding. It's only been two very long months since I told her. I have no intention to either give her up or give up who I am. She feels the same, but very scared. (She is a pretty independent woman, guys, so she could pack it up & go any time she wants.) Just a thought for all you guys who necessarily are scared shitless about the process—just as I am.

From: Gripp

I have always appreciated your posts. Your depth of experience and understanding always speak to me. I am sorry that things are going badly for you right now. . . . glad that you found my post encouraging. It is indeed easy to become overwhelmed by all the confusing and confused issues. I have only been out 14 weeks now. I believe that you wrote me and prayed a bit during my September coming-out time. Thank you. I am grateful that my wife loved/loves me. I am grateful that she wants to be married—to me. I am grateful that she is emotionally rather healthy and does not have a lot of dreadful "baggage" that has to be dragged around and worked on. My "baggage" is enough. For all of those reasons, life has been fairly easy on me these last 14 weeks.

Other generalizations that came to mind were that some men perceive of themselves as gay and seem to want to be able to devote themselves to their M/M relationship/s. I also hear some men talk about their wives as "soulmates," by which I think some of them mean "nonsexual partners." I somewhat desperately hang onto the term "bisexual" for myself, although many times I think that it is not the most accurate term for me.

Sometimes, it seems, that the wives have some issues that get in the way. It seems that sex has little to do with it. It doesn't seem to matter whether the man thinks of himself as BI or gay. Things just don't work out. I wonder if some men don't give up too easily or too soon. I don't know when "too soon" is, but I also remember being disappointed that it seemed that many were "throwing in the towel" and moving out and on.

Why do I want to keep it so badly, I ask myself—often. Developing another relationship would be unencumbered if there were no marriage, but I have no assurance that there would be another M/M relationship, or that if there were, that it would be as stable as our marriage. I do love the stability of marriage—economic as well as emotional. I don't want to have to time-share the kids with my wife, although they are both becoming adults. That sounds as if I am a mercenary for economic stability.

When I am at a low in believing that marriage is the best for me, my wife goes out of town and I find that I miss her when she is gone; that I talk about her a lot; that I want to be with her; that I want sex with her, often! That she is willing still, with what she now knows about me, to keep me, makes her love even more dear to me.

I see a therapist twice a week. She comes along when it is convenient, which is not very often, but when she does, she needs all the time for herself. I'm glad when she comes. She acknowledges her own needs very seldom. At these sessions, I realize that I am not exactly the person she thinks I am. She doesn't know how much I fantasize about other men. I see someone who appeals to me while shopping with her at the supermarket. If I want to talk about it, she is uncomfortable. I think things are safer for me (I am less likely to "stray") if I am able to talk to her about things like this. At any rate I want to be able to talk with her about me rather than only with the therapist.

I am glad my case did NOT happen earlier. Things might be a lot different. She might not have married me. She might not have stayed married to me. She might not have been as secure/mature as now and things would have been more strained. I guess I feel this way because I want to stay in the marriage; I don't want the insecurity of an earlier disclosure.

Let your bitterness find expression with me or us. Maybe it will allow you to expend that bitterness and be more positive in your relationship with your wife. We can't beat ourselves forever. At some point there has to be enough apologizing/groveling. There has to be some positive purpose in our lives; discovering what that is is a part of learning not to feel victimized. You said the big one, "unlucky." Is it luck or is there a plan? Do these things have a way they are "supposed to play out"?

>*The remarkable thing, I keep reminding myself, is NOT that at one point in my life I ever lied to myself or to others about my orientation. The remarkable thing is that I finally told the truth.*<

Had Clinton only followed our examples and told the truth! Big sigh!

From: Andy

There are several reasons why coming out as BI/gay can spur fresh intimacy with one's spouse. Yes, you are more with your true self and stretched by paradox. Yes, a decent spouse will not only be upset but also sympathetic with you as you struggle to reveal yourself (painfully)—my wife was also relieved that what she had felt for quite some time was deficient in our marriage now had a name and did not result from a deficiency in herself. Yes, his joy at "Finally" being transported by a sexual M2M relationship, it is a good time to fill the cup of the spouse as well. Letting go in loving a man can naturally make you more loving in general. Coming out can unlock the stifling of feelings that cramped you.

From: Kenneth

I just sent a generic letter to four of my relatives telling about the end of my 24-year marriage and that the reason is my own homosexuality. It was very lovingly and carefully worded. My wife read it and said she felt very taken care of by my words. I think it is legitimate to send such a letter to multiple recipients—of differing ages and emotional closeness—and await their varied responses. After all, how many ways can you say, "I am gay"? That is all some of them are going to digest at first in any event.

JEREMY'S PROZAC FEVER

From: Jeremy

It's another snowy day, and I stayed out sick today, so I've had too much time to ruminate. I noticed several recent posts in which guys wrote about feeling liberated and alive after coming out, and I wonder what's wrong with me. Like all of us, I had to make many difficult preparations just to be able to come out—for example, I had to switch jobs and ditch my military career. But during all of those difficulties, I just kept on going and tried to maintain myself. Don't know how I did it all in retrospect.

But now that I'm out, it's as if I've had a lobotomy or gone catatonic. I cannot focus at work, and it's all I can do to get out of bed in the morning. Maybe my professional ambition was somehow tied to my "dark secret." Now that the secret's out, I need to find something new to motivate me.

I look at my job, my vanilla suburban lifestyle, and it all looks like an outdated prop to help perpetrate my former deception. It seems purposeless, needlessly expensive (in many ways), and now that I have nothing to run from, the desire to maintain it all has nearly vanished. A few weeks ago, I started fantasizing about leaving my lucrative but insane job and becoming a street person or something. In more realistic moments, I consider simply taking a pay cut for more reasonable hours or even trying to use my skills in support of the gay community.

I just don't wanna be The Man anymore—let Mrs. Cleaver get a job too. I'm turning into what I would've called a "bum" just a few months ago—a trait that would not be desirable to any mate, male or female. Where has my work ethic gone? Where has my MIND gone? I used to have so many ways to motivate myself, and they don't work anymore.

I do see a therapist, but have had to cancel most of my appointments because of the work schedule. He prescribed an antidepressant, which I thought would help shake me out of this. I took it for five days and became irresistibly sleepy all day. Curious if anyone else has any experience with SSRI antidepressants (Prozac, Celexa) and whether the side effects ever subside. They just made me depressed AND comatose.

From: Joey

Mind you I am not a professional but I would guess that you are experiencing grief. I suspect that you grieve for the easier life in the closet. Making the transition is a quite the experience. Being out is, in fact, quite the let down in comparison. Now, I think in your post you struck on something that you might consider seriously:

This to me is what you are crying out to do. You have made a major proclamation to yourself and the whole damn world. Now, sit back a minute or two and let it sink in. Now I, for one, am clearly NOT Mr. Impatient. But the guys in this team have been so instrumental in advising me. So, here is my couple cents' worth. Take time off. Go on a trip to someplace interesting, if you can afford it. Frankly, find the nearest gay community. Get to know some guys and start getting into your new life. It will be a roller coaster. Count on that. But try to enjoy the ride.

I hope this doesn't sound trite and easy. It is not easy, but don't be so hard on yourself. Get your ass back to counseling, by the way. Your therapist has to be able to advise you better. But, in the meantime . . . keep us posted. We are always happy to advise!!!

From: Brian

The feelings you describe sound like depression to me (although I'm not a psychologist). I've had some of those same feelings so I think I know what you're going through. I too am on antidepressants. I was on Prozac and had some of the same side effects, sleepiness for one. I felt like my head was in a fog and I really had to make an effort to concentrate. Although this eventually subsided a little, it never went away completely and eventually I told my doc I wanted to try something else. There are lots of antidepressants available, and each one will affect different people differently. You need to explain how you're feeling to your doctor and ask him to try something different for you. You don't have to feel like you do. I'd suggest you stop canceling your Dr. appointments because of work and get yourself there. Work is work. This is your life. Good luck.

From: Carl

A few years ago I had my worst bout ever with depression (the only one that led to suicidal intent) and got chemical help in climbing back out. The most helpful and least prone to unwanted side effects in my case turned out to be Wellbutrin. From discussions both with the psychiatrist who prescribed for me and with two doctors who are particularly focused on the problems of depression, I gather that there are a great many antidepressants out there with widely varying properties—and with widely varying effects from patient to patient.

THOUGHT FOR ME . . .

From: David

Meditation yesterday really "spoke" to me. It concerned the word "congruency" and its use in a field I know little about—psychology.

Apparently when one is "congruent" it means that one's outward being is matched to his/her inner self. And I had to think about my str8 outside and gay inside in these terms. And wondered.

I have long stated that even as "out" as I am that I feel unfulfilled . . . but am unsure of what I need to do the filling. And maybe what I meant really is what do I need to do to get my inner me and outer me congruent . . . which, it seems to me, might be somewhat different from fulfilling. There have been times in the past couple years when I had a sense of harmony between outer/inner me . . . but could not express it or preserve it. It was like str8/gay for ME at least, was/is/ever will be a "meant to be"!

A quote (source forgotten) I keep here at my PC seems to apply (once again, for ME if not others): "Some things you cannot or will not believe are really true!"

From: Mike

Yes, congruency is the key to well-being. To get the outside you in sync with the inside you is a worthy goal in this life. I've been a student of psychology most of my life, and I've learned from personal experience that any time I am in Distress, I discover some element of incongruity between my inner and my outer life . . . The process works on all levels . . . individual, interpersonal, group, organizations, society . . . disjunction at any of these levels can usually be traced to a basic incongruity between espoused values and actual behavior. I think this is a very useful construct . . . it has helped me be more authentic . . . or at least to recognize my own bullshit ;-).

From: Joe

As someone who has a math background I'm (Intimately?) familiar with the concept of "congruency." Some might call it a kind of "integrity." For me, lately, the congruency happens only when I'm in the company of my boyfriend (there HAS to be a better word for him than that). And—my experience of being with him in a relationship of mutual love and care has begun to move me toward a sort of personal integrity I've not experienced before. "God moves in mysterious ways, his wonders to perform."

IN THE CLOSET

From: Dan

That was a great answer you gave to Jean-Paul, who—in my estimation—is loaded with homophobia (internalized against himself). Heck we all hate/dislike certain aspects of being gay (or BI) but it IS who we are and that's more HONEST, and that is liberating.

The counterbalance against this is that society doesn't like same-sex orientation. So on one hand we get increase self-acceptance but we get a decrease of esteem from family and loved ones. Therein, I think, lies the quandary that many men on the list feel. They have a NEED to be honest with themselves, yet they don't want to have to deal with all the junk society loads on them as a result. No wonder so many people stay in the closet.

I see people on this list who give a lot of other reasons (rationalizations?) such as "Stay together for the kids" (been there, done that), "my wife is my best friend" (oh yeah? is she REALLY ? if so, WONDERFUL! but is she manipulating you so you'll feel guilty?), "I love my wife and she loves me" (that, methinks, is the VALID reason for staying together), whereas the hidden reason is ("what will society/relatives/the church think of me if I reveal this private part of me?")—what people find out—SURPRISE!—is that a lot of relatives and society ALREADY KNEW they were gay, and actually its no big deal. The most CREATIVE people in the world are gay (musicians, artists, theatrical people, architects, designers, computer programmers, writers, etc.) Unless people like US are visible to society, and show them the good that we do (and are), society will continue to have a bad impression of gays and bisexuals. Most of us are really great people—and all the warmth and brotherhood on this list proves it!

From: Gabe

I am glad to see you like the answer and to be frank I was expecting to be criticized at some point for what I said :-). You seem to believe I am in the closet, which is not true. I am quite open with all my family, colleagues, and students. My point is that rather than "coming out," which is by the way such an American concept, what is important is "coming in," meaning to explore yourself, and gain self acceptance, get to know yourself.

My feeling is that some men take the "coming out" process like a religious crusade (very much like the "born-again Christians" in the States, which is why I said it is such an American concept). And, like any religious sect, it offers a lot of comfort if you go through all the rituals, but it can also generate a lot of intolerance, not to mention the fear of excommunication. I understand the need, I have been there, and probably am still there in part. To validate ourselves we tend to overemphasize our love for men, and relate everything to it. Well, it does pay to step back a little and get a bigger picture of life.

Probably what I am saying doesn't make much sense, but then what could you expect from an internalized homophobic atheist! :->

From: Kenneth

Floyd wrote: >*Are there positive reasons to staying in the closet or only half-reasons to do so?*<

There are certainly valid reasons to do so, as I and others have pointed out before. They are all negative, however, because they are fundamentally attempts to avoid negative consequences. It is never positive to hide part of your true nature. It is, at best, a lesser evil, hiding your candle under a bushel, a compromise, a promise deferred, a resignation to the status quo, in short, the existential equivalent of an, "Oh, well!"

From: Dan

There are, at times, some valid reasons for staying "in the closet" but I think NEVER permanently staying there.

First, you (everybody) must accept yourself AS YOU REALLY ARE. You have strengths and weaknesses. You have a basic orientation (or perhaps if you're BI, a dual orientation) or preference.

I denied myself for DECADES. Turns out the biggest person I HURT was myself for doing that. When I see posts about people on this list having m2m desires and staying CELIBATE as far as m2m contact, I see my OLD self in that.

I see many on this list, also the gaydads list, using drugs to combat depression. DUH! Anybody here see a LINK to people NOT ACCEPTING themselves and DENYING things and being in the CLOSET and the depression? Doesn't take a rocket scientist, does it? (Not to say that's always the case, oftentimes depression is chemical based.)

Perhaps you, like myself, see no way out but to GRIN AND BEAR IT. That's OK, but there are consequences. You choose your path, but be aware of where the path leads and what the journey along that path is likely to be.

But I assure you there are other ways, and ways as numerous as people on this list. Many different paths.

What was/is the answer for ME may or may not be right for you. I was OUTED by people at my work, and also my wife, to other people. I must say it was the BEST thing that happened to me. I have a very homophobic wife, parents, and brother. Right now, it's important for ME to acknowledge what I am.

Stonewall was very important. But all of us have our own STONE WALL to knock down. Some of us hide behind that wall. It shields us from the storm and wind. But the wall needs to come down. Some of us will never have the courage to do it. Others will chip away a block or brick at a time. Still others will just smash that wall quickly. But there will be an aftermath. Methinks if we are to grow and be healthy, the wall must come down.

HONESTY with oneself AND others is the most important thing, and it is rightly written "the TRUTH shall make you free!"

Treating others with love and compassion (as well as ourselves, I see many on this list beating themselves up over the bad feelings they have "caused" for their wives, kids, parents, etc.)—so when/if you come out of the closet—and for most of us it is WAY past time—we need to do it with compassion for the OTHER person.

When we come out we are going to "lose" some "friends" and even relatives. Some will hold US in lower esteem. But we must not lose our own SELF esteem. We will learn who our TRUE friends are.

And if some of your friends or relatives turn AGAINST you, as some WILL, when you come out, all you have to do is say "Father, forgive them, they know not what they do." But press on to make new friends and pursue the NEW life you will obtain/receive.

Should we come out everywhere?

Please accept there are places NOT to come out of the closet. I run/manage large projects for a large corporation, and most of my projects need the approval of a Vice President before they are started. I prepare all the paperwork, and especially the justification, cost/benefit analysis, etc. Now the VP may or may not know that I'm gay. But it is immaterial because my being gay does not have any bearing on the correctness or the execution of the project.

Let your creativity, hard work, attention to detail, artistry, etc. be the way you express yourself. Many people "in the know" understand these good characteristics are related to being gay or bisexual. Smart companies want people with these characteristics.

DOUBLE CLOSET

From: Pan

After I had come out to my wife and to some other people I thought that the worst was over and that I could now start living my life without having to hide any side of my true being. After all, now I was out of the closet in which I had been for so many years. [When I started,] I cried against my wife's shoulder and she was very understanding. And again I was ashamed that I had to do that (involve my wife).

This is the strongest rebound I have felt after my coming-out. I find myself in some kind of a double closet: I can't be wholly out as gay/BI to all I'd like to and I can't be wholly out as a married man to all those people whose companionship I desire. Now I see that my expectations of coming out have been perhaps too high and that there's a lot of work still to do.

From: Kenneth

Thanks for sharing so openly your feelings on this issue. I'm heartened (and I suppose shouldn't be all that surprised) to find that I'm not the only one in the group facing some of these feelings. There was a pretty wide range of ages in the group I shared dinner with (ranging from some high energy twenty-somethings who are up-and-coming employees at Microsoft to one guy who is 40-ish as I am), so some of what I was feeling may have been related to that diversity as well as marital status. I was left with this strange feeling that the younger guys might not have shared so openly the stories of their ski exploits from their recent trip if they "knew" about me. But what the hay, they were stories (and entertaining ones too!) being told in a public setting, so I'm concluding that the problem, if any, is with *my* outlook, not theirs.

Having read some of the other posts and given it some more thought, especially within the context of your very apt "double closet" notion, I'm left with the sense that we need to do our best to make sure we don't participate in building that second closet ourselves. Funny, I just had this flashback to being a toddler and hiding in the closet for fun . . . as limiting as it was (is), being in a closet has a certain sense of security about it, at least initially. But over time, claustrophobia sets in, and I think the lesson for me is that having ONE closet to bust out of is more than enough.

From: Andy

I don't know when I've felt as "at home" as I did last night at the Over-40 Fellowship potluck. Talked fairly nonstop with a very interesting multi-racial (black, white, red) counseling grad student and saw several old friends as well. The subject of the sons of those of us who had them (and by implication were or are married) came up—but not in any distancing way. It's a gay group but my being BI and married has never made me feel unwelcome. But the gay community can be pretty restrictive, not just in terms of folks like us. I loved Bruce Bawer's "Stealing Jesus" and now am reading (borrowed from our Indy Diversity Center library) his "A Place at the Table." He speaks of people who are rather conservative, middle-class, professional gay people being forced to enter a second closet of shaping themselves otherwise if they want to be accepted in the gay subculture (New York variety). How sad!

From: Pan

I'm at the moment out only to a few people, including my wife, my brother and a few others. So I'm not too familiar with the attitude that people in general take when somebody comes out. In my case the people to whom I've told have responded positively and understandingly. The same with the gay people I've told about my marriage and children. The response has been mainly positive and some have been genuinely interested in my life. So I guess I have paid too much attention to some negative feedback I've received.

And it's amazing how these few negative attitudes can reinforce my closets. Every time I feel I've made huge progress in accepting myself, some tiny incident can suddenly break that all. Just a week ago I experienced one of these incidents that made me feel my marriage as a burden and then I thought I'll never again have anything to do with "those people" that make me feel that way. Well, I've come over that already and I'm making progress again.

From David

Yes, I, too, feel like being in a double closet. But, at least, I feel like I have some company in each/both! Before 1992 I was alone in "my" closet. After 1992 I was "out" to a degree and my wife, sons and a few others were "in." THEN I really thought/felt I was the only gay guy with a family in some sense . . . and BMMA [BiMarried Men of America], and Spouse Support came along . . . then this group . . . and I found I had company there, too. I might prefer some sort of all the way out and no closet (if I knew what that meant), but I am very pleased for the present to at least not be so very lonely! And I owe thanks for being here with my brothers on this list.

PICKING A TIME

From: Jos

My suggestion would be that you pick a time when your wife will have a day or two after you tell her to just absorb what you've said. Be prepared to have to spend some time with her and know that she'll be angry and hurt. The first few days will suck more than you can imagine (you might as well prepare yourself).

As for leaving her, well let me tell you about my situation.

I too had a "friend" when I came out to my wife about 10 weeks ago. I could no longer deal with the pain of not being honest about who I was and also about deceiving someone I truly loved (my wife) so I came out to her. What a relief! I was SURE that once I told her that we would separate and that my friend and I could move forward with our lives because she would never allow herself to stay with me—she deserved more (my thoughts). WRONG!!! Not only are we still together but we've worked out a compromise that allows me to still see my friend or others a few times a week.

My point is, DON'T BE SO SURE THE MARRIAGE IS OVER ONCE YOU TELL HER, THINGS MAY TURN OUT MUCH, MUCH DIFFERENT THAN YOU THINK and you may discover it's not so bad, at least for a while.

From: Clem

How frequently we find ourselves saying this to ourselves and others on the list! For those who are hearing this (central) theme for, maybe, the first time, I want to emphasize that the "things that turn out differently" have to do with a lot more than whether or not you stay married.

I have hung on to my relationship with my wife now for 8 months since coming out. After a period of terrible misery, my wife is much, much happier than she's been in years. And yet we both know that whether or not we'll be together a year from now is still an open question.

The experience you're going through, unpleasant though it is, will turn out to be, possibly, THE "defining" experience, not only of YOUR life but your wife's—regardless of the final outcome (which may, in fact, be a "happy" one).

You will find that coming to terms with the gay or BI side of your personality—and its implications for your marriage—will yield an enormous amount of understanding about life in general.

But you need to "work" the issues to achieve this understanding, which is why it's not a good idea to give up—on anything— too quickly. When and if the time comes to separate, I bet you'll know—just don't trust your early reactions too much. It's hard to sketch the floor plan of a house that has just been hit by a bomb.

LOSS OF INNOCENCE—INNOCENCE RECOVERED

From: Clark

We have had both our adult children home this weekend, and the two people that they love: one married and the other perhaps will be. What a joy! Today was a dream come true: Sunday dinner with all of us at the table, together with a grandmother.

I weep inwardly when I think of the loss of all that, if we should opt for divorce, or even separation. Yet, the loss of innocence is so marked that I realize that there is no way we can revert to what was once there but no longer exists. The price we have paid is awful pain on everyone's part. The joy is that at least life is being lived authentically, and we are no longer deluding ourselves as to what was there once nor what is absent now. Were there no fall (from innocence) there would be no redemption.

From: David

But, when it was "inauthentic," was it innocence?

I feel so exonerated by being simple, by being real, by being without subterfuge. I had no innocence when I was in hiding. If anything, I am now—after all of this knowledge, awareness, and experience—ARRIVING at innocence, maybe for the first time since I was a child.

Innocence—is a mental construction—is an attitude of "yes"—is being where one is with all one's might.

From: Andy

Yes, getting beyond innocence is good (as I tried to say in my previous post)! Moving beyond their idyllic marriage (and presumed heterosexuality), couples who honestly work on improving their relationship after the husband comes out are being more conscious and more authentic, working on their marriage, realizing it, becoming more attentive to their own and each other's needs. Maintaining innocence is so self-centered and consumes so much energy (especially since it is impossible) detracting from healthy relationships. I am reminded of a phrase from (Jewish theologian) Martin Buber: "If there is nothing that can so hide the face of our fellow man as morality can . . . (nothing can so hide the face of God as revelation can)." When we are liberated from self-justification, we are more free to love.

From: Andy

I loved your image of the blessed Sunday dinner. I am just back from a week vacation with my wife, two kids, their wives, and a grandchild (and posting too much) :-). The joy of family life is plentiful, and I wonder if it is a kind of blessing that I myself and the world I live in came so late to consciousness of being BI and in a way that does not preclude family life (maybe gays will be entitled to more of this once gay marriages and gay adoptions are more legitimized). I will not be giving up wife or family so the loss that worries you does not seem to loom for me. Having been out for a decade to wife, sons, and their wives, my being BI is not denied, but it is largely ignored and is not a problem.

STRAIGHT SPOUSE SUPPORT GROUP

From: Buck

I went last night to an open meeting of the Boston Straight Spouse Support Group at which Amity Buxton, author of "The Other Side of the Closet," spoke about her book and her ongoing interviews with wives and husbands in preparation for her next book. I felt glad to be attending with a half-dozen friends, fellow members of the Gay Fathers of Greater Boston and of the Gay & Bisexual Married Men's Support Group. The Straight Spouses were very welcoming to us (especially the women in the group: the few scattered husbands of lesbian spouses seemed more nervous), and we were all glad to make the effort to communicate. But it was clear that they were there to support each other, and throughout the evening there were many reminders of the anguish in their lives that we had caused. We, on our part, couldn't help feeling defensive on occasion, and (speaking for myself) sometimes lapsed into attempts to give advice and fix other people's lives in that tiresome male way. But we listened carefully and spoke as well as we could out of our own experience

Amity was wonderful: a small, rufous, sparrow of a woman fixing us each in her glance and telling one simple truth after another. A third of the marriages break up immediately, another third undergo a longer breakup punctuated by attempts to heal and rescue what had been broken or discarded, and to protect the children. Another third try more heroically to stay together, and of those perhaps half succeed in strengthening the marriage and continuing. The process of coming out proceeds in waves; first the gay spouse comes out, then the straight spouse undergoes a curiously parallel process; then the children adjust (but maybe they know the important parts all along: there was much discussion on this issue). The coming-out process involves a reassessment of sexuality and selfhood, on both sides of the marriage. Lives change in complicated ways. Anger takes a long time to heal. But in the end people survive and find new faith.

For me, and I think the other men in our group, it was a fresh experience to hear the women speak of their experience. I'm sure we all felt echoes of old quarrels. Why can't he recognize how much this hurts me? (from one woman, why can't he help with my 13-month daughter so I can find the time to get my hair cut?) Why can't he tell me his truth in a way that lets me know how he feels? It seems so unfair that he has all that freedom and I'm stuck with all the responsibility and loneliness. Above all, there were the big words over and over: betrayal, abandonment, secrets, lies. Sometimes not the words, but the meanings were there.

But these weren't our own wives, after all, so we could listen without feeling quite so defensive. And we could tell some truths of our own. It's hard keeping secrets, including the secrets one keeps oneself. It's true we made promises, but we're not the same person any longer. Our lives have changed in ways that make us want to be more honest with ourselves, as hard as that may be on our wives and children. Some of the men were there with their wives or their ex-wives, the current presidents, respectively, of the Straight Spouses and the Gay Fathers. Another woman, representing a group called Alternative Family Matters, talked about lesbian moms coming out. There was a lot of bravery and well-wishing in the air, even while we talked about volcanic emotional landscapes where not much, for the moment, could grow or thrive. There were exchanges of information about support group meetings, websites, e-mail lists, national organizations. And people exchanged phone numbers at the end in ways that seemed more than polite.

Above all, we listened and talked to each other as clearly as we could, and I think we felt heard. I don't think many felt that these groups should meet together often, but we were glad that Amity had brought us together, and glad, as we left in our separate cars, that we had our own friends to help us find ourselves and feel safe in new ways.

SUPPORT

From: Mike

You really sound like you need a hug. . . . so here's a cyber hug {{{{{{{Jim}}}}}}}

I've been out to my wife for several years now. We went through a long period of "grieving" the marriage we once had before we were able to build a new kind of relationship. We went through all the typical stages of grieving I'm sure you've heard about . . . denial, anger, depression, acceptance, growth. We are closer now than ever in our 28 years together. We have found room in our relationship to allow me to express my full nature. For the past 5 years, with my wife's knowledge and support, I have been able to find and maintain healthy, intimate relationships (including sex) with a few other married men, who like me, hold their marriages primary while honoring their full natures by sharing intimacy with a man.

Given that you've just experienced a close family member's death, I would wait until you've had a chance to move through your grief about that before you come out to your wife. As I said above, and as I have heard many other men in our situation describe . . . the process that begins after coming out to your spouse is very much like grieving a loss. . . . the loss of the idealized version of marriage that you and she were raised to believe in. Grieving one significant loss is difficult enough—adding another loss, even if only symbolic, can only complicate your lives now.

This is just my perspective. I can't know your circumstances, nor can I know the best path for you. I can only share my experience and hope it gives you some options to consider during a time when you may feel your options are limited. One thing I have learned is that our options are only limited by our imaginations, and our faith in ourselves, our spouses, and our higher power.

CHANCE MEETING

From: George

Saturday night my "friend" and I went to dinner and then to a gay house party. The party was in honor of a fella who moved to live with his lover. There was a mix of guys there, mostly gay, but also a fair number who consider themselves BI. It really is a great group and since I came out to my wife this past July I feel quite at home there, and not guilty as I have in the past.

We were there for about an hour when a young fella came in that I had recognized as being with the company I used to work for. He did everything but crawl under the rug to avoid being noticed by me. When he realized that it was obvious that I must have seen him he generated enough courage to come up and talk to me. The first thing he said was, "I never in a million years had the slightest notion you were gay. And, I suspect, or at least hope you never had the slightest notion that I was gay either."

He was correct, I never had reason to think of him as gay or BI. He is an extremely handsome guy—swimmers build—and carries himself like a movie star. He was always very popular with the girls around the office. Many were always conniving on ways of getting him to ask them out.

He told my friend and I that he just recently accepted himself as gay. There was a girl he dated occasionally, a lesbian, in order to quell any suspicions that he might be gay. He actually was very much in love with a fellow he went to college with that recently relocated to our area to accept a job here. He said he has had other lovers in the past but never allowed himself to be with any one guy for any extended length of time because it might cause people to think he is a gay. He is really concerned about his relationship with his college friend because he is very much in love with him and wants to maintain a live-in relationship. He is scared to death that if anyone where he works suspects he is gay they will find a way of making life unpleasant for him to the degree where he would have to leave. He said this has happened in the past to others.

He, my friend, and I talked at great length about his situation. It also made us wonder if that fear, the fear of being exposed when one cannot afford to have it happen, is the reason that so many of our gay and BI brothers do tend to have many relationships, rather than one lasting one. In the predominately twisted straight world in which we live few would accept two guys living together for any length of time before coming to the conclusion that something might be amiss.

We all walked away from that party realizing that coming out, letting the world know we aren't really bad guys after all, is what must happen to attain a greater degree of acceptance. Here we are, three guys that feel that that is the only way guys like us can eventually live in relative peace, and yet we are, for a variety of personal reasons, afraid to come out any further than we have.

Yes guys, I know this is a sad commentary.

INFATUATION

From: Jock

I am a 31-year-old white male. Actually, it was my wife that referred me to you! I'd be very interested in sharing experiences, and having a "support group"of men in the same situation. To know that I'm not alone.

I came out to her last year after 13 years of marriage. I came out because I met a boyfriend, and I was flipped over him. I was so infatuated, in fact, that I just plain "gave it away." I started dressing differently, shaving every day, talked about him too often, was a bit tooooo eager to check my e-mail box, etc. My body language just gave my secret away. She asked point blank if I was having an affair with him, and I said yes I was. I was prepared to be thrown out, but that was better than continuing the charade. For years I've been having random encounters in parked cars and trying to get gay sex when I could in secret. This often meant finding other cheating spouses who understood the need to be discreet, who weren't bothered by meeting only on certain days and at certain times, and so on.

I just got tired of it all. I found a guy, I enjoyed him, I'm no longer a shy, naive boy anymore. I am BI-sexual and I must admit that to myself, and to my spouse. She has a right to know. But, instead of divorcing me, she is willing to tolerate it within guidelines. We are in marriage counseling—not to cure me, but to help her cope and understand my boyfriend is not a threat to our relationship.

She was surfing the Internet, probably in search of information about BI-sexuality—and found your mailing list and support groups. She subscribed to Wives of Out Husbands or something and e-mailed me your list.

Chapter 2
Sexual Orientation

YOU ARE NOT ALONE

From: Mandy

Bill wrote: >*I am a gay man, who was once married (before coming out to myself and to the world). When I came out to myself and the world, my marriage (such as it was) ended by mutual agreement. I now live as an openly gay man. That's my brief background, sparing you the details.*<

I have been reading with interest and curiosity the posts of you who are married but wish to have sexual contact or relationships with other men, yet still wish to remain married. Many of you express frustration that your wives are less than happy or cooperative with that scenario.

Bill wrote:> *I sometimes question those men here who say that want to be with a man, yet remain married. Are these men truly BI-sexual, or are they telling themselves that they are just to cling on to the comfort and familiarity (and societal acceptance) of "being married." I am sure that I fell into that category myself—telling myself for a time that I was "at least BI-sexual" (as opposed to only gay), to allow myself to cling to the idea of "being married."*<

I have no problem with the concept of bisexuality—I'm sure there are many bisexual people out there—people who are sexually and/or romantically attracted to both sexes. Sometimes those attractions and relationships are monogamous, and sometimes they're polygamous (wanting contact with both sexes simultaneously). Perhaps what I'm referring to are the men I often see self-labeled as "BI-curious" in the personal ads. I could be wrong, but I generally conclude that these "BI-curious" folks are "closet-queens" (to use the familiar, if not PC, term), people who cannot bring themselves to just admit to themselves or others that they are gay. Somehow, being "BI-curious" makes it acceptable be to attracted to men. Now, I don't point a holier-than-thou finger—again, I was one of those men for some time. Anyway, I wonder what percentage of self-identified bisexual/BI-curious men here might fall into that category?

I'm also sometimes surprised that men here who are in the married situation, yet wanting their freedom to go date or have relationships with men, seem to be surprised or disappointed that their wives have a problem with this. Did the wife know what they were getting when they married you? If not, is it any surprise that they'd have a problem with this now?

If you presented yourself as a sexually monogamous heterosexual male and then you pulled the rug out from under your wife with the bombshell that you have been or would like to have 1:1 sex with men as well, or have a 3-way relationship, is it surprising that this would be a problem with your wife?

If the woman knows from the beginning that her husband is attracted to men, or will have contact with men, then that's another story. Whatever people are honest about and agree to up front is great—I'm all for alternative definitions of "family" and "marriage." I for one (despite my long-time association with a conservative religious organization) no longer believe in lifetime sexual monogamy—I personally believe this goes against our basic biology and innate beings as humans. Commitment to one or more partners, yes, but that's not defined by or limited to sexual monogamy. But, I think for a committed marriage-like relationship like this to work, the partners involved all have to have similar beliefs—and know what they are up front.

I think there's a lot of wasted years and energy put to trying to convince one partner (the wife) that they need to change and accept the other (the husband) for a person they didn't know they were marrying (a bisexual, "BI-curious," or gay man). Because of societal, familial, and religious pressures to maintain marriages at all costs, wives may initially seem to be receptive to the idea of maintaining the marriage under the revelation that their husbands have "changed the rules." But is this accommodation lasting? Is the wife truly happy under such a situation? What is she giving up of herself—her values—to make this happen? Is a marriage under such circumstances a "good" marriage?

I also have some concerns that some subscribers to this list are perpetuating in others a situation that's doomed for failure. Sure, it's initially great to find out that there are others out there who are married, yet are BI or gay, and wish to remain married. We talk about how supportive we are of one another, but unless the "support" is modeling successful examples of marriages that are thriving under these conditions, what kind of support is it to encourage one another to cling to a slowly sinking ship? How much of a favor are we doing to these men who are struggling/clinging to a marriage that may be best left behind, in light of new awareness that these men have about themselves and their sexuality?

From: James

You raise some valid points but you ignore one profile or scenario that certainly describes my situation and, I know, a few others within this group. For some of us it is our wives that strongly wish the marriage to continue and want it to work—with lots of energy, discussion, and the related ups and downs—to salvage the marriage even if it means accommodating the husband having a male relationship in addition to the marriage. When I came out, I was clear that I was not willing to continue without male intimacy. My willingness to remain married to a woman I love dearly was that I had to have the freedom to have a relationship with another guy or I wished to separate as best friends for each of us to continue our journeys apart.

It was my wife's decision to remain married more than mine—her decision to make freely—knowing that I understood fully if she did not wish to remain married. It makes perfect sense to me that she would not wish to remain married in a mixed-orientation marriage. And I questioned her on several occasions about why she wished to remain married knowing she might have to share my "inner" life with someone else. And I am prepared that as time and our relationship evolve, she may change her mind. I regret any pain she feels and try to nurture her and be there for her, but also know what price I am not willing to pay to remain married.

We have bonded more strongly than ever since the coming out, so it seems we will remain married. However, about once or twice a year we discuss whether we are making the right choice because we face so many challenges. However, it has been easier than expected for my wife because I have not found someone to establish a relationship with, so it remains to be seen what she feels if and when I ever do find a guy to share parts of my life with in a meaningful way. Though she has already had to work through my falling in love with another guy, which I seem to do rather easily (G . . . sigh). . . . And these circumstances have helped us grow and communicate better.

Hope my rambling is clear . . . I just don't see myself in your description.

From: James

I just walked home after sending my last response and I want to share another perspective to your post.

One of the joys, of the many, of facilitating this august list is that I have gotten to know so many guys personally. And one thing that is really obvious to me is that there is such diversity and variety among the men, their thoughts regarding their marriages, their motivations, their situations, etc. . . . I could give you names for several profiles that occur immediately to me. Some men in this group are clearly committed to their wives and their marriages above all else, especially as it relates to having an intimate relationship with another man. They hope to someday have an intimate relationship but they are willing to begin this ONLY after they are certain that their wives are ready to begin that phase of their marital journey. And they are very cautious as they proceed to discuss and explore this idea or desire.

Also, another important variable to the issue at hand is that some of the men in this group have been out to themselves all of their lives . . . and some of them have been out to their wives since before they married. Some of us have come out to ourselves much more recently and we are middle-aged and our priorities differ from other men in this group. I can think of men in this group who remain married only because of their children and they clearly plan to remain married until the last child has left home and no longer. And among this group are men who have communicated this to their wives . . . and further, this decision was a joint one in some cases.

The point of this post is that I know from my own experiences with so many men in this group who have shared aspects of their journeys at our various gatherings is that we are a very rich group in the variety of our marriages, attitudes, and priorities.

Again, I repeat what I said at the beginning of my earlier post—you have many valid points, but I wanted in this post to comment that you do not take into consideration the variety that we are.

From: Stephen

I am thriving in my relationship with my wife; it is deeper and more enduring than what I experienced with the gay men I chose. I am also sometimes longing to hear the other voices of men in this group who are happy and contented in their choice of a woman as life partner. Perhaps the thinking is, if you're happy, why post? But I do think we need to more actively model how these successful relationships work.

It's important to underscore that "any" long-term, intimate relationship is going to be fraught with complexity, ambivalence, and "issues" at times. It's the nature of intimacy, but it doesn't mean the relationship is "a sinking ship." But those are the hard periods where we do need support from others to sustain us (not life rafts to encourage us to jump ship).

From: Andy

It is good to hear from people whose marriages are thriving but maybe also from those whose marriages and personal lives are "good enough." Sure, my marriage is a "sinking ship," but so am I—and so are all of us. We are all slated to sink into the abyss of death, and those of us who are closer to that end (I'm pushing 60) :-) are understandably less interested in chucking our marriages and starting over regardless of our orientations. Besides good-enough sex (sex isn't everything?) :-}, there's companionship and running a household together and going to the symphony and relating to grown children (and grandchild), relatives, and friends (gay and straight). Of course, the two of us are not the same people we were when we were wed, nor is our marriage—nor is any marriage (even those without special accommodations for additional relationships). Even the ship that stays afloat plies not the same waters twice (thanks, Heraclitus, the ancient Greek proponent of the reality of change). The spouse who is flexible and resilient and can allow values to evolve is surely better able to weather the storms that come and sail beyond them.

Diversity is surely the name of the game (thanks). Undoubtedly, some who advertise as "BI-curious" are really "closet-queens," but some are probably genuinely BI-curious, wanting to explore but not sure where they are headed (or where they want to put their head) :-). Some outgrow being BI to become gay, and some move in the opposite direction, and some are rather stable gay or BI (in one of seven Kinsey flavors, doubled in attitudinal and behavioral dimensions—plus more in Klein's Grid). Some marriages are worth keeping, and some are worth scuttling—and some probably should have been scuttled long ago instead of prolonging the agony. Easy answers that suit everyone are simply not applicable—as everyone acknowledges. If we can hold hands while our ships sink (God asks Noah, "How long can you tread water?" in Bill Cosby's sketch) :-), that is support indeed. There may not be too many role models, but there are folks who mirror the Whiteheadian interjective nature of God (a fellow suffer who understands) When we get tired of "taking matters into our own hands" <G>, it is nice to know that there are other hands ready to help.

From: Carl

But the real point, I think, lies in the danger of labels. I called myself gay for nine years, and it was not an adequate definition. Nor was the definition I tried for many more years to maintain, as a married guy who . . . um . . . well . . . had this little problem with homosexuality from time to time. Sexuality is just too complex and too volatile to fit cut-and-dried definitions. I now prefer to call myself queer and let it go at that.

From: Sidney

I am out to my wonderful wife for one year this month. I have been gay about 100 years (hehehehe). It has been a most interesting year. We are getting along better than ever. She has been encouraging me and has NO problem with me seeing guys. Even if Mr. Right does come along we will stay married and will stay together. Something happened the other day that I thought you all might like to laugh at. Gayness can be fun if you drop your walls. This is what happened: I have two pairs of pants that were missing from their corresponding suits. I asked her if she knew their whereabouts. She said, "You need to keep track of where you took them off." I looked at her and laughed then she laughed so hard. It was a wonderful moment. We both glowed. We have laughed about this for over a week. I think this shows true acceptance and openness for me seeing guys.

From: Woody

Well, THIS guy was starting to feel depressed because online buddies like some of you were seeing their marriages disintegrate—would I be next? I've been out for about 15 months to my wonderful wife. Before that our life together was rather humdrum with virtually no sex, just "roommates" as she later put it. No more. My wife finds a lot of positives to balance the negatives. I could well be accused of leaving my pants somewhere else. She even called me once, waking my lover of the moment (I don't hide where I am, leave phone numbers—if the guy can't deal with that, tough), to talk with me about a minor house emergency. Of course this must take a psychological toll. But—I've been gay, just not out to myself, for "100 years, heh heh" and she knows I'm NOT going back. I'll separate if SHE wants me to, but at this point we have a MUCH closer (and, well, exciting!!) relationship than we ever did at any time in our nearly 28-year-old marriage.

From: Mandy

For years, I myself assumed love and sex were (or should be) one and the same. I couldn't allow myself to truly enjoy or accept sex as a pleasurable activity if it were not happening in the context of a loving relationship—which is what much of society and most religions teach. To the contrary, "recreational sex" is quite marginalized (overlooking, for a moment, the double standards that seem to apply to straight men versus women and homosexuals).

Oh yes, there can be (and inevitably is) change in all relationships. Probably the younger and more inexperienced the parties are, the more change there's likely to be. I think anyone marrying/partnering in their twenties takes a risk and has to know that they are going to be different people in their thirties and forties. Hopefully, couples can evolve in compatible directions, but sometimes that does not happen—and divorce/break-up is the result.

Yes, I think it's possible a man can come out to his wife as gay or BI, and that the wife can accept this new information, this change to their relationship. But probably more often than not, that's a "challenging" change for a "traditional" relationship to survive. It's all dependent on the uniqueness of the parties involved.

I question the usual societal assumption that sexual monogamy is "best." Best for whom? Why? Yes, I agree that we can control our biological impulses and can be sexually monogamous, and/or even celibate. But why? Why do we need to? Where has it been demonstrated that sexual monogamy is "best?" Best based on what? Where has it been demonstrated that sexual polygamy or recreational sex is "foolhardy?"

From: Gerald

Hi everybody. . . . My wife and I are celebrating our 32nd anniversary (and her birthday—a double celebration). I feel so blessed because my wife is my best friend and most of our socializing is with gay and compatible people. I have a lot of sex with a few men and never thought I would like to settle down with anyone other than my wife. We quit having sex about 20 years ago. In order for us to both have our freedom, we have lived in separate residences (although close together). Most of the men I really enjoy being around and spending any time with are married men (I have a thing for Bears and construction workers). My wife knew I was gay when we got married, at 40 years old. I said to her before we got married that if she was crazy enough to marry me knowing that after having sex for a couple of hours I might get up and go out and suck a dick then let's get married. She IS an exceptional woman. She has never indicated that she would have any desire to change me and in fact her only requirement (she didn't care how much sex I had with other men) was that I never become boring. . . . I have kept that promise. We have been through good times and bad and each time our bond has become greater. We have been around too long to give a shit what straights think about our arrangement (if they don't like it . . . it's their problem.) My wife has offspring (four grandchildren and one great grandchild). I don't label myself as gay or BI or purple—I just am—I love this group and have met (and gotten together with a few) some really neat people. I'm not offering any advice other than to say get your wife involved with your gay friends so she doesn't feel left out . . . you will be surprised how the relationship improves. Good luck to all you younger guys and hopefully the changes you make will add to adventure and not be a drag.

From: David

My life's experience has been that the things most worthwhile have not been all that easy . . . and many that were easy were sure not "all that great" later! It's been said here before, and I echo it again, that those of us who examine our sexuality . . . are we gay? BI? heterosexual? OR? . . . seem to dig a lot deeper into ourselves and the meanings of life than those who just "take it for granted" that they are like and a part of the majority! What moves us to examine ourselves seems quite different and can come at very different points in life.

Some, like me, started questioning before the word "sex" had any meaning . . . some when the guy next door got aroused as they wrestled . . . many when boyish cock sucking exploration just seemed so good! Most of us, it seems, went through years and years of real soul-searching and DENIAL . . . in fact, not wanting it to be true even though deep within we knew it was . . . "I'm queer!"

Born and raised in the society/church we were, how else could we feel?

But, as several of you have said (and in earlier notes), we each of us have our own inner definition of what being QUEER means to us . . . and how to handle it . . . AND those keep changing as we change from year to year and experience to experience.

At age 70, I have come to realize that life is NOT all about sex . . . nor is marriage all about sex either! At the same time, I surely know, that for me a "romp in the hay" with a guy is best! Hey, hay-rompers!

From: Mike

I read about there seeming not to be very many "husbands out to their spouses" left here, who are happy being married and who are committed to maintaining a strong relationship with their wives within that marriage. As one of the "silent majority" of men on this list who DO fit the original profile described in the welcome message James sends out, I want to apologize for lurking too long and thereby contributing to the impression that our group's mission statement has become "outdated."

I can see why someone might get that impression lately. I have also noticed a preponderance of messages lately from men who are divorcing, separating, or otherwise ending the marriage to pursue life as single gay or BI men. I applaud them for their courage, for I have followed their struggles posted here, as they tried to "make it work" but for various reasons have found it necessary to move on and away from marriage. That is an honorable choice for them.

But I want to remind other observers that there are many of us out here who are choosing to stay in our marriages because, for us, at this time, this is an honorable choice for us. We love our spouses and they love us. We are doing the work of integrating our "other" sexuality into our relationships with our wives. And we are doing this in diverse ways. In my case, with my wife's loving support, I have been able to establish emotionally and physically intimate relationships with a few very special men over the past 3 years since joining this list. I have experienced a "wholeness" that transcends any words I could write here. I can tell you that I just spent the weekend with 4 other couples like us who are equally committed to their marriages and to supporting them.

How affirming to commune with others who have enough love and courage to face their own and each others' deepest fears, and leave the comfort of social norms to become architects of their own destinies . . . as individuals and as couples. And then to be so generous as to share their "prouds and sorrys" with other couples.

I am sorry that I have not written more often nor shared more of our experience on this list lately. I seem to have more motivation to write when things are not going well. And to lay back as an observer when things seem less urgent. Writing for me is therapy. I guess I write more often when I need to work through something. I selfishly forget that part of the value of this forum for me has been "hearing" the encouraging stories of men who are having some success in creating an authentic life. So I will try to remember to share the sun and the rain of my journey, so that others might take heart and feel they have company in all kinds of weather ;-).

From: Clark

I can attest that a number of people are in my situation: happily married.

My wife knew about my bisexuality from the get-go. We lived with varying degrees of comfort with that during 27 years of marriage. Even though we have had all grades of problems, I would have to characterize our relationship as quite good, healthy, growing, and positive. I believe that our marriage is, all things considered, one of the best I know. I happen to value honesty and frankness more than tranquillity.

I have grown immensely during the last several years. When I began coming to terms with what my homosexuality really means for the rest of my life, and began quite early discussing this with my wife, we entered into a phase of exploring ourselves and our marriage that has been unexpectedly painful and tremendously enriching. Like many of us, I came to see that I could not continue without some relationship with men, or a man. The implications of that for me, as for nearly all of us, are explosive on a number of fronts. Whether our marriage can last remains to be seen, although both my wife and I confess that we deeply want it to. Whether it should last, absent a commitment to monogamy, is another question. How to sort out how to be who I am when wearing so many conflicting roles has been difficult. It still is. Right now, I have no long-term relationship with a guy. The brief one that came to be earlier in the year has now receded into a less passionate friendship—his choice.

It simply is not true that marriages cave in when one or both of the spouses no longer fit the usual mold. There is an enormous amount of social pressure, and doubtless other pressures too, which suggests that this is, or should be, the case. I would not for a minute want to return to the kinds of duplicity that were involved in, say, the Victorian era, when happily married Christian men frequently had mistresses that they somehow excused themselves for, but could never admit. But I must say that our age, even for all its excesses and profligacy, seems to have taken a far more self-righteous stance, replete with great blankets of guilt, than former ages have done in allowing for differences. We twist and turn and flounce and flop in tortured self-reflection about what we can and cannot live with, and beat ourselves up when we fail to meet the standards for marriage, or family, or job, or career. (Don't ask me how I know.) Nothing of this sounds like freedom to me. And it does not sound like health either. Or even responsible living. And, I might add, I think it is not what any religious tradition holds out as a desirable condition of being fully human.

Yet we are creatures of our culture and age, no doubt about it. We continue to confront the ironies of our lives, seeking to find some resolution. And one of those is that some of us, gay as daffodils in September, are happily married to women, who sometimes accept us beyond the bounds of all human expectation, and sometimes suffer silently a pain that sears our own guts as we watch in shame or horror.

Perhaps in the end we simply need to accept what we are and what we have. Whatever that is.

If that, in your case and mine, is a happy marriage, even though it should some day end, make the most of it. And be thankfully glad.

> I am the rest between two notes,
> which are somehow always in discord . . .
> but in the dark interval, reconciled,
> they stay there trembling.
> And the song goes on, beautiful.

Rainer Maria Rilke

From: Mandy

As someone who has lived in both worlds—first as a self-loathing, married, closeted gay man trying to fit into a heterosexual "lifestyle," and then later as a self-loving, out, gay man—I can tell you that the latter is much easier. Of course one cannot know that until one lives it. I was much more fearful and unhappy trying to live my life as someone I was not, always fearing being found out, and feeling very unauthentic as a person, and someone who was largely invisible to the world, the "me" I would allow no one to see.

I cannot pontificate and tell anyone else what's best for them. I fear my long post yesterday has been interpreted in many ways it was not intended. I think some have interpreted it as me telling all married men that they should divorce. Not so. For those for whom continuation of their marriage "makes sense," I say go for it. There is no single one-size-fits-all answer. I was merely addressing those situations (which are only a portion of all situations here) where there was not consensus, honesty, and realistic expectations among the husband and wife, and/or where the husband is projecting expectations into the situation that perhaps really aren't there.

BISEXUALITY

From: Mandy

As a (formerly married) now out-of-the-closet gay man, I have a question for the group that can perhaps help me understand my bisexual brethren here. I just realized that there's perhaps a point of confusion in our language.

When you (those of you who describe yourselves as bisexual married men) all use the word "bisexual," I realize that I don't know if you mean that you:

1. are bisexual in the sense that you could be sexually attracted to another man (this would be my minimum definition of being bisexual),
2. or, are bisexual in the sense that you could be sexually "and" romantically (as in "a relationship") attracted to another man,
3. and, can these gender-neutral attractions occur concurrently? Can you wish to have sexual contact (and also relationships) simultaneously with both a man and a woman?

I had occasion to have an online conversation with a man (not on this list) this weekend who identifies himself as "straight," but is sexually attracted to other men. It made me realize that the words and labels we use may have very different meanings from one person to the next.

On the concurrent relationships issue (which, it would appear, at least some are interested in here), it seems to me that we're going beyond a discussion about just being attracted to both sexes (i.e., not having a preference for either), but now we're entering the territory of issues of sexual monogamy and polygamy, which are not limited to just bisexuals, but are issues for straight and gay couples as well.

Seems to me there are married straight men who wish to have sexual encounters with other women on the side, in addition to their wives. Those who do it covertly, are "cheating on their wives" (according to "traditional values" about marriage). Some wives know and accept it (this is more common in Latino and other cultures), and then there are some marriages where the husband and wife both openly play around, called "swinging." (Please excuse me if I've over-generalized or not used the PC language to describe these positions.)

It seems that if bisexual men are interested in having dual or polygamous relationships with either or both sexes, then one just simply needs to find partners who share these values.

If we're talking about married men who just wish to "get a little on the side" with another man, then is this situation any different than what straight men face, who wish the same (but with women, obviously)? What support groups do straight men in those positions find? Perhaps the equivalent support group, were there one, would be CHOW—Cheating Husbands Out To Their Spouses. ("Cheating" implies this is happening behind their wives' backs, which is not always the case with them, nor with bisexuals here.)

I guess what I'm driving at here (and I can hear the flames coming already) is that I wonder if some bisexual married men don't think their situation (wanting a variety of sexual contact, not just with their wives) is somehow unique and different, because they're bisexual, and that this factor somehow licenses them or entitles them to go behind their wives' backs. If they were straight, society would simply see them as a horny man cheating on his wife.

I know this will fall on some deaf ears, but I am NOT one who advocates marital fidelity just for fidelity's sake, nor for reasons of traditional moral values, etc. My concerns are more about personal honesty and integrity. It's what you agreed to up front with your spouses. Yes, lives and relationships change, and certainly a partner in marriage on his wedding day may not realize what he'll want in twenty years. But when it becomes apparent that he has "changed his mind" about sexual monogamy, or even about wanting to love more than one person concurrently, then wouldn't the wife need to (1) know about that, and (2) agree to and accept that, in order for the marriage to be considered a good, healthy marriage?

I think many of you here *are* *out* to your wives, and are in the process of redefining your marriages with your wives' knowledge and input. And I think it's great to hear the stories where this is happening, where wives have grown in the relationship too, in the same direction, and are okay with "open marriages," and dual or multipartner relationships. I have to say that I am interested in the reactions of wives who never saw it coming, and who themselves are not interested in exploring sexuality with their own genders, or entering into other sexual relationships themselves. Interested in how they accept their husband's desire to seek out others. I think these are the stories that are too rarely posted here.

I hope my questions are not seen as "antibisexual–married men." Though I am not one, it is an issue I'd like to better understand, and that is why I ask the questions.

I'm also thinking about the individual who earlier today posted a message about his disappointment in the group session he went to, with all the unhappy husbands . . . Perhaps bisexual married men would find more in common and more support from straight "swingers" clubs and groups, or from polygamous groups?

I hope you'll forgive what to some will seem like obvious or dumb questions, in my process to better understand this issue.

From: Dale

Mandy wrote: >*Can a bisexual man be satisfied with one sex or the other, at any moment in time, or across a lifetime?*<

The "natural" man, as other kinds of natural creation, exists in wonderful and seemingly unending diversity as well as a good deal of concurrent uniformity. My understanding of personality issues supports that some people find the sexual part of their (bisexual) personality will be expressed serially (in sequence) and will vacillate between male and female but not necessarily both at the same time. Others will find equal attraction at all times to both genders at once. Yet others will hover (within a range) at some point between equally attracted to both genders and an attraction skewed to the male; others similarly hover (within a range) with the skew being toward female. I haven't seen much evidence that would support there's one "universally" correct or normal way to be bisexual.

>*Is it a matter of a bisexual man finding his one life partner (and whether that will be a woman or man, who knows), or, does bisexuality imply an attraction to both concurrently, and a need to satisfy both desires concurrently?*<

For a given personality it could well be expressed in that model. For another, not. Again—I believe profoundly diversity is the norm rather than binary absolutes.

One way of looking at the term BI-sexual is to recognize the prefix "BI" simply means two. So . . . BI-sexual can simply mean being somehow attracted to and able to have satisfying sexual relations with both genders. It doesn't HAVE to have a quantitative rating for the distribution of that attraction between the genders.

I happened to say in a therapy session early on in my wife's and my struggles with all of this "I'm a gay man who happens to be married." At that particular juncture it was a VERY threatening thing to my wife for me to say that because "gay" translated that she would ultimately be excluded from my life as time passed and I inhabited the M2M side of my personality more directly and openly. She needed at that juncture to label me "BI-sexual" because it supported there was an ongoing place in my life for her.

I, on the other hand, made the statement at that time (and possibly still now) because: I knew that I'm only about one woman short of gay! I don't feel sexual attraction to women in general and the logical side of my mind supports the concept that if I were truly "BI" sexual I'd be more broadly attracted to women.

Since that time I feel a little more comfortable acknowledging "BI" in its academic sense even if it's only ONE woman I'm attracted to . . . and my wife has become MUCH less threatened by the label "gay." We both find honesty and comfort, though, saying that I'm "not straight." The one thing certain about us is that both individually and as a couple we continue to be works in progress!

My self-analysis and description of my personal status: I am attracted to ONE woman in the universe (my wife) and to men more broadly. I feel profoundly "connected" to my wife as my female life partner . . . can't conceive of myself being so attached to any other female so long as she's alive. I would LIKE to find a male with whom I also can feel this kind of "life partner" connection. I/we (my wife and I) continue in a kind of search mode with a variety of exploratory contacts happening as time passes but so far haven't found what feels to be a personality interested in "coming in" to my/our life in that fashion for an extended period of time. The one thing certain about the search is that if I/we stopped looking we're certain NOT to find anyone!

My recommendation is to explore and experience as best you can, all the while paying close attention to what strikes the most resonance with your underlying personality and personal style. As you collect a variety of experiences you should find your most positive responses to "cluster" together, which will give you the most reliable insight into what your personal realities are. I think you'll find the most reliable definition of yourself within yourself. What I think you'll find about yourself is that you are both different from and similar to a lot of other guys . . . but not ever a carbon copy of another personality! That's just the way God made us all, I think!

From: Chukky

Funny, but I disagree with most of what was written. I don't have sex with my wife since my coming out a year ago. Ummm, actually I never enjoyed sex with her or any girl I dated and slept with . . . but performed more to keep up the appearance. In my relationship now . . . the sex is wonderful . . . and words can't describe the feelings I have for him . . . in bed and away. Looking back, even on my honeymoon, I remember walking the beach and looking at the guys . . . and never felt the same about the women. In addition, I remember being friends with a few guys whom I really wanted . . . and hinted to but didn't come out directly because of their being straight . . . however, I thought they weren't . . . or let me say . . . I hoped they weren't. I would masturbate thinking about them . . . or a handsome stranger who I met or spoke briefly to. I cannot believe that a guy can be attracted to and love a guy and girl the same. . . . I know I am going to get blasted for that statement . . . but I just don't think it is possible. One has to be stronger than the other . . . and/or the people that say that are lying to themselves—either out of not being able to face the true fact or just being merely afraid.

I know in my situation, I lived knowing my true feelings since I was 18, (I am 40 now) but would NEVER admit to anyone I was gay—no, not BI — Gay! I always thought as a kid gay was feminine . . . and tried to repress my feelings for men. . . . It does not go away. In addition, because of the relationship I am in with my wife . . . and my lover, I realize I was never able to love a woman or feel the things toward her that I can and do feel for a man. I was never the guy who had a one night stand with anyone, in my gay or straight life. I was never able to be affectionate unless I felt warmth or, in this instance deep love. Thus, for me, I could never understand cruising the forest preserve or bookstores, etc. Before I had anyone, I would rather masturbate to my fantasy than be with a stranger. For me, the feelings, the emotional was far more important than the sex. However, the sex is so great due to the emotions—if that makes any sense. I hope I didn't offend anyone . . . just my own views I had to share. I guess in my own way, gay or straight, I'm untraditionally traditional!

From: Dale

Chukky wrote: >*I cannot believe that a guy can be attracted to and love a guy and girl the same . . . .* <

Based on your personal experience, I agree it would be impossible for YOU to be attracted to and love a guy and girl the same and/or that you may have some company in your position. You have no authority, though, to project your personal experience onto the rest of the universe as a given. I wouldn't deny you whatever your experience and insight is . . . but neither would I deny the guy sitting next to you whose experience supports a slightly different convention. Just because you can't project yourself into another "flavor" of sexual orientation other than your own doesn't mean it doesn't exist or isn't likewise as undeniable a reality for THAT person as yours is for you.

I can't say I haven't ever indulged in black & white thinking—feeling there MUST be some kind of universal "right" or "only" way things must be. Time and again, though, just when I was certain I had seen or experienced all the diversity there was in the universe, and that there couldn't be anyone who was XXXXXX—wait a little while and sure enough—along would come someone whose reality is XXXXXX! So—I feel I've made some progress toward being a better citizen of the world as well as a less stressed personality by trying to learn to give others permission to be whatever way they need to be to express and affirm themselves. Where I begin to fight back is when someone else expects me to take on THEIR reality for no better reason than they can't understand or tolerate mine!

From: Kenneth

I am in a love relationship with a married man. I feel that it would be improper for me to attempt to tell him how to relate to his wife. All I can do is tell him what I want in terms of being with him; the rest is up to him. He is the only one who can possibly know what he wants. When he decides, he must tell me. I absolutely cannot be of support to his wife, since I am the very person who most threatens their relationship (from her point of view).

So, don't ignore your needs and wants—express them. Respect your lover's. Then decide where YOU will go from there. Forget about supporting them as a couple—the whole idea is completely noncongruent (unless you wish for them to succeed, in which case you will always be the "fifth wheel").

From: Dale

Kenneth wrote: >*Forget about supporting them as a couple—the whole idea is completely noncongruent*<

I would challenge the idea of framing the idea in a way that makes it seem as if it were a "given" for the universe! It may be a challenge to construct such an arrangement. From my own experience, I can say that if all the parties are present at the construction process and committed to the idea, it can be done . . . has been done . . . and is being done.

>*(unless you wish for them to succeed, in which case you will always be the "fifth wheel")*<

This feels to be another perception, perhaps grounded in your personal experience, but a perception nonetheless. Again—keeping all parties acknowledged and fulfilled in a triadic relationship is likely to be it's own set of "different" challenges — but no more inherently impossible than a dyadic relationship. In some ways working out a triadic relationship could be more challenging and more complex . . . in other ways it could well be an easier scene because of the resources the additional person brings with them.

It's been my experience that self-held perceptions can be an effective predictor of success (or lack of it). "The whole idea is completely noncongruent" and "you will always be the "fifth wheel" are perceptions that would preclude you (or anyone else who takes them on) from ever having much success trying to construct a triadic relationship. I see them to be examples of polarized (and polarizing) thinking.

From: Woody

Dale couldn't have echoed how I feel better! I came out to my wife as a bisexual, but four months later, and a lot of self analysis of my own feelings, I told her I felt I was gay, but leading a bisexual lifestyle. Now, THAT WAS threatening to her, for the same reasons it was to Dale's. I now use the "one woman short of gay" phrase also—it seems so descriptive. I have no sexual attraction to any other women. As a matter of fact, I don't have as much sexual attraction to her as to most men to whom I am attracted (this has been amazing . . . for a 59 year old!). But—I do love her. And want to stay with her as long as she wants me.

Yes, you have to decide in your own mind what you think you are, what best to label yourself and be comfortable with it if that's important to you. It doesn't matter what others think.

haiku:
blood on fence post
stonewalls echo
coyote-howls

From: Scotty

Wow . . . well, we are all entitled to our own opinions, and often they are based upon our experiences, but how can anyone make generalizations?

I view this situation not as one where I am competing for my boyfriend, but where he is fortunate enough to love and be loved by two people, and if those two people can come to care about each other, then we have created more love in the world and in our own hearts. I know this goes against the entire "scarcity paradigm" that our society is based upon, and that it is challenging, but I also believe that, if we want this, it is possible.

It is, in fact, entirely congruent for me to want their marriage to succeed AND my relationships with both of them to succeed. My self-interests are not only defined by what feels good to me but also by living out my ideals, which include a sense of fairness and caring for others as well as for myself.

I certainly question myself about this arrangement. There are emotional risks being taken by all of us, and that feels good . . . we all have much to lose and much to gain.

One of the things about being outside of the status quo is it gives one an opportunity to experience one's own life in different contexts. There isn't a lot of cultural support for that, as we all know, so we find it where we can. I like the idea that we are capable of creating support for each other.

From: Fritz

There are three groups that people fall into: BI-straight, BI-BI, and BI-gay.

Every combination is possible: there are men who find one partner and stay with them and not act on the attraction to the other gender, people who have sex with both concurrently, people whose attractions do change over time (even short periods), etc. No fast rules apply!!!

From: Fritz

Mandy wrote: >*can these gender-neutral attractions occur concurrently? Can you wish to have sexual contact (and also relationships) simultaneously with both a man and a woman?*<

From my experience these attractions can and do sometimes occur concurrently—but not always as well as having simultaneous contact and relationships with both genders—again only for some people at some time.

>*based upon my readings and understanding of the research that's been done the answer to the above is that there ISN'T an answer . . . actually as many answers as there are people who self-identify as bisexual . . . and secondly, not to sound glib, what difference does it make? whatever works for the 2 or 3 or 6 informed consenting adults works!*<

I agree with the above completely.

From: Fritz

Chukky wrote: >*I cannot believe that a guy can be attracted to and love a guy and girl the same.*<

Some people do lie to themselves but many do not. People are attracted to men and women in different ways—meaning sometimes one is stronger than the other, sometimes the attraction is different, sometimes the emotional component is different than the sexual one, etc. I have found from talking to thousands of bisexuals (and straights and gays) is that it is very difficult to understand another's sexuality (let alone your own):-). Most people make the mistake of generalizing from their own experience and feelings. But the world is broad and the variations are infinite.

From: Stephen

When someone gets critical of the goals (such as a triad or dual monogamous relationships) of those of us who are fully bisexual, they are operating out of ignorance and entirely from your own sexual perspective.

Someone being exclusively gay doesn't have a clue (based on their own emotional and sexual life) that we bisexuals can indeed be absolutely turned on and go into heat over both men and women at the same time, depending on the situation. But that, my friend, is the fact. I do it all the time:-). Like the song says, "Love the one you're with"—and I do.

I have actually left the arms of a great man and taken a shower then gone home only to find my wife to be so loving and desirable that my batteries take on a full charge and I do it all over again and fall asleep with my sexuality fully and completely realized. It's an absolutely wonderful feeling to have both parts of my sexuality satisfied. For me that is true contentment.

My ultimate goal is to find one loving man and make of him a lifetime lover while at the same time keeping the love and respect of the woman I am married to. This is not and never will be easy. I never expected that it would be. But it is what I want and what I am working to achieve. I know that my wife will be the least of my problems. She knows that I have dual needs and that I am not worth a shit unless they are both being met. Now, I need to find a man who is as willing to share me as my wife has told me that she is. She realizes that there is part of my soul that no man can ever reach. A part that is hers alone, and she is willing to give the part that does not belong to her back to me, so that I can share it with a man. The one thing that I know is that there is more than enough love in any human being to fill the entire universe. The only limitation on one's ability to love is in thinking that there is a limit.

And so my friends, instead of quarrelling with those of us who are switch hitters why not just continue on your own path of self-discovery like we all have to do? In the end each of us must be the judge of how he conducts his life. And, each of us must pay the price for doing so. There is no free lunch.:-)

Billy wrote: > *"Why is it that heterosexuals feel that they have the right to sit in judgment of us?" That is an interesting question. I myself am surrounded by extremely conservative fundamentalist Christians.<*

When I came out to my wife I told her to tell anyone she wanted to tell if she thought talking to that person would make it easier for her to cope with the news. She told a dear and long-time lady friend from church. She was met with absolute silence. She did not get the support she had thought would come. I was hurt for her because she thought her announcement had cost her a friend. I made up my mind to test that supposition. We were going to be near the home of the couple in question and I told her to call and tell them we were going to be in the area and to ask if they would like to see us. I was delighted to hear that they wanted very much to see BOTH of us.

My thought was that when my wife told her about me that the lady was so stunned that she didn't know what to say because the news was so far outside her experience in life. I was right. They were very gracious and welcomed us with great warmth. After dinner her husband (a member of The Promise Keepers) and I went for a walk. I got the "I hate the sin but love the sinner" spiel. And then I got the surprise of my life. The husband confessed to me that he was not in a position to throw rocks at me because he had had a thing for pornography all his life, and that it was a real struggle for him considering his religious life. So I guess that there are 2 lessons to be learned here.

1. Some people take comfort from despising the gay community because it makes their own emotional baggage feel lighter.
2. It is human nature that most people NEED someone to look down upon so that they can feel good about themselves. Which perhaps explains why so many straight and gay people have such a hard time even believing that there is such a thing as a bisexual. I have been told so many times that as a person who identifies as a bisexual I am really nothing more than a gay man living in denial that it doesn't usually even phase me anymore.

Although I would not expect such ignorance from anyone on this list. In all fairness I must tell you that the same bigoted remark was made to me by a top ranking official from the National Gay and Lesbian Coalition.

And so, with regard to people being judgmental about your life I say, "Fuck Em." This is your life, and your adventure. You KNOW what to do, JUST DO IT!

From: Kenneth

Frankly, I don't think I am operating out of my "sexual perspective," but out of a lifetime of learning about human nature and what works and what doesn't. Every reality isn't relative. I hope you believe that, too. For example, I would hope that you believe that honesty in relationships is always the best policy, regardless of whether there are two or three people involved. By the same token, the capacity of an individual for intimacy is limited, whether that person is BI or hetero or gay. We're all still people and limited in time and energy.

I would like to quote from a book called "Intimacy Between Men," by John H. Driggs and Stephen E. Finn. The book is based on a combined 14 years of experience as cotherapists leading short-term support groups for gay men in Minneapolis. They write, "There is the issue of time and energy. Intimacy is so challenging, especially in sexual relationships, that no one can simultaneously do justice to two intimate sexual relationships. One or both of the relationships must suffer."

That is all I was saying.

From: James

I have a different take on this. . . . I agree (oh, boy, do I agree) that we are people and limited in time and energy. But I have learned a wonderful thing (at least wonderful to me) since coming out 3 years ago. I have learned that I have an incredible ability to love . . . and to love a number of people. Recently, I was trying to explain to my wife why I can love a number of men . . . really love them . . . in very different ways. I have thought of the three words in Greek for love and appreciate the need for different words . . . and I might even add another one or two. But I do not find that my time or energy limits me in any way when it comes to loving. The heart . . . at least mine . . . has the ability to expand and expand and expand with love. It used to scare me how easily I love . . . but not anymore. Where I would introduce the word or concept of energy is how I relate to those I love. There is where my limitations kick in . . . but my ability to love seems to flow on endlessly . . . (sigh)

From: Stephen

I was openly gay before I decided to get married, so I think there are guys here who can relate to your situation. I pained over the decision for five years (we both did), had lots of couples' counseling, and finally decided it was right. While it is challenging sometimes, I have never regretted it. I do sometimes wonder if we "mixed-orientation couples" have any harder a time than any married couple. I just think marriage is challenging and requires tremendous maturity no matter what your background or history.

A big difference is that I grew up in a pretty liberal, accepting environment. I wasn't keeping secrets. I wasn't choosing marriage as a way of conforming to heterosexual norms. In fact, I still think my mom, to whom I'm quite close, would prefer me to be gay. Less competition. I chose heterosexual marriage because I loved my wife and felt we had more going for us than I had ever had with a guy. I wanted the challenge and surprise of heterosexuality after years of homosexual relationships, which for me were great but also predictable in a way. Undoubtedly that was the men I was attracted to, not generalizeable to all gay men's experiences. For me with guys the romantic spark was just never there, although they were great buddies and I still love some of them.

From: Scotty

I have been reading the posts of the last few days. The issues about whether a person is bisexual, or why stay married . . .

I think that fear is what we are really talking about. Fear of rejection. I can't judge someone for holding onto the cultural acceptance of (apparent) heterosexuality. There are a lot of goodies that go with that. One of them is that you don't have to deal with being a reviled person . . . no small thing.

Before I finally came out and stopped trying to be bisexual or heterosexual I was terrified that everyone would hate me if they knew. *I* hated me. I thought my feelings were disgusting. When I finally came out it was because I couldn't stand the pain of hiding anymore. I woke up in the middle of the night one night . . . in my sleep I had pushed the woman I lived with out of bed and was hitting her, all while asleep. I am not a batterer . . . I wasn't beating her up . . . no one was hurt . . . but the message couldn't have been clearer.

Since coming out a discovery I have made is . . . I HAVE the safety and approval I was afraid I would lose. No, I do not have a wife I walk arm and arm with . . . but I have my own approval and dignity in ways I didn't before and that is priceless to me. If someone yells "faggot" at me (which happened once) I just think they are an asshole . . . I don't feel ashamed of myself anymore.

Without going into my whole life story, I want to share with you all that the danger is FEAR, NOT LOVE. The more we trust our fears to guide us the more separated we are from our true loving nature. That doesn't mean you can come out to everyone and they will be delighted . . . but it means you have got to delight yourself by BEING yourself. Look at all the pain that comes from trying to be other than you are.

I do not presume to tell anyone what they should do. I do not mean to imply that any one course of action is best for everyone. I am just saying . . . look your fear in the face, remember who you really are inside, love yourself, and see where that leads you.

If the shoe fits, wear it. But if it doesn't fit, don't.

From: Shawn

The description of what it feels like to have the capacity to love both men and women erotically reminds me so much of my own experience. Some people don't want to believe that we are BI simply because they have not had this experience. The thinking seems to go . . . "if I have not experienced it, then it must not be for real. Thus, I will ridicule and doubt the word of those who say they are BI." BI-the way, have you read, "BI Any Other Name"? Recommended reading.

I have come to the conclusion that I will not accept the fear and prejudice that might be hurled at me by anyone, whether it is because they hate my bisexuality, dislike my hazel-green eyes, dislike my Jewish great grandparents who hardly spoke English, or whatever it is about me that someone might fear or misunderstand. Life is too short for all that foolishness and a lot of us are moving on. The fearful and hateful and judgmental can stay behind in the dust if they so choose. I wish that they wouldn't. They're missing such a good time and I do wish them well. They are, after all, still our brothers and sisters. The Rev. Dr. Martin Luther King Jr. said it so well when he referred to the white hate-mongers (who were so busy shedding innocent blood) as "our sick white brothers and sisters." He still called them brothers and sisters!!!

To some degree we all choose our spiritual, emotional, and relational destinies by the attitudes we adopt and cling to. We all have been given the choice, however, to move on to a higher level. My hope and prayer is that the cultural shift now occurring will take our society to a better place than we've ever been heretofore.

MAN OF PARTS?

From: Carl

I came out to my sister recently. She sent me a letter including the following passage:

"My own impression (for what it's worth) is that your wife could accept a complicated arrangement in which she and a male partner each have your love—but not one in which she feels she'd have to compete with him for the same part of you."

This may be nonsense or may be wisdom—I can't tell which. Sex is not an issue, and my sister knows that. So how do I slice myself to accommodate this bifurcation? I'd appreciate comments.

From: Brandon

I have been with my partner now for 7 years and I have been married to my wife for 38 years. I love each of these two beautiful people such that sometimes I feel that my heart overflows. I have no difficulty separating the unique love that each brings into my life. I also seem to flourish with energy and excitement for life and the unique love that I have for each. It is similar (though more exuberant) to the love I have for my mother or father or for each of my individual children. Each is different and unique yet each is truly loved by me. It is also similar to the love that I individually feel for a few very close friends that bless my life. One of the big problems that I initially had, before I had come out to my wife, was: Could I separate this great need that I have to be physically, emotionally, and spiritually a part of another man and the great love, companionship, need, and commitment that I feel for my wife? I took my time finding this out about myself and eventually learned by trial and error that yes indeed I could separate out the two seeming opposites of my personality. I could accept and integrate all of my God-given needs. I answered my most basic question: "How is it possible for me to love this beautiful woman that blesses my life, yet be GAY?" I could not and still cannot split myself in two. There is only one of me—a Gay Married Male!

The fact that I have now been in a very loving and supportive relationship with my partner and still maintain a beautiful, fully rewarding marriage with my wife attests to the fact that it can be done. Life is not 100% perfect; but for each of the three of us, it is pretty darned good and each in our own way are very happy with our individual and shared lives!

I do know that if my male partner or my wife were competing for the same love within me that I could not handle life. I believe I would forever be torn apart, depressed, and frustrated with life—as I was before I came out to my wife and before my partner and I found each other.

How it works I do not know. My partner does not need to compete with my wife for my love and my wife does not need to compete with my partner. We do have a time problem though and only a time problem! I am with my partner two nights a week and one weekend a month. My wife is not an "alone" person so this is an ongoing dilemma that we continue to work upon. My partner on the other hand is an alone person and though he would like more time, he seems to accept the blessings that he has in our relationship as he fully understood that when we committed each other that I am truly a GAY MARRIED MAN.

From: Rodney

I'm new to this list and only recently (3 weeks) out to my wife and children. Although I'm 52, my first gay experience was about 18 months ago. My experience with gay sex has been limited to masseurs and escorts. Currently (while my wife and I try to come to terms with all this) I am abstinent with regard to men.

I was very interested in Brandon's response, because he describes himself as "gay." I hope you all will understand that my questions are not meant to be prying—I'm just trying to understand things better, and I can't always figure out a "polite" way to phrase my questions.

Do you continue to have sex with your wife?

I ask this, because several of the guys I've been with have told me I'm "really gay "because I enjoy having sex with them so much.

But I enjoy having sex with my wife, too, at least as much as with men.

For me, sex is like a radio with a bunch of channels. When I'm with a guy, I guess I'm tuned in to KGAY or something like that. If I take the time to "get my head in the right place," (i.e., to be wholly PRESENT with the guy), I can have a terrific time.

When I'm with my wife, I tune in to KBREED and also have a great time.

I don't usually get the channels confused or mixed, though I'd like some fine day to try tuning into KBI (my hottest fantasies are bisexual).

The radio analogy for me works with regard to things other than gay vs. straight sex. A couple of masseurs have helped me "tune in" to sexual experiences I wouldn't have thought I would enjoy. But with their guidance, I had a great time.

Does any of this make sense to you? How does it map onto your experience?

Now the issues with regard to Love are rather different, and (like you) I think she is really talking about the problem of monogamy for married BI- and gay guys. But as you can see, I am still struggling to understand the more fundamental issue of sex.

From: Henry

My wife and boyfriend do not compete for the same part of me. The two relationships are just different. My boyfriend, who's bisexual like me, understands this implicitly. My wife isn't so sure, but I told her, "If I had a girlfriend, then you and she would be competing for the same part of me." I know she'd be completely flipped (and I'd be thrown out on my ass) if I had a girlfriend on the side, and that's some acknowledgment that the relationships are different in kind.

From: Henry

I'm truly a novice here and struggling to understand a whole BUNCH of things, but I think your sister is trying to deal with the very unwieldy and confusing messages we have all been raised with concerning monogamous relationships.

In my own case, I know that it is possible to have SEXUAL relationships that are essentially devoid of intimacy, and that such experiences can be nonetheless positive and life-affirming. My wife, like most people (esp. women) in our culture, has a terrible time understanding this.

On the EMOTIONAL level, things get even murkier, because in one sense I fall in love all the time, with men as well as women. These are not sexual relationships, but if we work from the model that we all have a fixed amount of emotional energy, then I have hundreds of relationships in my life that "take away" from my relationship with my wife.

But I know it doesn't quite work like that. Loving people is to a certain extent like doing push-ups—the more you do it, the more of it you can do.

And although I know you can have great sex without intimacy, I also know that the greatest sex is that which is coupled with Love.

At present, my wife is the only person in my life with whom I have both sex and deep feelings of love. With this particular combination, you can go into some distant and wonderful places together.

But I don't see any reason in theory why you couldn't make this journey with more than one person. In fact, I suspect that the push-up analogy might even work here to some extent: the more you do it, the more of it you can do.

Having said that, I will also admit that it would make me very uncomfortable if my wife were to fall in love with another man.

So go figure. Thanks for letting me share my confusion with you.

From: Howard

How do you slice your love for your first child to make room for the second, or the third? It's not about love. That grows to fill the object(s) of your love. It is more about how you manage your time and energy. Consider those things carefully.

From: Carl

Thanks for your reply, Brandon. We have a lot in common. My wife and I have been married for 36 years. My male lover and I first were lovers 46 years ago, though when we fell into each other's arms it was the first time we'd seen each other in 40 years. I can't imagine anything that could be called living that doesn't include conscious love for both for whatever time remains to us all.

Certainly the precise quality of love for each is quite different. I love not only my wife, but the son and daughter-in-law and granddaughter that she made possible, and the composite family love is a very compelling force. At the same time, nothing within the family can compare with the depth and subtlety of the mutual understanding that exists between my boyfriend and me—nor with the support that I feel from my boyfriend in certain areas that we mutually value but my wife tends to ignore or even denigrate. I doubt that that sort of understanding could be available in a male-female relationship. Is this perhaps the key to offering "different parts" of myself to each?

SALVATION?

From: Gripp

I don't really, consciously, worry about salvation; but there are subconscious concerns which say, what if my dad is right, and I really will not "go to heaven" because of my sexuality. My upbringing is really a liability at times. I went through 18 years of church almost daily. I have been brainwashed from birth on—extremely conservative Christian fundamentalism. My parents said: "God is love." But at the same time they withheld their own love when I did not toe (tow?) their line, demonstrating that God did not love at all times.

My father tried to censure my reading. Fairy tales (Hans Christian Andersen) were not appropriate reading—sinful in fact. I had to ask God's forgiveness when he discovered that I was reading them. The Bible was all I needed. And the literal interpretation was expounded. He (my dad) taught salvation through works, although faith was mentioned. We had to "strive to be perfect as He is perfect." Imperfection was equated with sin. My "sin" of sexuality was not something I could "put behind me," so I never felt totally forgiven.

If I don't think about it (salvation) I don't worry. When I do think and talk, I worry about the differences between the interpretations that I was taught and the wonderful sermons and articles which I have read on your pages or from the likes of Bishop Spong and Bruce Bawer. They have helped me immensely. I still have a long way to go toward accepting me subconsciously and the fact that God loves me, unconditionally.

Actually I went almost 30 adult years without beginning to search out what I needed for myself. It began with my with my self-acknowledgement as a bisexual man leading to a relationship with my boyfriend. Coming out to my wife was the next logical step. Now I'm working on/for me, thinking out my issues.

Pray for me that I will continue to find a truth that God loves me just as he made me.

From: Andy

What an interesting life history you have! I find "bisexual" too confining (only two? two what? as if gender matters) :-). I prefer "omnisexual" or just "sexual." Buddha tells us to have compassion on all living critters. Of course, it's a delicious self-parody but the title of a bisexual magazine is "Anything That Moves." Isn't it a great and marvelous gift to be able to relate to all sorts of folks with our whole being, sexuality included? Come now, are you really worried about salvation as if it depended on some kind of purity? For me, pouring myself out in love is itself salvation. "Those who try to save their lives lose them, but those who lose their lives save them" (Jesus).

From: Brandon

Years ago I was lying on a rolling table covered in a cold cotton hospital blanket on my way into my 7th surgery in a year and a half. I had spent most of that previous year and a half in one hospital or another, away from my family and loved ones, and felt totally alone in a very cruel world. I was dying a slow death of excruciating pain, and a body that was disintegrating at an ever-accelerating speed. I had come to understand that even the God that I had so dearly loved and trusted had forsaken me.

Whether it was pure hallucination, a divine intervention, or my tired brain going crazy (I will never really know) but I heard these words as plain as any words that I have ever heard in my life:

"Brandon you are My miracle, I created you just the way I wanted you and I have no intention of undoing my original miracle!"

I knew instantly what was meant by this—as I had prayed all my life for a miracle to be "Straight," "Non-Gay," "Non-Queer," "Non-Homosexual," etc., etc.—It was at that instant that it dawned on me that God in all His glory and wisdom had indeed created me in His image and in His likeness. GOD LOVED ME FOR EXACTLY WHO I WAS!!! At that moment I stopped hating my very nature and truly started loving myself—this was a first for me.

Low and behold!!! That was my last surgery and afterward I started to regain my health and was soon out of the hospital and back home with my wife and family. Took years of in-depth therapy and counseling to get my self-esteem. I had it as a small child but lost it in early teens when I caught homophobia. Took me more years to learn who I really was by joining the Gay community and getting to know and love some truly good, loving, and holy Gay, BI, transgender, and transsexual persons. Also learned a lot about who I wasn't by a few real Shits out there.

I have now been out to my loving and supportive wife for 10 years. I have been with my loving and supportive male partner for 7 years. I have many loving gay and straight friends in this beautiful world. My life is full, good, and I go daily knowing that God truly loves me! Blessed is a good word!

My dear man—I can assure you that God created you just the way that he wanted you—Please graciously accept that gift of His love. The trick of a happy life is now to go forth and make yourself a happy person. If you do this then those that you love will see that happiness and goodness and it will truly rub off on all.

From: William

Yours is an incredible story. More amazing is that you have been able to "question authority" and come up with some answers you created for yourself. There is a strong spark of life in you which could not be extinguished with years of oppressive conditioning. Your sexuality is really a gift, one that enabled you to question more than your sexual orientation, but the way you were brought up, too. More power on your journey.

From: Gripp

Thank you Brandon! Yours is a marvelous story. I DO believe in miracles. I guess there is something God wants of me. It is certainly hard—trying—getting to that place.

Thanks for your help.

From: Floyd

Hey Brandon, what a wonderful story . . . it's totally inspiring. Yeah, god loves us all. Why the fuck doesn't everyone realize that and make the world peaceful?

From: Andy

My man lover —who saved his soul by not moving in with me—is a fundamentalist Christian, and he used to take in some TV shows and even a stray movie against the strictures of his elders. So I know the mentality well.

Our real story and the story we should be telling with our lives as well as lips—is the story of a prodigal God who pours out herself in love without measure and gladness above his fellows losing his very life in the process (in the "son" modality), confounding those who preach sin instead of love. Be assured, despite your subconscious doubts that are bound to bubble up, that God makes you and loves you and reaches out to you in acceptance even when you do not accept yourself.

From: David

Just about a half century after I really admitted to myself that I was a homosexual, and since being on this list, I finally stopped berating God, stopped begging God, and stopped being angry with God when it came to me that God had, as in COUNTLESS other cases, heard and ANSWERED my prayer: "David, I made you the way I did and that is the way you will stay." And I felt a strong "P.S." like "Now, what do you plan to do with this blessing?" First, I have learned to regularly thank God for two blessings:

1. Being gay
2. Being the patriarch of a growing, wonderful family (plus, of course, lesser blessings)

As most of you know, I still do not understand the WHY of 1 and 2 as a "given" . . . but that, too, is not uncommon in my life-long relationship with God. I get answers very often to what/where/when/who questions . . . and sometimes, even, to how. But God seems to refrain from answering "why?" most of the time for me! Maybe it is because my whys tend to be either in anger or just plain whining and self-pity . . .

But, at age 70+, I am sure now of the fact that being gay (or any flavor of "gayness") is a gift . . . and we are never rejected by the God of Love for being what we are!

HOW WE RESPOND

From: Marshall

How would you classify the married men that you (I don't necessarily mean YOU personally) might run across in the bathhouse, or the peep shows, or the truck stop along the highway? The married men that are looking for a little sucking (may or may not be reciprocal), fucking (may or may not be reciprocal) but NO kissing!—I am not gay!

I know from my own experience that:

- looking at a man was okay—that didn't make me gay!
- lusting for a man was okay—that didn't make me gay!
- being sucked by a man was okay—that didn't make me gay!
- sucking a man was okay—it was just returning a favor!—that didn't make me gay!
- fucking a man was okay—my eyes were closed and I couldn't even tell it was a man—that didn't make me gay
- being fucked by a man was okay—I just wanted to know what it felt like—that didn't make me gay!
- kissing a man would make me gay! Oops, I just kissed a man and I liked it.

So, are they gay/BI and in denial? Do they know they are gay/BI? Are they just deprived of sex at home and have found that some men (me for one) are sluts?

I wish I had the answers to my own questions. I don't, but I would sure like to hear your opinions.

From: Gripp

We have debated labels on this list many times and we seem to have agreed to disagree. And, the last word is not yet out. Labels don't say everything. Or they say a lot, but always with discrepancies. However, that is not what you want to hear. A person is what he calls himself, then. So one may be labeled as he chooses. But that is not what you want to hear either. What do we (in this case I) think about those who accept sexual satisfaction from men but don't want to return the favor? Well there have been times when I have been glad, even grateful, to have a cock to suck, regardless of how the person identified himself. I'm sure I have sucked many who did not think of themselves as gay, BI, or any other sexual minority term. And I didn't worry about what they thought of themselves while I was sucking them. But then I was not satisfied with myself or the unknown individual I was working on.

I imagine that I could say that there was a time when I was gay, because I didn't have sex with any women, just men. There was another very short time when I had sex with only women, mostly my wife. I guess I was heterosexual at that time. During my married and promiscuous time, I didn't think much about what I was. When I fell in love with a man and was faithful only to him and my wife, I began to think of myself as BI. And I worried about it, especially if I could easily get it up with one and not the other. I understand the need for a label for me; I agonize over it a lot. Do I really love my wife? All the time? (yes) Do I love my man to the exclusion of my wife? (no, I love her more, it seems, because I love him.) Does that make me BI? Well, I guess that BI is the closest label to my fluid sexuality. Right now I relate only to my wife. Am I now heterosexual? Well, no; I'm also tremendously attracted to some men. Am I attracted to other women? Yes, when I think about it, there are some women I get turned on by. Do I think about it a lot? Yes! I was reared in a negative fashion as far as any minority was concerned. Did I have low self-esteem? Yes. Do I still? Sometimes! I am still learning to accept me as I am, regardless of my current label. I still have trouble believing that God loves me, because I am not straight. Intellectually, I like me and believe in me, but subconsciously and sometimes consciously, I wonder if I will receive salvation; if others would love me if they knew about me; if God might really consign me to hell for the "wicked things" I have done.

All of that may seem off the subject of labeling myself and others. It is easiest for me to think that anyone who relates sexually to both sexes at any point in his lifetime is bisexual. That still doesn't satisfy me about me. What am I? Well, I am teaching myself to say that I am God's child; He made me therefore I AM!

From: Marvin

Count me amongst those who think it's bullshit! It has always AMAZED me that someone would suck my dick but not kiss me. They have no idea what they're missing!

From: Dale

Your question (and suggested thread) makes me think of the KSOG (Klein Sexual Orientation Grid) which is put forth in Fritz Klein's book, "The Bisexual Option." MUCH of the world tries to see sexual orientation and expression in a strictly binary format—gay/straight, male/female, etc. In reality even THAT part of the natural creation is as full of diversity as anyone can imagine.

Klein's concept with the KSOG is that sexual orientation/expression is not a matter of a two-dimensional, BI-polar spectrum. Rather, it is a composite of one's attractions, behaviors, sexual fantasies, emotional preference, social preference, lifestyle, and self-identification all set in a time context: past, present, and "ideal." The KSOG is set up visually on two poles—vertical and horizontal; the intersections in each category are rated numerically. What results is NOT a word or even a hyphenated word, but a string of numbers. This, of course, STILL leaves us outside the convention of having a neat, little label or "handle!" but is a more accurate measure, at that moment in time, of how we really are (and also partly how people may see us to be).

I've noticed the phenomenon of which you speak, of course. There is quite a general "wish," out there, I think, to avoid the label "homosexual" or "gay." There is good reason to avoid the labels . . . some pretty horrible things have happened to people who either take or are labeled gay or homosexual.

The labels BI and gay have never felt like they captured the complexity and diversity that is "me." I feel the most honest and comfortable saying I'm "not straight."

From: Joey

This reminds me of a conversation I had with a gay friend of mine. I mentioned someone who said he was bisexual. My friend's comment was, "Oh, hell, tell him to get off the fence and come on over here and kiss me!" I split a gut laughing.

From: Kenneth

The only thing I can suggest is that, of all the acts you mention, kissing is the only one that has a romantic component to it. In other words, even though kissing is erotic, it is intensely personal and, therefore, leaves very little room to maneuver if you are caught red-handed (red-lipped or red-tongued?) to say that you just were trying to get your rocks off and a guy was the only person within cum-shot. By the way, my companion taught me something called "toking." With mouths wide open, press the lips together, forming a seal all around the mouth. Then, one man exhales while the other breathes in, and vice versa for a minute or more. It's quite nice!

From: William

I've thought about similar things in relation to the consciousness of guys who dig m2m sexual activities but don't label themselves gay. And how come I have had a struggle labeling myself. However the real problem may be the American preoccupation with labeling everything, classifying, diagnosing, and then assigning value or worth to labels which really have no intrinsic value—Rolex vs. Timex. Guess vs. Gap. Kids at school get ostracized because they don't have the proper label on their jeans. And society labels and ostracizes men who suck cock now and then instead of sticking to sucking cunts. I think we should burn all labels.

From: Pan

When I'm in a gay bar I find it very uneasy to reveal to a gay man that I'm married. I always get a feeling that he thinks I'm only looking for a quickie in the bar toilet. So in a way I'm in a closet and denial but in this case it's my hetero side I'm hiding. And then I wonder when it would be safe to reveal myself. I hope I'm wrong and only being a little paranoid.

From: Kenneth

Boy can I ever relate to what you are saying! A friend of mine, who I originally met online and have had coffee/dinner with on a couple of occasions when I was in town, e-mailed to say he was on vacation and wanted to get together. He knows my situation as a married man who is struggling to find the "right" way to go on from here. Although I'm not sure exactly what he thinks of my situation, I *do* know that he is comfortable enough with me to suggest getting together. As it turned out, three of his other local friends joined us for dinner this week. I had a GREAT time, really enjoyed the fun & friendly conversation, but had the really odd, uncomfortable sensation of being ashamed of my status as a married (though I'm not sure for exactly how much longer) man. I wear a wedding ring, which of course isn't welded to my finger, but I left it on because it "is" who I am right now. It didn't occur to me to hide it until I was with the group and realized that I wasn't just "one of the guys." (I also recognize that some guys with male partners wear gold bands signifying their commitment, so don't get me wrong . . .)

Strange, I've finally just started getting over the deep shame I had felt for so long about my "gay" side, and now I find myself hung up over the "married" side. Sheesh! The "high" of a great time out on the town Tuesday night has been followed by some of the deepest lows I've felt in awhile . . . almost makes me want to burrow back into my closet, but I know I would suffocate in there if I did.

Has anybody else felt this kind of a "rebound" effect after something as simple as having dinner/drinks/coffee with some guys in the gang? Hell, I wasn't this conflicted after some episodes of sharing a hotel room with a friend on several occasions back more than a year ago. Of course, back then I would have probably classified myself as "gay-questioning," whereas by now I think there's not much doubt left. . . .

Maybe the universe is trying to tell me something, i.e., to just stop caring so damn much about what everyone ELSE thinks about my life and focus on what "I" want. But that seems to be an extra tough lesson for me to learn. Anyway, just wanted to say that I really know where you're coming from. Anyway, thanks for sharing. Your note really struck a chord with me.

From: Erin

I do not feel that is the case. I think that gay men, who are neither BI nor married, feel that a married gay or married BI is not fully honest with himself nor those around him. I also think that a fully gay, out man feels that the married man cannot be fully available to the out man. Being in a gay bar signals to others that one is available on some level. Marriage may add a note of furtiveness or unavailability gay men do not like. No one really wants to be "the other woman."

As one gay friend told me he was advised, when first coming out to himself, by another fully gay man: "Don't fall in love with a married man or a Catholic."

From: Marvin

What about someone (ME!?!?!) who's BOTH married and Catholic??????

It can be an issue with some gay men (married men) . . . and I can, on an intellectual level, understand the "bad rap" that we've got . . . there ARE a lot of guys out there who will engage in sex with another man and not consider themselves gay . . . or BI. . . .

There are also those of us who know who we are, are loving, passionate men, and have MUCH to offer a single gay man, while remaining married. Much as we all differ in our marriages, single men differ in their need for monogamous committed relationships . . . the key is having people involved in a relationship whose outlooks/beliefs all mesh.

From: Kenneth

My gay therapist has specialized in counseling gay men for several years now. He says that he has a number of straight clients that really enjoy getting blow jobs from anonymous gay men in public places. They are not gay at all! They're just in it for the pleasure of having another man fellate them! It would, therefore, be wrong to condemn them for not calling themselves something which they are not, i.e., gay. Labels can be misleading.

From: Stewart

So funny that you mentioned the "wedding ring" issue. I too have felt the same feelings. What puzzles me so much is that I have subconsciously felt "odd" for being with the gay crowd and being married. At times I felt as if I were a black sheep among society's black sheep.

All of my dear friends in the community I met via my local GAMMA chapter. We all have the same foundational issues at hand, but even when we walk through a club/bar, I feel as if my wedding ring is a bright neon target! I have now reached the point where I take it off when I go out. I have found, from my fellow buddies experiences, that the ring becomes too much of a conversation piece and it just gets exhausting to repeatedly explain.

I never realized I had an "issue" with this. I have not even shared that with my friends. This list just goes to prove once again, I am not the only one with these feelings!!

From: Marvin

Interesting twist on this thread. . . .

I used to always feel really uncomfortable wearing my ring when in the bars . . . not so much from what anyone ELSE might think, just didn't feel right to ME to wear it. . . .

Now I always leave it on . . . if someone immediately judges me by my jewelry I'm probably not interested anyway (besides . . . most of my friends would tell you that I'm a jewelry queen anyway)

From: Rodney

I am really struck by how much of our "struggle" derives from the need people have to apply labels to us (and our own need to apply them to ourselves). But no two straight guys are really all that much alike, when you get past their conventionalized surface, any more than any two gay guys are all that much alike, once you get beyond their surface.

And the real LOVE struggles—straight, bisexual, or gay—seem ultimately always to come back to the question of monogamy: how much we need it ourselves, how much our spouses and lovers need it. This has nothing to do with labels.

From: William

Right on Rodney. Since much of our struggle is a closeted one, it is lonely. Fortunate are they whose struggles are politically correct. The thinking public considers them to be role models and even heroes. Think of those who struggle for black identity, acceptance of a disability, for equal rights, women's rights, gay rights, etc. But how do we struggle for our place in the sun? The sun doesn't shine in the closet. Demanding to be considered equal to my brothers endangers my family and makes us all outcasts. Lucky are we to have each other through AOL and face-to-face support groups. All of us in this complicated world struggle with one thing or another. It's just that doing it in the closet makes it seem we are very different. But I don't think we are. It just seems that way. This is a very complicated life we have and all of us struggle to be complete and fulfilled human beings no matter what the struggle or who we are. If only we all realized this, the world would be a better place.

From: Kenneth

William wrote: >*Demanding to be considered equal to my brothers endangers my family and makes us all outcasts.*<

Your statement above is pretty gloomy. Could you explain what you mean by "brothers," "endangers my family," and "makes us all outcasts"? Aren't we already outcasts when we are in the closet? Struggling in a closet can only get you all tangled up amongst the coat hangers. . . .

From: William

Kenneth, I don't especially feel gloomy. First of all, all men (and women too) are my brothers. The statement above means that BI married men cannot demand equal rights without causing serious problems for their families. Think of what would happen to our kids at school if we came out publicly. I am not totally defined by my bisexuality. It's a piece of me only and that piece happens to be in the closet when it comes to the general public. Do you have a problem with that? Do me a similar favor and explain your last sentence.

From: Floyd

There are some positive things about the closet; it's not all black, as you seem to cast it !

From: Gabe

I do not wear a ring. We never have. But I have a friend who takes me out to the gay bars from time to time. The first thing he will say when we get there and we meet some of his friends, is that I am married and out to my family. It always makes me feel uncomfortable and angry. Not so much because I feel I should hide it, but because during the few moments I can enjoy out in a gay environment, I do not want to have to explain my situation, talk about the kids, etc. The reactions vary. Most of the time they don't care, or they think it's a weird European thing. Some guys are turned on by married guys. But most of the time I am the one that is uncomfortable, so obviously it is myself who still is not at ease with the whole situation.

From: Roy

It is pretty much similar to what I had gone through here in Singapore.

I started to mingle with the local gay communities. Each time I get to meet or am introduced to a new person, I will not mention anything about being married. Slowly throughout the friendship (real friendship, without getting physical), I told some of them that I am married and the reaction/acceptance varies.

Each time, when I attended a gay social gathering, one or two of the guys would ask after my family, which I think is really not appropriate and if they left the gathering before me, they would kind of remind me that my family is at home waiting. I really feel that they have gone beyond my level of comfort.

From: Miller

I was struck by the discussion about being out with a group of gay guys and wearing a wedding ring. It used to bother me enough that I took the ring off because I didn't want to go through all the explanations—now I leave it on because I see no reason to pretend I am something that I am not. I would rather be with someone who does not care that I am married than someone for whom it is a real problem. And I guess that every once in a while, we all need a "quickie" so that I would just as soon not send out wrong information to anyone, if that is what I am looking for at the time. (In other words, if someone would refuse to get together with me because I am married, I would just as soon know that right away). And if I'm not looking to have sex, I still feel that being honest is more appropriate.

It's true that some gays are pretty narrow minded (like some straight guys!). I've always felt that gay guys who feel there is no such thing as bisexuality, or who refuse to live in the straight world for one minute more than is necessary, are just cheating themselves out of experiencing life. While I fully understand the comfort level and nurturing that occurs in a "no straights allowed" existence, I also feel that exclusively living that life is somewhat childish—maybe refusing to deal with reality, perhaps, I don't know. That there is a need for a "gay world" underground is a sad comment on our society's refusal to accept gay men and women—but it's sort of like the old issue of the folks in the black community who refuse to deal with white people. I find that equally perplexing.

From: Floyd

This is an interesting issue and I'd love to hear more about it! I'm a married BI guy who has friendly relations with gay guys who seem to appreciate me without judging me. As far as commitment, yeah, I have a primary commitment to my wife and I'm clear about that from the beginning. Some of them also have primary commitments to their lovers or, in one case of a good friend, a long time (25 year) partner for whom there's no longer sexual attraction.

In these friendships, sex is *a* component, not the only component; I consider these to be friends, just like other friends within the context of marriage, and these may include sexual expression. My wife understands it as such, as my friendly lovers do.

From: Dale

Gay bias against men married to a female doesn't feel good whether it's on the street or here on this list. The thread about such bias has provoked my thought, and I think I've finally realized why it provokes such deep anger and sadness in me. I don't know whether bias in general is the same, but gay bias against married men seems often to be the personality pointing the finger of blame outward at married men rather than pointing the finger inward at prejudices lurking there. Each of us has tastes, tolerances, and limitations—I know *I* do. The dishonesty of overlooking our own prejudices and shunting the blame outward onto someone else is what drives me up the wall.

DISCLAIMER: There are "bad apples" in any group of people. Married guys DO deserve some of the bad press they have amongst their gay brothers. Some guys (gay or straight) go to great lengths to conceal their marriages or relationships and appear to be single because they feel their romantic prospects outside the marriage or relationship would be limited if their prospective partners knew they were "attached." I know of cases, too, where a married guy has become involved with another man to the point of having the other man leave a marriage, change locale, job, etc. . . . Along comes the wife finding out about the "entanglement," and rather than matching the commitment his lover has done (ditched the marriage, moved, new job) he succumbs to his marriage and bails leaving his lover high and dry. Very bad manners!!

My point is that no matter how many terrible tales there are that can be told, it's an injustice to the OTHER married guys who are honest, upright, straightforward, and a whole kitchen list of other traits, to universally label ALL married guys to be the same (that sameness being dishonest, cheats, liars, etc.).

Here are some "I" quotes from previous e-mail that seem to be more honest and truthful and don't point the finger of blame outward:

1. "I don't feel comfortable being around a gay or BI man who is married but whose wife or family doesn't know about his actions."
2. "I feel like a contributor to deceit and dishonesty if I date or have sex with a gay or BI man who is married. I don't like to feel like an accomplice."
3. "I can't visualize how a gay or BI man can be honest and open about his sexual orientation and still be married."
4. "I need to feel that a person who is in a relationship with me will demonstrate his commitment to me through sexual exclusivity."
5. "I don't want to try to do the work of dealing with the complexity of sharing someone I care for with anyone else."
6. "I want to have my lover devoted to just me, and I don't want to feel I have any competition for his time, effort, affections, energy, from anyone else."

When someone says "No one really wants to be the other woman," what they are really saying to me is "The only way I want to be in a relationship with another person is to own or possess them." If, for a given individual, a person must have that feeling of exclusivity with another person, I have no problem with that. I DO have a problem with someone projecting the strategy of exclusivity as being a universal given. Maybe people who can and do exist in a polyamorous situation are in a minority, but they do exist and there are any number of relationships satisfying and gratifying to their principals that aren't so tightly drawn into exclusivity.

The statement from Paul that: "Being in a gay bar signals one is available on some level. Marriage may add a note of furtiveness or unavailability gay men do not like" presumes that a gay bar is (or should be) some kind of private, membership-only club instead of a public place where ANYONE has the right of entry and service. In some communities the same bar serves both straight and gay clientele—the only thing different is that Tuesday night (or some other night) is designated "Gay Nite." If someone feels strongly about imposing strict limits on one's marital status, availability, sexual orientation, etc.—that's okay, too, but probably requires a private club setting.

I agree with the broad sentiment of the statement: "No one really wants to be the other woman." This metaphor "the other woman" represents being in a position of expendable, secondary importance in a context where the only position of worth or value is first place. It's a very short distance from "second place" to "second rate," which is not a very desirable state.

I hear people say, "My marriage is my primary relationship," or "I don't mind my husband having his boyfriend because he does things all the time that prove to me that I am his primary relationship." While I understand the sentiment of these statements, I feel our language fails us at this juncture. What I object to is the idea that one thing is "primary" which, by definition, means nothing else can be more important. If you're the one who is "primary" that may not be a problem. I also realize that some people may really need those words as a constant reassurance of their spouse's commitment to them. I wish we had words to use in these "duogamous" or polyamorous situations that could communicate the feeling of security and regard to all without inherently assigning rank, value, or weight to one unit over the other. I think it unfair to impose onto someone else you also care for and/or your relationship with that person (or persons) such polarized, denigrating language.

From: Marshall

When I started the thread of asking what you thought of married men hanging out in truckstops, bathhouses, etc. saying they were not gay or BI, I told you that this was a thread that had recently run on the Bear's Mailing List. Well, my survey of the results of the two lists is hardly scientific, but I can say without a doubt that these men did not take as much of a beating on the Bears list as they did here. Why is that?

Let me suggest a reason: the struggle to "come out" is like a "trial by fire"! Each group feels that until you have experienced this "trial by fire" you are not really a member of the group. We (as married men) are much closer to the married men at the truckstops and since our own personal "trial by fire" led us to where we are now we feel that they should have the same experience and then they can join our group; while the Bears (largely gay men) really can't relate to a married man wanting sex with another man, and so come up with much more tolerant reasons.

It would seem to me that we should all be very tolerant of any man who is experimenting with sex with another man. I think the more support that we can give these people, the more support they will give us, and I don't know about you but I sure appreciate any support that I can get in a difficult situation.

Flame away guys, but I really feel that intolerance is what we experience every day, and to turn around and be intolerant of others just doesn't seem to be a solution. It is kind of like the old story about the man that beats his kid, who in turn beats his dog.

From: William

I'm in it to my kids, family, and most friends. I believe in closet rights and often feel it equivalent to being a Jew in Nazi Germany. But we must be mindful of the effects of being in the closet—we often have paranoid feelings, are defensive, isolated, and distant from mainstream society. The struggle continues.

From: Gripp

Hey guys, I've been very frank with gay guys about my married (to a female) state and found that some guys don't want to mess with me, but lots of guys do; they like married guys for various reasons and fantasies, such as:

1. married guys have a certain sexuality and masculinity that appeals to them;
2. married guys are dads and husbands, have families, and that appeals to them;
3. married guys have commitments and therefore won't be as demanding (for gay guys who want to live alone but have sexual needs).

Should add, these gay guys are very solicitous of my wife and family, tell me they understand the importance of that commitment and don't want to disturb it, they just want to mess around with me whenever I can make it happen! Am I the only one with this experience??

From: George

Prior to the time when I was fortunate to develop a relationship with my friend who is also bisexual and married, I had a friendship, non-sexual, with a gay fella I used to work with. We got along well as just friends but I didn't want to get sexually involved with him because I knew of his desire to someday find someone to have a long term live-in monogamous relationship with. His attraction turned out to be more of an attraction for my family life and the relationship I had with my wife and our children.

Before I knew him and he finally accepted himself as fully gay he had tried various attempts at conversion to hetro via shrinks and religious organizations. When it was obvious to him that conversion wasn't a working solution he then attempted suicide. Thank goodness his attempt failed.

While he valued a family type of lifestyle he knew he couldn't accept an existence that called for living with a woman and couldn't imagine himself fathering children in spite of the fact that he really has a great deal of love for them. He admired my situation, even wished he were BI instead of gay.

When he finally did find someone to live with he still made every excuse to come and visit our home, usually at some period during the weekend when all of us were most likely to be home. He and his live-in lover were recently transferred to another city. Before he left, he told me that while it was very nice to have someone to love and cater to, he still had a big empty feeling and that empty feeling related to the need for family.

I found out that he came from a fairly large family, a family that apparently was full of love and devotion. He often told me how he felt that being gay was a curse and that he would trade places with me (and my family life) in a minute if he could.

So guys, I guess all is not rosy for everyone. I can remember that before I came out to my wife, I felt being BI was the worst possible curse. My wife now has accepted my orientation. We get along even better than before I came out, I guess maybe because I no longer have lengthy bouts of depression. I am a hell of a lot happier now than I ever have been.

BI VERSUS GAY

From: Marvin

BI vs. Gay! Why does it matter? What difference does it make?

From: Stephen

It ONLY matters when someone else tries to tell you that you are NOT who you know yourself to be, and then has the gall to tell you who THEY think you are, or should be. In the gay community where gay people and bisexual people (both men and women) co-exist side by side we must affirm and cherish one another's authenticity or we will all perish under the heel of the "Jerry Falwell" of the world—the kind of people who think that WE are all defective and substandard human beings. If WE cannot allow one another room to be ourselves then we are doomed. We must recognize and fight for not only our similarities, but our right to our differences as well. That is TRUE diversity.

Although bisexuality makes SOME gay people feel insecure; there is no inherent threat to the gay community because of the fact that being bisexual is a real sexual orientation. The fact that antigay people point, in their ignorance, to bisexuals as some sort of proof that being gay is not a fixed and true sexual orientation is just a matter of taking their single-minded stupidity one step further. It doesn't prove anything to those who are knowledgeable and WE MUST NOT ALLOW it to be used as a wedge to divide our community against itself. God knows, we are surrounded by enough enemies. We can't afford to turn on one another. Let's let the dogs that hate us squabble amongst themselves over who we are.

From: Marvin

My point EXACTLY Stephon! I'll grant you that my post came across as a bit flip—I wasn't up to a lengthy dissertation last night.

All too often labels serve only to divide . . . and it never ceases to amaze me that a "community" who preaches inclusion and acceptance of diversity can all too often be SOOOO exclusionary! I've been too out for too long—and have faced and dealt with the "get off the fence" attitudes that one so often runs into. . . . I've almost gotten to the point of not bothering to explain. . . . I am who I am—we are ALL diverse creatures—and should all accept each other for who and what we are.

From: Rodney

Obviously many of us DO "care about labels"; otherwise, we wouldn't spend so much time fussing over who's "BI" and who's "queer" and all the other nonsense.

At the risk of revealing more of my ignorance than I like to confess to, I would like to toss out the following observations.

The LEGITIMATE reason a "bisexual" cares about being called "BI" rather than "gay" is that this is his "invisibility" issue. It used to be, and still is, common for people who were solidly aligned with a sexual "pole" (i.e., people who were either exclusively straight or exclusively gay) to believe that a "BI" was actually either a "gay in transition" or a "gay in denial."

When I first started having sex with men, I frequently encountered this attitude, and for quite a long time thought I was losing my sanity when I would have sex with my wife and THOUGHT I was enjoying myself. It was only after I met a bisexual therapist (who had a great deal of experience with people who genuinely WERE in denial about their orientation) that I felt comfortable with the idea that I could REALLY enjoy sex with both men and women, just like I could REALLY enjoy both beef and sushi.

Now, of course, orientation is fluid, and I know I could move from time to time closer to one pole or the other, but right now I know I'm a "straightish" sort of "BI" (about a 3 on the "Klein Grid").

But it's been hard to find this position, because, again, Americans have so much trouble with ambiguity. And if you're bisexual, ambiguity is the name of the game.

I get really annoyed when I talk to someone who's straight about my bi-sexuality and he says, "That must be great—to have the opportunity of sex with ANYONE."

Actually, it sucks—because I'm desperately in love with a straight, monogamous woman. The only paths open to me right now SEEM to be heterosexual monogamy with her (repressing my gay side) or divorce, leading to my trying to find a woman pretty much like the one I left, but one who could "handle" my sexuality.

At one time it SEEMED to me that being gay would be much simpler. But on this list I have been reading all these posts from GAY guys who are desperately in love with straight, monogamous women. And I guess I've decided that their situation must suck even harder than the one I'm in.

Labels still bother me, because sometimes just below the surface of discussions of sexual labels there seems to be the aroma of statements like these: "You're afraid to admit you're gay" or "I'm not as gay as you are" or "You want to have the best of both worlds: make up your mind, Charley!" And when I smell this kind of stuff, I want to say, "Can't we all just grow up and get BEYOND all this bullshit?"

One of the great things about this group and its e-mails is that most of the guys here seem, indeed, to have gotten beyond all this.

Because, although we are all united in sharing sexual orientations that lie outside the "approved norms," we are all trying to keep our eye on the REAL ball, which is not sex, but love.

From: Moris

It only matters if you BELIEVE what THEY say . . . otherwise it does not. . . .
Moris, who no longer lives based on what others tell him, is right.

From: Ted

Right On! (I know this expression dates me!!)
I feel that the identity issue has to do more with politics than anything else. I feel that the gay activists are trying to force men & women who are bisexual into their circle to increase their influence.

I know that the Pat Robertsons & Jerry Falwells of the world have a word to describe both bisexuals & gays. And that word is deviant! Also queer, abnormal, sodomite and other pleasant terms.

We should remember, as should the activists, that bisexuals and gays are NOT the enemies. The enemies are the intolerant fascists who want to control all the aspects of your life!!

P.S. I like and enjoy sex with men and women (just not my wife!) I will continue to have sex with men & women. I am not going to let one group or another tell me who I can have sex with!!!

BISEXUAL ACCEPTANCE

From: Shawn

I am NOT bisexual by choice. It is at the very core of my nature. I have felt almost equally attracted to males and females for as long as I can remember. It is quite fundamental to who I am. I had no more choice in my being a bisexual man than I had about the mother who carried me or the color of my eyes.

From: Schuyler

I, too, prefer to label myself (if I MUST label my sexuality) as bisexual, with the full knowledge that my sexuality this lifetime has been VERY fluid. I am a "free agent" in my behavior, if not my "bent," and would like to celebrate all about myself that is affirming and not harmful to others.

From: Bart

I would like to add some thoughts concerning my experience as a somewhat, sometimes, bisexual who attended the Bisexual conference with my wife. I helped Amity Buxton, at a workshop at the conference on "Relationships w/partners of some sort of mixed orientation." What makes our relationship/arrangement/partnership work, and what are others in the workshops' current state and experience? This is long winded, but it was revelatory. Also, I would like to voice my view about bisexuality as a simple reality.

There were a good number of young people at the conference who seemed quite committed to the idea that their right to express their sexuality in any direction they wanted gave them a freedom that categorizing seemed not to give them. And they appeared comfortable feeling that they did not have to be labeled gay or strait. Our workshop revealed that individuals were dealing primarily with disclosure to a partner that they were "bisexual" and not "gay" or "lesbian." In one case two women had been partners and the one in the workshop had created a difficult situation by being attracted to a guy. In all it was impossible to observe that the attendees were necessarily experiencing bisexuality or the convenient use of the term as a way station on their way to becoming gay or strait. This is simply not fact. Though I consider myself primarily gay, but live with a woman, have sex with her (yes not as often as she would like) I believe my decision to remain in that relationship obliges me to consider myself bisexual. I don't sometimes feel like I want to do or be this, but I choose to do this for different reasons. We can have as many different reasons as we want for expressing love in whatever form of relationship we choose. This is not a political issue, it is a personal one. I think most of us agree on this.

Now who writes our agenda? Does the Right because they have a point of view? Fritz Klein was very specific in his analysis of bisexuality as the middle 3/5ths of a scale that simply allows us to understand ourselves as strait-BI, BI-BI, BI-gay/lesbian. In other words we all have degrees and tendencies. So aren't we born with these degrees in many cases as well as born with a clearly strait or gay orientation? What's the conflict or argument? There is power in individuality, not categorization. We are not all the same and we have to stand up as individuals. That is the real choice, to stand up or not. Let's write the agenda ourselves.

That is precisely what Lorraine Hutchins has in mind. Queers all over should applaud her courage to define the issue not in the simplistic terms of the Right. That will never get us anything real. Queers all over should drop this fear of subversion from within, and their own fear of "strait." It doesn't mean you have to act or be straight in any way. As gays we've lived under the yoke of not being able to simply be, in the same quality and degree as straight. Gay culture has been simply slow to accept that BI's are indeed as good an ally as they could find.

Promoting an acceptance and understanding of Bisexuality as its own orientation not only takes the thunder out of the Right's choice argument, it bolsters the fact that homosexuality is undeniably inborn to whatever degree the individual is drawn to express it. We are free and we must think and act freely!

From: Conrad

To me, that's not the issue. The label has a highly symbolic affect that means much to both my wife and I. My wife really has had difficulty letting go of BI. To her it means that I also find her attractive, that her sexuality is affirmed in our relationship, etc. When I started calling myself gay, she would not accept it.

I want to do all the things I need to do to affirm our relationship, and give my wife what she needs, including her sexuality. Yet, her inability to accept the gayness has led me to respond (clearly for the worse!) by "proving" to my wife just how gay I am—no sex for quite a while, even though I know I'm capable of enjoying it and how much it means to her.

I'm not talking about the word BI or gay. To me, its really getting that I'm attracted to men, not women, at least at this point in my life. The point I guess (if I really have one) is that its up to each to pick a word or not as needed to express, assert, symbolize, or whatever it is we need to do at the moment . . . .Words can help or get in the way sometimes.

From: Milton

I DO NOT consider myself BI-sexual (not that there's anything wrong with that) :-) because I live with a woman. Rather, I consider myself gay because I am exclusively attracted to men! Now I realize that there are those who consider a sexless marriage a parody, at best, of a marriage. My response to that is, if that's what's important for you, that's fine. Just don't try to define my marriage for me and my wife. We've reached our own definition, thank you very much.

I DO agree that we need to free ourselves from the assumptions and views of others and claim our own lives and then live them to the best of our ability. Some MAY BE calling themselves "BI" on the way to being "gay," some not. I've never figured out why it's so difficult to believe that people can fall anywhere on the spectrum, rather than being pulled to the poles. If you tell me you're "BI," that's great. But be sure you have a good idea about why you so identify, and don't be put there because you're living with a woman. I wouldn't even necessarily throw the enjoyment of sex with a woman into the mix. I used to enjoy sex with my wife. But I had to fantasize about a man to maintain an erection and reach orgasm. So, in this case, I DO NOT think that actions speak louder than words.

While sex is a good and a wholesome expression of intimacy, it's not the only expression of intimacy. And, in fact, can be a means of hiding from intimacy: "Oh no, I don't want to open myself up to you, so let's fuck instead."

From: Stephen

I beg to differ with Milton. You proved in your post that actions and the thoughts that precipitated those actions do speak louder than words. You proved that YOU are gay, and also proved to me that I am NOT!

I AM bisexual, and unlike you I DON'T have to, as you put it, "fantasize about a man to maintain an erection and reach orgasm." And, I am sure that you wouldn't "even necessarily throw the enjoyment of sex with a woman into the mix" since if you have to pretend that she's a man, then you aren't really relating to HER as your sexual partner. And therefore your claims for enjoyment of sex with women are suspect. For those of us who are truly bisexual the joy of having sex is NOT predicated on the perceived or pretended gender of one's partner but in the act of having sex all by itself. The difference between having sex with a man or a woman is one of the great joys of being bisexual.

To illustrate my point and the difference between us, let me tell you a story. Recently a friend of mine asked me to design an ad for the upcoming Pride at Work. He asked me if there were any universal symbols that the lesbian community would recognize. I told him that I know of two. The inverted black triangle and the "labris." He asked me what a labris was. I told him that it is a two headed medieval battle ax. The cutting edges of which are curved. He said, "I don't see the connection." I told him that to lesbians it looks like a woman's labia opened up. Being very gay, he turned a little green and said "Never mind. I don't want to talk about THAT." He couldn't relate to a woman's genitals and didn't want to talk about them. I, however, can relate to them. I love my wife's body and the way that it looks. All of it! I also love a man's body and the way it looks. All of it! So, I can relate to him and other men and their beauty as men, and also relate to my wife and other women and their beauty, because I love them both.

And that's how you tell if you are BI-sexual. When I have sex I never fantasize. I have never ever pretended that I was with anyone but the person I am with. I am right into the moment, and right into my partner no matter whom it is. The only thing that changes for me is the technique I need to use, not the thrill of being there, or the wonder and gratitude I feel at sharing my partner's body.

There is nothing philosophical about it. It is hot and sweaty and gritty and just plain great! I don't think that IT IS "what we say" OR "what we do." Both of those can be deceits brought about by expediency or necessity. It is what we truly THINK and FEEL that defines us as either Gay or Bisexual.

In the appreciation of Fine WOMEN, Fine MEN, Fine ART and LIFE!

From: Donald

Milton wrote: >*I consider myself gay because I am exclusively attracted to men!*<

And I agree! I personally describe myself as a married gay male. And though the BI/gay thing is a continuum kind of like your percentage of top/bottom (40% top/60% bottom), guess I feel if conditions were right with an ATTRACTIVE woman my odds of ending up in the sack with her would be about 1 in 100. But with an UNATTRACTIVE guy, in the same circumstances, my odds would be about 1 in 5.

From: Rodney

Milton wrote:>*Now I realize that there are those who consider a sexless marriage a parody, at best, of a marriage.*<

Though I would have some trouble, myself, living in a sexless marriage, I think it is interesting how little emphasis sex receives in some of the best "popular" books on love and marriage. "Getting the Love You Want" mentions it hardly at all, except at one point where "sexual incompatibility" is listed as one of the "surface" issues in a troubled marriage (i.e., an issue that draws attention away from the deeper, "real" relationship issues). Also, if I remember correctly, Scott Peck doesn't discuss sex at all in "The Road Less Traveled."

I have at last begun to make some progress, I think, in healing my relationship with my wife, BUT ONLY BECAUSE I THINK I'VE FINALLY CONVINCED HER THAT MY BISEXUALITY ISN'T REALLY THE ISSUE IN OUR RELATIONSHIP. Even if we end up parting ways because we can't find a "sexual accommodation," I'm now more optimistic than I've been in months that we'll part friends—very good friends. And this is critically important to me, because I think (after three kids and 34 years of marriage) that the FAMILY we created will continue to exist in some very fundamental sense, regardless of whether or not we're married.

It's worth reminding ourselves that in most of human history, the role of sex in marriage has been mainly procreative, and that "sex for pleasure" was in a different category (for men, anyway!).

What is a parody is not a marriage without sex but a marriage without love. And marriages without love are in great supply in our culture.

From: Rodney

My sense of sexuality is a radio with different channels. My queer sexual feelings seem to be somehow fundamentally DIFFERENT from my straight sexual feelings—in ways other than the obvious difference of the sex of the OBJECT.

In the past few days, I think I've begun to get a bead on this. It has to do with the NONSEXUAL feelings that the sexual drives have their ROOTS in.

For me, my erotic feelings for women have their roots in my PROTECTIVE instincts. A woman who seems slightly afraid or timid (of the world, not of me) is apt to turn me on. I see myself as being The Big Guard, and she as wanting me to penetrate her as a kind of "promise" to provide the maleness she lacks. I know this sounds stupid, but my straight sexual fantasies always seem to take place in a hidden corner somewhere, where (alone and safe at last) she surrenders to me with a delighted shudder.

Well, that's ONE fantasy, anyway . . .

With men, it's very different: my erotic feelings are tied in to ENVY. I am sexually attracted to men who seem to have "sorted out" some part of their lives where I feel I fall short. Typically, I like athletic men who are very confident about their bodies and who are upbeat and not overly intro-spective—just the opposite of me, in other words. They don't have to be young or good looking: just athletic and non-neurotic.

I think it's something like that that lies behind the kinds of icons you are describing: the macho stance, so totally UNqueer. (Though for me person-ally the "rough" image is a total turnoff—even with straight guys, this is bullshit. A REAL man has a certain calm confidence about him and doesn't flaunt it.)

In "Tonio Kroeger" I remember Thomas Mann's describing Tonio's crush on another boy, Hans. Tonio is sensitive and introspective and Hans is outgoing and athletic. Tonio at once wants Hans to enter his (Tonio's) intel-lectual and artistic world, in order to feel close to him; but he has also the pained awareness that if Hans enters Tonio's world, HE WILL CEASE BEING EXACTLY THE THING TONIO DESIRES.

Again, probably not worth talking about all this. Guess it's New Years blues.

DREAMS

From: Ray

For the longest time (maybe a year?), I haven't recalled any dreams. I used to, and wondered why I no longer seemed to remember whether they were romantic entanglements, dangerous pursuits, or recounts of everyday occurrences. And, certainly, my dreams, if they existed, weren't cast with the major people in my life at the current time. But the last two nights, I not only was aware of my dreaming. I recalled them upon waking, and knew that they were contemporary ones. On Sunday night, my dream took me to the symphony with a group of my dear gay/BI friends, many of whom had not met each other. During last night, I dreamt that my wife and I were leading an Adult Forum at our church about Mixed Orientation marriages (introducing the whole gay/BI topic into this religious culture). The audience was unexpectedly accepting.

Of course, my take on this is one of ever-growing self-acceptance. I'm finally integrating my daily life with my fantasy/dreamlike world. I'm becoming more whole, complete. Any thoughts, similar experiences? Just curious.

From: Clark

I spent three wonderful years in Jungian analysis in the late 80's, and learned that when you start recalling your dreams and writing them down they begin to flow at an astonishing rate.

I tried to keep it up for awhile when the analysis was finished, but gradually I tapered off, and thus quit recalling my dreams.

Lately, however, I have had the experience you describe. Not only am I recalling dreams (and writing them down), but they are dreams that bear to me a wonderful message about who I am. I told my brothers yesterday that my dreams don't lie, and they tell me I am a gay man. Dream after dream seems to indicate that I am on the verge of something new, challenging, wonderful. And many of those dreams leave little doubt that homosexuality is a big piece of it. Thanks for the post.

From: Daniel

Like you, I have not really dreamed for quite a while—just occasionally something happens, the most significant dream for me being what brought me out of my latent homosexuality some three years ago—dreaming that I was in bed with an attractive young man, many years younger than me. Unfortunately, he came into my office two weeks later and that is when I realized that I had to recognize myself for what I am, gay.

But since that time, I have rarely dreamed (or if I have, I don't remember it). It will be interesting to see whether my dreams will return as you suggest, through ever-growing self-acceptance—I hope so. I accept myself for what I am, but I am still, like so many others, not at rest in my circumstances.

From: David

I dream a lot. I often recall them. Usually one a night. SOME in great detail. And some repeat . . . same dream on different nights and I seem to know during the dream it is a repeat.

Many involve sex. Always m2m. Many exhibitionism . . . usually swimming nude in very clear water or standing on windy peaks/cliffs. Audiences always male. And, of course, dick rises to the occasion most of the times . . . moist sometimes but never in years and years the teenage wet dreams. More's the pity.

Almost always dreaming leaves me feeling good and well rested. If I don't dream, I feel like I am not slept-out on awakening.

WHAT DO WE CALL OURSELVES?

From: Carlos

What I am unclear about is what some of you call yourselves. I see the definition GAY being used often. I realize some of you have left marriage for a man to man relationship, probably realizing that you are in fact homosexual. I would have thought for those of you who remain married would consider yourselves bisexual. Clarification—Please?

From: Moris

I basically call myself a human, a man! But I do use Gay, but never gay, to refer to my sexual orientation. I also use the word bisexual. My sexual orientation is bisexual and I am a part of the Gay/Queer Community. That is why I use the Gay and not the gay. . . .

Bi, Gay, Male, and an All-American Man!

From: Jimmy

I guess there are about as many answers as there are guys on this list. For me, I am definitely gay. About 9.8 on the Kinsey scale I guess. And I am married. Our marriage is not sexually active, and hasn't been for years. My sexual activity, mental, solo and the (sadly) rare real stuff is all M2M.

We have been married for 27 years. Ours has been a loving, intense relationship. We have been through many bonding experiences together. What can I say? We love each other deeply, want to be together, and this happens not to include sex. It includes a lot of snuggling and huggies and affection. And for us, it is just what is. I guess it doesn't make sense to a lot of people. Well, I guess it doesn't have to make sense.

From: Gripp

It seems to me that there are as many expressions of sexuality as there are men on the list. Some of us have trouble finding a term to adequately identify our sexuality. There do seem to be some generalizations that are (only) generally true.

Some of us perceive of ourselves as being gay and married by "default" so to speak. "Society expected it of us" is a common thread. Some men realize that their marriage does not fulfill what they need in their "gayness." Working out the separation from the wife causes agony for many here. I have read many thoughtful responses to those suffering these separation anxieties. Others choose to remain married—and their wives choose to stay married to them. This creates issues to be worked on; this group is really good at helping here, also. The major issue seems to be "how to be successfully, happily married and yet meet our own sexual needs for a man or men in our lives." Working out issues with wives is an ongoing and constantly changing problem. For many of these men, their wife is the only female person they love, emotionally and physically. Sometimes the love is emotional only. (I personally can't imagine being in a sexless marriage with my wife, but I'm me, and only somewhat like others on the list.) Does that make these men bi?

Then there are others who are more evenly attracted to both men and women. I love reading these men's posts. (Polyamory is intriguing to me and seems "right." I like the thought of duogamy best!) Still the marriage seems to serve as the central focus in their lives.

I am always amazed at the number of men who married thinking it would "cure" their same-sex interests or that their homosexual side would disappear because their sexual needs were being met by their wife. We are taught that from youth on. Because I was not that way (that is, I wasn't satisfied with sex with my wife only), I don't see how some men get to their 50's before allowing their same-sex side to be expressed.

"Bi" is closest for me but it doesn't say everything.

From: Brandon

I refer to myself as a Gay Married Man. I have been married (39 years) to a very supportive woman—whom I love dearly. My wife and I have three great children and 4 wonderfully healthy grandchildren. I have a male partner with whom I have been committed to for 7 and a half years.

The reason that I use the word Gay and not BI is that my basic sexuality is homosexual and not Bisexual. Ever since I can remember my sexual, emotional, and spiritual attraction has been toward the male. Why I fell in love with and bonded to a female is a million-dollar question that nobody has yet been able to explain to me. Only guess is that one falls in love with a person and not a body type. I also have learned that I can genuinely love two people at one time—one male and one female. The two are not mutually exclusive. Only problem with having a wife and a partner is that of TIME MANAGEMENT.

Hope that this answers your question but it is only my definition of myself and really nobody needs to label themselves if they do not choose to. I only label myself "Gay Married Man" to get the conversation started. I really am much more complicated an individual than that and only getting to know me personally does one really get to know my multifaceted personality.

From: Gent

I am married also and consider myself to be a gay married man. My marriage does include sex with my wife, but it is enjoyable to me because of who my wife is probably more than the fact that she is a woman. I have no problem identifying with gay because of this reason: If something ever happened to my wife, I would never marry another woman or seek one for sex. I would seek a man. Therefore, I consider myself gay.

From: Clark

My experience is that labels are inadequate. And to the extent that they are helpful, my use of them has changed. I am still evolving sexually. I have come to conclude that I am 98% gay, or better. On the other hand, I still enjoy having sex with my wife from time to time. This is all Very confusing. Sexuality is so mysterious a thing that it refuses, like most mysteries, to be pinned down.

From: Willis

The men here cover a whole spectrum, and our views of ourselves likewise cover a whole perception. Generally, I view myself as bi. I have definite m2m leanings, though up to now it has been much more in the realm of fantasy than reality. It seems I am too shy or anxious or something to be relaxed about making connections with men. On the other hand, I have a good sexual relationship with my wife. Though I wish it were more frequent. I had many m/f sexual relationships before we got married. If for some reason I were apart from my wife, while I am pretty sure I would want to explore much more than I have on the m/m side, I think I would be just as happy to find a new girlfriend.

One of the things that kind of scares me about meeting and getting to know other BI or gay men is the fear that I will lose my wife and family. On another list, there were times when it seemed like everybody was posting about being outed by their wives, who then were throwing them out of the house, and these guys were all realizing for the first time that they weren't really bi, they'd been kidding themselves, they were in truth gay. That doesn't feel like it resonates with me, but then I'm not sure if I can trust my own feelings anyway, having kidded myself for so long about the possibility even of not being 100% hetero.

So, there's my self-label. But as to whether it's true or not—hell, I'd be the last to know!!

From: Chester

Your orientation is determined, not by what you do, but by how you think. If you fantasize only about sex with women, then you're straight. If you fantasize about sex with women and with men (in any proportion), then you're bi. If it's only about men, then you're gay.

If you fantasize about guys when you're having sex with your wife, then you're gay.

That's why straight men in prison who rape other inmates but fantasize about women while doing are still straight (thus, they don't "change" from str8 to gay in prison, then from gay to str8) and why one can be a virgin, but still be gay or straight. . . .

Fantasizing only about men, but being married and calling yourself bisexual is called denial.

From: Dern

I am married and in fact will celebrate my 23rd anniversary tomorrow. However I identify as gay. I met my wife in high school when I was aware of those feelings but did not understand them. Getting married was the right thing to do. We were and are very good friends and very compatible. If she were a man it would be complete for me. I am only attracted to men not women. This doesn't mean I don't have women friends or recognize a good-looking woman when I see one. However all my sexual fantasies are about men. I long to have a close emotional relationship with a man, never does a woman enter into these areas with the exception of my wife and my wife only. I see a bisexual as a person who is drawn to both women and men for close emotional bonding. If I had matured and accepted my sexuality when I was young I would be married to a man this day.

I also want to take exception (in a very light way) with your use of the term "gay lifestyle." A lifestyle implies choice. Gay men and lesbians live in varied manners as do heterosexuals. I am in the middle income bracket. I do not own expensive cars (well at least they are not Mercedes or BMWs). I am raising four kids. That is my lifestyle not expressing my gay side. In a day when there is such a big assault on the homosexual community over the argument that it is a choice, we have to choose our words very carefully as to not send mixed messages . . . IMHO. . . .

I make love to my wife: the person who happens to inhabit a woman's body. I do this out of love for her and make sure it is a very enjoyable experience for her. It is not enjoyable for me but just misses the mark. However the mark I set for my part is her complete enjoyment of the experience. She has come to accept that I do not get the same thing out of it. We are now free to initiate sex for ourselves for we now understand what it means to each of us and thus no more confusion.

From: James

At the 1998 Chicago Guy Gathering, Fritz Klein took us through his grid/matrix to determine one's BI-ness or gayness and all but one guy in the room was BI using his criteria. The fact that one lives a married existence with a wife is one criterion of bisexuality. . . . It is how we are living (at least to the world). But Fritz commented that his research and experience shows that men who are "BI" fall into three categories: (1) BI, but strong leaning toward heterosexual, (2) BI, but leaning toward gay, and (3) BI with equal interests in heterosexual and gay relationships.

But some guys in this group clearly feel they are gay and state that, and also seek no intimate relationship with their wives as far as physical intimacy goes. Others of us remain involved with physical intimacy with our wives. At the last Chicago gathering, we spent part of one session talking about the various ways to be intimate with our wives other than intercourse. And I see a strong relationship between how we see ourselves and how we relate to our wives.

From: Kallas

I am gay. I came to be involved in a marriage to a woman, through life's circumstances, and now have children, a mortgage, 2 cars, etc., etc. At my stage in life (53 years old and still an animal . . . heehee), I don't want to turn the clock back and start over . . . divorce, move, look for a partner, set up a new household, upset, then more upset. . . . My wife feels the same way. She doesn't want to be a single mother, look for a new straight husband, struggle with single-hood, no money, kids, etc.

But I am still gay and my wife and I are trying to make the best of it. For me, having sex with a guy is natural and fulfilling, and having sex with my wife is exotic, adventuresome, and strangely fulfilling. So we have exotic, adventuresome, and strangely fulfilling sex, whenever we feel the need.

From: Sam

I beg to differ about the being married and fantasizing about men only or primarily, and thus being gay instead of Bi. I'm BI and I like that conscious choice. I have been inactive the entirety of our marriage and have come to the realization that I am BI because I predominantly fantasize about being with a man, about 95% of the time. Sometimes I fantasize about my wife or another woman. But a fantasy is about having that which you cannot and about having it EXACTLY as you want it, when in reality, it rarely, if ever, works out to the perfection of your fantasy.

I love making love to my wife and we have REALLY great sex!! Love-making skills take work and conscious effort on both parties' part. Yes, sometimes one is more giving to the other and vice-versa, but in a long-term relationship you have to be creative and inventive to bring freshness to the moment. Sometimes planning and education are needed (i.e., Tantra workshops, etc.).

So, I am a conscious BI and have come to that awareness through my longing to be with another man through fantasy, excluding basic learning curve of pubescent youth. Yet, I know without the shadow of a doubt that I am Bi, and that had I explored being Gay for years, I still would have needed to bond with a woman to have that sense of balance within myself. And someday I do hope to connect with Mr. O-So-Right! and have a relationship. For me bonding is the CORE ISSUE!!

From: Willis

Sam wrote: >*But a fantasy is about having that which you cannot and about having it EXACTLY as you want it, when in reality, it rarely, if ever, works out to the perfection of your fantasy.*<

Yes. Yes indeed. I used to fantasize exclusively about straight sex, from adolescence, to almost exclusively about straight sex through just a few years ago. Looking back, there was a period, a long period, where I now believe I was suppressing fantasies, so a survey of my fantasies then would surely not have accurately reflected my orientation.

On the other hand, I think I fantasize more about men nowadays precisely because I am still very inactive with men, relatively speaking. In other words, I do fantasize about sex with my wife, as well as other women, and while I can't have sex with every woman I fantasize about, I can make love with my wife. That takes away some of the fantasy urge. Whereas up to now it's years between real-life expressions, with another live human being, of my m/m inclinations.

From: Clem

There was a time when I would have said that a guy who sometimes enjoyed sex with women but who thought of himself as "gay" was in denial. As long as a person KNOWS WHAT HE FEELS, then he should use whatever term seems best to him. And, as someone remarked, one's fantasy life actually isn't necessarily the best indication of his underlying "sexuality." I have a couple of times acted out fantasies and found them very disappointing in reality.

From: Neil

Most of us are not creatures that exist within certain commonly defined limits to which labels can be applied. We are certain ways under certain conditions. I fantasize mostly if not exclusively about men. Most of my friends, however, are women. My sexual attraction is very strong with men. The most satisfying sex I've ever had has been with women. I yearn to be with men. I am most at ease with women. My eyes go to men in restaurants and on the streets. I seek women out at parties. Sometimes I'm clearly gay. Other times I'm het. I identify as bi. So fantasizing exclusively does not make me gay. It just means I have exclusively gay fantasies.

From: Marvin

Everyone just needs to BE—call me whatever it makes you comfortable to call me, just don't expect me to BE anything based upon your definition of what you choose to label me.

From: Sheldon

Nothing is true except believing makes it so. All of this intense self-examination and labeling is something I have given up (or gotten past —whichever you prefer). I am perfectly happy to be me. I don't care to define myself as though I were some static thing—which will not be changed tomorrow. Isn't feeling enough justification for one to feel? Isn't BEING enough justification to just BE? Why must we punish ourselves by trying to push ourselves into some pseudo-intellectual pigeon hole and then put a label on it? For whom do we do this—society, our wives, our own insecurities? It seems to me that this goes nowhere. Rather like a dog chasing it's own tail. I'm just glad to be me.

I was appalled that some asshole has managed to get anyone to believe that he needs help because he likes having his cock sucked. I have NEVER met any man whether straight or gay who wasn't thrilled by the idea of a good blow job. And this poor man has quacks with shrunken heads tied to their belts dancing around him to cure him of being perfectly normal. I didn't read one single word except for the abuse stuff that was not normal. If it is his perception that this abuse has warped him into loving blow jobs then someone should tell him that every other man in the world has the same affliction.

And if his wife doesn't want to do it then it makes sense that he would find someone who does. I certainly would. If you have no more serious problems than those, cheer up because you're OK! It sounds like the abuse you're taking from the psychotherapeutic community is far greater than the free blow jobs you got as a kid.

Which brings me back to the original point which is that psychobabble is a dangerous thing. And so is labeling the thoughts, behavior, and feelings of others as "denial" when you don't really know enough about them to make that call.

From: Chester

Labels are just words we use to categorize things. When you label yourself with the term "I," I (my use of the term) understand what you mean. If that's an oversimplification of things and shouldn't be applied to people, then we should all stop typing on this list cuz how else can we communicate any ideas? :)

I'm not sure I understand why this particular label is such a bad thing. Maybe it's not the use of the terms, but the misuse of terms. When somebody is actually straight, all it means is that they desire to have sex with the opposite sex and not with the same sex. That's ALL it means.

From: Ted

I consider myself BI in that I enjoy having sex with both men & women. I enjoy looking at erotic pictures of men & women, probably more of women, since I don't get excited by the usual muscle men that make up gay porn.

On a scale of 1 to 10 (1 being 100% str8 & 10 being 100% gay) I range from a 4 to 6; maybe closer to a 6 since when I am sucking a cock, I find myself getting hard. While I am eating a woman, I rarely get an erection. (However, I REALLY enjoy both activities.)

I probably have had more m2m sexual activity than m2f activity (I have not had sex with my wife for several years). Since I am a bottom, in m2m sex I don't have to be active, while in m2f sex, I have to take the lead. Obviously, in male to female sex, the man has to perform. To really confuse things, the most erotic sex I have had is with SHEMALES! They incorporate the best of both worlds! The porn I really enjoy looking at is SHEMALES, particularly those with erections! I know that gay men are frequently antagonistic to TGs. So, I am not sure what I am. In a short period of time, I will have an opportunity to explore all sides of my sexuality since my wife & I are getting divorced & I will being moving out of the house soon. I guess that I would consider myself SEXUAL!

From: Dan

I learned in communications 101 that "Meanings are in PEOPLE, not in words." Methinks that's the problem when one says a word which is a label—the label may mean something different to you than it MEANS to me. Having said that, I agree MOST with the poster who said it is about ORIENTATION and not necessarily activity. Methinks if I THINK exclusively about men and want a MAN, then I'm gay. My activity might be bisexual, but my orientation is gay. I always look at men when walking down the street, and if they are cute/handsome think evil thoughts (actually they aren't evil, but they ARE sexy); whereas I never do that about women (and esp. lesbians!)

So, the NEXT time YOU are upset over some label somebody uses, think twice . . . it just might be YOU who has the problem . . . after all the meaning is IN you . . . what the word MEANS to somebody else, MAY be quite DIFFERENT.

From: Clem

On the off-chance there's still someone interested in the "labels" and "orientation" debate (in its current incarnation; as someone else noted, it's a topic that comes around on a fairly regular—seasonal? —basis)— I'll repeat the following material, which was sent to me in a post several months ago. I think it is completely correct, and merits repetition:

> "Sex between two men is different from sex between men and women and different again from sex between two women. The energies felt and exchanged between two men in sex are not cross-exchangeable with the energies he feels and exchanges with a woman. The feelings are different, the bodies feel differently, the procedures are different, the energies given and exchanged feel as if they come from a different part of the personality. A woman cannot provide her gay/bi partner the same kind of connection, arousal, satisfaction, etc. that a man can. Neither can the male partner provide the same kind of connection, arousal, satisfaction, etc. he experiences with his wife."

We've talked in the past about this strange sense (common, I suspect, among "bisexuals") that in m2m and hetero sex "the energies given and exchanged feel as if they come from a different part of the personality." I wish my wife and therapists understood this experience well enough to appreciate its implications.

From: Clem

The key to understanding is not so much to have this brilliant, perceptive, idiosyncratic mind. Interpreting literature usually comes down to UNDER-

STANDING THE IMPLICATIONS OF THE OBVIOUS. (For instance, you don't START by saying "Jay Gatsby's tragedy symbolizes the American tendency to confuse material values with spiritual values;" instead, you start by saying "Jay Gatsby wants Daisy, but when he gets her he finds he's somehow disappointed"—and you go from there.) As I get older, I find that more and more of life is like this. I can look "at the obvious" for months without seeing it, and then, having seen it, still have a terrible struggle "understanding its implications."

My therapist yesterday had me look HARD at one obvious fact: "Your wife is having trouble ACCEPTING WHO YOU ARE." As we say in the Valley, "No duh!"

But wait a minute . . . Ever since I came out, we haven't been discussing WHO I AM—we've been discussing what I DO with my various body parts.

No duh. No wonder we aren't making progress.

Then various kinds of lights and bombshells started coming on and going off (respectively).

One bombshell for me was a mind-boggling realization that my therapist led me to: I FEEL SAFER HAVING SEX WITH MEN THAN IN HAVING SEX WITH MY WIFE!!!

Isn't this counterintuitive? I mean, think of all the nasty diseases I might get from a guy.

But, so far, NO GUY HAS ASKED ME TO STOP BEING WHO I AM.

Denial of Self is the nastiest disease of them all. It kills you. Always.

So here's my wife, in her separate bedroom since my coming out, essentially holding her sexuality away from me until I'm ready to be someone else.

I experience this a little like the male spider, approaching a comely looking female, but sensing in her expression an unsettling message: "You can fuck me. But then I get to eat you." My therapist, by the way, is straight. I am an unusual case for him, judging from what he's told me. But my opinion of him keeps going up and up. He DOESN'T, by the way, think that homosexual abstinence is necessarily BAD for me. He just thinks it isn't really "the issue," and that my wife and I have been "putting the cart before the horse."

THE GAY THING, OR TGT

From: Woody

I've been looking at the label TGT (The Gay Thing) to put on and it keeps tugging at me . . . that thing that looks so much greener than the pasture I find myself in. In my "pre-realization" existence I knew very little about the gay world. Certainly I didn't imagine the fullness and richness that gays in general seem to have made of their . . . well, lifestyle? community? fabric of existence? . . . TGT seems so much an apt term.

It seems to me that shortly after establishing one's identity as gay, or perhaps BI, as I did for a short while, there come a couple of sirens (in the mythological sense) calling, serenading the ship you've embarked upon. The first is sexual freedom, and its corollary, the infamous "slut phase" (I'm still there!). The second is a realization that there is an entire lifestyle, an exciting, embracing, and enticing community to belong to. To someone who has been chafing with the feeling that they aren't really a member of the "hetero" community and that he is much more attracted to a host of guys than they ever have been to a woman, and is longing for understanding, male companionship opportunities, there is almost an irresistible urge to break away fairly completely and cleanly, and join—coming out in every way, perhaps, but also coming "in." (Your "Type A" response.)

But . . . I think few are able to join TGT completely, yet at the same time give what is necessary to maintain their relationships with their wives, their old friends, their family . . . and so many of the obligations we shouldered when we said "I do" and did TFT—The Family Thing. (Your "Type B" response). TGT then has to be something visited on occasions, or admired longingly from afar (often with a feeling of quiet desperation or worse, depression, affecting you).

Sometimes I'm almost overcome with jealousy—jealousy over those "freer" gay guys I know (most of my friends now are gay—mostly leather/bear types in my case) who can have guys over whenever they want, go to fun weekend events, cruise bars, attend gay parties, openly espouse gay causes, and in general just live it up in the style they want (though I've found so many of them can't, because they're broke).

I wonder, though, how many of them are occasionally jealous of their buddy, me, who heads back after one of my carefully spaced "get togethers" (we have a pretty good arrangement, for me anyway) and leather events to wife, home, kids, dog, and neighbors, not to mention financial security. I'm "out" only to my wife and family Dr.—out of employment necessity and also out of respect for my wife's wishes.

That doesn't mean I haven't dreamt . . . a LOT. . . . I've planned it out dozens of times. I'll tell my wife NEXT MONTH I'm leaving . . . for sure this time . . . gonna join TGT !! (now that I have a name for it): buy a truck with a fifth wheel trailer, put a sling next to the bed, and go visit all those guys who have invited me to come hang out with them . . . or: move into an apartment, find a lover I can really love (lost one recently . . . sigh) . . . or: move to the Castro, wear full leather out in public, hang out at the Sling or other places I've heard about in the gay ghetto . . . or: well, another dream tonight. Tomorrow I'll be up at 6, get ready to go to work, kiss my wife, pet the dog, download the stock prices, read some enticing e-mail . . . and think about TGT and another dream gay existence on the ride up the freeway to work. It's kept me going for years now. One of these days I've got to get around to it. One of these days . . .

From: Clark

I wrestle, as you know, with the same things. Although I have come NEARLY to conclude that I really must break out. The question is not whether but when.

I was just online chatting with a guy, a stranger, who asked me why I wouldn't want to remain married. Good question. I do. But the price, in my case of the sacrificed honesty, is just soul-searing. I can't stand what it is doing to me or to my wife. I don't know, I don't know. But I, for one, envy you, the dog, the wife, the stock prices, the career, even the freeway. And TGT as well.

From: Dern

You so spoke to many of my feelings lately. I have even considered going back into hiding. It hurts to try to step between both worlds. It creates a sadness that takes over. My wife and I were coming home from a PFLAG meeting last night. We had talked about stopping by a new rest/bar where we both had noticed a very cute bartender. I wanted to go back and flirt some more but looked at the time and the fact that my wife was there and would probably have a hard time with too much flirting and chose to go home instead. During that 35 minute ride I could feel the sadness taking over. My wife noticed it too. It is hard to talk about it with her for she then feels sad that she is holding me back which is true but not true at the same time.

Oh when will my bears-ship come in? :º(

From: James

Dern wrote:> *I have even considered going back into hiding. It hurts to try to step between both worlds.*<

I don't post much these days . . . not enough time . . . but your post really touches me. . . . have gone through so much yearning since coming out and at times had an incredible urgency about it . . . . and devoted so much energy to trying to resolve that yearning . . . and perhaps I'm reading too much into your post but it sounds like me much of the time. . . .

Trying to find peace . . . a sense of shalom . . . for some of us is a challenge. Fritz Klein gave me some great advice in Chicago a year ago saying that he has no expectations . . . and he shared that it took years to develop that . . . . and my wife and I try to "live the moment" or "live the day." Currently I am also trying to work on this philosophy since I love a guy who lives far from me. . . . so rest assured that some of the rest of us wrestle with the issue you express in this post. For me, though, I could never go back into the closet. . . . I tried it briefly and it left me totally without feeling . . . feeling totally asexual, which I still do sometimes. . . .

Before coming out, I masturbated frequently. . . . after coming out, I find little fulfillment in videos and only periodically am interested in masturbation. . . . I want the real thing! And increasingly since the incredible first six months of sexual activity with my wife (after coming out) I find I am less and less interested in intercourse with her . . . though we still do have intercourse and I do enjoy the other aspects of intimacy . . . and I drift towards asexuality and numbness if not in an ongoing intimate relationship with another guy.

To me, going to a gay bar, which I do weekly for dancing, is a very lonely experience—unless I go with someone. . . . . Your post reminds me of how I feel sometimes. . . .

I don't have any answers for you . . . (sigh) . . . just sharing that you are not alone.

From: Brett

I read your somewhat wistful e-mail about how things are with you right now and wanted to write and express my care for you and support through these difficult times.

I haven't posted in a long time since, as I think I told you, my life has gone in such a different direction than what I read on the list. Still, I hear you say that others need to hear about our individual journeys, so here's an update.

As you know, my wife and I have been separated for nearly two years now as we have tried to "reconfigure" our relationship to account for my being gay and our inability to live together as the married couple we had been.

Recently I met an incredibly wonderful man and have embarked on a new relationship with him. (It's a long but beautifully romantic story as to how we met.) Despite being over 2,000 miles apart we have managed to be together several times. This summer he's coming to live with me. What began as a passionate romance has evolved into a really deep, loving relationship . . . despite the distance . . . because we are both ready for it and we both work at it.

My point in sharing this with the list is I see so much despair from guys who can't imagine moving on from their current circumstance and "at our age" (I am early 50s after all) wonder how we can "start over" and whether we even want to. I love my wife of 25 years and our two children and I have absolutely no regret about those years. But I don't want to have any regret about the NEXT 50 years either and, at least in my case, that meant the painful but necessary steps of coming out, accepting myself, and having the courage to move on with my life. In so doing, I have cared for myself and am in the process of creating a life for myself that is more rich and fulfilling than I ever imagined.

My thoughts and prayers are with you as you work through what's ahead and I hope you can find the happiness and contentment you (and all of us) so richly deserve.

From: Boris

I'm in my mid-50's. The reality is: we "can" start over. It isn't easy, and it isn't without pain, but my wife and I have found separation, acceptance, and moving on is well worth it. After the fact (of) that it was the best thing that could have happened.

I would also add that in so doing, I have cared as much for my wife as for myself, and she is now free to create a life for herself that is as rich and fulfilling as mine. Of course we both miss much of what we once shared, but we both feel so much more that we are becoming our true selves, and thus we can relate to each other so much more real-ly than we could when we were trying to emulate a straight marriage.

SEXUAL PREFERENCE??

From: Gripp

In an article by Stephen Downing in the Duluth News Tribune, he discusses the term "sexual preference." What is your take on the term? Do we have a preference in our sexuality or not? A survey is going around on BMMA right now about whether we think our sexuality is chemical, biological, or environmental. Any discussion?

From: Boris

I, for one, do not have a "sexual preference." Preference implies choice. I never had a choice: I like men. After forty-one years of confusion on the matter, I think I side with those who hypothesize that there is a significant genetic component to being gay. I'm sure the environment contributes, too, but I wouldn't like to guess how much. My brother and I (21 months apart) were brought up more or less identically. Why am I gay and he's not?

I never use the term "preference"; I always say "orientation."

From: Archie

Whatever it is, it isn't "preference."

From: Clem

My inevitable crochet on all this is that all people are born with "bisexual potentiarust the "biological" and "chemical" arguments.

I thinl," but that their final (adult) "orientation" (SURELY not "preference," I think) is largely determined environmentally.

("I like guys sexually: I must be gay" vs. "This must not be sexual longing that I'm feeling: only queers feel that way!")

I am NOT saying that "everyone's BI." There's no meaningful sense in which that's a true statement for adults.

I distk one of the most interesting dimensions of this question is the one that seems to get ignored, however. Why is "gender orientation" such a tremendous fetish for us, among all the observable, variable dimensions of sexual behavior? It's because of its supreme importance among "fetishes" that I suspect there is something universal operating here (i.e., that at some point, EVERYONE confronts the orientation/identification conflict, whereas something less universal is involved, for instance, in one's interest in feet or anal play).

From: Boris

I have no evidence from my experience that I ever had bisexual potential. I liked my uncle when I was 4, I liked the boys I went to camp with when I was 7 (and on through 12), I liked the boys I went to school with when I was a teenager, etc. I never experienced a twinge of erotic interest, much less arousal, for anything female. I tried to make it happen, I tried to imagine it, I tried to fantasize it. Nothing. Ever.

I'm just gay. It's not a fetish, like leather or underwear. I do agree, though, that one's orientation (I think I even avoid the modifier 'sexual,' as I am emotionally and feelingly oriented toward men, which I think is as important (if not more so) as being sexually oriented toward them)—I do think that one's orientation is fundamental (universal?) in ways that fetishes are not. I don't worry much about how it came about that I'm gay, any more than I worry about the fact that I'm bald, or tall, or musical. I just am. And I'm glad of it.

From: Herman

Hmm, I would have to say the term "sexual preference" depends on where one is. For me, I am married and my sexual preference is with men. I also have sex with my wife, which is pleasurable but not my preference. Now sex with men is my PASSION—I get lost in it. It doesn't matter where I am or who I'm with I get immersed in the act and although aware of where I am and what I'm doing I feel complete and total. It matters not whether it is chemical, biological, or environmental. I love it. It beckons me. It arouses my senses. It makes me whole. It creates a feeling of well being. As I read somewhere I'm one woman short of being completely GAY. So in short, while I love my wife and am emotionally and intimately bound with her, I love men. Don't know if that answers any question but that is how I feel.

From: Lyndon

I couldn't agree more, and take it from me—you are a very intelligent and thoughtful man whose preference, oops!!! orientation, most decidedly leans toward men. And in spite of society's harassments ain't it great to be gay!

P.S. I finally got some new transportation and can you believe the only car with low mileage and a standard transmission in my price range ended up to be a deep purple fag mobile! Anyone got a Twinkie Winky I can put in the back window?

From: Dern

I prefer sexual orientation. Preference implies a choice, for me at least. I also believe it is more biological than any other.

From: Carl

I cannot speak for anyone but myself, but if I had a preference it certainly would not be to be BI. Sometimes I feel as though it's tearing me apart. I "opted" to be straight once I found out how great m2f sex was and how I could function perfectly well as a husband and a father. And what good did it do? For most of my life I have struggled to try to sweep my gay side under the rug and totally failed. No, preference has nothing whatever to do with it. How about psychological? Or spiritual? Or genealogical? And does it matter?

From: Marvin

I've always bristled at the term (much as I bristle at labels) for, as the author states, it does imply choice, in a very minimalist way. My preference is that my steak by prepared medium-rare. My preference is a baked potato with butter AND sour cream. My preference is honey mustard dressing on my salad.

Who I am is NOT a preference . . . it just is!

From: Joey

Pheromones! Perhaps we are not all aware, but many animals, including humans, produce and secrete pheromones. These are chemicals. I, for one, believe my gayness is biological. Therefore, being attracted to men included the scent they produce. Pheromones are detected by our brains through our olfactory sense. We can smell some but most are not detected in the form of an actual scent. No question, I love the husky smell of men. Ooooweeeee!

From: Clem

Boris wrote: > *I have no evidence from my experience that I ever had bisexual potential.*<

I have heard this from many gay men, which is why I call my opinion a "crochet." My analysis seems to answer some questions for me, but not others. I worked with an analyst once who said in a fairly convincing way that infants experience a kind of orgasm when they're nursing (even gay-to-be babies). The idea is sort of funny—but you might want to watch a nursing infant some day more closely, and I think you'll see what he means.

When I then use the language of a being capable of speech ("I like sex with guys; I must be gay . . . "), I give the impression that something is happening at a relatively late point in development that probably somehow begins much earlier and in a much less verbal way. Have you ever had an analyst ask you a question like, "What would your mother have done, do you think, if she had seen you get an erection as a baby? Or seen you playing with another little boy baby's private parts?" The analyst is trying to get at what I'm talking about.

I guess I'm mainly bothered by the "chemical" and "biological" arguments because they turn attention away from the crippling effect of institutionalized homophobia, which my guts tell me is at the heart of all this, insofar as "this" is a "problem."

If it weren't there, some of us would be focused quietly on eating pussy, wearing leather, sucking cock, licking feet. Some combination of the above? Whatever. Who cares?

>*It's not a fetish, like leather or underwear.*<

You're probably right; "fetish" is not commonly used the way I'm using it. I'm using it (perhaps less precisely) to mean "a dimension of life that has become eroticized, even though there is no 'natural' sexual content to the dimension." We sometimes forget that men really DON'T need men sexually, if you look at it from a strictly biological point of view (at least, if I'm right that this isn't a biological issue, which is of course an assumption on my part).

From: Boris

You know, I used to believe that no one "needs" sex. I don't any more. I know I *do* need it. I think *need* in the sense of nourishment and hydration limits the field to the physical. But I experience myself as one being—physical, psychological, and spiritual—and I know I have psychological needs. And I don't confuse them. And I consider my spiritual and psychological needs as natural as my physical needs. So I would never be convinced by an argument that none of us needs sex—in this context, at least.

From: Jimmy

Hmmm. I have quite a number of sexual preferences. But being gay isn't a preference any more than being two-eared is.

EARLY MARRIAGE

From: Nathan

I've been lurking for months and many of your letters have hit similar spots in my life but the discussion of marriage age, I think, is different for everyone. I guess I always knew I was different, but it took me a long time to figure out that I was gay. My first sexual experiences took place in men's rooms when I was in the Navy. Still, I thought I was straight and married my wife back in the late 50's when I was 21 and she was 25. She is my first and only woman, and I am her first and only man. Sex with her was wonderful in the early years and we produced four wonderful kids, who in turn have given us six wonderful granddaughters. If I hadn't married at an early age, I might never have had the pleasure of my granddaughters, the oldest of which is now a college freshman (and a lesbian). I may even live to see some great-grandchildren from the younger ones.

I realized that I was gay about 15 years ago and lost interest in sex with my wife, but she is my best friend and we are more like brother and sister now. When I came out to her last year, she told me that she had known it for years. She asked if I planned to leave her, and I told her that I did not plan to unless I became emotionally involved with a man, which so far has never happened. I know now that I could never leave her.

About four years ago, I discovered the local gay cruising place, a park near my house (this is a small town). Most of the men who go there are married bisexuals in the 30-60 age range. I know almost all of them and we chat and sometimes go off and have sex. They have become my friends. Sometimes I wish that I could meet that one special man, but this will have to do until he comes along.

HELLO BROTHERS

From: Shawn

I always knew I was "weird" from the age of 7. I had crushes on boys and girls. That was confusing. Somehow I knew it would be better to be fully in one camp or the other. Even in high school and college I was falling in love with women, but also had the hots for guys. I was very naive about sex so didn't know what to make of it all. Basically I was ashamed of my sexuality, both hetero and homo, but ESPECIALLY THE HOMO. "They" (society, parents, peers, clergy) certainly got that point across very well.

Before I married 23 years ago I did tell my wife that I was attracted to guys. However, I grossly minimized and underestimated the importance of that fact. I had no idea that this queer thing would never go away. I hoped that it would. I prayed that it would. Ultimately, my answer to prayer has been something like . . . God loves me just the way I am. If my creator made queer folks, then it must be ok for some of us to be queer. Because I was not "out to myself" when I met my wife, certainly she had no way of knowing the power of my attraction to other men.

About four years ago the pressure, confusion, and depression stemming from all the repressed libido started demanding attention. I told my wife I couldn't go on as if I were a completely "normal" heterosexual married man. You all know the feeling. I need not elaborate. I had never acted on my feelings. I still haven't done anything more than get a little cozy with a couple of guys . . . not very sexual or passionate, at least as far as my behavior.

I started going to support groups three years ago, met other gay/BI men, began letting others know (gradually) about the other me. The past four years have been very intense and scary, but also it's been a relief too. At least I don't have to hide anymore and I don't have to be ashamed. I don't have all the answers as a BI married man. My wife and I love each other and share a lot of passion. Also, we have an 11-and-a-half-year-old daughter. But we both know that I have to be involved with the gay community in order to be truly myself. The intimacy I experience with other men has been mostly emotional and social. I'm not a person that can be happily married and be free sexually with others. I couldn't deal with lying or sneaking around either. It just wouldn't work for me or for my wife. That's just who we are. Yes, I do desire the sexual experience, but I'm not willing to put my marriage on the line for the sake of having that experience.

It's still not easy being gay or BI, but it is better being openly BI than hiding in the closet of shame and self-hate.

Chapter 3
Male Relationships

CHICAGO, CHICAGO!

From: Pearly

Gary's posting of the song from Hercules touched me deeply. . . . . I went "home" to Chicago last weekend, to a community of beautiful men who all had an uncanny capacity for unconditional support and love. The following words are so relevant to my trip to the Chicago gathering (of gay and bisexual men out to their wives):

Brandon wrote: >*I have often dreamed of a far-off place Where a great warm welcome Will be waiting for me Where the crowds will cheer When they see my face And a voice keeps saying This is where I'm meant to be I know every mile Will be worth my while I would go most anywhere To feel like I belong*<

The "belongingness" in Chicago was an incredible feeling that sparked a new vitality and excitement in me. I brought home a piece of each of you who were there and I will draw on that to nurture myself for a long time. And thank you, Fritz, for bringing my self-analysis and awareness to a new level with your discussion of the orientation grid.

Warm hugs and thanks to the organizers—wonderful accommodations and events.

From: Andy

"While gentlemen in England were yet abed, we band of brothers, we happy few" (Shakespeare, "Henry V"—right, Henry?) gathered in Chicago. Not that heroic exploits are not also performed in bed <g>. Not that the brotherhood is not bigger than the gang gathered at that particular table (as someone on the list so eloquently posted). Not that there is not a continuity of interaction in cyberspace with Chicago fore and aft. Yet it was a special time, a time out of time (we took off our watches during a meditation period), an easy time when we could be ourselves without masks, a time when we could meet each other in the flesh and supplement our cyber hugs with real hugs (and kisses too). In the meditation, I ruminated on how good it was to have bodies, to be bodies, to be embodied. As we lay upon the carpet, feet touching, there was a sense of connectedness as we relaxed each part of our bodies (including both our brains).

When it was time to come back into the world of time and space, it was marvelous to be still connected by feet and to work that naturally into a series of hugs and then, refreshed, to take our chairs as the next full-group discussion began. When the time came for our parting group hug, I could think of nothing more salient in what the weekend meant to me than the realization in experience that we are truly a loving band of brothers.

MAN MEETS BOY

From: Stephen

Andy wrote: >*I have had a good 5-year love relation with a young man (me 43, Mark 19)*<

I'm sorry—I don't mean to be a prig—but this age difference really bothers me. He's a teenager! He's got so much growing up to do! I'm assuming that he was 19 when the relationship began, because otherwise it would have been child abuse. I have counseled so many men who thought they were mature enough when they were teenagers to handle a relationship with a much older gay man only to have to deal with the psychological residue for years afterwards. I think it's wrong. I think adults should know better. Am I the only one who thinks this way? Please don't toss out any romantic sentimentality about "true love" (unless it's about someone who's somewhat close to you in age).

From: Miles

I agree with you!!! I think a 19 year old can share many common interests with older men, such as religion, sports, etc., however—he is not in the same maturity category as an adult. And no matter how much he may say he doesn't feel exploited, I believe that such relationships are very very questionable. I don't get it, you guys—there are plenty of gorgeous twenty-somethings out there that you could form relationships with, why do you need 19 year olds?

From: Marvin

No . . . you're not the only one (and I'm not THAT old! <G> I'll grant that SOME people at 18 or 19 are mature enough to handle an adult relationship . . . . and some at 50 are not, but overall this age difference bothers me as well . . . not to mention that from personal experience I've yet to meet anyone younger than about 30 (give or take) with whom I have much in common—the life experiences are so different!

From: West

I agree with you that it is wrong for older guys to have a so-called love affair with "a very young boy." I think "love" in many cases is simply LUST. Why not call it that? I worked as a probation officer and as a school teacher for 35 years and never had sex with any of my charges. It wasn't that I wasn't turned on by any of them . . . I was, but did not pursue the attraction. 69 years old and proud of it!

From: Stan

I was wondering when the fun would start, and then I read the responses. What struck me most was how certain many of you are about the lack of maturity in a 19 year old. I think young adults today are a lot different than when I was 19. They've grown up in a world filled with a lot more information, risk, and decisions. I think we need to give them the benefit of the doubt when it comes to making these types of choices for themselves.

At the same time, I'll admit that when I was 17 I had a short relationship with a guy who was 27, and I had no business being with him because I lacked a sense of perspective on the relationship and how it figured into the rest of his life. I was falling head over heels and he was having a fling with a kid. I don't think I'd get involved with a younger guy now because I don't believe he could really understand the demands on me at home, at work, as a parent, etc., and I'd hate to unintentionally mislead him.

From: Dan

Does lust last over 4 years, as it has with me and my boyfriend? (61 vs 25). That's a 36-year-difference in age. I certainly don't try to act or dress like a 20 year old nor does he try to act like an ol' fart. I have made attempts to "loosen up" the relationship but he will have nothing to do with it. Oh well, let me enjoy it while I can. He knew I was married from the first date—I never made any promises to him of divorce, etc. He accepted and still does. I see him several times a week. I am, however, prepared for the day he may decide that he deserves something more "permanent." In the meantime, my Viagra sits on the shelf gathering dust. With him, I don't need it. <G> As someone said, there are 18-20 year olds who are mature enough and some 50 year olds who are not. Yeah, my boy may be a little immature in certain things but over the 4 years I've known him, he has made some changes (maturing).

From: Stephen

"My boy"? YEESH. Isn't that what you'd call a son? Would you have sex with your son? Shouldn't we treat all children as our children? Haven't gay youth been hurt enough, without sexual exploitation by one of the few adults who actually shows some caring? Why must they experience caring in a sexualized way?

From: Andy

Talk about ageism! Whew! I will agree that a wide age disparity makes sexploitation and imbalance likely, but I think it isn't necessarily so, and yes, "true love" (or true lust) :-) can bridge many gaps. I am not a chicken hawk (I have had sex with someone even older than I):-). I do not go looking for young things. It's just that age does not matter to me.

There may be some truth in my training people "under my tutelage" in the art of love. My most recent main boyfriend (in his 40s) was a virtual virgin when I first came on to him. We took it very slowly, and it was gratifying to receive notes from him exulting in the thrill of new experiences. I am a very affirming person and do a lot to reverse low self-esteem (even my wife's, according to my mother-in-law). If a lover wants to "use me" and then moves on—well, I don't mind (too much); it was good while it lasted. I do not rely on the love of other people for my own self-worth (and find clinging unworthy of a Buddhist).

Of course, lots of unhealthy relationships occur when there is a wide age disparity (and in lots of other cases as well). Sure, raise a red flag. But: "it depends."

From: Dan

I fell for a guy I met online who has a condo in the Mountains . . . he was 65 (I'm 52, but look a lot younger). . . . there are a lot of lesbigay folk in the Mountains . . . He was reluctant to tell me his age until I told him how it was a matter of basic honesty that I could care for him and love him no matter what the number was. About one week after I asked, I brought it up again and he gave me the answer. . . .

He had a beautiful spirit, and was warm and cuddly . . . sexually we were fundamentally incompatible (tops want bottoms, not other tops [go figure it out]) . . . in the final analysis it was not our age that did us in, it was being too rigid on important issues; also the distance, also the religion (he was Jewish) was a minor factor.

I guess "I" was the YOUNG BOY to him . . . he did say I brought out the "child" in him . . . which since I'm kinda playful too . . . we were both child-like. . . .

FINDING MALE RELATIONSHIPS

From: Stephen

Bear wrote: >*Seems like, because of all the loaded problems with male friendships, that it would be more common for a gay/BI husband and a straight wife (which is my case). Are there lots of us floating around out there? And just how do people go about living together in this kind of situation?*<

For me, the struggle with being bisexual is very rooted in my friendships with men. I was openly gay (not even very BI) before I met my wife. For the first five years we lived together, I was crazy about her, but I was also struggling with what to do with my gay identity. I hadn't had very satisfying relationships with gay men at all—it was like I was only attracted to men who were aloof and full of trouble. When I had an AIDS scare because of a boyfriend who wasn't up front with me (who had come down with HIV himself), I decided at 24 "enough."

I have noticed that when I really "work" my male friendships (and man does it take work sometimes!), my sexual urges towards men decrease. At these times I feel most balanced and fulfilled—I have a perfect complement of intimacy between my friends and my wife. For me the core of that need for men is for connection in some form, but when I deny and neglect, it gets pent up and sexualized. It becomes urgent and I act out. Now I have several really solid male friends who know all about me and its like we can't get enough of each other. We spend a lot of time together and I'm always amazed that it doesn't feel as awkward as it used to.

From: Schuyler

Andy wrote: >*The "high road" monogamy folks extol the satisfaction of friendship with men instead of overt sex (a valid option). Personally, I like both.*<

So do I.

>*Love and friendship is my first aim, but if sexual expression of it develops, all the better.*<

Intellectually, I entirely agree. A wonderful way to live, I believe, as long as we are conscious not to unnecessarily hurt others. The reality of my very busy life as well as the reality of the hurt that my infidelity, with ONE other person, causes my wife (and I know that I cannot "own" her hurt), however, convinces me that it is wise (for me, for now) to limit my overt activity in this area.

>*Hugging is also neat and so is sharing deep feelings—and we could use a lot more of both in our touch-phobic and emotion-phobic male culture.*<

Sharing deep feelings, emotionally and physically, is the primary benefit of my relationship with my male lover. As for hugging, I'm a shameless hugaholic. Thankfully, I'm acquainted with a large number of other hugaholics, male and female.

From: Kenneth

Schuyler wrote: >*Sharing deep feelings, emotionally and physically, is the primary benefit of my relationship with Robert. As for hugging, I'm a shameless hugaholic. Thankfully, I'm acquainted with a large number of other hugaholics, male and female.*<

You guys are singing my song. It means so much to me to hear you say how you are open to the sex acts with guys, but not as an end in itself. For a long time, I did not understand the affectionate component of homosexuality. Now I see that it is the intimacy that is the desire of gay men; when that is thwarted, the desire becomes sexualized. My boyfriend has been saying this, too, though he feels that the platonic friendship is enough for him.

I'm glad this kind of post is coming through. It would be educational for me to hear some experiences of guys who have found "the sharing of deep feelings, emotionally and physically" (I assume, non-sexually) with one or more straight men. It seems to me that Americans are so homophobic that it would take a VERY secure straight man to allow such closeness with a gay or bisexual man in one-on-one situations.

From: Stephen

I am just coming off a splendid weekend in which two of my male friends (both writers like me) and their wives spent the weekend with us. These guys are very special to me. Our spouses did "Race for the Cure" Sunday morning in Portland, and we went out, had breakfast, and talked for hours about our lives, our relationships, our plans, our fears. I felt so restored afterward, and my wife and I had amazing sex last evening—due, in some part, to having achieved that state of balance through my friendships.

I've had more of a sense of connection with these guys than I ever had with guys I used to have romantic relationships with. (Again that's just Me.) They're both very physically attractive (we all jog a lot) and at one point I was studying their bodies, aware that from an objective standpoint, they were very attractive, but that, subjectively, I had no desire to "have sex" with them. The same thing used to happen when I was more actively gay—the good guys didn't attract me, but the aloof, emotionally closed down intellectual powerhouses turned me on. Go figure.

From: Joey

It has finally happened. I met someone who is really the standard by which all others will be judged. When I was traveling last month a friend and I went out to a bar on my last night there. He introduced me to a man and there were sparks. This man and I have e-mailed each other daily since then and we talk on the phone at least twice a week. Well, he had to be in my city today on business. We met at his hotel on Saturday. OH MY GOD! I had thought that I had made love before. But he was so sensuous, gentle, and yet masculine, I have never felt so good.

We took our time and our bodies fit perfectly. We also went out to dinner, dancing, brunch, museums and shopping. We talked, laughed and I savored every moment. I hated to say good by. He walked me to the cab and waved good bye. Be still my beating heart. Well, I am writing this for two reasons. I can't really talk about this at home or work. So you guys have to put up with this. But, also, if any of us ever doubts why we are coming out I have the answer. I cannot express my affections or feel free of inhibitions like I was with him. It all becomes so clear. I am gay and I am finally happy. Thanks for letting me express myself.

DREAMTIME LOVER

From: Benny

Things haven't been going well for my wife and I lately. For me, I have been coming to a greater awareness of my erotic orientation lately and realize that in the long run, being gay will have a serious impact on my marriage with my wife. You see, it is not that I think that I need to be having sex with men, (though I can think of no better way to pass an evening) but rather that I am having seriously decreased desire for my wife. The reason that I see divorce as the only option for us is not that I want to enter a relationship with a man. The real reason is that I know that forcing my wife (and I realize that everyone is able to make their own decisions) to live in a basically sexless marriage would be wrong. After years of trying, I discovered, to my own dismay, that I am unable to make myself straight, or even to function that way very well. One reason that I came back to this board is that I needed a place to share my feelings with other people that have had similar experiences. And what follows, I have never been able to bring myself to share with anyone else. It makes me deeply ashamed to think of the kind of pain that this would cause my wife if she were to find out.

In the past nine months to a year, I have noticed that my sexual attraction to my wife has been waning. I began suppressing my sexual feeling for men to a terrible degree and I knew that eventually, I would not be able to keep up under the strain. To give a bit of history, I have always been a bit of a sleep walker and often talked in my sleep; this is what led me to know that a divorce was the only way to solve the problem. I began to have very vivid sexual dreams in which I would often be involved with attractive men that I knew. What I came to realize was that I was acting out those dreams with my wife, often waking up in the middle of a dream to find that I was actually kissing her and not the men in my dreams. I cannot begin to describe the guilt that I feel about those dreams. And to know that what she was experiencing during our sex was vastly different from what I was experiencing. This is something that I can never tell her, but makes me realize that I can't keep suppressing my sexuality.

I can't tell you how nice it is to be able to share that with someone. I doubt that this is a very commonly experienced side effect of being married and gay, but I would love it if someone could normalize this a bit for me. I hope that I am not the only one that has ever felt this way or had this happen.

From: Bear

While I'm not a sleepwalker, I did see some of my past behavior in your post. Sometimes, sexual performance with my wife has been difficult. There were a small handful of times when I'd close my eyes and imagine a man there instead—and, doing, instant performance. So once, instead of opening my eyes and enjoying myself with her, I kept them closed and enjoyed myself with Fantasy Man. The minute my heart rate slowed afterwards, I felt awful. Guilty, dishonest, filthy, disloyal, pathological—you name it, and I felt it. Of course I'm never going to tell her about it, at least now I don't plan to. She doesn't need to know. I think it would only be hurtful. But I did decide to never ever do it again. In the ensuing years, I haven't.

That's a difficult burden to accept. The only advice I can give is not to be too hard on yourself; to a certain extent, it was out of your control. I think we've all got enough difficulty in our lives over what we do when we're awake to abrade ourselves too harshly for what happens when we sleep.

A BIG THANK-YOU AND ANOTHER QUESTION

From: Skip

I just need to say THANK YOU to all who have shared their perspectives with the group and me over the last couple days. I am finding out that (for me) the power of this group is in the shared feelings, confusion, hopes, and struggles that so many of us are/have gone through. It truly is comforting to finally feel that I am not the only person to be going through this! I only wish I had allowed myself to take full advantage of the group a year ago when I joined . . . but I guess that just goes to show we all need to tackle issues when the time is right for each of us individually

I have another question to pose to the group. For the guys who identify themselves as gay and are staying in their marriages and making them WORK. Since I've started this sexual relationship with a guy (my first) I've found that at least as far as the sex goes I'm much more "into" his and my time together than I have been with my wife (that's not to say that she and I haven't continued our sex life, just that when I'm with him I feel more passionate than I routinely feel with her). I realize that a big reason for this is because it's new and exciting to me (kind of like the kid-in-the-candy-store scenario) and I recognized that part of my despair comes from feeling that I'm not experiencing the same level of passion with her as I do with him. I know I'm still attracted to her and there's no way to compare a 17 year relationship with a 3-week-old relationship (that's only based on sex at this point). Again, thanks to all who have shared, you ARE making a difference in someone's life!

From: Carl

Some of the guys in this enclave refer to their wives as "soulmates." Now that does strike me as a mite strange. My experience is that one of the attractions of the opposite sex, in either direction, is a certain sense of mystery. One is always at least slightly off-balance in dealing with the intricacies of the partner's thought processes. But in a same-sex coupling (including mine with my lover), there is, or at least can be, a very complete sense of empathy, of understanding, that I've never been able to attain with my wife even after 36 years of marriage.

This is true physically as well as psychically. With the opposite sex, you can guess what your partner experiences from the reactions you get, but with the same sex you know the feelings quite precisely, because you've been there more or less too. That near-identity of experience is impossible when the plumbing is different.

So to some extent loving another man is different in kind from loving a woman. Et vive les petites differences!

CHUMMINESS WITH GUYS

From: Stephen

Rodney wrote: > *I know I love my wife. I know I love having sex with her. I know I love having sex with guys. I know I would have trouble finding the same kind of closeness to a man that I have with my wife.*<

This issue raises another interesting issue for me. For bisexual men in committed heterosexual relationships, how do we get our need for intimacy with other men met without breaking our marriage vows?

I have thought about sexual intimacy as a continuum of behaviors bordered on the one side by full-fledged sexual intercourse and on the other side by simply hanging out. The interesting question for me has always been: on that vast continuum of behaviors, where do I draw the line? At what point does my behavior become unacceptable?

I watch my very heterosexual married brother for cues: he hugs and kisses his guy friends, flirts, pats their butts, pees together with them, showers together, hangs out naked in the sauna, etc., etc. All of this is done in the context of them being very straight guys together—so it's not threatening to anyone. I have found that many of these chummier behaviors meet my need, give me a feeling of closeness and intimacy with my male friends, although earlier in life I refrained from them because I didn't think I could "get away with them" without people thinking I had ulterior motives. But I find that experimenting with the line with my friends takes the edge off the desire for sexual intercourse. All I really need from my guy friends is a feeling of closeness and intimacy, and sex is no guarantee of that being met (although it has sometimes fooled me in the past). So I've experimented with the gradation of behaviors that are sexual and intimate without violating my marriage vows.

From: Rodney

My gay experience has been entirely with paid escorts and masseurs. It took me several months to realize I like masseurs much better than escorts, because so much of what I really want is simple animal, physical contact: it doesn't even always need to be sexual.

Sometimes I go to a masseur and don't get sexually aroused. But that's just fine: the massage is really all I need at that moment.

From: Rodney

I don't think I know how to have male friendships. I almost immediately begin to think of a physical relationship. My one, good male friend was my husbearcub lover. I used to be afraid to have male friends because I feared I would betray myself to them. Now that I am out to my wife, I don't care anymore, but I have long since cut myself off from friendships with most of my acquaintances because of my (self) homophobia. At any rate I have well over 50 years of non-experience making male friends. My relationship with women is the same, nonexistent, for fear (my own self-taught fear) of upsetting my wife.

I think of my brothers within this group as my best friends, and I long to meet some of you for the chance to learn to build a friendly relationship. Maybe someday. In the meantime, I am learning to reach out to be a friend to everyone here.

From: Miller

I think that my behaviors with close male friends run the gamut from hands-off to the occasional arm around the shoulders to hugs. Patting on the ass I do occasionally but I avoid it somewhat for the same reasons you mention, I don't want it to appear as if I have ulterior motives.

Even friends who know I am BI don't have problems with some of the more intimate behaviors such as hugging, peeing together, being naked together, etc. To me this perhaps suggests that the need for intimacy is innate and perhaps strong in straight men as well (but often not expressed due to our societal pressures).

I know that all of these behaviors—and friendships—have served to address my need for male intimacy. I have become much more comfortable with hugging men over time, for example; when I was younger, much like you, I hesitated to do that. The real friendships—the ones where you can discuss anything without fear—are important to me. And I have always nurtured those.

From: Max

When it comes to issues which are more emotional in nature (for example talking of one's feelings, like feeling sad, alone, etc.) then I tend to find that most guys (even quite a few gay guys) balk at the idea.

I find that my needs revolve around my wanting to get close and deep with a guy. To be able to lean over and hug him or touch him sincerely, and vice versa. Where I come a cropper is drawing the line on when it becomes more sexual. Sometimes I feel that it's "expected" of me, and other times it comes from within myself.

From: Rodney

Frankly, what bothers me a lot about "straight" male physical interaction is how much of the time it is (I think) tinged with a repressed sexuality. Sometimes, I want to say to my straight friends, "Why don't you guys just get down and suck each other off? You'd feel a lot better afterwards."

I have pictured myself in an ultra-male straight setting, like a poker game, putting my hand down, opening a beer and saying (with a "straight" face), "Well, guys, what do you think? Do guys REALLY give better head than women?"

Fortunately, I have successfully resisted these impulses so far.

But I have "macho" friends who tell me the most amazing stories without any apparent awareness of their sexual overtones. Swimming naked together (as adults), peeing in the pool, then swimming in the yellow cloud that gets formed. On a sports trip, shitting in the luggage of someone you're mad at and then having that guy smear cum all over your face in "revenge."

I'm not making these stories up. Nor am I making up the part about the fact that the guys telling these stories don't seem to see any sexual element in them. Sigh.

From: Rodney

I have some of the same trouble relaxing with men, wondering if I'm going to let some cat out of some bag. I think many of these difficulties have to do with the fact that we live in a culture where "sexuality" has become so intensely bound up with "identity."

In the heterosexual part of my life, I find myself frequently struggling to maintain a simple friendship with a woman, because of the societal expectation that men and women, put together and given the chance, will immediately fall to rutting. The tension seems always to be there, somehow, even when both the woman and I know that our relationship, consciously, is utterly nonsexual.

From: Stephen

I work in a plant with 400 other men. Within the plant there is a great deal of "talent." There are men who are breathtakingly beautiful. But! when I walk through those doors I leave my sexuality outside. I am there to do a job, not to shop for stick pussy. I have many good friendships. and a couple of dozen that are intimate. Intimate, in the sense that we share the details of one another's lives. I am "OUT" to my intimate friends and they know that I respect both them and their sexuality, and would NEVER hit on them or do anything that would make them feel personally threatened or uncomfortable. In each case when I have come out to my friends I have offered them the choice of breaking off the friendship. No one ever has. In most cases the man I came out to thanked me for sharing the confidence and felt honored that I had that much faith in him and his character. Since I believe that real friendship is based on SHARED experience, and not necessarily on SAMENESS of experience. I also tell them to feel free to ask me anything that they think they might want to know about the gay experience, and that if they ask me something I don't feel comfortable talking about I will tell them so. This makes them feel included, reinforces the bond of our friendship, and opens the door to dialogue. (Although when some of them have asked me specific questions about M2M sex and I told them the answer, sometimes they turn "beet red" and say "That's enough! Don't tell me any more right now." But, they always come back for more.)

As a bisexual man, and after having been married for 28 years, they know that I understand the problems of M2F relationships and marriage very well. I know when their wives are being a bitch and they are pissed. I know when they are so stressed by life that they feel sexually inadequate and can hardly get it up. I know which of them have women on the side. They in turn know about all the men I see. When I have a date they want to hear the all of the details. They are always fascinated by the gay experience. (My wife and I have a great sex life which many of my friends are already envious of, and when I go out with a man and don't get laid they howl with laughter, and they just love it. <G>) I am not out to everyone in my plant because quite frankly it's none of their fucking business. It IS the business of those men who are identified as my friends. The confidences which we share have only made our friendships better and more fun.

My being bisexual has given me the opportunity to remove some of the mystery of homosexual behavior and to educate my closest friends to the idea that the stereotypes about gay and bisexual men are horseshit, and that we are not so very different from everyone else.

In closing I would advise anyone who truly desires to make friends with straight men to be honest and straightforward in your dealings. Be a stand up guy, let your real integrity and character shine through. Be genuinely interested in them and their lives. Most importantly DO NOT to look upon them as potential dates. They are no more interested in you sexually than a lesbian is in a man. Just be open and be there for them. Let them know that you care about them as people and are willing to talk about their problems and that you can keep a confidence and not blab it all over the place. If you can do these things then the bonds of friendship will come and one day you will be able to share your sexuality with them and they won't give a shit.

From: Stephen

I've been reflecting on the whole concept of virtual support, meeting guys like all of you though the 'Net. My wife and the wife of one of my friends recently observed that men in our circle generally spend a lot of time corresponding on the Internet. That we live our friendships through e-mail. I mean it's so convenient for anyone socialized as male: no matter what risks of self-disclosure you take, there's distance and anonymity; there's that remove; there's the intellectualization behind a carefully composed sentence. The best of both worlds, I hazard to say.

Is surfing the Net and making friends through the Net a "guy thing?" And how much of the time I spend e-mailing is time I don't spend in the physical presence of my male friends? This is so safe and easy, but ultimately it's not real and perhaps it keeps me from "working" the "real" friendships I do have. Does anyone relate to this? Is anyone else starting to think that the time he spends corresponding to e-mail is a problem, is taking him away from his real relationships? It's not really chumminess, is it?

From: Bruce

Surfing the Net isn't necessarily a guy thing, but I do think that guys are more likely to use it as a place to meet friends. Several women that I know are avid Web surfers, but have never taken to the idea of using it as a place to meet others. There are exceptions though. Hot office gossip last week was a vendor's employee who was flying to Italy to meet the man she fell in love with over the 'Net!

Meeting people on the Net CAN be a substitute for face-to-face interaction, but it can also be used as a way just to take a first safe step. In the past I used the Net to meet other men, but I'd also try to attend a get together for online groups when I could, or to meet other men for dinner, a night on the town, etc.

From: Bear

Meeting people over the Internet should not be a substitute for spending time with non-virtual people (!), but there is a lot you can get out of it that is real and human and fills a need. There is a connection to another person—it's a fairly new medium, so it's hard to categorize it the way we do with other encounters (in person, phone, mail, etc.). If you find you are neglecting your other relationships, then obviously you might want to reconsider your relationship to e-mail. But where else could you find something as bizarrely specific as a list-served support group for married men who have come out to their spouses? When I found that this list of Gay/BI men existed, I was shocked—so many people, all with situations similar to me. What a luxury. Virtual chumminess can never replace face-to-face chumminess—but that makes it nothing more than a powerful addition to our lives, rather than a drain of energy.

From: David

My closest two male friends were both str8. The first I knew and loved over a dozen years . . . very intimate and close and never touched him sexually. Finally over 40 years later I came out via mail and told him how I had loved and longed for him. He was a real joy to know in our youth and young adult . . . and very kind now. Loving him was both a good feeling and very, very frustrating! "Look but don't touch" at that age is not easy at all.

The second followed a few years later and lasted over 20 years until he died. . . . Very close. Very intimate in all ways except I never came out to him. With him my love was different and had no sexual element. He has been dead 4 years now and I still miss him dearly and deeply. I feel blessed to have had these two in my life . . . plus some less close . . . mostly I have always had at least one close male chum . . . buddy . . . except the past 3 years there has been none other than some really dear ones I have met here on this list and we see each other way too seldom to have it be what I want/need! Caring male friends are a real blessing and asset in one's life! One of my books says we should each have at least one close, same-gender friend we could call at 4AM and say "I need to talk" and find an open ear and HEART! It's a thought . . .

From: Crawly

While I don't think I'm "addicted to the Internet," I can really relate to what you had to say about the anonymity of all this. There are a few guys I've said I'd like to meet in the group, but making the call is really scary. After the number exchange, I don't call, they don't call. I guess that's the way we are socialized. Part of the challenge for me is I have two small children and I work at night four days a week. I could plan I suppose but so many times I have the unexpected free time and I'm sure no one would want to just pick up and meet me.

PARTNERS, LOVERS, WIVES

From: Rodney

Several years ago, I visited an old college friend who, as it turns out, was gay, and who had a long term partner with whom he had been living (at the time) for ten years.

I took them to dinner and was amazed at the way in which they argued about EXACTLY the same things my wife and I did ("You know what your doctor says about eating red meat . . .").

DATING

From: Joey

Thus far, in my very brief exposure to other gay and BI men on the Internet, we seem to address issues primarily centered on home, specifically our wives. However, I would still like to open up a discussion of men dating men. Now, I have started to go out and, boy, do I feel insecure. I met a man on Friday night, for example. We seem to hit it off well, even exchanged e-mail addresses and kissed good night. (I felt very awkward about kissing him at his car on the street, by the way. I am nervous about bashers and was afraid to be seen.) I sent him an e-mail saying hi and that it was nice to see him. I haven't heard back from him yet and it has been a few days. Am I being over anxious? How do I just relax and be cool when I want to call him and say hi? Is it OK to call and say hi? I did ask him out, and he said yes but we didn't set a date as I am going out of town this week on business. I have had this before where I meet a guy and it is all hot and heavy and then, poof, it's over. Is it me? What should I be addressing with myself that may be at issue with the guys I am seeing? Mind you, I am not falling in love at the drop of a hat. I am not pushy or domineering. I am just looking for a guy to do things with and have fun. Thanks in advance for any advice or insight you may have for me.

From: Brandon

This was the hardest part of my coming out, as the insecurities of years and years of fighting my homosexuality had taken its toll. I was told early on that what I needed to do was take a stick and put a knife mark on it for every time that another male rejected me or left me high and dry after what I thought was a very nice date. I was then told to keep looking at that stick as my learning or experience marks. There was no guarantee as to how many marks I would have to place on this stick. I did not have a real stick but used this as my imaginary stability factor and sure enough the marks went on the stick at an ever decreasing rate.

I even put two deep groves on the stick, that each lasted 8 months, where I entered into two relationships with another man. I learned some very dear lessons from each of these relationships—all about who I was and who I was not. The old adage of having to kiss many a frog before ones finds their prince in life is so true. Only thing is we are the frog and it is up to us to find our true self as others kiss us.

My final mark was placed on the stick 6 years ago this coming Dec 9th. Met my man—I had learned lots about myself, as he had done about himself, and we clicked. He also had many tick marks for dates and two relationship marks on his stick. With his friendship, love, and support along with being accepted by many other wonderful loving gay men in this city, I now feel very secure and happy with my life as a gay married man. (Having a wonderful wife that accepted her husband's gay side did not hurt either.)

Last but not least: never ever forget that you are not alone in your journey of discovery. There are lots of us wonderful men out here that would have died for what you are trying to give another man—your love and companionship. We are truly out here. Thank God for this group of Gay and BI men on the Internet, where we can share and be honest with each other.

From: James

You have to be "you" and as long as you have a pretty good idea of who you are, then don't worry about whether it's OK to call or not. I recently met a guy and have had the same questions—we had a great evening together, then . . . nothing. When he declined to get together several times afterwards I simply asked him if he really wanted to get together again and he assured me that he does but his schedule wasn't allowing time to get together. . . . so we'll see. It's OK to ask him honestly if he wants to get together again. And tell him it's OK to say no. For me, I find it really difficult to say no to a guy because I don't want to hurt his feelings . . . but there comes a point, you have to be honest. I'm learning to be honest . . . even when it is awkward to be so. I try to be nice about it but not lead another guy on.

From: Josi

I have had the same experience you've had when I was dating. I think I'm open about who I am and what I want but there's no calling back. Even when I've overcome my self-doubt and followed through by making the second and sometimes third call, there's still no response, not even the courtesy of "Thanks, but not interested." There were three exceptions. One was a man I saw twice. He called to say he found someone who was a potential LTR and I clearly was not, by my own admission. The second man and I dated for a few months until he decided to return to his marriage and he did tell me so. And the third man I told that I was returning to my wife.

Although now that I want to date again, I'm afraid of facing what you've described. What you've talked about is captured in this joke a friend told me when I was bemoaning dating:

Did you hear about the two lesbians on their second date? They rented a truck and are moving in together. Did you hear about the two gays on their second date? What second date!

From: George

I have always had trouble dating. Not in finding someone to date, but in allowing myself to date comfortably. I came out, only to my wife, only recently. Assessing our situation since then, I can honestly say things are going well between us. We agreed right up front that I would NOT come out to anyone else. We both sincerely wanted it that way, knowing that each of our families and folks in our small community are accomplished (verbal) bashers.

I say things are going well since I came out to me wife because I know now that she accepts me as I am. She also knows that I need some sort of contact or relationship with other men. There is no question in either of our minds about wanting to stay married. We do truly love each other and hope to spend the rest of our days together.

At first we talked very little about it other than agree not to tell anyone else. For a while I tried to force us into conversation about the subject, but found that that was a mistake. Now we openly discuss it together, joke about it, and sometimes, though more rarely lately, cry about it.

I am bad at dating because when I do get together with a guy I am so damn nervous, afraid that someone will somehow suspect what we are up to. I am not a good date as a result. I always go home from these less-than-satisfying situations depressed and angry at myself. My wife knows that I am really interested in a very close friend of mine, also married, and whom I suspect very strongly is BI. She even has offered to set up a dinner with the other couple and arrange things so the guy and I can find some time to talk. She is doing this because she does love me and knows that in order for me to be totally happy and get rid of depression I have to satisfy my BI side.

I really appreciate you guys being there and sharing your situations. Before this group, I have to admit I considered doing myself in, convinced that I was among the very few, if any, guys who were married but still felt he needed other guys.

From: Joey

I happened to be online with a guy who broke up with me last month (we dated for about two months and, although I was not in love with him, I was surely in "like"—I enjoyed his company and the sex was good). In the course of our chat, I pushed him a bit and asked why it didn't work. Well, the first issue for him was my living arrangement with my wife. For him, this did not work. I am not perceived as really free, nor do I have a space to bring him to. Whenever we had a date, we ended up at his house. Now, guys, is this going to be an issue for us until we leave our spouses? I find this disconcerting.

The other thing I did was to call the guy who I met last Friday and hadn't called me. I am so glad I did. He seemed genuinely glad to hear from me. We chatted and bantered and the camaraderie was the same as when we first met. I asked him out and he said yes. I am psyched. BUT, is my living situation going to be at issue again? I guess the answer is to talk about it right away and see what he says.

From: Brent

A little over two weeks ago I had reached a real low point with the dating thing. It seemed like everyone I went out with was very quick to tell me that they "just wanted to be friends"—nothing romantic. I am willing to admit that, when I first began dating, I was going quickly—too quickly—to the romantic thing and, as someone pointed out to me, as a man who has been married for 27 years, long term, committed relationship is all I know and it's natural that I would want to go there. But I felt I had really pulled back from that; was trying to just "be;" was certainly not expecting much on the first date—or dates—just a chance to get to know someone and see if he was someone I wanted to pursue. Yet, I felt like I was getting "preemptive strikes" from all quarters.

There was one man I was seeing pretty regularly but found after a few dates that I was losing interest and was beginning to withdraw. He actually confronted me on this and noted that I was clearly not ready to commit; was not really making myself available for a relationship. ACKKK! Too available; not available enough—whatever I did seemed wrong!

I refocused my energies then on doing what I had originally set out to do when my wife and I separated, which was to explore and find ME and who that was and put my energies there. That helped me feel less "rejected" and, as you so eloquently stated with your message, acknowledge those marks on my stick as real learning experiences.

Happy ending . . .

Two weeks ago, one of my "just want to be friends" invited me to a party (not WITH him; just a fun gathering that he thought I might be interested in . . . gee thanks, buddy) and I almost didn't go but finally thought what the hell . . . and it was all women except for me, my "friend" and one other gay man. The three of us started talking and, surprise, surprise, the other man and I really hit it off. One thing led to another and it seems as if the potential for a really wonderful relationship exists here. I have made myself "available" to him and he has done the same and something seems to be growing between us. Guess what—he likes me for who I am, not for being someone I think he wants.

From: Marshall

I have been enjoying the Dating thread so let me add my comments: There are 4 types of men you can date (ignoring the frog and prince issue):

1. Another married man NOT out to his wife. I find this very tricky because you have to make sure you don't accidentally out him, and since my wife would probably want to meet him there is a pretty good chance that this might happen.
2. Another married man out to his wife. In my mind this is probably the ideal situation but from my own experience this is probably the hardest one to maintain. If you are both planning on staying married then there are always home commitments that must come first. When you are both keeping the home situation happy there isn't a lot of common time left.
3. A gay man who knows your situation. This should be a great situation but often the gay guy has to come second to the home obligations. After this happens a few times he has to be pretty committed to you or he is going to look elsewhere.
4. A gay guy that does not know your situation. This is one situation I have not found myself in because I am always very up-front about the fact that I am married.

There should be some sort of brilliant conclusion to this wisdom but I am afraid there isn't. I have found that many gay men are very unsupportive/unsympathetic to the problems that a BI man has but it seems to me that a BI-married man has much greater problems.

From: Sidney

I forwarded the e-mail on dating to my wife. I am out and dating. She said,

"This is interesting—it appears on the surface to be quite true and rather complete, and a problem. However, there is an option that I don't think he has explored. Take out the word dating and replace it with friend and see how true all of the sentences work out for men."

From: James

Thanks for sharing. . . . I agree with your comments . . . my wife's observation about your second category, which is what I seek (a married guy out to his wife) is that I'm looking for a needle in a haystack and she is probably right.

However, I had a fun evening last night and since my life has so few dating experiences anymore let alone positive ones, I wanted to share—just for the fun of it for me—something that happened last night.

One of my colleagues from this group and I go dancing at a gay dance club. Last night I danced 3 times in a row with a guy that had asked me to dance about a month ago (guy I am truly attracted to). I was really touched when the guy asked me to dance (that night) because until LAST night I have not had the gumption to ask another guy to dance. But last night I asked him to dance and we did. After the first dance, he kissed me and suggested we dance again, this time with him leading (a first experience with me) and though I found it was awkward following, I loved that he pressed his groin into mine as we danced . . . after that dance, he suggested we dance again, with me leading . . . and we kissed at the end . . . these are little things perhaps . . . but gee, I'll take all the little things I can at this point . . . left me "soaring" for the rest of the evening.

Another plus last night, it was fun to start to teach Joe to dance!! (<VBG> . . . he will kill me for this!) . . . he doesn't know it, but I expect that the two of us will give an exhibition dance at the next guy gathering

From: Carl

I wonder whether one can be very very happy without risking the pain. When my lover and I first started to re-establish our relationship, last winter, he wasn't at all sure he wanted to get that involved at this stage of his life and cautioned me that my want of circumspection might be setting me up for pain down the road. My reply then was that having made the horrendous mistake, almost 50 years ago, of trying to suppress my love for him I wanted to experience fully any of my feelings this time around, wherever they might lead. The result has been a richness like that of the sudden Technicolor, when Dorothy steps out the door of Auntie Em's house into Oz.

And there will be pain. Life is full of unpleasant surprises at this age. But for the time being I'm experiencing the most wonderful relationship of my life. That and being more thoroughly out than ever before have renewed the wonder of living, and I'll willingly pay the emotional bill when it comes due.

From: Woody

I've had the opposite experience. I have gotten together with only two married gay/BI's. All the rest were gay. I'm up front with the fact that I'm married, out to my wife, and don't take off the wedding ring. I've found that most are relieved to find a guy not looking for a deep emotional attachment. If you present yourself as looking for an emotional attachment—a one-on-one intense relationship—I wouldn't be surprised that one wouldn't have much luck with that approach. When I meet a guy I'm just looking for friendship—and (blush) hot sex if it happens (usually does). . . . And, a surprise to me, most have remained friends, though most are just casual friends, since.

From: Lyndon

This may be a little trite, and a little old and worn, but here it is: "It is better to have loved and lost than to never have loved at all."

How can we grow if we don't put ourselves out there for the experience? I am terrified that I will have gone through this emotional roller coaster and find that I am alone and unfulfilled in my true desires of a loving m2m relationship. There's always sex, and that can be obtained. But, a relationship? I am excited and scared, but I guess that's what makes it fun and why it's called living.

Part of me wants to find a relationship right now!!! But, I know that it has only been about 2 months since I really started this journey. I have to give myself more time to see who I am before I can share myself with another. Along the way I am making some friends to share stories and feelings.

WISH TO TURN CLOCK BACK

From: Marlin

I don't feel that I could stand to lose the emotional support of my wife and kids right now, so I am living that double life. On the one hand, I wish this relationship with my boyfriend had never happened and that I could turn back the clock to when I was just married and horny, but on the other, coming out feels like a primal and elemental force driving me to whatever conclusion it needs to come to, and that he is about the hottest and most amazing guy I ever met, that I can't give him up just yet. I got the tiger by the tail, like that old Buck Owens song says.

From: Chukky

I am 42 years old. My wife and I just live together . . . that's about it, and I am very discontent and not very happy. I am staying at home due to my financial debts and my children, both of whom are preteens. I have been involved with a man for the past year. Our wives do not know the extent of the relationship, wrong as it might be . . . but again due to life situations for both of us. He did not create the problems or the feelings I have toward my wife for they were there before he was. I am in love with him to no end . . . so much that it is often painful. I miss him terribly when I am not with him and cannot keep my hands off him when I am with him. I would have to say . . . he is the most important person in my life and there is nothing I wouldn't do for him. He did not complicate my life . . . but in fact for me . . . he is the proof that dreams do in fact come true . . . but I also realize that there may not be a happily ever after more due to him than to me. I cannot say I wish it all has not come about because that simply would not be true. He has made my life so rich . . . and come to life . . . feeling things I truly never felt . . . and sometimes the pressure he feels from his job, and from some of the thoughts I convey in regards to us and what I wish and hope the future will be. I've said for the past few months to friends of mine who know my entire situation . . . "right guy . . . wrong timing," yet I refer to him as my husband and he the same to me. I want us to be in a "marriage". He wants to be with his kids and is so afraid his children would resent him later . . . and I feel . . . the kids will always be our kids . . . and they might or might not hold resentment even if they never know the truth about their fathers. I feel we are both being cheated . . . . and I do not see things changing in any way for now . . . but I do know that I cannot see leading this double life thing indefinitely and what we feel just might not be enough.

GAY/BI RELATIONSHIP

From: George

I feel very fortunate in that I do have a monogamous relationship with my "friend," also married and BI. Frankly I wouldn't want it any other way, and neither would my friend. However, an acquaintance of mine I met via the Internet, had an experience that caused him to make an attempt on his own life. It was a situation where he, also married and BI, fell head over heels in love with another married BI guy. In spite of the fact that my acquaintance told his lover that he wanted to stay married he relented after repeated pleads from the lover, and finally agreed to negotiate a separation with his wife. The two rented an apartment together.

After a period of only three weeks his lover connected with a younger guy and left my friend to begin cohabitation with his new love.

My Internet friend was devastated and took an overdose of a variety of medications that nearly killed him. He did this because he gave up his wife and children for his lover only to be abandoned when his lover got the hots for another guy.

I guess if I wasn't able to have monogamous relationship I would avoid m2m contacts. As I have said in my earlier posts, I am out but only to my wife, and she knows of my relationship with my friend. I think the only reason she has been able to finally accept me having a m2m relationship is because it is monogamous.

From: Mike

Don't know who coined the word "duogamous," but we've been using it regularly on this forum since the beginning. I use it to describe my preferred situation. One man and One woman in my life at any one time. The woman in my life is my life partner, the man is an intimate friend/lover for a long as it is mutually affirming. I find maintaining true intimacy with anyone takes time, energy, and commitment. Two intimate relationships at one time seems to be my limit. I've been fortunate enough to have had 3 such m2m relationships over the past 3 years. Each exclusive while they lasted, each different in character and intensity . . . but each in their special way intimate and affirming.

My wife prefers my having ONE significant male other, mainly because of the risks involved with having multiple sex partners. The emotional component is sometimes threatening to her, but over these 3 years since I've been out and involved in m2m relationships, she is beginning to realize I have no intentions of leaving her for any man, no matter how much I may love him. No man can replace what I've shared with my wife for 27 years, no man could have given me 3 beautiful children. No man could love me as unconditionally as she does. I can't imagine any situation in which I would give up such a precious gift.

From: Clark

I have been going over these issues myself in the last few months. While I don't currently have a man in my life with whom I am actively sexual, I keep wondering whether it is a good thing to cultivate more than one male relationship which might be or become sexual.

Aside from the considerable issues of safe sex, which have been roundly debated and discussed in these posts, I wonder if the issues have to be put in terms of monogamy, duogamy, promiscuity, etc. I am beginning, barely beginning, to come to terms with the fact that I don't have to have every gay man who looks at me, or even all of those who are interested in me (as if there were a horde who were!). The issue is not just should there be one among many, but what is right and true for me in any relationship.

There is one thing of which I am thoroughly convinced: we do not involve ourselves sexually with another person and come away unchanged, untouched. Nor does the other person. We penetrate each other's auras, psyches, memories, when we come together. Which is why, I think, there is such lasting sadness from "one night stands." There is no such thing as a one night stand. That night reaches into days and weeks and probably years. And that is true of all human encounters.

Thus the issue for me seems to be more of whether it is timely, right, good for me to enter another's space, let alone his body. I have no categories in which to respond except to say that love, joy, play, and humor are signals of lasting significance. If they are present, and if I can be truly open to another human being, then perhaps what happens sexually will be an expression of something True. Maybe the bottom line is that it is all sacred.

From: Carl

This was the kind of post that makes this group of men such a great forum: thoughtful and provocative, sensitive, caring. Thanks.

When I was staggering through adolescence, my dad told me, "sex can be either very beautiful or very ugly, depending on whether it is the ultimate expression of intimacy between people who love each other, or something pursued for its own sake." If it wasn't the wisest thing he ever told me, then I've missed the point of some of his other dicta. And I'm satisfied that what he said is true irrespective of the sex of the "people who love each other"—or of those one with whom one pursues sex for its own sake.

From: Carl

I'm totally open with my wife about my relationship to my boyfriend—at least insofar as she'll let me talk about it at all—but that doesn't prevent her from being intensely jealous of him. In fact, that seems to be the crucial point in her refusal to discuss the situation with me or anyone else. Openness doesn't prevent jealousy. Period. But it may work in reverse: in our case, at least, jealousy seems to prevent openness.

My boyfriend came back into my life 15 months ago. I'd been quite clear that my romantic life was over, and suddenly I was head over heels in love like I hadn't been since I was in my twenties, when my boyfriend and I together first explored what it meant to make love in the fullest sense.

I was so grateful for the gift of love that it finally came home to me how important it is not to demand that the love be returned. Particularly since it was I who had left my boyfriend when I found that he wouldn't commit to sharing his life with me, all those years ago, I had no right to do more than exult in what I felt and let his feelings develop as they would. I dared not expect anything in return, and in retrospect I suspect that I would have smothered any feeling my boyfriend still harbored for me had I communicated the expectation that he should "love me back." That's how I discovered that this sort of love presents no opportunity for jealousy.

The result is that I've achieved what I could not have, had I set out to do so. Not only has my love for my boyfriend been deepening and mellowing over these months, but his love for me, so hesitant and defensive in the beginning, has been doing likewise.

From: Rodney

I keep wondering why it is that I end up sounding like the whore of the group, considering that I have now been CELIBATE now for four months, while my wife and I try desperately (and currently, not very successfully) to patch our marriage up.

Like you, I was raised with the idea that the "beauty" of sex has to do with love.

But I think it's only a half-truth. Unarguably, the most beautiful sex is that which is coupled with love.

But, in fact, sex without love can also be beautiful. Just as love without sex can be beautiful. As long as sex is consensual, it can be a lot more than just "popping a load."

Consensual sex points in the same direction as love: toward intimacy and toward unity. So we can have (1) love without sex, which is probably the least INTENSE form of connection, though it is much longer-lived than (2); (2) sex without love, which is typically more INTENSE than (1), but very short-lived; and (3) sex with love (combining the best features of 1 and 2).

I am going into this mild rant because I'm very tired of the notion that sex is somehow "ugly" and needs love to pretty it up. I disagree. Sex is beautiful.

From: Carl

I've been celibate for over a decade. My wife stopped having sex with me over 15 years ago because she could tell I was having sex with guys. And I voluntarily gave up guys because I thought anonymous sex was the only way of preserving my marriage and I was too afraid of AIDS to continue anonymous sex.

From: William

The business about love and sex is a liberal offshoot of love and marriage bull. The only problem with raw sex is possible STDs far as I'm concerned.

From my own experience, I have enjoyed every guy and every gal I've ever had sex with. Some I've loved, some I've liked, some I only liked while we fucked, some I didn't like while we weren't fucking, most I've loved while we fucked. And mostly I loved fucking. Does that make me a pervert, promiscuous, unfulfilled, shallow, or some other label? An interesting thing has happened, however. I met a man and fell in love. I discovered I loved him as much after I came as before (one of his tests for true love). My desire to get it on w/other guys is slowly dying. Travis is helping that to happen too since he really wants me to be monogamous. Being faithful to him is getting easier and easier. Maybe that happens when you fall in love. It certainly didn't happen because someone lectured on the evils of loveless sex.

From: Marvin

AMEN Brother! Sex in and of itself can be beautiful—as an expression of something deeper, as pure recreation, as a way of relating to another— WHATEVER! anytime it's between two consenting adults I feel no need to apologize or cheapen it in any way, even if a one night stand with someone I just met. . . .

From: William

Some of my greatest sexual experiences have been one night stands. What better way to break down conventional barriers to real intimacy and communication, if only for a few hours. Our society builds brick walls around each of us, obscuring the essential brotherhood of man and the possibilities of communion and mutual love. Hey man, sex for sex alone is great.

Uninhibited, liberated freedom to express oneself with another person, naked body to naked body is one of the joys of existence. Take advantage of it at every opportunity. Now . . . practical considerations of being married and gender differences or similarities make for some complications, but the rewards are worth the hassles dealing with these issues. Having good sex requires taking off more than your clothes. We have to remove hang-ups, religious prohibitions, society's taboos, useless conventional values, and ingrained personal fear and loathing. The journey is well worth it. Go to it with all the zest and energy u can muster and u will be eternally grateful.

ROAD TO DISCOVERY

From: Eric

As many of you may recall, I recently began a relationship with a man. This was my first boyfriend since my last male lover, the guy I had fallen in love with when I first acknowledged I was gay, almost 6 years ago. My wife dealt with the situation amazingly well—although from time to time she got really depressed—especially when she saw my male friend and I interacting. The problem was that although I enjoyed being with him—and the sex was fantastic—I didn't feel the excitement, the magic, the fireworks and the passion that I'd felt the first time I'd fallen in love with a guy. Friends told me that I'd never experience those things again—that the first time will always remain special. I'd grown to believe them.

Because of my move out of the house and to another state, as well as certain other issues, my boyfriend and I spent less and less time together and on several occasions I tried to break up, but he always persuaded me to continue. But deep down I realized that I just didn't love him.

A few weeks ago I met an Englishman who was vacationing here. We had the proverbial holiday romance—knowing that at the end of two weeks we'd part and go our own separate ways. But an amazing thing happened. We connected on an emotional level that I've only experienced with one other person—my wife. Suddenly the fireworks and passion were back and it seemed that it was even better than the first time round. For two weeks we spent almost every minute together. I didn't get much work done—but I kept telling myself that after the 2 weeks I would get back into my regular routine. It was like having a honeymoon in heaven. Romantic dinners, staying on the beach till sunset or getting there before dawn, a fair amount of partying and a lot of time alone in his hotel room. He wasn't embarrassed to show his affection and wherever we went we held hands, embraced, and kissed . . . regardless of whether people around us stared or not. That's part of the magic of South Beach I guess.

When we parted, unsure of what the future holds for us, I realized that if nothing else, this relationship has given me hope for the future and optimism that you can find that special magic again. . . . that there are people that make you feel absolutely incredible, full of joy and excitement.

I was able to end things with previous my boyfriend without causing him too much pain; I was able to share my feelings for my Englishman with my wife and children. And my English lover and I are making plans to get together at least one week each month for the foreseeable future. We're taking it one day at a time, but for now we're both on top of the world, happy, and dare I say it, in love.

My main reason for writing this is to remove the misconception that the first time remains the best. The fireworks and passion can hit you numerous times, often when you least expect it. Just be open to it.

From: Scott

I have been married for 3 years and have one kid, which I adore. I have been out to my wife for only a couple of months—she found a conversation in my history file in the computer and questioned me about it, I confessed. She is being really considerate and trying to understand. We are trying to work things out. I can't decide if I am gay or BI. I love my wife and enjoy sex with her, but I don't have any desire for any other women. Where is the line that says you are gay or BI? I met a guy who is my age and fell deeply in love with him. I talked to him every day, but only have seen him twice. He was the most wonderful person that I have ever met. He, at first, felt the same for me for a couple of months and then one day his feelings changed all of a sudden. He wanted us to be friends, just friends. I miss him so much and it is truly the deepest pain that I have ever felt in my life. This was the love that I have been searching for and when I found it now it's gone. I still talk to him every day holding on to a dream that someday he will feel the same once again. I talked to him today, and asked him if I would ever get to see him again and he said that he didn't think that it would be good for me right now that it would only hurt me to see him because of the way that I feel. I asked him if he thought that his feelings would ever grow back into the love that we had, and he said that he wasn't sure, but he didn't think so. This has left my heart broken and in pieces. All I can do is sit and cry and remember the meetings and all the talks that we have had. I love him and want him in my life. I guess a friend is more than nothing. He has just come out to his wife a few weeks ago himself and I hope that after his divorce and when things settle down in his life that he will realize how much I love him and what all I could give him.

Wow! I can't believe I have just sat here and rambled on.

From: Carl

If you'll accept the advice of someone who has often done a pretty poor job of managing his emotional life, you may be best served by trying to develop the stoicism to let go of him as a lover while retaining him as a friend. With my guy, I have to beware of open expressions of how much I love him, because that makes him nervous; he begins to feel boxed-in even though he knows how deep my love runs whether I express it or not. In your case, your friend seems even less willing to accept such expressions. If he knows that he can rely on you to keep your emotions reined in, he may relax enough to let his deeper feelings for you rekindle.

It may even take a disappointment with someone else before he accepts how sterling a virtue your loyalty is. And knowing that someone else is enjoying what you desperately desire can be very painful indeed. But even that can be coped with. Think of your love for him as a secret treasure, like having a gem tucked away in a pocket where you can feel it even though nobody else would be aware that it's there. If you focus on your feeling for him, rather than his feeling (or want of it) for you, I guarantee it will lessen the pain.

From: Anthony

With regard to your boyfriend and his lost love, I had the same happen to me a while back. It is very painful and we have to realize that this will happen in the future with whomever you meet and fall in love with. Just like any relationship, str8 or gay, you have to mourn for the loss of that love, like your wife who has to deal with that part of you she lost to men. And realize that you will find another person, not the same, but just as special, maybe even more, who will love you as much and not abandon you. It will take some time, but the pain does go away, and yes, a friendship is better than nothing with him right now. I still keep in touch with my ex-lover, and have met quite a lot of new friends who could be as special.

From: Travis

I disagree: that part of you that loved men was never open to the wife; after outing, she has the potential of getting to enjoy the whole of you, which is usually more than the sum of the parts. The wife can mourn the "old" relationship (before outing), but as soon as the couple can get into defining the "new" relationship, the better for all.

I FELL FOR A CO-WORKER

From: Corwin

I really began to question my sexuality when I fell head-over-heels for a co-worker and couldn't get him off my mind. Nothing ever came of that and he never knew of my feelings. Because of this I entered therapy, and it was the best thing I could ever have done. I was able to finally deal with and come to grips with my desires for and attractions to men. I think I was actually ready to admit I was gay at that time, but just needed someone impartial to talk to.

During this time life was very difficult for me. I was constantly grumpy and distant at home. My wife and children were constantly wondering what was wrong with me . . . why wasn't I happy anymore. I was having anxiety and panicky attacks constantly. That summer I had my first ever man-to-man experience with someone I grew to know over the summer via the Internet. It was a very wonderful and exciting experience for me. From that point on I knew what I had to do, and what path was laid out for me to follow. I definitely knew I was gay.

Shortly thereafter I came out to my wife. I anticipated the worst but received an uncanny amount of support from her that evening. Things have been up and down since then, but generally we are establishing a good friendship and co-parenting relationship. My children do not know yet, but we plan to tell them sometime in the next few months.

Our current plans include separation and divorce. For my health's sake I need to become the man I was meant to be. For me this means separate living environments. Both my wife and I have agreed that I will continue to be a supportive role and active participant in my children's lives. I will not disappear from their lives and will make this transition as easy for everyone as is possible.

I cannot continue to hide the fact that I am gay. It takes too much energy and is the sole reason for my anxiety and panicky attacks. This I know for I have not had any major attacks since coming out, and I have been emotionally healthier since. To the future.

From: Clark

I don't often respond, but this hits me squarely. I applaud you for the decisions you have made; for getting into therapy; for listening to our own heart and soul; for remaining firmly committed to your family; for having the courage to live the life you were dealt, and for making of it what you can and will.

Those, I among them, far beyond 30, can be cheered by that.

From: Constantine

My story is likewise very, very similar. I am now separated and becoming established in my own home. In spite of the rough times, I have never felt more energized and alive!

From: Kenneth

I know exactly what you mean, for I've been there, too. Only it took me until I was 48! I envy your precocity! :-) Best of luck to you. It will be emotionally very rough leaving your marriage, but in many ways it is true what they say about No Pain, No Gain.

BRINGING YOUR GUY HOME

From: Shawn

Re: "if your relationship became sexualized . . . how would she feel?"

My relationship is sexualized with my best BI-guy buddy, but we limit our physical involvement (keep pants on) for the sake of my marriage. We are infatuated . . . "in love" . . . and my wife accepts it. With the limits on our sexual involvement, my wife does ok with this. She really likes him a lot. She says, "I understand why you like to kiss and hug him; he's adorable." If my BI guy-friend needs more erotic excitement than I can provide, he knows he's free to seek it out. He doesn't mind telling me when/if he does that. I think the reason (or one of the reasons) this works is that my wife & I have a very passionate, close relationship, so she's not feeling excluded or threatened.

From: Shawn

YES . . . MAYBE SOMEDAY.
I never would have believed it four years ago if someone predicted I would bring a boyfriend home to my wife. However, as you see there are boundaries and limits that have been discussed and spelled out. It takes a lot of time, patience and effort on the part of all . . . and yes, LOVE.

From: Shawn

In view of that (your having sex with your man), it sounds like your wife is trying to live with this, but it's just too uncomfortable for her to FACE HIM in your house. I think my wife can FACE HIM in our house because she and I are still HAVING MORE than he and I! You know, everybody has different boundaries, opinions, perspectives and feelings about what they can and cannot tolerate. I'm missing out on some sexual pleasure with him, but for me it's worth it to be able to involve him more fully in my life in other ways. I love him and love her too much to have it any other way, right now. That's just me. As long as this works for everyone I guess I'll just have to keep my pants on. When/if I can no longer deal with that limit, I'm sure there will be a price to pay. Nothing is free in this world! Every freedom has a cost. Nothing is gained without losing something else; I am convinced that this is the nature of our life in this world. C'est la vie.

ROMANCE AND PANTS

From: Clark

This business of falling in love. I have now three guys in my life, all three different, and none of them by any stretch of the imagination more than great friends. I find myself in love at different levels with all three.
   When I shed myself of judgmental categories like "promiscuous" and "fickle" and take a look at my heart, I conclude that something is true and unavoidable about these relationships and the fact that I really have deep

love in my soul for all three. The programs I have lived by (and still do) try to preclude such a situation, it seems to me.

What say you? Is this the style of the male of the species? Abraham Verghese said as much at one point in "My Own Country." Methinks he may be right.

From: James

Coming out to myself four years ago led to a variety of feelings of love towards other guys . . . the Greeks had various words for the different types of love and I believe I have experienced all of them with other guys since coming out. I tried once to explain to my wife how I can love in a deep way several different men at the same time and I don't think she understands what I tried to explain . . . how one can feel a strong love towards someone else and yet it is very different from the love one feels for another person. We all understand the difference between loving a spouse and one's children. . . but the variety of shades of love towards other men is a wonder, a gift . . . but difficult to understand even within myself . . . so I stopped trying to understand it . . . now, I just accept it. And sometimes sex is a part of it and sometimes not at all.

BEAR BUDDY

From: Lyndon

Thought I would share what was one of the best evenings of my life, and particularly my life since coming out to the wife. Before coming out at home, I spent a day on the beach with some Bears at their "Bears At The Beach." While there I met or rather he introduced himself, one of the Bears organizers, who was making everyone welcome. We did not get really acquainted cause I am kind of shy, but later we began e-mailing after he read my post on the bears mailing list telling about my day at the beach. A lot has happened to me since then, but we had not seen each other since that day in July. Well out of the blue he responded to a note I had sent back on Saint Patrick's Day—it was kind of a "woe is me" note and I had figured I had scared him off what with all my baggage and coming out turmoil. Anyway, I got a note saying he was coming this way for a few days vacation and would I like to meet him for a drink? Well last night was the night and I had a blast, the wife knew where I was going and who I would be seeing and was probably the most cool ever about it. I found my buddy with no problem and I had no qualms about marching right up to the front desk of the hotel and asking for him! I got directions, seems he was at a condo in another building. Upon arrival I was introduced to his housemate, a priest. My buddy and I had a good time catching up, went swimming and jacuzzing. He is a very busy music director, organist, and a college professor. A bit younger then me, forties and handsome with a black hairy chest and black beard with a bit of gray, small features, beautiful hands . . . I digress . . . Before too long another priest arrived to visit, and the four of us went out to dinner. We found a good restaurant, not real crowded, and proceeded to liven up the place big time. I had an incredibly good time and arrived home tired but glowing—after midnight. The mood has remained up today. This last week I had been kind of unhappy and even gay men's chorus rehearsal did not lift my mood.

RELATIONSHIP MANAGER

From: Bruce

I came out to my wife 3 years ago after 14 years of marriage, and I tend to think of myself more as gay than BI. While there are still challenges we seem to have gotten beyond most of the initial coming-out stuff and have moved on to working out how to make things work on a day-to-day basis.

I used to feel that getting into a relationship with a single gay man was an invitation to disaster. Part of that was because one of my first experiences was a brief relationship with a single gay man. The relationship only lasted a couple of months before it broke up. He needed a full-time man and that was something I couldn't be for him.

My opinion started to change 7 months ago when I met a man that I was very interested in who was single and gay. We hit it off immediately and started going out. We talked honestly from the very beginning and decided that given the situation we would keep things casual. That lasted for two weeks until we both were forced to admit to each other that we were falling in love.

I worried at first that we were just setting ourselves up for a big fall, but little by little I've realized that it IS a situation that can work. Not every man is going to be happy with the type of relationship that we have, but it suits us perfectly.

Perhaps it works for us because both of us came into it after pretty much giving up on having a long-term relationship. I didn't think that another man could ever be happy with me while I remained with my family and he didn't think that he'd ever find someone whom he would be happy with who would still allow him his feeling of independence. He's lived alone for the last 15 years, and likes it. His home is the way that he wants it to be and he doesn't have to worry about how his wants might conflict with mine.

He's also very close to his family who lives nearby. They're very conservative Baptist, and while he's out to them and they accept that he's gay, they're a long way from being ready for him to show up for Christmas dinner with a lover in tow. Since I have a family too, he doesn't need to worry about going off to spend time with them and leaving me alone on holidays and other special occasions.

Family also enters into the picture because he loves children. He loves his nieces and nephews and dotes over them. He likes the fact that I have an 11-year-old for him to have in his life. He's always ready to attend recitals, spend a day at the amusement park, or day trip somewhere with us.

We make it a point to have at least one date every week where we go out for dinner, see a show, or just curl up on the couch with a movie. His condo is near my house, so it's very easy for me to drop in for a visit a couple of times a week. We've become involved in a lot of the same activities in the gay community, so we spend time together there. We also reserve one weekend each month just to be together. Those weekends are important to us not just because we have the chance to spend the night together, but also because we clear our schedules of almost everything else and just enjoy being together.

Perhaps most important to us is that even though we live separately and both have other commitments, we both know that the other is there at any time, day or night, if we're needed. I will admit that sometimes it gets difficult balancing everything, but when conflicts arise we've learned to sit down and work things out between him, my wife, and I. Both him and my wife sometimes have to do without me at times when they may want me around, but they know that I'm trying to be as fair as possible to both of them, and they're happy with that.

Our relationship isn't one that would work for everyone, but it works for us. We're both MUCH happier with our present arrangement than we were before we met.

GAY RUSSIA

From: Fernando

Two more things guys, I have been going through a living hell since I came out thirty months ago. I can honesty say if it wasn't for this group would have left this earth a long time ago. I am very serious about that.

I have been in out of a mental health facility for two years and had two suicide attempts. The marriage still survives—I want it to. However I have greatly mourned the loss of the experience of the love of another man. It is nothing like I have ever known. I dearly love my wife, but I have come to the realization that it's not the same. I don't have to tell you that we experience all kinds of different love and for us who love both men and sometimes a woman that presents some confusing issues.

I truly believe that from your mouths come the true words of wisdom. Such beautiful insight they have. Well enough of this shit. :).

I MET A GUY !!!! Several months ago. Not a planned sexual encounter. A mutual friend introduced us, Real nice guy. He is from Russia. My age, looks personality everything! Except . . . . Yes He is not GAY or BI. . . . We hung around a couple of times a week going to various places in museums, movies, etc. We went on a whale watch and he really loved that.

He enjoyed the boat ride so much he asked if there was some other excursion we could take like out to the harbor islands. Of course I immediately thought of San Francisco. So off we went two months ago. He seemed rather uncomfortable around the gay community. We were having lunch and in the middle of lunch he very nervously said there's something I must tell you. Please try to understand, I don't want to hurt you and maybe it would be best if we didn't continue our friendship. I was devastated. . . . He knows, by some action of mine that I am gay, I thought I would surely cry. He looked me in the eye and said. "I am GAY and I have the deepest feeling for you." God I said it! Well I won't continue with the rest . . . to make a long story short my GAYDAR really failed me guys. And I guess his did too. A few days later I knew what loving a man was like I believe for that first time in my life. . . . I am so happy it hurts. . . . I don't mean to be vulgar . . . but the sex is . . . there is no word.

His Name is Nicky and he is so cute :)
HUGS TO ALL GUYS—I AM IN LOVE

UPDATE

From: Chukky

Well, my lover and I made it a year and a month so far. I've come to the conclusion we are going to be forever. The past two weeks were difficult. He came out to his sister, because she asked me if I was gay . . . and I was not able to lie the way the conversation was headed over that night. She asked me about her brother . . . but before I said anything her remarks were "Don't answer, I knew from the time he was a little boy he was gay." He called her the following night and spilled it all to her. He was angry at me, her, and himself, however due to her support of he and I and her understanding of our wives and children, we all weathered the storm great. I am happy she knows the truth because now he has a family member he can turn to and talk with . . . and someone who will look out for him besides myself. They talked in great length since the initial conversation. He is calm and feels so good about himself, and the married situation. We are madly in love and come to realize that time will take it course and that no plans can be made at the present, even though we both know what it is we want and may or may not ever have. Our wives do not know the extent of our relationship for protection reasons of them and the kids . . . so many lives involved and no need to be upset at this time. When they grow up, perhaps things will change but for right now, we are both living for today. Its taken me a year to come to terms with not planning the future and this past month has been the first time I am so content with what is. He is the world to me . . . and I adore and love him as no other. I love my wife . . . but never was able to love her as a husband should love a wife but loved her the best I have been able to and will always love her and take care of her. Is she a victim . . . yeah. But it was not planned or charted out. I've come to realize I am what I am . . . and though I don't have to advertise . . . I am a man who is in love with another man and its taken me all these years to come to terms with it. (I knew in my late teens that I was gay.) I look forward to my life with my guy and all that comes thrown my way . . . ups and downs . . . and coming through each hurdle. Hope everyone feels at one time in their life, the wonderful, warm, loving thoughts and feelings that have been bestowed upon me this year as a result of my meeting the love I always imagined and thought I would never find. Dreams sometimes do in fact come true.

GAY PEN PAL

From: Kenneth

Hello men on the list. I am so excited about this I had to write. For you more experienced guys, this will probably sound very childish, but here goes.

About two weeks ago, I got a phone call from a gay pen pal with whom I have corresponded for several years but never gone all the way at work. He told me he was going to be in Minnesota and suggested that I try to rent a bed and breakfast with a fireplace so we could have a couple of days together! I said, "Yes, sure, OK, right!" Sooo . . . Monday and Tuesday are the days. I took vacation, rented the same cabin where he and I originally met (which has a wood-burning stove) and have spent many a spare moment fantasizing about what it will be like. He suggested that we not have any expectations, but just take it real slow, enjoy the moment and each other's company and see what develops. I'm thinking, "Yeah, but I better not come home a virgin!"

I told my wife exactly what was happening. She and I have always shared all. (We are gradually separating emotionally and will eventually divorce.)

Anyway, wish me luck! The guy called a little while ago and he is as excited as I am, though he is much older and more experienced (he's 70, I'm 50).

As I'm learning to believe, you're never too old!

GUESS WHAT

From: Max

Well guys, sometimes after the rain comes the sun.

I have to admit that, as many have advised me, it's best just hold on and when you're not looking the right guy will sneak up behind you and catch you off guard.

This is just what happened to me.

I'm stuck for words here but suffice to say that I met a guy who's been there for some time and both of us danced around the fence.

I certainly don't want to steal anyone's thunder but at last I've found a guy I can love deeply. I want it to last forever but know that the obstacles ahead are huge. I may even be berated for my decisions but I'm delighted by them.

RE: SIMPLE PHYSICAL CONTACT

From: Corwin

Someone wrote: >*what I most sense missing is just simple physical contact with another naked body—friendly contact, lying down together. To be sure, that kind of contact usually leads to some kind of sexual culmination. But I don't primarily miss the sense of "release." What I miss is the sense of contact.*<

Thanks for continuing to beat this one to death. Sometimes we all just connect with a particular piece of discussion. I almost deleted this without reading it, but I'm glad I did. Your synopsis about simple physical contact struck a cord with me.

I am currently seeing someone, but to be perfectly honest, it's not the sex that I really enjoy, it is the physical contact—warm skin to warm skin. I could actually do without the sex sometimes. Unfortunately, my lover doesn't see it that way. He wants and needs the sexual contact—but that's another story. There are times I just want to be held closely. Arms wrapped around, and feeling secure in someone else's grasp.

I actually read somewhere it's a good practice to have an occasional no-sex encounter with your lover/partner/significant other. You can do any kind of touching you want but no sex. Experience sensations with other parts of the body.

Chapter 4
Relationship with Wife

WHAT HAVE I DONE?

From: Steve

I can't describe the emotions I feeling these past few days. My wife's eyes and expression say it all. . . . I have destroyed her very being. Her face is a constant expression of pain, hurt, and disgust and it's all because of my need to be with a man . . . was it worth it? Was it worth the secrecy and betrayal? Was it worth the sneaking and the lies? I wonder sometimes. If it weren't for my uncontrollable urges would I be here right now? Even with the turmoil that my life has been in and the deep depression being experienced by my wife, I still find my thoughts wandering to my boyfriend . . . wanting to be with and hold him. Having these thoughts and feelings . . . what does that make me as my wife suffers with feelings of suicide? Never mind, don't answer that.

Her psychiatrist gave her a prescription for Prozac. . . . What have I done? The psychiatrist is concerned because she has no support system—no one to talk to but myself. She also made my wife run through the list of medications in the house. She also told her in graphic detail what happens to the children of suicide. . . not pretty.

I'm starting to feel the closet was the safest place for all involved. I called one of my wife's friends to ask her to help . . . support her and to let her know that someone cares. My wife invited her friend to spend a weekend with her soon . . . I hope she'll go.

My reassurance of my love continues, but I think to her it's beginning to sound false. I keep repeating the same song over and over: "I love you!"

I didn't do it because I was unhappy with my marriage, it was because I was unhappy with myself. No matter how hard my wife tries, she can't give me the feeling I get when I'm with a man . . . it's different. I am so sorry . . . and the list goes on.

I can't imagine how this is all going to work out and after only 5 weeks of this I don't expect to speculate, but for the guys going through this, or gone through this, I admire you all 'cause all I want to do right now is go off and hide.

From: Dale

When things broke loose over my sexual diversity (wife found a copy of something I had written to an online contact) we had a very difficult relationship crisis. I felt as if I was riding a wild horse, a merry-go-round, and a roller coaster AT THE SAME TIME! I had the some of the same messages to my wife but also some different ones:

> "I'm not going anywhere . . . unless you come to a point where you can't/won't/don't want to try to deal with the issues any more and want to send me away. "

> "I/we can't put the lid back on this box . . . the pieces just won't fit inside anymore. "

My reaction to Steve's message list:

1. I love you. I like it—say it often and MEAN it—but don't let it translate to "I love you therefore I won't do it again." The process you're going through isn't about you not doing "it" again—that's not an option. The process is about you both working hard and both stretching to find NEW common ground between you that allows for the WHOLE of your personality including acceptable expression of your WHOLE personality.

2. I didn't do it because I was unhappy with my marriage, but 'cause I was unhappy with myself. I like the first part—I'm not so sure the second part (however true) is productive. Having a gay/BI side to one's personality isn't something I ever remember feeling unhappy about—it's quite inconvenient at times because it just doesn't "fit" into society's scheme of things very well. Sending out the message "I don't like myself" (for ANY reason) is likely to proffer the response: "Well, if YOU don't like yourself, how can you expect ME to like/support you?" I don't think we are attracted to men because we are unhappy with ourselves—it's deeper than that. We are attracted to men because we are attracted to men. . . . PERIOD.

3. No matter how hard you try, you can't give me the feeling I get when I'm with a man . . it's different. Again—this is a pretty true statement—I don't know of a "sexually diverse" guy who wouldn't agree even before you have completed the sentence. BUT—it's not a very productive message for you to be saying AT THIS POINT. She needs reassurance—this statement isn't going to reassure her. Rather, it will further alarm her. It will translate to your wife that she's inadequate in some way or that she's being rejected. Later in the process when (if) you both can go forward and invest yourselves in finding common ground, it can be a helpful way to perceive things to diminish the sense of competition between your hetero side and your gay/BI side.

4. I am so sorry . . . and the list goes on. Better message: "I am sorry for the pain we both are going through." Try NOT to be sorry for the presence of your sexual diversity—it's not something you've deliberately chosen. "I'm sorry" tends to invoke "Well, if you're truly sorry, what are you going to do about it? What can you do to make me feel better?" Being sorry for the pain is an authentic, honest statement. You CAN do something about the pain. You can both become more familiar with the issues. You can talk about things to more effectively "metabolize" your feelings. You can learn about how and why gay/BI attractions come to be present in the personality. The more you know about things the more smoke and mirrors you'll remove and the less frightening it will all be to you both.

What you CAN'T do is remove her pain. SHE must/needs to work her way through it. She'll need your help, the help of a therapist if you can both go together, and she will need the help of outside support. Hopefully you/she can find support that knows about the issues and can acknowledge what she's feeling while at the same time advocate for you both and for the relationship.

This may NOT be the time to break out Amity's book ("The Other Side of the Closet") or the Gochros book ("When Husbands Come Out Of The Closet") because if you're both interested in trying to find success stories—you won't find many of them in those books. Read it yourself, maybe, but don't hand it to her as if it were the "Straight Wife's Guide to Understanding Her Gay Husband"! My wife couldn't read those books early on—I tried to read sections TO my wife and that helped some. I would hold her and read some of the explanatory/interpretive sections that were most encouraging. Even then she'd reach her saturation point in about 5 minutes! I think, though, the warmth of my body, my embrace, the vibration and resonance of my voice did as much to calm her than the words that were being formed by my mouth.

Realize that what you are going through isn't going to reach closure in 24 hrs. Our hard crisis time was 2 months—quite short by some accounts. Our hard crisis time came to an end because my wife came to a point where she realized she hadn't progressed anywhere, that she really didn't know much about gay/BI issues, and that she was getting dangerously near a point where SHE would be the one driving me away from the relationship rather than my being enticed away by a male love interest or some predatory gay/BI guy. She then, of her own volition, committed to herself to learn about the issues, to do whatever needed to be done, to go wherever she needed to go to find her own personal understanding and peace with the issues. THAT kingpin is something I don't often see or hear about in other wives' experience. More frequently it seems a straight wife will get to a point of panic and not ever come back.

Support for your wife? Yes—her psychiatrist is on the money when she talks about the need for support. The KIND of support she seeks (and gets) is important, though, for the prospects of success in your integrative efforts. My wife didn't reach out to other wives in general because she found most other women trying to deal with these things to be hostile and angry. In addition they felt they were victims and their husbands were the victimizers. My wife didn't like the presence of the hostility and anger. She also didn't feel herself to be a victim or myself to be a victimizer and didn't want anyone projecting those roles onto either of us.

J. S. Gochros puts it well in the conclusions (Starting on page 254) of her book, "When Husbands Come Out of the Closet:" Harrington Park Press pub: Haworth Press, Inc., 1989.

Don't be afraid to reach out. Either or both of us would welcome further contact—and would also be open for phone contact if you ask for our number.

GLAD FOR SUPPORTIVE COMMUNITY

From: Benny

I am so glad to have a supportive community. Things have once again become difficult between my wife and I. I am almost convinced that a divorce is the only solution that will help us. She however is not sure that she is ready to give up on us. I don't think that she understands that there are some REAL differences in the way that she and I go about being human. I can't even find the words to express this very visceral feeling to a group of married gay men, much less to her. We will probably attempt therapy again, hopefully with a more positive, final result.

I know this note rambles a bit and is not at all related to any of the threads, but I needed to scream something to someone. I was doing some research today, reading case studies of hate crimes and homophobia, as well as the Ode to Billy Joe in which the main character jumps from a bridge, when I was simply overcome with frustration with my situation. I sat there full of self pity for a few minutes until I realized that I needed to say to the world:

> You can beat me
> You can rob me of constitutional rights
> But you will NOT ignore me
> I am standing right in front of you and you WILL see me
> I am a human being regardless of what your prejudices are
> And if I can accept you then, you can do the same for me.

I want to thank you all for listening to me ramble and scream at the world and for welcoming me back to the fold with open, caring arms.

From: Eric

A few days ago I went to see the new Meryl Streep movie, "One True Thing," which tells the story of a daughter's relationship with her mother, who is dying of cancer. The movie opened many old wounds, but the scene that moved me the most was one where Meryl Streep talks about marriage and how, over time we become accepting of things. When we came home I looked at my wife's copy of the book to see if that scene was in it, and, unfortunately, the line I was looking for is not in the original, but basically it said that instead of worrying about those things that we don't have in life (and marriage) we should focus on the good things we do have.

For so long I obsessed about being gay in a straight marriage and how I'd never have certain things unless I were out of my marriage. What has kept me here (still married) is the realization that there are so many things I currently have that I'd taken for granted, and that once I took stock of my life I felt so much better. The funny thing is that once I became content with what I had, many of the things I yearned for (like a boyfriend) came my way.

From: James

Your comment reminds me about when I felt the same way right after coming out to my wife. Interestingly enough, she is the one who helped me verbalize my feelings. She commented to me one night that her self-image was intimately connected to our sex life. And I realized that my M2M needs were also connected to my self-image and the need for this special type of affirmation.

The one facet of this group . . . having someone or ones that you can say what you need to say . . . it is easy for us to get on the pity pot. . . . I have to work hard sometimes not to dwell on what I don't have. Fritz Klein has such a wonderful world view and has helped me enjoy the moment and, as he likes to say, "have no expectations then you are pleased when good things happen and not upset when they don't." (I'm paraphrasing here . . . <G)>

Love and light returned to you. My wife has a wonderful phrase about "seeing yourself reflected back to you" that I have come to understand and appreciate. Hope you see and feel love and light coming your way.

SILENT MAJORITY?

From: Berry

I feel that I am part of the "silent majority" of men on this list. I came out to my wife four years ago (I can tell you the hour and the minute), and since then we have had a singular purpose—to salvage our marriage. Neither of us could envision leading separate lives; after 26 years, she is an integral part of who I am . . . as I am of her.

I felt I was very lucky to have found this e-mail group. Like others, and I'm sure many others, I understood it to be a brotherhood of men who were out to their wives, but were committed to their marriage and their families. I thought I'd see more sharing of strategies and ways of coping with our "particular" situation. I thought I'd get advice on what works, and what might not work, on what to say and what not to say, on when to compromise and when not to. I even believed that I would forge some friendships with guys not too far away and we could get together with our wives for support and encouragement. To be perfectly honest, I really haven't found much of that. Yet. I, for one, get really discouraged to read over and over again of couples that are not going to make it . . . or already have called it quits.

I understand that some of our marriages just can't stand the strain of something like this and despite all the sincere efforts of both parties to make it they decide that divorce is the only option. I think we all know that what we are attempting is really bucking the odds . . . the dice aren't stacked in our favor. When these brothers are in that situation and are hurting and confused I think it's really heartening the way we all circle our wagons, and our "arms" about him and give him the support and encouragement he needs. But, once the crisis is over, once the separation and divorce is behind him . . . he should move on. I'm sure there are plenty of lists and support groups that can fit his needs better than ours.

At the risk of incurring a lot of wrath, I'd just like to state my opinion that I would like this list to get back to its original intention. I know that to many the word "exclusivity" is abhorrent, and I honestly respect your views. However this group was founded on exclusivity . . . for a very special population. A population that for so long had no support, no source of advice and certainly not much encouragement. I'm still looking for that guys. . . . I still need it.

From: James

Thank you very much for this reminder. I guess I should have participated more in contributing these types of posts and I regret now that I haven't after reading your comments. I have shared most of this type of info in private posts or at the various gatherings and I forget that there are men who may wish this type of interaction that cannot attend these meetings. Yes, we are diverse and enjoy a wide variety of posts . . . Humorous, reaching out for support, learning more about what you seek that you listed above, sharing our sorrows and tragedies, etc. But I need to be reminded, and thank you, about why we started this list and you are absolutely correct that the reasons you joined are the reasons we started the list. It is typical that guys join and if they post a few times will develop their own inner circle of friends with whom they interact privately . . . and for me most of the interaction for cop-

ing, growing, and sharing happens outside of the context of public posts. I
know it goes on, certainly it does for me and the men with whom I'm become the closest. But you are right that we need to share publicly more. I
know that some of us have commented to one another that we hate sharing
the "up" times and aspects because we fear it is like rubbing it in the face of
guys who have just shared about their sorrows or challenges as their marriages deteriorate but we need posts like yours and the others in this thread
to remind us that we have to share.

But always remember that the burden of what we discuss is shared by all
of us. If you have a question or concern, for goodness sake, ask it or share it
or request reactions. I'm not saying you haven't . . . but this list is in part the
sum of its parts . . . there are many strong marriages within this group and
many that continue to grow and blossom. I can immediately think of over a
dozen and I know there are many more . . . just need to think about it a minute . . . (gee I liked the idea of one of the members selecting a new guy . . . I
think I am ready for a new name . . . hymmmmmmmmm.....)

From: Pete

I hear you, and agree, perhaps those of us who are "making it work" are
not driven to write, but just read the posts and then close out for the night; I
know I do. Here is what has helped My wife and I make it and thrive in our
marriage of 18 years.

First it has helped that I was out to her since before we were married. Who
I was and who she was was established and discussed over and over in depth
before we decided that we had enough similarities to be able to compromise
on the differences. That life together could work out if we kept the communication open. She saw that the gay part of me was there for all time and that
those qualities were part of what she found attractive in me. Also we went
into marriage as a total commitment. Divorce has never been an option.

Secondly, we committed that our relationship was primary and that to
split affection would mean the beginning of the end. When I chose her for a
life partner, then romantically and affectionately we were bonded and monogamous, relationship wise. Sex and friendship we have viewed differently. It is ok for me to have sex with men (100% safe and regular HIV testing for both our sakes of course), and a buddy friendship here and there is
fine. But a lover, husband, special guy who would become integrated into
my ongoing life in a romantic way . . . no way! I know some have found the
need and ways to make this work. For us however we have seen this as a real
muddying of the waters that bind us—not possible if our relationship is to
survive. I can live with this without regrets, as I honestly don't understand
how anyone has the emotional energy to sustain 2 intense relationships, doing it right with one person is job enough for me. A trip to the baths a couple

of times a month or meeting someone from the local chat rooms, does me fine and knowing myself I must admit that when it comes to men, variety is my spice of life anyway!

We keep the communication open, she knows my secret screen name and password. She can read any of my e-mail and knows about everyone I have ever met. We are making our situation known to an increasingly larger number of our friends, and are close to the time I will share this part of myself with our teenager.

Other than these things the best help is to keep talking! Whenever I have something that I feel I want to hide from her it is my red flag that it is really something that needs to be discussed, not hidden. This is what has helped us, and I would love to hear similar thoughts from the rest of us in the "Silent Majority."

From: James

Berry wrote: >*thought I'd get advice on what works, and what might not work, on what to say and what not to say, and on when to compromise and when not to.*<

Pete responded: >*Here is what has helped my wife and I make it and thrive in our marriage of 18 years.*<

Thank you for sharing this. I find that different things help at different points in our journey or when I am at different points in my needs. . . .

This weekend at the couples gathering I was reminded that I need to remain focused on several things which really help me through the many challenges that my wife and I face:

1. To remember why I wish to be married. My love for and my bond with my wife is so strong that I need to remind myself of this at times. Also I seek only one spouse . . . my wife . . . and my male relationships thus fall into a secondary role. I will never be loved, cherished, cared for, and supported as I am by my wife and I try to return that gift back to her.
2. To identify those beliefs that are so strong that they live within me without question. As I work through all the changes since coming out 3 years ago and having to re-examine my values and belief system in the new context I am realizing slowly what I accept without question. One of them is that I trust totally my need for M2M intimacy. I cannot go back in the closet, I do not feel whole as a married man monogamous to my wife, and I am willing to risk my marriage—as wonderful as my wife is— to seek wholeness. My spiritual and religious beliefs

now are vital again but with many new variations, but the core is still there intact and firm.

3. To accept what I cannot change: risk, insecurity, loneliness, a future without shape or face.
4. To continue to communicate as fully as I can with my wife, despite my reservations, to help us grow together and not apart.

I'm still working on this . . . <BG> . . . thanks in great part from the influences gained within this group. . . .

SUPPORTIVE WIVES

From: Josi

I'm new to this list and so you may have covered this already: "how wives are/become supportive."

I came out to my wife a little over two years ago. At first she talked about being supportive of my bisexuality and even of my being with a man. Then she changed her mind, said she could accept my sexuality, but could not be married to me if I had sex with a man. It was important to me to explore my sexuality and I proceeded to do so. She became furious and moved on divorce. So after many battles and much money spent on lawyers, we have since divorced. But during that time I had chances to be with men and I learned that while I am clearly attracted to the same sex, I want to be in a primary relationship with a woman. I also had the opportunity to be with other women and realized that I loved my wife. So I proposed that we resume our relationship, which we have. We are living together and plan to remarry in the spring.

She has come to be much more accepting of my sexuality, as I go to a bisexual support group every week and go out socially with guys from that group. At my end, I have promised monogamy. At her end, she has agreed to look at some deep insecurities she has carried that transcend my sexuality.

In all this, I know that I am hoping and praying that with time she will come to further accept who I am and be supportive of my having a male lover.

For you guys who have supportive wives, what had to happen to gain that support? Are you just very lucky or what did you have to do to engender the support? Any help/suggestions you can offer would be greatly appreciated.

From: Moris

1. Your wife is tolerating your sexuality and not accepting it.
2. You have promised monogamy to her. By this I assume you mean no m2m sex. Right?

Umm, seems very unlikely that she will release you from your promise of no m2m sex. Therefore, there will be no lover in the future. I think (remember this is just ME!) that you should discuss this with her and with YOURSELF to see if you can live like this for the rest of your life because she may NEVER change her mind.

When I came out I did not express that I was sorry that I was bisexual. I made it understood clearly that I am and we needed to talk about what we were going to do from now on. She decided to accept me and she did. She helped me get ready for my dates, she knew when I needed to go out by myself or when she could go with me. She was the "Best Woman" when my boyfriend (now my husband) and I were married. I do feel very blessed to have a wonderful wife. I also know that you men here on the Internet helped me to accept myself and help me to give a positive image when I came out to her.

I strongly encourage you to decide for yourself if you can live monogamy with your wife forever! IF you cannot, then don't get married again until you know that your wife2b can accept your lover later. . . .

From: Stephen

Wow. Your wife already sounds like she's pretty supportive. I don't think any woman, no matter how unconditionally loving, can be supportive without some modicum of ambivalence around this issue. Just the fact that you two are talking so openly about the issues, and that you're both owning your "stuff" that you need to work on—sounds so hopeful to me. I think the big thing is not to rush her faster than she can digest and assimilate this stuff (maybe hold off on the boyfriend-on-the-side for a while). . . .

From: Henry

I haven't posted to the list since joining. A great deal has happened over the summer, in many ways so unusual as to be useless as a source of insight or advice, but the story may be worth reading as entertainment.

My correspondence with my friend J., which I began in June, was discovered by my wife. J. and I had no physical relationship—in fact we'd never even met in person—but my wife was very angry and upset nevertheless by the "emotional betrayal." However, even before she found out that J. and I were writing to one another, J. and I had already decided, for various good reasons, to crank the whole relationship down to the level of being just friends, although this wasn't easy. It just didn't seem as though things would ever work out any other way.

My wife finally decided to write to J. to tell him to buzz off and leave me alone. Well, J. wrote back, and soon they were corresponding regularly, and became friends. And then, they confessed to me, they had became more than friends. We arranged to meet, and J. has visited us a few times. Now I have the wife I still love like crazy, and a wonderful boyfriend; and my wife has a husband she still loves (thank god) and the same boyfriend. This arrangement gets tricky at times: I can tell it'll call for a lot of careful attention and tact—and it's still in an early stage of development—but so far things are working pretty well. We'll see.

So, some ridiculous advice for you guys who want to stay married to your wives and have a relationship with a man: first of all, pick a guy who's bisexual; then contrive to have your boyfriend and your wife fall madly in love with one another!

From: James

In my case, my wife and I had a strong marriage before I came out to her, she decided immediately that she thought she had more to gain remaining married and see how things progressed, and we both discovered that we bonded much more strongly after the coming out. . . . We have discussed briefly on several occasions about whether we are making the right decision to remain married but both of us always conclude that we are. . . .I don't know if this really answers your question or not. She keeps saying that her decision to stay was based primarily on the way I act and treat/nurture her.

From: James

I just read an e-mail response from my wife answering my question to her if she would be comfortable for me to be added to the gay/BI/lesbian mailing list here at work and would she be comfortable if I attended a social gathering of employees who are gay/BI. I didn't know her response because two years ago, she made it clear to me that she was NOT comfortable with me being out in our community. Her response today brought tears to my eyes . . . she has not come this far in our journey, she said, to stop now. She said yes to both questions and offered to go with me to the social event (at a local gay bar). So, we progress step by step . . . our "normalcy" grows more rich. We now worship at a gay-friendly church and now, my involvement with the on-campus group will communicate to many our "mixed orientation" status no doubt . . . which provides few, if any, problems for me but raises many issues that my wife will face no doubt.

From: Brent

Congratulations to you (James) and your wife for taking this step; and it's a big one. But at some level we all know that, once we open that closet door we can't close it again; just have to keep going, each at our own speed.

From my experience, I have received huge amounts of support from my Les/BI/Gay colleagues. Many people are "intrigued" at first by the mixed-orientation status; most are skeptical; all have accepted that there are "different strokes for different folks" and my wife and I have received TONS of support from people who admire the way we are proceeding in our relationship with integrity and love for each other.

As you go forward I believe you will find it an interesting process to decide how much of the details of your life you share with whom—I have to admit to taking the occasional bit of perverse pleasure in seeing the quizzical looks of folks who are DIEING to ask me "what's up" but can't quite bring themselves to ask the BIG question and for whom I feel no compelling need to explain myself.

SAVE MARRIAGE AND MAINTAIN OUR SEXUALITY

From: Phil

The situation is how do we save our marriage while maintaining our sexuality. If we can, what would the relationship look and feel like?

From: Dale

Both in response to your question—and as a way of providing an update of sorts from a couple who is staying together with no thought of splitting . . . here's the view from MY/OUR bridge:

ACADEMIC:

Research recently being done (and in progress) indicates that some of the most reliable predictors for success in crafting a mixed-orientation relationship and keeping it going lie in the quality and depth of the relationship to begin with. A good, strong, reliable relationship between the partners is more likely to weather the stresses and strains of adapting and changing the relationship to acknowledge sexual diversity than one that is (or has been) shaky and uncertain.

A study of 50 couples married from 10 to 50 (or so) years who self-identify as having a "good" marriage has been conducted and reported in a book by Judith Wallerstein called "The Good Marriage" (Houghton-Mifflin). Wallerstein identifies in the conclusion section of her book 8 tasks she found to be the "work" of a good marriage. While Wallerstein's book is a little "academic," I like to refer to it because if all you do is get it to read the conclusion section, it gives a sense of positive things to work toward rather than focusing on the dysfunction and what goes wrong in a marriage.

Back to part of your question: >*How do we save our marriage while maintaining our sexuality?*<

Here are two quotes from Ph.D. researchers in the field of mixed orientation marriages, J. S. Gochros and Amity P. Buxton. (disclaimer: No, my wife and I DON'T live our life out of books. We do, however, find resonance with what we feel works/has worked in OUR lives and what these gals have reported in more formalized ways.) WHEN HUSBANDS COME OUT OF THE CLOSET, by Jean Schaar Gochros, Harrington Park Press, Conclusions (p. 254):

> 4. Except for the possible need to work out a nonmonogamous sexual contract, the basic ingredients of a happy gay/straight marriage (i.e., mutual love, commitment, trust, shared interests, empathic communication, and some form of shared sexual gratification) are no different than they are for any other marriage.

Amity Buxton, THE OTHER SIDE OF THE CLOSET, p. 68 writes:

> Coping with the marriage issue will be a more constructive process with greater promise of success if the couple, rather than trying to preserve the traditional marriage arrangement, is willing to develop a relationship appropriate to the new circumstances. . . .

In summary, the research—and our personal experience—supports that the ongoing marriages that include sexual diversity issues will be similar . . . but DIFFERENT from a standard, conventional, heterosexual marriage. The couples who are having success keeping the marriage together and working are breaking the mold somehow. The "break-pattern" may be unique to each couple . . . but they're breaking away from society's off-the-shelf version of marriage each SOME way(s).

Gochros' list, above (mutual love, commitment, trust, shared interests, empathic communication, and some form of shared sexual gratification) have certainly proven to be key elements in our lives as we continue the process of constructing a relationship/marriage that is inclusive of the diversities found in both parties. Sexual diversity is a complicated and volatile set of issues, it takes a lot of skill and relationship capital to cope. But, you know what? There are OTHER issues in a successful marriage that are well-served by the adaptive skills learned from handling sexual diversity!

Gochros also writes:

> 3. Not only can marriages survive a disclosure of homosexuality, if the husband remains committed to the wife, they are apt to improve. Not only can homosexuality (or some degree of it) be compatible with heterosexual marriage, if the husband is capable of some degree of heterosexual satisfaction, gay/straight marriages can be unusually satisfying and stable.

PERSONAL/EXPERIENTIAL:

>If we can, what would the relationship look and feel like?<

1. Marriages accommodating sexual diversity (at least ours, anyway) don't look much different in MOST ways than "regular" marriages! That's the good news—because it's important to realize you don't have to "destruct," then "reconstruct" the whole universe!

2. Each "successful" mixed-orientation marriage will be a little different from the next one. All the things that work for one relationship will not probably work verbatim for the next. There isn't (yet, anyway) any sense of just one way these relationships work.

3. We have come to own a fairly extensive library of writings, manuals, books, etc., on gay and BI issues. We chose each title because it felt to be a resource we could use to help us understand ourselves or to help us develop strategies to deal with a mixed-orientation relationship. HOWEVER, in spite of all those written words, the most affirming and most helpful things have come from face-to-face interaction with others trying to deal with the same stuff! There's a much greater sense of immediacy about talking with someone face to face (or communicating with them directly online) than you can ever get in a book! Sometimes we find a strategy or set of strategies that helped us directly. Other times not. Even when another couple or individual doesn't have a direct contribution to make to our relationship we've ALWAYS felt encouraged that if THEY can do it however they're doing it, so, then, can we find our own way!

4. A working, successful mixed-orientation marriage isn't a "destination;" rather, it's a "process." We humans are ever-evolving and emerging beings. The agreements and strategies that keep us working well together need to reflect that sense of change, growth, renewal, and flexibility. Routines will occur that make the ongoing dynamics of managing a mixed-

orientation relationship easier and not such a "creating the wheel" task all the time . . . but it's ill-advised to ever put the strategies "to bed" and consider them to be on auto pilot.

5. A working, successful mixed-orientation marriage will be a more "open" place because it will be openly inclusive and acknowledging of more diversity (sexual and otherwise) and probably more personalities than a traditional, dyadic relationship. Without reneging on my statement, above: "There isn't (yet, anyway) any sense of just one way these relationships work," my observation is that there is a clustering of sorts towards a couple points of tangent so far as how the wife successfully deals with the expression of her husband's sexual diversity.

a. Autonomous: The wife comes to openly know about and accept the M-M side of her husband's personality. Ground rules are negotiated regarding various aspects of how he "inhabits" that part of his personality—things like how, when, how frequently, where, emotional involvement, etc. While these elements are known openly between the husband and wife, a strong sense of autonomy becomes part of the relationship and the wife doesn't feel a need to be personally and physically involved with her husband's M-M activities. At a tangent, the wife doesn't even know (or want to know) the name(s) of her husband's lover(s).

b. Inclusive: The wife comes to openly know about and accept the M-M side of her husband's personality. Ground rules are negotiated regarding various aspects of how he "inhabits" that part of his personality. However, THIS model has the wife being involved in some (or many) ways with the M-M side of her husband's life. At a tangent this could mean active, physical inclusion in triadic sexual activity. Shades of involvement less than that happen when the husband's lover(s) are known by the wife and inclusion can become very close and personal—a deep friendship—without crossing the line sexually.

Thinking about some of these more "open" strategies can feel scary and frightening as if one might lose the sense of boundaries surrounding the two of you that feel so protective, necessary, and reassuring. But, the boundaries only have to enlarge some. . .not be erased completely. The GOOD news in all of this is that the other personalities who come to be included in the relationship can be a real source of additional support, energy, fun, solace, creativity, and strength.

OUR OWN ODYSSEY

The "elephant was in the living room" from before the beginning of our marriage. I lost my virginity in jr. high with a male classmate. There were things along the way that gave my wife reason for "pause" but things never came to open discussion. In the early 90s my wife found out there were (and had been) casual encounters in my life since about my mid to late 30's. We had a relationship crisis at that time, couples counseling, etc. My wife stopped coming to counseling, however. Life was busy, kids in high school, etc. Two years ago my wife found a copy of something I had sent to an on-line contact. This blew the lid off good because it translated to her that I was trying to find a male romantic interest and leave the relationship. Not true, of course, but it was her perception . . . and perceptions fuel actions and re-actions.

We had a VERY hard relationship crisis at that time. She experienced bouts of depression, panic, nausea, insomnia—you name it. I described the situation for myself as trying to ride a wild horse, a rollercoaster, and a merry-go-round all at the same time. There were times when the only thing that seemed to help her find a bit of peace and reassurance was for me to take her in my arms and hold her.

At a point of about 2 months of the hard crisis time, my wife was ex-hausted, knew that I was tiring, and realized she was approaching some jeopardy of being the one, herself, who might drive me away from the rela-tionship rather than me being drawn away by a male love interest. That scared my wife a lot! In a span of about 24 hrs., then, she resolved with her-self to find out, learn, go, do—whatever it took for her to become more knowledgeable about gay/BI issues and to find (or try to find) her personal place in it all. After this point of personal commitment, the sensitivity to the mere presence of sexual diversity in my life faded almost instantly. The bot-tom-line issues revealed themselves to be a wish to be "INcluded" in the "whole" of my life rather than be "EXcluded." Thus began the new chapter in the odyssey of our married life.

Unless you wish to discuss specific strategies and personal details (feel free to ask), I will represent that we are very much an expression of #4-b In-clusive above. We do not now have what we would identify as a "Signifi-cant Other" in our lives—but HAVE had.

To represent our current status, let me borrow a little "galactic" imag-ery—we experience a number of contacts from fellows whose life's orbit whirls near ours for varying lengths of time. Any number of reasons exist that preclude them from joining OUR "magnetic field" on a more perma-nent or "regular" basis. Sometimes it's geographical inconvenience. Some-times it's a particular station or stage in life. However, while we wait for life's serendipity to bring us the opportunity to "dock" with another person-ality, we accept and treasure the times of resonance and shared experience we have opportunity to enjoy along the way. We continue to be a work in progress. . . and likely will remain so until they bring in the pine boxes!

From: Mike

Once again Dale demonstrated the real value of this forum. He and I have been on this list since its inception. Since the very beginning his posts have educated, inspired, amused, supported, and challenged all of us. He is a treasure. Thanks for sharing.

From: Bear

I really appreciated Dale's thoughtful and thought-provoking lengthy e-mail. He raised a lot of good points that have really helped me think through some of the questions and difficulties my wife and I are having. We've got a rock-solid relationship and are communicating well, but that doesn't mean that things are easy in dealing with all of this. Regardless, it is a pleasure to read such a well-thought approach to all of this. I, too, have a strong sense that the flexibilities involved in mixed-orientation marriages differ in each case, but the common points that are indicators of success are encouraging for me to read. It's nice to have SOMEONE letting me know that we're on the right track!

From: Brandon

My wife and I have always looked at the following paragraphs from the outstanding book "When Husbands Come Out of the Closet," pages 132 & 133, by Jean Schaar Gochros, Harrington Park Press, as fine examples of how our marriage seems to flourish through the years. Hope it sheds some light on the above question.

> There did, however, seem to be a few clear-cut answers. Rather than the degree of the husband's homosexuality, it seemed to be his degree of *heterosexuality*—or at least his ability to find heterosexual satisfaction, his love for his wife, and his ability to show empathy and regard for a wife's needs, rights, and feelings that were the crucial factors.
> Those marriages that seemed to flower rather than wither were marked by that ability. The husband retained a primary commitment to the wife both emotionally and sexually, no matter how homosexually active he might be. The wife felt listened to, heard, understood, loved, and treated fairly. Communication was increased. Displays of emotion—even overreactions, unanticipated reactions, and conflicts about homosexuality or stigma were tolerated, understood, and given empathic help.

The sexual relationship was maintained and was usually good. Even when problems occurred, the husband was committed to helping the wife obtain sexual satisfaction within the marriage, found some degree of satisfaction himself (as opposed to merely "servicing" his wife), and engaged in empathic problem solving rather than criticizing. Contracts were kept, and when minor problems arose, the husband was able to both assert his own needs and compromise to meet his wife's. The wife felt that she had a reasonable amount of power in the relationship and hence also had true choice.

No matter what the situation, the husband was empathic enough with the wife to know what she—as an individual—needed . . . Terri's lifestyle may have differed from other happy wives, but her stated feelings about her husband and the quality of her marriage spoke for all:

> Not a day goes by that my husband doesn't show me both verbally and nonverbally that he loves me. I know that if at some point I'm feeling especially vulnerable and tell him I'd prefer he not go out, he'll stay home willingly, without "punishing" me for it. Therefore I have real choice. I can *choose* to accept small hurts, knowing that I will be repaid over and over again with pleasure. And it's a two-way street: sometimes I do that for him, sometimes he does it for me. We care for each other and we care about each other.

From: Moris

Umm, not sure how to answer this. My wife lets me know when she is feeling bad about something and then we talk about it. I also maintain who I am during this talking. So she knows how I feel as well as how she feels. All feelings are valid. How she deals with her anxiety? Prayer! Lots of prayer! I know she falls back on God and His help.

From: Josi

I've grown into being quite convertible with maintaining who I am in our conversations/heated moments. My wife does not use prayer, however, to see herself through. But two things are happening that are increasingly mutually reinforcing: (1) I am doing better at letting her know I care, in the heated moment and in the many times in between; (2) she has found a therapist whom she trusts and who is helping her come to terms with some of the family-of-origin feelings that rear their ugly heads in the middle of our issues. The more I support her and express my love, the more she is willing to look at herself. The more she is willing to look at herself and not blame me for my sexuality, the more I can express my caring and love.

SHE'S NOT SUPPOSED TO SEE ME UPSET

From: Crawly

If you would prefer to just read positive mail, "erase" me now. :) I'm having a real blue morning and I think I could use a couple "it's okays," "hang in there's," etc. I'm regretting ever starting this because today it feels so hard. I'm crying for one of the first times.

Last night my wife and I talked and she said the hardest thing for her has been she hasn't gotten to see me upset at losing her and what we had. I didn't have an answer. It came this morning with my tears. She's not supposed to see me upset. That's not in my job description. I feel guilty for making her upset by my tears. Funny it made her feel less angry. She has been feeling mad lately and doesn't like it.

SO, I'm sorry for how pathetic this sounds, I just am feeling like I could use a hug. Even if it's just on the Internet. :)

From: Carl

You've given me a hug in a way, whether you know it or not. I've been more or less where you are emotionally (though so far it looks as though my wife and I will see things through), so that being reminded of it now, when the pain and the tears "haven't" come, feels good.

Friday morning (at 6:00, I hope) I'll set out for my third visit to my lover since we reconnected. It's now settling down to a trip every month or two, and I expected the usual foul mood from my wife when she learned that I would be going. But it hasn't happened. I guess she's getting used to the idea that I love both him and her and will be seeing him as often as I can manage despite my deep commitment to her.

This year has been full of emotional storm warnings for both my wife and me. El Niño of the soul, I guess. (My boyfriend never quite loses his cool, bless him!) But I feel so alive because of these emotional focal points that, in a way, I feel 10 years younger than I did a year ago.

So hang in. Some of the worst moments between my wife and I have ended with the two of us sobbing in each other's arms and protesting our mutual love. The problems often come out of left field, but so do the solutions. I used to think that every bad moment was "payment" for a good one in the past. Now it seems more like prepayments to me, and I look for the good to come out of the pain. It does. It really does.

From: Kenneth

I'm moved by your courage to be so open about your feelings of loss and grief. It is so healthy that you can let them be seen, both by your wife and by the men in this group. It is the beginning of the healing process. There is no need for you to feel embarrassed or shameful. Your are not pathetic, just real!!! Your wife was upset by your tears because they are rare; why, she probably felt a little guilty for causing them! The "job description" you mention is why men don't live as long as women. Celebrate that you do feel, and feel deeply—it means that you are really ALIVE! There are many of us men that would love to give you a real hug today. You'll have to settle for a virtual one.

MY THOUGHTS

From: Brian

I've been lurking on this list now for about 2 weeks or so, not really contributing much but just taking in others' thoughts and situations. It is truly amazing how much we all have in common. Most everything everyone has written about, I've been through. I really wish I had had this resource back then. Some of the posts brought tears to my eyes.

I came out to my wife 10 years ago. I had made the realization that I was gay about 3 years before. I sought counseling to try to come to terms with my feelings and really went through a bad time of it. My wife knew something was wrong but had no idea what. Finally, on our 13th wedding anniversary, my wife gave me a beautiful diamond ring telling me that I was the most wonderful man in the world and she would marry me again in a second. Suddenly, all of the emotion flooded through me. I felt like a heel keeping this secret from her. I broke down sobbing and shaking. With little coaxing on her part, I told her I was gay.

We (she) went through all of the emotions others have described their wives going through. First she accepted it, saying she still loved me. The following day she went through a deep depression and feelings of hopelessness. "What else don't I know about you?" "What will happen to me?" "Has our marriage been a lie?" I told her I truly loved her, and that I didn't realize I was gay when we married (I didn't!). I offered her all kinds of resources I had found to help her through this . . . books, counselor referrals, even the phone number of another woman married to a gay man that I had met through my counseling. She investigated each one (a little) but ultimately decided that she could "go this alone" and that's what she has continued to do for the past 10 years. She's sought no support whatsoever.

I'm very concerned for her. Eventually, we settled into the relationship that we now have. She allows me to have gay friends and "go out" as long as I don't tell her anything about it. As someone else said in a recent post, if I try to talk to her about my gay issues, she doesn't want to hear it. Although this arrangement has made the situation tolerable for her, I feel like I'm dying a slow death. I'm angry all the time. I don't feel I have any freedom to be me. I don't seem to fit in anywhere.

I guess the problem is that I truly love my wife. She's my best friend. I don't want to hurt her. I have offered to leave many times, telling her that we would both be happier. She says that she loves me more than she could ever love anyone else. It doesn't matter to her that I'm gay. I ask if she misses the sex (we haven't had sex in over 8 years!). She said yes, but as long as I come home to her, that's all she needs.

I'm now in counseling (again) and my counselor recommends couples counseling as a forum for us to say things to each other that are not being said now (we never really talk about this . . . it's too uncomfortable. We both hate confrontation). My counselor said this . . . my wife is in denial and that the couples counseling will help her to see the situation as it really is and will help us to finally be honest about it and do something about it. Has anyone else been through couples counseling? Did it help?

I was intrigued by the stories of couples still together where there was a "boyfriend" involved. I think that is ultimately what I would want for myself, but I honestly didn't think that that was a possibility. Every man I've ever met has run the other way once I tell them I'm married and have children.

To make things worse, I have a demanding job that requires me to be away from home a lot. So when I get home, instead of feeling I can go out by myself or to attend some gay social event (I'm a non-attending member of the local BEAR club—yes, I'm a bear!), I feel that since I've been away all week, I need to stay home and spend time with my wife. When I return from a trip, she follows me around the house asking for hugs. I feel so guilty if I want to do something by myself.

Well, I realize I've been rambling for too long. Sorry about that. I've just wanted to participate for awhile and this is the first chance I've had. Again, thanks for providing this forum for us (me!) and it is comforting to know that I'm not alone in this. I just feel like there is no resolution.

From: Rodney

You're a lot further along than I am. Your wife and you have at least reached an agreement that your relationship is tremendously important for you both and she has found a way (through denial) of coping with your sexuality. This may not be an OPTIMAL coping mechanism, but it IS a mechanism. You're still together and you haven't given up on your relationship. I think that's an achievement. Maybe we sometimes should "give denial a chance."

Right now, I am homo abstinent AND my wife is avoiding me: the worst of both possible (sexual) alternatives. I also don't yet have a high comfort level that when she comes back down to earth, she'll want me in her life.

I have been trying for a long time, unsuccessfully, to get my wife into couples counseling (long before I was out to her), originally for issues not having to do with sexuality.

But I can sure relate to that little razor that's going right through the middle of you: I love my wife AND I like sex with men. Even if I'm homo abstinent (and I'm not sure this is a viable long-term alternative for me), I have to insist that my wife see me clearly and accept what I am.

About counseling: an observation that may make your wife's wanting to "go it alone" more understandable. Many people, my wife included, distrust intervention by "outsiders" because they believe they are too easily swayed by other people. My wife rejected the idea of going, for instance, to PFLAG, because she "didn't want someone else telling her how to relate."

If you and your wife hate confrontation (this was also an issue in both my household and my wife's when we were growing up), you may both have difficulty knowing how to discuss difficult issues in "real time." On the other side of the fence, people who grew up learning how to hold their own in a fight sometimes have difficulty understanding how it's possible to be any other way.

Here's a totally off-the-wall thought: What if you were to tell your wife that you needed to talk to her more about your sexuality, and ASK her if she'd be more comfortable if you wrote her a letter, so she'd have time to digest what you had to say and decide what issues, if any, she felt ready to discuss, either in writing or face-to-face? You need to make it clear that you're thinking about a letter, NOT because your issues are "killer" issues, but simply because they are issues she may need time by herself to think about before responding (otherwise, the idea of a letter might cause her to panic). You would also have to be willing to let HER choose the timing and mode of the response—and make sure she understands you're willing to wait.

This seems awkward and unnatural, I know. But it might open up communication. And once open, who knows? Maybe the communication would start up in "real time" or even in front of a counselor.

Do you think you could at this point say something to your wife like this: "Right now, you want me to keep the gay part of my life hidden from you, and I respect that request. For this to work, however, I want the following:" (you supply this—is it to have one night when you're home-free to be "with the boy(s)" without hiding it or making apologies? Is it to go to your bear meeting? Some combination of these? Something else?)

If you do this, ask for EXACTLY what you want, not more, not less. And TELL her you're trying to be direct with her and that she has the right to say, "No, I can't go with A, but maybe I could accept B." This sounds more like a negotiation than it really is. You're simply trying to find some zone where you can BOTH be more comfortable. If you both get used to being up front about your needs and desires, I have to believe that will help, whether or not you're in counseling.

Note, too, that such an agreement may be nothing more than an interim solution as you work your way toward something better.

Another thought. Corny though it sounds, maybe when you're at home with your wife you should make your (all-too-little) time together more special. Go on dates. Maybe when you're out of town, send her flowers or little presents. She sounds like she above all simply needs proof of your love (we all need that—how much greater the need for a woman who KNOWS your love and sexual life are divided!).

From: Woody

I've been on this list of men for about a year, and I'm absolutely amazed at the variety of reactions wives have when trying to come to terms with their husband's sexuality once he's come out to her.

When I think about what it would feel like with the shoe on MY foot, I'm pretty certain I'd probably consider the same path that most wives have taken—a decision to separate—more because I don't think I could take the uncertainty the future might hold than because the marriage vows were broken. When I came out to my wife, I don't think I visited that viewpoint in my own mind like I have after some of the recent discussions on this list about what it would be like if the situation were reversed.

So how is it that some wives—mine included—are able to cope? I am allowed some freedom as long as I don't establish an emotional relationship (I did fall completely "in love" last spring [or was it "in lust"?—I still don't think so] and that has been the hardest part for me) or bring any kind of embarrassment to her (and being "out" in the community would do that for her). She demands a lot of personal attention in return. In everyday things as well as in the bedroom—very hard for me because with my rather intense gay/leather/bear orientation, my mind and lust always seem focussed on attracting and pleasing other men rather than on her. My wife WANTS to have frequent discussions of gay issues and of my "other" life. She rejects "don't ask, don't tell" so we talk about everything (yes, in some detail), including my "buds." I think she feels that if we are still talking, I'm not leaving—either physically or emotionally. "Modern Maturity" (we're both in our 50s) did not include being left alone at this stage in her life.

I'm grateful my wife has learned to accept that part of me and works very hard at keeping me around, but is it enough for me? Probably—but there is still the strong inner desire to be able, finally, after all those decades of suppression, to live my life openly and fully as a gay man. The grass is always greener. . . . At least being able to ventilate helps —thanks, guys.

THE ROLLER COASTER

From: Max

I've been keeping up with the postings to the group these past couple of weeks or so. It's funny how sometimes you read something and think "God, I could have written that. That's me!" and other times "What? Dunno about that!"

I think, for me, the most difficult part of all this is the roller coaster. It just throws everything else into confusion.

My wife and I have sat and talked MORE. Most of it is rehashing old stuff. Some of it was quoting what the other person had previously said. From time to time it would get more like a cross-party debate and other times there seemed a great empathy.

I'm myself, I find that I swing from absolute hopelessness to exhilaration.

When I was talking with my wife last night I mentioned how at times I'd get so low that if life were a light switch, I'd gladly switch it off. And yet, deep down I know there's a further distance to go before I get to that stage.

Last year I had a boyfriend for a couple of weeks. It was an unmitigated disaster. Love for all the wrong reasons. Top that with the fact that emotionally it really hurt my wife. Something which she largely kept from me. That is, until now.

I was talking with one of the guys I know last night. He wasn't impressed. More or less said that I've got to make up my mind and decide what it is I want for myself and just do it. Perfectly logical. Kind of ties in with one of the postings that's crossed in e-mail in the past day or so.

However, since when do relationships and marriage follow a logical progression? Logically speaking, I should have dealt with all this in my adolescence and not got married. Logically speaking I should have had a few gay relationships before making a decision. Logically, I probably should have saved my Communion Money. But there you go, there always was a hole in my pocket!

It's very true what was said in response to the postings on making a cold decision and following it. I love my family. Wife, kids, mortgage, budgie etc. etc. I don't want to leave that behind. I need the emotional bond of another man (or men). Sex isn't the greatest thing in my life. It never was. Somehow, the signals are that these two are incompatible. They cannot exist happily together. On the other hand, some have made a successful go of it. I take my hat off to those for whom this is so, and that includes their spouse(s).

Well, to my mind. Simple and all as it may be, it sits perfectly logically side by side. These feelings are mine. They are true and real. It's making these feelings come to life, to bring substance to them that's difficult. Someone once said to me (in relation to something completely different) "Make haste slowly." God, how I've tried. But how do you reign in the galloping horses when your heart and mind are so consumed with the need for affection with another man;? when it affects your daily living? (Did I hear someone shout "ECT, I'll bring the water and a tea-bag" ?)

To each and every one of us, our situation is different. What works for one, may not work in it's entirety for the rest of us. I think for most of us it's a case of plodding along like through a mine-field, tentatively taking steps. Each time breathing a sigh of relief when it doesn't blow up in your face and other times running for cover (in my case, internalizing) when it does. I enjoy reading others ventures through the mine-field. It gives me hope and comfort.

What I most like about this group, though, is that apart from the examples of other folks, the warmth, comfort, and love that comes across carries me over the glens of this enigmatic life.

From: Rodney

I know I love my wife. I know I love having sex with her. I know I love having sex with guys. I know I would have trouble finding the same kind of closeness to a man that I have with my wife.

Now this particular combination of feelings is not supposed to be possible in our culture. But I know they're possible: they're mine. Somehow or other, through some combination of genes and environment, that's how I ended up.

But because it's so hard for people to believe they're possible (it's at least hard for my WIFE to believe they're possible), I have a hell of a time, as you put it, bringing substance to them.

From: Henry

You sound just like me. Disbelief that men like us exist is an old problem for me. Before I was married, I told a few gay men I was involved with that I was bisexual. Now, 18 years or so later, I still remember their reactions vividly: contemptuous, incredulous, or sometimes patronizing of my "self-delusion." Well, those experiences taught me to shut up: I wasn't about to come out to any women I was involved with at the time, considering the reception I got from what I supposed would be a sympathetic audience. Maybe people's beliefs have changed since then—I don't know.

I've been out to my wife for 9 months now, and it's still something of an issue for her, I think. But for me, one thing's different now: I don't care quite so much whether people believe I exist, and that feels a lot better than some of the rather desperate attempts I've made in the past to convince people that I do. And as for bringing substance to those feelings, I've just begun to do that. It's not easy, and I don't know how it's going to turn out.

From: Clark

Funny that you all should be writing about this today.

I was thinking just this morning (in an intimate activity before rising!) that as gay as I feel most of the time, I am perfectly content expressing love with my wife. Sometimes I feel "tempted" to forego that—all for the sake of living a less complicated life, with the ability to come and go at will—yet I know that I would miss what gives me great joy: loving her and making love to her.

Strange how many of us are waking up to the realization that our realities, our feelings don't fit the prescribed notions that society and its guardians have mapped out. I don't know quite how to get to where I know I ought to be. But I know that there is "somewhere a place for us" who don't neatly fit the categories and profiles carefully laid out for us. I intend to keep going.

I had a dream last night in which I was trying to find a bridge across a waterway, and was stymied in my efforts to get across once I had found the structure. I could see through and reach through, but could not pass through a locked grid. How well my unconscious seems to know that something has to give. I must turn around and look for another way. And I shall. There!

SOME DEVELOPMENTS IN MARRIAGE

From: Kallas

I am living in a small city. My wife and have spent our married lives living in a fundamentalist Christian setting, expecting that I would be zapped and healed of my sin of homosexuality. We've been through the "ex-gay" mentality. Most of our 18 years of married life has been involved with some kind of marital counseling about our dysfunctional sex life. I have always been out to my wife. I am also out to my kids and most other people who know me. We have been through the mill about sexuality, guilt, etc., etc.

Anyway, the whole sexuality issue came to a head this past fall, when my wife filed separation papers. She said that she was lonely, and that our marriage was little more than a "room-mate marriage." For my part, I felt sexually repressed and inhibited by the church, and my wife gave me the message that I was unacceptable unless I was str8.

The announcement of a separation was a wake-up call for me. My wife had been complaining for years about our less-than-perfect marriage, and I always wrote it off as whining and non-acceptance.

So it looked like the inevitable would happen—that we would have to endure an expensive divorce, and live out our lives with not-enough-money, co-parenting, middle-aged misery, and all of that.

We were both emotionally exhausted, and I decided that I would set up an impromptu trip for the two of us, so that we could make some decisions about sexuality, and our future together, the kids, the house, etc. We took along a written list of issues and questions to discuss, and a notebook that we entitled "Final Decisions."

Well . . . magic happened. We fell in love, lost our inhibitions, shook off the censure of the church, accepted each other as we are, and returned home as "Mr. and Mrs. Smith—the mixed-orientation couple." It's been a month since we have been back home, and even the endless, gray, overcast days haven't diminished our renewed marriage. A one-week trip did more for us than years of marital counseling.

I proclaim myself 100% gay. And my wife accepts me. Hetero sex is exotic for me, but it is also wonderful. I place blame for our past difficulties, squarely at the feet of the Church.

MALE SOUL MATES AND WIFE

From: Shawn

Please share with me how you will have a male soul mate while preserving the marital relationship you so cherish. I really want to know what you have to say on this subject.

From: James

Well, I don't know if I can share "how," since I have not achieved this goal/desire. I knew when I came out to my wife that I was not willing to live without a M2M relationship . . . and that is a post/story in itself. We have worked very intentionally—my wife and me—to achieve a very bonded, close and loving relationship. But I know within that I need an intimate bond with another guy. What I HAVE achieved are wonderful friendships with other men, a first for me. Before coming out to myself, my close friendships were always with women, now they are exclusively with men. My wife thinks I seek a needle in a haystack . . . seeking another married man out to his wife or a single man interested in a relationship with a married man . . . but I take hope in the relationships that some of the guys here on this list have achieved that I may realize my goal. Since before coming out, my "real" life was one of fantasy, maybe this is the "post-coming out" fantasy . . . I don't know. But my wife is supportive and even helpful on occasion as I pursue this goal.

During the last three years I have had the good fortune twice to "practice" this type of relationship and now have a good idea why I have this need and have learned a lot about myself.

From: Moris

I assume you were talking to all of us that have a man and a woman in our lives. One way is that all three of us live together. Some do not do this, but for me, it helps. That way we (the three of us) become a family. My wife sees that he does not take me away and my husband sees that she does not take me away. I also treat both of them as my partner, my spouse. . . . I call him my husband. . . .

We (the three of us) worked out the sleeping arrangements. We work out our "dating" times. Times we do things as a triad and times she and I (and he and I) do things as a couple. My wife and I went to my husband's office Christmas party, . . . etc.

Be careful what you wish for, you just might get it!!!!

HAPPILY MARRIED?

From: Shawn

I'm wondering . . . are any of you saying that it's "ok" with your wife if you become sexually involved with another man? What are the boundaries that you two have agreed to and can you tell me how it was you two were able to agree to these boundaries? There's a difference between an intimate relationship between two men (emotionally) and one that has crossed the line to become sexual. Obviously I'm seeking some guidance and direction. It seems like walking a tightrope over Niagara Falls with a marriage potentially on the line. How many women, really, can tolerate their husbands getting sexual with other men? Not too many I suppose. Not my wife, I'm sure!

From: Brandon

The questions that you ask are not easy to answer with a few words or even a few pages of text. My wife and I have worked at and struggled with these questions everyday since I came out to her 10 years ago. Actually I struggled with them my entire life. I have posted a piece from "When Husbands Come Out of the Closet," pages 132 & 133, before and it is the only condensed version that best describes my wife's and my relationship. You need to understand that I describe myself as Gay (defiantly homosexual) though others would put me in the BI definition. I have been in a relationship (emotional, sexual, and very loving) with my male partner for 7 years while at the same time remaining in a wonderful, loving, supportive marriage to my wife of 38 years.

To answer your questions:

Shawn wrote:>*I'm still wondering, however . . . are you saying that it's "ok" with your wife if you become sexually involved with another man?*<

It is not OK as you put it—it is a necessity because of the fact that I absolutely have to have a man in my life. I cannot exist as a whole person without an emotional, spiritual, and physical relationship with another man (men). My life without a man was depression, sickness, withdrawal, and desperation. My life with a man is alive, well, and exciting! My wife knew and understood this early in the coming-out process. She understood that without my getting my basic human "NEEDS" met that she would lose everything that made her life whole and meaningful, including the husband that she had loved for so many many years.

>*What are the boundaries that you two have agreed to and can you tell me how it was you two were able to agree to these boundaries?*<

Our boundaries are love, honesty, openness, and trust. I also will do nothing that would jeopardize the safety of her or my health—which is the primary reason that my statement above read "Man" and not "Men." I am primarily a monogamous person, so this arrangement works best for us—though I could very easy be a slut if it weren't for the health issue. (Anonymous M2M SEX is like WOW!!! but that is another story!!!! and I do not profess to be a saint lest someone out there is getting the wrong idea.) We also have agreed to work on our marriage and good relationship every day for the rest of our lives. But this is what makes all good relationships!

>*There's a difference between an intimate relationship between two men (emotionally) and one that has crossed the line to become sexual.*<

My wife has more of a problem with the emotional and very little problem with the sexual!!!

>*How many women, really, can tolerate their husbands getting sexual with other men?*<

More than you would ever guess. The solutions to the equation of the mixed marriage are as numerous as there are couples. Every couple that decides to make a mixed marriage work must work through the particulars of their own unique relationship.

From: Gripp

Thanks for posting your reply. I can't wait for my wife to get home to show it to her. It says so well so many things that I want to gently express to her.

From: Rodney

Brandon wrote: >*It is not OK as you put it—it is a necessity because of the fact that I absolutely have to have a man in my life.*<

Your reply was very enlightening for me. Your comment above produced a kind of "aha!" reaction to me. I never really thought about it that way. It may not be POSSIBLE in one lifetime for my wife to get to a point where my sexual relations with men are "OK." But that may also not be necessary. This increases the POSSIBILITY of a solution.

From: James

Shawn wrote: >*Are you saying that it's "ok" with your wife if you become sexually involved with another man?*<

Yes, that is exactly what I am saying.

>*What are the boundaries that you two have agreed to and can you tell me how it was you two were able to agree to these boundaries?*<

Basically my condition to remain married was that I have a relationship—sexual and emotional—with another man if I ever find a male soul mate. My wife wants to remain married. We both love one another and decided to see if we could make this type of marriage work.

>*How many women, really, can tolerate their husbands getting sexual with other men? Not too many I suppose. Not my wife, I'm sure!*<

I guess I can think of about a dozen wives at least that are married to men on this list that do. Many others do not . . . and there are many that I have no idea whether they do or not. . . .

My wife has these boundaries: (1) that I may bring a man to our home when she is not here but may not use our bed, (2) I cannot see a guy intimately more than once a week . . . or even get together with him for non-intimate time, e.g., go to a concert or play, more than once a week . . . is too difficult for her she says, (3) I need to check with her about coming out within our own community (this is not an issue with a M2M relationship but is one of her boundaries) and she has become increasingly comfortable with me being more and more out . . . to the point of giving me the OK to join the university gay/BI/lesbian employee caucus this fall.

From: Boris

I resonate to James' exchange about how do you manage to preserve a (transformed) marriage and develop a complete relationship with a man.

In my case it was OK with my wife for me to become sexually involved with men when I came out. My wife knew that I'd lived with a (male) partner for 10 years before I met her, she knew I was gay, and she married me knowing she was marrying a gay man. When I told her three years ago that my coming out meant that I had to be with men (or a man), it was not a surprise to her.

She and I worked for two years to figure out how to integrate an authentic gay life, including male relationships, into our marriage. And part of that was her acceptance of the reality that I could function erotically only with men, never with her.

>*What are the boundaries that you two have agreed to and can you tell me how it was you two were able to agree to these boundaries?*<

Our boundaries weren't really boundaries. They were more like agreed principles. She asked me to move slowly, and I did. She asked me to pursue my path together with her, not separately, and I did. I shared with her whatever she wanted to know, but I never forced anything on her that she didn't want to know.

I made it clear from the start that we were not playing the permission game. I never asked her for concessions, and she never asked any from me. I told her what had to be, and I told her what I wanted. She told me the same things. Through it all, we communicated constantly.

>*There's a difference between an intimate relationship between two men (emotionally) and one that has crossed the line to become sexual.*<

Actually, my wife was more fearful of an emotional relationship than she was of a purely sexual one. Of course, for her the two were close to being the same thing. But she could distinguish between the two dimensions, or types of relationship. Fortunately or unfortunately (depending on your experience and point of view) I don't know how to be involved sexually with a man without being emotionally involved with him too (though the opposite is not the case: I can easily be emotionally involved with a man without having to be sexual with him).

>*How many women, really, can tolerate their husbands getting sexual with other men? Not too many I suppose.*<

As it happens, my wife couldn't tolerate it either. She desperately wanted to, and so did I. We tried. We did everything we could. There was a lot of tension while we did so, and a lot of suffering (more on her side than on mine), but a lot of love, caring, and understanding, too. In the end we agreed to separate. It turns out to have been the best thing for all of us, including our two grown kids. My wife loves being single, has no interest (currently) in pursuing a relationship with another man, is focussed on her work, her sons, and finishing her Ph.D. She and I are the best of warm, loving friends who share more than either of us will probably ever share with anyone else.

At the same time, even though I didn't want her to move out, now that she has, I'm loving being single (though it hasn't lasted very long), much more than I thought I would. The tension and the struggle are now over, and I have no baggage to carry with me into my new life. Our marriage was a good one, even troubled as it was, and our sons bear witness to that. Our family life and our relationships to one another have all undergone transformations, and we are all stronger, more real, and better persons for it.

And where I least expected to find it (being picked up in a bar!), I met a man who has grown to love me as I have grown to love him—a man who is so different from me that no one who knew both of us would ever have put us together! And, miracle of miracles, he doesn't live 3,000 miles away! I have much to be grateful for this Christmas.

From: Gripp

Welcome to the group and to as many different expressions of love and commitment as there are people in the group.

After coming out to my wife, I now wonder why I waited so long (25 years of marriage). She loves me and has been much more accepting and understanding than I could have imagined. She was reared in the Catholic church and had been taught that church's traditional, pre-Vatican II, paternalistic teachings.

Before we married, while dating, we were a part of a "dinner club" with the other single members. She and I were the only ones who married heterosexually, and, as it turns out, she is the only heterosexual one. All of this is to say that she knows many GLBT individuals, and has listened to them express all aspects of their lives, sexual and otherwise. One male couple of the group has been "married" longer than us. So while finding out that her husband (me) was not straight was a shock to her, she still had a very good understanding of what that meant. That probably helped in her acceptance of my disclosure.

She also knows that I love her and feel a great deal of passion for her. She would prefer that I not be BI, or whatever term I might call myself, but she still loves me and wants to remain married to me. I find that overwhelming sometimes—it's wonderful!

I was sexually and emotionally involved with another man for the two years before I came out to her. She knew him all along and was aware that I was rather "fond" of him. She was fond of him herself and often invited him to our house for dinner, parties, etc. My male lover has since moved away and I have gone to visit him, with her blessing. If she had her druthers, she would rather he still be here, than for me to be "anxious," "depressed," whatever it is. Because now that I know what it is to love and be loved completely by a man and a woman simultaneously, I am having a hard time accepting the loss of that missing part of me/us. She would also rather have the devil that she knows, rather than one unknown. (Me too!)

She remembers how happy and complete I was during that relationship. I was more overtly loving to her during that time. She says that she wants my happiness, that it is important to her happiness. She really loves me! I am sometimes overwhelmed by her love and what she is willing to accept.

>*There's a difference between an intimate relationship between two men (emotionally) and one that has crossed the line to become sexual.*<

I have never had an emotional-only relationship with a man. The relationship with my man became sexual immediately. I have been unable, in

the past, to separate emotion and sex. So I cannot relate there. We have recently had several days of discussions over M/M friendships, many of us
admitting that a friendship was hard for us to develop and sustain. (Others
have no difficulty maintaining friendships and emotional/sexual relationships with different people [men] at the same time.) My wife and I are still in
the middle of working out the "boundaries." She seems to be content to let
things lie until another relationship comes along, saying she will just have to
learn to accept it when it happens. I want to be proactive about it, and I bring
the subject up occasionally so that as many issues are discussed as we can
figure out to discuss. I desire to avoid hard feelings at that "sometime" in the
future, if it is possible to do so. (I need to avoid talking about sexuality all
the time, although it is what I am perpetually working on in my own head.
There are many other aspects to our marriage, including deepening our own
relationship, and parenting, among others, which also demand/command a
lot of time.) I let her in on my thoughts about m/m sex, and my attractions to
other men and women as I/we see them. She is becoming a bit more open
about her own feelings and attractions and is able to share those with me.
We can look at each other and smile when we see a man who is attractive to
both of us.

I regularly (more often than before) tell her how much I love her and need
her, how often I think of her, how I miss her when she is out of town on a
concert, how great sex is with her, etc!

She sometimes asks me if I think of him during sex. Once when she
asked, it was true; I had. Other times it is not. Sometimes I think of other
good-looking men or women during sex. At other times, it is not a part of
my conscious fantasies. I suspect that I should not always be open with my
fantasies—that there should be some perimeters or off-limits boundaries.
AND I am careful sometimes to ask if she REALLY wants to know.

Let me encourage you to gently and gradually explore your needs and desires with your wife. Is she your best friend? Mine is, so I want to discuss all
of this with my wife, as she wants to know, rather than be in the dark. I am
learning to trust her love of me and continue to depend on it.

I appreciate hearing about your concerns and the opportunity to respond
to them. It has helped me to formulate my own philosophy. My wife may
never be able to accept me as I would like to be accepted ideally, but then
again, I may never have an opportunity to live completely in that best of all
ideal worlds.

From: Lee

I read your post and thought I could maybe help a little by describing my
present relationship with both my wife and my boyfriend. My wife at first
disclosure was opposed to any extramarital relationship, especially one in-

cluding sex. After a period of time of having discrete sexual encounters and brief short-term relationships I met a young man with whom I fell madly in love. At this time I felt it necessary to disclose to my wife the full depth of my feelings for this man. This was a very difficult thing for me to do and I felt that it would most definitely end my marriage.

My wife was shocked about all my activity that occurred without her knowledge and then began to realize that the relationship I had with this young man was serious and most threatening to our marital relationship. She began to think about all her possible choices of action and decided that she wanted to remain in the marriage. In order for her to do this she had to understand my bisexuality or homosexuality and the need I have for a close loving relationship with a man. Throughout all this time I was able to tell my wife that I still loved her and cared for her deeply and that I could not imagine my life without her. This gave her some reassurance. She went online and met people through the straight spouse group and that was immensely helpful. Also she reached out to our minister and I must tell you he was open to the notion that we could maintain our marriage and encouraged my wife to try to find a way to accommodate my needs in our marriage.

So several months passed and my wife decided that she needed to meet my boyfriend. I was anxious about this but I felt it necessary in order to incorporate these two people in my life. So now my wife has met my man, likes him and loves to have him visit with us in our home. She even permits him to sleep over once or twice a week. This seems like a dream come true. I need to be somewhat reserved in demonstrating my affection for my male lover in front of her, but otherwise we all get along and enjoy each other's company. In addition, I have been able to have some quality time alone with both my wife and/or with him.

So each person must work all this out as best as they can. I give my wife all the credit for being open to all possibilities and recognizing that I would not be a happy husband if I had to deny these needs to myself. Also, she is understanding that I still love her a lot and do not want to leave her. She prefers that I am with my male partner because she likes him and feels he will be a good partner for me and I will not be out there having anonymous sex. She is concerned about my safety and hers. She also likes the idea that my man is respectful of her and cares for her as well.

Try to help your wife open her heart and mind to some other possibility other than all or none.

From: Joey

There is no question that each of us will achieve a different level of simpatico with our marriage and homosexuality. I can only speak for myself and my wife. She and I are interested in remaining married for as long as we can work together harmoniously to preserve that marriage. At the same time, I am out. I seek gay friendships and relationships. I believe that she is happier, as I am, in finding a one-at-a-time-type relationship with a man. (There is also in the wings her relationship with her new man (men) that she needs for her psyche.) So far, save a few occasions when she is in PMS or just having a hard time, it seems to be working. She knows I have sex with men. (NOT AT THE HOUSE . . . a clearly stated rule for us.) She seems totally accepting of this. Her philosophy is that she feels bad for me that I have not had sexual fulfillment until now. She was quite sexually active before I came along and she looks forward to being able to be out heterosexually. What she requires absolutely is open and honest communication, even about stuff that one would think would be painful for her. For example, this weekend I met a man who totally blew me away. I have a mad crush on this guy and I can't get him out of my mind. It threw me into a tailspin of desire and frustration. When I withdrew she became pretty shitty. When I told her that I was in pain because I didn't know what to do about this guy, her whole demeanor changed. Since I had finally included her in what was bothering me, she could deal with it. When she is excluded, she can't handle it. She has imaginings that are far worse than the reality.

So, I think for us, she will become my soul-mate and my new man/men will be my lovers and future significant others. She wants to be my sister. Even today at lunch I said, "Will you still care for me when I am old and decrepit?" Her answer, "Yes."

From: Milton

I wanted to share some thoughts with you all about marriage, especially in light of the threads that have been going around lately.

This past Sunday's New York Times Book Review had a review of John Bayley's "Elegy for Iris" (John Bayley, the English author, has been married to Iris Murdoch, probably one of the most influential English authors of the middle of the century for more than 40 years). The reviewer, Fay Gordon, talks about their marriage and there were some things about it that really resonated with me. I urged Sharon to read it and she felt the same. I suggest it to all of you who struggle with maintaining a marriage in spite of the fact that you're gay or BI.

Their story, very briefly, is that Iris Murdoch, who has written beautiful novels, is now suffering from Alzheimer's and Bayley is her sole care-provider.

Let me cite an excerpt from the review:

" 'To feel oneself held and cherished and accompanied, and yet to be alone. To be closely and physically entwined, and yet feel solitude's friendly presence, as warm and undesolating as contiguity itself.' " is one of the ways Bayley describes their relationship.

I wanted to share this with you because it holds meaning for me and you might find meaning in it as well, even if the only meaning for you is that there can be meaning in these queer relationships (double entendre intended).

My wife and I have been together 23 years and I've been out 14 of those years. So, yes, it is possible to stay married. Is it for everyone? No, definitely not. But I think that each of us must choose for ourselves and must find our own way. As a group, we can console, we can encourage, we can tell our own experiences, we can weep and laugh together.

From: Rodney

I continue to be intrigued by the posts from men who have wives who seem to have accepted the idea that their husbands will have sexual relations with other men.

I would like to pose the COMPLEMENTARY question—how many women can tolerate having their husbands' SEXUAL relationships "cross the line" and turn into EMOTIONAL ones?

If I were my wife, I think I'd actually find the sexual-emotional transformation more threatening than the emotional-sexual one. But maybe I'm being too theoretical.

BOUNDARIES?

From: Rodney

I see that other guys had ALREADY started posting about whether wives found the sexual or the emotional dimension of M2M relationships more threatening.

I'd really appreciate seeing more posts from guys who are comfortable discussing these boundary issues in what may seem them to be ridiculous detail. As a bisexual in a marriage that is currently not working very well, I find it tremendously helpful to read this detail, because it makes it much clearer for me how the THEORETICAL concept of a "nontraditional" relationship MIGHT work out in reality.

I also like the description of the boundaries regarding being OUT. They are very useful. It has only been in the last week or so (reading the "being

OUT" thread) that I realized that wives may have as complicated feelings about their husbands' being out as they have about their relationships (sexual and emotional) with other men.

From: Brandon

The ground rules (boundaries) in our relationship are (our refers to my wife and myself):

- Play safe!
- No threesomes (She is 100% monogamous by nature).
- Never have sex with a man in our bed or bedroom.
- Not share the motor home with another man (It is our very special place).
- Always let her know if I cannot keep an agreed-to time. (This is not being intrusive on her part but courtesy so that she does not have to worry.)
- Coordinate the time away from her so that she can plan ahead. This works both ways, so that when she has an appointment or plans, I can use that same time to be with my man or out with the guys.
- Be honest (This does not mean that I must share all with her. It does mean that I have the right to privacy as to what I do sexually with another man—she does have the right to know that I have been sexual and safe!) I also reserve the right to not answer questions that I feel are too invasive of my right to privacy—I have the right to say, "Are you sure that you really want to know the answer to that question?" In 10 years I have only had to evoke this agreed-to statement twice. Both times she realized that she had overstepped propriety and apologized for asking.
- Coordinate with her and she with me as to whom we come out to. This included coming out to our three children. This was interesting as both of us agreed, when I first came out to her, that we should wait to tell the kids. A year later, we both came to the same conclusion at the same time that it was now right to include the kids. As we were both emotionally and spiritually ready for coming out to them—it went very well. We were together, holding hands, when we included them. We were together and it helped the kids understand that this is our marriage, our relationship, and our love for each other. When they had been married for as many years as we had, then and only then, could they sit in judgment upon us.

>I'd also like that description of the boundaries regarding his being OUT.<

Yes indeed, wives do have a complicated array of feelings and most (for the first time in their lives) "Go into a Closet"! Most go through internal hell and have to reevaluate everything that they once believed to be true within their lives. Most deal with complete embarrassment as to why did they ever allow themselves to marry a gay man—"Am I so stupid and no good as a woman?" Most even have to dig so deep that they have to question everything (even their own sexuality and femininity), their husbands, and the world around them. They no longer even believe that they have the slightest idea as to whom they married. They even hate themselves and blame themselves for causing their husband's homosexuality. What most of us (Gay/BI) men have been struggling with all of our lives, they now get hit square over the eyes with a sledge hammer and somehow must now put their lives back together. This is a pretty daunting task!

All must deal mostly with themselves and their own insecurities and this is a very scary encounter for anyone. (Our being Gay/BI really has little to do with their own internal problems and demons.) Most take years to work though all of the confusion and frustration. Some never recover. Some never grow with the experience and forever blame everyone else, including mostly their husbands (former husbands) for their unhappiness.

Some (such as my wife) do indeed come through the experience and build for themselves a great and wonderfully supportive life (with or without their husbands). My wife, for instance, has learned to take charge of her own happiness and for the first time in her adult life is really, really happy. Yes indeed there are things about being married to a homosexual man that complicate her life and if she had a wish, she'd probably zap me "straight." She does understand that she fell in love with a homosexual man 38 years ago, has loved a homosexual man all this time and does want to continue loving a homosexual man until "death do us part." No, she had no idea that she was married to a homosexual man until I came out to her shortly after our 29th wedding anniversary. She has accepted me for exactly who I am and I do the same for her. She is a beautiful, loving, heterosexual female who also has many faults and brings difficulties into my life. By necessity, she accepts my homosexuality and I accept her faults and problems—including her horrible monthly cycles! That is who I am and that is how she is and that is who we are!

From: James

Rodney wrote: >—Wives may have as complicated feelings about their husbands' being out.<

This has been a topic of discussion at both couples gatherings and guy gatherings. But I'm not certain if we have ever discussed this online. Our wives may have as much or more concern about how "out" we are in the community as we do. Some of the wives have demanded that their husbands not be out to anyone else. My wife, for example, asked me initially not to come out within our own community because she did not want to deal with other women's pity. With time, she became comfortable with others knowing as she became stronger and self-confident about herself as well as confident about us.

From discussions at the gatherings, it seems that we men are in very different places about how out we wish to be within our family or profession, etc. In my case, I try to always check with my wife if I am interested in doing anything that might make others suspect anything. Our first trial balloon was when I wanted to take a bus to the New York Gay Pride parade 2 years ago. The bus was chartered for this purpose so we realized if I rode on it I might be coming out to those on the bus. As it turned out, the bus was filled 85% with women! . . . none of whom I knew. But this was a major step for my wife to accept. . . .

From: Stan

My wife and I have discussed some of the boundaries in detail, and I'm mildly surprised to find that they are very similar to those described by others. The first boundary is that if I'm with another guy, it will not be in our bed. The second is that my sexual encounters with other guys will be as safe as possible. The third is that I won't spend more time with him than I do with her, and that the time that I spend with her won't be just "family" time. We haven't explicitly discussed the coming-out issue, but I've always felt that I should check with her before coming out to others because every time I come out, she comes out, too.

Interestingly, we differ on the M2M emotional relationships being more threatening than the sexual ones. I've had several very close emotional relationships with other guys and this hasn't bothered her at all. The potential sexual relationship has always been much more threatening. Perhaps she feels she can compete on the emotional level, but not on the sexual? I'll have to ask her why it differs for her.

I echo the statements from others indicating that it is a very complicated subject for wives as it is for husbands. As soon I think I've understood all of her concerns, there appears a whole new slew of issues of which I hadn't thought. In addition to this, I find our emotional comfort level with discussing these topics to be very complicated and fluctuating. Sometimes we can have very detailed conversations about the how and wherefore of my potential interactions with other men without any emotional conflict at all, then at other times it seems that we can't discuss any of the issues without a heated argument.

This of course is not her fault; I'm as inconsistent as she with regard to my comfort levels with discussing the details. I have a difficult time figuring out what's an appropriate boundary to keep with regard to the amount of information I want to share. I want her to be adequately informed and well-respected, but I don't want her controlling what I do, with whom, etc., etc.

Sometimes this is a difficult balance to strike.

If others have found an easier (more consistent) way of dealing with these things, I'd very much like to know about it.

From: Andy

Good thread. Just a couple of comments. Not so much a boundary as a buffer: my wife likes me to do something else between M2M sex and being with her (so my glow will have diminished) :-). As for how out to be, she doesn't want me to leave gay community publications around where visitors might see them. In general, I am out on a need-to-know basis (and few indeed need to know). When I said to my doctor that my rash did not look like Kaposi's sarcoma, he asked if I was BI and I affirmed. When I shared an article I had written for a gay church publication about fellow bisexual married men with the pastor of the church I attend, he caught the drift and invited me to talk further with him about myself—which was open of him (though I have not felt a need to spell things out explicitly). At work at a staff meeting we were playing around with different waves, and I gave an effeminate one, which caused some laughter and friendly jibes (like everyone was going to avoid me as they left the room); kind of bold, I suppose, to parody the truth!

From: Bruce

We've had an interesting case here. A well-regarded judge dropped a bombshell several weeks ago when he came out of the closet as a gay man after 10 years of marriage and 2 children. The two separated, and in discussing it later in the press it seems to me that him being gay wasn't what caused the split, it was that circumstances forced him to do it publicly. As it is, she has still been the subject of a lot of "poor suffering wife" comments by some other political figures.

My wife and I have many of the same boundaries that many of the other couples do, but they have changed over the years. When I first came out she was really uncomfortable with the idea of me being out to anyone. Today I tend not to be out in situations where both of us are involved, like our church or the PTA. At work I'm pretty much out, and most people that are mainly my friends as opposed to family friends know. I can march in a Pride parade or take part in another public event even if it's going to be covered by the media, but try not to be where I'm going to be right in front of the camera.

I've had a somewhat similar experience with my lover too. At first neither of us was that open about me being married. The reason was the same as it was with my wife. . . . People outside the situation don't understand why he'd be willing to settle for a married man. Over time though we've gotten to the place where most of our friends know and seem to understand though.

From: James

Stan wrote: >—*The third is that I won't spend more time with him than I do with her, and that the time that I spend with her won't be just "family" time.*<

I personally feel it is very important to plan special time and special events with my wife so that she doesn't think that all special things are with a male friend. Though I did comment to her early on that I didn't want to get into a 'tit for tat' competition and asked her to plan things special for us also so that I didn't carry the total burden for "our" (meaning her and my) special time. My wife picks up very quickly (no matter how "low key" I may try to play it) when I'm excited about something coming up with a male friend.

From: Shawn

Stan's way of dealing with this complex situation sounds as thoughtful, reasonable, and balanced as any way I've heard; and perhaps even more so than some. After all, it might be simpler (but not easier) to keep everything to yourself. That's why others choose that path. You seem to balance privacy with honesty, etc., very well with your spouse. It's clearly an ongoing and complex process.

From: Henry

From my wife's point of view, my having an emotional connection with a male lover is far preferable to my having a sexual relationship without an emotional component. The context for her take on this is: the emotional connection between her and me is strong and she doesn't fear displacement;

and she knows I had lots of meaningless sex with men before we were married—she believes such relationships are dehumanizing and despicable.

From: Marlin

I think that our wives don't understand the concept of enjoying sex for it's own sake. Women seem to place sex in the context of romantic love that fits whatever frame of reference they associate with romance. To them, sex for it's own sake is cheap and trashy, and gay men might as well be whores.

I have been (fortunate?) in that just about all the men I have had sex with were friends or at least acquaintances before I had sex with them. When a close friend becomes a lover, there is an intimacy that borders upon that of a good marriage. I think that my wife would find such a relationship more threatening to her than just "buddy sex."

From: Rodney

I will risk what may be a minority opinion in this group. Though I am bisexual, rather than gay, I must confess that I find my gay encounters (which have been FOR PAY, no less!) neither cheap (!) nor trashy.

Certainly a casual sexual encounter lacks the resonance that an encounter with love CAN have, but I still "make a journey" with the guy I'm with. And a GOOD prostitute (let's call a spade a spade) can, on some level, "make the journey" with me. That's what it means to be "professional" in "the oldest profession."

I'm willing to announce to everyone on this list what a total whore I am because I think that the anti-sex conditioning that is (correctly) attributed to middle-class women raised in our culture indirectly supports homophobia. And homophobia is what we are ALL victims of in this group.

Let me restate that last sentence. Many of you think you have "victimized" your wives and children. That is simply wrong. We are ALL victims.

If it weren't for our culture's terror of sexuality, of which homophobia is merely a subclass, we would all be free to pursue our "higher" relationships (those including love) with much greater freedom and joy.

From: Gripp

I'm adding my thoughts to the survey. My wife and I have discussed my emotional attachment to a guy. (I'm still emotionally attached to my male lover even though he has now moved away and is physically out of my life.)

She prefers emotional attachment to sexual activity—she is afraid of disease, as am I.

We went to a wedding yesterday and she sat next to me. When the priest got to the place "forsaking all others, be faithful to him/her as long as you both shall live?" she admitted to being "uncomfortable" about that. We had attended a discussion on heterosexism at a recent PFLAG meeting; and she realized that the church was proposing heterosexism with this statement. That is quite a step for her to admit that and discuss it. She does still feel hurt that I have had sex anonymously with men in the past—during our marriage. She has never said anything negative about my emotional/sexual relationship with my male lover. She may be avoiding that because of my still-strong feelings for him. She still appreciates the honesty and we are dealing with issues proactively, for which I am glad.

So there! She prefers (encourages) emotional to sexual attachments and is working on heterosexism.

From: Travis

If you think of yourself as a victim, you cannot but treat the world as a victimizer; this is poison.

We are not "victims" any more than anyone else who has had ups and downs in life is.

What comes from you is pure and sacred . . . can you attest to that? . . . and if it is, how can you be a victim? . . . Who entitled "society" or "culture" to dictate your values, if not yourself? . . . Reevaluate these values and free yourself from that chain.

From: Rodney

I agree with the general principle that it is "poison" to see yourself as a victim—if you stop there and sink into self-pitying passivity (which is the image the word "victim" I suppose conjures up).

My point was more to question the notion that WE are victimizing our families, and I address this point mainly because I see posts that seem to reflect some such notion, and not infrequently.

Let me take my own case. The first obstacle I had to overcome in therapy was to get beyond the guilt that was paralyzing me. I was having horrifying nightmares, the obvious import of which was always that IF I HAD ANY LOVE FOR MY FAMILY, I WOULD FORCE THEM TO GET AWAY FROM ME. I was somehow hurting them, and (because of me) they were constantly exposed to danger.

My therapist helped me see that this was to a great extent a statement coming out of my own internalized homophobia (the phobic homo regarding whom I was, was, of course, myself).

Where did this homophobia come from? Where DOESN'T it come from? It is so deeply ingrained into our culture that we can hardly escape it. And homophobia hurts everyone, even (or maybe even particularly) straight people. It has the power to hurt to a great extent because we are not fully conscious of it. Everyone, in a sense, is a "victim" of his culture's unconsciousness, an unconsciousness he participates in. Until, of course, he becomes conscious of it! (I wish that last statement sounded a LITTLE less stupid.)

What I am trying to work through right now, for myself, is the degree to which in addressing my own personal issues and leading my own life I SHOULD or CAN work to demolish the homophobia of other people.

I hope that makes some sort of sense to someone. I certainly wasn't trying to advocate the cultivation of generalized bitterness.

From: Henry

Marlin wrote: >*Women seem to place sex in the context of romantic love that fits whatever frame of reference they associate with romance. To them, sex for it's own sake is cheap and trashy, and gay men might as well be whores.*<

Rodney commented: > *Though I am bisexual, rather than gay, I must confess that I find my gay encounters (which have been FOR PAY, no less!) neither cheap (!) nor trashy.*<

Before I was married, I spent a great deal of time and energy pursuing women, and was rarely successful at getting them into bed. At the same time, I spent virtually no time pursuing men and almost never failed to get them in bed. If women required as little courtship as men, I'm sure that straight guys would sleep with as many women as their energies permitted. I think the tendency toward casual sex has a lot to do with our gender and little to do with our sexual orientation. Incidentally, I never regretted casual encounters with men—they were often tons of fun—but they're not feasible for me any more.

From: Shawn

It's all really very simple; no matter what the sexual orientation, men are much more hot for sex than women. That's why (probably) gay and BI men are having much more sex than hetero men ever will.

From: Travis

Rodney wrote: >*My point was more to question the notion that WE are victimizing our families.*<

Perhaps "victimizing" is too strong of a word for me regarding BI/gayness, which is a natural flow surging from us; but I do agree with others—without feeling guilt for it—that we are putting our loved ones through some "paces" that are undeniably painful. And, as has been said often enough, there is no growth without pain; and pain, in this instance, comes from the revision of dead and outmoded mental structures; these are best discarded for newer ones filled with life. I admit to the pain my wife may feel from my outing, but I cannot feel guilt about it: my nature is not willed, it just is. She understands this.

The same goes for our own pain in coping with our "nature." As you rightly point out, this pain is totally derived from cultural stances. The remedy is the same for us as for our loved ones: discard outmoded mind-sets for more loving, useful ones. (I know—this is easier said than done.) But the point is, no one is going to do this for us: all challenges are painful and a new harmony takes time to evolve. I would rather live through the sweet pain I am enduring now than return to the dungeon where I dwelled before. The process is where life resides.

From: Dan

There are a lot of people on this list who are gay but are in love with their wives. Of course we do not want to intentionally HURT our wives or children, but also we do not need to beat OURSELVES up with our angst, pity, and remorse or guilt or other bad feelings.

When I was first questioning my orientation (and sanity) I went to a gay Roman Catholic priest (referred to me by Dignity) who counseled me in a marathon 3-hour session. One of his points was to: "beware of homophobia." He said that society is homophobic and that can marginalize us; but that also we ourselves are homophobic and we should beware of our OWN homophobia.

I do agree it is important to consider the feelings of our wives and children in whatever we do. What I think I am reading in many of the posts here is homophobia. And although I haven't read the BMMA list in awhile, it also used to be quite homophobic (and often the guys were downright nasty to each other.)

The second observation I have about homophobia is that to change society's opinions is up to US (at least in part). To deny or shirk this role is to guarantee the continuation of homophobia in society for our children and grandchildren. Society can, and must, learn from our example. Many think that to be gay is to be a fairy or "twinkle toes" or effeminate. If they only knew that many of us are Doctors, Lawyers (perhaps I shouldn't have listed that one), Teachers, Clergy, Priests, Engineers, Market Researchers, Editors, Statisticians, etc. in addition to the usual complement of Actors, Artists, Musicians, Hairdressers, Waiters, etc. What if society KNEW what we really are: tax-paying, child-rearing, voting, often God-fearing, upstanding members of society? Would its opinion be different?

The journey to self acceptance is not an easy one. But let me assure you what lies at the end of that rainbow is a peace and a joy and a relief!

From: Shawn

Just a brief comment on "where does homophobia come from?" I believe it comes from the same place that every other fear and prejudice comes from. They come from a low and darkened place where the light of love, acceptance, and compassion has not yet appeared. That place continues to exist because enough people have decided that they prefer the darkness of fear and hate to the light of knowledge, wisdom, and compassion. That preference is based on a lazy and selfish attitude of: "I'd rather cling to the ignorance that I know and hurt a lot of people (self included) than to grow up and go out on a limb to inquire about a higher, wider, and greater reality than the one that I know." I believe that fear and hate are choices, (infantile as they are) just as it is a choice to grow beyond one's human propensity to fear.

CELEBRATE COMING OUT TO WIVES

From: Moris

The anniversary of the day that I came out to my wife is Jan 17! Ummm . . . wonder if those who stay married celebrate the "Out" date?

From: James

Guys, the snow today may prevent my wife and me from celebrating my anniversary of coming out as we wished, but we will celebrate it at home in front of the fire with a bottle of wine nonetheless. I came out to her on January 6 (Epiphany) 3 years ago. Since we had family here until yesterday we could not celebrate it until this evening.

This anniversary has become as important if not more important to both of us than our "other" anniversary!

From: Brandon

Thank you for sharing. Interesting that my wife and I celebrate Oct 25th each year (This year will be our 10th) for the same reason. It is the renewal of our commitment to each other and our great respect for "In sickness and in health, till death do us part." This for us also includes accepting each other for exactly who we are as human beings and not as we wish the other to be!!

From: Bruce

We've celebrated my coming-out anniversary the last 3 years too in several different ways. The first year we did the traditional night on the town, and last year for number 3 we did dinner and a quiet evening at home.

My second anniversary was really special, for me at least. That weekend was the first time that my wife felt comfortable meeting the guy that I'd been telling her about for months. We met at his place, went to dinner, then to a quiet little place for drinks and to talk. The three of us had a great time, but more importantly he and my wife came away from the evening as good friends, and the relationship between he and I started to move from just dating to something a little more serious.

The date is an important one for my wife and I, since I'm sure if I hadn't come out we'd be divorced by now. It seems appropriate to include him in the celebration too, since our relationship took an important turn on that date too.

SEX WITH OUR WIVES

From: Dom

It seems like no one likes to have sex with their wives. I know this can't possibly be true, but everyone who writes seems to be in the "no more female sex" camp. I personally love having sex with my wife, and do so several times a week.

While I love playing with the bears (it's grrreat to see more fellas here identifying themselves as such), I still feel that the intimacy I have with my wife far exceeds anything I've ever experienced with a man. I'm not saying that it's not possible to have the same intimacy between 2 men (I know it is) but I personally haven't experienced it, nor do I really seek it.

I just want to fuck around (SAFELY) with a hairy bearded man on occasion. A great big friend if ya will, but I certainly don't want to give up what I have with my wife. We have an incredible sex life, an incredible life period.

I am just throwing that out there. Hoping to hear from the other side of the fence.

From: Joey

I am definitely one who would rather have sex with a man than my wife. Admittedly, we had a wonderful sex life. I have enjoyed sex with her for the last 15 years and with the women in my life that preceded her. But, the feeling I get when I am intimate with a man, well, ooo la la, it is truly indescribable. Because I am far more gay then hetero, my experience with men goes to the very core of my being. I have never felt that way with a woman. The best example I can give is when I was with my friend this weekend, we must have kissed for an hour. I was in complete ecstasy. I would have been totally impatient with kissing a woman after 10 minutes! For me, I am very lucky in that my wife comes easily. I have sought after highly sexually charged women for that reason. Frankly, I enjoy hetero sex enough so that we both can come and I have met my obligation. But, with a guy, I don't want it to end.

From: Marvin

Count me as one who enjoys FABULOUS sex with my wife! I can't imagine not loving her fully . . . and I know that if/when we ever DO stop being intimate I'm out. She won't tolerate a platonic relationship (nor should she) even though we are and always will be best friends. . . .

Having said that . . . I also should point out that I have ZERO interest in sex with any other woman! As one dear friend says, I'm "one woman short of gay."

From: Travis

Count me in this list!—my thoughts exactly!—although there are women that turn me on, I never think of acting on it; with men, on the other hand . . . but this could be a sign of starvation. . . .

I was also beginning to wonder if I was an isolated case. I could not live w/o the emotional involvement with my wife or w/o the intensity of our sex: she can match me stroke for stroke & I ain't giving that up! Sex with us had always been great, but now, after coming out, it is of an undreamt nature—I was "holding" her back!—not vice-versa. After coming out, I thought that sex with a man was more intense, but as she has uncoiled her passion, I am no longer sure.

And, for the purists (and this has been said before)—yes—sex with a woman is totally different from sex with a man. Someone in a recent e-mail here said once that these sex urges come from entirely different places in the brain. Nonetheless, to be whole, I still look to both types of love; she knows I need this, & that's where we are right now.

By the way, we just got back from a ten-day vacation, with no kids (thanks to grandparents!). We had a couple of rough days (emotionally), but these were nothing compared to the rest of those days. Alone, in constant communication, relaxing & having fun was a recipe for sheer renewal (& lots of—yes—sex).

From: Shawn

Just a quick note to let you know I have sex with my wife as often as possible and that I enjoy it tremendously (so does she!). Sex with men is just different and so exciting that I have to have it also. The question for me is how to indulge my needs while not destroying our relationship. She understands I need to be with men (left brain) but can't seem to take it emotionally (right brain). She is definitely a right-brainer so logic does not work well when we talk about this. Whence cometh our problems.

By the way, I am not a bear but sure can get it off with hairy guys!

From: Henry

I enjoy sex with my wife frequently, I fantasize about having sex with other women, and sometimes I even flirt with them. When I was younger (and unmarried), if I had a girlfriend, I'd enjoy the relationship, but after a while I'd look for a boyfriend. Then I'd get bored with men and look for a girlfriend. I think that this kind of oscillating orientation is a kind of bisexuality, so where I fit in on the gay-straight scale depends on what day you ask me. I wonder whether there are other guys like me; most seem to be in a steady state.

From: Moris

I sleep ("well, sleep afterwards!") with both my husband and wife. So I am not in the "no more female sex" camp.

From: Lou

My wife and I haven't had sex in nearly 8 years (married 20 years this week). She'd like to . . . but frankly, I'm not at all sexually attracted to her although she's a beautiful woman (if you like that sort of thing) :).

I have tried to make love to her, and can never stay hard. I don't have that problem with a male lover. My wife and I have talked openly and frankly about this (not my male lover involvement), but she knows I'm attracted to men and not women, so she's accepting it, but wishes we were intimate. At any rate, it just makes me long for the physical closeness with a man even more. . . .

From: Nathan

At the time that my wife found out that I was gay, we had been having sex maybe 4 times a year at the most. She was always too tired. Since then, we average 2 times a week. I enjoy sex with my wife and I don't have to pretend to be with another man in order to do so. But I prefer sex with men and before I was married often dreamed of settling down with another man. What this means for my marriage has yet to be worked out.

SINCE HER RETURN

From: Joey

Well, things between my wife and I have been very even-keeled since her return home. She has found the direction she needed to get her life back on track after I dropped the "Honey, I'm gay" bomb. Interestingly though, last night we had a moment that started out bad and ended good. We were watching Almodovar's latest film, "Live Flesh" (an excellent movie if you are into foreign films [Spanish]). In it, the young male lead wants to become a great lover and is befriended by an older woman who teaches him. When she is talking about what a woman wants, my wife chimed in with "See, this is what a woman wants, not what you do . . . blah, blah, blah. . . ." She continued the tease until I stopped her and snapped, "I know. I've heard this for 15 years now." The tirade stopped and we watched the movie. At one point, I realized that I was hurt. So, I turned to her and said that I did the best I could. I told her how I envied all the straight guys who had passion for women that I did not possess. How I envied being straight and how I hated not being the man for her. She sympathized with me and realized how I have not had sexual fulfillment until now. I tried to hold back the tears and she came over to me and hugged me. She admitted how awful it has been for me. We talked and agreed that we had a good sex life (and I do not think she was trying to pad my ego this time!). I think for the first time, she realized that she was not the only one who had to deal with hard issues from the untruth that existed between us. And that she was, in fact, sexually satisfied far more than I could have ever been.

Well, I am not sure I have much of a point for writing this. But, for me, I felt there was an understanding between the two of us that hadn't been there before. I guess the roles were reversed this time.

SHE WANTS DINNER WITH MY BOYFRIEND

From: Jos

My life just seems to get crazier by the day lately. Now my wife wants to go have dinner with my lover . . . JUST THE TWO OF THEM! She says it will help her to better understand the situation . . .whatever that means. I'm very uncomfortable with the entire situation. I fail to understand what possible benefit this dinner could provide except to cause more pain for all three of us. My wife and I are looking at all the options and as yet it is unknown whether we can make this marriage work. She does know that I can no longer be monogamous with her.

For those of you who don't know what's going on with me. I've come out to my wife just last month and have been involved with the same guy for about 6 months.

What should I say or do?

From: James

If you are uncomfortable with this, then I would say no. My wife has met each of the men I had a relationship with but we were always together . . . meaning all three of us. One guy came to my home for lunch after I told him that my wife wished to meet him. He was uncomfortable, and thus, so was I, but it went well.

From: Dale

I'm going to take the approach that not only should you LET your wife and your lover have dinner. . . .you should ENCOURAGE it!

It's good for your wife because the more she knows your lover the more she will see him as a person who lives, breathes, bleeds when he cuts his finger, has a personality, is vulnerable in some ways; all the things another, viable personality in the world is. The more you know someone else the harder it is to demonize them.

Besides our own experience the other "case in point" that comes to mind is a couple that we met recently.

We met the two of them in person VERY soon after his accidental disclosure a couple of years ago. His wife was having a VERY difficult time with things, yet had a lot of love and support for her husband. The two of them had a lot of history together, lots of good times, lots of "relationship capital!" She was in quite a quandary, however, and didn't like the place she found herself ONE BIT.

Last summer or fall, this guy became involved with a younger guy. Somehow his wife found it possible to know (and allow) her husband to spend a weekend with the fellow. I don't know all the incremental steps in-between, but it wasn't too long after that that she met the fellow. Once she met him she seemed to have very little trouble seeing him as a person, as someone who loved her husband but wasn't a threat to the relationship she and her husband had, and that she could (and did/does) like the guy quite a lot.

It might be good for your lover also because he may better understand the other "half" of you. He will be better able to relate to your wife as a personality rather than someone who is "hanging onto you" He may, in fact, be able to add HIS creativity and energies to helping you balance and juggle the complications of working within a triadic, mixed-orientation relationship.

It will be good for you—because if your wife and your lover are also your allies you receive energies from them both—as you give back energies to each of them, in turn. We've always found that the addition of another person's positive energies lifts the situation to a new level.

From: Mike

Interesting . . . I'd suggest you share your discomfort with your wife and maybe explore the reasons for it. How does your lover feel about it? Would she consider meeting him with you present instead of a private meeting? I agree that it is helpful for all concerned to meet each other as real people . . . when/if they are comfortable doing so. It doesn't mean everyone has to become close friends . . . once you have "pressed the flesh" so to speak (watch it guys) ;-) it is much more difficult to demonize the "other" and much more possible to empathize with the real human struggle to give and receive love unashamedly, in a culture that offers little support for those of us on the tail ends of the bell-shaped curve. Also, if your wife knows how uncomfortable you are about this—I would ask her why she feels she needs to do this now—and find out if she is willing to work through your discomfort with you and THEN possibly meet this guy when/if ALL parties consent. Just because you've finally found a way to be honest with yourself and your wife about your sexuality . . . and just because that has caused your wife (and you) some adjustment pains, does not mean you've given up your rights to boundaries and privacy. Assert yourself, man. And you might win the respect you deserve without depriving your wife of her rights in the process.

From: Gent

From someone who at times has given in to my wife's incessant questioning concerning intimate aspects of my sexual behavior, etc., I would suggest that you take it very slow and be careful insofar as you decide the degree to which you want your wife to be informed. A wife can take that which is revealed in an effort to be open and honest and then cut your throat with it and cause much pain for not only yourself but others. This is a lesson that I learned first hand several times. Be careful.

From: Bruce

If your suspicion is that your wife only wants to meet him to lambaste him for having "wronged" her then no, it's not a good idea for them to meet for dinner. I doubt if that's the case though because if that's what she wanted she'd figure out a way to contact him without you knowing about it.

It seems bizarre, I know, but I'm in a relationship with a man that we will be celebrating two years with in a couple of weeks. I arranged the first meeting between them after my lover and I had been seeing each other a couple of months, when it was clear that the relationship was going somewhere. It was the three of us that time, but after the ice had been broken I tried to keep a lower profile and let the two of them carry the conversation. Since then, the two of them have talked on the phone or seen each other without me several times.

It's easier for a long-term relationship to work if both your boyfriend and your wife have met and had a chance to talk. It made a difference to my wife meeting my boyfriend and seeing what a sweet guy he is. It helped him too to see me with my family, because he got a better idea of why all of us staying together means so much to me. Each of them understands the other one better and views them as less of a threat.

From: Jake

Some additional possibilities to consider: The wife may want to "size up" the "competition" (mine wanted to throw a birthday party for my lover). This is probably produced in part by the traditional idea imparted to her by the culture that she can "compete" and "win back her man." Wives when they first find out their husbands are gay/bi don't realize that the word "compete" doesn't really apply to such situations; it's like apples and oranges. The wife may want to meet the man to gently appeal to his sense of morals—from her point of view the lover is breaking up a family AND/OR she may come over as a very strong figure that will put up a definite and continual fight. . . . Any of these approaches could give the lover the idea that getting involved with this guy and his family may be more trouble than it's worth; there are a lot of other gay men out there without this baggage. (And of course there are those people who can work this out.)

From: Clem

Speaking (as usual, it seems) from the viewpoint of someone who's never been in a situation like this, I would apply a few principles from my understanding of how people relate in general.

First of all, I would ask your lover what HE thinks. He surely has a say in this, including a veto. He's a human being, just like you and your wife.

Has she met him before? If so, I guess I'd be less nervous. But it certainly sounds like an odd proposal for a FIRST encounter (if that's what it is), if there's no hidden agenda.

If she HASN'T met him before, I think I'd suggest that the three of you meet together FIRST. On the basis of that encounter, I think all three of you could make a smarter decision about the wisdom of having your wife and lover meet by themselves.

I agree that your wife's proposal sounds fishy. But I would let her take a private "crack" at the lover, if that's what she wants, and if you and your lover are comfortable with it. This is part of trust, and (as many on this list have commented recently), trust is a big issue for folks in our situation. I think WE need to "model" as much trust as we can!

From: Jos

Well, the dinner went well. My wife and my lover actually like each other and neither of them held back in their conversation. OH! the things they discussed . . . it ranged from her childhood to his previous relationships to whether or not he'd entertain the thought of a threesome . . . yep you heard right! (her idea) What the hell?

As well as their dinner went you'd think that maybe the roller-coaster ride would slow down right? Not on your life!

Today my wife got pissed off about the fact that my password on AOL has something to do with HIS name. OK I get it now, we can all three sleep together but heaven forbid I have his name as part of my password. That makes complete sense, silly me what was I thinking? (Stop laughing.)

We had a counseling appt. today, it was going pretty well until at the last second of the session she asks me "If you had to make a decision this moment, and you have to choose between being completely monogamous to me or to end the marriage, what would it be?" I said "I love you and I'll miss you." Let's just say that answer hurt her like hell and I knew that and felt terrible but it was honest.

OH! and the names she had for me today, holy shit! (After the counseling session.) I understand the anger but . . . this isn't what I would have chosen for my life either and I won't (can't) be completely degraded. Fifteen minutes later she calls my office and says she's sorry and that I don't have to move out. YEH! Lucky me.

OK. OK. Enough rambling! I'm sure plenty of you have been through this but it helps to just vent. Thanks for listening.

THOUGHTS AFTER A DIFFICULT WEEKEND

From: Shorty

My thoughts after a particularly difficult weekend . . . I do have fears, like all of us here, and this past weekend has been particularly hard on both my wife and I.

I hear so many here on the list who are trying to make it work. I am starting to wonder now if I am "fence sitting," and if I can make the marriage work or if it is me just trying to hold on to a safety net in this time of radical change. After a heart to heart on Saturday (one we should have had years ago), and many tears, I woke Sunday morning thinking, "Wait, did I just do a sell job to keep the marriage together (let's see if we can work this out . . .), or am I trying to hold on to this marriage because of my own fears of moving forward (a safety net to venture from), or do I want to make this work . . . do I want to stay with my wife? Do I want or can I remain in this lifestyle?"

I'm at the point of thinking, "how can I expect my wife to continue with me, and not grow and develop on her own, for her own personal development, growth, and happiness? Am I just being selfish, having my cake and eating it too, and not letting her move on?

Ha!, and add to all of that, I ended a cyber relationship yesterday, which was really hard . . . first time I have ever made a decision and pushed someone away in my life. Well, maybe I am finally reaching some point of personal growth, and strength within myself. To be a real person who is at one with himself, and can be happy with that. I have a long bumpy road to ride . . . but that is my journey in life, and I am beginning to accept that. I have a choice, to be unhappy and repressed, or take chances, and grow, and flower.

From: Dern

I hear you loud and clear. I have the same thoughts at times. I do have children but I think it has always been the family as a whole not just the kids and not just the wife. I feel my wife and I will know the day, if it comes, when it is over, when the good times will not outweigh the bad.

From: Floyd

You really focused on some hot buttons, some thoughts I've had, too, in my case as a 55 years old with a wife and children who are loving and supportive but troubled by my recently revealed bisexuality. Certainly having children makes for a stronger case to stay together and I wonder, as they grow older and are now fairly independent, am I holding on to an ideal of a family that is no longer relevant. And having a long history—in our case 28 years—is another factor; and I wonder if that, too, is history, an ideal, that shouldn't necessarily be supported any longer. So far, in both cases, I believe that neither is just an ideal, both are reasons to remain together; they are an investment worth maintaining in the future. Splitting would kill something that is of daily importance to me. I also believe that we are in a transition period that may result in my deciding otherwise.

We're trying to reconstruct our relationship because I believe that the essence of what we have is worth preserving. I also believe the essence of what we have may permit us to do that, to grow into a new relationship (or a relationship with a rebuilt but not entirely new foundation), and a relationship that supports my wife, as well as me, in new growth and development. It's certainly not going to be a "straight" lifestyle. I hope it will accommodate my needs for deep emotional relationships with men (I think the emotional attachment with a man/men is as threatening to my wife as sexual relations) and I hope it accommodates her needs for independent relations and a more individualized life as well.

OUR AGREEMENT

From: Clem

I must admit, I've pretty much been a lurker, but I've really appreciated reading the posts to the list so far. As so many have said before me, "It's nice to know you're not alone."

Although I only came out to my wife four months ago, we've talked quite a bit and are beginning discuss . . . well, I'll call them accommodations. I started seeing a therapist last fall, which was the catalyst for me coming out to my wife. Since then we've been seeing the therapist jointly and these sessions have been invaluable in keeping our discussions going.

Over this time we've forged a couple agreements. The first of which was a document that we both signed. It basically stated that as long as she accepted this side of me that I would never leave her and would support her. I also actually amended the opening of this agreement, which originally started out "No matter what . . ."

The second agreement was sort of a "Not in my house/Don't ask, Don't tell" kind of rule. I would only have contacts while traveling on business, which I will be doing extensively soon. And would also not engage in any "Internet affairs" except when out of the house. (This group is acceptable by the way.) Also, this is not going to be a topic of discussion between us, although I did offer that I would answer all questions. However, I told her to be sure she really wanted to know the answer. Thank you brothers for that piece of advice!

So, that's what we worked out. I can tell that my wife is still very uncomfortable with this, but she's also said that she still thinks there's a lot of good things about me and is basically willing to endure it. Comments, insights, questions? Thanks for listening.

From: Bruce

My wife and I started out with a series of agreements that sound a lot like the ones that you have with your wife. They suited us perfectly then, but over time things changed for both of us. I still intend to remain with her, but my orientation isn't something that we deal with by avoiding any longer.

Eighteen months ago I met a very special guy who I'm still with, and while that concerned her some at first, she ended up realizing that my male lover was very good for me and no threat to her. I come home when I go out for the evening, but she is now open to the idea of me spending the weekend with him on a regular basis. She ended up forming a friendship with him and going out of her way to include him in family events. None of these were things I could have even imagined years ago when I came out to her.

In short, I wouldn't worry about what will happen in a couple of years, because both of you will no doubt change in that amount of time. As long as you two are honest about your feelings, you're a long way toward working things out.

From: Daniel

I am about a year ahead of you but your situation and mine are not too different.

My wife and I also have some sort of signed agreement put together when I was deeply involved with another guy, which was mainly to safeguard the interests of my wife and the children in case I became "unstable." In my view it was not worth the paper it was written on but it gave her a little comfort at the time.

When it comes to rules, we also practice the never at home rule, and, in fact, I have never ever entertained someone in my own house. I, like you, travel a lot, and I meet up with friends along the way, mostly as a result of getting to know them through the Internet. But I also have a regular boyfriend who lives locally and whom I visit when I am at home. That is acceptable to my wife though I try to meet him discreetly when she is out at work or otherwise occupied. This seems to work. So, I guess the answer is to find a gay friend locally, and hope that he can accommodate you.

From: Woody

My wife and I worked out a similar agreement to the one you've written about, though we didn't put it into writing. I've found out we certainly didn't need to, because the female of the species has a mind like a tape recorder. Every single detail is engraved in stone, she feels. If I deviate just a little (well, that's the way it seems to me, but I'm the gay partner), the pertinent detail of the agreement is resurrected immediately. And always with a "we agreed" . . . where all the agreement was on my part, and the details were dictated by her. Just beware...in six or seven years, your wife may still feel the agreement must stand as written, when you and she may have moved on quite a bit.

I do have one leverage factor. My wife, now in her 50s, fears more of being abandoned at this stage in her life than I fear the consequences of moving out on my own. Eventually I usually win these minor tiffs, but at the price of some bitterness.

I've already decided to begin to do what you are doing now, travel . . . I will do this as a way of both working my way toward retirement AND being able to play "away" more (which is what I must do most of the time), as per agreement.

From: Clem

A couple of months ago I was pretty sure my wife and I were going to divorce, because she had a need for me to remain homosexually abstinent AND there were also a lot of nonsexual issues in our marriage—there still are.

My wife's behavior is very peculiar in many ways. But I am glad I listened to those guys on the list who encouraged me to "hang in there," NOT because I am now sure my marriage will survive (I still have strong doubts) OR because my wife is a pleasure to live with (she's far from being that), but because I think my wife and I have started to learn a lot about ourselves and each other in this (admittedly awful) period.

Though I still have serious doubts about the marriage, I'm beginning to think my wife and I are starting to be FRIENDS again after years of gradual alienation from one another. And things between myself, my wife, and our adult children are starting to assume new "adult" dimensions.

If you can follow the advice and "ride this period out a bit," you may find that your exercise of patience has a payoff. Maybe you'll even find yourself in the blessed state of some of the men on this list who have transformed their marriages into something that truly accommodates their sexuality.

But boy do you have my sympathy! I've been there. By the way, "being patient" does NOT include accepting her "take" on the situation or agreeing to ultimatums or one-sided contracts or any of that other bullshit. You are probably in a position to be the more adult person in the couple.

2 STEPS FORWARD, 1.9 BACK

From: Trevor

Last week she returned from the therapist and told me that she was beginning to understand that this "need" or "desire" that I had was not necessarily in conflict with my love for her and that she shouldn't try to compare them. We also discussed the ups and downs of emotional feelings that we have and will go through as we deal with this. I was feeling good.

Last night she tells me that she doesn't feel that I'm her friend anymore, that she's lost me. This hit me pretty hard. We then also began discussing the intimacy level of the relationships I would be having. She asked why I couldn't just do what I needed to do and not even talk to the other person. I didn't know what to say. I tried to explain that I would be having a relationship, but I would also tell this hypothetical person what my situation was from the beginning so he wouldn't get false expectations.

I think the real crux of the issue for her is a fear that I will fall in love with someone and leave her. What can I say or do to convince her that I won't leave her and that I still am her friend? Also any advice on staying out of the trap of discussing a relationship that doesn't exist?

From: Clem

I agree with you that this is probably her central fear. This fear is based on the assumption (very common among women) that you are more apt to fall in love with a person if you are having sex with this person.

Try to help her understand, first, that love and sex are not as intimately related for men (in general) as they are for women. She will need some help believing this (it would help if her therapist were a man). But you might point out that it is NOT a stereotype of the gay (or for that matter, the straight) male sexual experience that men fall in love after having sex. Quite to the contrary. If you are not looking for someone else to love, be sure she knows this. But you need to paint an honest picture. If you're NOT looking for a genuinely romantic (as opposed to a friendly) relationship with a man, she may eventually come to a point where she's comfortable with what you're doing. If her fear that you're looking for LOVE is well-grounded, well of course that's a different story. You need to be clear about your own expectations and motives.

From: James

I think the truth is that our wives are CORRECT to worry about our falling in love with a man. It is very difficult, if not impossible, for some of us (we romantic types especially) to prevent falling in love with another guy. I know it is really easy for me . . . sometimes I think I fall for about every third guy I meet <G> . . . but telling yourself (and your wife) what was suggested may or may not be realistic (from my perspective). We are vulnerable to falling in love. . . .

For me personally, it has worked best to admit this to my wife (hell, she brought it to my attention before I even admitted to myself how vulnerable I am to falling in love) but learn to live with this reality. And I mean I have learned to live with the fact that I may love some guy but am not leaving my wife for a relationship with him.

From: Trevor

You doubtless noticed my hedging. The hedging is due to my reading all these posts from the "romantic" types on the list (like you) who clearly ARE interested in love, despite what the stereotypes about men tell us. Such posts have been a real eye-opener to me. Now, I have not myself looked for love in my M2M relationships, but this may be, frankly, more a reflection of my lack of imagination than anything else (I just can't PICTURE it!). But out of morbid curiosity, let me ask you this: do you think that you are more apt to fall in love with a guy after having sex with him? Or does your romantic engine keep purring along even when your pants are up? The fear for women, specifically, is I think this sex→love connection. Is THAT fear well founded?

From: James

The "romantic engine" seems to function well in both circumstances (sigh). Do you have a remedy? <G>

From: Dern

Makes a lot of sense to me. For me I want a man to be in my everyday life. I need and want more than a fun time with an acquaintance. I want a "husbear" to grow old with and to share my life with wife and family with. I too will not have a man that won't accept the realities in my life. My wife and the kids are as much a part of me as my gay identity.

From: Marvin

BINGO! Speaks perfectly to the (societally imposed in many cases) assumption that each of us can only love one other at a time. . . . Why place the limits on our love?

From: Floyd

Interesting discussion; my wife and I are exploring the same avenues. One thing I wonder is, do you know you'll never leave her? It's impossible to say but the good news is that's always been a possibility and you've not left her yet, and that you intend never to leave her. Sounds like her insecurity is coming to the surface—naturally enough since you're talking about having intimacy with someone else which, for women, means the "ultimate" and which means a long-term relationship.

We're at the point, too, where it's meaningless to speak of hypothetical relationships. We're going back and forth now, and haven't resolved it yet. Should we discuss details of these relationships at all? Should we proceed with my having intimate relationships with her knowledge (maybe not all the details) so she can experience that, and decide from reality how it feels, whether she can take it?

From: Scott

I decided to reply to this post, because I fell in love with another guy. Things did not work out the way I would have liked. You all (excluding new members) have heard me speak of my boyfriend. He was and is still in my heart. I still and seems that I will always love him. I was with him only once, but knew I loved him way before then. What I feel for him is much more than sexual. I don't get to talk to him much anymore, just an e-mail every once and a while. Falling in love with another guy while you are married surely makes things more complicated than just having a sexual partner. The love I have for him completely fills my mind and my heart. It makes it harder at home to maintain an everyday life when my every thought is of another love. My relationship with my boyfriend has left me brokenhearted and un-wanting of another man in my life. Although my situation didn't turn out as I would have liked it, falling in love with another man is a wonderful and beautiful thing.

From: Miles

I guess that the only way my wife was ever able to make this work for her was the "don't ask/don't tell" approach. While not ideal, it works for her. She knows I am not about to go off and fall in love with another guy because it hasn't happened yet! Could it happen? Of course, it could happen to any of us, and if I were not so busy with work maybe it would happen to me. But if we envision our marriage as our primary emotional relationship and the linkage with another man as a secondary emotional relationship (or just a simply physical relationship), it can work. The only thing you can probably do to convince her is to continue to reinforce the emotional aspects of your existing relationship, and to explain to her that other men have made this work.

I agree that our narrow-minded society wants to insist that we can have only "one" emotional relationship, and some of us know that we are capable of maintaining more. The singular relationship limitation is not based on anything other than tradition, I suspect, but the sad fact is that most women not only cherish this notion, they really need it. Jealousy is a factor for some folks, let's face it, and not for others. So each of us is different in that regard.

Keep the dialog open with her. Keep talking it out, and do nothing in haste.

From: Conrad

We find the concept of "I'd never leave" doesn't get us anywhere. If we've learned anything, it is that things change. We try to focus on two alternatives. First, to build the trust and reliability and desire to meet the other's needs. Build the safety and love to let the risk of "what if" fade into the background. Second, we've come to really focus on the risk of not allowing the gay side into our lives. We're pretty convinced that the only alternatives (for us) are staying together miserably, with me angry and depressed, or the two of us separating, which neither wants. It's less risky to keep working on the range in the middle. Of course, there may be a time to give up and move on.

From: Marvin

This all brings back SO many memories of discussions early on in my coming-out process . . . some of the discussions still going on! We've had many lengthy discussions over the years as to whether she'd prefer me to have (a) one long term committed lover or (b) a series of (or concurrent) casual boyfriends. She's still not sure which she prefers . . . she sees risks to her (and me) in both scenarios.

The one thing that I promised my wife—years ago—and still live by is that I'll never leave her FOR SOMEONE ELSE—if I ever leave it will be because it's what right FOR ME. One of the greatest fears she's always faced (do I sense a trend here?) is that I'd fall in love with someone and leave . . . for her (unlike me) it isn't possible to love more than one person at a time. . . .

She felt ultimately more secure when I was involved in a four-year deep relationship a few years ago—I've told her since then if I didn't leave her to be with this man, chances are I'm not going to leave her to be with anyone—and I didn't "leave."

From: Bruce

Trevor wrote: >*What can I say or do to convince her that I won't leave her and that I still am her friend?*<

I don't know if there is anything that will convince her other than time. I had an experience in the past where a man that I was seeing broke up with me because he couldn't handle the situation. I don't think that my wife really believed that I wouldn't leave her for him until it came to the point where I had to make the decision and chose not to leave her. Looking back, while I was sure I loved him, I made the right decision.

When I met my male friend and started seeing him I'm sure that she felt some of the same uneasiness, but it was easier for both of us. Her acceptance came over time when she began to know him better and realize that he wasn't the type that was trying to get me away from her. I had told her that from the beginning, but it took her getting to know him and seeing how the relationship progressed for her to start believing it.

From: Trevor

Thanks again for the input on my situation. However, in subsequent conversations with my wife, I've found out that I've misread her feelings. Imagine that, a man misinterpreting a woman!!

I asked her again what her biggest, deepest fear/problem was with this whole situation. It wasn't that I would fall in love with someone and leave. She doesn't think I will. It's still the issue that she can't understand how the idea of sex with a person that I don't even know yet, and someone I'm not planning to commit to is more important than my love for her. She realizes intellectually (according to her/our conversations with the therapist) that they are two different things for me and she shouldn't try to hold them in comparison, but she still can't get past it emotionally. What is the key for her to understand or accept this?

I also got lambasted last night for not doing enough to help her deal with this issue. Although I've suggested the SOTTS list and a local support group, she has declined. I then proceeded to chide her, probably much too emphatically, about not trying to help herself enough through this situation. I was actually pretty pissed.

From: Clark

I am beginning to understand that there are just two humans on this planet, and only one story between them. I'll swear, everybody has the same story. This is RIGHT OUT of my wife's mouth: "How can you go for the unknown instead of me?" I keep protesting that that is not the way I am looking at it at all. Is this funny or tragic or both?

From: Marvin

IN general (and I hate to generalize) women have more trouble divorcing sex from love than men do. . . . As to why it's more important than your love for her . . . is it? Perhaps explain to her that it's NOT about what you do with your dick (sorry to be crass) but about WHO YOU ARE, a common misconception (damn . . . here I go generalizing again) amongst the str8 world is that homosexual feelings/identity/love are all about SEX, and that's only a small part of it—it's about WHO WE ARE—people need to quit focusing on what we do (or what they imagine we do). I think I was finally able to get this point across to my wife when I pointed out to her that if we were out for the evening with our closest str8 friends she didn't concern herself with what they may or may not do in their bedroom, so WHY the focus on what two men (or two women) do?

From: Clark

I am beginning to see the depth of social convention in all this. Allowing that social conventions come about because we need to protect ourselves, the point is even more poignant: monogamy has to do more with fear than with love. I don't begrudge anyone's being monogamous, and I suspect no one here does. It is just that monogamy doesn't quite cover the subject, does it? I happened to run across Bertrand Russell's Essays entitled, "Why I am Not a Christian" this morning. Read the essay on sexual ethics, written about 1936. It expresses the point quite well.

And, by the way, the reasons that Bertrand Russell was not a Christian are the same reasons, by and large, that I have a hard time being one. In other words, the God he doesn't believe in is the one I don't believe in either. The God I know is far larger than things like social conventions.

From: Daniel

It is perhaps far less misleading for us to call ourselves "men who have sex with men," "men who have sex with women," or "men who have sex with both men and women" rather than to brand ourselves as "gays," "straights," or "bisexuals"—all of which conjure up stereotypical images, that are often quite misleading. We are what we are, and I for one am glad that I am what I am! But it took forty-odd years to come to terms with it!

From: Clem

I agree with you about stereotypes and one-word labels. I also continue to puzzle about why sex is an identity issue, or why gender preference is so central. Why not call ourselves (as appropriate) "men who like oral sex" or "men who like butt play but not serious penetration, whether from men or women" or "men who like to lick feet" or "men who like to screw women who are straddling them and wearing bras" and so on. The answer to this question ultimately has to do with what our culture REJECTS. If we like something that is not "socially approved," then liking it becomes an identity issue, I guess. I'm surprised no one has come up with "pro-sex" as an identity label, because when you get down to it, an awful lot of homophobia is just specialized sex fear.

From: Amity P. Buxton <dir@ssnetwk.org

Interesting point. In my experience with these matters, it seems that we need backing for what is "different" until the point where our integrity is more important than culture or the "identity community.

From: Conrad

I agree about labels, but just as we have to end the simplistic labels like gay or straight, most of us probably would have to expand your description as well. For example, your schema might have described me as "a Man who has sex with both women and men." True enough, but incredibly simplistic as a description of who I am. . . .

I am a man who has (very little) sex with only one woman (provided she is my wife) and having a deeply emotional and intimate connection with her. In addition, I am always thinking about having sex with every man I pass on the street—but only actually having had sex with other men who have similar feelings, history, and approaches to sex with women and are also capable of having a not-too-intimate and emotional physical connection with a man also only one at a time—while fitting it into a ridiculous schedule of work, spouse, and kids, including hitting the right times to have the right amount of sexual, emotional, and spiritual connection, considering the same swings in the spouse, lover, and spouse of the lover. . . .

You get the idea. Seriously though, I find it very convenient to call myself gay, simply as "not straight." The real description just takes too long to work into a conversation. . . .

From: Andy

What a long and wonderful thread :-). I resonate with a lot you say in this and prior posts. The desire for monogamy is based on a need for security, for boundaries, for walls—much more than on love—perhaps because women (who champion monogamy more than men) have had less power, have been more home-bound, value marriage more, have more of their identity wrapped up in having a successful marriage. Interestingly enough, women have fewer children when they have an opportunity to work outside the home and to develop an identity other than full-time, life-long mother (so that redefining womanhood may be a key ingredient in curbing overpopulation). As for our seeking the unknown, this can be thrilling; my wife tells me that my potential beaux have an advantage since there is novelty there while she is "old shoe." Loving several fellows in different ways because they are different people who evoke different responses from me: yes! And the stupid linking of the divine with the conventional, Yuck! There are so many bad ideas of God out there—with plenty of backing. The distinction between normal and deviant could just as well be construed as a distinction between conventional and creative. I draw attention to Socrates, Jesus, and Joan of Arc as people who were condemned in their own time and canonized later as "different in a good way." Friend Jesus was surely plenty unconventional and even anticonventional—which is one of the reasons I like looking for God in his direction.

From: Clark

You have replaced Reinhold Niebuhr as my favorite theologian of all time, second only to Gregory of Nyssa. (And there is more truth to this than flippancy.)

RELIEF

From: Nick

Well, guys, I told my wife last night about joining this group and about my idea to start a live—in-person!—group. It precipitated a rather long discussion about where our marriage is going, and although my wife is hurting, I feel much better (that sounds terrible, doesn't it?). Even light and airy today! I don't want to cause her pain, but I also know that our marriage can't continue like it has been. Two years of anger/depression may finally be lifting. And I'm thinking that this group is a great way to reconnect with the gay/BI/questioning community and gain some friendship with men in similar situations. Whether this all leads to an open marriage, or the end of the marriage, we'll see. But at least there is m-o-v-e-m-e-n-t. Amazing what a computer, a phone line, and a bunch of great guys can do.

And I do have one word of advice for those of you who are just revealing to your wives: when opening up to her, don't underplay the intensity or significance of your attraction to men. When my wife and I were first dating 4 years ago, we discussed my bisexuality. But because I was falling in love with her and we were having great sex, and I hadn't had a relationship with a man in years, I think I let myself just gloss over much of the issue. As a result, she didn't think it was a very important part of my identity, and that's clearly a wrong impression.

Now she says had she known how significant my attraction to men was, she might have opted not to marry. Now she feels a bit deceived. And you know what? She's right.

From: Clem

Sounds like you're making progress! That's great! (I'm green with envy.)

Your advice about not misrepresenting your sexuality to a prospective wife is excellent advice. But as your post suggests, the problem for a (dare I use the word?) bisexual is that typically you don't YOURSELF fully understand your sexuality when you are busy falling in love with a woman—esp.

if you have not recently had sex with a man (or, as in my case when I was falling in love with my wife and have NEVER had sex with a man).

As usual, the core problem turns out to be generalized cultural homophobia coupled with our American desire to see things in sharp outline, preferably in black and white.

In sum, I doubt that your wife-to-be was much more deceived than you were.

From: Jim

A couple of weeks ago I joined looking for support and understanding. Since joining I have read some inspirational e-mails enabling me to come to terms with my BI sexual feelings. This past weekend I was able to sit down with my wife and explain to her how I have been feeling inside. I explained to her that I was BI sexual and had feelings for guys. I told her that in no way does this change how I feel for her and that I love her and my two sons very much and assured her that I would never leave her. She felt great pain but accepted that I was BI sexual. We are committed to keep our marriage together. In fact since I have told her our sex life has never been better, so far! I can totally open up to her without feeling guilt inside and able to show her how much I do love her. She is o.k. with the fact that I need to talk to other men about my situation and that I would let her know when I decided if I met the right person to have a relationship with so she could express her concerns. I am committed to keep an open dialog with her and to hold her in my arms until her grief if gone.

I don't think that I could have come out to her with out all your support and hugs. I truly am grateful for all who have touched my life to give me the strength to open up to her. Thanks again and I will keep you updated as things progress.

COUNSELING FINALLY

From: Phil

First I want to thank all of you who gave me the fine advice on how to find a counselor/therapist.

I found one through the local Gay and Lesbian Center; he is gay; he also does couples, if we are ready for that in the future.

I want to share with you the interesting question I was asked to ponder: "If you could solve all your problems, what would the situation look like?" I couldn't immediately answer that; can anyone? One thing is certain, once the toothpaste is out of the tube, you can't put it back in.

From: Rodney

This is a very interesting question. I think I COULD answer (have, in fact, already answered, for my wife's edification) the question, "What do I want?" I'm still waiting for my wife to tell me what SHE wants, in order to see if we can work something out. It's hard to answer the whole question about what the ideal situation would look like until I hear from her.

(What I want, is everything just the way it was, with one exception: I would be able to have sex with men without hiding the fact from my wife; I would practice scrupulously safe sex; but I want to continue having sex and a married life with my wife. What I HAVEN'T emphasized with her, because it's nothing new, is that, even more importantly for me, I want her to stop being angry all the time—at me, at our youngest, at the people at her work, at the world in general. This is a much bigger issue, in my mind, than my sexuality.)

From: Rodney

It still takes an amazing amount of effort for me to remember that the "sexual problems" in my life would simply vanish if my wife felt differently about my sexuality. As it is (because I want to save my marriage and because I can't directly change her feelings), I keep working on accommodations and compromises. When I'm in this mode, it's easy to forget that my sexuality isn't really the problem. I'm sure I'm not the only one who has had a Significant Other start talking about my sexuality in 12-Step terms ("First, I admitted I was powerless over my sexuality . . ."). I've even found myself going along with this for a while before I realized I needed to slam on the brakes, and say, "Wait a minute! I never agreed that my homosexuality was a Disease!"

WIFE REFUSES COUNSELING

From: Dan

Like the wives of several (many?) of you here, my wife also REFUSED to go to counseling . . . either jointly or singly. . . .To me, that signaled the DEATH bell for our marriage. Although we still have care and concern for each other, we really do not love each other. . . . For a marriage to stay together, it takes both parties working HARD for IT . . . if only one makes all the sacrifices it may stay afloat for a little while, but it may be somewhat awkward and 'atilt' . . . eventually the hole in the bottom (of the boat that is, you thought I meant something else ? <grin>) will let in enough water (and other emotional debris) to sink the operation, and down you go.

If she does NOT CARE enough to seek counseling, then methinks she does not really care enough to save our marriage . . . or she selfishly wants everything on her terms. . . .

My wife said my being m2m oriented was what shut down our marriage. I say yes that's a factor, but there are also other things going on. To her, being gay or BI is a disease, a sickness, and also a sin against nature.

I suspect that you can imagine that I am not thrilled to be around such a judgmental self-righteous person. So I avoid the conflict, and spend as little time with her as possible. Unfortunately that also limits my time with my kids.

Having said that we have much to be thankful for. We have our health. and we do care for each other.

One of the things I'm thankful for is all you other guys on the list and this opportunity to share our life stories!

From: Schuyler

My wife has also steadfastly refused (couples) counseling, or to consciously connect with other straight spouses. Nine months following my open (very compartmentalized, clearly secondary) relationship with another married man, however, I can no longer state that she neither cares about the relationship nor that she is inflexible. My wife had some very negative experiences with a counselor that we used for couples counseling several years ago (NOT related to the gay/BI issue). I also only recently learned that she feels like I "dominate" these type of sessions.

Over the nine-month period, things HAVE improved somewhat, although I would still characterize the relationship as very shaky. Any improvement is due more, I believe, to the following facts, which have played out over time:

1. I have not abandoned either her or the family, and have not made the "gay" issue the center of my life (neither do I deny my sexuality and I am out to my kids).
2. Whereas I don't lie about my "boyfriend" or the fact that I see him regularly, neither do I "advertise" the fact. I have learned that, at least for now, the preferred approach is "don't ask, don't tell." This is clearly made easier by the fact that I have chosen a relationship with another married man in a STRONG committed relationship, and that we have the option of meeting (primarily) during working hours.
3. I continue to tell her that I love and value her.

4. As I have become more accepting of my sexuality, more versed in the experience of male intimacy, and heartened by the positive role models of so many of my brothers, I have found that my commitment to the marriage relationship has actually increased over this nine-month period. As I am made more "whole" by these experiences I previously denied myself through fear and shame, I am able to better appreciate the (very different) value, strength, and commitment of my life partner. Although I have not expressed this DIRECTLY to my wife in these terms (much of which I don't think she wants to hear), I can't help but think that she is experiencing some of this in terms of my relative (to the pre-boyfriend depression) happiness and stability.

All this being said, I cannot, in good conscience, say that we are a mixed-orientation couple "success." There are SERIOUS issues that separate us, and our lives together may not last after the last child leaves home. All I am saying is that I no longer have any clear picture as to what my wife should or should not do, particularly as this concerns counseling or connection with other people in similar circumstances. I believe that my willingness to give up any notion of how my wife should act or process the changes that I have unilaterally made in our marriage contract is more or less directly related to the likelihood for survival of the relationship.

From: Andy

Perhaps your wife should seek a counselor better suited to herself, going on her own at first, later dealing with your domination in the therapeutic process itself. However, there is also something to be said for your letting your relationship with your wife develop over time, to humor her denial, to give her reassurances, to keep your gay life a minor obbligato, to present her with a self which is more whole and happy. As the rappers might put it, "You can lead a ho to water but you can't make her drink <G>."

From: Lobo

Why haven't you told your wife that you value her and that you appreciate her strength and commitment? Are you still interested in couple's therapy with your wife? If so, she might be able to find a therapist she would like. She could talk to a prospective counselor alone and then decide, on the basis of rapport, whether or not to continue as a couple.

Then if counseling is resumed, you could check out the domination issue by observing yourself in a session and learning how the therapist views your interactions. You could also try talking less in a session to see if this changes your wife's participation.

This raises the question, has your wife felt dominated by you in other areas of your life together? If so, how does she respond to this. What is her method of dealing with the "oppressor"?

From: Rodney

This is a tough one for me, too, because I think couples therapy would be very helpful for myself and my wife. But as some other members of this group of gay and BI men have pointed out—you really can't hope to accomplish much by FORCING another person into therapy.

I think I hear in your comments an echo of my own special concern: at this point, I wish my wife were in a certain kind of therapy that would help her deal with some of her OWN issues that are larger than our marriage. If our marriage didn't survive my coming out, I would feel pretty much OK if my wife and I parted friends, and I would feel MORE than OK if I felt she came out of it all a happier person.

We all want our marriages to work out, but I think we need to keep reminding ourselves that there are issues that may be even more important than the survival of the marriage itself. Marriage CAN actually stand in the way of "growing up." I, at least, think it's time for my wife and I to grow up. Well, now I'm starting to ramble and rant.

From: Lee

Rodney wrote: >*I would feel MORE than OK if I felt she came out of it all a happier person.*<

This has been my goal all along this journey. I came out totally to my wife about all my activity and my current love interest several months ago. It was shocking to say the least. She has eventually accepted all and continues to want to work on keeping our marriage together. She has met my lover and has invited him into our home for dinner. We all get along and they are currently becoming good friends. I did not expect this at all. It just happened. So be patient. You have no idea how your wife will take all of this as time allows her to digest it all.

From: Andy

I had three counselors, third one was the charm! I set up the first counselor to help ease the pain for my wife as I was preparing to leave her (as I thought I would have to once I disclosed my alleged orientation and secret involvement). Well, my wife wanted to keep me anyway (to my surprise) :-) and it turns out that I'm BI more than gay. My first counselor never made the switch to the new state of affairs and my wife resented him (probably unfairly) because he was allied in her mind with the effort to ditch her. Second counselor, just for me, was gay, but that was rather irrelevant; he had little understanding of bisexuality (at least he let stand the notion that bisexuality did not exist in a support group he ran, according to a friend), seemed distant; we never clicked. The third counselor is someone my wife came up with—recommended by a friend. She took the position that we could make our marriage work if my M2M involvement were allowed but limited—something which has worked for us. The moral of the story? Perhaps it is that if the counselor you start with does not work well for both of you (after a reasonable try), try another!

From: Marvin

It is strange for a counselor to take ANY position!

We were lucky . . . immediately after coming out, we saw a counselor, jointly and individually (first time either of us had seen a counselor for anything) to help us deal with things . . . in our search for one I checked two sources: (1) a local G/L referral line and (2) a personal friend of mine, a counselor, who happens to be a lesbian.

They both offered several options . . . and the counselor we chose was on both "referral" lists. . . .

We also (my wife and I) had LONG conversations about WHO to choose as a counselor. I didn't particularly want a str8 man . . . she didn't want a gay man . . . neither of us particularly wanted a lesbian (we felt that any of the above would potentially create issues with understanding, acceptance, and overcoming biases) so we decided on a straight woman. Turned out to be a PERFECT choice for us . . . she helped us to frame our issues, keep the discussions on topic and heading forward, and NEVER offered opinions or options on her own, instead helping to direct conversation so we could explore options/alternatives on our own. . . . We saw her for about 9 months . . . and to this day I consider her to be one of the most special people I've ever met.

From: Walter

A professor of mine once said two things that I have always carried with me:

1. There is no growth without pain.
2. In any creation of beauty, there is some sort of destruction first.

Growth, at any time, is uncomfortable. However, the rewards are well worth the effort.

From: Joel

I would like to give my appreciation to this net and all of you guys that make this net, after all you guys are this net. Many thanks for all you have done for me directly or indirectly. In one week's time I was at the end of the world. Tired of living lies and not being open. Hiding my feelings from my wife. I had enough of cheating myself let alone my wife.

First step, I told my wife I am tired and need to change by coming out. Second step to was to get some professional help. I am still screening and trying to make initial contact with some therapist. Third step was to join this list. Best thing that happened to me. Fourth step was to continue the line of communication with my wife and tell her how much I do love her. Fifth step was to let go of our marriage, if that was where the pieces where bound to fall. I had to for my survival as a person. I had to ask myself what I wanted and my wife what she wanted.

There was no way that she was going to stay with me I knew deep inside of myself. She told me Friday night that she was not going to do any type of open marriage. It is not her, with the type of morals and family values she has. She is very conservative. We fell into a silence from Friday night and all day Saturday. Saturday evening I reinforced I did love her while she read more and more on the subject of gay men and straight women, "Uncommon Lives." She did start talking with anger, hate, belittlement. It was a communication line again all and all.

To my surprise she agreed to stay together and give it a try. We may not save our marriage but it is a effort to try and save it. I know we have to work a lot of sharp corners out, but it is a beginning.

I felt sad and hurt when I made a decision to come out but at the same time I felt a rebirth, which made me feel good. When she agreed to some form of open marriage I have that same ecstatic feeling last night and today.

Many thanks to ALL of you who were in communication with me directly and those of you who were posting as I have been reading all your letters.

MARRIAGE IN CRISIS

From: Gaard

The time has come for Gaard to post. Right now as I write this I feel my marriage is in crisis. So many people have told me that the life Laura and I have built together will ultimately come to and end. How much I want to prove them all wrong. I am crying and a mess as I write this. Please bear with me as these words are not premeditated, rather they are coming from a very hurting heart.

I do not know where to start so here goes. As most of you know I came out to my wife last spring. I was at the point of breakdown when it all started. So much hurt, confusion, pain, uncertainty, lust, denial, all compounded in my heart. I became impotent. The night I came out my wife and I tried to make love and I could not get it up. I told her I needed to leave our bed and go downstairs and smoke a cigarette. She knew then that the time had come that whatever was bothering me was about to come out. She followed and I basically had my first major meltdown.

Since that time we have come so very far in our quest to figure out what the hell is going on with my sexuality. She accepts my sexuality, for which I am eternally grateful. I love who I am and what I am all about, and have managed to keep my self-esteem in check. We have however come to a brick wall in our quest to deal with all this. We have, all the way through this, worked as a team to communicate, express our thoughts and pain, to come to understandings that we both feel comfortable with. We have agreed that I may pursue friendships with males of like persuasion. We have also agreed that these friendships are to remain nonsexual. I have no problems with this. I have, however, expressed to my wife that, ultimately my desires at some point will be to have an emotional and physical relationship with a man. Our struggle at this point is monogamy. We or I have agreed to honor monogamy in my marriage until we can work through this issue. However, my wife feels we are not working together to that end. She wants and should expect as a str8 hetero female, monogamy in her marriage. This should not be much for a woman to ask of her husband. Her question to me was: Is the lovely home and family life that we have built together over these years worth sacrificing for an intimate relationship with another man? A loaded question indeed.

GREAT TIMES TOGETHER

From: Schuyler

I who am SO grateful to you, your wife, and your partner for allowing me to be a part of your day on Wednesday. It was really good to experience ALL of you, and I can unreservedly say that I, too, liked all of you very much (not to mention your wife's wonderful cookies—yummy). I would say that you are a very lucky man, except that I know that luck has very little to do with it. My meeting with both your partner and your wife, as well as the time we spent together alone at your home and in your car, gave me a much better sense of what a very special man you are and your (often painful) courageous journey to this point. Although we shared when we first met that your arrangement is not "perfect," from where I am sitting it seems pretty darn near. I would give my left nut to have my wife be one-tenth as accepting (perhaps one-tenth as SECURE may be more accurate) as yours is. And your partner is just the dearest, sweetest, most gentle guy.

CHOICES

From: Brent

I have been reading with great interest many of the recent comments about the choices available to us as gay/bisexual men in relationships with wives we love. For what it's worth, my wife and I have been working on this for eighteen months and here are some of the ways we have responded to this; perhaps they will help.

1. We did get a counselor—a good one—and she has helped immensely. Yes it cost money we thought we didn't have; what's your relationship worth to you? As much as your car, furniture, etc.??? We continue to see her jointly though I am happy to report that at our last visit she suggested we didn't need to come as often, as we seemed to have worked through the most difficult aspects of our crisis with great love for each other and for ourselves too.

2. VERY early on our counselor pushed us to write down our truths—to separately acknowledge (BOTH of us) what our core values were; lines that we absolutely could not cross because to do so would cause serious damage to each of us as an individual. It was a great experience in stripping away the layers of stuff we had created over 30 years of a REALLY GREAT marriage that was primarily about accommodating each others' needs.

Of course, one of my bottom lines was that I was out and could not go back in the closet and that I needed to experience sex with men which had been at the core of my desire for as long as I could remember. At 51 I could no longer deny who I was without damaging myself even more than I already had.

One of my wife's core values was that she could only live with me in a monogamous relationship; that it was simply impossible for her to live in a nonmonogamous relationship with me; that much as she wanted to accommodate my needs, this was too much for her.

I expect many wives are at this point when I read guys saying, "My wife won't let me have sex with men." It's not about YOU, it's about her; as it should be.

A core value we both held was that we deeply loved (and love) each other. A way had to be found to accommodate what appeared to be diametrically opposed needs.

For us that took the form of a separation and with it a release of the monogamy issue for BOTH of us. In this way, I remain true to my need to explore being a gay man; she remains true to her value that, if we are to live together we are to remain monogamous. On some level it may seem like we are splitting hairs since we are officially married and nonmonogamous but so what; it is what works for us and that's what counts.

3. After a year of separation we know some things we didn't a year ago. We know that we will always be connected on some deep level no matter what—even if we don't look like a conventionally married couple we are connected in ways MANY married couples are not. We also know (now) we will not return to the "marriage" we once had. This was NOT a foregone conclusion when we separated but we have both evolved to a point at which we have to say this is a truth for us as a couple. And make no mistake, we have grieved the loss of that even as we work to create a new relationship for ourselves. We are still grieving it, no question. But given who we each are and what our core values are, it's not something we can have. That's a tough one, but we are working on it with equal parts of love for ourselves and each other.

4. What we don't know of course is what will happen in the future. Our counselor however pointed out to us that we are both capable of loving more than one person at a time; that these loves are "different"—parents, kids, siblings, etc. but still we can do it. Why would a new partner for either or both of us be any different?

5. Finally, we have learned to view our relationship as a PROCESS rather than an ENDPOINT. We know that we will remain connected, in some way and on an extraordinarily deep level, "until death do us part. "

On this list I have read many stories; many of which seem workable for the parties involved but unworkable for us. If this helps any of you, then it was worth writing and (I hope) worth your time to read.

SUMMER BY THE GAY BAY

From: Schuyler

I'd LOVE to go to the guy gathering AND I'm just not sure that's the right thing to do at THIS stage. It's still very much a day-to-day thing with my wife, and I don't want to be purposely hurtful. I went out to dinner and a movie with my lover last Wednesday—the first time that we have been out "socially" in the evening—we usually meet for lunch or at his house during working hours only. I was honest with my wife about where I was going and with whom, and made a point of being back home by 11 p.m. Still, my wife was noticeably cool for SEVERAL days, made several oblique comments. She keeps saying that all this (our lives together) is temporary, that as soon as our youngest (now 17) is out of the nest, she wants HER own life. On the other hand, we often have periods of relative calm, usually when the fact that I'm seeing my lover is not "in her face". I'm on the roller coaster big time, my friend. I think I've told you that my wife absolutely wants to have nothing to do with either therapy or other straight wives.

Who knows what the future will bring. I really very consciously try to take it "a day at a time". SO . . . although I HAVE thought about the guy gathering, I'm not ready to commit.

My relationship with my partner is going VERY well. He is smart, incredibly attractive, sweet, kind, caring, and considerate, besides being a VERY hot lover. He is very patient and understanding, and I feel free to share EVERYTHING with him. I typically talk to him every other day or so during the week (this week he's back East). During weekends he is usually with his wife at his second home in the country a couple of hours from the City. I truly believe that IF I am to have a partner to meet my needs for male intimacy AND maintain a marriage/family commitment, that I could not have chosen a better person than my partner. This relationship has been going on for almost six months now, and it (intimacy, trust, comfortability) just keeps getting better and better. I love him very much. I keep pinching myself. There's no going back.

LIFE CHANGED SINCE COMING OUT

From: James

Everything changed two years ago when I came out to my wife, and definitely for the better. Neither of us would go back to life before that. Sexuality became the focus of our thoughts, our conversations, our being. I knew that when my wife said she loved me, she knew the "real" me, and I loved her all the more for it. Communication became crucial and we talked and talked, between two and four hours a day, for about three weeks . . . it was exhausting but we covered a lot of emotions . . . cried together often, made passionate love often . . . read "The Good Marriage" by Judith Wallerstein, and discussed it together. We had a rich and wild honeymoon period for about six months. In the two years after the honeymoon, we tend to go through cycles of a couple of months of good times and brief periods of a couple of days to a week of "down" times. We tend to recover quickly and heal. At least twice during this period we were not certain that our marriage would survive. Now, that possibility is a shadow only. But we quickly became very tightly bonded. For us, we did not consider counseling until this past spring, but I know that for many couples it has been crucial to seek good counseling immediately. My wife and I find that time apart is healthy also . . . she recently went to the beach with a group of women, and I go to New York City for a couple of days during the summer to attend some gay plays. Our most recent phase was deciding to be totally honest about what is going on inside us rather than try to protect the other one. I would not suggest this type of sharing immediately after coming out . . . for us it took two years before we were ready. We had to learn first not to take on the pain of the other partner, which is a tough challenge when you love someone deeply. We're still here, together, but we are still vulnerable. We live each day and try not to worry about tomorrow . . . let go and be.

My wife's Perspective:

When presented with the question of how life has changed since James's coming out, my first response would be that life hasn't changed, but how I live it sure has! There have been some obvious changes:

- We've opened our marriage to allow James to express himself more completely in intimate relationships with other men.
- Our style of relating has become more open and honest.
- We live more in the present, trying not to assume too much about the future. By dealing with such a complex issue, we've taken on a depth of relationship that could never have been possible within the dynamics of our old marriage.
- Our friendships have shifted . . . the most satisfying ones are with other mixed-orientation couples and with friends who "know."
- We've become more understanding and open to change, realizing our marriage will continue to be challenged for the rest of our lives.
- On a personal level, the biggest impacts on me (besides sharing James with other men) are the subtle changes in the way we respond to life and to each other: I've learned the real difference between being honest and living honestly. As a result of addressing James's sexuality, I'm learning to be less concerned about resolution and more "tuned in" to the process.

TRUST

From: Stephen

Once the "cat" is out of the bag and everyone knows what you've been doing in secret, trust is certainly damaged for a while. My way of dealing with it was head on. To graphically tell my wife just as much as she could handle, and then say, "That's what I have been doing. Now that I am out to you, sneaking around to meet a man is in the past. I am NOT going to apologize for what has been done, any more than I expect you to apologize to me for every time you have failed me, and disappointed me, by being human and by NOT being the wife that I needed at the time. But, this is ALL true . . . I did it. Now what? What are YOU going to do with this information? I will promise you that from now on if I say to you I am going to do something that that is what I will be doing. I will NEVER hide what I am doing from you again. I know that you have no reason to believe that statement but I also have no reason to believe that you will not go nuts on me like the wives of some of these poor guys on the list and throw my ass out, or attempt to 'get even with me' by making my life a hell on earth. I would DIE for you in a heart beat, but I will not LIVE as your emotional whipping boy. So, now there is going to have to be a NEW element of trust on both our sides based on the fact that if we are going to survive we have to make every effort to tell it exactly like it is in ALL aspects of our life together. I think that by deconstructing our marriage and rebuilding it from the ground up we can not only re-establish trust between us, but make the marriage better than it was. I see my sexuality as OUR problem, not just my problem. We both have to learn to live with this or we are doomed as a couple. I have to learn to respect and stay within your level of comfort, which I expect to expand as you grow in understanding. You have to learn that my sexual horizons are much broader than yours, and that you can only fence me in long enough for me to accommodate your current feelings of insecurity. What do you say? Are you willing to work on this with me or shall I pack my shit and walk away?" At this point you must be willing to walk. There is no room for bluffing here. That is how I handled the problem of trust, both broken and rebuilt. I am sure that my marriage is now stronger and much more honest than it has ever been. This is just one man's approach to the problem. Total honesty, and a refusal to do anything less than honestly face who and what I am, together with my wife. The inherent risk to my approach for re-establishing trust is that putting all your cards on the table at once will be rejected by the straight spouse in the heat of the moment.

For myself I have no doubt that our level of trust is in point of fact much higher now than it ever was before. This is because we "cleaned house" and much of the old emotional crap from our relationship was brought into the light and resolved where possible. It is easier to be loving and trusting when you are carrying less old emotional baggage. I have noticed that a lot of the misery that is experienced by SOME of the people on ALL of the lists sounds like redirected anger from other parts of the marriage. That stuff must be dealt with or "That Gay Thing" will become a convenient excuse for creating a disaster. On the SSML list every time some STR8 spouse wailed "Our marriage was wonderful and everything was perfect until this happened" I had to take that with a huge grain of salt. I think that all relationships need constant attention and that "TGT" forces that issue and makes it imperative that we concentrate on the real issues. These are my thoughts and experiences with trust and trying to keep my marriage from getting fixated on one aspect of our life. My wife and I are both bigger people than the question of whether either of us is going to exercise our gonads.

A STUMBLE IN MY JOURNEY

From: Mike

For a long time after my wife and I began dealing honestly with "The Gay Thing," I found myself struggling with "how much honesty is TOO much honesty?" I could see the pain of her struggle to accept our reality every time she knew I was planning to see my lover. The leaving and the "re-entry" periods were very tense and uncomfortable for both of us.

The ground rules we had negotiated included "You can ask anything you want and I will answer honestly." "Don't ask anything to which you're not ready to hear the answer." An honest answer COULD be "I'm not ready or comfortable talking about that now." In most circumstances, that is working very well for us. In fact, I have never yet had to invoke my "I'm not ready or comfortable" clause ;-) .

Typically, if I was planning to see my lover, it had been in the evening, and so I would let my wife know a few days ahead of time and ask if my going out would be a problem. I would be willing to change plans if I was negatively impacting a family event or if my wife felt particularly vulnerable and needed me to be home. (Trying to be Soooooooooo sensitive .);-)

Most of the time, she would say it was OK, even though her discomfort was palpable. I would go and we'd both go through a short period awkwardness upon my return. But a few months ago, I had what for me was an important insight. I had made plans to take a half-day vacation from work so I could spend an afternoon with my lover and be home in time for dinner as usual. I wondered to myself if I should let my wife know about my plans.

But, I rationalized that since I would not be disrupting her sense of "normal" schedule and family routine, that I could "spare" HER the discomfort this time. So I didn't tell her what I was planning. I certainly didn't feel I was being dishonest. . . . I told myself I was being "considerate" and I was "protecting" her from unnecessary distress.

WRONG !!!!!! When I got home, she told me that my boss from work had called me and left a message at 2:30 in the afternoon. I was shocked. Even though she didn't ask why my boss would be calling me at home in the middle of the afternoon . . . I KNEW she HAD to be wondering. Within 10 minutes of my homecoming . . . I called her into our bedroom (the kids were home and we needed privacy) and explained to her that I had taken the afternoon off to be with my lover. I explained that I didn't think it was necessary to tell her since it didn't disrupt our normal routine and I know how uncomfortable it is for HER when she knows I'm going to be with him. Her only response was, "I wish you would NOT try to manage MY feelings for me or PROTECT me from my own feelings."

In a flash I knew they were not HER feelings I was trying to protect. They were MINE. I was trying to avoid the discomfort I FEEL when I talk to her about my plans to be with my lover. I am still uncomfortable reconciling my role as husband and father with my role as another man's lover. For me this was an important realization. I could stop bullshitting myself about whose feelings I was trying to be so "considerate" of. My wife is much stronger than I give her credit for being . . . and I do NOT need to "protect" her from our reality. I DO, however, need to resolve my own conflicts over our reality. This insight, for me, was an important step in the direction of personal authenticity. And this is an ideal toward which I have decided to spend the rest of my life working.

So when I consider withholding, or "spinning" a truth in the name of "protecting" someone else . . . I ask myself, "Who am I really trying to protect anyway? From what? and For what reasons?" The answers usually lead me to a greater understanding of myself and the work I have left to do.

Yes, I have stumbled in my journey . . . and may well stumble again . . . but each time I hope to get up and continue my journey a bit wiser. This "authenticity" thing is really tough. :-)

FIGURE LIFE OUT?

From: Gent

Just when you think you are about to get your life figured out, then . . . well, you know what happens! This is definitely the case with me. You will recall the immense pain and hard times that I had coming to grips with my wife finding out that I was gay. She told anyone who would listen and when

I found it difficult not to act on it, asked me to move out and she filed for divorce against me. After six months, we reconciled and I have been back here at home since late last year.

Well, the story wouldn't end there. Less than two days ago, my wife shared with me her reason for never in her life being able to have close female friends . . . you probably guessed it . . . she has always had homosexual feelings towards women. She says she prefers men though. Well, this certainly adds a new dynamic to my life that has to be processed.

RE: HUSBAND AND WIFE

From: Brandon

I'll have to say that my relationship with my male lover is quite different than any other relationship I've had with a woman.

From: Dale

The key operative word here is "different!" It has come in to quite sharp focus for both myself and my wife that there really IS a difference in this matter of men relating together and men relating with women. Our therapist worked with my wife quite a long time to get the concept of "different" established and to move away from some kind of perception that was value judgment-based—words like better, worse, more, less, etc. The things one exchanges with a man in a relationship—sex included—are NOT the same as what flows between a man and a woman in relationship—and the two aren't cross-exchangeable. Being able to understand this concept has helped my wife (in our relationship anyway) feel less diminished by my emotional/sexual interest in men. It's not so easy to feel loss if you know that what you're grieving over wasn't yours in the first place—and couldn't have ever been!

WIFE'S SEXUAL CREATIVITY

From: Floyd

MY wife's gotten much more creative and active sexually since I came out a year ago. Is this common with other guys ? Does the heat last??!

From: Conrad

Common, absolutely. It's not just the spouse, either, we suddenly have dropped a whole lot of repression, too. . . .

Lasting? For some, I do not think so for most. For us, a long period of drought followed, from which we are just now emerging because I have my second lover. . . . It's perhaps the first time again.

From: Gripp

It has been five months now that I am out to my wife, and I would say that "creative" in sex is a very good term. Actually, I think that she thinks that if she keeps me sexually exhausted, I'll not have other thoughts or feelings. We'll have to talk about that sometime, but not right now. :o)

From: Marvin

Interesting. . . . Shortly after my coming out my wife became an absolute ANIMAL sexually! At times, I've thought she was trying to "convert" me. <G> After about 8 months our sex life settled down to pretty much what it'd always been—not as often as I'd like! She is, however, still MUCH more adventurous than she ever used to be.

From: Woody

The heat has lasted almost two years in my case. Before coming out: perfunctory sex no more than once or twice a year for some years. Never very hot before that.

Things improved right after coming out to my wife . . . not only coming out about being gay, but also about my identification with the "bottom" position, which I'd never heard of before being exposed to the gay/leather community. What an epiphany. Suddenly I could understand where at least part of the sexual conflict was coming from. My wife thought she wanted a dominant husband sexually, but her husband wanted to be a submissive guy who was being "used" sexually (well, it's an old erotic fantasy with me anyway—and of course it's always with a man, but I'm not married to one). We've talked, explored our sexuality in literature, in bed . . . and (hang on to your seats, guys) watched gay videos together (bear and leather ones in my case—some frisky, some pretty hardcore as far as male sexual and bondage, dominance, and SM practices). I can still be in the "dominant" role only with the help of Viagra, but when my wife is feeling frisky and dominant we can really "get it on," and we do frequently now. Yes, she knows I'm deep in a fantasy, but I think she is too—and what's so bad about that? We just hope the neighbors don't complain about the noise from next door <G>.

From: Moris

Mine was the SAME WAY! I thought she was trying to f*** me str8! Fun while it lasted.

From: Daniel

I suspect that this is true for many of us—I think it releases something in both husband and wife—who in a normal sexual relationship are perhaps not particularly adventurous. Discovering that the husband is adventurous and may even talk about some of his sexual activities with his male friends—such as oral sex, may encourage the wife to try these out for herself if she is minded to do so. Partly because she might have always wanted to do so, and was afraid to suggest it before, partly because in so doing, she may think that she is obviating the need for her husband to go with men who are giving them similar sexual experiences. Unfortunately, the latter does not work for me. I find I have to be with a man from time to time—he has something that a wife does not have . . . hairy chest. . . . !!

From: Bruce

One of my roommates in college used to say that "Men trade love for sex, Women trade sex for love." While that is an oversimplification, I've always found that there is some truth to that in a lot of cases.

Physical displays of affection such as hugging, kissing, etc. were always more important than sex was to my wife. After I came out, the hugging and kissing seemed to become more important, and the sex became less important. At one time I thought that it might be due to worries about HIV and other STDs, but she knows that I have been in a mutually monogamous relationship with another man for two years now, and she trusts him as much as I do. I still love her very much, and I show her in lots of other ways, and that seems to satisfy her.

We have talked about it, and she knows that if she wants sex that I am more than willing, and I am also open to her seeing someone else if that's what she wants. She says that she is perfectly happy with the way things are. (And believe me, she has no problems letting me know when I've screwed up or when I'm doing something that she doesn't like).

I don't think that you can EXPECT your wife to agree to a relationship if it isn't what she wants. It wouldn't work any better for me to expect her to agree to that type of relationship if it wasn't what she wanted than it would be for her to expect me to deny my sexuality.

Chapter 5
Our Kids

PROBLEMS OUR KIDS FACE

From: Joe

I didn't respond to your original post but cried nevertheless when I read it. So sad that relationships go ad—especially when being gay/BI is no one's fault but just is. God created this diversity and made each of us just the way that he wanted us! Why can't the world of man just accept God's plans?

There is one additional concern I have that I failed to address in my other post. As I said before, one of the issues that concerns me and others, is what effect telling my children that I am gay will have on them. The unanimous opinion of the group is that kids are resilient and as long as it is handled properly, it should not be anything that we cannot work through together.

From: Brandon

After working with some 300 married men (or previously married) here in this local area and talking with PFLAG members and many gay fathers in all parts of the country, the opinion is that kids are indeed very resilient. A few pieces of good advice:

Be totally honest with them but never crude or vulgar. Only tell them as much as they can comprehend. Answer all questions openly and in kind (Don't tell them more than they asked for). Keep answers simple and to the point. They have no right or need to know the details of any sexual intimacy. Let them know you love them and your sexuality is not their fault. When they are old enough, asssure them that your sexuality has nothing to do with theirs. Reassure them that they can ask you any questions. Try to reestablish a good working relationship with their mother. Don't make too much of the issue as kids really don't believe that parents are sexual beings anyway. The sexual orientation of the parent is not that big a deal with children. Spend as much time with the kids as you can and have fun together. Remain a good and just disciplinarian. Get involved with a Gay-Dads group. Let your kids see and share your happiness in life—be a good role model. Take total charge of your own happiness and they will love you for it! Somehow instill in each of them a sense of spirituality. The younger the kids find out, the easier it is on their acceptance and understanding.

Taking this a step further: what about the reactions of their friends and acquaintances to this news? It is all well and good to tell them that it's OK for them to keep it to themselves if they want, but eventually word will get around, via parents, etc., and it may come back to them. What happens when some kid comes up to one of my children and says, "So I hear your dad is a fag"? Kids can be very cruel. I know for a fact that some kids believe the ultimate insult they can hurl at another child is to call him gay—probably not even knowing what it means. I want to project my homosexuality in a good way to my kids. I've always taught them to be tolerant (what a surprise!), but I just dreaded them being teased and caused pain because of me.

I can assure you that your kids love you dearly and they will find the strength to deal with these problems—provided you give them the love and support they need. You'll find out that each of your children will soon tell at least one of their friends. (Even our twenty-year-old did this.) This has something to do with making it real to them. Don't be too concerned with this as once shared it most likely will no longer be an issue with them.

Advice for you—Quit second -guessing and trying to control your kid's lives.

From Joe:

I am currently apartment hunting. There is a complex about 2 blocks from my house that has units available. I like the fact that it is close, for the kids' sake. It might make the moving out a little easier to swallow knowing that I am so close. Is this a good idea, bad idea, or does it not matter?

From: Brandon

Doesn't matter—other than how it affects your relationship with your wife. Kids will adapt but not if you and their mother are constantly fighting. If that is the case, I'd opt for some distance emotionally and physically.

From: Amity P. Buxton <dir@ssnetwk.org>

Having talked with hundreds of spouses over the past 12 years, I'd like to share what I've observed in relation to your situation.

First, regarding your children, they will honor your trusting them enough to be honest. Your eight-year-old was telling you that being gay's okay. The children I've interviewed say pretty unanimously that the sooner the parents tell them, the better. One way parents have handled the "family secrets" bit (a negative situation for all family members affected) is to make a distinction between "secrets," which term connotes shame, and "private family affairs"—no one else's business—not even a grandfather's.

As for your father-in-law... only you know the situation. Honesty is, to me, however, the name of the game—also respect for someone's being hurt or made ill by the news. Trying to protect oneself is another matter. On the other hand, his wife says not to. Personally and professionally, I feel that, in the long run, family secrets only corrode family relationships. Much depends what you're going to do about your orientation: family breakup, hanging in, having your wife accept your dating or finding a man, fulfilling your same-sex needs in other ways. All these factors need to be weighed.

From: Brandon

One's only job as a parent is to feed, clothe, love, protect their defenselessness, enjoy them, give them some sense of spirituality and some early training.

You are 100% correct about the honest relationship. I found that one has to give that age group lots of time. If we are absolutely honest with them from here on in and treat them like adults (like one of your dearest friends and not like children) they will eventually come to love the real gay/BI us and give us the respect that we deserve. Please be open and vigilant for the least spark of their opening the communication process with you. Never ever criticize them for their initial reaction to your coming out. My daughter reacted like your youngest girl and has not been a problem. My two boys took longer to accept me and come to the point that they can joke and tease me playfully about their gay dad. My two boys initially took to defending my wife and trying to protect her. They also both took the religious homophobic understanding of our situation. Both after reading all the books I could provide for them on the subject, talking to their friends and getting encouragement from my wife and I—came to really understand and appreciate their gay father. Both are now open and honest about who they are and about their feelings. All three kids say that the best thing that ever happened to our family was my coming out. They see the beautiful relationship and support that my wife and I give each other—this has been an inspiration in their own relationships.

SON'S OFFHAND REMARKS

From: Schuyler

Last Thursday evening, after work, I went out to meet a new friend I became acquainted with from this group for dinner in the City. I had informed my wife that I was meeting a new friend, and she knows that I am expanding my contacts with other BI guys. That morning I had also told my 15-year-old son that I was meeting a friend for dinner and would be home late (and don't forget to put out the garbage!).

While I was out Thursday night my son asked my wife where I was and she told him that I had told her I was meeting a friend for dinner. He then made the "offhand" remark that I was meeting my lover, and that, "You probably think he's going to the 'Y' (meaning the gym) when he says that too." These remarks were not only painful to my wife (who is, understandably, sensitive to my meeting other men), but made her think that my son knew more than SHE knew about where I was going and what I was doing that evening. When I got home late that evening, she was very upset. My wife and I have been in the process of discussing whether or not I should come out to the children, since my therapist has been strongly advising this for a couple of weeks. My wife asked me to talk to my son about his comments, and I told her that I would do so the next day.

As soon as he was home on Friday, I calmly confronted him about his comments, which he said were a "joke." When it was clear that he would offer no other insight into why he made the comments, I told him that I was bisexual, and that I thought his comments to his mother might have something to do with his knowledge of that. He had very little reaction (this is typical for him), other than to deny that it was other than a joke. He was smiling the whole time, but he wouldn't look me in the eye. His only response, after I asked him what he thought of my revelation, was "I think it's gross." He didn't seem surprised, he didn't seem particularly "grossed out," and he didn't seem angry. I continued by explaining to him that I thought it was time that he knew, that his mother has known for several years, that this was something I had been struggling with for a long time, and that I didn't want this to continue to be a secret. I also explained to him that my wife and I were not planning on separating (at least for now) or making any other major changes, and that this was something neither myself nor the family needed to feel ashamed of. After explaining all this, and asking him if he had any questions, his only reaction was "Are we done?" (also typical).

My 18-year-old living away from home is taking the knowledge that her old dad is gay/BI the hardest. I came out to her on Friday afternoon by telephone. This knowledge came out of the blue (according to her) and she was in shock (and tears). I reassured her that this didn't affect how I felt about her, and gave her the same reassurances that I gave my son. I also told her that I would like to have her support, and that this wasn't a tragedy. Since she was so obviously upset, I called her again on Saturday, and she expressed that she is angry that I had told her and that she would rather not have known. She, of my three kids, is the one most likely to be concerned about what other people think, and admitted that she thought it was something that she had to be ashamed of. My wife talked to her on Sunday and was VERY sensitive—told her that this wasn't something that I chose or could change and that it wasn't anything that any of us had to be ashamed of. She also told her that it wasn't something anyone else (outside the family) had to have knowledge of, while suggesting to her that it might be good to take advantage of the counseling service at University if she continues to be really upset about this. I was very grateful for my wife's support and the sensitive way she handled this. I think she is as relieved as I am that this is out in the open (at least within our family), although she is concerned with how these two kids are handling the knowledge.

I talked to my married 21-year-old by phone on Saturday, and she was great. She admitted that she "knew" based on her intuition and perceptiveness. I told her that I believed that she knew, that it has been difficult for me to come to terms with my sexuality, and that I was only now (after 4 years) at the point where I could be this open. She said that she was proud of me (for coming out) which felt really affirming. At the same time, we sort of skirted the issue of where this left my wife. I KNOW my daughter would not approve of my having extramarital sex, straight or gay, and this is obviously (from my point of view) not an appropriate subject for conversation between father and daughter. I'm especially happy to be out to my daughter because I think she can be of great support to my wife, who does not easily avail herself of support.

Although it may be difficult (particularly for youngest two kids), I believe that this disclosure happened about as perfectly as it could have. The fact that my son "forced the issue," got me "off the dime" with my wife's support at a time when I don't have a boyfriend/lover and can honestly tell everyone that (should they ask). This was a subject (telling the kids) that was very much on my mind, so my wife and I had already been somewhat prepared. I had prayed for guidance, and I choose to believe that this is how my prayer was answered.

I am sharing all this because I want to express gratitude to the group. I don't think I could have had the courage to do this without your experience, strength, and support. I am relieved to be OUT. Over the short term, it may create some upheaval. I can't help but believe that, in the long run, it is best for the entire family. I think it will be helpful to my wife to have the support of our kids (especially my daughter) and to no longer feel that she has to keep this "secret." It should also help the kids prepare for their parents' eventual separation, which, although not imminent, is probably how this will ultimately play out.

From: Jud

In my son's case there's one consideration you need to take into account; he may be concerned that he, also is BI/gay and not know how to deal with that.

Because of the publicity a genetic basis for homosexuality has received, as well as the lack of actual knowledge about the topic by the press or public, many people are convinced that "like father like son." Thus, if my son is at the sexually insecure stage typical of youths his age, he may be seriously questioning his own orientation, even if he is 100% straight!

With my son in particular, one should point out that all theories which address a genetic basis for homosexuality emphasize the fact that the gene involved is sex-linked and passed by the mother, not the father. Thus, from my son's perspective, the fact you are BI/gay (sorry, I'm new on the list and not sure who is gay and who is BI here yet) makes no difference whatever as far as his own genetic predisposition goes.

You'll be doing him a real service now and in the future in addition to relieving an enormous amount of stress for both of you by taking the time to reassure him that any insecurities he is experiencing are normal for healthy young men of ANY orientation, and help him to understand that same-sex relationships aren't the "dirty" or "disgusting" activities he is currently imagining them to be—they are as sincere and deep as heterosexual ones.

One thought you do need to consider is the way in which you are simultaneously coming out yet remaining "safe." It's obvious from your comments, as well as those above, that you are raising your children to view sexual relationships outside of—or in addition to—marriage as "wrong," and thus are attempting to conceal from them the fact that you do, in fact, participate in such activities. In a very real sense you have come out as a BI/gay man but you remain closeted in terms of your relationships themselves. It would benefit both you and your kids if you were able to help them to accept the fact that for some individuals (married bisexual men and women prominent among them) a poly, versus monogamous, type of relationship is often both more rewarding and capable of contributing to the stability of the primary relationship. Don't let them see you as either sexually frustrated (which they can't help but feel if they think you are drawn to men sexually but can't allow yourself to act on that attraction) or as "sneaking" behind their mother's back (which may be the feeling your son is expressing in his comments to your SO) and "cheating" on her with men. Instead let them develop the concept that a bisexual/gay married man is not only capable of sustaining two very different types of relationships simultaneously, but that each relationship can contribute to the stability of the other. They need to understand that bisexuality/homosexuality goes beyond sexual activities and involves relationships, a wide range of emotional responses, and sincere commitments, just as heterosexuality does.

From: Amity Buxton <dir@ssnetwk.org>

Based on the research I've done for 12 years with children's reactions, it is wonderful that you were honest with yours as soon as you and your wife were strong enough to support them in their coming to terms with new information.

As for your college daughter's concerns, you may want to suggest that she get in touch with COLAGE (Children of Lesbians and Gays Everywhere). It's a project of Gay and Lesbian Parents Coalition, [now called Family Pride Coalition] International (on whose board I sit, actually) and run by adult children for children of all ages. It has support groups, e-mail lists, a summer conference for children to share concerns, etc.

The COLAGE home page is <http://www/colage.org> and direct e-mail address for the director is <director@colage.org>.

Children seem to find and feel more support with peers in situations as close to theirs as possible. The COLAGE kids whom I know are really great. A lot of what they do is simply "hang out" together, with the result that gay/BI/les/trans issues are put into the wider perspective of their whole lives.

From: James

I do have a couple of thoughts to share from my own experience . . . both in telling my children and repeating what Amity Buxton's research interviewing 20 children with a gay/BI parent:

1. It helps when the wife is in a good place about the issue and can be present when you tell the child. One issue with your child will be "how's mom?" and another will be, "Are you divorcing?" If both of you present this information in a positive way it certainly helps. My daughter, whom I came out to one week before coming out to my son, asked if she could be present also when I told my son, which she was.
2. Amity's research shows that age is not a factor. Children told her they want to know as early as possible. What is an issue you guys have already addressed: (a) how much to tell him/her, (b) let him/her ask questions, (c) don't discuss sex per se . . . kids never want to know about what you do sexually (until adults, then some of them still don't want to know. . . . my daughter, e.g., DOES want to know . . . which caused me to do a lot of thinking before I could comfortably share

some things with her). She wasn't being nosey, she simply loved me and wanted to share in discussing this aspect of my life.

3. For my wife and me, it was important that we not tell one child and not tell another because we didn't want one child to find out from a sibling or otherwise and be angry that a sister or brother knew but he/she didn't. So once my daughter learned by accident, we discussed it with her then told our son the very next weekend when he happened to be home for a visit. How much you tell one child would depend on age.

4. Important thing is that you and your wife agree beforehand, what she discusses, e.g., what she feels and her reactions, and what you discuss.

From: Buck

I'm adding below a wonderful piece that was contributed to GayDads a couple of years ago, on the subject of Long Distance Dads.

Circumstances and jobs resulted in my ex-wife and I settling far apart after the divorce five years ago. She has primary custody of our two daughters, 7 and 15. We agreed from the beginning that co-custody could not work in our situation.

Now my kids and I are separated by 3 time zones. Nevertheless, we stay actively involved with one another. They travel as often as school schedules and finances permit, spending most of the summer with me. Maybe even more important is the daily contact. I use the telephone, fax, mail, FedEx and computer to try to keep a constant presence in their lives.

My ex and I have always agreed on the importance of the girls having two parents, even in the bitter days around the divorce. I'm lucky there. She has put no obstacle in the way of my relationship with the kids. To the contrary, she laid down an early rule for her household: When Dad calls, whatever we're doing stops, even if it's dinner, or playing with friends, etc.

Here are some suggestions from my experience:

Vow to come as close to daily contact as you possibly can.

Set a regular telephone time that works for them (somewhere between school and dinnertime is good). Then make it work for you, even if it means darting out of a meeting and having a quick conversation.

Follow school progress carefully. Make notes if necessary. Ask "What's happening tomorrow at school?" Then be sure to ask about that event after the fact. Meet with the school principal, explain your situation and ask to receive duplicate mailings of ALL communications, from report cards to fundraising flyers (they'll be glad to send those). Make sure you meet each year's teachers. If nothing else, it gives you the basis of something in common to joke about. "Does she still dye her hair bright pink?"

When schedules conflict and you can't talk in person, leave a long, silly message on the answering machine.

The fax is terrific. Set up with auto dial, even a young child can put a drawing in and push one button. You can get a copy of an exam, an essay or whatever. You can send a cartoon or whatever will provoke conversation.

Do not take "nothing" for an answer, as in "What did you do today?" "What are your plans for the weekend?" etc. Drag it out of them! Remember, part of what you're doing is teaching them to become adults, and eloquent conversation is a rich gift for any child. This is usually not much of a problem if you have daily contact because your questions are specific: "What happened when you read the frog essay to the class?"

Conversation is a two-way street. Even if they don't ask, talk about what's happening in your life. My girls really like my lover and show it . . . when they are in Oregon. It's as if he doesn't exist when they're back in Indianapolis. So, I introduce him into the conversation: "Guess what my silly husband did today?"

E-mail is a great supplement to the telephone. It's fun for them, and can work from as young as five, as long as they know how to get in. Separated kids are just waiting for some demonstration that your love has faded.

I have to confess that mail has been my least successful tool. I can't get them to respond, even when I send pre-addressed, stamped envelopes!

My final point is that I'm not sure how much it matters what either you or your kids say in a conversation compared to the fact that you are talking. My seven-year-old and I tell a lot of riddles and make up silly words. We always end our calls with a two-minute "battle of the good-byes" in which we race through "good-bye" in every language, plus some translations not previously known, like "tiger-head." It never fails to crack us up and end the call on a high note.

I hope this helps.

From: James

—Forwarded message—
GAMMA Newsletter
by Amity Pierce Buxton, PhD

How and when does a father come out to his child or children? The answer depends so much on the particular father, his children, and their heterosexual mother—not to mention in-laws, playmates, neighbors, classmates, church or temple congregation, and community. No one answer fits all dads or all children. However, some general thoughts from my research, including interviews with children, might help a gay father decide the best way to come out to his children.

From the children's point of view, the task which challenges them most is simply growing up. To cope with each stage of development, they need and want a supportive and stable family environment in which to grow physically, cognitively, psychologically, morally, and socially. They want to know their parents love them and care enough to spend time with them, to let them explore the world around them as well as set limits, and to be there when they get hurt or fail to meet expectations. When things get rough "out there," they want to be able to "come home" to their safety net. Finding out this new information about their father shakes up their picture of the family and adds another challenge with which to cope alongside those of growing up.

Prior to telling his children, a husband's disclosure to his wife has already changed the family constellation in a small or large way, no matter how loving and close the couple are. Whether the wife quietly tries to understand her husband's new identity or erupts in anger, some degree of tension reverberates in the household. Children, closely tuned into the family ethos, often become aware that something is different even before they are told.

The question then is when to come out to them and how. The bottom line is to tell the children with love with a goal of helping them understand, more than of fulfilling the father's need to tell. A relaxed, intimate atmosphere, freed of household chores, perhaps in a setting away from the house, helps create the kind of intimate framework that will best convey a loving and caring meaning of the disclosure. A simple introduction and then a statement with room for reactions and reflection are really all that is needed.

Some fathers tell the children separately or all of them at once—with or without their wives—in person or in a letter followed up by a face-to-face conversation. Telephone calls have not proved to be effective. Looking back, children say the sooner they are told the better, or they feel they were not trusted to handle the truth. A rule of thumb that seems to work is to wait until both parents are comfortable enough with the gayness to be able to support their children as they process the disclosure. If the couple plans to separate, it is not helpful to come out at the same time. The breakup poses a worse crisis for the children than the coming out, though both events are upsetting. Coming out some time before or after the divorce will also help the children understand a reason for the break-up other than their being its cause. Despite planned timing, some children, having observed changes in the father's appearance or social activities, precipitate the disclosure. Seeing the father's new partner may also lead to direct questioning. No matter when the father tells the children, the mother's explicit respect of his perspective makes it easier for children to accept the disclosure.

Each age brings its particular reactions and expressed needs. Young children, not knowing much about sexuality much less homosexuality, take the announcement as a matter of fact, as long as they are assured that both parents continue to love them and will be there for them. Older, school-age children may fear taunts from classmates. Teenagers, who do not want to appear different from peers and whose own sexuality is emerging, have the hardest time accepting the news. They face many of the same challenges their gay father faced in his coming out: identity, integrity, sexuality, and life plan. Even children who were told when they were young have to process the information all over again when they become adolescents. Some wonder if they might be gay, lesbian, or bisexual. Others wonder if they, too, might marry someone who will turn out to be gay. Adult children tend to make moral judgments, and some feel angry at the impact on their mother. No matter at what age children are told, the telling is only the first step.

It helps when parents have factual information about homosexuality and resources available as they ask further questions in keeping with their age and stage of development. For instance, teenagers may want to know other teens with gay or lesbian parents, and you can refer them to COLAGE, Children of Lesbians and Gays Everywhere.

When children are encouraged to talk about such worries, the hurtful events become a source of learning as the gay father and straight mother explain that name-calling stems from ignorance. Parents can also give children tools to handle future problems. For example, if a child were ridiculed at school for having a gay dad, they can suggest retorts such as, "Hey, you're talking about my dad," or "He's still the same old dad, you know." Keeping children's possible reactions in mind, a gay father can come out to his children with honesty and love, confident that they will at some point accept him in his new identity. This means assuring the children that his relationship with them will not change, that he and their mother both love them, that they will lose neither parent because of this, and that both parents are there to answer questions and help them deal with whatever concerns come up.

Some children take months to accept the disclosure. If for example, the father leaves the household to live alone or with a partner, one or more children may be reluctant to visit him. Advice offered by many fathers includes: Give the children time. Let them ask all the questions they want. Introduce them to changes in your life slowly, one by one. Avoid putting them in situations beyond the sensitivity level of a particular child or the general maturity limitations of this or that age group. Listen to their anger, tears, and accusations without putting up walls to defend yourself. Wipe their tears and cry with them. Show you understand their anger. Explain with confidence your new identity, don't argue. Coming out requires time, patience, and love. Most children take the news in their stride, if allowed to come to terms with it on their own terms. Being a good parent doesn't stop with coming out. In some cases, the communication initiated by the coming out improves the parent-child bond. Throughout the process, their love for their father remains very much alive, even if not shown. Coming out to them gently and honestly gains their respect.

From: Roland

I finally feel prepared to write of my recent coming-out to my son. Following the extraordinarily powerful Chicago Guys Gathering and the coming-out of a dear friend to his children, I felt a peace and strength in my own position. As some of you may know, my situation and relationship is different than many of you have experienced. I left my wife for a separation 10 months ago, after discovering that she had never seen our marriage as anything but a convenience for dealing with her chronic depression and inability to face the world. We did go into counseling and I discovered that there was no way to continue any kind of marriage with her unless I could finally actualize my bisexuality within the relationship. We spent six months working at this until my own confusion and anger and resentment over our marriage convinced me that the only way to heal was to separate and gain clarity.

It has been a remarkable life I have found. I have gained love and acceptance and affirmation at every turn. In a totally unexpected turn of events, I fell in love. All of this took place within the context of still being legally married and very much attached to my three children. My one groaning and great regret has been my distance from my (almost) 16-year-old daughter, and she and I have worked mightily to maintain our relationship.

I have always maintained that when the time came, I would speak privately to my children about my sexuality, no one else. My wife and I would, together, address them about the divorce, and we would include sexuality as merely one of the many obstacles in a marriage rife with problems.

My son turned 21. Saturday evening I went to his place with birthday gifts. We sat and he opened gifts and then we went to the kitchen so that he could make me a pot of fresh Guatemalan Antigua in his new coffee pot. We sat while the water heated and I knew the time was right.

I reminded my son of when he was 10 and he told me that talking about my college drug days was more information than he wanted to know. I also told him that now, at 21, there was information that I felt I needed to share. Over the years all of my children have become aware, to some extent, of the physical and emotional abuse I suffered as I grew up. I explained that sharing this information would help his understanding of some of my motivations and reasons for handling my life in that way I had. He listened intently, never interrupting, never showing boredom. I told him one of my greatest fears in all of this was my fear of losing him, his siblings. I explained my determination to try to help them understand my nature, and the complexity of our marriage. I told him of my brother's comment when I came out to him last summer and he thought I was going to tell him I had cancer. I said that I could handle death; it was rejection I had a tough time with. And then I told my son that whether he could understand me as bisexual or gay, he did need to know that I wasn't heterosexual. And then I took a really big gulp of coffee.

My son asked me if I was going to take a break now. I said yes. He then looked at me with a half grin and said, "You know, I've been waiting for this conversation. Specifically, I have been waiting since last July for this conversation." He explained that last July while I was staying with him before moving, he tripped over an e-mail while doing a "Find" request for another item. After reading the letter 3 times and wondering why a person he didn't recognize was writing to his father about whether bisexuality existed, it all finally clicked. He acknowledged he was floored and his world was turned upside down. He knew he needed to speak with someone about this and chose not to talk to me or my wife. He chose, maturely, wisely, a trusted friend whose older sister is lesbian. They talked at length, and my son came out of this realizing that while his awareness of me had changed, my behavior wasn't changed one iota. He said he watched me and wondered how I was handling my life. He admitted to wondering how much of the separation was due to the sexual issues. But out of his own sense of respect, he did not ask me about it. First, he felt he had inappropriately accessed private mail on my laptop. Second, he is simply respectful of other's space.

Then he stunned me by talking about his recent accident. He said, "You know, Dad, I don't like to talk about the accident much. But I really am aware that you never left my side for 3 weeks." He told me of waking up in the morphine haze while I was stroking his hair or holding his hand, fighting the nurses over little things to make him more comfortable, and that if he hadn't been aware of it before then how could he possibly ignore how much I loved him? He then went on to tell me how much he appreciated me, how much he loved me, and how little my sexual orientation mattered to him. His exact phrase was that it was a "non-issue."

Our conversation covered over 3 hours that night. My son told me of meeting my friends and knowing from the moment I had introduced them as being part of a support group. He knew more about them than I had ever told him. He told me that when he had met my "roommate," he looked at him and wondered just how this man would fit in with mine-and-his life. Beautifully, the two have since built a caring and respectful and possibly even loving relationship between them.

He asked more about the situations I found of other peers in this group and said that while some fathers may have lost a great deal in coming out, that this was OUR family; he, and speaking for his siblings, they, were MY children. And as far as the risk of losing them, "Well, Dad, that ain't gonna happen. It just AIN'T gonna happen."

As I was preparing to leave at 1:30 AM, he asked if I had anything else to share. I laughed and said that I thought that might be enough for one night. He laughed and thought so as well, just wanting me to have a sense of closure before I left. At that point, he hobbled over to me (day after surgery, mind you), and didn't so much hug me, as held me. The holding went on for a good five minutes and he stroked my hair and patted my back, and over and over said that he loved me. A crying jag tore through me for a minute and he held on. When I finally pulled away I told him again how much I loved him as well, how proud of him I was, and headed out the door. I got into the car, started the engine, and felt the release and rush of emotion and gratefulness overtake me. I sat there in the car sobbing; joyful and more in love with that child, perhaps, than ever before.

Almost a month has gone by since then. Our communications have increased in not only frequency but depth. The curtain is finally down and he has been able to open up to me in all sorts of new ways. He never told his mother of our conversation, though I did share a good bit of it with her. I will speak to my oldest daughter in the very near future. I am waiting to speak to our youngest child until some other issues are dealt with having to do with our her peer group, support, and the rural environment in which they live. I have been a very firm believer that each one of us MUST make the decision to come out to our children at a time WE think is appropriate. As I have said before, the support and integrity and maturity of this group has been a lifeline for all of us. Yes, sometimes we have to select and sort through the amount of info, but that is OUR responsibility. Thank you, again, to each and every one of you for what you give.

DON'T TAKE KIDS FOR GRANTED

From: Bib

I wanted to let everyone know that reality has set in a bit on me about this divorce. I met with my man about 1:00 yesterday afternoon and spent the night with him. Yesterday evening we talked a little about what it's going to be like when I move out of the house. Although I was feeling joy and relief over being able to finally be free, I realized how much I am going to miss my children. I feel as though I am leaving them. I'm going to miss my five-year-old daughter giving me a kiss and hug before she goes to bed each night. I'm going to miss telling my 11-year-old son to stop slamming the doors. I'm going to miss the day-to-day things a father grows to love about his children. Although I will be having them one night a week and every other weekend, I still feel as though I am losing them. It hurts deeply! I lay there and cried in my man's arms last night as this reality finally came down on me. I felt so hurt over what this is going to do between me and my children that I laid there and cried and wished that I had never been born.

My friends, if you have children, don't take them for granted. Love them, spend time with them, and collect those memories each and every day.

HAVEN'T YET COME OUT TO KIDS

From: Joey

I came out to my wife 5 months ago and she has been very supportive. She has her days, mind you, when it is very hard on both of us. But, my point is, we waited until she was ready before we approached our 11-year-old son. When she could handle the scene, then "we" talked to him. It was important in our minds that we were handling the situation. Since then, he has witnessed less than great moments. But, being aware that this is difficult for both of us and that we are talking our way through it, is beneficial for him to see. No marriage is without strain no matter what. For him to see that we both still care about each other above all, is leaving a positive mark for him.

To let you know how good things have gone for me and my son, this is what he wrote in my birthday card: "Even though you are gay, I still will love you for the rest of my life. For that's what friendship is for (or in this case Father-son-hood)." I started to read this out loud and couldn't finish as I got so choked up.

From: Farran

I am blessed with a great wife who said to my own parents, as they were condemning me for both being gay and for "walking out," that if they loved their grandchildren and ever wanted to see them again they would deal with this constructively. She told them it is "their problem, not Farran's."

From: Garner

I am a pediatrician and deal with kids and all the problems associated with them, both emotional and medical. My wife and I are coming to terms with my being gay and as for the moment our sons have no idea there is even an issue.

Children have a tough enough time with divorce and the following opinion is mine and mine alone. I feel sexuality in general is something to be
open about but we never discuss sexual activity with our wives to our children, they don't really want to know when or even if we have sex :). To tell
our children we are gay is a heavy trip and divorce is difficult enough.

My general feelings are if I meet someone I truly care about and love and
a relationship is established then by all means I will tell my sons. However
until the point arrives I don't see the need. If our marriage ends it will be
enough to explain. Children will love us as long as we have given them the
love and best nurturing we can. It may not be immediate but I think almost
all will come around and love us even though we don't fit the mold of heterosexual couples anymore.

From: Brandon

After working with nearly 300 or so men in the local area who are gay fathers (from GAMMA, Gay Fathers, Northwest AIDS' Foundation, Chicken
Soup, & Dignity) I do not find that your observations are correct. In the instances where a parent has come out to their children, where the relationship
was a good one before coming out, the children handle the news of a Gay or
BI father quite well. In most instances the relationship between parent and
child improves after some initial reservations. It does make a difference if
the spouse or former spouse is supportive. It also helps that the spouse (former spouse) be present during the revelation of homosexuality or Bisexuality. It is also advantageous to tell all of the children so that a later disclosure
to one does not make that person feel like they could not be trusted, feel left
out of family decisions, or that one is to embarrassed to include them.

Also, it helps to only include in the coming-out information to the extent
that it is appropriate to the ages of the children. One's personal sexual practices are never appropriate.

If the child is old enough, it is wise to include a discussion of SAFE SEX.
With AIDS information everywhere they know the risks and will be worried
about you and whether you been safe. A simple: "I have always practiced
and will continue to practice SAFE SEX" will do!

From: James

I hope that Amity Buxton will respond to your post. I'm not a pediatrician, but I disagree with you. Hopefully Amity will share that her research
in talking to 20 children with a gay/BI parent revealed they were unanimous
that you should tell your children and tell them soon regardless of age.

My two cents (or so).

From: Archie

I agree that "coming out" to our children is not something we should reveal unless it becomes absolutely necessary. My wife and I have been separated almost three years now. Our five children have had a hard enough time trying to adjust and deal with the emotional baggage that comes with such a separation without having to have the complications of their father's "gayness" added to their troubles.

My wife believes I wronged her and the children because of my gayness and that there would be no benefit served in revealing the truth to our children. I don't agree with her for this reason. I "outed" myself to her prior to getting married so that she would have the opportunity to say "nay" or "yeah" to the further establishment of our relationship. She chose to stay. In so doing she also chose to accept me as I was: loyal, faithful, true, supportive, caring, and gay. I'm still that same man today only freed from the burden of a marriage gone awry. I'm sure that the children will learn the truth in time, but when they do it will come from me as I view the truth—not by someone's distorted view—and the truth be known my only clear and present objective is to be the best father I can to five wonderful, beautiful children.

From: Alex

I don't see how I can attempt to hide the fact that I'm gay from the kids any longer—if I don't tell them, they are likely to find out about it from someone else and that's the last thing I want to happen. It is likely my wife and I will be separating sometime in the new year—I am thinking it would be better for them to find out while I am still at home—for at least a short period of time. . . .

Continuing on, deceiving them isn't going to benefit anyone that I can see—only make matters worse in the long run. I realize that a separation/divorce is a lot for them to handle on its own and finding out that I am gay will only compound the issue for them but I have heard many others who have had their kids go through similar situations and still end up managing to cope with the situation—albeit not an easy one to deal with.

From: Dalas

For those of you with kids whom you have/will come out to, the link below may be a helpful site to bookmark/favorite. The acronym stands for Children of Lesbians And Gays Everywhere. Visit it and consider giving the address to your children. Kids who have gone through the same situation can often be very helpful and good role models.

And kids can really surprise you. I remember I was driving my older daughter and some kids someplace when one of the guys made an anti-gay remark. She stopped him in his track by saying in a very confrontational tone, "You have a problem with gay people?" Then there is my other daughter who is co veep [co-vice president] of her high school Gay-Str8 Alliance. . . .

http://www.colage.org

From: Jonathon

The chilliest word in many of these letters is HIDING. Come out come out wherever you are. Hiding suggests you have something (shameful, unacceptable) to conceal.

Kids will surprise you.

From: Amity Buxton <dir@ssnetwk.org>

You're right to go slow and easy—even though kids have told me that the sooner the better. But "sooner" does not mean immediately, rather, sooner rather than later. Many were referring specifically to their parent's hiding and lying.

As you know from your work and mine from teaching, so much depends on the circumstances of each family—age of kids, etc., etc. Moreover, both parents need to be at ease enough with the new information and how it's impacting the family that they can provide the kind of support that's needed when the kids learn about their parent's new identity and orientation. So if they aren't at ease, the kids will be even more confused.

Just take it slow and easy . . . but not so long that the kids figure out something's amiss and dream up all sorts of scary, unreal things.

CONVERSATION WITH SON

From: Joey

I have to recount to you a conversation that I had with my son this past weekend. This is one of those moments that dwarfs all others and makes you realize what the true meaning of life is.

He and I were having dinner together and he brought up the subject of my youth. You know, "Dad, when you were my age . . ." In the course of my response about my eating habits, he commented, "Oh I didn't know you lived with your mom. I thought you lived with your dad." I responded with a bit of surprise and realized that my youth was really an unknown to him. So, I gave him the abbreviated history of my father's 5 marriages and my mother's 3. I also recounted with a little detail about the day my dad left my mom for wife #4. He smiled, as most do when they hear about the passions of my parents and who begot whom. After I finished, he said, "Wow, you know you and mom are so great. The way you are dealing with this situation and how you came to me. I don't know how to say it but you two are such a terrific couple." (Mind you, this guy is 12.) Then he said, "I can't imagine you two apart." I took the opportunity and said, "Well, what if a man should come into my life?" He looked at me without a change of expression. (I was waiting for him to react negatively.) He said, "You know I went to my sex education teacher and said that I was offended by the way kids say bad things about gays. My dad is gay." I was stunned. I asked what did she say. He said, she said that without naming names, she would address this with the class. I looked at him and told him how very proud of him I am. (I can't even write this without filling up with tears.) I started to cry and told him how very much I loved him and I was so glad that he was my son. He filled up with tears as well and said that he was so happy that I was his dad. We stood up from the table and hugged. Guys, this is the most wonderful child, so accepting, so loving. Nothing I can think of will ever replace that moment as being the heart of my existence. To be able to tell him the truth and have him love me for who I am makes all of this worth it.

From: Lou

That's SO wonderful!!! Wow . . . what a blessing, eh? I know you feel a million pounds lighter to know how accepted you are by your son!!! Too cool!

SON MEETING FRIEND?

From: Joey

My wife and I have been debating how to best handle my son meeting my gay friends. A new friend of mine has expressed an interest in going out to a play and would like our son to join us. (I think that this invitation is remarkable since all of the other guys I have met have not expressed more than a casual interest in my wife or son. So, for someone to want to include my son to attend a local event is a shocker! This guy, by the way, is very nice, professional and we have only been out once. I think he is trying to be forthcoming and show his acceptance of my fatherhood.) My wife has heard that when it appears to be a dating situation, then the kids should not be involved—ever. That seeing a parent in what is perceived to be a date sends a very confusing message to the kid, confused allegiance, etc. I have no problem conforming to this, I see her point completely. But, today, my friend has made yet another suggestion on something the three of us can do together. How have the other parents here handled this kind of a situation? I fully respect what my wife wants here but are we being too narrow in our approach?

From: Marvin

My immediate impression is that attending a play, with you and a man he's never met, sounds a bit strained . . . how old is your son? Has he met your friend, even briefly? I would think that you'd be better introducing the two of them in a less structured environment first . . . and seeing where it goes.

My children know most of my gay friends . . . and were well acquainted with (one of) my lovers. We let it happen naturally—things like my lover just stopping by to chat when the kids were home, running into each other out & about—that type of thing—short-term, very natural meetings—then moved more naturally into doing things together . . . it worked.

From: Bruce

You could try to just make excuses every time this guy makes an invitation, but I really don't know that it's a good idea, especially if he seems like he may be someone who you may be interested in having a long-term relationship with. (He apparently has that idea in mind or he probably wouldn't be so interested in meeting your wife and son.) Depending on the age of the child, though, your wife might be right about not taking him along on anything that resembles a date. Besides being confused, unless the play is really geared to a child his age he's probably not going to warm up to this guy very well.

I introduced my lover to my daughter (She was 9 at the time) by arranging a day at the amusement park for the 3 of us one Saturday when my wife was away. It was something that both of them enjoyed, and a very relaxed atmosphere. It didn't really seem like a date since it was really HER day and we were just tagging along.

My wife and I had gone to dinner with him several weeks before, and I think THAT went better than if my daughter had been along too. She seemed to be more open and ready to talk than if our daughter had been there. Later, we added events for the entire family, but only after everyone was comfortable with each other.

From: Greg

Would it really be a "date" or a "night out with the boys?" Obviously the context makes a big difference in the conduct exhibited. I think it would be great for your son to see that two gay men can be just as fun to be around as all those str8 guys at a game. Just save the kissing, hand holding, etc., for a more intimate time or when you think your son is ready to handle this other reality.

From: Joey

Thanks for the valuable input. A couple of things. First, my wife sent along the following as an addendum. I think this will better present the point of view that was given us. Second, my son is 11. He has met my boyfriend at a dinner party (the infamous dinner party back in December that some of you will remember started WWIII, the short war.) My son remembers my friend from that evening.

I would like to add that I would NEVER have my friend join me on a date. That is totally inappropriate. I was just trying to get a sense of what would a kid consider a date and what he/she would not. If any time I am with a friend particularly one who I am not dating, will that still be perceived by him/her as a date anyway? That is the crux of the issue for us. Thanks again all.

Brenda wrote: >*What I have heard, re friends of either the gay spouse or the straight spouse, is that any dating or one-on-one friendship should be completely invisible to kids. The kids need to feel that they are number one in their parents' world and that their parents revolve around them. Introduction to single outsiders sends the possible message that this is who their mom/dad is now interested in. Even if this is not confusing, I've heard that kids spend a lot of time/energy trying to figure out what this person means to them, trying to please them, get to know them, put them into some context. If this person is not a significant other, then the kid has to go through the whole process all over again (and again) with other insignificant others. I've been told that, unless there is a compelling reason to introduce this person to your kid, better leave well enough alone.*>

From: Bruce

All kids are different, but I don't think that my daughter has ever considered any of the activities that she's taken part in as being a date, and the activities have included everything from the day at the park I mentioned to dinner and a movie, to lunch and shopping. My lover and I are probably not as attentive to each other on those occasions as we might be if we were out alone, but that's about the only difference.

My guess is that, at 11, your son will probably take his queue on whether the person is a romantic partner from the way that you act around him. If you treat him as simply a friend, he'll probably pick up on that.

From: Bruce

My relationship to my lover IS invisible to my daughter in that she's never been told that we're anything other than friends. Introducing him has made it easier to include him as one of the family, and she seems to like that. I'm fairly sure that she's made some type of connection that he and I have something more than a simple friendship, but I've tried to make sure that she isn't assaulted with more information than she can handle. She still knows that she's very special in my life and I think that she ALSO thinks that she's very special to him.

My daughter has been introduced to a number of my friends over the last several years, and many of them are my gay friends. . . single and couples. For the most part, she's enjoyed meeting them and I think that it helps when I mention their names at home that she knows who I'm talking about. It was much more uncomfortable for both of us when I was being closed lipped about where I was going and what I was doing. She seemed to know that I wasn't being entirely honest with her. I hated that because it made her feel more left out, and seemed to say that it's OK not to tell the whole truth. Age has a lot to do with it though. At 12, she seems able to handle most things and know the difference between being evasive and protecting one's privacy. She's at an age when she's not wanting Mom and Dad hovering over her all the time, so me being away with friends isn't that big of a deal.

From: Moris

Won't it be nice when can hold hands in public!!! And that it would not be demeaned as something inappropriate for a kid to see?

At home, my boyfriend gives me a kiss (not a deep kiss) when he gets home just as I give my wife a kiss when I get home REGARDLESS OF WHO IS THERE!

My 3-year-old grandson thinks nothing of my husband and I kissing! and holding hands!

We teach our kids about proper str8 contact from the time they are born. Why do we wait until the kids are ready to teach them proper gay contact?

DISTRESSED ABOUT GAY FATHERS

From: George

I didn't want to upset the system by putting "help" in the subject line, but this is a situation that calls for my (our) help to a young person who is terribly emotionally distressed upon hearing his father is BI(gay). My lover last week came out to his wife, daughter 20, and his son 12. This was a surprise move to me since he has always been determined not to come out to anyone. He told me Sunday night that his depression re: being dishonest with his wife and family combined with his guilt caused him to make the move. He did not however, tell his wife or children that he and I are lovers. My wife and I have known his family for years, double dated, etc. and as most of you older members know, my lover is also my best friend. To make things more complicated and, yes, depressing for me and my lover is the fact that Sunday afternoon his son came to me totally confused and depressed. He rambled on and on about his concern for his father and mother, will they divorce, etc. Then after an hour or more of sobbing, rambling, etc., he came out with a fear that is terribly real to him, "Because my father is gay, does that mean that I will be gay too?" This is a real concern for him, he can't stomach the thought of being gay, of losing his friends, being condemned by his peers at school. Our community is very homophobic, a fact that is obvious to this young man. This is a concern that I cannot answer. I told him that I would find, and pay for a counselor to see him, that it would be private, and that no one needed to know about his seeing him. He, as I said, has no idea of the relationship that his father and I have. I already talked to my counselor today about the situation and he feels that to let the boy know of our relationship, at least at this point, would just add to his disillusion. The help I need from my fellow brothers is information about existing online groups that the boy can hook up with. Right now, he doesn't want to talk to anybody other than the counselor I told him about. He is so afraid that others, his friends and relatives, will find out about his father. His father, my friend, has promised his wife and children that he will not come out any further, that he will do nothing to publicly embarrass his family. But, the boy is going to need support and when he is ready for it, it would be nice if I had the names of groups for him to contact. Right now, I am his only support and, under the circumstances, I feel like the world's biggest heel right now. My friend never expected this result. He came out because he felt the need for honesty. I guess one never knows what the impact the orientation bombshell will have when finally dropped. As most of you know, I came out to my wife a year ago. After much anger, sorrow, all of the usual responses to the coming-out event, we are presently doing quite well. I am confident that our marriage will last. But, after this experience with my friend's son, I doubt seriously that I will ever come out to my children, or any further than I already am. The uncertainty of it all is too scary. Thanks for listening, and thanks for your anticipated help in providing me with the online locations where my friend's son can seek support when he is ready to accept it.

From: Mike

Try a Web search for PFLAG (parents and friends of lesbian and gays) and/or COLAGE (Children of Lesbian and Gays Everywhere). I'm sure that will lead you to some online support for this young man. I think it's wonderful that he chose to come to you for support. Obviously he thinks a lot of you. I know it must put you in an awkward position now . . . but when the dust settles . . . and he knows the whole story . . . he may see that you and his father are still the loving supportive men you've always been to him. Hopefully, he will see that his knowing now that you and/or his father are gay, does not change any of the qualities about you and his dad that nourished him in the first place.

From: Homer

My first marriage ended because my first wife suspected me of having an affair with a gay friend from high school. My two sons, who also have a gay out uncle (my ex's brother), have grown up to be very normal and healthy young men. The oldest is 18. The youngest is still in high school. Do not worry about your children finding out you are gay affecting them. If anything, my sons finding out that their mother thought I was gay and having a gay affair, and that their uncle is gay has made the boys much more tolerant and they now know that gay men are not out to try to molest them. Having a gay father and a gay uncle has made them much more well-rounded where they now know not to jump to the assumption that gays are bad and that being gay is a horrible thing. Keep the faith and trust your children to know that you love them no matter if your are gay or straight.

There is a lot of love in this group and support for you and our many other members.

From: Dern

Every one is different, including children. I have three boys. I came out to them one year after I told my wife. We waited for Linda to be over most of the shock. We figured it would be easier for them to see a united front and also for them not to see their mother falling apart. That was two years ago. The boys were taken aback but they have not changed their ways of interacting with me. Their schooling was not affected much. The youngest had more concerns than the others. He was 13 at the time—a very hard age anyway. The other two were in college and a senior in high school. I have found it nice to be able to talk and move in complete honesty in my house and so does my wife.

From: Max

The only input I feel I can make on this is your more than generous offer to pay for the lad to have counseling.

While it is a noble and charitable deed, I would fear that in time it may cause more problems than it would solve. Also, I feel it would interfere with what is currently a weakened father-son relationship.

Please, in reading this just see what I'm writing. At no point am I either criticizing or second-guessing your judgment.

However, although the "problem" stems from the lad's perception of being gay, etc. I would feel that dealing with it and seeking counseling should be done through his parents.

If the nature of your relationship with his father were to come out later (and so far he's surprised you by outing himself to his family), then how would this alter the lad's perception of you and the reason(s) why you comforted him and suggested counseling. While I find reading your letter really heart-warming and humbling, there really does appear to be a conflict of interest (to the outside observer).

The reason why I've copied this to the group as opposed to my usual method of posting privately is that I feel my making the above comments deserves fair and due criticism. I am just one voice. A father and a son but nonetheless, one voice with one person's experience. I would hope to provoke thought, not to cause an immediate about-turn.

WHEN TO TELL THE KIDS?

From: Sidney

I am living with my wife and this will stay the same. At some time in the future a cute guy may move in. Our 25-year-old she lives at home and is finishing college and will be leaving home shortly. My 18-year-old child is away at college. Any thoughts? Two of my best gay friends think I must tell them ASAP. Another says never—NO. My wife says they need to be told but when I am stronger.

Any Ideas?

From: Moris

Your wife is right. When you are stronger. That is when you no longer feel guilty or bad because you are gay. When you know and ACCEPT!

without guilt who you are. Then tell. That is when I did to mine . . . Found that to be the best for me.

From: Gent

The most important consideration should probably be that your kids find out from you or someone else of your choosing at the time that you feel best based on what's best for you and for them. The hard part, and one I can't answer either, is WHEN. I don't know when, but if you think they will learn it from some other source that is either hostile or unfriendly to you, then I would make plans to tell them sooner than later. My own kids are pre-teen, so I haven't crossed this bridge yet. I am basically planning on letting it be a matter-of-fact thing based on their ages and then let them ask questions as they may arise.

From: Brandon

I would vote with your wife on this one and yes you absolutely need to include them in who you really are as a person; but you MUST tell them from a position of strength (i.e., stronger). The more that you truly love yourself the more they will appreciate their real father. From the sounds of your e-mail, I say you are about there. Be advised that your outing can go many ways with them and you need to be prepared for the eventual outcome no matter what that should be. It is best that you be the one that tells them and the sooner the better.

Also be advised that in most of cases where the father comes out to his children, it goes remarkably well. There are usually some reservations early on but generally the relationship with the child improves remarkably. You must prepare yourself for the eventuality of losing one or both of your children if the coming-out goes badly with them. Always remember you are not responsible for their happiness or their reaction.

Also, your wife's attitude and acceptance of herself as the spouse of a Gay/Bi man has a big influence on how the children react to the revelation of being the child of a Gay/Bi parent. It is a very good thing to have your wife in the room with you when you tell them. She doesn't necessarily have to even say anything, but if she does, she, like you, must be open and honest about her feelings and reservations on being or remaining married to you.

I came out to my three children (your kids' ages when I came out to them) and it went very well after some early reservations on both of my son's parts. Daughter had no problem and said that she always suspected that I was gay.

From: Dern

All the suggestions are good. My wife and I provided a united front when we told the kids. We told all of them together because we felt is was not fair to have anyone carry the burden of the others not knowing. We also felt it would be best for another reason and that was so they would have each other to talk to about it. We waited until my wife was through most of the initial pain so she could be on my side and assure the children that nothing was different about their father. My three children are all teenagers. It has made our relationship better and now my wife and I can talk about things openly, not in couched words. It went very well for me. The one fact in your favor is that they are older. The youngest had the biggest concern and was afraid of being an outcast for having a gay father. We have had some things happen but all was resolved and my youngest was stronger for it.

From: Joey

I told my 12-year-old about myself shortly after telling my wife. We decided to wait until we were both ready to approach him when we were BOTH strong. We felt that he needed to see that we were both OK with my being gay. It seemed to work well. At the time, I just said I had something important to share. He froze in anticipation. I told him that I loved him more than the stars and moon. I then told him that I had been dealing with my sexual orientation since I was a teenager but was afraid. I told him I was gay. He thought about what I said and said, well, at least you are not dying and you and mommy are not getting a divorce. He went on to say, this is how I was born and it is OK that I am gay. We cried and hugged and professed our love for each other. I know he does not understand the intimacy of gay love, hell he can't even imagine why anyone has sex at all. But, the point is, you both should tell your children. They are adults now and your revelation will have less impact on them than if they are teens.

Chapter 6
Advice and Comments

GETTING OFF THE CAROUSEL

From: Rolf

I've grown accustomed to the ups and downs of being out and married. Every so often, however, I am faced with a knot in the Slinky, as it were. It was one thing to make the mistake of falling in love with a married man who is not out to his wife. Strike one . . . got in and out with a minimum of emotional damage (Damn, he was GIB). Then to meet a younger military man who showed some interest in pursuing a relationship, but crumbled when his ex entered the picture.

OK, so far. Then, to meet a single man, very attentive, no sex yet, but lots of heat, chemistry, and shared intimacy. Until . . . he finds out, on a second meeting, I am in an open married relationship. Then the morality and the "A" word come up. Very respectful, not totally dismissive, but certainly more discomfort on his part than I feel safe with. He's "thinking about it" and so am I.

Three questions occur to me, for those men who are in open marriages and have successfully established and maintained a relationship with a male lover (not involving your spouse):

1. Where did you meet these men? What venues have not been productive?
2. When and how to disclose? I certainly don't feel comfortable discussing my family with every man I am "involved" with. But, if you wait to see if it has potential, then it looks as if you have withheld info.
3. What are the chances of maintaining a balanced relationship with a spouse with whom you have shared history/companionship and a man with whom you have intimacy, Eros and a hope of building something meaningful?

This is the first time I have put out real stuff, so I would ask you to be gentle. On the other hand I want answers. To be honest, I am feeling very dubious, a little numb and somewhat helpless. It just seems like more than I can manage, but I am lonely. Anonymous or meaningless liaisons don't cut it anymore. I need more. . . .

From: Mitch

I have one ongoing relationship of three years duration . . . another crashed and burned after about 1.5 years . . . two others are still working on their first year. Another man evolved into a close friend of both me and my wife after about a year (his and my sexual relationship ended at about that time); he has been in our life for 5 years now. I leave it to you do decide whether this is success by your own feelings; I am only counting the men with whom I share a strong emotional bond; fuck-buddies and fun flings are a whole other question.

One thing that is both a great stress creator and reliever in my case is that these are all long-distance relationships. This demands a lot of effort and creates a special kind of loneliness that folks not in the same situation rarely understand. BUT it also helps keep my wife from feeling constantly encroached upon by my male friends. I do not want to always have the men I love living 400-1,500 miles away (ye gods but I want that to be able to change some day!), but it has been working so far for us. It's not for everyone!

As for where I have met men: Online (hence the long distance thing) and friends-of-friends have been best for me. Social functions that were NOT first-and-foremost about sex (like hikes and outings with the local bear club) I have also found sometimes introduce me to men with whom I become good friends. Worst place to meet a man for a longer-term relationship in my experience: BARS! Just not a good place to find guys who will be interested in relating closely to someone in our special sorts of circumstances; as soon as they hear the word "wife" they'll probably be out the door and cursing you and all other bisexuals under their breath.

My advice (worth the electrons it is printed with) is this: If your gut tells you that this man might possibly be someone you'd want to have an ongoing emotional relationship with, not only a short-term or casual fling, disclose your marital status AS SOON AS POSSIBLE. Before the first roll in the hay is good, I think. I always wear my wedding ring, and if I get that "good man, possible boyfriend" vibe from a man I try to mention my wife somehow very early on. It keeps bad scenes from happening later. And if he runs . . . well, he runs. Next!

Oh man, I sure wish I knew the answer to the chances of maintaining a balanced relationship with a spouse and a man with whom you have intimacy! Some men on this list have worked this out in various ways for various lengths of time. As for having it work indefinitely, I sure hope it can be done because I am presently involved with a man I would love to remain intimate with till death do we part. It seems the way to do this is unique for every marriage and every man friend.

Good luck! We're all trying to figure these same things out ourselves.

From: Bruce

OK, I've been seeing a man for a year now, I guess it's time to admit to those who don't know it how our relationship started. We actually spoke to each other for the first time one fine spring day when we saw each other at the airport overlook, one of this city's most notorious gay cruising spots. NOT a place I would suggest going if you were interested in anything more than a quickie.

All in all, I think that involvement in community activities is probably the best place to meet other men. The reason that I asked this man out on a date that day when we met probably had more to do with the fact that I'd seen him at a number of events in the gay community over the previous 18 months than anything that happened watching planes land. At community events you're exposed to a broad cross section of the community, and have a chance to get to know them in a fairly low-pressure environment. And even if there's nobody there that you hit it off with, most gay men just LOVE playing matchmaker, and everybody has a couple of unattached friends.<G>

I had also tried meeting men in bars and online, and while I do know cases where both have developed into serious relationships, neither ever worked for me.

I told him I was married the first time we talked. I had gotten to a point of being rebuffed so often by guys that I told that I wanted to get it out of the way as soon as possible. If it was something that they couldn't accept, then I wanted to know that before I started getting too emotionally involved.

I didn't go into a great deal of detail when we talked the first time other than to say I was married and out. A week later when we went on our first date I mentioned that I had a daughter but didn't volunteer much more information. Several days after that though, we both felt a need to get together for a "where is this thing going" talk, and THEN I went into things in quite a bit of detail.

It's not easy but yes, it is possible to maintain a balanced relationship with your spouse and a man with whom you have intimacy. As mentioned, my male lover and I have now been together for a year, and it has been a relationship that has been fulfilling beyond my wildest dreams. The two of us really never intended for the relationship to be anything beyond something very casual, but within a month after our first date we had fallen in love.

For us one thing that has helped enormously is that soon after we began to get serious about the relationship I started making plans to get my lover and my wife together to meet each other. Fortunately they liked each other from the start. He does things with my family and I on occasion, which helps me avoid having to choose between them for certain events. The two of them being on friendly terms has also made them feel less that they're in competition for me. They each know that the other has everybody's best interests at heart.

Building a loving relationship has presented some challenges to be sure, but that's true in almost every relationship, gay, straight, or bisexual. There are barriers that we face because (as he's known from the start) I have no plans to leave my family. We've worked around that though, and through trial and error found what works for us. It's difficult sometimes not being able to spend the night when I want, but we've hit on an arrangement where one weekend a month I spend with him, either at his place or traveling somewhere. On other occasions I may stay and "tuck him in," kissing him goodnight, then turning out the lights and locking up as I let myself out as he falls asleep. I know it's corny, but for us it works.

Although we do not live together we are able to be pretty much the same as couples who do. We volunteer and contribute to different causes in the community together, support each other when we need it, and try to spend as much time as we can together even if it's just cuddled up on the couch watching TV. My wife can accept this because she knows that I'm doing the same for her and our daughter. They are both very accepting of the fact that there are some times when it's important that I be with the other one, and know that I'll try to balance my time as much as possible. For example, I'm getting ready now to attend Church with my wife and daughter. This evening I'll be in Church again, only this time I'll be at MCC.

Most of us here at some time or another have felt exactly like you do now. If it's any consolation, a little over a year ago I was feeling so depressed that one of my friends on this list was ready to hop a plane and fly halfway across the country to see what he could do to pull me out of it. Two weeks later I was looking across a restaurant table at this man, wondering why I was starting to feel so funny. . . .<G>

BACK TO BUSINESS

From: James

Lenny wrote: >*BUT here's my all-absorbing question: is it realistic to think that one can truly lead a full, active life as a gay man AND a successful mar-*

ried life. Can there really, really be a balance? How in the hell do you split the two? It seems to me that we as a group are a bit selfish in wanting both. If you had to give us new just-muddlin-through-it-now newcomers one GOOD SOLID piece of advice PERIOD what would it be?<

It is my style to usually respond to this type of post privately but you ask such a central question, one many of us face, have faced, and will continue to face, that I'm going to respond publicly. I guess I respond in irritation first . . . at the suggestion that I am selfish to want both. . . . because I know that my wife wishes to remain married and I gave her the option of not remaining married when I came out to her. And I believe she has the right to seek a separation or divorce anytime that is the best decision for her to live honestly and fulfilled and true to herself. Also, I know to be true to myself, I cannot promise to avoid a male friendship that includes intimacy. This is a crucial issue for every couple represented by the membership of this list.

And it IS hard for the wife and it IS hard for the husband also. Yes, you bet, I feel torn. . . . I felt torn when I was in a relationship and I feel torn in times like now when I am not in a relationship. It is a balancing act to be sure. . . . I want my wife to feel nurtured, loved, and special and enjoy an active sex life so it means being certain that happens and if I do something with another guy, there also has to be things planned with her in mind, and I need to be sensitive to the day before and the day after I spend time with a guy because she needs that attention at those times . . . your implication that this is not easy is correct but it is a choice some of us have made. You ask is it possible to maintain an active gay life and an active married life . . . this is THE question we men face . . . for me, the active gay life has not really happened, but the successful married life has. . . . I, for one, cannot say that both can happen but my impression is that it has happened for two of the guys on this list for sure. . . . I try not to envy both these guys (<G> . . .) and some days I'm successful. . . . and some days not . . . (<G> . . . like today). . . .

I don't have an active gay life . . . rather, I have periodic moments and as many of us have shared after our guy gatherings, . . . there is a definite withdrawal afterwards because the quality of the talk and bonding is so stimulating and rewarding that it is sorely missed . . . my philosophy or rationalization, as the case may be, is that life is always a balancing act . . . we balance our professional time with our family time, we balance the time we spend working on our houses or our cars or our yards or whatever with other issues . . . so now, we work this aspect into our lives . . . gee, thinking about this makes me tired. . . .

This is my perspective on your rainy-day question . . . now, back to my green banana!

From: Schuyler

What a wonderful post, James. You are so articulate, and you always seem to hit just at the heart of the matter. I'd like to use your comments as a reference point for some of my thoughts and personal situation.

I must continually remind myself that my recent choices have created an ethical/moral dilemma for my wife that is HERS ALONE to deal with. I know that she is struggling with it, and I have also learned that there is very little or nothing that I can do to "convince" her that the "correctness" of MY choice is the correct choice for HER.

It has taken years (and much therapy) for me to recognize my need for an intimate male relationship, and to realize that being true to myself is CRITICAL to my self-esteem and happiness, whether or not the marriage is to survive. AND I am in an intimate male relationship that continues to astonish and fulfill me in so many ways that I could only imagine before. Unlike your wife, my wife does not necessarily wish to remain married—at least not to ME. I KNOW that she would MUCH prefer to have a relationship with a man for whom she is ENOUGH. This fact causes pain for BOTH of us. We stay together for reasons that are quite different for each of us. I believe that there is a love and commitment (perhaps on different levels) from each of us, as well as very practical reasons (finances, kids, etc.) that make staying together easier than the alternative. And NO, it is NOT easy.

Learning how to better achieve this balance is what this group is all about for me.

Boy, oh Boy, being sensitive to her is the REALLY tough one for me. Knowing how to be sensitive around this issue is really tough. For the most part, although I don't make a POINT of telling her when I'm going to be with my boyfriend (we meet ALMOST exclusively during our regular work hours), she has an uncanny way of "figuring it out" and typically responds with a decidedly cool manner and clear signals NOT to attempt (even NON-sexually) intimacy. I have found that it is usually best just to let the storm pass, while respecting her right to withdraw within herself. Sometimes this backfires, though, and she's hurt by the inattention. It can be really tough to read when this mood has begun and ended. There's no MANUAL for this stuff.

I do want to live an authentic and honest life, and for me that means not only not denying, but EXPERIENCING my need for BOTH male and female intimacy (from ONE person of EACH sex). I am very close to having what I want (or think I want for now) in terms of male intimacy, AND it comes at a very GREAT price in terms of my marriage, which clearly, at this point, is NOT successful.

Even with the wife and the boyfriend, there are MANY more "green banana days" than any other kind <VBG>.

I NEED A LITTLE ADVICE

From: Stephen

I have reached the portal and am afraid to go through it. I have found the answer to my bisexual needs and am afraid to embrace it. I need help and advice to know what to do. What you people have done in your lives may hold the key to helping me decide on a course of action. I am either going to create a dream come true or hell on Earth as I destroy my marriage. I can't tell which, and of course you can't either. But you CAN tell me how you have, or are handling the problems I am facing.

First of all we should get straight that my wife is NOT the problem. Her love and support for me has been beyond belief, and certainly more than I ever expected of her. My wife has made fantastic progress in dealing with my bisexuality. But, this love and need I have for men is REAL, and not some stupid mind game or something that is going to go away. She fully knows and realizes the implications of that fact, and that even if I promised her (in good faith) that I would be monogamous and faithful to her, that it would be a lie, and that sooner or later my body, my hormones, my feelings, and my sex drive would force me out into the world to be what I am, and do what my nature compels me to do, and what I NEED to do. To be with a man!

I am about to form a "friendship" with a man and that will put me into 2 separate monogamous relationships. What I am worried about, and afraid of are those "special days," as well as the general logistics of being in 2 loving relationships at once. I am especially worried since even though my wife accepts my need for such a relationship, she does not (at this time) feel comfortable with the idea of meeting or interacting with the man I choose. She prefers that I compartmentalize that part of my psyche and keep most of it to myself.

This is also a little more complicated by the fact that I am seeing two great men right now. Anyway, both of these men are wonderful, each in his own way, and I can't choose between them at this point. Sometimes I feel like some air-headed cheerleader playing the field and fucking everything in sight. I want them both. One is an executive with a major airline and the other is an ex-minister working as a psychologist. They are both special men and not to be taken lightly. Each of them gives nourishment to a different part of my mind and soul. And then of course there is my wife, whom I worship and adore, and who nourishes my heterosexual self, and those needs, with skill and love beyond compare. How does one balance a three-some like this? Or, if I can cut it down to only one man, how do you balance the world's greatest wife and a fantastic lover and make them both feel loved and keep the lover from feeling like he's getting screwed on special days and by life in general? I am really afraid to make the commitment to my man because I am afraid that I will hurt him and God knows that is not my intention. They both know that I cannot and will not ever leave my wife. She has the power to ask me to leave, and I would go, but I will never leave her loving arms willingly. I want to be, and do, what is honorable within the parameters of this highly unusual marital situation. . . . HELP! How do you guys make this work?

From: Bart

I haven't usually (have I ever?) written into this list, but it's not a bad time for me to get some help with a similar situation. I have some definite and not so definite ideas about threesomes. My wife and I are good friends with Amity Buxton whom we recently met up with for the Gay Parents weekend. My wife has been doing outstanding work with the strait spouse side with her own support group locally. We've advanced tremendously in the five years since I came out. I've had a friend (eventually became my male lover) whom I met over 5 years ago at our nearby famous beach, we started going out, had a relationship on and off for well over 2 years. My wife did everything in her power to know him and demystify the ideas and blocks she experienced in herself, mostly societal conceptions and earlier personal abuse injuries.

They became instant friends, though he himself wrestles mostly with not wanting to be responsible for my wife and my break up, especially over him. He was in that situation as a young man in which his older partner left his wife precipitously and uncomfortably. We've sort of taken our situation and turned it inside out. He, 2 1/2 years ago moved away from here but I visited there, then last summer he came back and we spent such a tumultuous time trying to sort out just who the three of us were and what our needs were.

I don't think I ever had to let go of so much stuff, all of us for that matter, but the parting was always bittersweet. He and I have tried to phone each other every week (mostly every two), and simply live our lives. Now he is arriving again on Friday. I'm a basket case, because I know we might have to let our illusions dissolve, certainly mine. Where I have maintained or tried to, the responsibility I've felt for our mutual feelings, my life has changed a lot over the past year, including a good start in my own catering business and a lot of ground covered in my ever changing more open relationship with my wife; do I really want to work out a future where we're all together? When we parted last year, we had come to the realization that we all had a strong and specific task together, revolutionary if you will, because really, what road maps were there? We're all very freedom-loving souls, adventuresome, but tied to our established lives like anyone else might be. It was a chance to see how something unconventional could work. How the growth of each of us was influenced as well as handled by the other.

From: Kramer

I am compelled to jump in here and share, as this is a bit close to home for me as well.

For me, reinforcing the primacy of our marital union is key to my wife's security. What we decided together at the onset of my coming out was that pursuit of a relationship with another married man, who is also out to his spouse, who's spouse is also supportive of his sexuality, would lie within acceptable boundaries of our new paradigm.

And yes, our need for love/intimacy from other men is indeed real, and we must never underestimate how important this need is to our self-esteem. Like you, and many others I'm sure, I could not promise my wife monogamy. I made it quite clear to her that I love her, cherish her, she is the center of my universe, and that if ever she could not deal with the circumstances that go with my sexuality and wanted me to leave I would respect her wishes. Then and only then would I ever leave our marriage.

I have decided to live a duogamous lifestyle. I am a one woman man and a one man man. I sought and met my lover P last February. He and I live in cities that are 600 miles apart. We try to see one another a minimum of every 8 weeks. Also, P's wife has become a very good friend to me and she and my wife do get along very well. My wife and P get along very well also, they have built a brother/sister relationship with one another. We, all of us, are there for one another. What has helped tremendously is keeping the channels of communication very OPEN, and honest. If an issue comes up, we all try to iron it out together. And trust me, the issues do come up.

Special times and holiday's can be challenging, but that is where the creativity and flexibility come in. We have discussed holidays, and came to the conclusion that our families must come first. P and I will have our special times throughout the year. Also our distance from one another make dealing with holidays all that much easier.

What has been most challenging for my wife and I is the sleeping arrangements when P and I are able to be together. This has been the roughest on my wife. That final hurdle in sharing the one she loves with someone else. What has worked thus far is in each of our homes, we have a room designated as our room. When P comes to spend time with me we sleep in our guest room. On my end we must exercise great care in this respect as my wife and I do have two young children. We also have a room in P's home. The difficult part is when we (all 4 of us) are together. For instance, my wife and I are spending our vacation in September with them in his city. Of course P and I want to be together as much as feasibly possible, however we must work the feelings of all concerned into the equation. Again, this is where frank, open communication is so very important.

Naturally, we do not have all the answers, probably never will.

I hope it has helped you a little. I pray you find the happiness and fulfillment you seek.

I NEED HELP

From: See

I had a bit of a rough night in marital counseling tonight. We see a husband and wife couple for therapy (they're both licensed). I like the extra perspective of a male and a female in our sessions.

Tonight the male counselor said something to the effect of "Well are you gay or BI?" I said that where I am right now I'm not sure about those labels. He said, "well, it sorta makes a difference: if you were just BI, then you could be as happy with a man as a woman, and it really wouldn't be a sexuality issue, it would only be a monogamy issue. If you were gay, then it would be a different thing and you could never be happy sexually with your wife."

I felt pretty panicky on the drive home. I truly enjoy my relationship with my wife, including the sex, and she says I'm a pretty good lover by her standards. However, she is the only woman I have ever enjoyed having sex with (I've dated other women during high school and college, but remained a technical virgin until my marriage to my wife). There are many men that I've enjoyed sexual relationships with (after I was married to my wife). While I was explaining what I was feeling to my wife on the way home she said, "You sound like the comment I saw on SSML 'one woman shy of gay.'"

I'm not sure I agree with his comment that just because I feel I'm BI, I could be totally content sexually with only my wife. For me, I don't care about the label. I'm just interested in feedback if other folks have ever felt confused like this or uncomfortable with selecting a label to tattoo on their head <g>.

From: Dale

I'm a "one woman short of gay" kind of guy—not sexually attracted to women except my wife but more broadly attracted to males (though not

EVERY male!). The labels BI and gay have never felt like they captured the complexity and diversity that is "me." I feel the most honest and comfortable saying I'm "not straight."

My first reaction is that the male therapist is focused on his need to label you. I suspect he feels he needs to label you because he has a preconceived paradigm of treatment and suggested therapies if the label is "gay" and a different set of "instructions" if you are "bi." It feels like a therapist-centered approach rather than a client-centered approach.

My wife and I have been in therapy quite a long time. Our therapist has never tried to impose on us her "solutions" or her philosophy or some prepackaged therapy set forth for a given situation by her training. Rather, she has worked very hard to help us figure out what WE wanted to do with ourselves—and each other—and then help us find ways to make it come to pass. My wife, for example, came to therapy feeling emotionally threatened. She was certain I was probably trying to leave the marriage for a male love interest. So. . . . a lot of work was spent trying to reframe the universe in ways that would allow her to see that I WASN'T about to leave her as a life partner. That meant our carving out a different (new? maybe) reality for ourselves. Another "for example"—when my wife began to get some closer, more direct and personal insight and experience with the realities of me and male-to-male sex, it felt threatening to her. Male sex was "better" for me . . . therefore sex with her must be "worse." My reaction to/with a man felt "strong" to her . . . therefore my feelings for her must be "weak." Do you get the picture? The work of our therapist, then, was to help her to begin to understand that male-to-male sex is "different" in many ways from male-to-female sex . . . and different again from female-to-female sex. Being able to see things in THAT light helped her not to feel so competitive or to feel so diminished by the presence of male-to-male sex in my life.

It feels to me like your male therapist may academically know about gay/BI issues but that he comes with personal and/or training biases that "front-load" his ability to really help you address YOUR agenda as individuals and as a couple.

That's the view from MY bridge!

From: Rodger

The main problem becomes will your wife understand, let you seek outside male partners and will she feel secure in you being safe (sexually) and will she feel secure in knowing you are not trying to replace her with a man?

I go through this with my wife. She knew I was BI prior to marriage. But I did not act on my "other" sexuality till many years later. We do the rollercoaster ride. Great times . . . some lows. . . . She feels I am seeking another to replace her at times . . . It is a continuous labor of love to let her know I am not, and do not intend to leave her. Love is a strange thing. I love my wife . . . I love my lover. But in a different way.

I wish you and your wife luck. You are on the right track. It has been only 6 month for me. It is getting better. Smile. There is light at the end of the tunnel—just keep chugging along.

From: Lobo

Being aware of the danger of making a judgment call on a comment about a therapist, I will do so anyway. Trying to define what is gay and what is BI is baloney, as far as I'm concerned. This guy really doesn't understand the picture. Finding someone who does is the first order of business. As a psychiatrist, this is an informed opinion (not necessarily correct of course). We are all rooting for you.

From: James

I would be cautious in letting him influence you or your wife. Each couple has to establish what works for them. And the labels thing is like all labels, it helps in conversation, but often limits the reality of who people are. And there are GAY men who are married by choice . . . so let this couple help you where they can and "flush" the rest!

Might be helpful for you and your wife to attend a couples gathering at some point . . . will give you the perspective of other couples meeting many of the same challenges that face you and your wife . . . a thought . . . also a way to affirm who you are and your goals . . . thanks for sharing. . . .

From: Brandon

I am totally dumbfounded by what your counselor said!!!!

First of all his definition of BI is totally foreign to me. My definition of BI is someone that needs or fantasizes about a relationship (sexual, emotional and spiritual) with both male and female. For him to mislead you into thinking that you have a choice in your needs is bewildering to me. Only you can determine what your needs and thoughts are! It is not an either/or situation for most BI men that I have talked to.

Second of all I call myself Gay (that is where my primary eroticism lies), yet, I have and maintain a wonderful loving and mutually supportive relationship and marriage with my wife for 38 years now. We maintain a very active and mutually rewarding sex life that is both emotionally fulfilling and inventive because of the mixed nature of our sexuality. For him to tell you that you could never be happy sexually with your wife is bullshit at it's worst. Again only you and your wife (each in your own way and in your togetherness) can make the statements that he is trying to force you to believe.

From: Walter

I too would be classified as "one woman short."Although this situation is a lot more complex than that, I am still in love with my wife. I find her sexually attractive; we have a good sex life. Now, if you take the attraction to males away, yes, I am still attracted to other women, but I love my wife too much to want to destroy what we have.

Okay, now bring the male attraction back in. See how complex it is? Amity put it very well when she indicated that there is so much more to all of us. Love is a very strong thing! Try and find some stuff by Dr. Fritz Klein. His book BISEXUAL OPTION can really help with some more understanding about you, by using a grid instead of a scale like the Kinsey scale. Sort of gives us dimension as a person.

I'VE DISCOVERED SOMETHING

From: Skip

3 weeks ago I met the man who has turned out to be essentially my first M2M relationship as an adult and since coming out to my wife a year and a half ago.

I've discovered something that I probably knew in the back of my mind—that being with a man has made me feel complete—however our relationship is strictly for each other's sexual needs and our "game rule" is that there is no emotional connection between the 2 of us (he is a single gay male and that is his wish and at this point in my life that suits me fine). My wife has stood by my side since I came out to her, she is aware of the guy I'm seeing and our arrangement and we're both trying to figure out ways to redefine our marriage to incorporate my gay side. In her words she's "tolerating it and on the way to accepting it." In this last year of my being "out" to her, (selfishly) my main focus has been in finding a male lover. Consequently, our sex life and to some degree our intimacy level has suffered. However, our communication has never been better.

My questions that I need help with are for the guys who are married and had their first M2M relationship after they'd been in their marriage for awhile (we're at 12 years):

1. Did you know without question that you wanted, needed to stay in your marriage?

2. Did feelings of wondering if you could be strictly gay and thoughts of ending your marriages sometimes take over?
3. Is it possible to rebuild a marriage, make it stronger and keep the 2 sides of me separate?

Since this is all new to me (the experience) I have been feeling way more overwhelmed and confused by all the feelings that I've been experiencing than I ever could have imagined. Besides taking things very slow, any other advice that can be given would be appreciated. Also my wife is wanting to talk to any other wife who's making this type of relationship work.

From: Bruce

My case doesn't totally match yours, since I did have M2M sexual encounters in college, though I wouldn't class any of them as a relationship. After I married, though, there was a long period (12 years) when I did my best to be straight. I came out to my wife over 3 years ago and since then have had my first real relationships. The first lasted several months and my current lover and I have been together for over a year and a half.

My wife and I decided that we both wanted to remain a family (We have 1 daughter) if at all possible. So far, nothing has come up that has changed our minds about that. We do still love each other, enjoy being a family and want to stay together.

Over time I have come to identify as gay. That still hasn't ended up in me feeling that I wanted to end my marriage. There are times when I DO feel exhausted at maintaining two relationships, times when I don't feel like I have any time for myself, etc. but I doubt if it's any more frequently than most straight men who have similar feelings.

There are times when I wish I could be with him and I can't, but we try to work around that. We arrange all of the family schedules so that there are as few conflicts as possible, and my man and I spend one weekend every month together, either traveling or at his place. It's also understood that if I'm needed more either at home or at his place we'll arrange it somehow. So far we've always managed to work things out.

Our marriage is much stronger today than it was before I came out, primarily because we're now much more honest with each other. Before I was suffering through this alone, and was so afraid of spilling the beans that I ended up just not saying anything to anyone. My feeling has always been that we were much closer to a divorce before I came out than we are now.

I can't really speak to keeping two sides of my life separate, because I don't. All of my friends and family have met my man, and he takes part in our family events. My wife is the only one that knows for sure that we're lovers, but my feeling is that both her mother and our daughter have figured out that my man and I are something more than just friends. Having them all at least aware of him has helped, because it would be difficult to keep so big of a part of my life secret from everyone. It also helps that he and my wife truly like one another, because it makes it more difficult for them to be jealous of each other based on the time and attention the other one gets.

From: Dale

I've been married 30 years—-all of which had "the elephant in the living room." My M-M activities, attractions, etc. have NEVER been about trying (or wanting to) to find a substitute or replacement for my marriage. Whatever it is I feel/get through M-M contact is different from what I get from my wife and my family. I can't cross-exchange the M-M with my wife/family issues. When we finally began to deal openly and directly with the M-M side of my personality a little over 2 years ago I was very firm that this wasn't about my wanting to go away from my wife and family . . . unless she sent me away. Now, after these three years of openness and my living the position that I'm staying around . . . my wife feels much less in jeopardy of losing me over gay issues.

I have wondered whether I would have married had I not met the woman I'm married to. Since I can't back up and replay life's choices, I'll never know because the fact of the matter is that I DID marry her and she IS my female life partner.

I feel our marriage/relationship is stronger now because openness and honesty (which feel good and don't hinder energy) has largely replaced the fear and secrecy (which don't feel good . . . and SAP time, energy, and effort. We have "adjusted" a number of elements in our relationship (not many) to allow for more openly acknowledging and expressing my sexual diversity within the relationship rather than outside of it. That was the "magic" elixir in OUR relationship . . . in other's it works out sometimes to have an agreement providing much more autonomy for each partner. (The "I understand and accept the gay part of your personality, but don't have to be a part of any of it" position.) The deciding difference, though, was my wife . . . it was HER bottom line to be INcluded rather than EXcluded by the gay part of my personality.

From: Peter

My first adult M2M relationship began about 3 years ago, after 13 years of marriage. The sex was great, but I couldn't stick to the rule of "no emotional attachment." It would have been much more convenient to be able to stay emotionally unattached, but I couldn't do it. Not with a guy I regularly have sex with. Still can't. And it does get stressful and complicated, for me.

When that relationship ended, after about a year, I quickly got into another M2M situation. During that relationship, I came out to my wife. I thought that being exclusively with a man was the way I needed to live my life. That turned out to be wrong. My wife and I got back together, before the divorce was final. We have 2 children, and after being separated for a while, I found that our family life together is as much a part of who I am as my own sexuality is. Our goal was, and is, to find an open way to deal with my M2M needs and desires, which is comfortable for both of us. So we decided to try finding a guy we both like, and sleeping with him together. We did, and still do, and that works well for us. We've been seeing the same man for over a year now, and it works well for all three of us. I realize this is an unconventional solution, but it works for us. I never imagined this could work out so well, until we tried it. My wife and I now have an intimacy level far better than it ever was before, whether we are with our special guy, or just the 2 of us.

For me, coming out has been an ongoing process, during which my perspectives and sense of self are changing.

To answer your questions, as they apply to my life:

1. At one time during my process, I didn't know without question whether I needed or wanted to stay married. We HAD TO separate for a time before the answer became clear to me.
2. For a time, I didn't wonder whether I was strictly gay—I was convinced of it. I needed to experience living with my lover, as a gay couple, before I could conclude that wasn't the solution for me. That living situation quickly brought me to the realization that my life was empty without my wife and kids.

After those experiences, my wife and I have rebuilt our marriage fully. Our relationship is stronger than ever, based on love, honesty, communication, and respect for each other's needs and desires. And we are having FUN, together. I have not been able to keep "the 2 sides of me" separate. For me, it has proven to be far less stressful sharing everything with my wife. I consider myself to be very lucky that the woman I love is so open-minded.

From: Woody

I Hope I can help. I'm 58, came out to my wife 5 months after my first "contact," about a year after the big realization that I was at least "BI curious." (BTW I consider myself "one woman short of gay" now—Gay is my identity and I'm happy with that). We will celebrate our 27th anniversary soon. But—I never had any real interest sexually in women, got married at

28 after about 5 years of off-and-on bland courtship, been guy watching and fantasizing since teens. Just somehow never made the obvious connection, partly because my attraction is to the masculine gay side (leather and bears)—not interested in 80% or more of gay guys, though I respect them as part of the "family."

I didn't at that time think of myself as strictly gay, did not really think I'd end the marriage at the point of first experience, was afraid of coming out because I was sure ending the marriage would happen (it didn't!). I was even in an online support group, but protesting that I should contact the attorney before coming out. (I didn't.)

I don't keep the two sides separate very well, as my wife can attest. She would like me to, but it's TOO STRONG. I'm gay 100% of the time, just live a bisexual lifestyle. And play a lot with a string of "buddies" here and there. She's the one who "compartmentalizes." I can't do that.

From: Chukky

1. About wanting/needing to stay in my marriage. Right now my place is here due to my children. My wife and I have a nice (non-sexual) relationship, she has no idea of any other kind of involvement on my part. If she did, she would have me out of here. I love her as a friend and my "husband" as a spouse. If he were to say . . . let's leave and live as one, I would. For me to leave until it has to be, (if ever) would cause many people's lives to change drastically. When the time comes for me to go, I will know it. And if I leave because of a new love, I will leave for ME . . . not for him . . . but because of him and I.

2. I know I am gay, I know I always have been. I thought I would be able to live with my secret forever . . . just didn't happen that way. I thought hard and long of ending my marriage but again, because of mainly the children . . . . I cannot do that right now. I've learned because of all this Life is sacrifices and compromises . . . and that's how I am living right now. I am making the best out of my situation in a way that I think is best for everyone—fair or unfair as it may be.

3. As far as my wife understanding . . . she would NEVER go for me having another relationship no matter what I was.

From: Mike

I am not str8 and I must express my whole sexuality. I feel strongly that I want to stay in my marriage. I like my role as husband and father. It satisfies an important part of me. But 3 years ago when I came out (again) after 15 years of repression, depression, and no sex (at all), I was prepared to lose my marriage if my wife could not accept me as I am. Happily, she loves me and accepts me as I am. She is learning (as I am) to integrate my full sexuality into our marriage. Not easy at all . . . .for either of us . . . .but well worth the effort. Neither one of us would turn back now. We were both miserable most of the time before I came out. Now we are alive, and experiencing the full range of emotions, ups and downs. Sure beats the flatline numbness of the prior 15 years.

There were times when I worried that I was forcing myself (and my wife) to accept the choices we made before we were conscious (to be married, to be parents) when we really should have just done what so many other couples in our situation have done . . . . . . go with convention and split. I have no doubt . . . . .and I have said this to my wife . . . .that if we divorced, I doubt I would ever enter into such an intimate relationship with a woman again. I would most likely seek that with a man. I guess that makes me gay. . . . living a bisexual life . . . .as another brother from this list said recently. But the fact is, I AM married, I DO love my wife, and my sense of self includes my roles as husband, father, lover. . . . I would be wounded deeply if we were to divorce. I worry much less about that. We are living in the present . . . trying not to second guess the past and predict or worry about the future.

Integration is my goal. It is the only thing that makes me happy now. And I know it makes my family happier too. The fact is, and my wife would agree, the more integrated I become, the MORE available to her and the kids I am. The more of ME that I bring to the roles I play (husband, father, lover, manager, musician, etc.) the better able I am to make a positive difference in my life and in those lives I touch.

ARE THEY ALL LIKE THIS?

From: Rodney

I came out five weeks ago. At first, she was alternately compassionate and furious (actually punched me out at one point!). But after a few days, she let me get back closer to her. We even had sex a few times (much to my surprise, these encounters were terrific).

But then she started saying that she felt "vulnerable" and "exposed" after lovemaking, and told me she "needed some space." So she's started sleeping in another part of the house and fairly pointedly stopped talking about my orientation issues. At first, this didn't bother me too much—I can understand the need for going off in a corner to try to figure out where you're "at."

But lately, it seems to me that she is more than usually irritable with me. Almost any issue can set off a fight (last one was over why we spent so much money on dry-cleaning last month—I'm not making this up!). And wow! does she seem distant.

I've mentioned in my bio and (I think) in other posts that our marriage had hit some rocky passages in the past few years, long before I came out, and over issues that were totally unrelated to sexuality. But I feel more at sea than I ever have before.

Does my wife's behavior sound familiar to you? Does it go on like this forever? Any suggestions or thoughts?

From: Dale

Try not to despair as she struggles with things and goes through many stages in her effort to process it all.

My read on all of this is that the additional load of trying to process what she perceives the disclosure of your sexual diversity means to her and to the marriage has really burdened her coping abilities. Little things (like the dry-cleaning bill) are much more likely to exceed the coping limit and flare into a "fight." The dry-cleaning isn't important . . . coping with all of these issues is! Helping her process and resolve the issues (your patience and understanding, talking with her when she wants to talk, counseling, etc) will help give her coping mechanisms more headroom to deal with the day-to-day milieu without flaring.

Research going on into the strategies of keeping a mixed-orientation marriage together indicates the most reliable predictor for success in keeping the marriage together has to do with the depth and quality of the relationship outside of the sexual-orientation issues. In other words—does the relationship have "capital" to give it the resilience it needs to cope with the throes of metabolizing the new issues of mixed sexual orientation? There is some advantage to the new openness and honesty that comes with disclosure of the presence of sexual diversity rather than hiding it. Along with this advantage, however, there is a whole load of stresses and challenges that can easily outweigh the advantage—at least temporarily. That's where the "capital" of the relationship has the opportunity to kick in to help carry the relationship while you all readjust, renegotiate, etc.

Each relationship is different. Some straight wives go to a place of panic and are never able to return. Some gay/BI guys figuratively go to a "desert isle" somewhere and never seriously consider trying to open up enough to let their straight spouses into the M-M part of their personality. Some couples try for a while to integrate the issues but eventually tire of the complexity and hard work necessary to keep the relationship together. Lest you lose hope—there ARE couples out there who DO find their way through the thickets, keep the marriage together (and the relationship) and even strengthen it!

Here's a quote from the conclusions section of the Gochros book: "When Husbands Come Out of the Closet"

> 3. Not only can marriages survive a disclosure of homosexuality, if the husband remains committed to the wife, they are apt to improve. Not only can homosexuality (or some degree of it) be compatible with heterosexual marriage, if the husband is capable of some degree of heterosexual satisfaction, gay/straight marriages can be unusually satisfying and stable.

In my own case I have seen our experience with these issues go through stages. The first stage was the hard relationship crisis. Following that we entered an integrative period characterized by a lot of exploration, experimentation, learning, research, etc. Now, a little over three years after final, full disclosure, we are not exploring and experimenting so much . . . but are more in a stage where we are practicing things that we have found help us or are good for us. At the same time we try to stay open for new ideas and new strategies and insight, too. I would represent the process to be ongoing and dynamic, never something finally static and resolved.

From: Carl

The insecurity element that your wife feels could have to do with the possibility that you will leave her for a guy (pretty hard on the feminine ego) or with worry about AIDS—a subject on which my wife is totally paranoid. Your wife's removal to elsewhere to sleep and her complete avoidance of sex suggest that this may be an issue.

Several folks in this forum (and also my wife, unprompted) have used the term "roller coaster" to describe the unpredictability of domestic mood swings following unexpected revelations. In our household, things go through discernable periods. The last two months were dominated by my wife's denial. "I don't understand it," she said over and over, apparently meaning that she didn't want to address the possibility that any man (let alone her husband) could literally "love" another. Last fall, when she realized that my lover had cleaned out a room in his house for my use, it became insecurity of the "Is he going to leave me for that creep and what will I tell my friends if he does?" variety. The following month, the mood was saccharine: "be sure he knows how sweet you can be and what he'll have to give up if he leaves me for that creep." That was scary—like living in the eye of a hurricane and not knowing when the winds might suddenly hit again.

Now things are much more positive, following a major crisis over money matters. She seems to appreciate whatever we do together the way she did last summer, and far from pulling away when I try to touch her, as she does during her negative periods, she actually reaches out to me.

It's all rather like downhill skiing: things change pretty fast, and your posture had better be very flexible and resilient or you can really wipe out. . . .

From: Brown

My wife used almost the exact same words when she told me that lovemaking between us had become more than she could handle. At that time we both had to look at where we headed. Just as you describe, our sex life had returned after she found out I had been sleeping with the boys. At first there was intense pain, but after a short while we were better in bed than we had been for some time.

I had promised to come clean and I did. Whatever she asked of me I responded with the truth. Even when I knew I told too much, I could not hold back. My wife by then could tell if I wasn't coming forth with the whole truth. When she knew in her heart that I was a gay man, lovemaking with me became too painful for her. During that period of time I didn't touch another man.

It wasn't long before she told me that what she wanted was a monogamous relationship with a str8 man. What you are going through is not uncommon at all. It can be an emotional roller coaster for both of you. However, if you can keep the lines open and can talk to her, please do it. The only way for you to know what's happening in the process is if she tells you.

For us, the process had lead to our separation. I moved out of the house last week. I hope that my wife and I become friends again. My kids keep us from not losing contact with each other, but she is understandably still upset and angry.

And for the first time in months my own tension level has dropped. I don't have a clue about the future. But I will live my life as a gay man. It is not a forgone conclusion that your path leads this way, but if you don't get in touch with your wife you can expect the roller coaster to be even more wild.

From: George

I am out only to my wife and I find that I must from time to time initiate "light banter" on the subject as a means of trying to assess her attitude toward the real me, and in regard to the BI/gay orientation in general. I do this since once we had our initial discussion (that is putting it mildly) on the subject when I came out to her, she seems to have taken the stance that if she ignores it, IT will go away.

When we were with a few other couples the other night someone enlightened the group with the news that one of our local married doctors apparently came out to some of his close friends that he was BI. The news generated a lot of comments, unfortunately mostly negative, but the comment that hit me the hardest was when my wife referred to the doctor as a "sexual misfit."

On the way home I asked her if this is how she viewed me, "a sexual misfit." She said she was tired of the subject and preferred not to discuss it any further.

Although when I originally came out to her, after much discussion, Q & A, etc., she finally indicated very strongly that she had hoped we would stay married, I am not sure now whether it is to save face or that she still might have some degree of love in her heart for me. I tend to doubt the latter at this point.

Can we ever be sure where we really stand with those we love?

From: Rodney

I keep going through the same kind of questioning of the REAL foundations of my relationship to my wife that you describe in your post. Sometimes, I'm optimistic; sometimes, I'm not.

The "sexual misfit" line really strikes a chord with me. What if you were to ask your wife about whether Bill Cosby is a "racial misfit" or Ben Stiller a "religious misfit"?

I have never been a highly politicized person, but I remember joking to my therapist the day after I came out to my wife, "You know, when I came out to my wife I instantaneously realized the dream of every middle-class Anglo male with vaguely leftist politics: I became the member of a minority group."

My therapist laughed, but I have subsequently begun to realize how painfully true this is. I consider this learning part of the "meaning" all this has for me.

From: Clark

Reading this puts me in mind of how very similar our journeys sometimes are. If only my wife knew how much she has in common with other spouses. But some people don't realize the value of mutual support (or don't need it, or don't want it).

The business about coming to the point of bringing "it" up to assess feelings, etc., rings so true. And the matter of dropping it because we get tired of discussing "it" rings equally true.

I have also found that usually when I bring "it" up, I am rather disappointed in the long and endless conversation that follows. I find myself just editing out more and more. And that bothers me.

From: Brian

Just a couple of comments on what you wrote here:

My wife too never wants to discuss "it." If we don't talk about "it," "it" will go away.

What she doesn't understand is that for me, "it" is always omnipresent. I think about this night and day. I'm living my life waiting for my life to start. (Does that make sense?) I can't ignore "it." As far as wanting to stay married, my wife also says that as long as I don't leave her, she can accept me. She has this need to stay married regardless of what the situation is. I finally realized that this is what she grew up with. Her parents stayed married for 49 years (until her Dad's death) even though they absolutely HATED each other. I guess to her, separating would be admitting failure for some reason.

Guys, how can I get my wife to go to counseling with me? She just won't go.

From: Josi

As for getting your wife to go to counseling, two things come to me: (1) Talk in terms of your needs, asking her to help you address your issues; don't put it in terms of what she needs or how she would benefit. (2) Find a female counselor so your wife will feel some hope for an ally; going to a man she's likely to feel ganged up on even if he's straight.

From: Rodney

The problem I'm having is that I can't seem to bring the discussion with my wife around to anything that seems to approximate "communication." For the past three weeks (I came out about six weeks ago), she has simply refused to discuss the issues. She has taken to sleeping in another room. She announced to me a couple of days ago that she "finally thought of something good about me" (which was, that I used to fix breakfast for her when our kids were little so she'd have time to read to them in the morning). She has almost (but not quite) indicated that she might be willing to start having sex with me again if I'm SURE I can keep my commitment to remain abstinent with regard to men (in other words, it's OK if I'm a bisexual, as long as I don't do the kinds of things bisexuals do).

My youngest, still living at home, has begun applying pressure to my wife to go with me for couples therapy, threatening to move out if things don't get better. I'm not sure my daughter fully understands that going to couples therapy is no guaranteed route to a continued marriage—that, indeed, therapy might lead to divorce.

I feel stuck. I can't tell how much of my wife's behavior is normal shock, how much is conscious manipulation, and so on. Getting into therapy seems to me the only way to move forward. But maybe there's something here I'm missing.

As you may have inferred, our marriage was going through a hard time for years before my coming out. But, in any case, do you have any thoughts on my situation?

From: David

In Amity Buxton's words, when the hubbie comes out of the closet, the wife goes in.

When my wife went through this "phase," I advised her to observe the FACTS of her life, not the conditioned meanings. 99% of the facts of her life are totally unchanged by the revelation. We eat out, we talk on the phone with the college kids, we pay bills, we go to shows, we snuggle all night and get up and go to work, stopping off at Starbuck's together on the way. This is what we've always done. Occasionally I go out with a friend.

She could choose to live "totally" and miserably in the 1% that's new and different, or she could live predominantly in the 99% that's familiar and comfortable.

The facts of our lives are generally gentle. Violence erupts from minds and meanings. We benefit much from a simpler, less "meaningful" life.

Regarding her going to therapy, you are requesting her to respect YOUR autonomy in exploring what you must explore. You can set the example by not trying to make her do what she doesn't want to do. In fact, you canNOT MAKE any other person do what they don't want to do. Relationships structured around spouses controlling the other are a competition, not a partnership. It is sufficient for you to say—ONCE—"It would benefit me, and I think it would benefit YOU to join me in therapy. Please consider trying it. I know you'll survive it if you do. It's your OPPORTUNITY, and mine, but I leave it to you, and I respect YOUR decision, and I won't badger you about it" (and then, OF COURSE, keep your word by not badgering).

HELL ON EARTH

From: Lyndon

In response to some of the posts I have been seeing lately all I can say is I am out about a month to my wife and after feeling tremendously relieved I now feel totally abysmally shitty. I am full of rage, and deep sadness. My wife is coping as best she knows how, loves me and really wants to make our marriage work, On one level I want that too, but feel very strongly that it would be impossible. I identify myself totally as a gay man and want to be my own free person, not still hiding in a marriage where I cannot be me. I am the primary provider of my family, we are not well off by any stretch of the imagination and my spouse earns very little. In many ways I feel even more trapped then I was before; I have never been so miserable. I just want to scream. If it were not for my responsibilities and my deep belief that suicide solves nothing I would walk in front of a truck. I should not be angry at my wife for loving me but I am, it is as if she has not heard a word I have said. She at one point said she had unconditional love, and if it were truly unconditional she would release me from this torture I am in. She says that upon rethinking her love is conditional, that I must be honest with her and stay with her. I wish I could figure how to be happy within those constraints, I do not think I can.

On top of everything else my youngest son is harassed at school, is called a faggot and worse by other students and my bringing this up at a meeting with his teachers resulted in nothing but dead silence. The fact that I am a teacher in the same district does not help either.

Can I learn how to be happy in this marriage? We have agreed in principal that I can have time away. I thought that would be sufficient but I do not think it is as I am a hopeless romantic and cannot be satisfied by sex alone; I need an emotional bond with another man and that includes living with him, not just on scheduled occasions. I also think I need time as a single gay man, not jump from one marriage into another. I want everything now and am so damn sick of hearing advice like one step at a time.

Originally my wife had agreed the children should know, now she does not. So I get to be out only to her and a few other family members, how nice.

How many of us have completely ruined our own lives simply by trying to do the right thing and to be accepted and liked? I thought I had finally learned to love and accept myself, so why is it so hard for me to move forward?

From: Bib

I know exactly what you are talking about when you say you feel "trapped." That was the only way I could describe how I felt in my marriage, absolutely, tee-totally TRAPPED! Every little thing my wife did or did not do would send me into a rage. I spent most of our 13-year marriage in depression. When I finally sat down and told her I was leaving, I felt so much better. Our relationship is better, I'm happier, and she seems happier and ready to get on with her life as well.

I had told her I was gay over a year ago, and thought that would be enough to alleviate the depression and the feeling of being trapped. But I soon realized it was not enough.

I'm not saying you have to leave your wife to be happy. I'm just saying carefully examine where you are, what you want, and what it's going to take to get you to that point.

From: Brian

I have been where you are now. I know the feeling of relief at coming out, finally getting it over with, only to have nothing change. Although it's wonderful that your wife still loves you and wants you, in many ways her acceptance makes it so much harder when what you really need is to be able to be out to everyone and to live your life as you need to. I'm going through the same thing. It would have been so much easier if she got really mad and just threw you out, right? If you're not already in counseling I recommend that you find a therapist immediately. With the rage that I detected in your post I think it is an absolute necessity. My counselor has really helped me to see things in a more positive light and has helped me understand WHY my wife is responding the way she is. Although therapists cannot tell you what to do in your life, they are able to help your see things more clearly, and at least for me, to be able to see a resolution—however far off that may be. No situation is hopeless. You can work this out over time. It will be painful . . . most changes involve some pain . . . but it can be done. And remember you are not alone in this. Please get yourself into counseling as soon as possible.

From: Rodney

I relate totally with the ambivalence. I don't think it's all that easy just to walk out of ANY marriage. First of all, there was SOME reason we got married in the first place.

Second, we're all of us in a situation which is truly pretty much out of the mainstream. And who is going to give us guidance here? I consider myself PHENOMENALLY lucky in that I have found a therapist who is bisexual and is married (but even HE is not really in a "mixed orientation" marriage, because his wife is also bisexual).

I sure wish I had found this group of Gay/BI men a few years ago.

I don't really know what my wife thinks yet, because SHE doesn't know. And part of the "responsibility" of being in a 29-year marriage is, I think, not to leave it too quickly.

From: Rodney

I have been out to my wife about five weeks now and, like you, have moments of the blackest imaginable despair. But since I'm bisexual, I at least have been spared the kind of total denial you have been subjected to. (I

GUESS it's better to have only one half of one's sexual reality rejected, anyway . . .). I also have a lesbian daughter, and another straight daughter is totally "cool" with my orientation, so that's made me feel less at sea than someone in your situation, who is so totally stranded.

The notion that you were SELFISH in coming out would be funny, if it weren't so awful. My wife accused me of COWARDICE in coming out to her (I wonder why it was so damned hard to do!).

I guess the best thing to remember is at first that coming out is like throwing a bomb right on top of your wife. Attitudes are bizarre in the extreme. Some people have told me it takes at least three months before ANYTHING reasonable begins to happen. (Three months?!!!!!!). People keep telling me that somehow or other things get more bearable.

But you need to keep reminding yourself that you are a human being with as much right to happiness as anyone else. It HAS to be ultimately your decision regarding who you are out to, though you may want to take your wife's desires into account (though, quite frankly, I can see NO defensible reason for remaining FOREVER closeted to your children, for Heaven's sake! I guess I'd have to HEAR the reason, anyway).

When I'm tired, I even find MYSELF accusing myself of being a worthless, lying philanderer ("couldn't it at least have been women?" . . . though my messing around with women would probably ACTUALLY have been much harder for my wife to deal with).

I wish I could say something more positive. It sucks. But you HAVEN'T ruined your life. Remember that you AREN'T really the heavy in this, that your wife is struggling to deal with a situation she doesn't really understand, that any "position" she takes right now will probably change in the next few days. And, after all is said and done, HER desires in all this are only HALF of the equation. It isn't as though it's your job (as the heavy) to take anything that gets dished out to you.

As my therapist is always reminding me, relationships are voluntary. And they have to work for BOTH people. Or they have to be terminated.

From: James

Reading your post reminds me of the saying that things must still get worse before they can get better. The feelings that you are having are obviously taking an emotional toll on you. But it will be those same feelings which will bring you to the place in your own life where you will have the grit and determination to do whatever it is that you end up believing that you need to do for your own sanity. In the end, I believe that you will be in a position to seek what it seems to me that you want—a committed emotional and sexual relationship with another man.

My own experience has shown me that once just a few people know it is hard to contain that information and keep it from spreading even if that were your desire. No doubt, your objective of your children knowing that you are gay will be accomplished one way or another. It seems to me more of a question of timing and who they hear it from. As for your wife, I believe you set her out upon her own journey when you began your own. All will likely happen in due time.

PLEASE, know that I care what happens to you. You are in my thoughts and I wish you the very best. Believe that things will get better eventually. I wish you all the best!

ROUGH TIME RIGHT NOW

From: Bear

Boy, I'm having such a rough time right now. My wife and I are talking a LOT, about the possibilities of an open/flexible marriage. She's trying so hard to be so supportive, wanting to do everything right, and I'm just terrified that it is hurting her too much. Saturday night, she suggested I go out to bars by myself. We both felt awkward about it, but she gave me a few limits (talking is okay, kissing is okay, no more), and I departed, feeling good about us. Going out by myself was okay—I went to a few bars, spoke to no one, felt very alone and ridiculous about the whole thing. It was such an unnatural thing for me to do, to try and go out and just meet people. I recognized that I was putting a lot of pressure on myself, and I just tried to relax and enjoy being out and exploring all of this. I had a good time but was so overwhelmed with the strangeness of it all that I don't know if I'll do it again.

My wife is supportive of the idea of me looking for gay relationships outside of our marriage, but talking about anything more than the idea of it hurts her so much. I am getting to the point of stopping feeling guilty for her hurt—but she is in pain, and that is the last thing I want. I acknowledge that it's my fault, but I also acknowledge that I can't do anything about it. So I end up feeling rotten, for both of us. And so does she, and I just hate it.

I feel so very alone much of the time—I moved two years ago, leaving behind a town full of friends I'd made over a decade. We know very few people here in the city . . . so I don't have any opportunity to meet friends through friends—the way I've become accustomed to meeting people throughout my life. The last thing I want is to continue the anonymous sex I've had over the past sixteen years, but it just seems it would be so much easier to go out, find a quickie, and have it be done with.

There are all these things I want to say to someone, anyone—that I've never kissed a man but want to, that I want someone I can just throw my arms around and not feel nervous or awkward, that I want to explore my gay sexual side in a new way, to discuss my attractions—and my wife can't hear any of it and it's not really all that fruitful to discuss with my therapist and then there's no one else. It's just so hard to feel capable of fixing any of this when I feel so alone. Sorry to vent—I'm hoping that this will fall on some ears that might make me feel a little less alone and hopeless.

From: Eric

While I love going out dancing, I really hate the bars. I'm not comfortable going up and chatting to total strangers, although if someone approaches me I'm always prepared to talk for a while.

I found that I recognized a lot of the guys at my gym from the dance clubs and eventually began talking to some of them—for me it's much easier talking to "strangers" in the gym or on the beach, but also through the Net as opposed to a bar.

Don't worry about venting online; that's what we are here for and this group has helped me get over numerous hurdles on this path.

From: Max

Hang in there my friend. The ride may be a bit rough but the going looks firm.

One thing I have learned, and God knows I'm a slow learner, is that there are two sets of enjoyment in exploring the "gay" world out there. The first is the things you've wanted to do but didn't (couldn't) because of fear or whatever. The second is having your needs met in terms of friendship and solidarity more so than (but not excluding) sex.

Enjoy them both, but see them for what they are. Two separate needs or whatever. If you try to mix the two I find that both of them fail to live up to expectations and leave (if you'll pardon the pun) somewhat of a bitter taste in your mouth (cough!).

My first voyage to a gay pub on my own was nerve wracking. I insisted (to myself) on going alone. I sat up at the bar and sipped my pint. For quite a while my heart was pounding and I was sure it could be heard above the din. Anyhow, after the few pints, the visual undressing, the longer-than-comfortable eye contact and the thirty-something also making his way down the line of guys at the bar I decided to head for home.

I'm glad I did it that way. I had only one thing to concentrate on. I didn't risk making a horse's collar of myself in front of anyone I knew or wanted to know.

Start small and build from there.

From: Stephen

One of the greatest myths of the gay community is that going to gay bars is a necessary rite of passage. It's not. The only time I've ever enjoyed going to gay bars is when I had a bunch of friends with me. I'd much prefer to join a queer community group, or volunteer, or go to readings by gay and lesbian writers. The best experience I've had meeting other queers was when I was consulting at a volunteer agency that worked with sexual-minority teens. It was a blast! What a great excuse to get together and meet like-minded (truly like-minded!) others! And we had structured activities to ease the way of making connections. Going alone to gay bars will not put you in touch with what is great about being gay. It's no surprise you didn't have a good time. Hang in there. It'll get better!

From: Carl

Man, do I ever know how you feel! Last spring, when I went to my hometown to sell my parent's house, I went to a gay bar for the first time in years. Like you, I felt very strange and out of it, but what made it wonderful was seeing other guys with their arms around each other's shoulders, and occasionally a couple guys kissing. Like you, I didn't talk to anyone. But I did really dig watching other guys express uninhibited affection. Back in the late seventies I used to write for a raunchy little gay review. One piece, comparing sitting in a toilet stall with a glory hole to the confessional, attracted the attention of one man, who had been brought up Catholic. He assumed I had been, too, and he wrote to me via the editor.

Shortly after receiving his note, I had to go to a convention in the city where he lived, and one dull afternoon I called him. He invited me down to his place for a beer, and we hit it off immediately. We became fast friends and I stayed with him every time I went to New York until his death. He was strictly gay (I'm BI), and partly because of the way we met I immediately felt that there was nothing in me I needed to "protect," which wasn't true with any of my friends, and certainly not with my wife.

That friendship was enormously important to me at the time and seems even more important in retrospect. To unwind from the tensions of married life with him every time I went to New York (and I did so for two or three days a week at one point while working for a magazine that had been moved there) was a marvelous outlet. We would kiss and hug hello when I arrived and when I departed and often in between.

We tried sex once. We never repeated the experiment, but we remained close friends for well over a decade—the closest friend I'd ever had up to that time.

Part of the beauty of the relationship was that we could disagree without the slightest rancor. An edge came into a disagreement only once, when he referred to us as "lovers." "We aren't lovers," I countered. "Lovers have sex!" "We're lovers," he reaffirmed. "No we're not!" "We're lovers," he said, looking at me steadily. I realized that there would be no resolution, and I half realized that he was saying he loved me. I looked away and we never mentioned the matter again.

Were we lovers? I really don't know. Do any of these distinctions really matter? Probably not. What matters is that this sort of relationship with a gay man can be enormously fulfilling for a married man, even when there is no sex involved.

And there is none between my new lover and me, either, these days. When I arrive at my boyfriend's home, the first thing I always want to do is put my arms around him and kiss him. God that feels wonderful! I put my arms around my wife and kiss her a lot, too, but it's very different. Affirming in both cases, but affirming different things.

Surely living in a large metropolitan area you have far more opportunities to meet gay guys than I do, living in the country. You will sooner or later meet someone with whom you can be completely yourself and live out the gay side of your nature in unselfconscious freedom. Go for it.

IT CAN BE SO DIFFICULT

From: Crawly

I'm not sure exactly why I'm writing this but I am suddenly so blue. My wife and I stayed up until three talking last night, and while it could be described as a very loving talk, the reality of what was said has reared its ugly head today. I think we are over as a married couple.

Although no one is filing for a divorce, (we are not in any rush) she says that she's coming to grips with the idea that she can't work on this marriage even if I decide I want to after our separation. I guess I'm feeling a bit guilty because although I feel right now its over, I've never lived alone before and the future of what I want is down the road a ways. Everyone says this is the hard part and down the road is a happiness I can only imagine, but today I don't know if I can hang in there until that day arrives.

I'm sorry if this sounds like a big pity party. I just needed to talk to someone and I don't want to start crying. This is safer right now.

From: Kramer

Hang in there babe! We are all here to support you. I must tell you, however, that you and I are pretty much at the same fork in the road. My wife and I have decided mutually and very lovingly to end our married relationship as well. It is very frightening yes, but I am holding on real tight to my rainbow. My rainbow brings me much comfort and security. We have far to go with this. We do not know where to start. We have never had to deal with this before, and unfortunately life does not come with an instruction manual.

We are not rushing into our divorce, we are going to let it evolve. We have two small children. We have not discussed this with them yet either. As I said, we do not know where to go with this or how to start. We are initially going to start with an in-home separation, and work the details out as they arise.

It is so difficult sitting down and planning our Thanksgiving, and forthcoming Christmas as these with be the last holidays we plan together as a married couple. But I find strength when I look to the light as I know complete fulfillment for both my wife and I will be found when we let go and walk down our respective tines of the fork.

That's all for now, trying to be strong as I celebrate life "somewhere over the rainbow."

From: Carl

Maybe it's in the air. My wife hit me with a negative gust last night, when for the last few weeks I had thought the worst was past and our marriage was saved. This morning I woke up wondering whether I should just call it quits. I'm sick of being the only one to work on the marriage. I'm disturbed by the idea that she will never countenance my coming out to our friends or, indeed, anyone in our local community, because she would be ashamed to admit she's married to a queer.

Having visited my lover three times in the past three months, I've found out once again how much it means to me to be with guys who understand the gay in me. All of our local gay friends have died or moved away, and if I'm to sustain my marriage I realize I absolutely need some local gay connections.

I guess I'll stay with her. I can't stand the thought of cutting myself off from her and my family. But . . .

From: Mike

I definitely resonate with your feelings of frustration over your wife's discomfort with you being "out" to others in your community. And if I had my "druthers," I'd force the issue here too. BUT . . . I am reminded that I have had 43 years to get "comfortable" with my own nature in a society that disdains the very core of ME. And while I've made significant progress in the past few years, I still have a lot of work to do. I don't know how long your wife has known about your "other" sexuality, but I'm assuming that in comparison to YOUR "knowing," she has had less time to process or integrate the meaning of this to herself as a WOMAN and a WIFE. I hope you can respect HER process long enough to find out if there is a chance that your marriage can survive the "authentic YOU."

From: George

In our community, which is super anti gay/BI anything, my wife would be totally ostracized if I came out. Because of this, when I came out to her, I assured her that I would not take it any further.

I'm still working on gaining her total acceptance, and if I can achieve that, I'll be happy as a clam.

I don't think hiding my orientation from the community in general will at all hamper my ability to meet other BI guys. We live in a very small community, but there is still the library, swim and exercise club, and other places where I have been successful in carefully applying my gaydar. In fact, it was at our local library where I met my very close BI married friend.

From: Brandon

Take heart, as I know exactly where you are in this journey. During the first year after coming out to my wife, we went through these same gyrations. (I have now been out for over 9 years.) We went through some very agonizing discussions and I put up with many of her tantrums of self-doubt and insecurities. She put up with lots of my righteous indignation for the world's homophobia. It was not easy but somehow we conquered and continued on as a couple that survived and flourished within our relationship and committed marriage. I kept telling myself that it took me 49 years to come out and I had to also give my wife time to learn and grow as I did.

One thing that also helped me along the way was something I learned in 5 years of intensive counseling. "I did not take responsibility for my wife's unhappiness." "I did not take responsibility for her insecurities." Those were hers and hers alone to deal with. She for the first time in her life had to conquer her own demons and dragons of life. After about a year of her own counseling and my constant reassurance that I loved and needed her; After many, many tantrums on her part; After some stupid moves on my part; etc., she started to mature emotionally and spiritually. For the first time in our married life she started to act and conduct herself like a grown-up human. She started to take responsibility for her own happiness in life. She learned, as I did, that she had to stop blaming others (including my gayness) for everything that was wrong with herself or our relationship. I also have maintained from the moment that I came out to my wife that I was who I was—her "Gay Married Husband." I let her know that being a part of another male was a very important part of who I am and I would never ever compromise that beautiful part of myself.

In retrospect, the journey that my wife and I continue on, after my coming out, is a rich and productive time in our lives. We remain to this day the best of friends, the best of companions, the best of soul mates, etc. Our marriage is stronger than it has ever been. Our commitment to each other appears secure—to death do us part!

Would my wife go back to the days before I came out to her? Yes! She still sometimes fantasizes about the days of her innocence but she no longer reads "Romance Novels." We do still curl up under a down comforter in front of a good "Rock Hudson/Doris Day" movie and cry for some of the lost innocence of our early married years.

HOW DO I HANDLE THIS ONE?

From: Travis

Having just come out to my wife two months ago, I have very little experience on how to handle anything! But, the ups and downs!—yes, we are having those.

I have trouble with the unexpected nature of her reactions; I am slowly learning that they point to something that suddenly has made her insecure: it could be a little pun, misplaced humor, or even a glance in the wrong direction. At the bottom, I'm finding that she feels the threat of not being able to fulfill all of my needs or desires, emotional or otherwise.

What do I do? I listen; I ask what brought the reaction about & then we talk . . . and talk . . . & I gain insights into this new set of reactions that she is experiencing . . . so I try to prevent stepping on the same bristles next time . . . except next time there will be a new set of bristles. I am hoping to get better at this.

From: Lyndon

I too am a little new at this, but my wife and I have had ups and downs before. What I may not have learned before I am trying to learn now. This is the big one!

There are days where I can work myself into a happy mood only to be broad-sided by the emotion locomotive. She's not driving the train but is a passenger. It's hard because there are so many angry feelings and statements pouring out of her that I just can't handle it. She is accepting of me, and wishes me the best, but it is hard for her with all the hurt she is feeling. Someone mentioned you have to make anger acceptable, but I need to know how. What can I do to steel her anger? How can I help make it go away or so that she can handle it?

I figure I have 2 ways to deal with this. (1) move out and stop dragging it out for her, or, (2) stay here and work it out so she has the support that she offers me. I gotta try and work this out, not to save the marriage, but just help get her through this, as her friend. She has panic attacks about where I am and what I am doing. She too becomes unreasonable and lashes out, I should know that she is trying to heal, but it hurts me too much when she does. Then I lose it and I feel like I have failed at doing the one thing I need to do for her—to help her heal. What a strange trip it's been. Thanks guys :)

From: Lyndon

It is interesting that many of us are going through a similar time right now. My wife and I are at a new level. My first real relationship with another gay dad is now over, and my wife thought this would be a good time to reevaluate our relationship and make some guidelines. We have had a couple of knockdown drag outs but the results have been positive, and my mental state is the best in years.

My wife also does not handle my being away well, but it has gotten better with time. Surprisingly, I am more content about being at home with less panic about the future. So hang in there guys, if I can reach this point anyone can.

From: James

One of the comments that has been shared again and again on all of your e-mail and needs to be said often is that we have to be prepared for our wives to need lots and lots of reassurance. This is really difficult for them and little things and incidents can trigger insecurity. My wife would cycle through periods of peace and stability alternating with periods of great insecurity and it amazed me that she needed so much reassurance. Also, the difference between accepting something intellectually and emotionally has been discussed in e-mail from you guys lots of times but needs repeating also. And we guys also find that we can accept some things intellectually but find it very different when our emotions "kick in." Fortunately, with time, at least for us, the cycles become fewer, further between, and shorter in duration.

From: Jerry

This is the first time I have posted, but have learned a great deal from everyone's insights, and have made some really great friends among our gang of gay/BI married brothers. I related to so much in your post. I have been out to my wife for only 3 months, and our road has been rocky to say the least.

I'm 33, and have been married 13 years. We have two wonderful teenage daughters. My wife and I have been in counseling together and myself individually. (She refuses individual counseling thus far, i.e., It's MY problem, and I need to deal with it!)

I have found a support group for gay married men, have been attending the group twice a month, and have really benefited from the experience. I have not ventured into the arena of m2m sex (at least not since I have been married), as I don't really know what I want. My issues, however, are related to my coming to grips with my sexuality, and as I have come to discover, my need to assert my independence within my marriage. My wife and I have been immersed in each other. Does codependence ring a bell? As she defines a marriage, the spouse should be EVERYTHING to the other person. If that's not the case, then what's the point? (Her exact words!) I feel that I have been just as guilty in forming this definition. If I could totally lose myself in the woman I love, then I don't have to look at me. And feeling this way sure made it a lot easier to suppress my homosexual inclinations. It was smooth easy seas, till the "gay thing" reached up and grabbed me by the balls! Now I am taking a good hard look at myself and I'm not crazy about what I see. I see a lot of weakness, and avoidance, and a great deal of anger buried deep inside. But I am changing, I am growing, and I have made the decision to do so. But this is not a choice my wife has made.

What I am discovering is that whenever I make any attempt to have some autonomy, I am met with anger and hurt. "How can you do this to me?" I respond with a tremendous amount of guilt, and close myself off from her, leave out details, and scurry back into my closet of shame. When I think of redefining our marriage to include sexual relationships outside of the marriage, I don't see this as a possibility for us, as she can't handle my attending a support group. And if sitting in a room with a group of men causes this reaction, then how would she feel about an outside relationship?

How can we expect to work on ourselves if we are met with resistance at every turn? Am I delaying the inevitable by staying in the relationship? Am I causing more pain for her in the long run? I truly love my wife, and she is the last person in the world I would want to hurt, but I can only change myself! And if she is unwilling to look at other options, then what choices are left for me?

I have no answers, and that just kills me. I have always been Mr. Fix-it! So talented in analyzing others' problems, and giving sage advice. Now faced with my own dilemmas, I feel utterly powerless and lost!

From: Clark

You know, I read messages like this, and I find that there is hope for the world after all.

What a neat statement of someone who is growing, changing, stretching, practicing being loving. And I don't mean to sound patronizing by saying any of that. I have been working on just such basics as these for the past 26 years, and I find myself as much a neophyte as ever. Just to hear someone articulating this kind of basic communication effort is refreshing.

From: Joey

Since I wrote a few days ago, my wife and I have talked a lot. I also conferred with my counselor as well. But I have to say, the input from this group of men is just fantastic. What seems to be working for my wife and me is patience, from both of us. A challenge, to say the least. But, as angry as I was when she spoke to me and sent me e-mails, I tried very hard not to turn the tables on her. I know I did a bit. And each time we go through these episodes, I am less inclined to get angry. I am starting to use my head and not my tongue. (I will try to ignore double meaning. . . .) But, I think she made an extremely valid point. She needed to vent and boy did she vent. But it is over. I sense no residual hostility.

From: Travis

Thanks for your reply; trivial as it may seem, these posts form the basis of the reassurance that I would not get from anywhere else . . . and you are right: the wives' issues are at the forefront of our challenges; otherwise, we wouldn't be here, would we?

SHARDS OF LIFE PUT TOGETHER

From: Bear

Hey guys—I've been silent here for a while as the strange shards of my life have been slowly been put back together as my wife and I are making things work out. I needed to write this morning to vent some strong feelings that I can't share with her. Last night, for the first time, I went out on a date with a guy I've been talking to lately. She was aware of it from the start, supportive at first but slowly growing colder and more unhappy as the date approached. I'm just trying to let her sort out her hard feelings about all of this—because it was so apparent to me that last night was great, something I've been cheating myself out of for the past 15 years, and something I want again. Flirting, talking, kissing, being in bed together—this was a real date, a real encounter with another man, not the quickie, anonymous, shame-inducing sex I've had in the past. I was in heaven, blissful and feeling whole for the first time in my life. I'm very BI, so it's not like I haven't had a satisfying sex life, but this was so different. It wasn't even great sex, just really amazing connecting with a man in such an intimate way, feeling good and intimate and excited.

So, feeling this great this morning and then facing the stony, hurt face of my wife (I actually saw her at 2:00 when I came in last night, as I was showering off after the date . . . a most awkward of moments), I needed to say this all to SOMEBODY, because I haven't ever felt this good about something, EVER, that felt so good to me and is so hurtful to the person I most love in the world. I'm not doubting that things will work out between us, I'm just wishing it didn't have to be so damn hard for her. Because what became so very apparent to me last night was that this is RIGHT, this is GOOD, and this is what I've spent my entire adult life wanting but not letting myself have.

Life is just a freaky, inexplicable grab bag.

From: Sidney

Well I know what you felt and mean about dating. The agreement my wife, and wonderful she is, and I have is as follows: Here's my frame of reference (these are my wife's words):

> Premise #1: I consider the people you are "going to see" to be your friends.
> Premise #2: I have friends that I go to see also.
> The sameness: We have friends because we enjoy others company, and there is no way either of us can meet each other's entire needs.
> The difference: You have sex with your friends, I don't have sex with mine.
> Therefore: When I go to see my friends, I tell you "I am going to my friend Julia Friday night I will leave about 6:30 or so, and be home somewhere around 10:30 or so."
> When you go see your friends you can tell me the same.

I also discuss the guys with her. No not the sex part, but other stuff. She is supportive and when I say I feel a guy is boring she knows what I mean.

From: Josi

My heart leaps at your joy. At the same time (having been there myself), that this is now a time to show your wife that your having relations with a man will now enhance your relationship to her. Now that you are filled with the experience with this other man, let your cup runneth over and fill the cup of the "one you most love" as you put it. Then she will begin to associate the best love and attention that she ever got with the great love and attention you received from this man.

NOW WHAT?

From: Sidney

I have been out to my wife for 2 years. In this time she encouraged me to see other bears (I am a real bear). We have had guys over, etc. We both have been in therapy separately. She always said she wanted to stay married, and I wanted to stay married, but also have a cute cub around. This was fine by her. But today she sent me an e-mail note below:

>*I suspect in my own heart the plain truth is that you are in serious conflict about being gay and being married to me. Your loyalty and heart and head are all telling you different messages. If I am right then we need to talk about it just like that. I will take a big chance here and say that I believe your conflict to be that you don't want a "married to a woman" relationship with me. The kids are growing older and it is your time to become who it is you are just as it is mine. I think that remaining in our relationship the way it is is very unsatisfactory for both you and for me. I think we need to create something workable for both of us. Honestly.<*

Well I am crushed to say the least. Any ideas?

From: Shawn

My guess is that your arrangement has been working for both of you, to a degree. Now your wife evidently feels that you have one foot in the married world and one in the gay world. She seems to be saying that's it's time to reevaluate this arrangement you have. I think she's suggesting that perhaps you are not fully acknowledging your "gayness" for fear of losing what you know.

You probably need to be willing to hear her out and take what she says seriously. Sometimes our wives know us better than we know ourselves. She might be right and that might just be scaring you right now. Don't let your fear keep you from really listening to what she has to say. Did you honestly believe you could have both relationships as such in the context of your marriage forever? Well, it is a nice thought in a way, but it might be hindering both of you from growing and moving on with your lives more fully.

From: Kenneth

Believe me I can relate. My wife dropped the bomb on me 2 weeks ago. I think the fact that she sent you an e-mail rather than tell you in person is very telling. I hate to say it, because I am still coming to grips with the same situation, but she has sent you on your way.

I am the last person to give you advice to salvage your marriage, I haven't been able to salvage mine! What I would say however, is that if your wife felt that communication was so bad that she had to send you an e-mail, means that there is probably nothing left to salvage. I am sorry to say that bluntly.

My current goal is to arrange for the most amiable separation possible to maintain a good relationship with my kids. Which also means maintain a good relationship with my wife (soon to be ex).

Good luck on your new journey. If you want to talk to a pilgrim who is a few days further down the path than you, please e-mail me.

From: Lou

My wedding anniversary is coming up soon, and I'm not looking forward to it. I'm totally out to my wife (since before we were married over 20 years ago), and we've been talking separation and divorce the last few months, although lately the waters have been much calmer. . . .

I know I should just go out and celebrate the years we've had, and the great friendship we still have, but I can't help but mourn a little.. you know? I feel like I'm denying what's going on by going out and acting like nothing is wrong.

From: Ted

My wife and I celebrated our 25th anniversary by going out to dinner. I had just completed a two-day tryst with my male lover. My wife asked me if I had "a good time."I knew what she meant. I replied in the affirmative. She said she was happy for me. (Later she partially recanted that remark.) We even laughed and cried over the food because we both knew that this would be our last anniversary celebration. No need to deny any of your feelings in these moments. In fact, it's a more sacred occasion if you don't . . . even in public.

From: Carl

With respect to the e-mail, if she's wrong, there is nothing to be crushed about. If she's right, and you're clinging to the marriage for the wrong reasons, it's important that you explore yourself and find out what the truth is. Either way, she's opening up a subject that, it seems to me, "should" be discussed between the two of you.

In fact, I envy you a wife who can be that direct and talk about her worries. Don't let her and yourself down. Find out where the truth is, and build on it.

From: Joey

I think your wife just read my mind. I would suggest that you really listen to what she is saying here. My wife asks me repeatedly, in so many words or less, do you really want to be here; because if you don't then you have to go. I always answer that I want to be here at home. But to be perfectly honest, No, I don't. I have just started to admit that to myself. In some way it makes it easier. After all, one of the things we married gay/BI guys are trying to espouse is the truth. We want to be true to ourselves. So, it might hurt her, it might hurt you. But the truth is what it is. You have to be honest with yourself and quit playing the game of being the dutiful husband when your heart and mind are not in it. No one wins that game. I am not trying to be hard on you and I hope you don't take it that way. Do I make sense here? You have to know what is right for you, then the two of you can work in unison because that is what a marriage is all about. Even if the united effort will ultimately split you up. Good luck my dear friend. I am there too.

From: Brian

I think your wife is EITHER saying that SHE is no longer comfortable with the your arrangement OR she truly believes that YOU are not truly comfortable with it and for some reason are not expressing your true feelings and desires. Whatever is the case, she has some doubts about the validity and honesty of the present arrangement and needs (and wants) to talk honestly about it. (I wish my wife would be so open . . . I envy you). If I were you, I would honestly evaluate your true feelings yourself, then talk to her about them. If you are really happy with your present arrangement and want to stay married, then you can tell her that. If you consciously or unconsciously are not (and you're just saying you are so as not to hurt her) then you need to say that too. She is giving you an opportunity here. Be honest with yourself and with her. Treasure her, she sounds wonderful.

HELP ME FIGURE MY LIFE OUT

From: Rodney

Sorry all, I've been quite quiet up to now, still trying to figure my life out and where to go from here. Is there sex with our wives after coming out to them? This is the major problem right know. For her, she wants it—I do not.

Am I wrong to stand my ground on this? Maybe it is my way of pulling away from her. No, I did not enjoy that part of our marriage, just went along like all good husbands should.

From: Boris

The euphoria that set in when I came out was so great, my entire emotional life went into overdrive. For a number of complex reasons I had not been sexually active with my wife for 11 years, so it was a major event when we started having (very good) sex in the wake of my coming out. But it didn't last. After my first male/male affair (after 23 years), my wife and I both knew that sex between us made no sense. She wanted it, of course; I didn't—I lost "all" interest.

My experience of sex with a man is different in kind from sex with a woman, and (again, for me) that difference is determined by the erotic dimension being totally lacking with a woman. Physiologically and sexually all the plumbing worked, and it was intensely pleasurable. But there was no attraction whatsoever to her femaleness. Once that became clear, the jig was up. We stopped having sex by mutual agreement and consent, to her great sorrow and my great relief.

From: Marlin

I think if our wives want sex, we should give it to them, even if we aren't "turned on." If they are willing to stay married to us and provide us with our emotional support and raise our kids, then we can turn to them with willingness and do our best and take pleasure in their satisfaction. Surely women put up with our desires and satisfy us when they aren't in the mood, so why can't we do the same? I haven't seen it carved in stone that we are entitled to sex lives in perfect congruence with our deepest desires at all times, so we should be willing to do our duty and take our comfort for good service willingly rendered with love.

From: Shawn

What you said about sex with our wives seems to come from the heart of a guy who cares about the well-being and satisfaction of his mate. I liked your question about why do we think that we are always entitled to flawless sexual satisfaction for ourselves without more regard for the needs of our wives. Some of this attitude I think is reactive to the fact that we are men who have repressed and hidden our desires for so long. Still I believe yours is a mature, responsible, and loving attitude that guys should strive for if they want to stay in their marriages.

From: Floyd

Just want to double what you guys are talking about; for me, the crux of a happy BI-married life is maintaining a respectful, generous, loving relationship with my wife. She accepts my need to express myself erotically, intimately, and emotionally with men, but it's not easy! If I keep that in mind, I'm able to understand her reactions at low moments when she's feeling vulnerable and needy, and I can find a way to help her as a best friend and lover should. We all have such moments, and we all need help like that; but it easily becomes twisted and confused when sex and insecurity are involved.

From: Kenneth

I must take issue with you here. Sex with one's wife shouldn't be part of the division of labor, like taking out the garbage or washing the dishes. Even if you are willing to make the sacrifice of real pleasure for the sake of obligation or altruism, isn't your wife deserving of a sexual partner who is thoroughly desirous of her? Should the world's most singular sensual delight be reduced to the status of a quid pro quo?

From: Ted

Let me put my two cents in here. (About what it is worth!!)

Unfortunately, for men to be able to perform, we must be turned on. Now for you younger guys, that may not be a problem, but as we get into our 40s, it gets harder to get up (PUN INTENDED) to the task.

If a woman isn't in the mood, but decides to go through the motions, all she has to do is to lay there. Men have to be active. It gets harder to fake desire as you get older!

From: Gabe

It would be difficult to stay with my wife if I had to fake sex with her. I think that could be totally unfair to her. I think that we display also a kind of machismo in such an attitude. The issue is sharing knowledge, hence decision, hence power: If you were to acknowledge lack of desire, then she will have equal knowledge, and she will be able to make the decision to leave. Although we might not do it consciously, many times we conceal our behavior, actions, or thoughts to maintain control. Does it make sense? :-)

From: Mike

You said all: we really owe our spouses . . . and all we should expect from them is honest sharing of information . . . hence each can make informed decisions in their own best interests. No one is held hostage in that case.

I wrote a while back that I discovered something about myself that I did not like, but that I was glad to have learned. When I withhold information from my wife "to protect her from the pain of knowing" . . . I am really only trying to protect MYSELF from the pain of TELLING.

From: Marlin

I wish I was getting more sex with my wife, but we just don't seem to be able to connect. I'm usually willing at the drop of a hat, but she so rarely is. If I had been getting more at home, I might not have had the energy to pursue my boyfriend in the first place. Who knows how things might have turned out otherwise? Oh well, that's blood under the bridge. . . .

From: Ted

I have not had sex with my wife for 7 years. I have lost interest, but so had she. In fact, we didn't have sex on a regular basis, except when we were trying to conceive. After we succeeded, our sex life diminished!!!

Even when we were younger, my sex drive was much stronger than hers. She was never very interested in experimentation.

P.S. Where are all those women our mothers warned us about!!!

From: Willis

Sometimes when my wife and I make love, she's obviously just taking care of me, my "needs." I love her for that. Sometimes, she wants it as much as I do. I love her for that. Sometimes, she flat out refuses to take me on. I'm no saint; I don't love her for that. But I do RESPECT her for that, and I love her for being a person I can respect.

If she only gave it to me to satisfy me, to do her wifely duty, quite frankly, I would not respect her. If I only gave it to her to satisfy her, to do my husbandly duty, I hope that she would have the self-respect not to settle for that.

Unlike the workplace world, where I claim the freedom to reveal as much or as little of my private self as I feel comfortable, depending on the person, in the home with one's wife, I feel that honesty and being true to oneself is the way to go. That's not to say that I would never make love to my wife unless I absolutely wanted to. But if satisfying her were what it was pretty much all about . . . to me, seems kind of depressing.

From: John

I'm 52 and so far haven't had any major problems remaining sexually interested in my wife (knock on wood), even though she's not letting me touch her these days.

Though I've been catching up after being offline for a couple of weeks, I've been interested in the discussion of one's sexual "responsibilities" to one's wife. Since I may not be married much longer, this may be a wholly academic question for me, but I think that if, for some reason, I were to be in a marriage in which I didn't have major sexual interest in my wife, I'd still be concerned to provide her with sexual gratification. (I'm assuming that there are strong Nonsexual reasons for continuing the relationship—why else would you bother?).

If the wife doesn't take a lover (certainly a possibility), then why not learn how to give her erotic massage? Toys and oral sex could probably also be applied to good effect. I can easily imagine a completely gay man being able to drive his wife to heights of ecstasy that many wives in heterosexual marriages never experience! As a bisexual, I think I would venture a guess that gay men, on the whole, are CONSIDERABLY less selfish, sexually, than straight men are. You could prove this to your wives.

No sexual arousal required on hubby's part—just a commitment to provide a good time! And that's an expression of love, isn't it?

(I chuckle to myself at the thought of a gay man stealing the wife of a straight man because the gay man is a better lover. I in fact think this scenario is utterly possible.)

Hey, relax! It's just sex!

From: Ted

I agree with you that there are many ways that a man can sexually satisfy a woman besides penile intercourse.

However, that assumes the wife is receptive to those methods. Without going into explicit detail, let me say, that my wife ISN'T!

She is in many ways a woman of the 1950s. So, if you have women who ENJOY!! sex, consider yourselves very fortunate. I think my wife considered it her DUTY.

After a while, it is no fun to have sex with a mannequin or blow-up doll; even if she does breathe & have a pulse!

LOVE & SEX

From: William

The important thing is not what we label ourselves, gay, str8, bisexual but what is needed in the marriage between the husband and wife. Just because u r gay or just because u r poor, or whatever, doesn't determine the success or failure of that marriage. What do the husband and wife want from each other and can the other person give it, is a part of the big question. To me, the other vital ingredient is love. The label is unimportant if there is compelling love. Without love issues of race, looks, religion, sexual interests, etc. become the focus.

From: Gabe

I guess you are right from your frame of reference. Mine is different as is becoming apparent from the responses to my statements. I guess I am speaking as a bisexual man. The struggle for a gay man in a marriage is very different. Still in certain circumstances marriage to a gay man is possible. Depending on the couple, anything is possible. Compatibility is the key.

From: William

I still feel that the key ingredient is love. If you really love your partner, everything else falls into place. Unconventional sexuality is just another obstacle in a marriage. And I don't mean to minimize it. But so are different religions, races, disabilities, abilities, ages, classes, etc. If two people really love each other, they can figure out how to make things work. Leave out the gay variable and put in one of the previously mentioned variables and you have the same obstacles to overcome and the same questions. "How do I deal with my self-esteem marrying someone from a lower class?" "How do I face my family marrying someone so much older?" etc.

What do u think guys? Am I simplifying things too much?

From: Ben

I think you've described the struggle for most of us beautifully. Mine was similar, although I consider myself bisexual. I found the two struggles you describe were very related. One was my struggle for personal identity the other was the struggle to have a good marriage. My stubborn nature would not let me compromise on either. Each struggle is shaped and resolved depending on the other. My unavoidable struggle with my sexuality made me a better person. The love between my wife and I made our marriage work. No deep love, no marriage. No acceptance of who I am, no ability to accept myself and love fully in return. Without love, no "method" of making a marriage work will succeed.

From: Boris

William wrote: >*Unconventional sexuality is just another obstacle in a marriage.*<

I think it depends on the kind of sexuality. My being gay is not just another obstacle, it is fundamental. Once my wife realized I could never desire her as a straight man desires a woman, she knew our marriage as we'd always thought it was, was over. But she also knew I love her as much now as I did when we first met.

Again, "real love" is not a clear idea to me here. My wife and I have figured out that to make things work for herself, for me, and for us, we need to live apart from each other. This is the only way we can continue to really love each other, and we do.

My being gay is not a variable, it is not an attribute of my person. It defines who and what I am, it is part of the essence of who I am. It is not like a belief system that I can choose or change. It is not like a disability that I have to learn to cope with.

I am not and never have been in any way bisexual. I have never erotically desired my wife of 20 years. Does this mean I don't and never did love her? I know better.

From: Gabe

What we want and our uncertainties and/or certainties is only half of the picture. The other half is what does *she* want?

In fact, my wife and I had an hour and a half on the subject last night. She does love me, I am her best friend, we have a good time together, we are a parenting team, but I am not what she wants. She agrees I am a better individual since I came out, and she is happy about that, but she does not like my being with men. She might not know what she wants, but she is certain about what she does not want or what she does not like. She is clear that if I had told her at the beginning she wouldn't have chosen to marry me. And she feels a crisis of self-esteem for staying with me. In some way she feels like being in a closet. She hates the whole idea of me being with another guy. We are making plans all the time for the future, like we had a future together as a couple, but the issue is always there.

I guess that is probably no help at all. Maybe a solution could be to separate for a while, and then restart as a couple if we chose to, both of us. That could be a way to clear once and for all the issue of betrayal.

WHAT'S HIS NAME?

From: Carl

After having written that life was good because of the warmth that seemed to have developed between my wife and me, today she referred to my boyfriend as "what's-his-name." I was crushed. I've mentioned him hundreds of times over the last year and more. Is she really that far into denial? Is she really that insensitive? Is there any hope that the roller coaster will ever glide to a stop? I think I'm gonna be sick. . . .

From: Felix

Your wife is not in denial. I have learned from my wife that what you are describing as your wife's denial, is her way of trying not to snap. Women have much better constitution than we men do. If she refers to your lover as "what's-his-name" ask her why she feels the need not to speak of him in the first person. You will get a lot further than if you attack her for being in denial. Don't forget that our wives put up with A LOT. They have made HUGE concessions to stay with us. We have no right to get pissed at them for being mad that we are gay/bisexual. We have to love and support them no matter what, as they do us. DO NOT assume to know what your wife is feeling when she calls him "what's-his-name." She probably never thought she'd be married to a gay man, and an occasional slip is permissible.

From: George

Many of the members on this list let their wives know before marriage that they were either gay or BI. There are some, maybe many that did not. I am sure there are some who didn't know, or probably didn't admit to even themselves that they were gay or BI until well into their marriage. Many of us felt that maybe the magic of marriage would cause our closet identities to go away completely. Boy, were we fooled.

I think if a guy really knew he was BI or gay prior to marriage and didn't let his wife know of his feelings or attraction to men, then the wife has cause to get pissed now and then. Yes, many of these wives are trying to make the marriage work, I suspect for a variety of reasons, like financial, shame, or whatever, and some are trying to make it work because they truly love us and know that we love them. I know my wife didn't know I was BI before we married, and I never really knew, or probably admitted it to myself until well into our marriage. As a teenager and young adult I was even on the homophobic side (I am not proud of this), never thought of guys as a sex object. But even though in my situation this is the case, and I really did not think of myself as BI or gay prior to marriage, I cannot get uptight at the few times my wife gets pissed or maybe lets hurt show through.

I have been lucky. I only came out to my wife last year. She has made remarkable strides in acceptance. At first I thought she would show me the door, I was even ready for it. But, after a few weeks of quiet reflection she came around, and our relationship started back on track until at this point I think it is better than ever. She even kids around with me about my attractions, like nudging me when there is a cute guy in sight, and then passing me that sly smile because she knows the type of guy that turns me on.

Just this weekend when my "friend" asked me to go away for a vacation week with him she completely surprised me by taking a positive attitude right up front. First thing on Monday morning she made arrangements to go visit our daughter while I will be away saying this way she would be visiting our grandkids and wouldn't miss me so much.

I personally think that a wife who entered marriage thinking that her man was straight has the right to let off steam now and then. When I came out to my wife she was plenty steamed, but then realized, as I did, what a wonderful life we had had up until this point and felt it would be a crime to waste what we had.

Sorry for running off at the mouth, but I am so damn happy the way my situation has turned out that I have to stick up for what I think is right in this situation.

From: Willis

First: wow, I'm really glad for how things are working out with your wife. Some time ago when we talked, I recall that you had very little hope for the future. Apparently your wife has come through for you in a big way that you had not thought was possible. I for one take that as a lesson that there is always hope and possibility of good things.

I think maybe the problem, if any, with what he said was just the way it was phrased as a universal thing. I don't feel like my wife is any kind of victim in our relationship, at least not based on my bisexuality. I don't think that she feels betrayed or anything like that about it. Not to say that she is 100% comfortable about it, by any means, but it has not been a kick in the teeth for her, either.

From: Rodney

I'm also in favor of not directing too much anger toward ourselves because of ANY secret we hide or lie we tell when that secret or lie is a response to the pervasive homophobia in society. Remember that we are ALL victims of this homophobia, and we need to listen to our wives' anger with this in mind. Is it US who is victimizing them or a more general social attitude?

From: Carl

My wife knew before we were married in 1958 that I had spent 10 years thinking of myself as gay, and by about 1961 we had both realized that my expectation of needing men no longer once we were married was a hollow hope. She knows, all right. And the "slips" are far more than occasional.

What causes the problem is her inconsistency and her refusal to talk about or work on the marriage. I don't know what to expect from one day to the next. Being at peace with myself because of finally accepting myself for what I am has given me a lot more patience with her than I used to have, but Job I ain't. And every time she slaps me in the face with one of these peevish or vitriolic or self-pitying behavior patterns, after a period of warmth and apparent acceptance, all I can think of is, "Who needs it!"

From: Felix

I'm not saying at all that our wives are victims. Granted all the love and support we have for each other is presupposed to be inherited, however, I maintain that we have to be a little more sensitive to our wives' situation. In short, they are married to gay men, some of them knew it going into the relationship, others did not. This does not mean we can flaunt our gayness to them. We need to be who we are, and we cannot expect that our wives are completely at peace with this. We need to talk it through with them and make sure that neither one of us is harboring any hostility. My wife is very open and honest about her feelings, but I still sense sometimes that she is holding back for my sake. I try to gently remind her that I love her and I need her and that I am not leaving her just because I am bisexual. Our monogamy is a testimony to that.

From: Moris

Just wonder that don't we (the gay one) also "put up with A LOT"? My wife has made HUGE concessions, but I know that she has done that because (1) she loves me, (2) she believes that my being BI is not wrong, (3) she lives what she believes. Why should a wife (or anyone), that believes being gay is not someone's fault, get mad at them for being gay?

Once we outed ourselves, we both have a choice: stay or leave. I do understand that time needs to be given and time MUST be given. After all, we had time to adjust. So I agree that we MUST give our wives time to adjust . . . and each person adjusts at different rates . . . so we should not get mad at our wives while they are ADJUSTING to our being Gay.

From: Carl

What is so angry-making about my desire to spend one evening a month in a church, hanging out with a bunch of gays and lesbians, if that can help to save me from the kind of depression and despair—and irascibility and hostility—I went through after my last close male friend died and before I re-established the connection with my love? And if it helps me avoid driving to see "whatshisname" so often, why should she be angry about that? Yet it is my commitment to attend that dinner this evening—a plan to which she gave her blessing last Thursday—that put her into her present self-pitying sulk.

Perhaps the fact that I spent an hour on the phone last evening with "what's-his-name" has something to do with it. She may have got wind of the warmth and joy of that conversation. . . .Man, it's wearing me down. . . .

From: Carl

We've just got to find ways of building on the parts they support and workarounds for the parts they don't. Not easy sometimes . . .

From: George

Great hearing from you. I miss not having chatted with you in a while. I have always felt we have enjoyed a special kind of a bonding since we first started chatting many months ago. Yes, my wife has come a long way. We have had some pretty lengthy and very serious discussions about my orientation. We sat many a night into the wee hours of the morning going over old photo albums of family, vacations, and other interest areas. We obviously had a lot going for us and she, thank God, felt that she would be a fool to toss everything to the winds.

When I came out to my wife, I guess part of the reason she took it so hard, was so despondent, and very distant for weeks was because she was blaming herself for my interests turning to men. There was no way that her lack of enjoyment of sex pushed me into a bisexual mode and I assured her of that in every way I could. I wouldn't want to end our marriage and I am happy as I can possibly be that now she doesn't either. I don't want to sound corny, but I believe that a marriage built entirely on sex is destined to crash. Ours certainly was not built solely on sex and it is a damn good thing it wasn't because we have so much else that is helping to hold it together. The only thing my wife has asked me to promise her is that I not come out to our children or anyone else. She is fair in asking this for we live in what I feel is a very homophobic community and coming out to the world would only tend to isolate us, and this, she nor I need.

MARRIED GUYS, HELP ME!!!

From: Carpenter

I really need some input from you guys who are gay, out to your wives, and staying married—I'm having a really bad time of it right now—Deep

Depression and the most Profound Sadness I have ever experienced in my life—far sadder than the day I came out to my wife. What I would like to know if this is a phase that I must pass through, or if it will take a divorce to cure . . .

From: Brandon

Hang in there, as I recognize your dilemma as similar to my own Deep Depression. I lived through it and with it for many years. I knew for many years that suicide was the only out of that deep hole I had dug in life for myself.

I have been on depression medication for years now (It, for me, runs in the family—father and grandfather suffered severe bouts of it for years. Both tried to destroy themselves on numerous occasions.)

The REALLY-REALLY good news is there are few if any side effects and they do help!!!!! There are many different kinds of antidepressants out on the market and sometimes it takes trial and error to find just the right one for each individual. It took two different medications before they found the correct one for me. I have been functioning as a very happy gay married person with much joy in my life for many years now.

Let me assure you that this is not a phase that you must pass through and a divorce will absolutely not cure you. I recommend that you take your time and let the medication work, find a really good counselor and work diligently on learning to love yourself. When both of you become very strong and self loving; then and only then, decide whether a divorce is the best for either or both of you.

From: David

Patience! Accept any/all support you can get . . . wife, shrink, others, here . . . and wait . . . The best book I ever read on depression had one key phrase in it: "You will get better . . . you really will." . . . At the time I read it and decided to use its author as my shrink I really didn't believe it but adopted the safety step of "wait and see." Waiting and patience paid off!!! Fortunately BMMA and spouse support came into my life in time to make the waiting and SHOPPING around easier. . . . Without naming names, many of them are now on this list and they are still a help.

From: Sterling

I see you are hurting, so I'll toss my two cents' worth your way, for whatever its worth to you. First, I am confirmed as a bisexual, not gay, and I am out to my wife for a little over a year now.

Depression—I think I know where you are at, but I have been fortunate to keep out of the "pit" for the most part. My times when I felt most "sad" and depressed were transitory, but it never feels that way at the time. I know it seems like it will never ever end.

There's the rub. I too have felt that if I were able to just up and run away to the "gay" life that's waiting for me, I would survive and so would my wife and kids. When I recently inherited some money, I could have done just that. My wife was the first one to suggest that now I had the ability to go off and live my other life, and I had to face up to it. I have felt aloof and separate from my wife at times, because there are a lot of things I have been thinking about, and they are obviously private. But as we have struggled to make things work, it's become clear to me that I have to decide what I want! And I have decided that I like what I have built since I have been with my wife. I like my place in the community, where I have been a cub leader, chair of the elementary school council, and marginally involved in municipal politics. I love my wife and cherish what we have had—honesty, mutual support, and deep friendship . . . and there it is: my wife as a friend, my kids, whom I love (and to whom I have a responsibility). As for focusing at work, that comes and goes depending on my energy level and the depth of the crisis. The more urgent something is, the better I am able to pull it together. So most things are going ok, those that aren't probably don't matter, and some things are going great. I am glad I don't get a weekly report card. . . .

When I first signed on the Internet when I was 37 (God—it seems like so long ago now [39 now]), I went onto the #gay help channel and asked about what I could expect. The fellers on there let me know plain and simple that were I to leave my family for the gay life, I'd be entering a world where I'd be a minority that suffered intolerance from the majority of society, if not outright hostility. I'd have to leave the community where I presently live (small rural town that is not very GLBT-tolerant). I moved out into the country to enjoy the lifestyle. I have no permanent boyfriend at the moment and as an overweight and somewhat shy man, I would have to find some way to gain entrance to a community that is, naturally enough, kind-of closed and sheltered. In other words, they were careful to point out that the nirvana I expected was not what I was going to experience. And it made me think about what I wanted—really wanted.

No one can answer whether the situation works for you, but you!

So guys, there's my story. I am working with a shrink—in fact, my wife put a call in to him earlier today (Sat) to let him know that it's getting worse. Starting next week, I'll be on antidepressants, like so many other gay men I know. Anyway, if you've been here, please let me know how it ends.

It hasn't ended for me yet. And, you know, I'm not sure it ever will. . . . I think maybe I am starting to come to terms with that. I guess you're going to have to travel the same road yourself. It's long, and winding, and scary more often than not. But stay in touch with your friends on the list and elsewhere. And have faith in your ability to make the choice that's right for you. I'm pulling for you, bud.

AGE REALLY BITES

From: Art

Although I have come to appreciate the wisdom and insight that age and maturity brings to this whole issue of gay/BI-marriages, it would be nice to hear from some of the younger guys facing this issue in their lives. I sometimes feel that I'll have to wait until both my wife and I are in our 40+ years in order to "cope better" with ourselves, each other, and our marriage. Please tell me this isn't the case. Am I capable of suppressing feelings and desires of being with another male?

I guess what the real issue here is that it appears most of you have had time to experience your "gay side," while I on the other hand have only had very few gay experiences. How do I explore that part of me? Is it really necessary to do so? Is it really possible to do so while maintaining a "heterosexual style" marriage?

I realize that since both my wife and I are relatively young (29 years old), it's really not fair for her to basically put her life, dreams, and desires on hold waiting for me to decide what I want out of this relationship. In the meantime, what is she really getting out of it? A good friend, a father for our son, or what? The fact that we just had a baby and my wife had a complicated pregnancy has helped put the whole issue of sex between the two of us, or lack thereof, on hold. But what happens when neither of us can use those excuses any more? Then what?

I hope that my questions, concerns, and words don't offend anyone, but these are just some of the things that I'm trying to put into perspective. The immature side of me is screaming to get out, while the mature, rational side is saying, "Hang up your dancing shoes buddy, time to grow up." Age definitely changes one's perspective. . . .

From: Mike

I hope the younger guys on this list will respond with their perspectives as you hoped. I am one of those "40 something" guys that we seem to hear more from on this forum. My wife and I enjoy a deeper love and intimacy now than we ever imagined as younger people. There is something very wonderful that happens when two people (m/f, m/m, or f/f) who love each other, journey together through life. It is especially "growth-full" when neither of them avoid the trials and tribulations of trying to live life authentically. This is anything but a "passive" experience. In our case we have "CHOSEN" to face life and all of its challenges together. Each time we make this conscious choice . . . we grow in our self esteem and our appreciation of the other. Yes . . . we have "grown accustomed" to one another . . . and I LOVE it.

Can you imagine embracing your sexuality AND expressing it with your wife's support? Many of us can and do. Age, in my opinion, is not the most important factor here . . . it is MATURITY.

Others, having embraced their own natures, find it necessary to move away from relationships/partners that have become TOXIC to both parties, because of one or the other's insistence on suppressing nature. This too is a choice that honors nature . . . that nurtures the authentic soul.

I have been pleasantly surprised at my wife's capacity to make her own decisions (as long as she has all the facts available) and to take responsibility for her own happiness. Things work so much better for both of us when we avoid taking on the others' pain, confusion, decisions. That does not mean we don't have empathy and compassion for each other, or that to see the other in pain is easy . . . it just means we trust that each of us will have the courage and the honesty to honor our own and each other's authentic NATURE, and that as long as we do that . . . we will be OK (i.e., right with the universe).

I can appreciate your frustrations . . . .God knows I have heard the same contradictory voices inside of me that you describe . . . the battle with ourselves is THE POINT of this life . . . regardless of one's age. Embrace it. Learn from it. Paradox is always present in a "SOULFUL" moment. Going back up to my cave to meditate now. . . . ;-)

From: Pancho

You are exactly where I am . . . yet I am 40, not 29. This whole coming-out to your spouse is a process. . . . one that takes time. We all do it in different ways, and at different speeds. I don't think age has a whole lot to do with it. . . . I am just as lost and confused and don't have answers either. As you indicated, you and your wife have an "excuse" for not having sex currently. So do I . . . but I also fear what happens when that is gone. I've been out about 6 months . . . in the beginning, our relationship was almost finished. It took a therapist to help us get to the real bottom of any relationship . . . do we love each other, do we have enough in common—trust, respect, friendship, etc.—to make anything work? I say "anything" because we didn't have a clue what our relationship was going to evolve into.

I didn't know for sure if I was gay or BI or what (don't want to get into that long-running philosophical discussion again here! LOL!) At that point, I only wanted men. I have had an affair, earlier, with a woman. I've had periods I wanted both. Right now, I am heavily into men. Our therapist helped us both understand that we do love each other. I learned for the first time in 19 years of marriage that my wife really did love me. . . . for me. She has opened up and accepted me for who I am. I never felt like I ever had that before . . . our marriage is more of a partnership, than me being the head of it and her dependent upon me.

I have been open and honest with her, trying to help her understand what it is I need and want from another man. I am honest with me. I accept me for the first time in my life. I am ok in my own skin. Coming out actually fixed a lot of things in the past 6 months.

Don't get me wrong, there are still issues and probably will be. I was in a long-distance relationship when I came out to my wife. That just ended and she has been so comforting of my loss. She knows it is something I need and something that she can't give me. She isn't threatened by him (or wasn't) and I was honest with her about him. She knew when I saw him. He was also married and not ever going to leave his wife. My lover was a safe (out of town) way for her to accept this. It worked for everyone until my lover got a serious case of guilt (his wife got suspicious). We are on hiatus waiting for him to realize his denial! I may never have him back.

We aren't having sex much. We did during the fall and it was good. I was into sex with her. I didn't fantasize about a man during sex with her. Since December, I have no desire to have sex with her (grieving the loss of my guy!). The couple of times we did have sex, I fantasized about him. Then I felt guilty! It may be months or years or never before my lover comes around. I am at a serious crossroads and so is my wife. Will I have someone else? Probably, I am just terrified of going down that road right now. The important thing is to talk . . . keep that communication open. I found my wife and I will continue to have a marriage . . . at least in the foreseeable future. It is based on a deep love, 4 kids, and a lifestyle that we both enjoy. We truly like each other. I am sure there will be periods of more and less sex. There always has been during the past 19 years when there wasn't another "man" in my life. The most important aspect of navigating the communication is knowing where your wife is during all this. I know my wife. I know how she thinks, how she processes. Bringing up issues and blurting out feelings at a time when she isn't ready for it will spell doom in the relationship. Don't rush. Take your time.

You have your brothers on this group and others to talk to. She probably has no one. My wife didn't have anyone but our therapist. Good luck. There are lots of us out there in the exact same place.

From: Chukky

I am one of those forty year olds you speak of. I am gay and married with children. I came out to my wife two years ago and remained monogamous to her up till that time for the past 19 years. I have a lover, she knows the guy but not the situation. Truthfully, I am sure she knows the truth but we have three children and we are a family. My wife and I have a very nice "friendship."We have not had sex since my coming out basically for two reasons. The first being I don't want to with her (or any women I can think of) and the second is because I am the type of guy that can only be in love and have sex with one person and that person is my lover, who I have been involved with for the past 17 months. He too, is married with two kids—preteens. I would like nothing more than for things to be different. I would love my life to be with him in a "marriage." We give each other the support, the love, the passion neither of us has ever felt . . . but because of commitment, we have to stay where we are. For now I am content with it . . . frustrated too . . . but do believe we will be together on a live-in basis sometime. I love him as I would a spouse and he feels the same. From each other, unlike with our wives, we have nothing to hide . . . and that is a wonderful feeling.

From: Andy

It is never time to hang up your dancing shoes. Life is a dance! And age doesn't bite. I have never been happier, more productive, more athletic (though I lost at tennis tonight—opponent said, "There aren't any balls you don't try to go after, are there?" with some amazement; it's true) than I am now, and I'm pushing 60. As for your wife being cheated by you being you, that's up to her to decide. I would think it reasonable for you to ask her for a little time while you figure out who you are and what you need and want. After all, a marriage is not something that people "get something out of" (sounds too utilitarian) but a relationship. It certainly is possible for a M-F marriage to accommodate a man expressing his gay side—we have several examples here—but a marriage is less likely to continue when the parties are younger and sex is absent.

From: Sherman

I understand what you are going through, but have learned that all is not hopeless. I am 27 years old and came out to my wife recently. Coming out to her, I think, saved our marriage. For a few months beforehand I was moody, quiet, uncommunicative . . . just plain miserable as I faced the fact that my sexuality could not be changed by ignoring it. Our relationship would not last under these circumstances, I knew that. If it was going to end, I wanted the real reason to be known. I came out to her knowing that she would probably not accept the situation. She was more accepting and understanding than I could ever have imagined. Yes, things are sometimes bad, there are answers that we both want that just don't seem to come, but open communication can't be emphasized enough.

The situation has forced both of us to look at ourselves, who we are, what we want, where we're going, etc., all of the questions you bring up. We have the advantage of youth, not being so set in our ways. This is a good thing. Right now we want to be together, to really get to know each other and at the same time find out who we really are. For me part of finding out who I am is exploring my sexuality since my experience with men has been so limited. We both agree that ultimately it can only help our relationship; I can't imagine being 50 years old and still wondering, "Is this the right thing for me?" This is not putting our relationship on hold; it continues to grow and develop as we both find out answers. The relationship may change, but isn't that what relationships are supposed to do?

My point here is don't wait to deal with this and don't expect that it will go away. You ask many good questions, questions that there are not immediate answers to. I have learned to live with that, but have become very proactive in finding the answers, even if they aren't the answers I wanted.

Don't know if this helps at all; just wanted to let you know you're not alone here and offer my limited experience dealing with this. I think it even helped me to say all this. . . .

From: Scott

My wife and I are both 23. We are having some of these same issues to deal with. Our intimate bedroom relationship has become almost nonexistent. My problem now is, What do I do with my gay feelings now that my wife knows? How do I act? Just general and total confusion cloud my mind. It is very difficult to deal with everyday life. I want to be able to be myself, be comfortable and not pretend anymore, that is what my wife wants for me also. On the other hand, she can't take me going out to a bar or anywhere else. We have ruled out the possibility (for now) of having an open relationship. She can't take me being with another man, and the man in me can't take her being with another man either. My general daily thoughts are WHAT THE HELL DO I DO NOW?

Are you in therapy? I know that it is helping me to be able to go in and talk to my therapist about anything. The only thing that I can say to you is GOOD LUCK, you're not alone!

From: Scott

I know that I still love my wife and am attracted to her sexually. I also have discovered and admitted to myself that I am a lot more gay than bisexual. She is the only exception to me being completely gay. My wife and I don't have a strong sexual relationship right now, I think, because of her suppressed anger toward me. I do enjoy being with her, but I know that I would never marry another woman again, simply out of the fact that I am not attracted to any other women. Throughout the day on campus, I find myself rating the guys that I see and checking them out. I have also come to the conclusion that if someone asked me now if I was gay, I think that I could be honest and tell the truth. However, I have also found that I have become more homophobic since my coming out to my wife. I try so hard to not have the "tell-tale" signs of a gay man. I feel that because of my problems here with my wife, the problems that I have had with my love for my boyfriend, and his not returning that love, and then my parents, that I am just not wanted anywhere. How do I cope with these feelings? I sometimes feel that I should just move out and explore my gay feelings and the culture that I am so wanting to find out, but then I also find that I don't want to be without my wife. I am so confused about my gayness and how I am supposed to deal with it and incorporate it into my life. I know that I can't just put it away again, but my wife says that she can't live with me having a relationship with another man. She wants me to be "me" and happy, but how do I do that when I know that she can't handle me loving another man?

From: Shawn

You said your wife says she could NEVER deal with you loving another person (man). My wife said she could NEVER deal with my loving a man. Well, now she IS dealing with it. True, I've been sexual with him without "going all the way" and maybe that has helped a little. I've made some concessions for the sake of our marriage. HOWEVER, the point being, I do love another man and my wife and I ARE dealing with it. It has taken years to get this far. She and my man friend are becoming friends. It has taken difficult conversations, arguing, crying, compromise, prayer, love, commitment to each other. . . . Also, my man friend is a healthy and beautiful human being who knows the meaning of love. WHAT I AM SAYING IS—SHE MIGHT BE SAYING NEVER, BUT THAT DOES NOT MEAN IT CAN

NEVER HAPPEN! But, it will take a long process. We Americans need to understand; real life is not Instant Breakfast!

From: Shawn

If you're married, but want a man too, I think there are some basic questions to ask and answer:

1. Are you genuinely still attracted to your wife sexually? Are you really BI or are you really gay?
2. What "arrangement" can you both agree to and actually live with if there's still enough mutual passion to warrant staying together?

It seems to me that if you are sexually attracted to your wife, then the marriage can withstand change and maybe even a gay relationship (to the degree you both can live with).

On the other hand, if you don't really have a loving and sexual passion for your wife, then I believe you have to face that. A passionless marriage cannot withstand the pressures placed on it by the man having gay desires. In that case I think the couple has to work on dealing with reality and letting go of each other while still being friends, if possible.

From: Conrad

Your comment concerning the need for passion in your post really struck a cord for me, but I can't tell if its because I disagree or because you hit the nail on the head.

For much of our lives, I maintained sexual passion for my wife, but I don't think it was (usually) what I know can be real sexual passion. We always accepted our sex life as OK, which it was. No more, but rarely less.

But does no sexual passion really mean no loving relationship? Purely, as a matter of fact, it's just not true. Lot's of couples have little, if any sexual passion in their marriage, yet truly love each other and stay together. These are healthy relationships as well as neurotic, old, sick, or mixed orientation. I know several mixed-orientation couples who really do fine without sex.

But, it certainly doesn't work fine for us. The difference, I guess, is that my wife wants sex and passionate love. She deserves it. She deserves her sexuality as much as I deserve mine. I've been trying to make myself able to give her what she wants and needs, not only because I love her and want her to be fulfilled, but because I accept that it is good, if not a prerequisite, for our relationship. I know I could do so before, but can I now? I'm not sure I can.

HOW MUCH IS TOO MUCH TO ASK?

From: Jos

My wife is considering trying an "open" relationship approach in our marriage. She knows I'm not willing or able to be monogamous to her and so is thinking of trying a compromise. I'm not sure it will work for either one of us but I think we (especially she) are worth the shot.

Here's my dilemma. She wants a list, a specific list of what I want in this hypothetical agreement. Yikes! . . . I feel like I'm setting myself up for just another outburst. (You may remember how she reacted to my kissing my friend, she thought it was treason, for me it was just a kiss.) I think we have different expectations on this subject.

Well it doesn't make a difference how scared I am; I guess I need to provide the list. I have a few ideas of my own but I'd like to know what arrangements some of you have made with your wives. Please don't tell me it depends on my needs, etc. I know that! I just want to open myself up to suggestions I may not have thought of and then I'll decide if they apply to my situation.

From: Rodney

Once again, I find myself talking about situations that are wildly different from mine. Part of me is green with envy that your wife is even able to have this kind of discussion with you. But I know it is never that easy. . . .

I have a couple of suggestions. First of all, keep absolutely clear in your mind that you're NOT going to agree to some kind of "legal" document which commits either of you once and for all to a code of behavior. No one ever knows himself well enough at any given moment to know what will be hard or easy to do in the future. This is especially true in matters of the heart . . . and the groin. THIS IS AS TRUE FOR YOUR WIFE AS IT IS FOR YOU. So if this is a ploy on your wife's part to avoid uncertainty, I'd make it clear that you think it won't do that.

HOWEVER, let's take a more optimistic outlook. Let's say your wife is just asking you to be as clear to her (and to yourself) about WHAT YOU REALLY WANT. . . (as long as she has the option of not granting all your wishes). Now, communication like that is a totally different matter, and I think an excellent idea.

Keep this discussion open as a TWO-WAY dialogue in which you are BOTH trying to understand what you need, what you want, what you can tolerate. Accept the idea that EITHER of you might find out later on that something you thought WOULD work WON'T. In other words, turn this into an EXPLORATION rather than a NEGOTIATION and it might be a very good thing for BOTH of you.

From: George

At the time I came out to my wife I was (and still am) in a relationship with a fella who also happens to be my best friend. He is married and, like me, wishes to stay that way. My desire was not, and is not, to play the field. I am very satisfied with having a steady lover. My situation, for me, couldn't be better. My guy and his wife have been our friends for many years. We live in a very homophobic setting which dictates remaining in the closet to the rest of the world.

When I came out to my wife, this past July, we had a very turbulent two or three weeks. I was convinced our marriage was at an end. Then, all of a sudden, we became somewhat rational and sat and talked, and talked, and talked some more. We both realized that we had had a pretty damn good relationship through the years. There was a lot we enjoyed doing together, much we liked and loved about each other. We are proud of our children and enjoy a close relationship with them.

When I dumped this BI thing on her, the fact that I found that I was also attracted to men, I did so because I had to be honest with her. I know to some degree, she felt that my friend and I are unusually close and wanted to know just how close we really were. I told her all about our relationship, how long we have been lovers. I admitted that we hugged, kissed, and had sex, safe sex, with one another. I even startled her by admitting that at times we just sat and held hands while we talked. I verified that while I was attracted to, or noticed, other guys, I had no desire to expand my BI involvements.

Once this confession period was out of the way I naturally felt one hell of a lot better about me and my relationship with my wife. For the first time, in a long time, we had an honest, above-board relationship, a damn good feeling. Now came the rules session. This was inspired by my wife. She informed me that on such-and-such an evening, she wanted to sit down and discuss the rules that she would expect me to live by (or BI):) now that our marriage has taken a different turn. She suggested that in the meantime I think about it, so that when we sit down we can have a meaningful discussion. When the night came to have our discussion we were both a bit fidgety. She started out by saying that she didn't want me playing the field, engaging in one night stands, and felt it imperative that I limit my involvement to another married man. This kind of arrangement, she felt, would be more apt to ensure that I continue to value our relationship and from a STD point of view be safer. She then informed me that she didn't want me to come out to anyone else, family or friends. Lastly, she did not want to know what we did emotionally or sexually.

Wow—the rules she wanted enforced are exactly as it has always been, except now she knows about me, the real, honest-to-goodness me.

I know she would rather have me be totally straight, but I am not, and I know she does now accept me, and that is what is really important to me.

I strongly advise anyone in this position, a BI or gay married man, who really loves his wife and wishes to remain married to talk it out, and talk it out calmly.

From: James

I suggest you talk about a time frame . . . i.e., how frequently she is OK with you seeing someone else or you tell her . . . once a week is my agreement with my wife, which may include overnight. Assure her that you will practice safe sex, then the rest should be left to trust . . . you need to consider the dignity of the other man involved and I think it's best that you two not get into exactly what you do . . . though it may be helpful to state what you do not do . . . if you know that for yourself.

From: Brandon

Remember always that the only reason for an agreement between the two of you is to rebuild and then maintain the MARRIAGE TRUST and nothing more! This keeps the agreement out of the realm of CONTROL!

!!!!!!!!!KEEP YOUR AGREEMENT (to rebuild and maintain trust) SIMPLE!!!!!!

Do not agree to anything that you know that you cannot live with—only you know yourself. Assure her that you will always practice "Safer Sex" and if you fail—you must let her know immediately.

Agree to keeping her informed as to where you will be and when she can expect you home. This is only for your safety and her piece of mind. If you are ever late, a call is an absolute must no matter where you are or who you are with.

Assure your wife that you will always tell her the truth from this point on in your relationship. Truth does not mean that you must or should tell her everything. My wife knows that I have sex with other men but she has no right to know what I or the other man do in bed. It does mean that if she asks you a question you must answer her honestly and straightforwardly. You must insist that she understands that you retain the right to tell her (If she asks you an embarrassing question): "Are you sure that you want to hear the answer?" If she says: "Yes," then tell her. This helps build up the trust between both of you and makes the long-term relationship work. In the 9 years since coming out to my wife I have only had to ask my wife "are you sure that you want to hear the answer" on two occasions and both times she said: "NO." But the trust factor remained intact! We both retained our dignity and honesty!

Agree to the amount of time that you will be away from the family but insist that you have the right to renegotiate. This is important because at some point you may get a monogamous male partner and you will have to accommodate his needs with your wife's for both relationships to grow and prosper.

DAZED AND CONFUSED HERE

From: Jos

Here's my situation: I'm 38, wife is 31, kids involved, and I've only been out for a little over 2 weeks to my wife. Told my wife also about my male-to-male experiences. To say the least we are on this wild roller-coaster ride with our emotions. I've shattered her world and I feel awful, I love her very much. She is a wonderful person, but . . . TGT!

She knows that I have a friend/lover currently who has been in my life for the past 7-8 months. I've promised not to "do anything" with him or anyone else until we figure out how the two of us are going to deal with this situation (divorce, open relationship, whatever). I've told her that I don't think I can be monogamous any longer but could put myself on hold for now. The thing is that I love this guy, he's my best friend too. She has let me go out with him a few times and this week when I left him I kissed and hugged him goodbye. Not a peck either, a real kiss.

My wife asked me what we did and did I kiss and hug him; I told the truth. She's furious, says I broke the promise not to have sex. Hey, she's the one who thinks she might be willing to live with a compromise in our marriage; what's so wrong about a kiss? It's not like she believes I'll never be with this man again. She says it would have been easier if I had never told her, just kept cheating and lying and that I should just lie to her now. What's that about? At this moment it seems that leaving her for the gay life is my best option but I don't want to hurt anyone. I also feel it's too early to make such a monumental decision.

Anyway, I know it's very soon for us. We are early in the game. She is crushed and I don't want to underestimate her pain but I've been living with this for 25 years. The shame and secrecy have taken a toll on me and I refuse to keep lying to her and others. No more denying who I am! I'm not ready to shout it from the rooftop but I won't hide anymore either.

I'm considering a hiatus on my relationship with my friend but I know I'll resent my wife for making me do that. I'll miss the hell out of him and very well may lose him as a lover. Any advice guys?

From: *Moris*

When I came out to my wife, I told her who I was and that she had the choice of staying or leaving. Sounds about the same for you.

Yes, it will take time for your wife if she wants to adjust to who you are. Just as it took time for you to adjust! Give her the time.

But she cannot adjust if you behave "str8." But then on the other hand you won't be giving her time to adjust if you push the gay on her too fast.

Between a rock and a hard place.

FOR ME!!—I would not give up the lover, but may hold off a while (you define "a while" with your lover and wife) with the lover. My wife did not like my first boyfriend (the first one she knew of), but I continued to date him and wife and I talked about what problems she had with him. One cannot work through something that does not exist. She did a lot of talking about me being able to date, but when I did, she still had to work through it.

Like you said, two weeks is too soon! Do work on it with your wife. As long as BOTH of you are working on it, it will happen. And if your lover sees that you are working on it, he may stay around for "a while" to be a part of your life.

From: *Brandon*

Your spouse is going through exactly what my wife did for the first year or so after I came out. She'd be very supportive of our relationship and seemed to totally accept and understand my commitments to her and our marriage for many days and then all of a sudden all hell would break loose.

I have been out to my wife now for over 9 years and she still has moments of self-doubt about herself and about our relationship. For the most part, our friendship, love, and commitments to each other thrive and she expresses that she is one very happy woman. She still insists that if she could have a wish, it would be to have me a normal heterosexual male husband and she could have continued to live within the innocence before the coming-out. She claims to understand in her heart that she has always loved me as a gay man (that is who I have always been).

My only advice (I usually don't give advice but you asked) to you for your wife can be: Let her communicate her feelings openly and honestly, Acknowledge her feelings, Give her time, Give her love, Give her your constant assurance of how you feel, Always be honest with her (this is the only way that the trust can be rebuilt between both of you), and Get her involved with a support group or other wives that have (are going) through what she is experiencing (my wife would be delighted to correspond with her).

Look after and pamper your own needs. Ignoring them will really get you into emotional hot water! If you would like a dissertation on the hell I lived through for almost 50 years before coming out—let me know. Look after your own happiness first—If you are not happy—how can you project happiness into your marriage?

I went to a counselor for 5 years and came to find out my true self is a Gay Married Man. I have been out to my loving wife for 9 years, have had a male partner whom I love dearly for 6 years, and I am basically a very happy man in life. Good luck to both of you and hope that this helps.

From: Daniel

Welcome to the group and to the roller coaster—I guess most of us if not all have experienced what you are going through, though in different ways, and there are no standard solutions to the problem.

I came out to my wife early last year and then unwittingly embarked on an intense love affair with a guy whom I still love, but am not *in love* with now. It nearly destroyed my marriage but it says something for the resilience of many wives that if they love you enough, they will stand by you as long as they can and try to rescue the situation. One thing which is nice to realize is that you are not alone—there are many of us out there in a similar situation, all trying to get to grips with the problem. The basic problem, I guess, is that marriage and homosexuality are not good bed partners.

ADVICE PLEASE!

From: Conrad

At my turtle-like pace, I've come to a decision, I believe, and would like some advice before I do anything. I want to tell my wife that I don't want to be lovers anymore, that I don't want to try, that I want us to be great, loving, intimate friends, raising our children and sharing our daily lives.

I know that it means a great deal to her for us to be lovers, passionate and romantic. But I just can't do it. It's keeping me from getting where I want to be in my gayness. I just can't stand to hurt her and really don't believe that our personalities are able to pull off the multi-loving sexual relationships approach, which has been my goal. I'm concluding that we're on a track based on real love and commitment, but nevertheless leading to a split and probably one that will occur after our relationship has really deteriorated. In other words, calling it quits on the current path is at least partly an attempt to salvage and expand on the part of our lives and our relationship that we both want. I just can't spend all our energy focusing on what we can't do for each other!

I expect that her answer will be a flat no, stating a preference just to separate. I really don't want to physically separate. I really want to be in the daily lives of my four boys, 16, 15, 11, and 7. I love the house; my office is here. I think that her let's just separate response will soften, much as she once thought she could never deal with my having sex with another man. She really wants the family to be intact. We really love each other, and have always had a great, great relationship, until recently.

We have a space that even could be my separate bedroom. I don't particularly want to move out of our bedroom (I do still really like cuddling!) but think it might be a good way to define our new relationship.

Any thoughts?

From: Clark

Gee, you sound like me. To a point.

Last week I was all ready to do the same thing, minus the separate bedroom. That is, move out and move on at some appropriate, and possible, time.

I think my wife came to a conclusion, however, that she simply didn't want me to leave. When she knew I really had come to the point of leaving, at least emotionally, she began to, to use her words, "fight for me." It is far from clear to either of us what this might involve and produce. But so far it has yielded a more intense and passionate relationship. And for me, a little freedom. I don't like ultimatums; but I think it was actually good for me to say, "Here is where I stand, and I can't stand living this way any longer."

The bottom line that I am trying to get to is to define where you want to be and decide to be there.

I am beginning to think that a common thread that runs through many of our lives and stories is that we are a sensitive, loving bunch of guys that can't stand to see our wives in pain that we feel we have caused. So we dog-gnaw the situation on and on and on some more when "fish or cut bait" might be the kinder thing to do. In other words, decide. Let the ramifications follow, as assuredly they will and must.

From: Rodney

At the risk of stating the obvious, I would point out that your wife will of course be anxious to get on with her own life, once she understands that your prognosis for the relationship isn't very good. I assume you already understand this and can appreciate why she'd want a decision. It doesn't sound as though she's going to ask you to make an IMPOSSIBLE "decision," the way some of the wives of other guys on this list have done.

I would vote in favor mainly of being totally up front with her. Ask her what she wants. Explore unconventional alternatives. Maybe there IS some possibility for two logically semi-separate families (yours and your wife's) to live together under one roof. But that sounds like what you're essentially asking for.

But try as hard as you can to put yourself in her shoes. There's a limit to what anyone can ask somebody else to do. I don't think you can ask your wife to put her life on hold because of your attachment to your kids and (especially!) your house. THAT sort of expectation is what will destroy your relationship.

From: Andy

I think you should explore options more before making a proposal. You are approaching some rather delicate negotiations which could result in someone not getting their needs and wants met, which could mean some real pain (more so than revealing another side of yourself or disclosing extra activities). I think you may need to find out more from your wife about her needs and desires, what she wants from you, what forms of sexual and sensual expression she treasures or could do without. And perhaps you could do more of that with yourself as well. I don't see how being sexy with your wife in some form inhibits you from searching for or relating to a man as a lover (but, then, I'm BI):-).

QUESTION ABOUT INCLUSION

From: Sidney

Do any of you have or know of a relationship where the wife, husband and boyfriend have relationship. Inclusion where all live together or something like that? I am not thinking of sexual threesomes, but where the guys are separate but the wife is also present for things around the house and for social relationships and issues of that nature?

From: Brandon

I do not know if this is what you are after but here goes:

I've been married to my wife for 38 years and I live part time with her here at our home in the suburbs. I've been with my partner for 7 years. I am with him two days a week and one weekend a month at his and my apartment in the city. In addition we spend two 1 week vacations together each year. My partner is gay, single, and never married. The rest of the time I am with my wife and love it. We are not a sexual threesome. The three of us do go to many social events, Broadway musicals, concerts, and church together. My partner also attends many of the family gatherings with my wife, my grown children, and young grandkids such as birthdays, Thanksgiving, Christmas Eve, etc.

From: Bruce

I have a relationship similar to that one with my wife and lover. I've been with my guy for 2 years. My wife met him not long afterward, as soon as I felt that the relationship was going somewhere. Luckily for me they both liked each other from the start. Not long afterward he began being included with the family in different things like attending shows together, being invited to birthday parties, etc. He would probably be around for more things, like Christmas, Thanksgivings, etc. but he spends those with his. My 13 year old considers him a favorite uncle. In addition, I normally spend either Friday or Saturday evening with my male lover on what most would call a date . . . going to a movie or out dancing or having dinner with friends. We see each other at least a couple of times during the week, even if it's just to meet at the Y to work out together. I spend one weekend a month with him, and we normally take at least one or two short trips together during the year. Most Sundays I go to morning services with my wife and our 13 year old at the church we belong to, then attend evening services with my lover at the MCC where he is a member. There is no type of 3-way romantically or sexually between my wife, my lover, and I, nor is there any chance that there ever will be. My wife does consider him a very close friend though, and has no problem calling on him if she needs to. There have been very few conflicts so far with our schedules since we're all pretty much in agreement as to what events take precedence. If there is a conflict, we're usually able to talk it out and come up with a compromise that everyone is happy with.

From: Moris

You describe what I have. My wife, husband, and I live together. We just got back from a musical recital of a friend of ours. We do things together. I do things with just my wife. I do things with just my husband. I sleep with my wife for 2 nights, and then 2 nights with my husband. It took a while to adjust to changing beds. But I did!

From: Daniel

I am aware of a couple where the husband came out to his wife about a year ago, and fell in love with a man half his age. His wife was distraught but after a great deal of discussion, decided to get to know the young man, whom she now loves, not sexually, but as a person. I don't think that they live together but the mixture seems to be working quite well.

From: Shawn

In answer to your question, much to my surprise (in the last two months) my boyfriend, wife, and myself have developed an inclusive threesome relationship! We and our children spend regular time together as a "family." I can hardly believe that it has happened, but it has. It is a very complex situation and we are working hard to make it work well. We all have a lot to learn, but are willing.

From: Joey

I had to respond to this one. I have starting seeing someone who is becoming important to me. This weekend he will be heading this way to spend the weekend. He is ever so interested in being a part of my existing family dynamics. My wife, my new male friend, and I will be having dinner on Saturday night. We are all looking forward to it. I have no idea how it will really go, but I think we will have a good time and lots of laughs. What is so vital here, is that my wife remains a part of my life and this man is willing to include my family in on our relationship. He is a delight and a surprise. I will keep you all posted on how it all pans out.

From: Shawn

I'm no expert on this type of arrangement. There is only one wife involved in our situation since my male friend is divorced. We all get together with our two children on weekends. Usually, my wife spends an evening a week with him and so do I . . . we both date him so to speak. (He's bi; so am I). The three of us get together for a "family meeting" weekly (no children) to talk through the adult issues. Also, I see him a lot during the week because our offices are close and in the same town . . . very convenient. We all share a lot in common spiritually which really helps. Sometimes we talk together with God about our concerns and ask for help.

I hope this information is helpful to you and others. We're new at this, but so far it's working for all of us. There have been some problems and snags, but we've worked through them lovingly while praying for help from above! The help does come because we're all asking for it.

WHAT A DIFFERENCE A WEEK MAKES

From: Conrad

Thank you all, for your responses to my plea for advice a few weeks ago. You helped more than you may think, and perhaps in a different way than you intended.

Briefly, I was ready to give up on trying to make marriage and gayness work together. While I started this new coming out about five years ago to expand my experience of self, my sexuality, and my life, I mostly had reverted into a different style of shut down. I couldn't bring myself to have a successful relationship with a man, hurting my wife. I couldn't bring myself to maintain a successful relationship with my wife, feeling as if that was denying myself.

We both understood why and how to do what we needed to do, we just couldn't do it. . . .

So I posted my "I'm ready to give up."

Bluntly, several of you laughed at me. God, Conrad snap out of it! I was pretty pissed off at the time. Several of you said, "Yea, you've tried, not everyone can pull that off, time to move on." I was pretty angry at that. I can't have expressed how deeply I feel about wanting my wife, my children, my dogs, my home, to stay part of my daily life more or less as they are now. It would be denying myself just as much as denying my sexuality . . . .

Several of you said keep plugging. Yea right. Five more years of working so hard and getting nowhere?

I was able to laugh at myself in response. I physically slapped myself (lightly—no S&M) repeatedly and said really trite phrases like "Snap out of it" and "Just do it." Forget the past. Look forward. Make everything how you want it to be. Don't think so much. Feel it. Do it.

I was open as I have not been in a long time. I immediately met just the person I was looking for. I immediately felt renewed love and respect and appreciation for my wife. Feeling real love, not just to minimize her pain. We made great love. Really hot, not just to please her. Really expressing myself and my love for her.

My wife hurts, but she's OK. She knows we can't nurture our love denying our lovingness. . . . She knows we can do this. She knows we do not have the option of not trying. . . .

My boyfriend is 38 (I'm 44) 3 young kids, and in a profession, really built, the softest voice, the sweetest smile, just right. He lives about within an hour's drive. He came out to himself about a year ago when he started a relationship with another married man. They stopped seeing each other a few months ago. I'm his second. He's my second, after a first that was so wonderful, but so hard to make work. I could not do or be now what I am and need without that support.

I know that (at least some of you) remember what's it's like to feel that amazing peace and flow of emotion when this starts. . . . I'm going through my days amazingly happy. . . .

I feel that maybe I, and we, have learned enough to pursue our love instinctively, trusting and built on the foundation of love and experience that have meant and still mean so much to us.

From: Sidney

This morning, while looking in the mirror, I said to myself, "I am a gay male who is married to a wonderful, beautiful, caring, and loving woman. I want to maintain the closeness and the wonder of that partnership with her. I want her and my gayness. I have children and have responsibility to them—responsibility to be open with them and to be a father to them. I have not really been as happy as I am now, accepting my own gayness. While at the same time I am a little confused. But this is getting better and will pass.

From: Neil

I haven't written very much or been very supportive of others in the past few months. It has been a time of much pain and rapid transition as my marriage ended and I moved out and moved on. In the process I left the Midwest and moved to San Francisco, a decision made and accomplished in six weeks. The move was very successful and I get to start life afresh from a new place.

I want to thank all of you for the help along the way. Your comments were very insightful in making me realize that I could not continue in a marriage that would not allow me expression of who I am. Even if I had remained monogamous, there was still no support for my sexuality. And your comments woke me up to the fact that I could not continue to bury that part of myself. I feel very liberated and paradoxically, while alone, I feel more connected than I have in a very long time. That's a real surprise because I was afraid of the loneliness.

TELL ME HOW TO COPE

From: Jos

What a bad day I'm having. Woke up feeling pretty good (even choked the chicken with my wife present) but it sure went downhill quickly after that. Yesterday was awful. My wife has absolutely no trust in me anymore (I had a boyfriend for 8 months prior to coming out so I understand her pain). I worked late Thursday evening and she assumed I was out f*****g around of course and to make a long story short let's just say neither of us were very understanding of what the other might be feeling (huge understatement) when I came home.

I'm getting such mixed messages from her that I don't know how or what to do anymore. She says:

> Thursday night: "I can't trust you, you lied to me for ten months; why would I believe you were at the office?"
> Friday morning: "Don't tell me the truth even when I ask, lie to me, protect me."
>
> Thursday Night: "Tell me how much money I get, I want a six-month separation."
> Friday Morning: "I'm so afraid that you'll meet someone other than your boyfriend and then you'll leave me. You'd never leave me for your boyfriend. [She's mistaken.] Please don't leave."
>
> Yesterday: "You disgust me!" (ouch)
> Today: "I love you and I'm here to take care of you" (during one of my sadder moments).

OK guys, you get the picture. I told her today that all my instincts are telling me, what would be "natural" for me is to quit fighting this, the gay life is what I need/desire. Part of me feels like I'm fighting a losing battle. I'm thinking it's just me continuing (as I've done for 22 years) to deny who I really am.

The other part of me says you have a great life here with a wonderful woman that truly is your best friend and that you love. I feel very alone. The person I need/want to support me is my wife. The person who can't/won't because it's too painful for her is my wife.

Shit!!!!! Hopefully tomorrow will be better.

From: Moris

Been there, done that. Many of us have and the outcome is also different for different people. Yes, the roller coaster ride is not so good. What I did was not to take EVERYTHING my wife said while in one of her down sides as the way she really felt. I took it as that is how she is releasing her pain and nothing against me. As a matter of fact, it was good that she released her pain.

I think you and your wife (the up wife, not the down wife) need to really sit and talk about the "cheating" thing. Your wife had one man, your one boyfriend, to forgive you for. My wife had 17 men to forgive me for. But she does need to forgive and allow you to build the trust back with her. How do you do that? That is the question you two must come to terms with. And yes, she really has no say in you seeing your boyfriend. So you both, you three, must go from here!

From: Woody

I can't tell you how to cope. I haven't found the answer to THAT either. But . . . my wife and I are still together almost two years after I came out to her. That may be because we have regular discussions when both of us are in a neutral mood over a little wine or Scotch, followed by dinner.

From: Mike

Hopefully tomorrow will be better. Well, you're close, I'd say "Tomorrow will be different" . . . and that MIGHT be better. The point I'm trying to make is . . . nothing lasts forever . . . not your anxiety, your wife's anger, the guilt you feel for having betrayed her trust . . . all feelings . . . no matter how intense . . . will pass . . . if they are allowed to "BE." So patience is the thing . . . and faith . . . that you will "know" what to do . . . and "when" to do it. If, as you say, your wife is the ONE from whom you NEED love and support . . . give the same to her . . . and you will get it back exponentially. A wise friend once told me . . . "You can't comb your hair while the wind is blowing." There's alot of truth in that for me (at least it did when I still had my hair). ;-)

From: Miles

I do think that wives calm down after a while. I would not make any definite moves toward separation for several months; or at least, if you do separate, don't formalize it legally right away. She may find she can live with this situation over the long run. She may find she cannot, but it is way too early to force the choice.

Continue to be open with her and remember to occasionally tell her that you understand how conflicted, frustrated, and upset she must be.

From: Dern

Just as it took you many years to come to terms with who you are, so will it take time for your wife to sort out her emotions. It has been a couple of years since I came out to my wife and we still have those kinds of days. They are fewer and further apart, but still they come. Always remember that her feelings are just as valid as yours. You need to validate what she is feeling not minimize it. Then when you understand what she is feeling you can respond in a caring and accepting way.

My wife feels that me finding someone will make me want to leave her too. It is the hardest thing she has to face. My infidelities were easily forgiven but this having a special man is the hardest for her too. I understand where she is coming from and reassure her that I do not plan to leave her.

From: Clem

You've gotten a lot of good feedback, I think, from the other guys. Bear in mind that your wife's concern that you might leave her for a man are in many ways the same as ANY wife's fear that her husband might leave her for another partner—female or male. The SPECIAL issue for the wife of a gay/bi married guy is that his sexuality might force him "naturally" toward a MALE partner—which the wife, unfortunately, is not. This adds a special—and perfectly reasonable—dimension to her fear of abandonment. That's why YOU need to know where YOU'RE coming from. I think women can sense the uncertainty, if it exists, and this uncertainty will produce wild shifts of mood. Perfectly understandable.

For this reason, I would also underscore the theme that has come up in several posts of trying to enter into your wife's emotional situation and help her know that you understand it. This sort of thing, sometimes called "active listening," will also help you understand what you need to do to make her feel more at ease.

From: Marvin

I know early on in our process we discussed the fact that my wife felt that if I were seeing another women she'd know how to "compete" . . . but that she had no idea how to "compete" with a man . . . took us a long time to work through the "competition" idea and to get to the point where she truly understood that I wasn't looking to replace her and was perfectly capable of having concurrent relationships . . . we also BOTH felt FORTUNATE (believe it or not) that our "issues" were out in the open—both of us realizing that in ANY relationship there is a risk of "leaving for another" and that by us having it out in the open we have "one up" on most other couples where it may be hidden. . . .

Probably the biggest assurance for my wife, and something I VERY firmly believe, is that I'll NEVER leave her FOR anyone. If I leave it's because that's what's right FOR ME—FOR US—I think she finally truly believed this when I was involved, deeply, with another man for three years and didn't leave. If I were ever going to leave her "for someone" he would've been the one and since I didn't she doesn't worry so much anymore that I will.

SHOULD I STAY OR SHOULD I GO?

From: Albie

It's been three weeks since I told my wife my need to have a relationship
with a man, and asked for her consideration of an open marriage. And except for a moderate shower last week (no lightning yet) it remains very calm
on the home front.

I was out of town all last week and Friday night when I returned I was
very much in the mood to make love. When I first started caressing her, she
kind of grumbled "I don't understand how this is supposed to work" which I
took as a positive that she's thinking about an open relationship. After that
she warmed up very quickly and we had a wonderful time together in bed.

As I've mentioned before, my wife is very nonconfrontational, repressing her feelings until she snaps. This usually happens at the marriage counselor's office. Next appointment: Tomorrow.

I'm just curious, how many of you men are currently working through
the issue of asking for your wife's approval to have a relationship with a
man? How long have you been talking, and how has it been going?

From: Mike

I remember early on feeling like I was "asking for my wife's approval." I
quickly learned that framing it this way was disempowering for me and put
us in a "one up-one down position." Neither of us has any responsibility to
seek approval from the other. We owe each other honesty and consideration. I soon worked it out in my own head, and found a more equitable way
to frame the situation. I was unequivocal about living authentically as a bisexual man. Someone said recently on this forum. . . . it's the uncertainty,
and ambiguity that many wives sense. . . . and when they sense that, they
find us unpredictable, and therefore threatening. As compassionately as I
can, I leave no doubt that I intend to live fully as a bisexual man AND that
I prefer to do that in the context of a loving and intimate relationship with
my wife. With that information, she can make a fully informed CHOICE as
to whether she wants to be married to me as I am. I do, however, want to be
considerate of my wife's feelings, plans, and family obligations. SO, whenever I want to go out to be with a man, rather than ask for permission or approval, I state what I want to do and when I want to do it, and ask if there is
any reason that particular time is not good for her or the kids. I am open to
adjusting my schedule to give preference to her and the kids . . . .whether her
reason is emotional (I just need you to hold me tonight) or practical (honey,
we invited your parents to dinner that night). I have never felt that she took
advantage of that during the 5 years we've been actively integrating my bi-

sexuality into our relationship. And I have tried not to take advantage of her either. I am no longer in need of anyone's "approval" to do what comes so naturally to me (thank God). I just try my best to conduct myself in a considerate and trustworthy way. That's just one man's way. . . .

From: Dern

I have been working on getting my wife to allow me to find a man for 4 years.

From: Marvin

You so beautifully stated the key is to quit seeking "permission." NO ONE should need permission to be who they are. I remember vividly a conversation of almost 8 years ago where my wife was dancing around verbally . . . afraid to ask what she really wanted to . . . when I finally said, "If you're asking can I live the rest of my life without being with a man the answer is no, I don't think I could even if I wanted to."

Amazing how things changed once that line was drawn in the sand . . . up to that point it HAD been "dancing around" on both our parts, but caught up in the "what do you need" "what do you want" type discussions . . . a classic catch-22 where all of our individual decisions hinged on a yet-to-be-made decision of the other. . . .

From: Sherman

Funny, before I read your post I never thought of my situation as an open relationship . . . but I guess when it comes down to it, that's what it is. After months of seeing how miserable I was without that missing part of me, my wife agreed that it would actually be best for me to actively seek someone out. I have met the most incredible man, and we've been seeing each other for a few weeks. He is amazing, the relationship is amazing and finally I am truly happy. For now, anyway. It is terribly rough at times—the wife feels that she's competing, she questions how I can really care for two people—the whole idea of bisexuality, etc. But overall she is great. She hasn't met this guy yet, but asks a lot of questions about him, about what we do . . . and has been calm considering. Luckily, I have a woman and man who understand and are willing to work a little (ok, A LOT). I'm still slightly dazed at the whole thing . . . I never thought it really possible for things to work out so well. . . .

From: Dern

I guess I should have phrased that a bit different. I have told my wife the same thing. I cannot and will not deny that I am gay again. To ask me to deny that would be death for me as a person. I told her that I had tried to deny for many years and I turned into something I didn't even like. I will not be totally who I am for anybody that includes her or the kids and I have put it in those words.

I should have phrased it like . . . I have been waiting for her to come to terms with the view I have of our future. This view includes a man as a full-fledged partner in a three-way emotional family. As it includes my wife, I have to help her out of love through her growth and understanding. I do not waffle on the things that are important for me but I do always consider the total family in all my decisions. My responsibilities are to myself and my family for they are what I want in my life too.

From: Bib

I don't think the issue is to seek permission or not, but to get your wife to understand, and then accept or not, who you are. So I am not working on getting her approval, because whether I get it or not won't change my desires, and besides that would be manipulative at best. But rather I am trying to see if both of us can be satisfied with the situation. It's been 5 years now that we are dealing with it. Right now she has hit a wall, which mainly is a problem of self-esteem, and recognizing her own needs.

From: Herman

Up until yesterday I would have said that my marriage is my most important priority. I truly love my wife intimately and emotionally. However, I am also GAY. Hmm, funny only four short months ago I could not have said that. However, that is what I am. Now what? I received a reply to an earlier post that said "I feel it would tear me apart stepping between two worlds, not complete in either." That is how I am feeling. My wife is very understanding about my sexuality. My problem is that I don't feel complete jumping between my two lifestyles. I don't think I can keep this open-ended marriage and feel complete. Yet, I love my wife. This all seems too difficult for me. I want to leave and be myself with no boundaries and no guilt. Yet I know if I do I would cause pain. I would cause heartache. My therapist say's I'm trying to move too fast and to take things one day at a time. I feel like I'm somehow giving my wife a false sense of security when I don't think there is security at all. Family, obligations, vows, love, I'm very confused. Yet, not confused. Hmm, this sure sounds confusing. Should I stay or should I go?

From: Dern

Your therapist is right—you are moving too fast. Stop and rediscover yourself and make sure what you want is what you want not just the thrill of being truthful about yourself. I have a hard time stepping between the two worlds but I know that someday I will not have to. I am working at widening my wife's and my circle to include a third. When this happens I will have one world consisting of all the aspects important to me, Str8 and gay!! I have to move slowly in order for my wife to catch up. I also have to move slowly in order to make sure my wants and desires are true and not just some whim. I have to move myself back to the man I always thought I would be. Those years of hiding and lying have twisted me and my thinking and that has to be untwisted.

WHERE DO WE GO FROM HERE?

From: Herman

I've been wondering if someone could explain a few things for me. My wife confronted me last June. I came out to her in Dec. As I go forward with my life I am quite confused with how I will approach our newly redefined marriage as I see it. Prior to my wife's confrontation I was out of control with my anonymous sexual behavior with men. I believe I was using my behavior as some sort of sexual fix. To cover my depression, denial, shame, and low self-esteem. Of course the more depressed I got the more sex I sought. Which became a vicious cycle I got wrapped up in. With therapy and open communications with my wife I now have a new-found freedom I never had before. The problem is I'm not sure how to go forward. Reading the various posts here has led me to see how different and alike we are. When I go out now usually twice a week, I have been very comfortable with myself and have in fact not jumped into bed with anyone even when sexual opportunities have presented themselves. Just being able to be comfortable with who, what, and where I am makes a profound difference in my sexual behavior. Funny, some of the people I've been with, as I see them now, makes me see how out of control I was. Hmm, talk about depression or how much did I have to drink? I am emotionally and intimately bound with my wife and I am scared of falling in love with a man. How do any of you handle this? How do you deal with loving two people? This one thing weighs heavily on my mind. Do any of you feel torn between loving two people and two sexes at that? How do you deal with the guilt or isn't there any? I don't just want to have sex but I'm not sure what I'm looking for. Can anyone explain this difference I'm experiencing? Maybe I'm looking for love and just don't want to admit it because it scares me. In any case I've rambled on enough for now. "Where do I go from here?"

From: Sam

Someone else replied that the heart has the capacity to love greatly. I would like to address this.

Many years ago I took initiation from a real saint from India. They are not interested in connecting you to themselves, only in giving you the real inner connection to the AUTHENTIC SELF. This authentic self loves you and all, always in the present moment, for it only exists in the ever present moment. It is ABSOLUTE PURE UNCONDITIONAL LOVE FOREVER and that is the experience that this conscious state, called Christ Consciousness in the Western vernacular is. It isn't about anything else. Not about JUDGMENT, or GUILT or SIN, which is a man-created concept to impart fear and to gain control. What is wrong with loving another as long as it truly is love? Love is of its own dimension, it stands within its own TOTALITY.

Some of us human beings, in this particular case, MEN, feel, want, and need to bond on an INTIMATE level with other men. Some men perhaps can get to this bond without sex, others of us choose to go through that doorway of experience because there is something about the ecstatic experience of eroticism and coupling to orgasm that steps past or beyond the mind and mental faculty, beyond just talking and words right to the CORE FEELING. Raw primal emotional energy expressing itself DIRECTLY. That's why in all these life cycles, sex has always hung out. It is so immediate, bypassing the EXTERNAL. We are not just the external but are very deep INTERNAL BEINGS.

I believe it is our God-given right to love whomever we choose and that we can even love more then one sexually in a harmonious way.

From: Moris

I fell in love with a man and I still love him; I always will. But he could not accept me as a bisexual. He wanted me to be a gay man. "Hiding" my str8ness would be just as bad as hiding my gayness. I want my wife to accept me as a bisexual and I and want my husband to accept me as a bisexual. So I made a very hard decision, but a good one, to be just friends with him and move on with my life. I found another man. The three of us are living together and my first lover was the Best Man at our wedding.

Sometimes good decisions are the hard ones to make. . . .

From: James

I know of no way to avoid falling in love. . . . I have fallen in love with another man probably 4 times by now, but only recently so deeply that it equals the love I have for my wife . . . yes, you will feel torn . . . but my wife and I love each other so much that I can share with her about my love for the other guy. We talk about it, cry about it, and share as much as I can without being hurtful to her. I feel no guilt other than the regret of my wife knowing she cannot fulfill all of me. And this saddens both of us. But I do not consider this "guilt" per se because I cannot help it. But I try to acknowledge it and keep my relationship with my wife open . . . if you are the romantic type, as am I, I think you are very vulnerable to falling in love and I've learned to live with it and not try to avoid it.

I find the heart has an infinite capacity to love. It isn't the loving that proves problematic to me but the energy it takes if I am in a male "relationship" when I am trying to connect, nurture, and love two individuals. But I know of no way to avoid that if you intend to interact with another man intimately. And I realize there are many shades of "intimacy" also. . . .

We are reminded over and over and over again about the multiple aspects of the journey we gay/bi married men are experiencing . . . and how much we have to learn to live the moment, cherish the "now"/the day and try to strengthen ourselves from within . . . this journey is not easy for us or for our wives but I truly believe it is rich and worthwhile even though we have some definite "down periods."

From: Chester

I haven't actually been in love with a guy yet. I've only let myself get involved on an emotional level (conceptually) with another guy this past year.

I'm just wondering though, if you really fall hard, what happens to the marriage? Anybody had any real experience with this?

From: Shep

Nuthin' deep or introspective here. I'm "in love" with my fuck buddy. He's the greatest.

But he too is in a relationship. It is what it is. My heart goes pitter patter when I'm with him, and I get so excited when I see e-mail from him.

But can I "see" him more often? No.

Can I "be" with him more often? No.

Can I call him as often as I'd like? No.

My wife is my primary care provider. While his partner is his. We see each other as often as we can without "rocking the boat." It hurts.

But for me—and for him I suspect—this is the fun of it. And why it's lasted so long—we don't see each other full time. We give each other that "thrill" our partners aren't willing to provide. I'm his bottom, for example—his partner ALWAYS wants to be the top. He and I join a third for a threesome—neither his partner nor my wife would ever do that.

So maybe that's just something to think about. Sure you're in love, and it's exciting, and you want to spend all your time with this guy, but ask yourself if you did would it get old, routine, boring, and then you'd be stepping out on him.

It's best we just stay fuck buddies. It's hard, and yet easier. The thrill hasn't faded with time as it has with the wife. Absence makes the heart grow fonder and all that.

See him as much as you can that your wife will allow. Make the most of that time.

From: Gripp

It seems that when I loved a man, I loved my wife more.

From: Dern

I too went through that vicious cycle of anonymous sex. When I came out that stopped almost completely. I still had all those triggers inside and needed to recognize them and reprogram myself. As my wife and I work through this my self-esteem and self-acceptance have grown by leaps and bounds. I have "taken back" my physical sexuality and now understand that it is something I want to freely give to a man who also knows me and cares for the person in the body. I love the quiet that this has produced in my soul. Those quiet times when I sat and contemplated the self were times or torment and confusion. They are now times of peace and acceptance. I am me. Finally!!!!

I have the vision of having a man in our life (my wife's and mine). I can love two people but that man has to be part of my everyday existence, not someone to visit a couple of times a week. I know that for me that will not work, it will tear me apart stepping between two worlds and not really feeling completely part of either. Now I have to just help my wife to that understanding and acceptance.

From: Murry

During the long process of coming out to myself, I eased the pain by telling myself that I was bi, and that lessened the guilt for me as I operated a curious logic which ran like this—I am not betraying my wife's trust going for a man as a man is not in competition with a woman.

More recently, as I have met more men I realize that my sexual desire for my wife (never very strong) has vanished and that I was deceiving myself with my curious logic—in fact, many men really turn me on and it is M2M sexual contact and intimacy that I crave.

Like many of the guys in this group I dearly love my wife and wish to retain the connections and the history that we have shared over the years. What I am still finding hardest to deal with is to admit to my wife about my M2M sexual needs—I feel I am letting her down. These include what I have been discovering for myself about my own sexual preferences and turn-ons like being attracted to chubby guys and wearing leather. Like you I find the prospect of falling in love with another guy pretty daunting—I feel as though I've failed and can I juggle a double relationship? When I first came out to my wife about five years ago, it was because I could no longer play games of deception any more. Yet this initial talking openly with my wife was not a once-and-for-all thing. I find it really difficult to keep her up-to-date with my making contact with guys and I always give myself a hard time after I've been with a guy, whether my wife knows or not.

When I'm feeling good about myself, I believe that when the time is right I will meet someone. It's the hopeless, lonely place where I was a couple of days ago which are the hardest places to endure. I wish you well on your journey and know that you are in good company.

FEEDBACK PLEASE

From: Joel

I have some questions for you fellow brothers. First some short history; My wife and I are just going to start counseling in the near future. I do want to stay with her and be able to deal with my bisexuality. Bottom line I am sure in our situation, I cannot have my cake and eat it too. I will be able to do the things I want to interact with other guys but I know she will "NOT" stand for me to be sexual with men. Crossroad—Be married or be allowed to have sex?

I know every couple is unique but how have some of you guys dealt with this in the same situation?

1. Can a marriage survive with a spouse that has such strong convictions with a bi-sexual man?
2. Men that can separate physical needs with emotional love for a spouse live a dual life?
3. Will I have to make a choice between men (my honest sexuality) and my wife?

Any of you guys that have been down this road I would appreciate any feedback. I could use some help and a guiding hand down this dark corridor.

From: Dale

Any number of marriages (I'm using the term broadly here to represent an ongoing, "permanent" relationship between two people) exist and are very viable without sexual exclusivity between heterosexual partners, homosexual partners, or mixed-orientation partners. While sexual exclusivity is a very strong convention in our society, many marriages and relationships exist and flourish quite nicely without it. It may even be possible for YOUR marriage to open up and broaden its horizons given the right amount of support, information, and work from both partners. It's for sure, however, it can't be done unilaterally.

It is my personal opinion and conviction that denial and suppression of one's sexual orientation (be it straight, gay, or somewhere in the middle) is NOT a good option.

Here's an anecdote from a recent posting:

Jane wrote: >*When my husband was 42 years old, he went through what I can only describe as a nervous breakdown; pacing and crying at night, agitated and antsy during the day. I kept begging him to tell me what was wrong, but it took about 3 months for him to finally tell me. He told me he was gay.*<

LESSON: In my personal opinion the best, most humane, and most efficient way of dealing with one's sexual orientation is to find open, direct, and acceptable expression.

Some guys do the "dual life" thing for long periods of time. There is no guarantee, however, that rigid compartmentalizing and separation of physical expression/experience away from emotional involvement can be maintained any more than one's mind can be separated from one's body!

From: Clem

My current position with my wife is that I will remain homosexually abstinent. I SUSPECT this position won't work in the long run, for all the reasons you listed, but I needed to "shelve" the sex issue in order for my wife and me to work on our more fundamental relationship issues. I wouldn't even attempt this if I weren't as deeply in love with her as I am, and if I didn't sense and respect the enormous amount of growth she needs to attain in order to deal better with many, many issues in her life.

My wife seems to have made enormous progress in the past few weeks and seems gradually digging herself out of the "victim's pit" she had been living in for decades. She is beginning (without my even forcing the issue) to ask me questions about my bisexuality, which may indicate that ultimately we MIGHT be in a position to "redefine our marriage," which I think would be unarguably the most healthy outcome.

I think you may hear these points frequently in the next few weeks, and I think they're important: (1) go slowly; these things take time, and you may be surprised how it all plays out, if you give it time; (2) be prepared for some really crazy shit as your wife's psyche tries to reconstruct itself after your revelation; a certain amount of "crazy" behavior is pretty "normal" for people in your situation; you will probably repeatedly be absolutely convinced you can't take it any more; always count to 10 before you call your lawyer.

My favorite therapist in fact says, "When you get deep enough, the issue is NEVER sex." This of course turns Freud on his head. As time passes, I am also more and more convinced it's true.

In my own case, I think it's entirely possible that my wife and I will end up separating, though the process we're going through right now will I think make it more likely that we will end up being good friends, at least.

And, as time goes on, I actually feel more optimistic that the outcome might be a lot "happier" than that. But I'm past the "panicky" point, and am myself able to work on the parts of my life that don't depend on my wife. And the marriage itself no longer seems to be the only reality in my life.

And it is wonderful, wonderful, wonderful, to have stopped lying to her (and to me) about who I am.

WHY AM I IN THE DUMPS THIS MORNING?

From: Corwin

I'm just really out of it today. Need to vent and release the emotional buildup. Had a rough night with my wife. I'm supposed to be going to an all day conference today but I'm not really looking forward to it.

To bring everyone up to date, a few weeks back I came out to my parents and my brother. It went really well. General acceptance and love all around. Mom's not totally there yet, but is still talking to me. For this I am thankful and surprised.

Last week my wife and I decided we were going to tell the kids about the divorce and my being gay. As far as we're concerned, the two go hand in hand and you can't tell one without the other. Apparently she had a really rough day yesterday thinking about it all, and really unloaded on me last night. Apparently finally realizing that once we tell the kids, and it is all out in the open, that we will actually move forward to the divorce.

I can't find any way to convince her to see a counselor or talk to anyone else about this. I know that is what she needs. She needs to blow up at someone other than me, that is for sure. I can't take that stuff anymore.

It just ripped me apart. We both know this needs to be done. She doesn't want to turn back the clocks and forget it all. She doesn't want to ignore it. She still wants to tell the kids, even after saying all that she has.

So I guess this weekend is out. Which means we move it out another 3- 4 weeks, maybe even until after school is out.

Thanks for being my sounding board guys. I'm not sure what happens next. I was all prepared to get myself psyched up to tell the kids on Friday, now I don't know where I'm headed.

From: Carl

Man, this all sounds familiar. I went through more than a year of it. The first few months there was just sort of a numbness to it all. Then I went to see my guy (for the first time in 40 years) and it started sinking in with her that this wasn't just some sort of extravagant gesture, but a serious thing. The late fall, after two or three of my visits to Toronto, was loveydoveyness interspersed with violently homophobic outbursts. This last visit, just after Easter, she accepted with relative equanimity. I think we're getting somewhere. But we don't have the problem of young children (our son is 35), and I think she accepts that I really am BI, rather than gay and that my relationship with my lover is no longer sexual, and hasn't been since before we were married. That can make a lot of difference. In fact, it should make all the difference. So I can't presume to say to anyone in this situation, "just hang in there, and things should eventually start getting better, the way they have for me." But since I've had much of the same shit flung at me by my wife in her moments of despair, and we finally appear to be moving beyond that, there is hope.

From: Shawn

I think you are trying to deal with too many M A J O R issues and decisions all at once. Try to step back, take a deep breath and do some prioritizing and limit-setting. You're in an emotional turmoil frantically trying to balance two relationships. I think you need to focus on how to deal with your wife of 33-some years first. Ask your man to please bear with you while you get your balance and wits about you. If he loves you he'll give you some time and space to deal with your family issues. If he pushes and pressures and makes you feel bad about having to do that . . . well, then . . . I don't think that's love and I would take a second look at that man. If he's pushing and pressuring you when he knows you have a long list of complex family matters to deal with; who is he thinking about? . . . himself or the turmoil you find yourself in? You need and deserve some time to work things out at a reasonable pace. These are major life decisions that can't be made overnight.

Why is he angry with you? Can't he see you're in pain and you've been married lots of years?! If he can't deal with that and with you, without being angry; there is something that sounds real selfish about that attitude in my mind. Besides, you have this wild crush on this guy (your first). Try to see it in perspective if you can. He'll either wait a little while until the dust settles, or maybe he just isn't the guy to run off with and "marry."

I hope this doesn't sound too overbearing. I'm trying to help. Perhaps I said too much. Hope not.

RE: JOURNEYS!
POLY-VERSUS MONOGAMOUS RELATIONSHIP

From: Peter

My wife and I are married now for 27 years. We have seen one another through some really tough stuff. We love each other very, very much. Besides that, I sort of feel as if I am a monogamous personality type (if there were such a thing). I am not at all certain I would be able to handle parallel relationships.

The complication is that I am (two years out) decidedly, completely happily, (but nonpracticing) gay. So there is no sex in our relationship. Just everything else, which is much. And there is a large amount of frustration, abated only partially by voracious reading of gay fiction and nonfiction, Internet erotica, and pleasant masturbation<

From: Jud

If it helps, I can provide a bit of feedback from the opposite perspective as a balance.

I've always been out to myself, and for nearly all of my life to those around me. I tend to fall just slightly to the heterosexual side of middle on the Kinsey scale (about a 2.5, with 3.0 being dead center), a point that tends to fluctuate a bit to both sides. My wife (who is also bisexual, although inexperienced in same-sex relations and a bit more "heterosexual" than myself) has always known my orientation and supported it completely. Like yourself, I'm in a long-term (18 years) marriage that has grown richer, not poorer, over the years.

Unlike yourself, I have always had a poly orientation, as does my wife. While (as yet) we have not acted on that in our marriage (we aren't swingers, rather we hope to add one or more members to our relationship on a long-term basis—and since we're both bisexual that leaves a VERY wide range of opportunities :-), it's been strictly a matter of lack of opportunity. Both of us have been part of open and/or poly relationships before (her first husband was BI and very open and I've been part of two different group marriages—one heterosexual and the other completely bisexual). Right now we have an open relationship in which either of us is perfectly free to develop outside relationships w/o any threat to our marriage with or without telling the other about them.

From the perspective of having been a part of multiple relationships in a group marriage, I can definitely address the question of parallel relationships from a somewhat different perspective. From every experience I've had—and seen others have—in such relationships, it is not only easy to maintain the "balance" that people fear will be lost in such a relationship, but they can actually help you to actually grow even closer to a primary partner as a result as well. If your spouse is comfortable with you becoming involved with someone outside your home sexually, and you do decide to explore the option, you may very well find that your relationship with her is enhanced as well. A good friend of mine is a gay man who has been in precisely the same situation with his wife for the last five years—and according to him, they are vastly happier together now than they were before he became sexually active outside his home—with his wife's knowledge and approval, of course.

Poly relationships can open entire new dimensions of experience for you, particularly if they are more than just casual sexual encounters (nothing wrong with those either, but they don't have the depth or stability of a longer term relationship). Many people feel that it is impossible to actually love more than one person at a time—something that anyone who has been part of a poly relationship knows to be false. It is not only perfectly possible to feel deep emotional commitments (and sexual attractions) for more than one person at a time, each relationship seems to add a new dimension to the other(s).

You state that you are experiencing "a large amount of frustration, abated only partially by voracious reading of gay fiction and non-fiction, Internet erotica, and pleasant masturbation." All these are helpful if they excite you (although most of the explicit public sites are pretty poorly done—that's bias, btw, among other things I have designed Web sites—and unlike the private, explicit, personal sites many men maintain for the enjoyment of friends and lovers, tend to lack any sensuality, sensitivity, or even taste!), but none is a satisfactory permanent replacement for a relationship with another man. One of the greatest problems with using erotica, fantasy, and masturbation as your only sexual outlets is that you tend to be exposed to only a very limited (and exaggerated—most humans just aren't "assembled" like the men in most porn, as you know) range of same-sex activities. Porn and adult sites emphasize only the very basic sexual activities, they ignore the range of experience available to a bisexual/gay man. Most porn focuses on a "quick" or totally physical sexual experience, where in real life same-sex experiences, like opposite-sex ones, involve intense emotions, lengthy and erotic foreplay, concern for the partner's pleasure, sincere friendship and a deep and sincere caring that just doesn't appear in masturbatory literature, rather than just "one-stop orgasms."

Even if your personal values prevent you from engaging in outside sexual relationships, you still can profit from expanding beyond your present boundaries by forming relationships with other bi/gay men that stop short of actual sexual activities. Being BI or gay is about more than defining your desire for sexual pleasures with a member of your own sex (although that's one of the nicer parts about it) :); it's about defining your emotional needs as well. So long as those needs remain unmet, you will always find the kind of frustrations you describe in your message. Anyone, male OR female (yourself included, obviously), can provide you with the physical stimulus you need to achieve an orgasm; but without meeting your emotional needs it isn't likely to be enough to eliminate the frustration.

I'm not suggesting that you "jump in" and start up a relationship with someone. But I am suggesting that—if it is something that would not violate your personal values and that your wife would support—you think about it as a potential alternative. Masturbation can be a great experience, but it's MUCH more fun to share it with a friend! :)

RE: COPING

From: Dale

Close after my accidental disclosure four years ago it felt as if I were riding a roller coaster, a wild horse, and a merry-go-round all at the same time. I know it doesn't change things or make things any easier, but try to find some comfort in knowing that the wild fluctuations of mood and reaction are sort of inherent at this particular stage of the "process." Time and personal investment on BOTH yours and your wife's part will help you get through this stage.

Regarding betrayal, jealousy, and trust: These issues can feel interwoven—maybe they can be. However, there are really two separate issues amongst the three words, and it may be helpful to think about their differences because healing each issue can be a slightly different strategy:

Jealousy (which you didn't mention directly) comes from the fear of losing one's love object.

Betrayal and trust come from feeling an agreement (real or implied) has been breached or violated.

The implication is that healing jealousy will probably involve finding ways to reassure your wife/lover/friend that you DO love them, that you WILL respond romantically to them, that you DO care for them, that your loving and romantic attentions to them are still THERE!

Betrayal and trust have to do with how you handle real and implied agreements.

While it may feel to be an additional burden, trust is something that has to be rebuilt incrementally over time. If you're serious about rebuilding the trust that she feels has been compromised, you are going to have to faithfully invest in strategies that trace and retrace the idea that you ARE trustworthy, that you DO and WILL keep her informed, that indeed she CAN trust you again as she did before.

When my wife found a copy of something I had sent to an online contact it translated to her that I was looking for a male love relationship that would replace my relationship and marriage with her. That WASN'T my agenda . . . it was her perception. Her perceptions fueled her anger, fear, reactions, hostility, mistrust—the whole ball of wax!! It did NO good to ignore, deny, or minimize her perceptions. It worked best to acknowledge her perception ("If someone had treated me the way you say you are feeling, I would feel the same way you do—maybe even stronger!) and then find ways to demonstrate in real life and in real time there was reason to move away from those perceptions towards perceptions that were more aligned with what my wishes really were. It's been almost 4 years since that accidental disclosure. Partly because I've been here, STAYED here, kept her informed, included, etc. over these years she doesn't have the sense of betrayal and mistrust she had back then.

Both of us carry personal pagers. When I go out on an errand, it's not at all unusual for my original agenda to expand to include other things that seem to naturally branch off the original list. Even though we hadn't discussed an ETA (estimated time of arrival) back home, time would stretch on. When I got home, then, I would come to a wife burning in the window in addition to the traditional candle!

I don't know how many times both I and our consoler traced this message: "I carry a pager. You know the number. PLEASE page me the first moment you feel yourself begin to wonder about things."

The caveat here is that your wife has to be willing to recognize and acknowledge she's feeling uncertain and vulnerable at that moment. It's easy, though, to cross-transfer feelings of uncertainty and vulnerability outside ourselves onto someone else. "If XXX loved me he wouldn't be gone so long. He would know how fearful I feel when he doesn't come home on time." (sound familiar?)

I would further say: "It's much more fair to us both for you to call me to give me the opportunity to communicate what the REAL situation is than to have you launch into uncertainty where we're both at the mercy of your imaginations." Of course. . . . if I would remember to be proactive and call her even before she paged I think I got even MORE points for doing that!

If we are sincere about R&R (repair and restoration) of some of these issues with our spouse, I don't know of any antidote besides commitment to communication, being absolutely dependable, meaning what you say and saying what you mean.

Here is a question I'll pose that could help you clarify the uncertainties you struggle with in this anecdote:

In your heart of hearts, can you find what The Gay Thing (TGT) is all about?

A. Is it about reassigning TGT a kind of primary status in your life.? Are you wanting to move into a new kind of life, to inhabit a part of your personality you haven't lived in heretofore? Does it feel unavoidable that you will need to let (or encourage . . . or force) the status quo to downsize however it may be necessary to reflect the new primary status of TGT (even if it's only a temporary primacy)?
B. Is it about expanding your life and your horizons so that you can be more openly inclusive of TGT without losing contact with your current life, relationships, lifestyle, etc.?

If, in your heart of hearts, your response to TGT is "type A" (above) you aren't likely to be satisfied until you have moved out of and away from all or part of your current life, and into a different kind of life space. The circle of this new space will likely exist in about the same "net" effort as your life always has. To make room for the new things, some of the old will (of necessity) get lain aside. You are likely to feel personal "stretching" involved in assuming a new/different personal profile than before, but the "string" that traces the boundary of that profile probably won't lengthen much. The energies to make these changes will partially come from new elements being included, but you will also lose the resources of some of the elements that evolve away from you.

If, in your heart of hearts, your response to TGT is "type B" (above), the "rest of your life" isn't in so much jeopardy of abandonment. Priorities will shift some, of course, but there will be a greater need for you to open yourself up more, to stretch around more complexity, more issues, and be more inclusive of a broader spectrum of behaviors, people, strategies, etc. Realize, however, that the energies to make some of these changes will come from the new elements being included.

Simplistically this could be like staying in your current house but doing a remodel. Maybe you'll build a studio over the garage where you will have a wonderful view of your yard and the neighborhood as you finally provide a place to humor your talent for ceramics. . . .and to write. You might build on a new, larger master bedroom/bath "suite" to provide a roomy, comfortable sanctuary in which you can pursue the intimacies and passions of your life. And. . . .the existing master bedroom could get transformed into an enticing and inviting guest room reflecting your new commitment to hospitality!

Answering the question, "In your heart of hearts, can you find what The Gay Thing (TGT) is all about?" can be discovered through introspection and soul searching, then acknowledged by both you and your spouse. The "A" response (above) can be imposed unilaterally by either partner. The "B" response (above) requires consensus from all the parties and elements involved.

That's the view from MY bridge!

Chapter 7
Moral Issues

HOMOSEXUAL ABSTINENCE

From: Rodney

(A) How well does it work, in the long run, for a bisexual man to remain in a mixed-orientation marriage with the understanding that he will remain abstinent with regard to men? (B) What has been the experience of you guys who are in my situation? (C) How does abstinence work out, in the long run? (D) Do you ever reach a point where your wife stops worrying constantly about whether you're keeping this "new vow"? (E) Is there something a little immoral, almost, in the "homo-abstinent" solution, because it IS, after all, based on denial? (F) And doesn't one's denial on this level almost GUARANTEE that our culture will never come to terms with the problem of bisexuality and monogamy, REGARDLESS of how much progress it makes with regard to homosexuality more generally?

From: Brandon

After years of utter desperation for the touch of another male and the complete feeling of aloneness because of my desperate need to be physically, emotionally, and spiritually a part of another male, I have come to terms with the issues that you are facing. My life was pure hell (depression, loneliness, physical illness, feeling that I was not real, knowing that I was going crazy, feeling my life was a total lie, etc., etc.) without the physical intimacy with other males. I knew that when I came out to my wife that I could never ever take another vow of remaining abstinent concerning a relationship and sex with men.

(A) Since I have come out to my wife and my homosexual needs are now getting met on a regular basis, I feel alive, well, and very happy in life. I cannot vouch for anyone else.

(B & C) I have met and worked with many many other men (now close to 300 here in the local area) in your and my situation and I have only met one other person that seems to have been able to stick to his vow of no physical contact with other males. I have been friends with this beautiful man for almost 11 years and he ages far too fast. He is desperate for contact and the stress of it all has taken its toll both physically and mentally. He even moved out of his home for a while but desperately missed his home, garden, and wife so he moved back in with the understanding that he would forgo any further sex with men. He is an honest man who loves his wife and one who lives in quiet desperation. The stress is taking its toll!

(D) I have been out to my wife for 10 years and no the wife never stops worrying—but then the same thing goes for women that are married to heterosexual men. It goes with the territory. I have been with my present partner for 7 years and my wife still worries about my leaving her for Mister Right!

(E) For some reason our society has not yet matured to the point of seeing beyond most moral issues as either black or white. Placing people in categories and placing labels is easier than trying to understand the complexities of the human soul. You are 100% correct and stereotyping is indeed a sign of profound cultural immaturity!

From: Henry

(A) I can't say for sure how well abstinence works in the long run, but I'm a bit skeptical. When I got married 15 years ago, I gave up all girlfriends and boyfriends. Then, something about hitting 43, and having another kid, and being on the Dad/paycheck treadmill set off a powerful escapist "nostalgia" for my younger self, who had lots of girlfriends and boyfriends. I was seriously thinking about looking for a boyfriend, but nothing came of it. Well, it didn't matter that nothing happened: when my wife found out, her trust had been broken. Now, much later, things have changed. I have a boyfriend my wife approves of (in fact, they also have a close relationship). Both think I can now be trusted, and I think they're right about that.

(C) The immorality of abstinence is another question. All morally mature adults abstain from all sorts of things that could damage their lives or the lives of others. In my case, it has involved a lot of patience and forbearance—showing my wife that I'm the same guy she fell in love with, that I planned on sticking around, that I still wanted to make love to her, that I had no intention of giving up my responsibilities to her and our kids, and then letting her decide whether she was going to throw me out because she couldn't stand the idea of me. This went on for many months. It took time for things to evolve to the present state of affairs and the way things turned out was a big surprise to me.

(E) I'm much more aware of the monosexual vs. bisexual polarity than the Les-BI-Gay-Transgendered (LBGT) vs. straight polarity. I've experienced blatant prejudice from gays, something that surprised me until I realized that nonstraight solidarity might be a rather flimsy, opportunistic, and maybe temporary political coalition. And I know liberal-minded straight people often associate bisexuals, but not necessarily gays and lesbians, with libertines, orgiasts, etc. So, there's some crap there to get past.

One last remark—I'm not a therapist or counselor, so it's just my opinion—I think that in general there has to be more than one thing that's broken with a marriage for it to end. Bisexuality is a spectacular, compelling issue that can divert attention from other problems in a marriage. Maybe working on those other problems can make even more apparent to our wives that all the noise and smoke of the bisexuality issue is, well . . mostly noise and smoke.

From: Boris

My response is probably not all that relevant to your question, as I am gay, not bisexual. From the moment I took responsibility for fully becoming the gay man I am, I knew unequivocally that I could not be abstinent in my mixed-orientation marriage. I lived with a guy for 8 years before I met the woman I married. Yet during the 19 years of our marriage, I never touched a man. The cost? 19 years of chronic neurosis, anger, irritation, and even emotionally abusive behavior. Yes, it's a moral issue!

I was out to my wife before we married, and she married me as a gay man. Once I came fully out (3 years ago), I lost *all* interest in having sex with her. I never stopped loving her, however. That was my dilemma.

(A) In my experience? BADLY!

(D) Quite the opposite. When I told my wife my life had changed, I made it crystal clear to her that the only way I could continue my life was to be in relationships with men. I knew there was no way I could honor the letter of my marriage vow, and I was certainly not about to take any new vows.

(E) I can't speak to the political and cultural issue directly, but I can certainly speak to the personal moral dimension of my own experience. I was not a nice, or "good," or "moral" person for many years, and my unpleasantness is directly attributable to my denial of my true self and my true nature. I actually love my wife more fully now than I ever could during my neurotic period, because my love for her is more grounded in honesty and reality than it ever was before. The inability of our culture to grasp and accept, even when it doesn't understand, the unique differences of who we "actually" are rather than the categories we're supposed to fit into or the roles we're supposed to play—this inability is based on a low level of consciousness that is collective and conventional.

From: Dale

(A) seems to me to have two elements to it so I separated them thusly:
(1) How productive/effective/possible is it for a bisexual man to totally deny expression of the duality of his sexual attractions and sexual orientation?

People of any sexual orientation can forego direct sexual expression and be celibate to observe religious vows and living in a religious order, for personal reasons, as a result of catastrophic events and illness, etc. How and why they do this is a topic all by itself.

For the more "ordinary" amongst us, though, expression of our sexual selves isn't something we are very successful casually suppressing or denying. Whether it's sexual orientation or some other major personality issue, we manage our energies and our lives better when we are able to be authentic to and expressive of our true, underlying self.

Suppression and denial can work for some people for long periods of time. However, when some important life issue begins to be "on the move," the mind's capacity to suppress and deny seems finite. The literature in gay/BI writings as well as personal anecdotes on support lists like this are FULL of stories of guys who have gone to herculean effort to not engage in homosexual behaviors but have had NO luck at removing the curiosities, urges, and attractions. In fact, rather than diminish, they seem to accumulate and build up with suppression and denial.

The literature then reports the expression of these pent-up energies often goes SOMEWHERE if not provided direct, acceptable expression. Anxiety disorders, depression, abusive behaviors, impulsive behaviors, even thoughts of suicide and suicide attempts in some cases can happen. I have issue with the "love the sinner/hate the sin" strategy here. Expecting someone to be something they aren't or not to be something they are imposes a kind of "sentence" on that person to be at jeopardy for some of the disorders I mentioned above. To me that's an unreasonable thing to do.

(2) Can a bisexual man stay in a mixed-orientation marriage if the conditions of his being in the marriage are that he totally and successfully deny his sexual diversity?

(a) Yes, it IS possible for a M-F marriage to last and work AND acknowledge sexual diversity in one of the partners. . . .but it will be a "different" kind of marriage. A number of gay and BI men on this group (and others) are doing it now.

Amity Buxton ("The Other Side of the Closet") writes:

> Coping with the marriage issue will be a more constructive process with greater promise of success if the couple, rather than trying to pre-

serve the traditional marriage arrangement, is willing to develop a relationship appropriate to the new circumstances.

J. S. Gochros ("When Husbands Come Out of the Closet") writes:

Not only can marriages survive a disclosure of homosexuality, if the husband remains committed to the wife, they are apt to improve. Not only can homosexuality (or some degree of it) be compatible with heterosexual marriage, if the husband is capable of some degree of heterosexual satisfaction, gay/straight marriages can be unusually satisfying and stable.

(b) If the partners each have the commitment to the relationship and the resources both individually and relationship-wise from which to draw I wouldn't preclude ANY arrangement between two people from the potential to last and work. Mostly, though, a really successful, working, mixed-orientation marriage isn't going to be just a "regular" marriage in which the straight wife gives lip service by "loving the sinner but hating the sin."

(D) This translates to issues of healing a perceived breach of confidence and/or betrayal. So long as the view of a gay/BI husband's desire and need for contact with men is seen by the straight wife as "breaking the promise" or "cheating" and the "vow" is NOT to cheat or break the promise—-it's a cul-de-sac! (A place where one goes around in circles without going anywhere!)

Here are a couple of points of perspective that are more likely to bring about a more empathic response:

Commitment and devotion to the marriage can be demonstrated and expressed in a spectrum of ways. Sex does not have to be the defining factor that determines whether there is fidelity (keeping promises) in a relationship, commitment or devotion.

Sex between two men is different from sex between men and women and different again from sex between two women. The energies felt and exchanged between two men in sex are not cross-exchangeable with the energies he feels and exchanges with a woman. The feelings are different, the bodies feel differently, the procedures are different, the energies given and exchanged feel as if they come from a different part of the personality. A woman cannot provide her gay/BI partner the same kind of connection, arousal, satisfaction, etc. that a man can. Neither can the male partner provide the same kind of connection, arousal, satisfaction, etc. he experiences with his wife.

(E) Just as a motor works with the most efficiency and the most power when all its pistons are tuned and working well, so are we humans the most powerful, creative, and efficient when we are able to be "authentic" to our whole personality.

(F) The easiest person to hate or to have bias against is someone whom you don't know and whom you can dehumanize. People you know and feel connected with/to seem to have some kind of "insurance" against our bias against them. Soooo, the more people know us—ALL parts of us—the less likely they are to find reason to express prejudice, hatred, bias, etc. Frequency and repetition are factors, too—the more of us are "out" and open—the greater frequency society comes in knowing contact with us and has opportunity to develop familiarity and tolerance.

From: Andy

(A) Yes, there are some who practice homosexual abstinence with equanimity. It would be good if they would post on this. Especially the two of you who lived for some years as gay men before opting for monogamous marriages, so they "had their fill" before abstaining and anyone who has found relations with men rather wanting and not what he really wanted :-).

(E) As for sexual politics: You are quite right that we bisexuals need to confront binary (bipolar?) thinking. The Kinsey scale makes it quite clear that there are lots of gradations in attitudes and behavior between the exclusive homo and hetero poles. It is also interesting that some of the heroes claimed by gays (such as Alexander the Great and Oscar Wilde) were bisexual (or at least married fathers). Maybe we need BI Pride—though I am happy just to be queer!

From: Dale

There have been "pockets" of times of M2M abstinence for me, too. Usually they have been associated with times of some kind of "peak activity" elsewhere in my life. One I can remember in sharp detail was when my wife found out there were casual M-M encounters in my life. (This was before the "finale-ultimo" outing that happened when she found a copy of something I had sent to an online contact.) I had been in counseling at that time . . . and when this happened, of course she joined me for couples counseling.

Also, for the first half of our marriage I wasn't sexually active with guys—not because I hadn't been or wouldn't have . . . but because I didn't have opportunity. I didn't have guys coming on to me . . . and didn't know where to go and find contact. If things would have spontaneously worked for me to have opportunity, I think I would have participated. In my mid- to late 30s however, I had a pivotal experience in a restaurant restroom. A fellow exposed himself to me as an "invitation to dance." I didn't touch him, I didn't talk with him, but it was a very unsettling experience. I didn't sleep well that night—and the next day went to a department store restroom nearby and had my first BJ! It was as if scales had fallen from my eyes and I could see where and how men were finding each other. As I look back, one of the ways I analyze the situation was that my "cup" of suppression and denial had finally gotten full. A "trigger" had occurred to break open previous patterns of awareness and behavior, and I was "on my way," in a certain way.

From: Andy

(A) Most interesting thread. You know my motto used as my signature: "the more loving I do, the more loving I am." I do think when one is being whole-hearted and sexy that affection for wife and for men can flourish while, conversely, when one is crimped both can suffer (especially if the wife is being aloof). Therapists have a slogan: "When you stifle bad feelings, you stifle all feelings—including good ones," and one of the aims of therapy is to get you in touch with all your feelings, including those socially disapproved (not something men socialized in our culture tend to be good at ;-). We have seen lots of folks rendered nasty, angry, depressed (anger turns inwards) by denial. And one of the questions to be raised in a culture which tends to exalt sexual sins above others is whether being "good" sexually though nasty is not worse than acting sexy in forbidden contexts as a good-hearted person.

(B) Having said that, I hasten to add that there are people who practice homosexual abstinence without scarring their personalities. They may well identify as gay/BI, acknowledge feelings of attraction for men, fantasize about men while engaging in sex with self or wife, take part in the gay community—or not—but do not engage in overtly sexual behavior with men. Perhaps because that works well for them (good chance of success) or because of belief in monogamy or a deal worked out with the wife (a vow—less chance of success). This is not to say that deals and compromises are not a good thing in a mixed-orientation marriage, but temperance rather than abstinence might be a more reasonable and sane accommodation.

(F) I love the political argument: I will be letting down the queer community if I allow straights to dodge the gay question by not having sex with men! I'll have to use this <VBG>. What is true here is that it is part of our (political) rights as gay/BI men to figure out for ourselves what is right for us in expressing ourselves given our orientation—in the face of social conventions (and sometimes laws) that would discourage us.

From: Rodney

Andy wrote: >*There are people who practice homosexual abstinence without scarring their personalities.*<

Believe it or not, you're the first person who's responded so far with even the slightest suggestion that homosexual abstinence CAN work under any circumstances without producing nasty side effects. So the discussion gets more complicated.

>*I love the political argument: I will be letting down the queer community if I allow straights to dodge the gay question by not having sex with men!*<

I'm not quite sure what your tone here is, but I hope I managed (despite myself) to communicate my thought that the REAL community to be benefited by honesty is the STRAIGHT community. I think the gay community has made some significant progress toward establishing its rights and validity in the eyes of the world. But I think there is nothing quite comparable among bisexuals. And (as a result) many (most?) bisexuals spend most of their lives not realizing that they are bisexual, saying, "I like women, so I know I'm not gay, so I guess I'm just one of those straight guys who likes/would like to have sex with men"! At the very least, this is a block to consciousness; at worst, it encourages the ugliest form of bigotry (I bet there are at least a few homosexually active bisexuals who spend a fair amount of their time gay-bashing). But I think, on the simplest level, bisexuals have a certain responsibility to challenge the bipolar thinking that is so pervasive in, and so damaging to, our cultural health.

From: Rodney

Thanks for the support and validation. I'm trying now to help my wife see that what I am facing and what SHE is facing, too, though I'm not sure she fully understands this yet, and what we are BOTH facing, is something much larger than a sexual issue, and that to ignore this fact is probably to deny its "meaning."

She and I are of course aware, first of all, of the impact of my coming out on our marriage. Our marriage had already been under tremendous strain, and frankly my coming out to her has had MAINLY the effect of bringing all SORTS of issues into much clearer focus. Will we remain married? I don't know. But I am much more optimistic than I have been for years that we will at least end up FRIENDS. And it is surely better to be CONSCOUSLY UNMARRIED FRIENDS than UNCONSCIOUSLY MARRIED ENEMIES.

("Enemy" is much too strong a word here; I use it mainly for rhetorical purposes. The emphasis is meant to be on the issue of CONSCIOUSNESS.)

The responses I've been receiving on my post regarding "homosexual abstinence" have been enormously helpful to me in helping me understand WHY, at this comparatively late stage in my life, all this has happened to me. Though I'm on the left side of the political spectrum, personally I am fairly reserved. I don't like to "make a fuss," and I instinctively distrust people with Programs, political or whatever.

So here I am, having gone through the pain of coming out and NOW finding that I just might be able to pass, thank you, on having more homosexual experiences. But something tells me that this is not the right way for me to go, either for me or for my family.

We all saw the movie "Pleasantville" on the weekend, and, yes, it gets pretty heavy-handed toward the end. But toward the end, one of the characters says something like, "Once you've changed, it's not so easy to go back." I think I, my wife, and my two children (who are thoroughly informed about the issues between me and my wife)—I think all four of us had a more sharply-edged response than most of the other people in the theater did.

SEX BEHIND WIFE'S BACK

From: Scott

I would appreciate hearing thoughts from other married men on whether it is sinful to have sex with men behind their wife's back.

From: Carl

"Sinful" implies a specific moral code against which to measure what you do, and therefore its interpretation depends on the belief system you bring to the marriage. But for me—and I've been there—it's psychologically and practically unsatisfactory, whatever your moral outlook.

For maybe 26 of the almost 37 years I've been married I had casual, furtive sex in parks and rest stops and trucks and back rooms. And I'd go home and feel like a shit, and my wife would guess why. Furthermore it was like eating pretzels: unsatisfying, so the more you have the more you want. It often was exciting at the time, but it meant nothing. More like a game of pinball than the sort of fulfillment I really was looking for.

The only memorable sex I had with anyone except my wife in those years was when I let my guard down and got emotionally involved with one guy and broke my cardinal rule never to sleep with another man for purposes of sex. That affair was a disaster, because he finally demanded that I leave my wife and family, and I refused.

My present lover—who also was my very first lover when I was a teenager and almost miraculously stepped back into my life—is deeply fulfilling though there is no sex between us this time around. Our relationship is intimate, companionable, loving, caring, understanding, supportive, and (for me, at least) energizing. Perhaps that would have been the solution for me all along if I could only have seen it. But would I have been able to get along without male sex? I really don't know.

From: Joe

Guys—at the risk of sounding like a broken record (remember those?), I still recommend picking up a copy of "Embodiment" by James B. Nelson (Augsburg Publishing). The chapter on marriage and fidelity was eye-opening for me and put that issue in a deeply (as opposed to shallow) Christian and liberating perspective for me. (Now, if I could only get my wife to read it. . . .) Personally, I think that chapter should be on the suggested reading list along with "When Husbands Come Out of the Closet," etc.

From: Lou

My two cents . . . (I'm gonna run outta pennies soon) :)

I've struggled with the question of "sin" as relating to having sex with men while married (I'm still married) . . . and I've come to a couple of conclusions. . . . Like someone earlier pointed out, "sin" relates to the morals you bring to your marriage. In my case, being a born-again Christian, the matter of being promiscuous has always been a sin in my mind, I somehow managed to rationalize away my actions with men as NOT being infidelity as far as my marriage was concerned, because I was having affairs with MEN and NOT WOMEN. So it really wasn't cheating on my wife . . . geesh . . . the lengths we'll go to . . .

So my conclusion is that any sex outside of that with my wife is sin for me, according to what I believe . . . if for no other reason, it breaks my vows with my wife to be her faithful lover. Does that mean I'm successful? No . . . does it cause me tremendous pain and guilt? Yes . . . I'm in the midst of trying to work through all of this, and find some resolve without having to leave my wife.

I wonder if having an intimate emotional relationship with a man without sex is enough for me. I don't know . . . I'm looking for it . . . I can't imagine it would be . . . but who knows . . . that's my thoughts for the day :).

From: Rodney

Though my point of reference is NOT that of a born-again Christian, I struggle with this issue constantly. Like you, I have tried various imaginative "redefinitions" of my marriage vows and tried to convince myself that having sex with men wasn't a violation of my promise to "forsake all others" but my wife. And, like you, I could never bring this off. Bottom line, one has to ask oneself, "What does my wife think that promise means?"; otherwise, you get involved in endless word games, which ultimately ARE only word games, regardless of how much sanction they may seem to receive from our national leaders.

This is ultimately not a LEGAL issue, after all. It's an issue of love and trust.

I think the only way out of this maze is the direction pointed to in various posts I have read on this list—you have to try to determine what vows you COULD make and COULD be faithful to. And then you have to see if your wife could accept them, also. I don't know if your church sanctions nontraditional vows, but I would myself have no trouble living in a nontraditional marriage (one that permitted some degree of openness to accommodate my homosexuality). Whether my wife could tolerate such an arrangement is quite another matter.

There are many parts of my traditional vows that I would never break—a commitment to be there for my wife "in sickness, in health, for better, for worse, for richer, for poorer, till death do us part" (I probably garbled it, but I think it goes something like that). And surely that kind of commitment is not a trivial thing in a world, like ours, so filled with uncertainty.

But my wife is not inside my head and surely can't imagine what kind of faith she can place in ANY of my promises now, since I have so extravagantly violated my vow of fidelity.

Coming out to one's wife is to make an enormous commitment to honesty, and OUGHT to actually INCREASE trust, not DECREASE it. But it doesn't seem to work quite like that from my wife's viewpoint.

You and I may know or suspect that for every man on this list there are a hundred, maybe a thousand, maybe a hundred thousand men who are following the only route our culture really leaves open for men who love both men and women: hidden infidelity to someone, somehow.

Rereading this message, I'm not wholly sure why I wrote it. I doubt there's anything here you don't already know and haven't spent hours thinking about. But maybe it's worth emphasizing that the pain we feel when we are not honest, which is both admirable and (unfortunately) not all that common these days.

And it is a function of love: you finally realized you loved your wife too much to keep up the charade. Sigh. We could all have avoided so much trouble if we were a little bit better at lying. And a little bit less in love with our wives.

From: Peter

I'm married, have 4 kids, and am sexually attracted to men. (To what "degree," or whether that makes me "gay" or "BI" is not important to me. I know what I like) I can only speak for myself. For me, the only "sin" is that it took me a lifetime to finally confront, explore, experience, and become OK with the fact that I am attracted to men. To me, any positive feelings that come from within can't be a sin. Those feelings are part of who I am, part of my nature. To me, my sexual experiences with other men have been very positive experiences. I find, in retrospect, that it was absolutely necessary for me to have MM sex behind my wife's back. I needed to experience that, as part of coming out to myself. I could not have shared it with her, back then. You see, I didn't even understand it myself, so I could not have hoped that my wife would understand my MM needs/desires. I was not able to stay emotionally uninvolved with the guys I was sexually involved with. In fact, I was emotionally involved before becoming sexually involved. So the relationships I've had with men have been long term and involved.

During my second long-term MM relationship, I came out to my wife. We separated briefly; almost got divorced. She asked me to leave. Not because I like guys, but because I was still LYING to her about being sexually involved with my "friend."

During our brief separation, I learned that my wife and kids are as much a part of me as my own sexuality is. Living an exclusively gay lifestyle, although briefly, was not a fulfilling experience for me. By some miracle, my wife and I reconciled. With me out to her, we knew things would have to be different. Although my wife is straight, she understands that sexual orientation is not a choice, but a fact. And she does not want to see me deprived of fulfilling my MM needs and desires. Yet she was not comfortable with the idea that I would be out dating and having sex with other guys. So her idea was to try finding a guy we both like. It never occurred to me, but I figured it was worth a try. So we looked, and met a few guys, and had sexual encounters with a few of them, until we met one that we REALLY both like. And he REALLY likes both of us. The three of us have been seeing each other for many months. The sex is great! We have fun together, and enjoy our weekly encounters, thoroughly. The friendship is complicated; he is also married, and his wife knows nothing about our true involvement. But that is a whole "nother story."

I truly believe I could never have gotten comfortable with my sexual orientation if I had not experienced my true desires. And I believe it was necessary to do that behind my wife's back, at least to begin with. It was very stressful living a double life. I did not feel good about sneaking around, but I also did not know what else to do. My answers came gradually, after much turmoil. I never asked to desire men; it is just the way I am. So I figure it is absolutely necessary to try very hard to figure out what to do with that. For me, it would be a sin not to.

From: Henry

How often the same things happen to us, but at different times of our lives. I came out to myself long before I was married, had relationships with men and women. I decided that the exclusively gay life wasn't what I wanted. I believe, though, that if I hadn't slept with a lot of men before I got married, I would have experimented while I was married. As you say, you have to find out about yourself. But I knew what TGT was all about before getting married, and what were, for me, its limitations; so it wasn't difficult to remain faithful throughout our marriage.

Then (thanks to one of these damned BI/gay "support" lists, that was "supposed" to help me keep my zipper up) I formed I strong emotional attachment to another married guy. We had no physical relationship, but that didn't matter to my wife: to her I had been unfaithful and she was POd big time. So fidelity means different things to our different wives, I suppose.

Since then, much has changed. This almost-divorced guy is my lover now, and my wife is very fond of him, as he is of her. It is ironic to me that, when the "infidelity" trouble started, I assumed that I'd make do with some gay/BI men friends and porn, because I thought that's what my wife would allow. But it turned out that she didn't like the idea of me going around with a gang of platonic gay/BI friends—knowing my premarital history, she suspected that that would lead to trouble—and she passionately detests all pornography. She's more comfortable seeing me involved with one guy she knows and trusts, where there is a real human connection, than for me to be tempted to have meaningless relationships or look at porn. So I'd say to guys, don't assume you know what your wife thinks is right or wrong: find out.

From: Peter

As much as we all have in common, it always fascinates me to see/hear how our solutions are different. It is another reminder that it helps to hear other guys' perspectives, but we each must find what is best for his own situation.

Just a couple of years ago, I was convinced my wife would hate me if I came out to her. Now, being attracted to men is something my wife and I have in common. It is fun to discover where our tastes are the same, and where they are different.

I guess it is important to point out—nobody can possibly know better than you, if or when you ought to come out to your wife. For some guys, the best solution is not to.

FIDELITY TO THE WIFE

From: Lou

My wife and I have had a LOT of discussion these last few weeks (I was out to her before we were married 19 years ago), on what is "acceptable" to her within the bounds of our marriage, and she has finally landed in the "no sex with men" zone. . . .

I can "date" . . . meaning . . . have coffee . . . go to dinner . . . have friends . . . like I do now with straight friends . . . but no sex. Even then, she feels like it's only a matter of time until I find her replacement. For me . . . I think realistically, it means I still hide a part of my life from her . . . the part that needs intimate male relationships. . . . I've done it my whole marriage. . . . I can keep doing it . . . . I don't want to. It's not how I want to live my life . . . but it's a compromise I have to make now, and can hopefully do it without injuring her emotionally. I still wrestle with reconciling my "faith" with the whole sexuality issue . . . but that's a WHOLE other story. . . .

It still comes down to—do I complete the commitment I've made to my wife and sons to be husband/father. If I don't, does that mean I'm NOT keeping my commitment to GOD when I made that original commitment to my wife?

Big questions . . . no easy answers . . . but glad you and the other guys are here to shed light along the path.

From: Dale

Fidelity (in my book, anyway) refers to an agreement into which both/all parties are (and stay) in agreement. Generically speaking, then, agreements of fidelity occur between people, between businesses, between businesses and individuals . . . lots of permutations.

The "arrangement" you describe is totally understandable. It's how LOTS and LOTS of guys live their lives for years and years at a time. However, the arrangement cited above is not, in my mind, a "fidelitous" agreement because one party (you, as the gay/BI-male member) is at some level not in agreement with your wife, the other party to the agreement. As patently satisfied as your wife might feel that she has "succeeded" in retaining or imposing her perimeters on the relationship, I couldn't say she has achieved "fidelity." I sincerely wish she could find a clearer, more realistic vision of not only her world . . . but YOURS!

Should it be true that "Even then, she feels like it's only a matter of time until I find her replacement," I would say she is the one who will have set the scene for the relationship breaking down because she couldn't find a way to find a place for the "whole" of your personality. You can hardly be expected to excise and divorce yourself from such a profound part of your personality. Rejecting a part of your personality as she does so profoundly most certainly presents the tip of a wedge between the two of you. While that wedge (in concept) might lay dormant for a period of time . . . long periods of time, even . . . it can never be deemed a "dead" issue.

In pressing for "fidelity" so exclusively on HER terms, she has, in fact, lost it at the threshold that separates the present from the future.

From: Rodney

Brother, does this sound familiar!

The form this issue of fidelity takes for me is that it seems my bisexuality is OK with my wife, but only as long as I don't do the kinds of things bisexuals do. Now, I can understand and sympathize with (especially) the practical concerns my wife has about my homosexuality, but there is (an increasingly vocal) part of me that asks, "When you blow the smoke away, isn't this about being INVISIBLE in the same sense racial minorities and (yes!) feminists talk about their "constituents" being invisible to the primary culture?"

As you may have figured out by now, MY "faith" issue is that I believe my sexuality is a creation of God. It has somehow to "make sense" in terms of my life "story"—but I haven't quite yet figured out what the meaning of it all is.

From: Jud

Not to be the devil's advocate here, but thought I'd interject an alternative point of view to this thread. It seems as though there are some of us (me included) who have placed the commitments we've made to others (our wives, our families, our God) above that of our own happiness and self fulfillment. None of us is getting any younger, and do we really always have to follow the tenets of the Judeo/Christian ethical code? Are we going to buy into society's rule that we must deny (and some might argue punish) ourselves in order to look proudly into the eyes of our wives and our maker when we are called home? Is there no legitimate way that we can feel good about ourselves and our decisions in life if we do the things we have to do to satisfy our urges in this heterosexual and monogamous society that we were all raised in?

Although I was brought up in the Christian tradition, and still honor most of its tenets, I still try to live my life by an equally powerful (and yes, sometimes conflicting) rule to try to live my life without regrets. You know that bumper sticker that says, "The guy who dies with the most toys wins"? Well mine would read, "The guy who dies with the least regrets wins." But regret is a deeply personal measuring stick. Sometimes it's more practical not to beat yourself up over causing pain to others and just focus your energy on how to stop the pain and move on to a situation that you can do the things you want and need to do in a supportive environment.

Yeah, yeah, I know this all sounds like a very easy way of justifying the committing of "sins" and there are plenty of terrible axe murderers out there that have absolutely no regrets for what they've done to others. And I'm DEFINITELY not advocating that everyone just switch to using their own consciousness as the only guide to their behavior. But what I am suggesting is that some of us need to look at the mistakes and the wrongs we've done in our life with a little bit more forgiving heart. How can we ask our wives and families to forgive us if we can't forgive ourselves first?

From: Kenneth

Jud wrote: >*Is there no legitimate way that we can feel good about ourselves and our decisions in life if we do the things we have to do to satisfy our . . . ?*<

Yes, there is at least one. It would be to tell our wives that we love them too much to deceive them and pretend we're faithful when we're not. That our own integrity means that we choose not to manipulate others, nor deny ourselves our basic need for man-love. If that means divorce, at least we are free to be ourselves without deceiving ourselves that we are being kind by lying when actually we are protecting ourselves from the pain of separation from our familiar and safe source of emotional support.

From: Cleff

You all have given me so much to think about. I have come to some conclusions about fidelity to my wife. I am unsatisfied and wanting more. I need to really begin to nourish my soul if I am to be satisfied. I'm not sure if an intimate friend without sex will be enough, but I want to try. I made a commitment to my wife and, yes, to God.

I have justified having sex with men by telling myself that my wife wouldn't be as threatened by another man. I don't want her to know that I have been unfaithful to her. That would only hurt her. My infidelity has put a distance between my relationship with God. I want to move closer to God with love, not lust.

I am not filled with guilt at all. I really do celebrate my bisexuality. I love who I am. My sin separates me from God. I understand that God loves me as I am. Maybe more when I sin? I really feel I need to be faithful if I am going to love myself more.

I really do love myself. I am not going to tell my wife about any need I may have for sex with men. I'm just not convinced that it is a need. A desire indeed! I believe that my desire to have sex with men is no different than another husbands desire to have sex with another women. I desire other women, too.

I don't need to ask my wife about what she thinks.

You were all so helpful to me. I don't need to ask my wife about fidelity, because I know what our vows meant to her. I really agree. It doesn't matter how I define fidelity in my marriage. The only definition that matters to me is my wife's. My wife knows that I am BI sexual, but she does not expect me to have sex with men. For many of you sex with men is not sin. For me sex with anyone outside my marriage is sin. I appreciate all of your help. I would appreciate any help you can give me as I begin to be faithful to what my wife expects from me.

God Bless you all! Pray for me.

P.S. doesn't mean I can't look! Doesn't mean I won't flirt with you! KISS KISS . . .

HONESTY

From: Marlin

I have been beating myself up over being dishonest with my wife. First, it was dishonest of me not to tell her from the start before we were married that I was gay (or at least BI).

I can rationalize this matter somewhat, due to my own denial of my homosexuality (there—I used the word) so that "bisexual" (and basically str8) was as far as I could admit to myself. My level of self-esteem has never been very high, and to identify myself as gay, much less to be out, required more courage than I had or have now. When you hate yourself, it is hard to do anything that might subject you to the disgust and disapproval of others from whom you draw whatever sense of well-being that you have. This is my excuse on the first count.

As far as sneaking around my wife's back in this relationship that I just got into less than 2 weeks ago, I cannot excuse myself. The temptation was simply more than I could resist, and I felt that if I withdrew, I would never have such an opportunity again. My own thinking is probably so warped at this point that I have no good way to test the truth of this. It is morning and this is the time of day when I am at my lowest spirits, so my feelings are filtered through a mess of shit.

There is a self-destructive streak in me that I fear may be calling the shots right now when I feel under the gun. So I must be careful what I do or say so as not to satisfy that dark force within me that needs to "burn down the house" in order to justify self-destruction. I know this sounds like some sick shit, but I am what I am.

The posts of this list have been a lot of help in this, as has GAMMA. I don't feel like I am totally unique in my situation, but rather just another confused asshole with a lot of emotional baggage. If other people can get through this, so can I. Perhaps what I am afraid of most here is fear itself.

From: Moris

We all have been there. One thing I had to do was forgive myself before I could even ask my wife to forgive. I did and she did.

From: Marlin

Right now I'm feeling like maybe I've had my little fling and that returning to the fold and not straying again is a possibility, and may be the only route to recovering what little peace of mind I had before I let temptation turn my life upside down. I want to be back where I was before I sinned against my wife's love and trust. I suppose I rationalized her shortcomings as an excuse, but we have both been acting and feeling goofy for some time. I was the one who did the unthinkable. The more I'm around my boyfriend, the more I feel like I had to have been out of my mind to risk losing all that is important to me just for the excitement of gay sex. Besides, it is not fair to him. If I am committed to my wife, then there is no future for him in a relationship with me—only random meetings for sex and the odd dates. He is very unstable now and I fear that getting involved with him isn't helping his state of mind any. Besides, he's jealous of my wife and cracks bad jokes about her. My main concern now seems to be how to salvage my marriage and try to get my head together as best I can, perhaps utilizing a therapist. I can't deal with all this double life stuff, and I don't want to go through the whole process of poisoning my marriage, divorce, property settlement, etc. I want my quiet little life back, but I'm afraid I've lit the fire that will ultimately burn down the house.

THOUGHTS/FEELINGS ON MONOGAMY

From: Felix

I want to talk about thoughts and feelings on the monogamy issue. I really love my wife and can't handle being in more than one relationship; neither can she. My problem is that I always figured that whatever sex I ended up with, it would all just come out in the wash. I figured, though, that it would be a man I'd spend my life with. Then I met my wife, and everything changed. She is the only person I ever considered being with forever. She is everything. But I am from time to time really frustrated with my gay needs and denying them. She says that she leaves her needs for a "straight" man at the door because she loves me. And that I can be selfish sometimes about my needs. Maybe I am, but I know I am gay yet I need her in my life, and no one else. Is it a matter of letting myself be loved by her, and looking in my own backyard for the things I want instead of elsewhere?

From: Shawn

If only the matter were so simple as just getting your needs met in your own backyard. Unless you have a fantastic, supernatural ability to deny the man-needing side of you, you'll chronically be "bothered" by it. My wife recently said that she denies all others for the sake of us. I said, yes, dear, but you don't have a need to be with a woman like I do to be snuggled up close to a man. She agreed that my needs are greater and more complex in that sense and that there are no simple solutions.

Keep attempting to gently remind your wife of your realities while loving her as much as you can. It will take a lot of time, communication, patience, tears, etc. but eventually she might become more understanding of your dilemma. Keep being honest. That can be very hard and painful at times, but in my opinion it is the only way to go.

From: Miller

Well, this is a pretty complicated situation! You say that you can't handle being in more than one relationship, yet you are gay, and you are in a hetero relationship. Eventually, I suspect, the dichotomy of that scenario will be so frustrating it will become a major impairment to your psychological well-being. Your choices are to leave her (probably unacceptable to you), to avoid forming another relationship but just having occasional sex with men (might work, but that too has its limitations obviously), or to learn to live with polyamory and multiple relationships. Perhaps you can work through this by eliminating those things you absolutely will not consider but leaving yourself open to solutions you "might" consider in time. Since you are in this relationship with your wife I am going to presume you are at least somewhat bisexual and not 100% exclusively attracted to men. To me, bisexuality by definition almost requires that we be very flexible. So perhaps you might benefit by bending your assumptions and absolutes just a bit.

From: Marlin

I'm not sure monogamy is the problem. I think one's degree of monogamy depends upon how close and committed a couple is, whether the commitment is explicit or implicit. So far I have yet to achieve that level of closeness with any of my m2m relationships, even lifelong friendships that turned sexual. Perhaps if my wife and I were less closely committed and in love with each other, I would not be so out of sorts over my "slip." I seem to be disengaging myself from my boyfriend now, as he flounders with his alcoholism and drug addictions. He needs support in maintaining sobriety that I cannot give him due to the relationship. He needs time and space to work on himself, and I need it to restore what remains of my sanity.

From: Mike

In all of your posts I can "hear" that this relationship with this boyfriend has you feeling out of alignment with your core values. That is always disconcerting . . . and I believe that's for a good reason. I think it is this feeling that, if we are "listening" helps guide us, helps us to find OUR OWN way. Follow your instincts. Alignment, integration, values, authenticity . . . these are important elements of peace. Going in the direction of these can never be wrong in my opinion. Peace to you and all of our online family.

From: Shawn

I think a gay man needs to be honest with his wife and remind her that his homosexual desires aren't going to just disappear because he is married. If he doesn't express it at all to her I think it becomes misleading. The wife could begin resting in the delusion that her husband has none of these desires and fantasies building up inside. Years later, when he might be at risk for acting out, it could be more destructive because an atmosphere of dishonesty has been established. Our silence about our real desires can be dangerously misleading, setting the wives up with a false sense of security that the gay husband no longer desires anyone/anything else. I don't think that kind of silence is a favor to the wife of a gay man; although it might make her feel better in the short run.

From: Marvin

Truer words were never spoken (typed?).

One of the things that I've always been EXTREMELY careful about is, in addition to honesty, not setting unreasonable expectations. . . .

I vividly remember a conversation with my wife shortly after my coming out (damn . . . almost 6 years ago now!) wherein she was dancing around the sexual exclusivity question—almost afraid to actually ask. When I finally said, "If you're asking if I can go the rest of my life without ever being with a man, the answer is no. I don't think I could even if I wanted to, and I don't want to." Looking back now it may have been a bit harsh, but it was honest. While my wife doesn't always know of all of my "activities" she DOES know that I have a strong physical and emotional attraction to men, that I can and do readily fall in love with them and that I WILL have sexual relationships with them. She also knows, which is more important to her, that I'm not actively seeking to "replace" her. . . .

From: Felix

Wow! I never thought I would elicit such response with my query. Let me lay your questions to rest:

1. I LOVE my wife. She is my best friend and I trust her and need her.
2. She is very accepting of who I am as I am of her.
3. We have great sex.
4. I am attracted to men but I have decided that I need her more than I need to find a man with whom I am potentially compatible.
5. When I proposed to my wife she said she would marry me if I promised to take out the garbage every night, and I have kept that promise.
6. I have no intention of leaving her 'cause who will take out the trash?
7. I still need sexual and emotional closeness with a man despite all of this.

Question is, how can I truly be a success if I can't keep my promise to her and myself: that is to say, I need to come up with a way to let her love me enough to be satisfied with her gender. How do I look in my own backyard for this? Am I complete in this union with a woman, even if I love her more than I ever loved any man I was ever with?

From: Shawn

Thanks for the feedback and encouragement. As I think back over the past five years I am astounded at how far forward my wife and I have traveled. There have been some terrible and hurtful times, but we are still together loving each other and I have a liberty and self-acceptance I never dreamed possible. All things are possible, though, for those who persist in believing!

Today my best BI guy friend came over for lunch and hanging out with us. It's the first time he's been to my house. He's the man with whom I share the most emotional and physical intimacy (still with clothes on to date). He and my wife really liked each other and we all had a good time together. I was sort of teasing him when I said, "see, you're the kind of man a guy can bring home to his wife!" . . . and he is.

From: Andy

Sounds like being with a man is a want, not a need, for you so you can do without it. At least, that seems like what you would like to convince yourself. That way you can take the trash to the can in your own backyard and practice "peter monogamy." When I first saw the title of this thread, I thought it meant a monogamy limited to not using your peter so that maybe kissing, etc., was OK, not a violation, as long as your penis stayed in its scabbard :-). Personally, I think monogamy is overrated.

I PROMISED MONOGAMY

From: Stewart

I came out to my wife 18 months ago, and overall it has been very favorable. We go through the routines of life: kids, career, etc, but we can't seem to overcome the "what's next" issue that seems to linger over our heads. My wife and I seem to move about our suburban lifestyles as good as the neighbors next door. The only difference, as you might expect, is our situation. In the beginning my wife basically forced me to promise that I would never leave her for another man and that I would certainly never pursue a sexual relationship of any kind. With all of the hype of coming out, I told her that I could in fact take this "catholic priest" lifestyle and it would not be an issue.

As I grow in realizing who I really am, I have come to see that this is something that I really don't know if I can do. I have addressed this concern with her, and it was almost like coming out again. Needless to say, it caused a great deal of pain . . . all over again. My therapist said it was wrong of her to ever "pigeon-hole" me to make that commitment, but I can't blame her for trying to do so.

Up until about 2 months ago, my wife has refused therapy. She recently started seeing and is building a rapport with a counselor who I feel will greatly benefit her. She was so resistant because she thought I wanted her to go so that the therapist would talk her into having an open marriage. The open marriage concept was discussed, but she is grounded to the fact that she would never entertain the idea.

So here we are now. I feel that this is the next MAJOR hurdle for us to jump. Problem is . . . I don't know how to push it forward. She is in a state of mind where I don't want to throw a great deal at her since she is so new in her own therapy. . . . Plus she is now pregnant! You just can't bring up the topic of "can I fuck another man . . . PLEASE?" at the drop of a hat. However, if I wait for her to broach the subject, I will be waiting for the rest of my life! Whenever the topic is brought to surface, understandably it is a heated FIGHT. I just don't know how to "grow" in our relationship if we don't pursue this topic! I've held so much in for the past 27 years, I am just growing tired of having to keep certain feelings cooped up!

Sorry so long, but I have wanted to write this for days, but just could not muster up the gumption. Any words of wisdom would be greatly appreciated.

From: Max

That was a very interesting e-mail. God, did it ever sound like me? I'm not so sure any more that there are rights and wrongs in this for either partner in terms of one making a request of the other. The only thing I know is that, for the most part, my wife and I are exactly where you and your better half seem to be. We just don't talk about it anymore. Also, my wife has abandoned the idea of counseling, which we both attended initially and then she attended on her own (counselor's decision). I had my own counselor, whom I haven't seen in a year or so.

Deceptive as it may be, I've had to make decisions for myself alone to have relationships with other men. I've not made these very lightly and I'm fully aware of the consequences. However, I can't in all honesty put my wife, nor myself for that matter, through the pain and torture that we went through last year.

I can't and won't advise anyone in this position. All I can do is state what I'm doing and hopefully express the reasons why I'm doing it with clarity and fairness.

My thoughts are with you on this one, if (but not) only because I'm there too.

At the end of the day, as I've said privately to others in this group, you're entitled to your own feelings and needs. Sure, sometimes they can't all be met 100%. But it is reasonable, and may be necessary, that the majority of them are met.

From: Mike

Your post comes across as genuine, compassionate toward your wife, and respectful of the feelings that you BOTH have in this situation.

Would you consider sharing it with HER? Perhaps writing back and forth on this issue for a while will take some of the fire out of the "heated fights" that occur in your face-to-face attempts to discuss this with her.

My wife and I kept a journal for months when we first began to deal with these issues. For both of us, it was a tool to help us get our thoughts out without the dynamic of "live" conversation that sometimes takes you down a road you don't want to go.

From: Shawn

My wife was just asking me tonight about some playing around I had done on one occasion with some friends. Not being good at lying, I told her that we had done a lot of massaging and fondling. She felt quite upset and offended by my need to do this sort of thing occasionally. It usually ends unpleasantly when she starts asking questions and I start telling the truth. I'd rather that she didn't ask at all, but she says, "You know that's not me."

My dilemma is that my honesty seems to just take us down that unpleasant road to all the hurt feelings on her part and my guilt about her feeling hurt. I know it angers her if I'm physical with another man. I stifled myself for so many years; it just made me miserable. I'd rather withhold information given the negative outcomes of these discussions. But then I feel I'm a deceiver and she accuses me of being a sneaky sleaze. It feels so condemning!

I don't know what to do. I feel like refusing to talk about the details of my affections toward others. What good does it do to confess? I could use some support and input. She stayed on the couch tonight. I'm going to bed alone! I don't like this outcome. I'm sorry now that we even talked about it. These discussions never seem to get us anywhere and don't do our relationship any good as far as I can tell.

BI/GAY M2M MONOGAMY

From: Scotty

Hi guys. I haven't posted in a while but I have an issue that I want to put out for discussion/support/feedback.

I am involved with a married man. He is out to his wife, she and I are becoming friends. That aspect of things is generally good and sometimes wonderful.

The challenge I am facing is this. The man I am involved with has a capacity for many loving sexual relationships with men. He assures me that I am his primary male partner, but he has friendships that have or can include sexual expression. This pushes my buttons big time. I know, from my experience, that the connection we share is deep and strong, but when he is with another guy I feel very threatened on a gut level, even though I understand in my head that I am loved. I have been with other guys too and the experiences, while pleasurable, don't measure up to emotional quality I feel with the man I am in love with. Right now, after a tumultuous couple of days, we have agreed not to be sexual with other guys until such time as we both agree to, or perhaps together with a third if we both want to.

I am looking for ideas and support because I have been working on this issue for a while and I have not been able to move past the emotions. Maybe I don't need to? Maybe we aren't compatible? Maybe I need to just suck it up and let him do what he wants. I am struggling, as you see.

How are other people dealing with these issues? How do people move past the feelings of abandonment that are triggered by their lover being with another?

From: Shawn

There is nothing wrong with your feelings. They are yours and they are understandable. The thing is, you cannot control what your lover does. You can only tell him how his behavior makes you feel. You can ask him for reassurance. You can discuss the matter together. You can continue to love him and derive what joy you can from the relationship. But, ultimately, in a loving relationship, you cannot make demands of him or attempt to control him. That would only diminish the quality of the love you two evidently have been sharing. Try to let it go and let him be who he is, as long as he is still being loving and considerate toward you. Your feelings may or may not change. The feelings are important and must be acknowledged, but they are only secondary in the scheme of things.

From: Andy

Open relationships? I wrote the book on that <G>! I think it is a tribute to your love that you have decided not to have additional liaisons for now, but I don't think it is necessary in the long run. As you intimate, his being with another guy does not detract from you. He may even learn some arts of loving that he can try out on you. My main boyfriend, who is a little shy and taciturn, surprised me tonight by asking—while we were making love—about others I had been with (and it turned him on all the more) :-). He also wondered whether we might like to do some different things and what my fantasies were—moving us to another level of communication (he also expressed interest in the gay baths). You do well not to suppress feelings of jealousy/abandonment but as you get more secure in your love perhaps you can learn to disregard them more.

From: Joey

Boy do I ever understand. We married guys who are heading into gay relationships may have a rude awakening. Monogamy is NOT a standard in gay relationships. We who have been married tend to be geared towards monogamous relationships or at least we are relationship-oriented. Now, depending on the guy you meet, his history, and his attitude on that day, you may find one who is totally into monogamy. I think the range is from a monogamous-oriented guy to one who is like: "Hey look, I need variety to keep me happy." I recently fell for a guy who rejected me because I have only recently come out. He claimed that I am not ready for a monogamous relationship. My feeling in retrospect is, fuck you . . . I just spend almost 20 years being faithful to my wife . . . what was your longest relationship, 4 years . . . 5 years . . . tops. Frankly, I should have told him off, but I was too infatuated.

Anyway, the point is that some guys are going to require variety and you may or may not wish to deal with this. You must be true to yourself. Even if you are totally in love with him, you have to decide if his wandering or if his need for threesomes is acceptable to you. DO NOT, DO NOT get into a relationship that is in anyway destructive to you. Love will not necessarily conquer all. Be careful. I am glad that he was up front with you. I have talked to too many guys who were terribly wounded when they caught their lover with someone.

From: Moris

Joey wrote: >*Monogamy is NOT a standard in gay relationships.*<

Yes, I know it is not a standard . . . but it can be . . . and with some it IS the standard. I would say keep looking until you find someone that meets your standard. That is what I did. . . . Feb. 22 will be 1 year for my husband and I.

From: Chukky

I am a married guy, involved with a married guy and we are/have COMPLETE monogamy to one another. We have our own adaptation of a marriage . . . for the best it can be right now, since we are living with our wives and raising our children. No, they do not know the extent of our relationship other than that of "like brothers." If he did not have the same beliefs in monogamy as I do, I would not be with him because some of the most important values I hold are trust, monogamy, honesty, and unconditional love, even though this is contradictory of how I am in my marriage to my wife. I know when the time comes for me and my wife to divorce, (which I have no doubt will happen because I want to take charge of my own life), I will still stay monogamous in a gay relationship. For myself, there is no other way. Someone wrote a few days ago about how challenging it is having another relationship. I agree and disagree with this statement. My lover and I have been together 16 months . . . long time. . . . We have had our share of ups and downs—however, because of communication, we have weathered all that has come our way, in addition to learning about each other through the relationship process. We are at a point in our relationship that his friends (who are gay) and a few family members know about us, that we are husband and husband. My friends—all straight—know what we are to each other, and have socialized with us, going to dinner, gay piano bar, movies, etc. My mother and my sister know of our relationship as well and even though they do not condone it, everyone has been very supportive not only on my behalf, but on the behalf of both of us.

So . . . yes . . . depending on the individuals involved . . . it is very possible and it is also very fulfilling. Just a side note, I came out to my wife 2 years ago about my identity. We have a very nice, nonsexual relationship. When we do happen to get divorced, when the kids are a bit older, we will remain very good friends, since she is so innocent in all that has happened. We went through that roller coaster stuff of her feeling cheated and lied to, even though that was not the case on my part. I felt I could take this big secret of what I am to my grave. For me, it did not work out that way.

From: Chukky

I would go crazy if I knew that my lover would "possibly" be with other guys. God love you . . . I know I would not be able to handle that one at all!

From: Mike

As you so often do . . . .you've raised some very significant points here. I too wonder if gay/BI or mixed-orientation relationships would fare differently if they received the same social support that str8 relationships receive. Some of those social support systems act as "golden handcuffs" keeping many str8 marriages together much beyond their natural shelf life, I suspect.

As for monogamy . . . I believe it's more of a male/female difference than a gay/str8 difference.

I do know that I sometimes approach my m2m relationships from a str8 model (the only one I've really known most of my life). It causes me to have expectations that may be unrealistic. I am trying to re-examine and reconstruct my attitudes and expectations based on a new understanding of myself and my sexuality. It is sometimes confusing, because under stress I revert back to the old familiar patterns . . . which, in my case, no longer fit.

Oh it's so wonderful and yet so frustrating to be a 14-year-old in a 44-year-old body.

From: Carl

Chukky wrote: >*I would go crazy*—<

Just as my wife goes crazy from time to time about "that creep"—who happens to be the greatest guy I ever met. But note that we are talking about "unconditional love." It's only when we look for a return on the emotional investment of love, and thus pose "conditions" on it—that we create jealousy. Love that demands nothing of the other person, love that is nurtured as its own reward, exists whether or not it is returned and whether or not the beloved is faithful.

My boyfriend ("that creep") has had a lover of sorts for 15 years, and that lover is the only person my boyfriend will allow in his bed—and it can only be rarely and briefly. Okay, so be it. I sit in the kitchen at my boyfriend's place and look at the lover's pictures on the wall and am deeply touched by their relationship. I would love to be to my boyfriend what the lover is, but I know I can't any more than my wife can be to me what my boyfriend is. The lover is much, much younger than I and much smaller; more to the point, he's local. He watches out for my boyfriend and calls him daily.

I love my boyfriend deeply. I want him to have the relationship that I can't give him. I'm delighted to find that he also loves me—again in a way totally different from his relationship to the lover. And he understands my need for the connection with my wife, which is to say that he isn't jealous of her any more than I am of his lover. Indeed, he's very compassionate about what she is going through because of my having openly declared my sexuality and my love for him.

But admittedly I had to live to age 69 (no cracks, guys!) before I thoroughly understood how all this works. I remember my jealousy of my boyfriend's roommate (who turned out to be straight—well, sort of) when I first met my boyfriend. So I've been there too. Thank God I stayed around long enough to learn better!

From: Marvin

Do NOT just "suck it up and let him do what he wants" unless that's what's right for YOU. Each of us is different in our needs/desires for monogamy. You may require it. It IS something that's worth examining . . . and determining if it's a core value of yours and necessary in a relationship or not.

For some it is. For others no. I don't for a minute buy the gay/straight dichotomy here—the need/desire for a monogamous (or sexually exclusive, which is what we're really talking about here and a totally different topic) relationship has NOTHING to do with orientation.

I determined long ago . . . after MUCH soul searching, that for ME sexual exclusivity is not required, or even necessarily desirable. I just need to know that I'm loved, and that my partner is there for me emotionally—that doesn't require exclusivity. In the early stages of my examination of the issue I remember thinking, how can I possibly expect my lover to be exclusive, when by virtue of the fact that I'm having sex with my wife, whom I also love, I'm NOT being exclusive to him?

Don't get me wrong . . . this isn't something that I arrived at lightly—or quickly. It probably realistically took me a couple of years to sort it out and arrive at my current position. It of course helps that I've NEVER been the jealous or possessive type. . . . I've known for some time that the perfect situation for me (and I haven't found it since the end 3 years ago of a 4-year relationship) would be my relationship with my wife, a loving committed sexual relationship with a special man, and a number of occasional playmates (yes, I've been called a slut! <G>).

Bottom line: you have to do what's right for YOU—not letting societal "norms" and the way you've been raised and living dictate what you do. Spend the time necessary in solitary soul searching . . . talking with your man . . . talking with your wife . . . counselor if you have one—whatever you decide is right for YOU is right . . . period. Don't let anyone tell you otherwise.

From: Rodney

Marvin wrote: *the need/desire for a monogamous . . . has NOTHING to do with orientation.<*

This point can't be made too frequently, I think, because it's so easy to lose sight of. It's also easy to lose sight of the related fact that some women can handle our orientation issues much more easily than they can the nonmonogamous requirements of being actively gay or bisexual in a heterosexual marriage. I suspect, in fact, that is the TYPICAL profile of the wives of the gay and BI men in this group.

It's hard for me to "enter into" my wife's pain on this score, because I don't think I'd have any difficulty accepting the idea that she was having sex with other women, but I would have trouble accepting the idea she was having sex with other men. This is probably a wildly irrational form of "semimonogamy" on my part, because I suspect there would be a greater likelihood that her female lovers (more than her male ones) would require a love relationship, not just a sexual one. (In fact, my wife has never expressed an interest in having affairs of ANY kind, and I think she's being honest with me.)

In counseling with my wife, I find myself frequently slipping into the error of thinking that our problems have to do with my orientation, BUT ONLY INDIRECTLY.

From: Scotty

I wanted to thank the men who took the time to respond to me. I appreciate your thoughts and your support. Here is what I have come up with as a way to handle the situation. I told my lover to do what he wants and needs to do, that I honor his being, and don't want to set restrictions on his self-expression. I also told him that I don't want to know about his encounters with other men. I also resolved within myself to not have sexual experiences with other people unless my heart is involved. I think part of the wounding for me has been from my own sexual play when it has lacked connection at a heart level.

I feel good about this course of action.

STAY BECAUSE OF LOVE?

From: Shawn

My wife and I continued our discussion this morning after a night of her sleeping on the couch. We are both feeling less emotional this morning, I am glad to report. It seems we stay married because we are still very much in love with each other and enjoy a passionate sexual relationship. We have no other major issues except my bisexuality and need for intimacy with at least one special man. I don't feel a need for lots of sex with many guys.

My wife understands that it is hurtful when she withdraws and gets depressed. She asks me to be more understanding of that since she is trying to accept my bisexuality—ok . . . that's fair enough. It just felt like she was angry and pushing me away. But she was feeling rejected and down . . . for which I am sorry. I do love her passionately and have for 24 years! She is a beautiful woman in every way. I couldn't ask for more in a wife. She's wonderful and kind and committed to me.

Actually, I only desire to be intimate with one man who is also in a committed heterosexual relationship with his fiancée. He and I have not gone too far yet with our physical affections except to kiss and hold and lie together with our clothes on. I haven't known him long, but we certainly fell for each other. We're both basically virgins when it comes to homosex. Our feelings for each other run a lot deeper than just the physical stuff. I find him to be an incredibly beautiful human being . . . the content of his heart and character. He feels exactly that way about me. My wife knows how we feel.

I'm so new to this situation I find myself in. Please guys, keep writing to me. I cannot begin to express the magnitude and depth of my appreciation for all your input. You guys are lifesavers. This online support is an incredible Godsend! Please keep it up. Because of you, talking to my wife again this a.m. and the beauty of God, I am feeling more hopeful today. Thank you, thank you, from the depths of my heart for your love and concern. I've enjoyed giving it out and it's wonderful to receive it back!!!

From: Scotty

Sounds like you and your wife need to discuss, when the issue is NOT "up," what kind of boundaries you both need and how to deal with the feelings that come up when they do come up. If she were able to share her hurt and anger with you, and you could listen without defending or stopping her in any way, and without castigating yourself, you two might be able to stay more connected through the process.

From: Joey

The next time that happens remind her first how she reacts. Tell her that you want to be honest and open but her reactions do not lend themselves for you to be so. I would definitely hold back on telling much until she is able to handle it. I know I can be open about all this stuff to my wife but I think she is extraordinary. So, as a friend of my wife's said to her, "I admire your ability not to have sexual jealousy." For most of us, this jealousy will be the seed for many an argument. Good luck.

Yes, I have been in that "bouncing off the wall" syndrome of "I'm going to stay/how can I, I'm gay!" In fact, I got indignant about the whole thing and said something like, "I finally had the courage and insight to state who I am, now I have to leave." Well, my friend, I won't tell you what to do, but I can tell you what I have learned for me in my own journey. I learned that there is much unknown territory in this particular journey and it served me well to make friends with "uncertainty." I drove myself crazy with the back and forth stay/go routine. I learned that for me I was desperate to have some certainty in my life and that it was uncomfortable to "not know" what would happen. The bouncing back and forth gave me momentary glimmers of security . . . saying in my head something like "ok, at least now I know where I'm going" only to be swept away in the cycle again. I learned that I needed to be in that unknown space and that trying to force an answer only intensified the struggle and issue and made me less clear on what I really wanted . . . i.e., what my truth was and is. For me, I now know (and feel CONSISTENTLY strong about this) that I will be with my wife forever. . . . I love her and she is my life partner. Fortunately, she is very supportive and is coping well with my relationship with my partner. I hope this helps in at least some small way. . . . "Acceptance" of where I am at any particular place seems so often to be the key to my clarity—whether it's about "the gay thing" or an every day occurrence (and acceptance doesn't always mean I like it!!).

From: Kenneth

You asked for advice, so here goes. Your wife gets upset when she finds out that you have been physical with another man. You are miserable when you aren't. You are taking care of yourself when you "massage and fondle" other guys. Perhaps she is taking care of herself when she asks you about it (you said that she claims that that is the way she is made—to have to know). So, try not to feel guilty when she asks you about something that will surely upset her if you tell her the truth and divulge what makes you happy. If she cannot accept you for who you are, she should know better than to ask! Keep focusing in on your happiness, and let her find hers. :-)

From: Moris

I told my wife NOT to ask any questions that she was not ready for the answer . . . which way it might go. She once tried to sleep on the couch, but I would not let her.

Just because she asks you a question does not mean you have to answer it. Ask her if she is ready to hear the answer regardless of what the answer will be. Discuss the possible reactions to your answer before giving the answer. Maybe she is not ready to hear the answer, so you can just ignore the question. This did help me sometimes. But one thing for sure . . . don't start to lie . . . do be truthful. But remember that being truthful is not the same as TELLING EVERYTHING. My wife knows that I have been with a few—well, ok a lot—of men. She does NOT know who they are even though she does know most of them. She does not know that I was involved with them sexually. When she used to ask me who, I would tell her that I will not reveal their names. Some are married and wish to stay that way. I was honest with her and did not reveal their names. She no longer asks who.

From: Clark

It is this point that seems to keep me stagnant.

I have said before in these posts that the change for me began coming around when I was confronted with the reality that I was trying to protect everyone else from their own pain.

Still, I have to admit that I am the occasion, if not the cause, of a lot of my wife's pain. While both she and I are getting clearer about what we can and can't do about that, it still hangs me up. Though I want, in many ways, to remain married, it is precisely the dilemma of being honest or dishonest that causes me to wonder about the wisdom of it. If I only did what I could honestly report without jerking her around, I would do nothing, at least not actively and sexually.

For example, last night I wanted to go to meet a guy that I'd like to get to know. For a variety of reasons, my wife would have had to know the facts of the matter, or else I would have had to lie. I hate the deception that comes from it. But telling the truth doesn't necessarily cause fewer problems. I have tried telling "only what is needed." Those of you who are married to intuitive women, and those to boot with an insatiable curiosity, might know I am speaking truthfully when I say that there is no such thing as "a little information." Even if there is, there are silences, depressions, all sorts of things to deal with.

Right now, I am not in a relationship with anyone. I have met a guy that I want to get to know. The other night, sensing that something is different with me, my wife woke me up to the question, "Is there someone else in your life?" I said no. She then asked, "Is there somebody you would like to have a relationship with?" What to say? If I say no, I am not telling the truth. If I say yes, I am in for God knows how long a conversation. And where would we come out? Where we always do. Raising the same questions about how our needs are different and wondering whether we can work it out. I said no again.

What I would like is to have a marriage in which I could tell the truth and not wreck her emotionally in the process. Some of you have that, and I envy you. I have a wonderful wife. Whether it will ever work so that we can enter a phase that can adapt to m2m relationships for me, openly and candidly, I rather doubt at this point.

Clarity, anyone?

From: Schuyler

I can't clarify much, but boy, can I relate. Our situations are that I AM involved with someone, and I feel very fortunate in that respect. I don't have to go out on "dates", and we only meet one another during work hours when I'm already normally away from home.

I know how hard it is to know when to be truthful or not. It's not an easy choice. Honesty without compassion is NOT a virtue—what virtue is there in pointedly or brutally hurting someone you love? I have been guilty of that a lot, and I don't feel proud of it. On the other hand, I also know from experience that when I lie, it is a disease that eats away at me until sometimes I don't even know wherein lies the truth. I've been that route too.

I have come to believe that it is absolutely essential to be honest with MYSELF, but that complete and total honesty with others (including my wife) is not ALWAYS the best route. I need to examine my motives. If my motive is to protect, to heal, to love, I need to consciously attempt to choose whichever route (honesty or dishonesty) will take me there. It's not always an easy choice. If my motive is to hurt, I try (not always successfully) not to go that route. Sometimes the objective truth takes me on the hurtful path, and I consciously choose to be dishonest (usually by omission rather than an outright boldfaced lie). Sometimes I just blurt out the objective truth, and hurt is what follows—I make no pretense of perfection in ANY of this.

Right now I'm trying to muster the courage to tell my wife that I'm going to the March guys gathering. Not looking forward to the fallout.

From: Clark

Schuyler wrote: >*Right now I'm trying to muster the courage to tell my wife that I'm going to the March guys gathering. Not looking forward to the fallout.*<

I understand all too well. I can't tell you how many things I have scrapped just because it wasn't worth it. But it takes its toll. I get to the place where I hate the "game" so much that I just want to throw in the towel and leave. Sometimes I wonder why we try so hard.

Then I look at my wife, whom I love, and who loves me, and I know.

From: Carl

Clark wrote: >*I can't tell you how many things I have scrapped just because it wasn't worth it.*<

Exactly!

A week ago, I went away, partly on family business, but obviously also to see my guy and spend a few days with him. I left behind a rather despairing letter, pointing out to my wife that she sometimes behaves as though she just would like me to get out of her life. With it I also left some e-mail printouts by way of demonstrating that I'm not just being dramatic when I say such things, but that many of my brothers here go through much the same sort of torture.

When I got back, all was serene. It was Wednesday—my day to take my wife out to dinner because she has worked all day. We chatted comfortably and warmly, but avoided THE subject. I kept wondering how to ask her whether she would mind if I skipped one of our Wednesdays so that I could go to the gay and lesbian potluck at the church next week. I decided to postpone the question.

On Thursday, my wife asked me to take her to dinner. I almost begged off because of all I had to do after being away for five days, but in the end I went. I felt so comfortable during dinner that I asked her whether she would mind eating with me every Wednesday but one a month, pointing out that the potluck occurs the first Wednesday of each month. Her response astonished me: "Oh, I'll get something at home; I don't like to eat here alone. But that's no problem. You go to the potluck." And said without a hint of sarcasm or self-pity or reproach!

I was very proud of my wife. After we got home, we let the dogs out to pee and stood watching them through the storm door with our arms around each other. Life is good. . . .

From: Shawn

A short term solution might be something like this . . .

I met a guy I want to know better & go out with. I told my wife. We agreed I can go out one night/week without taking too much time from home, hearth, and family so to speak. I agreed that I may get affectionate with him and get very close physically and emotionally, but I will keep my clothes on. This enabled us both to have the sense that I can pursue the relationship without things developing too quickly. That might not be a bad thing you know. Do we really require instant physical gratification?

I admit, this might only be a short-term solution, but it helps me to be able to spend time with him while my wife is feeling less threatened. I don't have the pressures now of having to cover up or fearing interrogation. It's not a perfect idea, but are there any perfect arrangements or decisions in this life? If you want to stay married, I think compromise may be the only way.

From: William

You know, u might have a marriage in which u could tell the truth. U won't know until u tell the truth. And that takes courage, faith and a willingness to face the unknown. I think wives and our marriages are stronger than we often think (when they are weaker, they are either not keeping or are illusions we refuse to give up). We have to give up control when we speak the truth. Tell the truth, let the chips fall where they may, and then pick them up to play a new, exciting, and never before played game of life.

From: Max

My experience, FWIW, was that my wife said "Everything is OK." This was her way of trying to stabilize the situation while she found her feet. Then the brown stuff hit the air conditioning. I tried the dating thing and it was that which brought calamity. Having said all that, from reading other guys' notes, some have had great success. To each his own eh?

TELL HER BEFORE OR AFTER THE FACT?

From: Floyd

My situation is this: I'm out to my wife and she's accepted it, including my stated intention to be physical with men . . . and she says, okay, but tell me when you're going to do it. How do I get from here to dating? Does it work in any of your experiences to tell your wife you've met a guy and you want to have sex with him? Does it work to tell her after the fact? Any experiences, or advice, are welcome!

From: Brandon

When I came out to my wife it was a forgone conclusion that I was going to start dating and would end up in bed with some man. Yes I told my wife. Best to tell her beforehand as to what your intentions are and deal with the truth up front. After the fact—only tell her that you did have sex and that you practiced safe sex. If you are interested in some of the past posts on safe sex, let me know and I'll send you the "threads." My experience is to let my wife know my intentions and honesty is the best in the long run. I am presently in a relationship with a man and we have been partners for 9 years. Wife knows that we have sex but has no right to know what we do in bed together. God speed to you in your journey.

From: William

What works for me is to tell my wife as little as possible without lying. A white lie now and then doesn't hurt, but any real lies only lead to trouble.

My wife has told me that the way she deals with my sexuality is to think about it and to be confronted by it as little as possible. And she is not in denial. She accepts me fully and we have a wonderful relationship.

When she first found out about me, 17 years ago, she had to confront my lover, who was my ex by that time. I don't think she could have met him if we were still involved. They had lunch together. My boyfriend tried to reassure her that my primary interest was her and my family. He said she should look at my sexual encounters with men as if I went bowling with the guys every so often. She laughed, thinking his suggestion was insensitive to the significance of my having sex with others. Since then, however, referring to my encounters with men as "bowling" has been a neutral unthreatening way of confronting me, being honest with me, and not making all those emotional connections to using the word sex or making love. So, if she has to know where I'm going when she won't accept a weak excuse, she asks "Are you going bowling?" When she thinks I'm being irritable of late she says, "Not enough bowling? or "Maybe u should go bowling." When she says "I bet you've been going bowling" or refers to bowling, or gets angry about my bowling, we can laugh, or discuss it in a neutral way. She can smirk or I can giggle about it and we can move on, knowing we are honest even though we don't go into details about my bowling technique.

From: Bruce

My wife is pretty much the same. Since we both came to terms with my being gay, she has always been interested in who I was seeing, how serious it was, and the like. When I began seeing one person regularly, she went out of her way to meet him and to include him in things. When I had to be rushed from work to the hospital this summer, the two calls that she made from the emergency room were to her mother and to my lover.

She is fully aware that our relationship has a sexual side, but she doesn't want to hear the details of it any more than she wants me to tell him the intimate details of my life with her. The exception to that is that we HAVE had several talks about HIV and other STDs and what steps I was taking to avoid them. She was also told when both my lover and I tested negative after we'd been seeing each other exclusively for over 6 months. The few times (back when I was playing the field) that I told her more, she made it QUITE clear that she didn't really want to hear it.

She knows that if there is anything she wants to know she just has to ask, and I will do my best to tell her everything that doesn't compromise somebody else's right to privacy.

ABSTINENCE REVISITED

From: Clem

I am sexually abstinent with men, and I would like to share some of my thoughts on this issue with the rest of you.

First of all, I should mention for those of you who don't know or remember this detail about me—I'm bisexual (about a "3" on the Klein scale). I really enjoy sex with women and I really enjoy sex with men. When I'm with a woman I am, for all intents and purposes, straight—I don't fantasize about men. On the other hand, when I'm with a man I am, for all intents and purposes, gay—I don't fantasize about women.

I try to tell my wife she's getting "two for the price of one," but she doesn't find this remark funny. (My joke is also not entirely honest, as I will explain later . . .)

My bi-ness is relevant only because I ASSUME that the option of homosexual abstinence is feasible only if you are genuinely bi. It would be self-destructive folly to attempt homosexual abstinence if you are gay.

What has only very, very gradually become clear to me is that the issue of homosexual abstinence for a bisexual IS NOT ULTIMATELY A SEXUAL ISSUE.

It is an identity issue.

I CAN remain reasonably happy not having sex with men (except in fantasy j.o. sessions), as long as I insist that my wife understand I AM BISEXUAL AND I WOULD **LOVE** TO BE HAVING **REAL** SEX WITH GUYS. At a minimum, it has to be an acknowledged FACT in our relationship (acknowledged by my wife) that there is a part of me that is repressed through a conscious choice.

I currently insist on this acknowledgement and I am living in the hope that this acknowledgement will eventually lead on my wife's part to a willingness to let me actively express the bisexuality in my personality. But this is merely a hope.

What if she never reaches a point where she's letting me be my true bisexual self? If the nonsexual relationship falters, well, of course, it's a no-brainer. We split. But what if we succeed in rekindling our old relationship—maybe even coming closer in a conventional hetero relationship than we did before my coming out?

Well, there's a PROCESS here (this is what I didn't understand three months ago). The CORE issues between myself and my wife have NEVER been sexual. By putting the sexuality on the back burner, I have successfully focused our attention on the nonsexual parts of our relationship. And we are at last beginning to make progress in these areas.

And, guess what? This process is leading to changes in her sexual awareness—without my ever forcing it. She will occasionally do things like ask
me if I think a particular guy in a restaurant is attractive. Now, I don't talk
much about sexuality—SHE does. But she's clearly thinking about the issues: she doesn't think the sexuality has entirely been "handled." And, for
me, that's a critical shift in awareness on her part.

I HAVE insisted, again, that my bisexuality is real and it is THERE—it is
just repressed. In the current setup, the "gay" part of me is simply CLOSED to
her, because we are denying it—and this denial PERMANENTLY
COMPROMISES THE POSSIBILITY OF OUR BEING "FULLY" INTI-
MATE.

(Actually, it's worse than that because, despite what I've suggested
above, I don't really think bisexuality is actually something "in between"
being straight and gay—I think it's fundamentally different than either.)

If you are bisexual and CONSCIOUSLY choose homosexual abstinence, you must do so CONSCIOUSLY and you must insist that your
spouse acknowledge what is being done. And you must insist that what is
being done is NOT good, but is really a concession to your limitations as
homophobics living in a homophobic culture.

After all, what if activating your bisexuality would ACTUALLY BE A
GOOD THING, opening the possibility of rich levels of connection between
both men and women that are fundamentally closed to nonbisexuals?

From: Archie

You wrote about your commitment to homosexual abstinence. More
power to you, if you can pull it off (pun intended) without weakening or it
making you bitter. I couldn't do it. If I could, then I wouldn't even have
come out to anybody, it would still be my secret. Had my wife asked me for
such a commitment when I came out to her, I could have only agreed to it as
a temporary condition. I went through too much pain admitting my homosexuality to myself, my wife, and my family to turn back now. Fortunately
everybody has been supportive. Perhaps twenty years ago they wouldn't
have. Good luck however it turns out.

From: Clark

This is a subject that I would like to write on at length.
I'd like to respond to two things: one explicit and one implicit in your
comments.
The explicit piece is what you say about conscious choice and the fact
that the conscious choice is not fundamentally about sex, but rather about
identity. I agree with that. I am more and more mindful that the "correct"

choice or course of action for any one of us is something that is peculiar to that constellation of things that comprise our stories, our selves. To the world in general, celibacy makes no sense. To the celibate, however, it makes a good deal of sense. If one has the grace or, if you will, the gift of celibacy, it is clearly possible, and indeed right to exercise it. To live in a monastery when one is not celibate, however, is somehow at the least a deviation from the ideal, if not a betrayal of the values one affirms. The same is true for you. From what you say, it seems to me that you have the gift, the power, the will to do what you have chosen.

So I affirm and applaud what you have chosen. Indeed, it is what I chose for over a quarter of a century. (And I count myself richer for having chosen it somehow.)

The other thing, the implicit piece, of what you said has to do with the fluid nature of our lives. We simply are not static. We are, in the nearly hackneyed phrase of Tennyson, "a part of all that we have met." We change. I find that today, homosexual abstinence, while it might make a good deal of sense on one level, simply does not accord with who I am. And that despite the labels I might apply to myself: bi (which I could defend) or gay (which I think is more nearly accurate). It seems to me that, despite all, we continually look for norms, for correct ways of doing this or that. Which is natural enough, to be sure. We want to establish the right time to "tell the kids." We want to decide on the right way to behave if we are married and bi. We want to establish the correct approach to divorcing, if divorce we must. We need to have a consensus (don't we?) on the subject of how best to approach same-sex relationships if we are married and gay.

The main thing that the last four years have taught me is that there is no one correct way to do any of this. Of course there are norms. There are even absolutes ("in omnibus caritas," in all things, love; "do unto others as you would have them do unto you"). But the norms are simply that: norms. They are not prescriptive for every life, nor for any individual life as long as it is fluid and changing. So I conclude that one must decide these things in the context of the highly individualized situations in which we find ourselves. You are doing, and have done that. I am doing it too, though coming to different conclusions: conclusions that I would not have dreamed of a mere two years ago. We have to keep trying to figure out not the correct way to live life, but the right way to live OUR lives. And that involves, I think, listening to the deep truth within us. And that may well be different for you or me or someone else than it is for the majority.

It all amounts to living with judgment suspended, with our deepest selves affirmed, and with a conviction to take our individual lives quite lightly, though very seriously too. We are nothing more nor less than our stories—our combined experiences, sense impressions, bodily realities, spiritual selves. Nothing less than listening to the inner heartbeat of all that will tell us what to do or where to go.

Or so it seems to me.

Thanks for writing. A part of my own story, I have learned, is that I live my life best when I am in dialogue with others such as you who will tell me theirs and listen to mine.

From: Clem

Thanks for your reply. "Pulling it off" (as you punningly put it) is of course what my life is all about these days.

Your remarks make me wonder if I made it clear in my original post that I'm NOT in favor of "marriage at all costs, even if it means repressing my bisexuality."

Abstinence is NOT a good solution, because it compromises too much that is valuable (one's identity, not just one's sexual life). It makes sense ONLY if one's wife simply can't handle the sexual issues, but the marriage is very strong in every other regard.

Ultimately, however, I believe that not being able to "handle the sexual issues" is a sign of immaturity, so I suspect that abstinence is not actually part of a viable LONG-TERM solution. (Could a marriage be "very strong" and still encompass immaturity like this?)

In my own case, I think the outcome will ACTUALLY be one of these—in order of decreasing desirability: (1) my wife will reach a point in her own development where she will see that my bisexuality is actually a GOOD thing for our relationship and should be permitted to find expression somehow; (2) my wife and I will arrive at a better, more adult place in our relationship and THEN decide that we need to separate (remaining connected as FRIENDS) in order to proceed in our life's business; or (3) my wife and I will not be able to fix our NONSEXUAL problems and will opt for a less-friendly divorce.

The fourth possibility (that we will achieve a dramatically improved interpersonal relationship that will make it "worthwhile" for me to remain homosexually abstinent) actually seems unlikely to me, though I have to believe it is at least POSSIBLE.

Right now, the key thing is MOVEMENT. If I didn't believe my wife was changing, I'd simply leave the relationship. After all, it was significantly broken long before I had any sex with men. But she IS changing, so I want to hang around to see how things turn out.

Why wait around? Well, there's still enough love going on between myself and my wife to keep me hoping. And the connection seems to be getting decidedly stronger as time passes, which is the opposite of what it was doing before I came out to her.

Hope this clarifies things.

CELIBACY

From: Dern

I have told my wife that if she expects me to remain celibate in my gay side, I would have to be celibate with her too. I don't think I could handle the longing that the sex used to churn up. I say used to churn up because at the present time I am not engaging in any M2M sexual activity but believe it is a temporary state. I know I would resent the fact that she was being satisfied and I would feel short-changed. For those who may choose to remain celibate, is that in both departments? Do you refrain from sex with your wife too?

From: Conrad

We've hit this topic like a stone wall. . . . I continually find that sexuality/asexuality is one and the same and not susceptible to division into gay and straight components. If I'm open to sexuality with a man, I'm open to sexuality with my wife. If I'm shut down, I'm just shut and dead.

Really accepting this connection is making a difference. We both realize that I didn't go through everything we've gone through so that I could ALSO shut down my sexuality with my wife (with the gay sexuality long dormant). I must now accept and nurture my gay sexuality if I am to have anyone sexuality at all, with my wife or otherwise.

It's still difficult, of course. We just try to focus on being open to all our love and sexuality with each other, and not just what is going on elsewhere or what we're not getting from our spouse. I'm really optimistic that this is the only way that can possibly work for us. God knows we've tried everything else!

From: Clem

I am currently celibate with my wife, too, but this is emphatically NOT my choice. She just hasn't gotten to a point where she can "handle" having sex with me. This should change shortly.

You make an interesting point, however, that is consistent with my experience: the more STRAIGHT sex I have, the more NON-STRAIGHT sex I would LIKE to have. My sexual engine gets going, and it wants to do ALL the things it wants to do.

When I was younger, I didn't think it would work like this. But experience has taught me differently.

From: Dern

I don't see it as a power play. It is a matter of survival for me. I do enjoy sex with my wife but it does leave a small hollow in my emotions (for a lack of a better way to term it). I am able at the present to cope with it because for now my M2M celibacy is viewed by me as temporary. To ask me to remain celibate for the rest of my life in that department is to ask me to deny my gayness. I know what effect that hole had when I was in hiding and feel that it would lead to a deep resentment of my wife if she were to ask me to remain celibate in the M2M dept. No power play for me, I see it as a reality. I am gay, not bi, just happened to be married. If it weren't for my wife there would be no woman in my life as a partner.

From: Dern

My wife has accepted my being gay. When I say I enjoy sex with my wife I mean that it isn't a chore, it isn't un-pleasurable. The satisfaction that comes from sex with my wife is making sure she enjoys the experience totally. I do cum but the intensity is not there.

I am sure I am gay because women do not attract me in any way. My wife was my first female and only female sexual experience. My wife and I dated quite a while before we started the petting and sexual stuff.

What I want from a man is the closeness, the touching, and yes the sex. I have no desire to get this from a woman. There is something about a stocky hairy man that just drives me insane!!! My wife and I have a very healthy emotional relationship, especially now after I came out. I too have joked about sending her for a sexual reassignment operation. She, however, could not pull it off she is too much a woman; not in a frilly sense of the word. I want the same type of relationship with a man. I do not want the one nighters, the anonymous stuff. I want a bearded fool to come home to, to spend the ordinary day-to-day living with, but I also see my wife in the very same picture for she too is a part of me.

I no longer struggle with the fact that I am gay. I never considered myself bi. I view sex with my wife as sex with my wife the person and not a woman. Her mechanics are different. I do not fantasize about men because my wife is my love and I am there to make her happy because I love her. The hard part for her is that she knows she cannot completely do the same for me.

From: Mike

My experience exactly . . . when I was suppressing/denying expression to my gay sexuality, I lost access to my str8 sexuality. In fact it went further than sexuality. I was less "available" in every way . . . physically, emotionally, spiritually . . . to myself and all others. Once I found authentic self-expression . . . with the continued love of my wife . . . and then with a special guy with whom I could express my long suppressed need for male intimacy . . . I was reborn. I was, perhaps for the first time, totally alive . . . totally expressive . . . sexually, emotionally, physically, and spiritually "available" to ALL of my LOVED ones. This miracle was not lost on my wife, for she then had MORE of me . . . even though, paradoxically, she had to "let go" of her attachment to me, only to discover that in so doing, my love and commitment to her increased exponentially. The paradox for me was . . . the more I was able to share my love freely . . . the more love I had to share. But when my love affair with that special guy was over . . . and I felt I had no outlet for expressing intimacy with a man . . . I soon sunk back into my "half living" state. The light had gone out . . . and I became remote again . . . even to myself. Celibate . . . but not really by choice. I just lost all interest, all desire. I temporarily forgot who I was.

Happily, even in my darkest days, I knew, that having once experienced the light of love and full self expression, that I could find it in myself again. I was never hopeless (as I had been in the years prior to my awakening). I just needed some time to heal, to learn, to open myself again. I knew there was NO WAY I could go back to those dark days of suppression and denial. My faith and courage prevailed. Eventually I began to open myself to intimacy again.

My wife, having seen the difference in me, and having experienced the joy of being with me as a WHOLE man, has continued to support my desire to express myself intimately with a man. She knows from experience now that my loving a man does not diminish my love for her . . . in fact it enables me to express my love for her and our kids even more so. I think this is what has made it possible for her to CHOOSE freely to stay in this unconventional marriage with me. My experience has affirmed my belief that I MUST express myself authentically . . . as God made me. Any attempt I make to suppress or deny ANY PART of my nature . . . brings unhealthy consequences to ALL PARTS of my nature. Sometimes celibacy is a free and healthy choice . . . other times it is the unintended consequence of trying to suppress one's nature.

From: Dern

Just a thought. Is it really celibacy when you choose not to have casual recreational or anonymous sex? I haven't chosen to be celibate. I have just chosen to keep my physical sex as a gift that will go along with an emotional relationship. For me the casual sex does not fulfill the true longing in me. I long to have that LTR love and the truly electric sex that goes along with it.

WHAT TO TELL WIFE

From: James

I believe in honesty and my wife knows when and with whom I'm intimate but I feel a commitment to the integrity and privacy of the other guy also. My wife said that she understood that so I do not share details. I was surprised when she shared what she thought I was doing, etc., ... gee, I wished my intimate life was as active and exciting as she thought . . . so it was helpful for us to share general information but I don't share details at all . . . and don't plan to do so.

From: Woody

I don't always volunteer all. But if asked, I fill my wife in completely about whatever I'm doing and whatever I've got planned. I tend to play somewhat more than my wife is comfortable with, and sometimes find I have to intrude on "her time" (mainly weekends) but when we have our regular cocktail hour or breakfasttime chats, I've promised to hold back no details if that's what she wants. For some reason she's happier with a blow-by-blow (well, YES . . .) account the next day than wondering what went on while I was gone. She still prefers this to separation.

From: Moris

My wife knew when I slept with men (during my dating phase) because they were there at the house. But she did not want details. And she does not get details.

From: Bruce

That was my experience as well as James. . . . It AMAZED me to find out how successful she thought I was! We have only discussed sex in very general terms, primarily as it relates to risk of HIV and other STDs. She knew what steps I was taking when I was seeing other men casually, and once I was in a relationship she knew when we'd both tested negative twice after almost a year together. She knows that my sex life today involves a lot more touching, holding, and cuddling because we talked about that when we discussed my need to spend the night with my male friend on occasion. In general though she doesn't want me to discuss my sex life with my male lover with her any more than she wanted me to discuss that part of our life with him.

She IS interested in finding out what's going on between us though, but in nonsexual terms. I spent the weekend with my lover this past weekend and I spent the better part of an hour with her last night talking about where we'd gone, what we did, and the like. She's interested in what's going on in the gay community because that's a very big part of my life, just as I listen to her talk about her work and her activities.

From: Mike

Good thread . . . and a challenging issue. My wife has expressed her need to feel "included." And even though we are both a little awkward about how we share TGT . . . it works best when I let her lead with questions. Our ONLY rule is . . . we will ALWAYS answer each other's questions honestly . . . even if the answer is, "I don't feel comfortable sharing that right now." It was only in the beginning (first 2 yrs.) that I felt a need to invoke that response to her questions. Now we have come to a middle ground where I am more comfortable sharing more about my m2m relationships and she is asking less "personal" questions. I agree with James about respecting the privacy of any man with whom I become involved. So I never share details about him without his permission. Her main interests are (1) to feel included in my life and (2) that I conduct my m2m intimacies in a safe and healthy manner and with discretion as to avoid undue social embarrassment for her and the kids. That does NOT mean I can't be authentic . . . it just means I don't scream "I'm gay" in a public place. I am happy to meet her needs in this regard.

We have agreed that we both have a right to expect HONESTY from each other AND we BOTH have a right to PRIVACY. They are not entirely mutually exclusive but they ARE different I think.

BOUNDARIES WITH OUTSIDE RELATIONSHIPS

From: Nick

My wife and I, after 5 years of marriage, are just now beginning to discuss the possibility of me (and maybe or maybe not her) having sexual relations with men outside of the marriage. She's known about my bisexuality since very early in the relationship and has always seemed fine with it because I wasn't seeking sex outside the relationship—and because we had a sex life. But that has dwindled away, and now I've realized I deceived her in some ways by underplaying my attraction to men (I prefer men to women probably 95-5) throughout the relationship.

Now the reckoning has come. After three years of on-and-off depression, I've figured out that part of it might be caused by the fact that one whole part of me—the part that likes guys!—is pretty much shut down. I know things have to change, and so does my wife. The question is: how do we do it? Perhaps having more contact with the gay/bi community will do it for me (clubs, activities, etc.). Perhaps it will take more, like having some kind of sexual relationship outside the marriage. We'll see.

In any case, I'm curious to hear from other guys about how you've set boundaries with your spouse on those outside sexual relationships (re: whether she knows or not, how far it can go, sexplay rules, etc.). I know everyone has a different situation, but any thoughts and feedback are appreciated. I'm so delighted to be a part of this group!

From: Steve

In my situation it works like this . . .

As long as I tell her when I'm going to see him and when I plan to be home (must be within the same day) she's "ok" with it. She doesn't accept me, understand me, or approve of my behavior. But as long as I tell her when I plan on seeing my lover, the thoughts in her mind, and her accusations of me cavorting around behind her back blowin' every guy in town, are kept at a minimum. She doesn't ask what we do and I don't volunteer the information. I have no set of rules on what form of sex I can and cannot partake in. I do practice safe sex and to decrease her fears of me (or herself) contracting HIV, I get myself tested every 6 months. As far as the other STD's and Hep (A, B, and C, etc.) I have to know the guy very well before I shed my "second skin."

Once you start engaging in m2m sex, it is a very secure, self-confident, self-assured woman that won't question "where" you've been and "who" were you with every time you go out to get a loaf of bread. I hope you are able to explore your total self in a manner that is nonthreatening to your marriage.

From: Dilbert

Although I'm probably about as 50-50 as you can get in terms of my sexual attractions, I certainly empathize with your conundrum about negotiating sex outside the marriage. I've been out to my wife for over seventeen years and having friendships including sex with other men with my wife's support for quite a while. I stress the word support, which is quite different than grudging tolerance. My wife has never had a problem with my bisexuality (actually, she finds it quite erotic); she did initially have a problem with any sex outside the marriage. Initially, we agreed that, while we were deciding the issue, I wouldn't have sex with men (although I appreciate other women's beauty, I've never had the inclination to have an affair with a woman). We acknowledged that there might come a point where I couldn't wait any longer and she couldn't support my activity with men. If that had happened, we would have parted company. I think that both of us took the problem of the other (my need for sexual expression with men and her views on monogamy) very seriously. We both had a lot at risk in terms of our marriage. We had repeated discussions of the same issues, raising the same points. We have always had excellent communication with each other and both have good conflict resolution skills, which helps a lot.

Finally, I think my wife just realized that I wasn't going to be really happy until I could express that part of my sexuality. We negotiated a set of guidelines for both of us. First, I share all of my correspondence and communication with other men (after letting them know I will do so). We agreed that, since my relationship with her was primary, time spent with my friends would reflect that commitment. For myself, friendships and sex with other married BI men (who have similar home lives) has worked best. We agreed to safer sex guidelines, because I'm not interested in bringing anything home. We also agreed to renegotiate if either of us found the agreement intolerable. Fortunately, that hasn't happened.

Experience is the great teacher. Initially, my wife was somewhat anxious about what would happen when I first hooked up with someone. After a while my behavior taught her that I wasn't trying to find something missing in her and that I wasn't trying to escape. Our sex remained outstanding (with the added sharing of my experiences raising the temperature). Now this part of our life is as comfortable and normal as all the others.

I'm sure that how you work this issue out depends a lot on how you approach problems together in general. I can only tell you that if the love and commitment is there, you can find a way to make your bisexuality a gift to your marriage.

From: Marvin

1. NOT IN OUR HOUSE!!!!!!!!!!!!!!!!!—this is one of the BIGGEST of "the rules."
2. I WILL come home every night (this one is still in the negotiation stages, and has been somewhat flexible from time to time).
3. She wants to know about it (not details, but generalities—as in when I'm seeing someone. I generally follow this—if I'm seeing someone

seriously she knows—if I go out to the clubs with friends and sleep with someone she may not).
4. Practice ONLY safe(r) sex (again—this is a HUGE one—only intelligent way to be, and we've discussed what that term means).

That's really pretty much it for us . . . and as an FYI, I've been out for nearly 6 years, and with the exception of #'s 1 and 4 (which were carved in stone immediately) the other guidelines are changeable.

From: Bruce

Setting the rules for my wife and I was mainly a matter of sitting down and talking things out, and the rules have changed as other situations changed. When I first started seeing other guys, one of her biggest concerns was that I always came home every night. That agreement still holds, but now that I'm in a long-term relationship with another guy she understands the need for me to be able to occasionally spend the night with him, which I do about once a month. She likes knowing in general where I'm going, not to keep tabs on me but so she knows that she can reach me if necessary. I carry my pager or our cell phone too in case she needs me, even though she's only used them once.

We do not discuss the details of my sex life with other men, but she knows that if there are any questions that she wants to ask I will do my best to answer them. She has met most of my friends, but has no idea which of any of them I had sex with before I met my lover. The exception to this is that when someone looked like they were becoming more than a casual fling, I told her. We have talked about HIV and other STDs and what I was doing to avoid infection.

Above all we have agreed to keep the lines of communication open. This not only refers to the big things, but also to setting down with the Day-Timers once a week to review what time commitments we both have and schedule things out. Trying to balance my time between wife, our children, and a lover is probably the biggest challenge, but we've done fairly well so far. We have agreed that if conflicts do arise we will sit down and talk them out.

ARE WIVES SEEING OTHER MEN?

From: Brandon

Of the guys who are having sex with other men outside of your marriages, are your wives free to also have sex with other men? Do they do it?

How many wives have even considered it? And how has that affected your relationship?

From: Sheldon

In the past seven years I have had sex with more than 100 men. Right now having sex with men is currently on hold for me (but not dead). I am looking for a good relationship and friendship with just ONE man (I have one in mind but this is slow going.) My wife knows of my search for one special "friend." She is supportive of that search.

My wife is free to take a lover if she wishes. My only request in this area is that I not be the last one to know about it if she decided to do so. Just as she knows all about my decision to stop picking strangers up, and search for just one good man to have fun with. In all other things relating to such an eventuality I trust her judgment completely. It's funny but several months ago she said practically the same thing to me. She said that she KNOWS that any man I decide to make my "special friend" is going to be a very good person.

Up to this point she has told me that I am all that she desires, that her needs are satisfied sexually, and that she does not want another man. That could change. But after 29 years of marriage if either of us needs to exercise our gonads what is the big deal? It does not affect our bond or love for one another. We both already have deep friendships and emotional bonds with our closest friends. Some of her closest friends are people that I do not know well at all, and vice versa. So, combining sexuality with deep emotionality outside the marriage is just one step further toward being able to give and receive love wherever it is found. Probably not the worst way to live one's life.

From: Wise

We're still trying to figure this out for ourselves. I'm pretty far on the gay end of the spectrum and, although we continue to have sex together, my wife and I have both acknowledged that it's not the most satisfying sex either one of us could have. Whether we'll ever make the leap to both having separate male lovers or not, I don't know.

From: Gent

This is a valid point and one that I personally have had and sometimes continue to have trouble with. At one point, we opted to get together with a third person—a man. I was okay the first time, but I was an integral part of what was going on and it didn't go but just so far. The second time, I wasn't an integral part and I guess I had more time as well to focus on her reaction to the other man's attentions. The green-eyed monster bit me! After I thought about it, I think what really bothered me was that since I do still function sexually with my wife, it was hard for me to conceptualize why she would have the same need to be with another man since I am a man. In my pursuit for fulfillment, I wanted to be with a man—something that she is not. I know this is faulty reasoning and shows selfishness on my part, but it sure caused problems for me. Just thought I would relate my experience.

From: Boris

Sheldon wrote:>—*Are your wives free to also have sex with other men?*<

When my wife and I were still living together, I was having sex with men. I made it clear to her that if she wanted and chose to have a relationship (or relationships) with other men, she was free to. I figured what was sauce for the goose was also sauce for the gander.

>*How many wives have even considered it?*<

My wife considered it but realized it was not what she wanted at that point (or now, for that matter, and we've been living apart for almost a year).

My wife and I stopped having sex soon after I came fully out three and a half years ago. Before that we hadn't had sex for about 13 years (many reasons for this, not just my being gay). Once I came out and started seeing men, I knew my days as a pseudoheteroerotic were over for good!

From: Floyd

Two things on my mind when I think about this issue:

My wife invests sex with greater significance and symbolism than I do, so what does it mean if she transfers that investment to another man ? Is it going to have a significantly bigger impact, and be a deeper and more committed relationship than one I would have with a man?

If my wife were having sex with another woman—it would be comparable to my having sex with a man. If she ever needed sexual closeness with a woman, it not being something I can provide, and I think I could tolerate it.

From: Nick

This raises an interesting point about the wife's outside relationship being potentially more threatening to the marriage.

My wife, too, imbues sex with more meaning and isn't really interested in sex for sex's sake (outside the marriage). Yet, since we have basically no sexual relationship at this point, I couldn't deprive her of seeking outside sex if that's what we decide is OK for me. And I guess I'd have to accept the risk that she'd find some guy who pushes all of her buttons (sexual, emotional, spiritual, etc.). That's probably a risk I'd be willing to take.

At the same time, I think it is much easier for men looking for casual male partners to find some, uh, ACTION than it is for women looking for casual male partners. Just look at the online personals! Wouldn't most of you agree?

Chapter 8
Miscellaneous

ACCEPTANCE

From: Cary

I have realized a lot about my gay feelings. Before coming out I found my release by going to wooded rest areas and such to find guys to share in mutual masturbation, a very temporary satisfaction. I was at the point of looking for that stimulation about 4 days a week. Since opening up to my wife and friends, and being able to have an emotional, intimate relationship with a man those cheap thrills have for the most part diminished. Although my male lover and I can only be together a few times a month, those precious moments outweigh all those cheap unfulfilling moments of the past.

I guess as to the title of this note, "acceptance," I have accepted my inner need. Someday I will be by the side of my lover, living out who I am and giving up the things that I had set up along the way to cover my true self. My wife will always be my best friend, and my kids will always be my kids. I hope and pray that when this day comes, that my wife will still be able to understand and not despise me for the actions I have to take to truly be happy. I found my peace with God and no longer feel judged as I have in the past. He created me with the desire to love another man, I no longer question that, just accept it. I think the doubt and hurt I put myself through along this discovery was the only thing that was distancing me from His love. I remember someone once saying "God will never be more than an arms length away, as that is as far as anyone of us can push him away from us."

So here I am, Gay, loved by God, and ready to live life as it presents itself to me. I hope that my loved ones will be able to really understand all this, and be able to understand.

MONOGAMY/BISEXUALITY IN ANOTHER SOCIETY

From: Rudy

I can only speak from my first-hand knowledge, but: it didn't matter, doesn't matter, did matter, and does matter. It all depends on the individuals involved. I come from a culture where a man was allowed to have as many wives as he desired and could feed. Surprisingly though, it is a matriarchal society. The first wife was the primary one when it came to control issues. She would accept the other wives as her husband would take them, and treat them as family. There really isn't a lot of jealousy, in fact it is rare. We (and I mean my people) know that one heart can love many other hearts, without the love for one interfering with the love for another. We recognized that the love we feel for one person is different than the love that we feel for another one, and accept this as one of our basic truisms. We do not incur any difficulties in making sure that all of everyone's needs and, wherever possible, all of their wants are met.

Like I said, the first wife held the primary position when it came to control issues, but it was and is the husband's choice as to who he is going to sleep with, and when. We do not take a new wife until such time as we, individually, are ready to, and there are some of us that remain monogamous, by choice, while others will have several wives. My grandfather had three. There is very little discord in our community.

The husband's choice as to who he was going to sleep with and when also carried farther than just their own lodge in only one respect. My people do not condemn homosexuality. They accept it as being part of one's nature, and by being something that the Great Everlasting Spirit gave each one of us as part of nature itself. If a man wants to sleep with another man, then he goes to his lodge, and they sleep together. Many of our children will have homosexual experiences as teenagers, and go on to a heterosexual lifestyle for the rest of their lives. Others will remain bisexual, and some that are truly homosexual will live their lives as that, and they will all have rich full lives. And, there is no shame. Our men treat their various partners with the respect that each one deserves, and also tries to fulfill their needs. As far as who is the number one in any of these relationships, they all are number one. Each one holds a distinctly different position in their man's heart, which will not be replaced by anyone else, and also that they will not replace the feelings that their man has for someone else.

It is ironic that I do not have to hide myself in my world, but I must hide myself in yours because your world cannot accept the realism that we are all creatures that were made by the Great Everlasting Spirit in accordance with what he wanted each of us to be. As I pass between both cultures, I realize that the Great Everlasting Spirit is the same Spirit that your world calls God. What I have the most difficulty with is that your world cannot accept the gift that has been given, and given so freely, and allow it to blossom and come into full bloom so a person can realize their full potential. Please don't misunderstand me and think that I am referring to this group when I say you, I am referring to the general culture and society that you all are just small members of. You fight the same battles with that society that I fight, but in so many ways you have a head start because you have more knowledge of the intricacies of this society than I have.

The cohesiveness that holds my people together is a bond of love and the acceptance of the capability of one person to love more than just one other person. Perhaps it is because we are so bonded with Grandmother Earth who has taught each of us that we are free beings, and that we should find peace and joy in our lives instead of strife and discord. For us, it is a matter of survival. It's funny, the white man always called us "savages."

UPDATE ON GENT

From: Gent

I am a native and continuing resident of Mississippi, I was married in 1991. We had our first child in late 1992 and our second in 1993. I always knew that I was attracted to men, but I didn't allow myself to explore that until I was 42 years old. My wife found out that I was "exploring"—a day which shall forever be vivid in my memory. The next three days were horrible. I finally admitted to her that I was attracted to men and had indeed acted on my attractions.

We tried to work things out through the months that followed until we separated last year pending a divorce. Before we separated, we tried negotiating arrangements where I would see someone who was partnered, someone on a certain day of the week. Oh the things I promised trying to make it work! But it didn't. The bottom line was that my wife couldn't live with the thought of my seeing anyone—even if I promised not to leave, etc. I couldn't blame her for feeling that way, yet at the same time I felt that I needed to be able to explore this side of me in order to be truly happy or else be miserable for the remainder of my life. I did not want a divorce, yet my wife wanted me out if I was not going to be monogamous. Therefore, I moved out.

Some months later, and after lots of reevaluation, but before the divorce became final, I decided to try to work things out with her in order that we might maintain our marriage. I loved my wife then and love her now, but then, as I feel now, I know that I want more and have a very great desire to have a special man in my life.

My wife better understands my need to have a man in my life now. She socializes with some of my gay friends. She has been into their homes. She has even been to a gay club with me. She is trying very hard to understand. I am able to go out at times with my friends, but she feels much better if they are partnered, which most of them are.

That which is not so easy is staying faithful to her demand that I be monogamous. It is very hard and excruciatingly difficult to keep that promise. I am happier than I ever was in my entire life now that I have some very good gay friends. I connect with like-minded men on a level I never before thought possible. It is great. Since "coming out" to myself, along with having my "closet" involuntarily blown open by others, I am happier than before. But it has had its ups and downs.

I won't belabor how my "closet" was blown open, but imagine having your wife and even your own family members tell many, many, many people. Then multiply it by the people that they tell. Initially, it was embarrassing. But eventually, that embarrassment turned to exhilaration which now expresses itself as freedom to be more of who I want to be than I ever before thought possible. As a teacher who is very public in several organizations (all but one very str8 organizations), I have enjoyed support or at least acceptance by those who have been made aware.

Where do I go from here? I don't see a win-win situation for me in my life. I want my wife to be happy; my children to be happy; and for me to be as happy as humanly possible given the obligations and commitments that I have made to them and to myself. How that is to be accomplished, or what the end result may be, is yet to be determined.

MUSINGS

From: Marvin

Don't know why . . . but just want to share a couple of things that have happened in the past few days. . . .

1. Last week one night I started chatting with a guy, married, in an AOL m4m chatroom—even though I rarely do so, I offered to meet him for a drink after work since it seemed like he was a nice, genuine guy who was struggling with his sexuality in the confines of his marriage . . . overall a nice visit, until he made the comment that he didn't really think of himself as BI or gay . . . that he was just "infatuated with dick." I commented that every dick I'd ever seen was attached to a MAN. I'm not sure he understood me . . . and the more I think about it really bothers me . . . no wonder that married men have the reputation that we so often do . . . and have thrown in our face . . . that we're just interested in m2m sex and nothing more, and that we're all "hiding" in our marriages. . . .

2. Was out to lunch with a group of co-workers on Thursday—group of six of us (two in the group who I'm out to) . . . anyway . . . while eating lunch there was this guy, alone, about 25, eating at the same restaurant . . . he and I VERY briefly exchanged knowing looks. . . .(I've always known that I have very well functioning gaydar, and that while I sometimes miss it, if I think so I'm rarely wrong. . . .) during the course of lunch I had to use the men's room . . . said guy comes in while I'm in there and hands me a sugar packet (guess he didn't' have anything to write on!) with his name and number on it! Hehehhehehehehe . . . kinda cracked me up—
and no . . . I didn't call him . . . although I was tempted! kinda cute . . . made me feel good! <G>
Just random ramblings . . .

RE: HEAR WHAT I DON'T SAY!

From: Mike

Don't be fooled by me. Don't be fooled by the face I wear. For I wear a thousand masks, masks that I'm afraid to take off and none of them is me. Pretending is an art that's second nature with me but don't be fooled. For God's sake don't be fooled. I give the impression that I'm secure, that all is sunny with me, within as well as without, that confidence is my name and coolness my game; that the water's calm and I'm in command and that I need no one. But don't believe me, PLEASE!

My surface may seem smooth, But my surface is my mask. Beneath this lies no complacence. Beneath dwells the real me, in confusion, in fear and aloneness. But I hide this. I don't want anybody to know it. I panic at the thoughts of my weakness and fear of being exposed. That's why I frantically create a mask to hide behind, a nonchalant, sophisticated facade to help me pretend, to shield me from the glance that knows. But such a glance is precisely my salvation. My only salvation. And I know it. That is, if it's followed by acceptance, if it's followed by love. It's the only thing that will assure me of what I can't assure myself, that I am worth something.

But I don't tell you this. I don't dare. I'm afraid to. I'm afraid your glance will not be followed by acceptance and love. I'm afraid you'll think less of me, that your laugh would kill me. I'm afraid that deep down I'm nothing, that I'm no good, and that you will see this and reject me. So I play my game, my desperate game, with a facade of assurance without and a trembling child within. And so begins the parade of masks. And my life becomes a front.

I idly chatter to you in the suave tones of surface talk. I tell you everything that is really nothing and nothing of what's everything, of what's crying within me; so when I'm going through my routine, do not be fooled by what I'm saying. Please listen carefully and try to hear what I am not saying. What I'd like to be able to say, what for survival I need to say. But what I can't say.

RE: EMOTIONAL OBSERVATION

From: Clark

I have always been, as my mother puts it, 2/3 water. Yet, when I reached high school, I found that I could no longer cry. I am not sure whether it was cultural conditioning or what. At any rate, I remember crying when the mother of a dear friend lay dying. I was a freshman in college. The tears felt so good, although my grief was real and deep. Since then, I have cried, indeed wept bitterly, many times over many things.

As recently as last night, when my wife and children and I were sitting around the dining table talking about all the stuff around my coming out, etc., my wife commented that she was surprised that I had not shed any tears during the conversation. Sometimes our psyches are all locked up, I suppose. I also know that for me, anger seems to be antithetical to tears. When my defenses are up, I think I never cry. It is only when I am interiorly soft, malleable, that I can cry. Never thought about that before. (And I had a good deal of anger last night. That was, I suspect, why I didn't cry.)

Once again, I am amazed at how this sexuality thing flows through so many of us who have strong religious inclinations. Many have commented on that before. It strikes me that the connection is borne out among a fair number of us on this list. Even some of our group who say that they are not religious say that they are spiritual. I think, for whatever it is worth, I'd opt for the latter if I felt I had to make a choice. Alas, like gayness, it is not apparently a choice that I can make.

Chapter 9
Leaving the Marriage

LOOKING FOR APARTMENT

From: Bib

The other day, I blew up at my wife over her lack of housekeeping. I told her it was the last straw. Last night she and I had a long talk about us. She asked me if I was planning to leave, and I told her I was. She did not cry and carry on as I expected, but was already prepared to hear that I was. I have moved into an extra room we have (where my computer is set up), and am sleeping on a mat on the floor. I did tell her that my reason for leaving was not the housekeeping, but that that was the catalyst that brought this decision to the foreground. I told her I have been very depressed for most of the 16 years we've been together. It was not anything she had or had not done, but it was because I was trying to avoid who I truly am. She said she knew it and she also knew I could no longer be happy here. I also told her about my lover. He and I have been seeing one another for the last month. I'm spending the night with him tonight and he and I are planning an out-of-town weekend trip in two weeks (I can hardly wait). She didn't say it, but I could tell by her lack of reaction that she knew I was seeing someone.

I'm planning to find an apartment as soon as possible and get things started on the divorce. It's going to be rough financially, but I know it's the best decision for me and for her. I told her I want her to start living her life, not to be shut up in this house all the time. I want her to find her a man who will treat her right and be good with the kids. (Stepfather is an issue I'm going to have to deal with another time, I guess.) I told her I will remain in town to help her with the kids and anything around the house that she needs help with.

My son is aware that I'm leaving and doesn't seem to be very upset about it. I think he has been expecting it. My five-year-old daughter is not aware of my leaving and I'm not sure how she's going to take the news. They seemed to be more upset about me taking the computer with me when I move than they were over the fact that I'm moving out.

Even though things between my wife and I have not been good for many years, it's still difficult to end an almost-15-year relationship. She and I agree that we don't want to become enemies because of this divorce. We want to be there to help each other when needed. To me, one of the strangest things about all of this is how free I feel now. I told my lover last night (as well as one of our brothers) that I feel as though a great weight has been lifted from me.

I do ask that each of you keep me in your thoughts for the weeks ahead as I try to work things out financially and find a place of my own and start learning how to live again. It's been too long since I've been on my own. Thanks for listening.

From: Steve

I am so very happy for you in that you have at last released yourself from a situation that, in the past, brought you great unhappiness. However, along with that comes extreme inner turmoil. As time passes in our marriages, the deeper the anguish becomes because of TGT storm brewing within. I am envious of your courage to break the ties and of the support you receive from your boyfriend. I am certain that you have made the right decision at this juncture in your life . . . you will never regret it. You are at last free to be the person that has been deep within. You are now allowed to join the severed pieces of your being. To at last be a whole. Your children will always love you, for you will always be their father. Not even you can take that away. They will hurt and you will be there to support and reassure them that Daddy will always and forever love them . . . support them . . . protect them. They may not fully understand, and they may even blame themselves for your departure. You will guide them through their pain and grief and they will love you all the more for it. You do not have to be living in the same house for your children to feel your love and support. I wish you well in this new journey. I wish you all that you dream,

From: Kenneth

You didn't say how old your son is. Old enough to have learned that "real men" don't show pain or hurt or fear, I'll bet. Please don't assume that your leaving his home does not upset him. He may not want to be a bother to you. Believe me, he will take your moving out very hard, whether he shows it or not. He may even think it is somehow his fault . . . e.g., if he had been a better (nicer, more obedient, courteous, etc.) son, you might not have left HIM (and he will see it as leaving him, not just his mother). I hope that you will take him aside and tell him that sometimes things do not work out between a husband and wife as far as living together goes, though the two of you still love and respect each other and intend to continue as friends. Tell him that you love him very much and that he is NOT responsible for what happened, nor was his sister. Even though you and your wife are distancing from each other emotionally, that does not mean the same must be true for your children. I think that it would be easier for them to accept a gay dad than to lose him for reasons that they are never told. Perhaps your boyfriend can be like a "second dad" to your kids. Wouldn't that be neat (assuming other factors do not interfere).

I hope this note doesn't sound too preachy. If so, I apologize. I hope it all works out for you. It must be nice to have a lover who means so much to you.:-)

From: Bib

I'm sure you're all getting tired of hearing the soap opera of my life. Things here have not worked out quite as I thought they would. My lover and I split up yesterday. He and I spent the night together this past weekend and I found myself pulling away from him early Sunday morning. I thought maybe I needed to time to think things over and examine my feelings for him, but after talking with him last night, I have come to realize that a full relationship with him would not work out. Perhaps my boyfriend and I will see one another every now and then, I don't know. I do know that I could not be with him as a "husband," as he and I had discussed before.

I'm not sure what my future is going to hold, but I do know that I'm still going through with the divorce from my wife. I cannot go back to being a husband to her, and she knows that. I've been unhappy in the relationship for far too long.

WIFE IS LEAVING!

From: Carpenter

Although I thought I was prepared for this, I know now that I was not. My wife and the kids will be leaving this house for a new one. Although they are still here, I am already seeing "ghosts" that will be left behind when they are gone. I am already dreading being alone in a house that has for so many years been filled with the sound of kids laughing, crying, and playing. I'll miss the sound of the washer and dryer going at all hours of the day and night, the smell of food cooking when I walk in the door. I'll miss tripping over the kids toys that are every where. I'll even miss tripping over my son's bike every time I try to get to the trash can in the garage.

Since I knew this was coming, I made a commitment to myself that I would not try to stop or delay our separation. I knew it was to be in everyone's ultimate best interest. I'm glad I made that commitment in a less emotional state. Otherwise, in order to keep my marriage together, I would now be making promises and compromises that I would later be unable to keep.

This is a very hard post to compose as I am writing it through tears. At this point, I wish I had never discovered the joy of a man's love. Rather, had I kept my homosexuality strictly in the physical, rather than emotional (sex in the bookstores only), I would never have discovered that two men could love one another, and ended up loving my wife as a sister, rather than a wife. In other words, I would not have known what I was missing.

From: Mandy

I am very sorry for the very difficult times you are experiencing right now. Straight, BI, or gay, married or not, the break up of any relationship is difficult. Certainly a committed relationship where children are involved, and where expectations of "forever" where perhaps once held, can be devastating.

I remember those very ghosts you describe. I remember being in utter despair around the time of my separation from my wife. I remember thinking, "What HAVE I done?"

But, you have to remember to take things one day at a time. It's cliche, to be sure, but "this too shall pass." And it does. In time, you will learn that you made decisions in your past based on what you knew to be true at the time—marriage seemed like a great idea at the time, or "the right" decision, whatever. But when our information about ourselves and our world changes, we can't be held to or tied to decisions based on old, outdated assumptions and information. I think commitment for commitment's sake is empty. I think commitment is based upon complex givens and assumptions. When those change, you have to reconsider those commitments.

It sounds like you know this break-up, your own personal situation, is going to be best in the long run. But you are understandably caught up in the memory and emotion of it all. I know. It WILL get better. Surround yourself with those who love and understand you. Use their support.

One day at a time. Don't try to fix everything all at once. Have a goal to work on or fix only one thing at a time, one day at a time. At the end of the day, look back and think about and appreciate that one thing you accomplished that day.

From: Farran

I haven't said a whole lot lately and figured it was time for an update. This will give another perspective to those new guys who just signed on to this Club.

Just some background. I'm 34, married 11 years, two kids and live near a very large metropolitan area. I have always known I liked guys and had a few minor experiences up to marriage. After getting married, I shared that interest with my wife and she was cool with it but nothing happened. Over the past 2 years the pressure built and came to a head. After much soul searching WE decided that I couldn't stay a gay guy in a str8 marriage. I have moved out to my own apt. We are doing everything we can to remain best-friends, co-parent, and not turn life entirely on its head.

We have told our families. My wife's, although religious, was very cool with it. Mine, who are not religious, flipped. My mom is still struggling with it in a textbook sort of way. She's convinced she knows how she caused this. She will get over it in time.

Since then it has gone good. I do enjoy my own place. We have each found more time to do things we didn't otherwise do. While I saw this as a "gay issue" about identity, freedom, expression, experience, and love . . . she saw it as a spiritual quest with her spiritual identity and fulfilling her needs on that level. Both of us have gone out some with other people but I'm far from eager to "settle down" since there is so much to explore . . . and I don't mean just different sizes and shapes. :-) Similarly, I knew I couldn't just "put the genie in the bottle" and pretend I wasn't attracted to guys. MANY guys do that . . . and unfortunately . . . that often means they don't talk about it.

While sometimes I do wonder "what have I done" I know that a great deal of thought went into this and it is the right thing to do. While some of you can do the "double spouse thing" we couldn't. Hurray that it works for you. For some, you have a buddy on the side and more power to you. I fall too hard and completely to do that. And for some of you its a sex thing and going to the rest stop and getting blown every so often works. Hurray for you also. While I might call that the Bill Clinton approach to marital fidelity, it works. My dick and my heart were always too linked to do that. (Still doesn't mean I would save the dress!!!)

I have enjoyed reading what others write and struggle with as time goes on. To the newbies, you have my empathy. This is not easy and there is no right answer. Talk with people here and in other places. Make sure you talk with people in different stages. It will be hard to find those that successfully put the genie in the bottle . . . they are still in the closet. Don't get me wrong . . . that's ok, if it works for them.

I hope that this has helped some of you and been interesting to others. To those who it wasn't . . . sorry. You all were very helpful to me as I made it through various milestones.

From: Mike

I'm sorry you feel like you wish you had never discovered the joy of a man's love. I hope you meant that figuratively and that at some point you will allow yourself to feel that joy without guilt or shame. I know it must be difficult to end your marriage too, regardless of whether you both feel it's the best choice under the circumstances. I'm sure neither one of you expected this when you got married. You will both certainly grieve the dream you once had during your innocence. I hope someday though you will both be able to look back and see the gifts that you have been to each other despite the current pain of the situation. Growth and learning are often accompanied by pain and sadness.

I was so numb for so many years before I allowed myself to love a man, that even the pain of losing him, and the pain I know my wife and I feel while grieving our former innocence, I embrace now as a blessing. A reminder that after all those years of walking death I am truly ALIVE. Reminds me of the tin man in the Wizard of OZ when he said through his tears, "Now I know I have a heart . . . because it's breaking."

From: Brown

I'm with you here buddy. In a couple of weeks I will be moving out myself. This signals the end of my marriage. While we are not working on divorce terms as of now, we both know that will be the outcome. My kids are aware of all that is happening and know their world is changing rapidly. The 18-year-old told me that she finds the change is coming too fast. Her comments were how I used to be her father and now I'm her gay dad. In her eyes the two don't seem to mesh.

Every day a thought crosses my mind. I wonder if I'm doing the right thing. But each time I look at recent events (within the last 2 years), I have to admit that men are more than a sexual fling with me. A few weeks ago I had the most wonderful time with a man I love. I learned beyond a doubt that I had missed this kind of connection in my life. The experience went way beyond anything I ever felt before. So, I know my doubts come from my fears about the unknown. What will my life be like as a gay man?

I only know I can't live with my wife as we are now. It's too painful for both of us. I can't be what she wants and seeing me come out is driving her nuts. Tonight she told me the door is still open. If I find that living as a gay man is not what I want, then she will still be waiting. I said thanks, but dear please don't expect this to happen. I know how much this hurts you and yours. My prayers are with you.

CAN I SAVE THIS MARRIAGE? SHOULD I?

From: Lou

I haven't posted here yet, but I've had contact with a couple of you who've been really supportive! (Thanks)

Even though I'm going to my local GAMMA meeting this Thursday, I just needed to post. . . .

My wife and I had a very long and frank discussion to talk about dealing with my depression over this whole deal. (btw., I've been out to my wife since before we were married 19 years ago) . . . but our discussion came down to:

1. I'm not in the process of coming toward her, but going away.
2. There's a silent unspoken thing that says to her "she's not what I want."
3. She doesn't want to be 50 and get dumped. If it's going to happen, it should happen now and we get on with our lives.

I don't know how to walk away after all these years together—or even if I should. She said that everything she's built her life for doesn't count anymore. . . . There's no joy in keeping the household together. I can't argue with ANY of what she said.

She's definite that I can't have a relationship with someone outside our marriage . . . that if that's what I want, I have to leave. Even if I don't enter into a relationship for a long time with someone, the fact that I'm looking is enough for her to want me out.

She's being very rational . . . we don't scream and argue. . . . We're best friends . . . but the whole situation has led me into a deep depression (although the medications are starting to kick in). . . .

She's right about not being what I want, even though she's the most wonderful person (woman or otherwise) you would want to meet. If you were going to be married to a woman, you couldn't do better. But, if it weren't for my two boys, I know I'd be gone in a heartbeat.

There's so much at stake. . . . Don't know if I should continue to deny needing to live as a gay man until the kids are gone (God . . . 6 more years?). . . . I know many of you are in this same place . . . or have been there . . . if you're someone who prays, I'd appreciate your prayers . . . this is the toughest thing I've EVER faced. . . .

From: Derrik

I know exactly how you feel, medications and all. This is my entire dilemma. I just have come out to my wife after 13 years of marriage and 3 kids (youngest is only 5!). We have had more frank discussions in the last several weeks than in our entire marriage. I've done my best to make her understand that this is not about HER, but about ME and what I need.

I would love to stay married to her, and be with my sons. There's no other woman I'd want to spend my life with! Aside from the social and financial benefits of remaining married, I do love her. But perhaps not enough, or in the right manner, to have her as a wife.

The ideal situation would be for her to allow me to enter into some long-term relationship with another man (I don't want to whore around with anyone, man or woman). She may come around to that, but I doubt it. In the meantime, I still make contacts with other guys and sneak behind her back. It's almost as if I can't help myself.

My wife said she feels as if she is in a play and she knows how it will end, but doesn't know the in-between parts of the storyline. I'm not even sure how it will end. I am one who always seeks resolution to problems, and hope it comes quickly. This is a problem that isn't going to be resolved quickly, and that adds to my frustrations over who I am and what I want.

Please, guys, pray for me, too. I've never felt so much pain. Thanks for listening, and for your support.

From: Boris

Lou, your statistics are very close to mine: married nearly 22 years, wife pushing 50s. My wife married me as a gay man—she's has always known my whole life's history.

My wife felt, and said, almost exactly the same thing to me for the two years we struggled to find a way to continue living together in a wholly re-defined and transformed relationship. We didn't think we could continue to call it marriage. What eventually changed for my wife was the realization that she "did" have a life of her own that was not defined in terms of some-one else, such as her mother, her sister, her husband, her children. . . . At the cost of great pain and suffering, she found her own inner strength to accept the fact that our marriage was not and never had been what she thought it was. Yes, I love her—I love her as much as I'm capable of loving anyone. But I cannot love her as a man loves a woman. I never could, I never did, even though it looked as if I did, even to myself (after all, the plumbing worked as advertised!). That was the hardest thing for her to accept, and it took her two years to work through to acceptance. Once she'd done that, she knew she could not be what Amity Pierce Buxton calls "superwoman." She wanted to be. She wanted to continue living with me as her partner and soul mate (but not bedmate), but my active involvement with men was too much for her. She just couldn't do it.

In my case it was my wife who left. She moved to her own place last spring. It was not what I thought I wanted. I wanted to try to make it work just as much as she did. But when she was clear she had to move, I acquiesced. Now that it's happened, I've discovered it was the best thing for all of us: for my wife first, for me, and for our sons. After my wife moved, the tension between us began to ease up, and now there's none at all. She's very happy in her new life, however radically different it is from anything she'd anticipated, and so am I. We continue to be the very best of loving, close friends, in constant contact. We see each other regularly without any awkwardness, and she continues to have a real interest in my developing relationships with the men I'm involved with.

I don't think I ever became depressed at this stage of things. (It was quite another matter just before I finally came out fully and publicly!) I do feel sadness and regret at the loss of what was a wonderfully rich and complex marriage relationship, but my real, personal relationship with my wife has suffered no diminishing results. It's stronger, in fact, because both of us are becoming ever realer to ourselves, to each other, and to everyone else. Yes, it comes at the cost of considerable and real sacrifice, but the outcome is more than worth it. I've never felt more alive.

I know just how you feel! I can say exactly the same thing about my wife (though she's the most wonderful person you would want to meet). As for my boys (20 and 16), they have been an integral part of this whole coming-out crisis for the last three years, they know everything from both my wife's and my perspectives, and they fully love and support us both. My relationship to the boys has never been stronger or deeper.

I'm writing to you to say that if it's right for you, *don't* deny who you are! Dare to live it and pay the price. It's worth it. It is not easy, and it will cost you some tears and anguish as you go through it, but in the end it will all come right—at least, it did for me. And I never thought when I started on this path that I would be where I am now. But I wouldn't be anywhere else.

OUT OF A THIRTY-TWO-YEAR MARRIAGE

From: Brett

I had come out to my wife in the fall—something I was prepared to do a year and a half ago BUT she had gone into depression and still is not out of it. I also had seen a lawyer about separation and told her about it. Since then she has been badgering me. She denied outright my gayness and wants to move wherever I move and stay with me. Last night I could not get to sleep since she disturbed me so.

On top of it I fell in love head over heals for the first time in my life. He is perfect for me. My first overnight with him was the night I told my wife we were getting a separation. It put me at peace. Now, he is angry because I have not made more progress on the separation and feels he is getting shunted aside (not true).

I need some cyberhugs and some advice—(a) how to deal with getting out of a 30+ year marriage without losing my own sanity and (b) how to make my love know I care and plan to spend life as a gay male with him.

From: Joey

I recommend you deal with each person one at a time. Your wife has to come first since she deserves no less. If she is not at counseling, get her there. If she is not on STR8s or SSML, get her on it. Have the heart to heart and make sure she gets it. I know all of this is much easier said than done. But, even if you are leaving her, you have to be there for her. She still needs you. She may also need medication. BUT, please make sure she gets the right stuff. I would hate to hear that she went downhill because her doctor was too by-the-book to give her proper medication.

Now for your boyfriend—I do not have much patience for him at this point. If you are his Mr. Right, then he should be more understanding and considerate of the whole of you INCLUDING YOUR WIFE, TO WHOM YOU ARE STILL MARRIED. I have yet to meet a man who did not express concern for my wife and son. He needs to give you what you need. It will come back to him in spades. Well, I have no idea if any of this will work but, above all, here is one thing you do need:

{{{{{{Brett}}}}}}

My heart and prayers are with you. Best of luck buddy. We're rooting for you.

From: Josi

In response to how to get out of a 30 year marriage:

Imagine a lightbulb. It has two wires, a positive and a negative pole, not in the sense of good and bad, but in the sense of directing energy and receiving energy. That's like all of us—we want to receive others' positive energy, especially in this time of coming out and separating from our wives.

I have found out about this coming-out and separation process is that I get rewards from the relationship by giving back. What I mean is that in coming out, I was hungry to be recognized for who I was, after all these years of being buried. I wanted my wife to accept me. Instead, I had to learn to accept her and show that acceptance. After a two-year struggle to remain together, we will end this relationship within a month. At the same time, we will end as very good friends. She is no more accepting of me than she was two years ago. But I AM MORE ACCEPTING OF HER.

Instead of feeling resentment when she either gets clingy or tries to beat me up verbally, I tell her (most of the time) that I understand her pain. I give back to her and then the universe gives back to me, although she does not.

As for part b, how to make your love know you are with him for life: be careful of rebound relationships. Give it time. If it's meant to be it will.

TODAY IS MOVING DAY

From: Crawly

I'm not exactly sure why I'm writing today, except that I know you all will understand the feeling coming up today. I'm moving out for real today. It's been postponed many times but today is the day. I'm okay but I'm having my really sad moments as well. This isn't how I thought my life would play out. (Who ever does!) I feel a bit foolish that I'm sad today because I still am going to watch my kids three days a week here, it's just that now this isn't my house.

Last night my wife made me my favorite dinner, but we really didn't have the time to talk like we would've liked. Our toddler who doesn't want to go to bed didn't help. I was really touched that even on the night before I leave she was taking care of me—I have a cold. I guess there is so much more I wanted to say before I left but right now its too painful. I love her, just not the way I should to be her husband. Hell, we haven't had sex in months. My choice.

The funny thing is I know we will be all right in the future, but this distancing thing is a real bitch. How have some of you guys in this situation felt when this happened? Any sage advice would be greatly appreciated. I'm sorry to rant, its just nice to know I can here.

From: Shawn

It sounds like you two really love each other. After all, there are different ways for people to love each other. But who wouldn't be grieving at a time like this? It is the ending of the relationship such as it was or as you had hoped it might be. You're wise, even in your grief, to be looking forward to a time when you'll both be past the acute hurting phase. Then, hopefully, you both can heal and learn to love each other in whatever way you're able. You'll always be family, in a sense, once you've already been family to each other and had your children together. It is an ending and it is sad;

there's no denying that. Hopefully you'll be able to create a different loving relationship with each other. I know others who have been able to do it. Hang on to hope, brother, the best you can. That's all any of us can do in the more painful and sad times of our lives. Your feelings of sadness are not "foolish" as you implied . . . just very human.

From: Kenneth

I also never thought our marriage would turn out this way. Today I ran across some long-term goals that I wrote out 5 years ago, and my wife was part of them all. Now I know that in approximately 60 days I will be a single man again (albeit living with my boyfriend). It feels like a real adventure, yet tempered by grief over the loss of my relationship with my wife and lover of 23 years (we haven't had sex in six months).

My wife's therapist (whom I know and trust) gave us an exercise called "The Goodbye Process." My therapist also recommends it, describing it as tough but important. Just reading it over now causes me to burst out in tears. I would like to describe it to you, however, as I think it can help structure your saying what you want to say to your spouse.

This process is founded in a branch of therapy known as Imago. It teaches tools for effective dialogue in intimate relationships. The "Sender" is the person talking. The "Receiver" is the person listening. The two parties take turns being the Sender and Receiver. Mirroring is repeating back to the Sender, as closely in verbiage and tone as the Receiver can, the words just spoken. Do not change the meaning or manner of the expression.

> Sender: Send global memories and say good-bye to each memory. For example, "Living with you was mostly awful, and I say goodbye to . . . ." Or, "Living and being in relationship with you was . . . ."

> Receiver: Mirror each global memory and then say, "Did I get it?"

> Sender: State each negative experience and/or trait and say good-bye good-bye to each. For example, "You never listened to me. I say good-bye to that." State each negative experience one by one and let your partner mirror each one separately.

> Receiver: Mirror and then say, "Did I get it?

> Sender: State each positive experience and/or trait and say good-bye to each.

> Receiver: Mirror and say, "Did I get it?"

> Sender: Say good-bye to each part of the dream that will never be. Al-

low receiver to mirror after each separate part of your dream that will never be.

Receiver: Mirror and say, "Did I get it?"

Sender: Say good-bye to the entire dream.

Receiver: Mirror and say, "Did I get it?"

Sender: Say good-bye to the person by name.

Receiver: Silently acknowledge Sender.

Sender: I am released from my past with you, [person's name], and ready to enter my future.

Switch roles and repeat.

My wife and I plan to do this exercise. I know it will be very painful. But afterwards, I feel that I can move on to my new life freely and with little regret. That's a price worth paying. :)

From: Josi

Many thanks for sharing this exercise. I will be moving out by the end of February and I think this will be a very valuable tool in the transition. I started crying just reading the instructions.

From: Carpenter

It's now going on 4 weeks since my wife and kids moved out. She left because she didn't want to be the one left behind. Believe me, it gets better. Looking back a few weeks, I now realize I was operating on automatic pilot. I was pretty numb, and cried several times a day. I still tear up once in a while.

Once you get settled in your new home, and get into a routine with your wife and kids, it will get easier, and you will begin having brief moments of happiness. These moments of happiness will start lasting longer and longer.

Like you, I also have a young child. My other child is early teens. Today, we went to the kid shrink and found that we have been overcompensating with them. We've been eating dinner together nearly every night at one house or the other, and I usually stay through bath time when I'm there. According to the therapist, this is confusing the younger child, and creating false hope for the oldest. Our intention with all this togetherness was to help minimize the effects on the kids. Like you and your wife, we get along fine, and the kids' welfare is our common goal.

At this point, try to live in "day tight" compartments, and just concentrate on accomplishing something positive each day—even if it's just going to work. I know I didn't feel much like being around other people those first few days. However, I made myself go in, and have only told a few people what's going on at home.

From: Ted

I have just seen my future in your post. My wife recently told me (Merry Christmas!) that she wants a divorce. The last 10 days have been something else. I am stalling for time right now, but I imagine I will be packing sooner, rather than later!

I am reminded of the T.S. Eliot poem "The Hollow Men": "This is the way the world ends/Not with a bang, but a whimper!"

Believe me, I really feel that way! Good Luck! At Least you are not going to be alone!!

From: Ted

When I joined this group, about a week ago, I thought that I was the only person having this problem; a marriage of many years dissolving. It saddens me to learn that I am not unique. However, having this group for support is a great blessing!!!

This is the real benefit of the Internet. Frankly, who cares about all this e-commerce crap & porno sites. The major benefit of the Internet is the ability to create virtual communities where people of similar interests, problems can get together.

It is said that computers create isolation. I think it is just the opposite. It allows us to express thoughts that we would be reluctant to tell our brothers or best friends to others with whom with very much in common. Thank you all for being here!!

From: Carl

A-men! A number of brothers were very supportive in the recent crisis in my marriage. For a day or so there, I wondered whether it was ending. But things seem to be back on track. You're terrific, guys!

IRRECONCILABLE DIFFERENCE

From: Rodney

My issues with my wife go far beyond my sexual orientation, though my wife seems to be in denial about this fact and acts as though my orientation is THE issue. I think I have finally realized, after considerable internal debate, that we don't have the "emotional capital" left in our relationship to carry us through resolving BOTH our mixed-orientation AND our other (actually more difficult) issues.

This morning it seems to me that it might be wiser simply to explain this to my wife and suggest that we attempt to achieve a friendly divorce, one in which we would remain connected (as we are now) more as brother and sister than as man and wife. I think continuing this struggle on its current terms will merely continue to alienate us further, and diminish the love for each other that we still have. The sexual orientation issue is, after all, a "clean" issue—can be seen simply as an "irreconcilable difference."

I feel sad at this thought, because I had finally decided that I CAN continue to practice homosexual abstinence. I haven't found it actually that difficult. But even though I have yielded that ground to my wife, she continues to rant about how she doesn't think she can "trust" me any more. And, having been simply celibate now for three months, I'm not sure I care any more about continuing a sexual relation with my wife, even though it had been quite good, actually, prior to my coming out (when she retreated to a separate bedroom).

I will of course discuss all this with my therapist before proceeding, but I thought there might be among you someone who has been in the "place" I'm describing here. I'd welcome any input.

From: Max

This is the one issue that runs around and around in my mind. I love my wife but not in the way I used to. Also, over the past few months I feel she feels the same way. This is unspoken, for the most part, between us and I suppose it's some place we don't want to go because to acknowledge it would probably be to sound the death knell of our relationship.

There are times when I feel all is going well and we're "relatively" happy. This is an insecure happiness, as from one moment to the next I don't know if it's going to last. I can in some way see myself coping with single life and in another way, not coping. I would see this for my wife too. However, it's the total effect on our kids that would worry me.

I've tried to deal with the "other" issues that are involved in our marriage but find that my wife just sees the sexuality as the issue.

The one area where I differ is that I cannot practice abstinence when it comes to my homosexuality and I can when it comes to my heterosexuality. Does it mean that I'm gay as opposed to BI? I don't know and don't really care at this stage. I know that my wife has let herself go and in doing so has become far less "appealing" to me. (Horrible word but I can't think of another one more suitable at the moment.)

After all this I'm afraid I don't have any sage advice. All I can do is say that I know where you are and probably what you feel. Hang in there my friend. At this moment I live day by day. When things get rough I put a limit of 3-5 days on it before I'm going to confront it. (When I do confront it, my wife says, "It's nothing. There's nothing wrong. It's all in your mind!") That's what's kept me going.

From: Ted

There is a French adage which goes "To leave is to die a little" (I must give credit to a column in the Chicago Tribune for the quote!).

In facing my impending divorce, I have been much more introspective. We have all experienced leaving the familiar and the fear & uncertainty it created. Be it going to kindergarten and being away from home for the first time, going to high school, moving out of the house & going to college, etc.

When we were young(er) it was easier to get over the fear & we recovered much quicker. Now, it is admittedly more difficult. I know that on MY moving day, something inside of me will die. But I (and we) must go on. The only good news is that there is this group to share with.

From: Erin

I think our wives would feel a lot more confident if they felt at home with our sexual instincts. They cannot, for it is very difficult to "compete" with gay instincts when one is in a heterosexual marriage. Thus our spouses must feel uncomfortable and therefore somewhat untrusting. And I think it is going to manifest as irritability, or denial, or some other form of agitation.

As for relationships—every long-term relationship experiences the kinds of pressure and anxieties we experience. I do not think there is anything so extraordinary just because we add the factor of sexual orientation. Yes, we have called it what it is, so that raises it to a new level of consciousness for us and our spouses, but that does not mean that we will not have the same ups and downs of any LTR.

For me a key to keeping going is dialog and counseling when needed—by both and for both parties. Things break down when one refuses to go into counseling if the other asks her or him to.

From: Ted

I too am facing the prospect of a divorce of a long-term marriage (18 years). I have 3 young kids. I thought that my wife and I would stay together for the sake of the kids. We have not had sex for over 7 years. More from mutual agreement, frankly lack of desire on my part, I approached the idea of staying together in the status quo.

Unknown to me, my wife has been seeing a therapist who, along with a group of women friends have encouraged my wife to get a divorce. She thinks that she can find a new Mr. Right. She wants nothing to do with the status quo. Her attitude is that of Henry V to Falstaff: "Make less thy body hence, and more thy beauty," or in other words, "Hit the road Jack, and don't you come back no more, etc." So now I am starting to negotiate the timing of the separation & all the other fun stuff that goes along with a divorce.

From: Kenneth

My wife feels that her overeating was a reaction to my rejection of her body as an object of sexual desire. (I told her I was gay before we were married and have always exhibited passivity when it came to having sex with her.) I tend to trust her judgment on this (that is not to say that I assume responsibility for her being that way). There are many overweight, middle-aged people in heterosexual marriages, also. Perhaps the indicator is being in the position of feeling that how one looks just doesn't matter anymore, either because your partner is indifferent, is also overweight, or finds the other sex more attractive. Since I began husband hunting, I have lost 20 pounds! Could the secret of eternal beauty lie in continuously being "in the meat market"?

From: Marvin

I'll have to admit "being in the meat market" is a STRONG motivator to stay in shape! <G> I don't, however, think your observation(s) on our wives are valid, any more than the oft-banted-about supposition that our wives stay with us for financial reasons . . . may be true in some cases but not in all. . . .

For the record: at 38, with two teenage children, my wife is 5'9", approximately 125 lbs. and a perfect size 7, with legs that go on forever—in other words sexier than hell! <G> She's also a successful professional woman, earning easily twice what I do—why does she stay with me and "put up with" a less-than-straight husband? Her answer (and I quote), "because I love you, Dummy."

From: Marlin

I wish my wife was long and tall (my B/F is, though). She is overweight, is depressed and a rotten housekeeper. She's also rarely interested in sex.

Unfortunately, she so rarely gets the urge for sex in the mornings when I am ready (and most able). I really get disgusted and fed up with my life, and if it weren't for my kids (who can be really loud and obnoxious a lot of the time) I'd just load a few family keepsakes into my truck and head for Key West (the end of the line). I'm so used to not getting what I REALLY want out of life that I've settled for whatever mess of shit of a life provides emotional security (or the illusion thereof). Sometimes I just feel like shooting myself in the head to shut up the goddamn brass band that always seems to be playing in there. Such thoughts seem to surface like drowned winos from the river bottom from time to time, and I'm not trying to make anyone else depressed, but there are times I feel like I'm gonna end up like my dad, sitting on the sofa with a glass of whiskey in his hand saying "its a goddamn crock of shit." What's that they say, "life sucks and then you die?" I should get down on my knees and ask JESUS to fix my sorry ass and help me improve my outlook on life but, since I cheated on my wife, every time I try to pray it's like a broken radio, nothing but dead air. I suppose I will get up in the morning and go to work and keep putting one foot in front of the other. This too shall pass.

From: James

Even for we men committed to our marriages . . . meaning committed to remain married . . . separation and divorce are thoughts that come and go or ebb and flow as things change within our marriages.

One of the things my wife and I realized several years ago is that—just like ALL married couples everywhere—we cannot anticipate the future. But what we can do, is live the moment, enjoy the process of being, and try to nurture one another and love one another as much as possible or as much as our relationship allows. . . . This helps her and me let go of the worry about tomorrow. My wife has said several times . . . including recently . . . that she does not know what the future holds for her nor can she say how she will feel tomorrow . . . and Fritz Klein has a wonderful suggestion about letting go of expectations . . . "have no expectations" and you will be happier he says . . . I have tried—often unsuccessfully—to apply his suggestion.

So for you new guys, I hope you can enjoy the present and let go of tomorrow . . . to improve your quality of existence. It is working for some of us . . . or at least it helps us work through our stuff. . . .

For my wife and I, the talks about divorce or "are we doing the right thing in trying to remain together" . . . come fewer and farther apart the longer we remain together . . . and the couples gatherings really help affirm our attempt to remain married. Please understand I am not suggesting to anybody that you need to remain married. . . . Each of us must do what appears to be best for all involved. The only caution I would share . . . is that I've been in this situation now long enough to have heard several men share that they made decisions to divorce too hastily. . . .

From: Erin

And as Blake Pirsig wrote in the 70s: "Expectations are a trap."

From: Joe

As a musician I have a different perspective; I believe that for a relationship to work you don't need to work in "unison," like the Rockettes, but in "harmony" like gymnasts who support one another.

CAN WE LEAVE OUR LOVING WIVES?

From: Lou

While I love my wife (more as a sister, NOT in love, per se), I'm not the husband she needs. Her only crime was to fall in love with me and want to build a life. . . . Am I knowingly and willingly holding her hostage? Well . . . I was at one point, but now that she and I have talked openly about everything, and have talked about separating or divorcing, and have decided, for now, to stay together, then she's staying of her own accord knowing fully where I am.

Yes, of course, she's stuck because she doesn't want to lose her marriage of 20 years and she doesn't want to lose her life, and her family as she knows it . . . and she's also unprepared to re-enter the work force . . . so . . . she doesn't have a choice really, without a great deal of pain for her. It also means a great deal of pain for me as well . . . but not as much as for her.

I feel for my wife, and all our wives. I wouldn't want to be in her position. Hell, I don't want to be in MY position, but here I am . . . trying to make the best of it. This is as unfair as hell for my wife. She's definitely the loser. For me . . . if you're going to be married to a woman, you couldn't do better than my wife. She's been as loving and supportive of my coming out as anyone could ever be . . . but it's at a price for her . . . she and I are no longer "lovers" . . . my choice, not hers.

I wish it weren't so . . . I'm trying to be loving and affectionate with her . . . but as you guys know . . . that becomes increasingly tough for some of us who only now have realized the mistake we made when getting married.

From: Dan

Just a quick observation which may be appropriate for some of us. Here he is with a wife who wants to have sex with him and he does not!!! Is he actually unwittingly or unknowingly holding her HOSTAGE? She wants to live the fantasy of being a happily married couple. Yet at least in the bedroom dept., he cannot provide that. Apparently she has been willing to live without. Wonder what this is doing to HER and HER self-esteem. Many of us beat ourselves us over our m2m desires. Or we are secretly compulsive about satisfying them. While our spouses sit on the side . . . think about it. How fair is this to them?

Sorry to single out one man, actually there appear to be many others in this situation, and in fact I have been there too. My failure to get a divorce has on one hand delayed her getting on with her life and on the other has financially supported her pretty well.

It would be easy for me to rationalize about my wife's homophobia and condemn her judgment. She has caused me much harm and grief, but in my own self-acceptance process, she has been denied sex and cuddles and I wonder what this is doing/has done to/for her? I want her to move on peacefully and not harbor resentment. This is a pretty tall order! Our divorce proceedings are still ahead of us. Wish us luck! I guess what I'm really trying to say is WHATEVER you/we do, let's try to do it with compassion and consideration—at least more than I've shown thus far.

From: Clark

As I continue to move through this process, thoughts of my wife's pain are with me constantly, yet knowing that there is nothing you can really do to assuage it. I keep coming to the conclusion that I cannot protect people from their own pain, even if I am partly the occasion or cause of it—or all of it, for that matter.

I keep believing that the issue really is, after all is said and done, "What is Truth?" What is THE truth? And there is no way that I know of that we can generalize and say that that Truth is the same for everybody, at least as regards the exigencies of individual lives. But I do think it is the right question, perhaps the only one.

From: Max

I read with interest the e-mails on this subject. I never ever wanted to hurt my wife but that is just what I did. I was open and honest with her, but more than she was ready for. I was not able to judge that.

Again, I would echo what was (I believe) said about no longer being "in lov" with his wife. There's been too much water under the bridge between us. We've hurt each other. I still love her but in a deep caring way and no longer in a sexual way.

I'd love if we could separate without the problems and pain but I don't think that would be possible. And even sometimes when things get good I don't even want to contemplate separating.

From: James

I have shared this comment many times before . . . my wife and I agreed early on after my coming out that we would each try not to take on the other's pain . . . otherwise it became overwhelming . . . and caused us to share less and less, which was the opposite of my wife's desire. It is not possible for two loving people to avoid this totally but it really helped us to talk about it, acknowledge it, and understand when the other one listened but didn't respond as before he/she did before the agreement.

From: Lou

Yah, truth is THE question . . . and what I'm trying to do is live at the "ground zero" of honesty. It's tough . . . I'm not successful all the time, but I'm working at it . . . held back by the pain that the truth causes my wife . . .

From: Ted

I will be celebrating (noting??) my 23 (and LAST wedding anniversary).

My wife wants a divorce & we are starting the procedure now; I will probably be on my own soon. If we do go out, what I would like to celebrate & remember are the good times we have had together. We have grown together for many of those years & over the last few years, we have grown apart. That is life! Mostly, I would like to celebrate the 2 great kids we have made together. Because they are a combination of both of us I will mourn a little (maybe a lot!!) but life does go on. I will TRY to focus on the positive. Talk to me in a year & I will tell you how successful I have been!!

From: Lou

Today is my 20th wedding anniversary. When I hugged my wife this morning and wished her a happy anniversary on my way out the door, the words rang so hollow.

How could I wish her the opportunity to celebrate a union which has caused her more pain than joy because I'm gay, and not the devoted husband she needs? Which threatens now to upturn her life, and leave her alone in what should be the prime of her life?

I'm really down about this. I'm planning dinner and a movie out tonight, and my heart is not in it. I don't think hers is either, she just wants it to be "alright" between us.

God, this is the shits. Thanks for your love and support brothers.

From: Joey

Don't be so hard on yourself. Go out and ignore the obvious. Just be good to her. Love her in the best way you can. You will be true to yourself and she will love you for it. Despite what is transpiring, you do still love her and tell her so. There are no lies anymore. Let that fact elevate you. Good luck and have a lovely evening. For one night, don't worry about tomorrow.

From: Lou

Yah . . . you hit the nail on the head . . . I also wonder . . . will I find a man who loves me as much as my wife does? And can I see myself sitting on the front porch with him in my 70s?

I'm told I shouldn't impose the hetero model of marriage on a gay marriage . . . but that's all I know, and it's hard to imagine myself in the twilight years with a man who loves me as much as this woman does . . . thoughts?

Yah. . . . it's only dinner! Not really, of course . . . but I'll try to find a way to express to her the way I love her, and help her to feel valued. This just takes a lot of energy, you know? I'm not sure how much longer I can try to spare her feelings, and delay what seems to be inevitable. But in the meantime . . . we'll do dinner and a movie, and may even pretend there's nothing wrong, just like we've done for the last 20 years. . . .

From: Lou

You hit it RIGHT on the head. . . . I DIDN'T come out because I wanted to have sex with men. . . . I was already doing THAT!!!! I want a relationship . . . man you're so right . . . now to find that relationship.

From: Nathan

For me it has been difficult to be honest with my wife and just as difficult to be dishonest since we don't communicate that much. Yes, we talk about how our day went, what the kids are up to at school and girl scouts, but the communication has always been superficial. We rarely talk about our feelings and have not talked about my being gay since our first lengthy and tear-filled discussion in June. Even before joining this online group and going to GAMMA meetings, I have wanted a closer relationship with my wife. I think it is quite a tightrope to walk between being honest and telling everything to our wives, and the balancing act will vary from couple to couple. The question of who's being spared by not sharing with our wives is not easy to answer. Sometimes it is ourselves we really want to spare the pain of telling, but sometimes it may be our wives we really spare by not sharing some things. It's quite a process to discern which motivation is at work when we decide to share or not share.

From: Ted

My wife & I will soon celebrate (?) our 23 and probably last wedding anniversary. She has told me she wants a divorce. I haven't even thought about doing anything for the anniversary yet (way too far in advance). If we do decide to go out for dinner, I would like to celebrate the good times we have over the years and the 2 great kids we have made!

It will also be a melancholy, if not a sad occasion because it will mark an end to a relationship and the start of a new life.

From: Brian

Lou wrote: >*"I wonder . . . will I ever find a man who loves me as much as my wife does?"*<

This is the question that I ask myself over and over. How can I give up a woman who loves me so much? I must be an idiot!

From: Kenneth

I think I have an answer for Brian. Just as we must leave our mother in order to grow as adults, we gay or BI men must sometimes (not always) leave our wives or risk being stuck where we are. Just as crops must be rotated or the land will become less productive, the influential people in our lives must sometimes change to allow for undeveloped parts of ourselves to emerge. :-)

From: Marlin

I think that if you feel that way about your wife, don't give her up. I haven't "officially" come out to my wife yet, and haven't mainly because it would make explicit the nature of my relationship with a certain male friend. I think that people require a certain amount of plausible deniability in order to handle inconsistencies that might pop up from time to time in any relationship. Making grand, official announcements about one's sexuality might prove liberating for a time, but the net damage to primary relationships could outweigh any possible benefit in the long run. My relationships with men have a history of being transitory, so while I might revel in fleshly pleasures for a time, the nuts and bolts of fitting together two personalities into a meaningful arrangement have proven beyond my grasp, with the sole exception of my wife.

Dropping the bomb might clear the air in one sense, but might also lay waste with poison to that fragile landscape of love.

From: Paul

I'm 41 and just came out about 7 months ago. Also forced the divorce as it would be a joke to stay together. God how can a couple stay together when one is gay . . . the entire relationship becomes a joke.

Now it was tough when it all blew up in my face last year, and believe me it really BLEW UP. Wife was so shocked she OUTed me to everyone in ear-shot. But now I don't care. It actually saved me having to do it. I've lost heaps of friends but making new ones. Most of the agony is behind both of us and the wife is now JUST talking to me, though the kids are a different matter.

Now I don't give a fuck what others may say . . . I did the correct thing for myself, my wife, and my kids. The X2b is now starting to get on with her life, the kids never really saw us fight and now I'm starting my life again. Not to have been honest and open and end the marriage would have been a crime against the wife; she has a right to restart her life also.

From: Rodney

You express that keen sense of pain that I, too, can't quite escape, even though my marriage has been troubled for a long time by issues OTHER than my sexuality. Sex has just brought everything to a head. The fact that you feel this pain demonstrates more clearly than anything else that the life you have had together has had meaning, great meaning, even if you see it beginning to end.

Many people never find love in their lives. Many heterosexual couples never feel what the two of you have felt. I would suggest that you share your pain with each other and take a new kind of vow: to transform what you have into the best UNMARRIED relationship you possibly can.

There are more relationships possible between a man and a woman than a married one. And what you end up with might STILL be better than what most people ever find. Once you pass through the grief, the new relationship will almost certainly be better than what you have now because it will be based on truth and not be contaminated by your sense that you SHOULD be

able to give each other something you CAN'T give—simply because of the cards Fate has dealt you.
I say this, and find myself talking to myself. It is, as you say, the shits.

From: Roland

It has been a long time since I felt a sense of direct connection with a theme or comment here. Please understand, it is not the lack of similar issues we all face, but my own unique conditions that have often put me at arm's length from many of you. For example, I had so very little in common with those of you who felt the anguish of what cruelties you were heaping on your loving wives by making decisions that caused them harm, over your sexual needs. It wasn't that I doubted even a single one of you, or the intensity of your pain and confusion; it was simply that after a short time of reflection early on in my own situation, I ceased feeling guilty for making decisions that had nothing to do with my sexuality.

After 22 years of marriage and finally realizing that she no longer had my unconditional support for her codependence and dysfunctional usury, my wife accepted medical treatment for her depression. Finally finding a drug that worked wonders with her system, she made steady improvement and began, daily, to discover the enormous depths of the cruelty she heaped on me over the years. After announcing that she had come to the conclusion that I and the marriage had been a convenience for her, I lost my grip on my own marital perceptions, and the life I thought I had lived ceased to exist. My wife acknowledged that my bisexuality, of which I had proclaimed months before our marriage, was something she had used against me as a way to keep me from accessing her own sexually dysfunctional resources.

I left my wife four months after her revelations because I could no longer figure out how to love her and resent her at the same time. I had lost my concept of marriage (not to mention love, for that matter), and I found I could not trust her after all the years of deceit. I had remained faithful to her all those years, with both men and women, and she had not one idea of the strength and commitment it took to do so. I left my wife almost two years ago because after all those years, she acknowledged that it was easier for me to take care of everything than for the "little girl inside of her" to grow up. And when issues of my sexuality, and my need to finally access and actualize my full sexuality came to the foreground, she quaked and talked about how much that frightened her. I realized I was not longer willing to be controlled by her fear.

I too found a remarkable man upon leaving my wife. Solely by happenstance, I sought out assistance from my friends and male brethren when I returned here to relocate my business. I felt that of all the places I could look, this group of men would understand me better than most. I was fascinated but also frightened by the gay community at large, and I was so terribly vulnerable when it came to hetero relationships. One previous member of this group had a large home, an ex wife who was leaving for the West Coast, and was away for days at a time each week with his job. He basically opened his home to me. Months later, we realized our hearts were also opened as well, and we have enjoyed a loving relationship unlike I have ever known, or could have suspected based on my only other long-term relationship. The reciprocity and depth of love and kindness astonishes me and enriches everything in my life.

A dear friend recently asked me if I still considered myself bisexual. I was surprised by the question, but I easily said "yes," I still did. Some things don't change after this long. I still find women sexually and fantasy attractive. But, what I cannot say anymore is how much of the love and naturalness I feel for my partner is in great part because he is a man or because he is a human being who has loved me so unconditionally and with such intensity. After such a deficit in my life, to find this in a human caused all my buttons to be pushed and my triggers to be tripped. And yes, it scared the hell out of me and I insisted that we move slowly. Would this have happened had it come from a woman? Intellectually, I would like to think so, but as it didn't happen that way, I can't say that with any certainty. What I do know is that I have been blessed.

My children have not only accepted the changes in my life, they have enthusiastically embraced them. In the words of my almost-20-year-old daughter a couple months ago, my partner and I have "shown her more about love in the last 6 months than she had learned in the last 17 years." Strong words, and a stunning affirmation. All three of my children care for and, in their own way, love this person who makes me so happy. And all three children, having grown up in a home with a chronically depressed parent, have made it clear privately that they supported my choices, although it has taken awhile to adjust and acclimate. That is natural. But we never lost communication, and the children now have two homes to call their own, and do so.

Folks, so often we take on a huge load of the guilt that can be so devastating in this drama of life. When I made my decision to leave, my wife accused me of leaving to seek out "my gay identity." It was too easy for me to accept that until reality set in and I took a good look at my internal motivations, not based on her fear and anger, but on my own feelings and independence. Those who are chronically depressed have an uncanny ability to not only always be victims, but also play havoc with revisionism history.

Congratulations on being able to move forward, find love, and begin life anew. I salute your ability to survive. I empathize with the fear and loss and pain both you and your wife will encounter, but if both of you can't be happy, you might as well seek it on your own.

From: Gripp

Those of us who are "in love" with our wives are in the minority when thought of in historical perspective. Marriages throughout history in most cultures of the world were arranged. Love was not considered (Idealized) until the late 1800's. Occasionally throughout history it happened, often it did not. Hollywood has glamorized it. So forming bonds with our women, providing a family, a household, and economic stability is what has been expected throughout the ages, not loving. Think of Tevya in Fiddler on the Roof. "Do I love you?" "Do you love me?" Love was not considered at all. John Boswell discusses this in "Same Sex-Unions in PremodernEurope."

Many of us have found love, with our wives or our male loves, so we know what it is and are concerned that it be experienced in all of our sexual alliances. That is not a historical reality.

OUT SIX WEEKS AND SEPARATING

From: Trent

After being out to my wife for nearly 6 weeks now we have come to a decision that we should separate. I spent a few days away to meet other like guys and even though there was no sex I had a fantastic time and felt so comfortable. I told my wife that this was something that I couldn't ignore. She is not comfortable with this and does not want these influences around our children. They know that we have been having problems and the situation as it is now has got to have an negative impact on them. We have told our parents about our impending separation and they support us but think we should stay together and work it out but we have not told them the real reason. I have not told them about my sexual preferences yet, as I think it will hurt them more but I know I must sooner or later. My greatest fear is what the separation will do to the kids. Our marriage counselor said that mixed-orientation marriages seldom work so I hope she is right for the kids' sake. They missed me the few days I spent away so this is going to be really hard on them. Why are the kids the ones that have to suffer the most?

From: Travis

SIX WEEKS IS JUST TOO SHORT A TIME!!!!

Regardless of the future outcome, I would believe that relationships—especially with kids involved—are worth more than six weeks' time.

And frankly, I find it a bit misleading—if not irresponsible—for your counselor to use a statistic to imply that your marriage has a good chance of failing.

Had you been on this list *longer,* you would have read over and over again how every situation IS different, yours included.

Frankly, the number of "observations"—relative to the undiscovered or revealed mixed marriages in the general population—are, at this moment, way too few for anyone to make sweeping statements about the success rate of mixed marriages or their statistical significance.

Change counselors. From previous posts here and my own personal experience, I get the feeling that most "counselors" know little about the bisexual and use the situation to learn about bisexuality themselves, if they are interested and unbiased.

On these grounds alone—the fact that it seems that you and your wife have barely skimmed over the alternatives—you may want to reconsider the separation decision.

I believe a wife (of SCOTTS) made a good suggestion when she proposed a "time frame" for working this out. Turns out that that was very agreeable to my wife. One week after my coming out to her, she was absolutely definite & clear that we should separate—the sooner the better. I believe this is a standard reaction. After four months, we're very together. The future is uncertain, but it is always so anyway, no matter what sort of marriage you have.

The benefits of reconsidering the separation over a longer period so much overwhelm the costs to either of you, that it seems certain that it should be given a longer time frame for resolution.

You have my best wishes & any support I may be able to give you both.

From: Amity Buxton <dir@ssnetwk.org>

Yes, yes . . . Slowly, slowly. That's a resounding cry from all couples and spouses I've interviewed.

From: Rodney

I am very nearly at the same point myself, so I certainly don't want to suggest you're making a big mistake. However, at the strong recommendation of a friend, I just read Hendrix's book, "Getting the Love You Want." I hated the title, because it seems so self-centered and simplistic. But the book itself is very thought provoking and well written. I am moving a little more slowly now in my decision to separate, encouraging my wife to read the book, and wondering if maybe there's a path out of this darkness that I hadn't seen before.

What if the real issue in a marriage is NEVER sexuality? What if people who marry BECAUSE THEY ARE IN LOVE are DOOMED to enter a period of profound conflict unless they fail to come to a deeper understanding of how love works and what marriage is really all about?

What if marriage, in the final analysis, is really a path to self-awareness that INEVITABLY goes through a forest of pain?

What if therapists who confidently tell you that "marriages like this rarely work out" are correct only because, these days, "marriages IN GENERAL rarely (really) work out"?

From: Henry

Unless there are lots of other problems with your marriage, I think your decision is way premature. And assuming there aren't lots of other serious problems with your marriage, I think your marriage counselor is incompetent to endorse this decision.

From: Marvin

I'll chime in agreement here—6 weeks is no where NEAR long enough to make such a decision.

My wife and I were fortunate in that the counselor we found, very shortly after my coming out, told us very early on to pledge that we'd do NOTHING long term for at least six MONTHS! She was right . . . almost 6 years later and we're together, our marriage stronger than ever.

A counselor's place is to HELP guide discussion and to facilitate the communication necessary between spouses . . . helping to keep you on track, NOT to make sweeping pronouncements based upon assumed generalities . . . I'm suspect of any counselor who would make such a black & white statement.

From: Trent

My wife and I were separating. Our relationship has been pretty rocky for the last 12 months. This has a lot to do with the growing awareness of my sexuality. My wife actually discovered one of my ICQ contacts 3 months ago which is when she suggested we both have counseling. Later we went away on holidays and that is about the only time that things seemed to be a little better. It has been the last few weeks that things seemed to get worse; we have not had sex for nearly 3 weeks now and then it was seldom before that and she would get angry whenever I got on the Net to chat with someone. I now realize that I don't love her anymore or even desire to have sex with her at all. She wants me to completely turn my back on my sexuality and it is something that I have done once but it is so much stronger now and I don't think I could do it again. It was after we decided to separate that the counselor said that marriages in this situation seldom work. She never at any stage put the idea into our heads to separate. Since we have made the decision we have got on a lot better than we have over the last 6 months.

We told our kids yesterday that Daddy was moving out and they took it so much better than we anticipated. They actually think it is a great idea that I have found a place close to the swimming pool and they would be able to spend Friday nights with me. It is our parents who didn't take it well and my father, who I thought wouldn't really care—is devastated. It seems like the kids are stronger than we gave them credit or they just don't fully understand. We have decided to give the separation a 6 months trial and then we will decide if it is to be permanent or not. We didn't tell our parents about my sexual preferences, as we thought they had enough to deal with us separating. If we don't get back together after the 6 months then I will tell them and hopefully they will be able to fully understand our decision.

Thank you all for listening and it just helps to write it all down. It somehow helps to get my thoughts into order.

MY WIFE WANTS A DECISION

From: Lou

My wife wants a commitment and a decision from me on: "whether I'm going to continue to live with her, or separate or get divorced." We've been married 20 years last month, and have two boys, 12 and 17. I love her deeply, but am not in love with her. Been out to her since before we were married, but my growing unhappiness being a gay man in a hetero marriage has come to the forefront this past year. I don't want to leave my boys. If it weren't for them, I would have moved on long ago, and she knows it. She feels like it's just a matter of time until I find her replacement. I've hurt her so badly, and don't want to hurt her anymore, but I'm not prepared to live on my own, or find a relationship with a man. I feel stuck. And, despite the antidepressants, am again suicidal. Nothing seems to help the pain. Am I just being a chicken shit by not moving out and taking my lumps? Does it make any sense for me to try to salvage this 20-year relationship with this wonderful person? If anyone has a life preserver they're not using, I'm here floating in the North Atlantic.

From: Stephen

She has a right to at least that much of a commitment from you. Decide what you want to do with your life and MAKE that happen. Your ambivalence is what's killing you. You will feel better once you make up your mind. Just make a decision.

Your children will survive no matter what you decide . . . you and your wife may not. I came out to my children immediately after I came out to my wife. Even though they both feel loved by me and we are close, they have ALWAYS known that I see them as a byproduct of my marriage and NOT the primary focus of either my emotional or marital life. The current idea that one's children are an altar upon which everything else in one's life must be sacrificed is wrong. This idea causes one to put all of his eggs in the wrong emotional basket. This path leads to self-destruction.

Believe it or not your children do not (or shortly will not) want to be your primary emotional focus. Children are very observant and if you dote on them and despise your wife, the kids will resent it. It puts pressure on them to cater to your emotional needs and it will make them feel insecure knowing that you have no use for their mother. Being in puberty and beginning to socialize soon you will have to make an appointment just to talk with them. And, more and more you will find that they don't want to share much of their lives with you. Having come from a scenario where everything was done "for my kids," I can tell you first hand that my siblings and I hated that mantra. We all still think it was bullshit (a refusal to face life). I myself had children because I got married. I DID NOT get married in order to have children.

It's just my opinion but that is how I see it, and do it. I hope you can find the strength to find balance in your life.

From: James

It would help to know more why you feel you are not prepared to live on your own. If that is the major reason that you are staying with your wife, then it isn't fair to her.

From: Lou

The reason I'm not ready to live on my own is because of my boys. I want to live with them. I can't bear the thought of NOT living with them everyday. The perfect solution would be for my wife to move out, but that would make me a total shit to ask her to leave her home and family. Having a male lover on the side is not going to work for us, because it means more lying and deceit on my part because she won't stand for it, so I'd have to keep it hidden. I'm confused, as you can probably tell.

From: Joey

It goes without saying that you do not have an easy situation. However, I have a few thoughts. Please pardon what may appear to be harshness on my part, but . . . it sounds like your wife can no longer tolerate the uncertainty. She probably feels that this feeling of uncertainty has just gone on too long for her. Perhaps, it is fair for you to now live awhile in uncertainty. You can't hide behind the boys. Of course, you love them, but you are letting yourself use them to promote your indecisiveness. I don't think you can do that anymore. You may have to seriously consider biting the big one (and not the one we prefer) and do the honorable thing.

I thought I was in the same place last Monday night when my wife and I had our absolute worst fight in our married lives. But, by time we went to bed, I was not moving out. But, I was ready to do so, to do the right thing. Good luck. We are pulling for you.

From: Lou

I appreciate your comments, and you're right . . . I shouldn't make the boys the primary focus of my married life. I don't think I'm doing that. . . . What I can't bear is to not have them in my life everyday, living with me, sharing their lives with me like they do now. I couldn't abide even just living down the street and seeing them whenever I want . . . I want to see their puffy faces in the morning when they wake up, and kiss the youngest one awake when he oversleeps his alarm, and be down the hall when they have a homework question, or need 10 bucks to go out with buds to get a burger . . . that's the part of "living between the lines" I don't want to give up. Unfortunately, this scenario also comes with a wife, whom I'm not able to satisfy emotionally or physically . . . a condition she would be willing to accept if I was able to make a commitment to be at least faithful to her, and not have a lover on the side. . . . I know that leaving their mother will be traumatic for the boys, no doubt. There will be pain. Their lives will be fucked over. Am I willing to do that to them for MY happiness? Isn't that the ultimate in selfishness? The jury is out, but fortunately, it's hung :) .

From: Clark

I resonate with what you are saying.

First things first. When suicidal (and most of us probably have been to some degree), get help. If you are not seeing a counselor, get to one. Check the local resources. Call a gay hotline. Go to the Web. Call your local HELP line if you have one. Do something. Don't waste your life, and don't make things worse by staying stuck. Many of us on here are available for telephone support, counseling, etc. I would encourage you to contact any one of us by phone without delay.

Second, I will do what most of us rely on: share where your story parallels my own, in hopes that I might add some light. I have come to the same conclusion about myself: that I am a gay man in a hetero marriage. While I DO love my wife, and even make love with her enjoyably, I now KNOW, after experience and experimentation, that it is as a gay man that I am most myself. Either that, or I am going through a phase, and I definitely don't think this 53-year stint is a phase. My observation is that to stay in such a relationship, under circumstances that you describe, and without the umbrella of mutual agreement and support, is to continue to do untold damage to ourselves and our families and even should you not be out to your boys, they are bound to be picking up on your spiritual and mental state. So the whole system, the whole family, is affected. You don't want to leave any more than I do. But, weighing all things, it might be best for your mental health. And for your family's eventual healing. You will never know how it might work until you DO leave. Believe me, I know how hard it is: emotionally, financially, psychologically. (And I am equivocating about doing it myself.)

Remember a couple of things. First, it is quite likely that you will continue to have deep relationships with your sons. Even if there is a hiatus of a year or two, things will even out in the long run. At least that is a possibility, and in my opinion, a risk worth taking. Second, you do not have to divorce simply to get out. You can separate. A good mediation lawyer may be the way to go in talking through those possibilities, including an amicable divorce settlement, should that option be appropriate.

Let me be clear. Again, I KNOW from experience how hard this is. And how scary. But I also KNOW how tremendously draining it is to be hamstrung on the horns of dilemmas that won't resolve themselves. If it is your wife who wants a decision, make one. Trust. Let go. Do what you must.

And be aware in the midst of it that you are loved, and that you do love. The North Atlantic is cold this time of year. But lifeboats are near, the night will soon be over, and you will survive. Believe it. Now, get thee to a counselor!

From: Conrad

You are not alone, many of us are now or have been in the same place. There's just not an easy answer. That's why we're so special!

We're not at the brink right now, although we have been before, and I think we will be there again soon. I, too, am absolutely in love with my family and my wife although without any romantic or sexual passion. I really can't imagine choosing to leave our wonderful home and wonderful life, but not because I'm chicken shit. It's because I get so much out of what I do have here, even if I know that such a huge, really gay piece is missing.

Where we are now is unacceptable to both of us. Last night as we went to bed, she said, "will you ever kiss me again?" I leaned over and gave my presently standard loving but not passionate kiss. Major disappointment. I'm just not able to bring myself to give her the love and passion she wants and needs with such a gaping whole in my sexuality. Yet, I'm not able to bring myself to have the kind of relationship I want with a man while she is feeling such a lack, a gaping hole in ours. In response, we're just stuck for several years. We're just shut down, busy with challenging careers and busy lives and kids, and festering holes.

I still believe that it's preferable and possible to open up our relationship and have loving M2M at the same time as a full, satisfying relationship with my wife. Many men seem to be doing it. But I'm not sure we can do it. Sometimes I think that staying in this purgatory of trying without getting there is worse for our relationship (and the kids—8, 12, 15) than acknowledging reality and splitting. We're 39. We're both folks who demand quite a lot from our lives. Maybe its so much easier without a good relationship. I appreciate too deeply what I have, while recognizing how much I miss.

For me, I think it comes down to a more spiritual transformation to accept that I deserve to have more. How I can I believe that (after the remnants of my childhood shit!) when I cause my wife so much pain? Doesn't that prove I don't deserve more?

From: Conrad

I didn't interpret the plea as "for the sake of the children," but for Ken's own needs and wants. My kids are a strong pull in staying in my marriage, too, and I don't think it has any aspect that is "married life is better for them than splitting." It's because I want them in my daily life and I want to be in theirs.

From: Lou

I think the "it doesn't have to be forever" is the key issue with my wife. We've talked about that if I don't leave now, she has no guarantee I won't leave her when the boys are grown . . . then where does that leave her? I'm the "breadwinner", and she hasn't worked outside the home for 18 years . . . so she feels that she's not marketable in a job that could pay her expenses. Bless her heart, she's asked me to teach her the computer so she could learn some skills in case she needs them . . . geesh.

It's the uncertainty that she feels I might leave at some point if I just can't "take it anymore." And, she's right, I can't guarantee that I won't leave after the boys are grown . . . or I won't leave in 6 months . . . or that I won't leave at all . . . So . . . having the option to reevaluate in 6 months, or a year, is really no help. Am I just delaying the inevitable?

From: Andy

Selfish is good. Pain is bearable. Indecision is confusing. Suicide is pathetic (and in the Atlantic: bathetic) :-). Get a grip (not the grippe). See a counselor! With help, try to figure out what your deepest needs are and honor them (that is being rightfully selfish) and listen to what your wife needs and worries about—without supposing that you can fully meet those needs or assuage those worries. My wife also relies on my income; I think she knew that I would support her financially if we parted (and indeed I did so while we were separated for a year), but if your wife worries about this, set her straight <G>. My wife was much more worried about her emotional future (which was a plenty reasonable worry). With help, I was able to reassure her as she left some latitude for my m2m adventures within our continuing relationship. Your wife may yet bend—then part of the "fault" for your break-up is hers. If she does not get what she needs from you (or will not let you meet your needs), then maybe it is she who needs to make a decision to end the current relationship. I would not let myself be pushed into a hasty decision. Your wish to be with your boys comes through loud and clear; it would not end if you lived down the street, but it would be greatly diminished. What is not clear (to me, to you?) is what your relationship is to your wife, a "wonderful" person, whom you have "pained" (how, really?), whom you do not "love." Do you feel some affection, sense of companionship, enough to continue to live with this person indefinitely with different expectations? It seems to me that you will be digging yourself out of your (suicide-considering) confusion if you work (with help) on clarifying self and relationships. More than that no one (including yourself) can ask at this point. We are here to hold your hand (or whatever else :-) as you journey on.

From: Stephen

I faced the same problem. Not because of being gay (that had not come up yet) but because I had my first major heart attack and didn't want to die and leave my wife with no way to make it through life. We put our heads together and assessed her skills and desires. She has always loved working with children so we opened a day care for her. (1) We incorporated, and made her President of her own corporation. (2) We gutted the basement and constructed a great day care for her. (3) She is licensed by the state for 12 kids, ages 5 and under. (4) She brings in about $1,200.00/week gross. Ironically, the day care and her knowledge that she doesn't NEED me has made going through my coming out much easier for her. Now all we have to deal with is our feelings and not paranoia about money and survival.

From: Rodney

Your situation is so wildly different from mine, I hesitate to say anything. You've gotten a lot of feedback from the men here who have been in your situation, and it all seems thoughtful and loving. But, I notice a couple of themes in your posts and in the replies you've received that I think need to be highlighted.

It is important in something so complex as this that you and your wife BOTH need to get beyond all the guilt. Are you being selfish? Not selfish? Don't waste your energy on this question. You're just trying to feel your way out of a messy situation that has no obvious answers. The PRACTICAL issues are so hard, you don't need to further confuse them by beating up on yourself.

Secondly, don't fall into the trap of thinking that your wife and family have been VICTIMIZED by you. Anyone whose sexuality lies outside the norms of our very sexually narrow culture is a victim of that culture (i.e., you're the "victim" every bit as much as she is). You made certain choices among those options provided ready-made by our culture. Unfortunately, our culture doesn't provide ANY options that really fit your situation. You're going to have to "roll your own."

Your wife HAS to be willing to accept some responsibility for this. I can sympathize with her pain: this isn't the tour she signed up for. But no, she's NOT simply your victim. This is where marriage counseling can help. Even if you can't save your marriage, you may be able to find ways out of the marriage that will help you BOTH find some significant degree of happiness.

There are some unconventional arrangements that might greatly ease the pain. You might choose for a while to be "virtually divorced," living together in the same house for mutual emotional and material support while you BOTH tried to start laying the groundwork for a separated life later on (maybe after the boys have left home). But this would require that your wife accept the idea that you would be pursuing sexual contacts with men outside the marriage (she would, of course, have a right to the same freedom). Maybe this would be acceptable to her if you kept it all discreetly invisible to the family. (This is why you need to talk: I'm assuming you're not having sex with her, so there must be some other reason "she won't stand" for your homosexual activities. Why is it SHE hasn't simply walked out?)

The point is that any WORKABLE solution will be UNCON-
VENTIONAL. Don't let your wife insist on your "making a decision" about
staying in a conventional marriage: THAT'S SIMPLY NOT AN OPTION.
Sorry. The only choice you COULD make is to leave, because you CAN'T
"choose" to be heterosexual or BI. So refuse to make a decision—that is,
REFUSE TO MAKE THE "CHOICE" AS SHE HAS FRAMED IT,
BECAUSE IT'S NOT REALLY A CHOICE.

Instead, rethink and reframe the nature of the choice itself. I think the
better path is to "deconstruct" your marriage, try to figure out what you
BOTH want and need, and then build a plan in which you BOTH get as
much as you can out of life. It might very well be a plan to separate over
time and in an orderly fashion. I'LL GUARANTEE WHAT YOU END UP
WITH WILL SEEM "WEIRD" TO YOUR NEIGHBORS. But fuck your
neighbors. They don't need to know. It's just between you and your wife.
And it is an issue that you SHARE, just as you share your sons.

Again, don't get sidetracked into the emotional guilt trip regarding who's
suffering the most. I bet there's a way where you can minimize the pain on
both sides if you BOTH accept responsibility for the problem. Good luck,
and take care of yourself!

From: Clem

You hit some really key themes right on. I think much of what you say is
true of people, life, and relationships in general. Being gay or BI and married just FORCES us to confront these issues, but I suspect they exist under
the surface of almost ANY relationship—married, gay, straight, or BI.

My therapist has helped me see that my current unwillingness to separate
from my wife is based largely on my fundamentally paternal sense of responsibility for her. I can see that now, and am willing to spend time working on our relationship, because she seems herself at last to be confronting
all kinds of things about us as a couple and herself as a person. I know more
clearly than she does that a possible outcome of all this pain (which is, after
all, the pain of growth)—a possible outcome is still divorce.

This is because we ARE in a sense dying as individuals and as a couple—but "dying" in a good sense. Something new is emerging, something
more conscious and mature. As we become these new individuals, will we
want to remain in a married relationship? Maybe. Maybe not. The point is
that any relationship we "remain" in will really be a totally new one.

As your remarks imply, it is sometimes very tempting to submerge one's
identity issues in a relationship. It's less difficult, for sure. Every guy on this
list is discovering that this form of escape just won't work in the long run.

So in one sense, our sexual "issues" become merely the particular individual force that drives us into growth (whether we really want it or not!).

WHEN ARE WE SEPARATING?

From: Shorty

I was posting this to another member and thought maybe I should share some of my experiences. I was asked when we are actually separating. . . . We have officially separated. Last night after our weekly counseling session, I moved into the other bedroom. I guess some realizations are hitting me. The night before, my wife said something to me which involved an age-old communication problem between us. We spoke about it; I was telling her that I was trying to figure out why I was angry with what she said (my issues with her over her "controlling attitude" with me). It dawned on me that while we were trying to resolve this between us, that there is no reason any longer to resolve some of these problems, because the marriage is over. Equally, she is not telling me things that we used to talk about (we grow apart I guess). I want to ask, but I think "what right do I have to know if she doesn't tell me?" It's kind of another stage in evolving this separation of two intimate close partners. It hurts so much after growing into this for many many years. I'm a mess!

When we left our marriage counseling session yesterday, I asked my wife to drive, since I was so down and weepy. Most of the session was about how we separate. There are no rule books here. We don't really know how to go about it. I was saying, "you know . . . how do we decide when to stop sleeping together." Our counselor said, "You just do it." So right there, I said, "Well, then tonight." I got in the car, started to cry and took off my wedding ring, and said to my wife that I don't think I can wear this anymore. I was hurting so much. I don't know whether I am doing the right thing or not (the ring thing). Later my wife said it seemed like I was doing it out of anger, but I corrected her that it was only out of the pain and loss that I am feeling. I gave her the ring later and said here, put it back on. This is really fucking confusing!

In the car on the way home we continued to talk as I leaked. I have a question! How do you pull back? I think maybe I should be pulling back and not letting her know ALL of my pain. Or do I tell her all? The pain we see in each other confuses me; is this part of moving away from each other? I said to her . . . when you broke up with past boyfriends, did you explain your pain to them, or avoid them to pull away and lick your wounds, and start mourning the loss of love? Do I need to do that to heal and move on AND to be able to start a new kind of relationship with her? I'm still processing this, so I don't have the answers yet.

Anyway, we got home and while my wife took the dog for a walk I moved a small night table, and clock radio to the other room. I was hurting so bad I just felt I had to do it. In retrospect, I should have told my wife first. I know this is just as difficult for her, and she was hurt when she saw what I had done. I fell down on the bed (my new bed) and sobbed like I have never sobbed (well at least it felt like it!). I needed comfort, and it is difficult to realize and accept that I won't be getting that comfort (as I have known it) from my life partner. Thank God she did come in and sit down. We talked more. We comforted each other, but there is definitely a feeling that we are pulling back a bit emotionally from each other. So, we slept apart last night. This is equally confusing for my wife as well, as last week we agreed to continue to sleep together (just friends) and then make the change when I move out (which could take months . . .). I asked if she would sleep over the first night at my new place, and then back to the old place the next night, then separate. It's hard.

It was a sad night emotionally for me. There were a lot of tears . . . shit this is difficult! The "evolution" of our separation.

Needless to say, this whole thing is VERY confusing to sort out. Am I doing the right thing? Am I going about it the right way? Is this happening too fast? Too slow? We'll see!

So anyone know of a "manual" on how to do this?! New title for a book . . . "Separation for Dummies" HA! (And I'm not implying I'm a dummy, just blonde!)

From: Brett

I read your post and wanted to reply immediately; been down that road and let me tell you there is no manual, there is no approved (or disapproved) way to do this. There is only one guiding principle and that is to listen to your heart and follow what it tells you to do. Much of the grief that we cause ourselves, and our wives, in these situations is when our heart is telling us one thing (I am a gay man; I need to fully understand what that means and love and accept myself for who I am not what I, and others, perhaps WISH I were) and our head is telling us another (I'm not "supposed" to do this; what about our years together, am I behaving selfishly, can this marriage be saved, are we trying hard enough, etc., etc.) all the questions we torment ourselves with.

I'm not saying making this decision is easy or uncomplicated. I'm simply saying that when you're all "muddled up" about it, take time to get away, meditate, get in touch with who you really are and what is really in your heart and soul and the answer will become clear. Obviously for some guys on this list the answer was to stay and work it out. For others, myself included, staying meant being inauthentic with myself. Not only do I hurt myself when I do that, I hurt my wife as well by taking us down a path that sooner or later is going to collapse anyway. Separation, after almost 30 years of marriage, was inconceivable to me but, finally, the only course of action I could take that was responsible to me.

Separating your heart from your head is tough and we all have a lifetime of social, religious, and familial messages telling us what to do (and mostly what not to do) that often go against who we are. Don't forget we live in a homophobic culture, so we don't get much support from the culture, from "society," for who we are. In the end, it's your life and your soul. Take care of it. Good luck in your journey. . . .

From: Clem

I just had a session with my therapist. One thing he's very good at is finding the central point in a mass of material. Today, he ended up something like this, "For your marriage to survive, your wife has to be able to ACCEPT WHO YOU ARE. Rather than STARTING with 'negotiations' (for instance, 'will you accept me if I am abstinent with men?'), you need to find out whether or not she fundamentally requires the 'annihilation' of your sexuality. You have no basis for a relationship if she finds your bisexuality too dangerous or destabilizing to live with—and this is a larger issue than your actual sexual behavior."

Now, it remains to be seen exactly what this means in practice. But I thought his analysis very sharp, despite its apparent superficiality. Anyway, it helped clarify for me the way in which my conflict with my wife is not ultimately a conflict over what I'm *doing* sexually. It's fundamentally a conflict about WHO I AM. "Who I am" is not negotiable—even if I WANTED to negotiate it, I couldn't.

From: Mike

Thanks for such a self-affirming, empowering point of view. I like to think that I too have found MY voice. But too often in the din of the majority culture (white, hetero, male) I forget that, . . . and retreat into my "if only I were 'normal' " mantra. Bullshit. God created a party mix of "mixed nuts" and I'm just one of 'em. Perhaps a bit saltier than most ;-). Better that . . . than a bland, "normal" nut. "Sometimes I feel like a nut . . . sometimes I don't" ;-) You go boy!!!

From: Clark

Have been away for a few days and so am just reading this thread.
This note gives me a chance to do a little reflection that parallels what
you write.

For over four years now I have been, in one degree or another, tormenting
myself around "the issue." Probably each of us has extenuating circumstances that color our lives a bit of a different shade from others. Mine is the
fact that I have been juggling sexuality, marriage, and career, which is—perhaps more than most—intricately linked to the place of others in my life.

In my office hangs a beautiful piece of cross-stitch which my wife did
and gave me nearly twenty years ago. It bears a quotation from a friend and
professor of mine. "Follow where your heart leads you and those obstacles
will melt as the snow in the spring sun."

Sometimes in these last few years, it has been, and still is, difficult to determine exactly where my heart is leading me. And I have to allow for the
fact that the heart, like any guide, can make mistakes from time to time. I
have come to conclude, however, that at least my dreams don't lie to me.
And in dream after dream I appear hungering for the love and touch of a
man. In a phrase of Clem Sanford, dreams are often "God's forgotten language." I know with assurance that on a profound level through the unconscious, the voice of Truth is speaking to me.

I have recently done some work with a counselor who gave me to read a
little tract by Emmet Fox, whom some of you may know. It is called, "The
Golden Key." The idea is a very simple one, and it has turned my life around
in some major ways. Fox says that the "Golden Key" to resolving any trouble is to quit thinking about it and to think instead of God. He argues that everything will work out one way or another when we do this. I read the tract
about three times, and shared it with my wife as well. I then decided that I
was going to stop thinking about specifically the questions of whether I am
doing the right thing, whether we should separate or not, whether I should
resign or remain in my position. Over and over I am letting things unfold as
they will, trying to be, in the term, "as loving as I can be." When I start
thinking about "it," I repeat to myself, at Fox's suggestion, "God is leading
me, guiding me. I am not alone. Truth is working itself out."

I can imagine that this kind of stuff does not make a particle of sense to
some of you, and you will understandably discard it as so much religious
clap-trap. I don't blame you. But I must say that it speaks to me. It all boils
down to believing that down deep, God is speaking to and through my heart,
and that when I follow where my heart leads me, I may be ever so lost or
confused, but ultimately I will arrive at a place of peace.

From: Mike

What you say here does not seem to me "religious" at all . . . spiritual? Yes. Clap-trap? NO. Every sage, prophet, poet, and philosopher whose words have resonated true enough to last throughout the ages . . . has said the very same thing. Follow your heart . . . it is that ALL KNOWING part of you that is pointing the way. Some may call that GOD, or the HIGHER POWER, or their INNER GUIDE, or insight, wisdom, or intuition . . . as we have discussed at great lengths recently . . . it matters not what label we use (as long as it's useful/meaningful to us and our correspondents) . . . what matters is that we TRUST the process and go . . . not blindly . . . but consciously . . . with the flow.

From: Clem

I'd like to mention a couple of things that have become really key ideas for me to cling to.

First, you are trying to understand where the gay side of your personality leaves you with regard to God. I think you really know the answer to that. ACTUALLY, you know that God is love, and that being able to love another man totally HAS to be part of God's plan. It's just a logical proposition, so try to approach it the way Aquinas would. You will probably arrive at a different conclusion but of course that's a problem in the scholastic method (SORRY, I just couldn't resist the dig). God sometimes has to resort to talking through us through visions and dreams because churches are so busy burying his Word under piles of very human prejudice and stupidity. Unfortunately, the process of misunderstanding had already progressed a long way BEFORE the Bible as we know it was codified.

Second, you are trying to understand where the gay side of your personality leaves you with regard to your wife. This is the hard one for me. Right now, I think I'm hanging on to a very simple idea: you may want with all your heart and soul NOT to have sexual feelings for men because these feelings screw up your ability to be in a loving relationship with her. But unfortunately, however much you might WANT not to have these feelings, you have them. Your wife, being after all merely a human being, and more specifically a middle class twentieth-century woman, may not be able to live with you if you have these feelings. You are a good man, so you should have no trouble forgiving her for this shortcoming—or even thinking "in her position, I wouldn't be able to be MARRIED to Gay/Bi man, however much I might LOVE him"—but ultimately YOU can't fix that problem. All you CAN do is PRETEND, for whatever agonizing period of time, that you are somebody other than who you are. But ultimately GOD won't let you get away with that. Sorry.

YOUR WIFE

From: Brett

I have just gone through a couple of months of having my wife "fight for me" and to some extent it is suddenly pleasant. However, I wonder if she really knows what "fighting for me" entails in the long run? I asked that of a counselor yesterday who is seeing both of us. I also know from past experience that this is temporary—or at least history suggests it is. Thus, again I worry that I have gotten myself to the point of finding an apartment, only to be outdone by a few strongly friendly tactics. I know I do not want to have to go through the past couple of months ever again or even anything remotely like them. Thus, I find myself seeking out encouragement to go it alone . . . weird isn't it when we really wanted it to work out and after 34 years I cannot say I haven't been really trying too.

WELL, THIS SUCKS!

From: Shorty

My wife has finally come out of her shell. She ran into a friend of ours on Sunday (gay ex-partner of a very good friend of mine) and spoke about our marriage and then of my newfound sexuality. (I don't mind at all that he knows . . . that is not a problem).

I was kind of glad she had finally *talked* to someone, as she has been in denial over the last four weeks, not even admitting this issue to herself, let alone talk to me or anyone else about it. A real step for her. I thought she was making progress.

So, yesterday she had a very teary session with her therapist in the morning, then we had our marriage counseling session later in the afternoon. It was there that she said that she now sees that there is no other option for her and I and wants to separate. She is supportive of me, and has come to know the difficulties I have suffered with in my life of repressing my sexuality, and is truly empathetic. That support is nice. She feels I can only go on and be the person I have to be only if we part. She wants me to be who I am, and not what I have repressed. Equally, she doesn't see how she can possibly fit into this model. I have my doubts, as well, about how she can be her own person unless I release her. So, I am dealing with the fear, that this is probably best for both of us.

I know, I've heard it all before from many here in the list, "hold on . . . give it time . . .," " but this is all screaming to an end. We both know this is the way to go. I am kind of disappointed that she didn't even pick up the book "Other side . . . " that I bought for her, and hasn't wanted at all to discuss options to our new relationship. She just doesn't see how she can fit in I suppose. Over the last few weeks I have been doing some reading, and reading posts, and thinking "what's in it for her?" She needs to grow just as I do, for her own self. I was having difficulty seeing how she was going to be able to do that.

Last night she placed the book "The Other Side" on my night table and I thought . . . wow, she didn't really even look at it and here she is (symbolically by putting it there) giving it back to me. After a terribly difficult teary, sobbing evening for both of us, I looked at this book which was being "given back to me" and thought . . . "wow! Isn't this the ultimate rejection of coming out and letting my wife (my closest friend) know about what I had repressed all my life. We all fear rejection when coming out, but I wasn't really expecting this. What a lonely feeling. My partner who has been with me for 19 years is rejecting me because I am gay. Well! . . . who else do I get to tell?! I can't wait! (just me verbalizing!) I know there is only one way for me to go . . . and I am heading there . . . it will be hard.

So, we have agreed in principle to separate, and we have now (today) told a few close friends, and some co-workers. What is most difficult is that we both have this love for each other. It's terribly sad, and we are both hurting. I know this will be an amicable split, but am prepared for difficult times in that process as well. I can't fathom the difficulties of splitting up the "things." Momentos that mean so much to me, of a shared connection with this woman I have been with for 19 years. She is equally devastated with this realization.

We live in a housing co-operative so we are now both going on a waiting list for our own smaller units. The availability of a unit may come quickly or may take some months. I am lucky to be living where I am. We will live close by and will be able to support each other in this move towards separate lives.

For today . . . I'm just in a complete fog, and trying to keep from falling apart.

RE: THERE'S A PLACE FOR US

From: Kenneth

Someone wrote: >*I cried then because I was afraid of being alone for the rest of my life. I cry now for the memory of all the years I lost in hiding and I cry for my wife because I know now that our marriage will end and she too will face being alone for the first time. I now cry too for all those people like us who are still out there isolated and desperate.*

Now, I have hope that when I get past the pain of losing the best friend I have ever had, that there will be a place for me somewhere out there. There will be someone to hold my hand again. Life has not ended because I am coming out all over the place, life is beginning again<

Thank you for a beautiful post. I identify with your sense of loneliness and fear of never being loved. I also know what it feels like to "lose the best friend I ever had," though I truly believe that my wife and I will remain best friends even after our divorce. Even more do I believe that we can find someone to hold our hand and lead us to that special place called Happiness. I have found such a man. His name is Peter and he and I just spent a heavenly week in Fort Walton Beach, where we decided to take up housekeeping together as soon as we both can wrap things up with our wives.

I would never have looked twice at my current male partner if I had clung to my image of "the right guy for me." For one thing, he is 22 years older than I. Giving up my fantasy of being in love with a young buck was not easy. But if I had not been willing to try, I might never have found the "Somewhere" I have found with my lover. So, my advice is to wear your heart on your sleeve, take every opportunity to meet gay or bisexual men, give all the love you can, and stand back, cause the world will come knocking at your door!

BROWN CHECKING IN

From: Brown

I'm moving out. What you are going through is much the same as events with me. The moment it became clear to my wife that I had found a place and would be moving, her anger has grown tremendously. I came out to my wife over a year and a half ago. This past summer my wife discovered I had been leading a double life. The weeks following that disclosure were intense and painful. But I have never seen my wife as angry as she is now.

Actually she outed me to members of my own family first and recently forced my hand in telling my own mother. I know she is terribly hurt and wants everyone to know this breakup is not her fault, not what she wants, and you my friend are the very bad man who is destroying her life and your kids lives and well just everything.

As the time for my move approaches, her anger takes new and unexpected turns. The only thing I can do is pray for better times. I know the reality of this step has her extremely upset. We both know it signals the end of us as husband and wife. Yet she holds on to the slim hope that I might see the error of my ways and want to come back. She has told me the door is still open. That is when she's not trying to slam it on my head. I have to go. We would both shortly be nuts if I stay any longer.

At the same time, I started feeling sad and down. I can't stay in my marriage as it is. I've been married 23 years. Gay or not, ending this hurts me too. My friends tell me to hang with this. In a while it will get better. I have to believe this. We can't do a whole lot to make this much easier for the parties involved. The only thing that has stopped me from reacting to her anger has been an awareness of her pain, the fact that I will always love her, and looking into the faces of my kids. I see her in them all time.

BROWN'S FAREWELL

From: Brown

My unsubscribing is permanent. My own focus has changed over the past few months. I've been out of my family's home for a month now. The process leading up to this event was extremely painful for all of us. Actually there are still issues that must be resolved, but my wife and I are not communicating much these days. I believe time will help heal some of our wounds. My kids seem to be rolling with all of it pretty well.

The truth is I just could not handle hearing the same or nearly same story from men on the list any more. I read and shake my head. Many of you are going to have so much pain as you work through this stuff. My own coming out has opened me up to loving myself as I am. I can hardly describe how good it has felt even with all the trauma it took to get here. The best thing I could do for my wife and kids was put an end to the tension in our home. I could not stay and become the gay man I am without causing more hurt, anger, and pain. I chose to respect my family as well as myself and get on with my process.

Having said that, I should also tell you that moving into the gay community is not easy. I'm in my early 50s and pretty clueless. In a month I've had both good and not-so-good experiences with gay men who are in the life. In the past I "dated" other married men most of the time. I make a point of not doing that now. No regrets about the things I have done or bad feelings about what has happened. I know I have a lot to learn. Leather bars may be exciting, but I'm out of my element there for sure. Call me Daddy Bear if you like, but I don't know what you really want from me. It will take time to determine where I'm heading with my gay sexuality and even what I like and don't like. There are many options available. Ah, so many men, not enough time.<BG> It's been one hell of a month.

Luckily I have friends who tell me to slow down, take a deep breath and let things happen as they will. I was in a kind of limbo for many years, so you can imagine the rush that came with allowing myself a lot more freedom. Attending a weekly coming-out group has also been a great help. Many of the men are like me, married or divorced with kids. I also have the love and support of another gay father, who gently pushes me to explore and become the best gay man I can be. I love it when he tells me that. I love knowing he understands what I need to do. Just between us, I also think he enjoys hearing about my adventures . . . just a tiny bit kinky Yep, a brand new fag can be as much of a bitch as he wants. It's in the handbook you know. Where would I be without a sense of humor? Guys you have to let it out, don't let it get you down all the time.

I guess I'm trying to say goodbye to the list now, in this note. Dear list men I hope you all have the best outcomes possible. A few of you will find ways to compromise and live your lives as you wish within your marriages. I found out I could not do so. My wife could not live with and I certainly could not blend my sexual orientation into our marriage. Ok . . . it's Ok to accept my gay self. In fact it feels wonderful. No illusions that my life will be coming up roses from now on. Believe me, the thorns are present and I bleed when they prick deeply.

Hugs to you all . . .

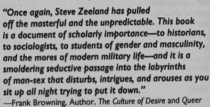